The Right to Refuse Mental Health Treatment

The LAW AND PUBLIC POLICY: PSYCHOLOGY AND THE SOCIAL SCIENCES series includes books in three domains:

Legal Studies—writings by legal scholars about issues of relevance to psychology and the other social sciences, or that employ social science information to advance the legal analysis;

Social Science Studies—writings by scientists from psychology and the other social sciences about issues of relevance to law and public policy; and

Forensic Studies—writings by psychologists and other mental health scientists and professionals about issues relevant to forensic mental health science and practice.

The series is guided by its editor, Bruce D. Sales, PhD, JD, University of Arizona; and coeditors, Stephen J. Ceci, PhD, Cornell University; Norman J. Finkel, PhD, Georgetown University; and Bruce J. Winick, JD, University of Miami.

The Right to Refuse Mental Health Treatment

BRUCE J. WINICK, JD

American Psychological Association • Washington, DC

Published by
American Psychological Association
750 First Street, NE
Washington, DC 20002

Copies may be ordered from
APA Order Department
P.O. Box 92984
Washington, DC 20090-2984

In the UK and Europe, copies may be ordered from
American Psychological Association
3 Henrietta Street
Covent Garden, London
WC2E 8LU England

Typeset in Times Roman by General Graphic Services

Cover designer: Berg Design, Albany, NY
Printer: Data Reproductions Corp., Rochester Hills, MI
Technical/production editor: Ida Audeh

Library of Congress Cataloging-in-Publication Data

Winick, Bruce J.
    The right to refuse mental health treatment / Bruce J. Winick.
        p.   cm.
    Includes index.
    ISBN 1-55798-369-0
    1. Mental health laws—United States.   2. Patients—Legal status, laws,
etc.—United States.   3. Mental illness—Treatment—United
States.   I. Title.
    KF3828.W57   1996
    344.73'0412—dc20
    [347.304412]   96-42913
                                                                          CIP

British Library Cataloguing-in-Publication Data

A CIP record is available from the British Library

Printed in the United States of America

For Patty
I have somewhere surely lived a life of joy with you

CONTENTS

DETAILED CONTENTS

ACKNOWLEDGMENTS

This book has been a journey of many years, and I am indebted to many people for their help along the way:

—to David Wexler, for his encouragement and for serving as a sounding board for many of the ideas;

—to a long list of research assistants at the University of Miami School of Law, including Douglas Stransky, Alina Perez, Bill Collins, Katherine Diamandis, and Karen Kaminsky;

—to the always helpful library staff at the University of Miami School of Law;

—to Lidia Grumberg, Trenesia Green, and Cynthia C. Lyons for typing and retyping the manuscript;

—to Deans Claude Sowle, Mary Doyle, and Sam Thompson, for their support and encouragement over the years;

—to the University of Miami School of Law for summer research support;

—to Ida Audeh, for superb yet gentle editing of the manuscript; and

—to my children and friends for their understanding of the time away from them that this project has necessitated.

To all these and many unnamed students and colleagues who were good enough to listen and offer helpful comments as I worked through these ideas, I am most grateful.

Chapter 1
INTRODUCTION

A. The Problem: Involuntary Mental Health Treatment and the Potential for Abuse

Except in an emergency, no physician would remove a patient's appendix, set a broken leg, or inject medication without first obtaining the patient's informed consent. So fundamental are the values of personal autonomy and bodily integrity that underlie this practice that medical ethics,[1] the American Hospital Association Patient's Bill of Rights,[2] and basic principles of tort law[3] all require it. As the United States Supreme Court has recognized, a logical corollary of the informed consent doctrine is that the patient has "the right not to consent, that is, to refuse treatment."[4] Indeed, the Court has found this common law right to be a constitutionally protected liberty.[5] Yet the members of one category of patients—those suffering from mental illness—have traditionally been subjected to treatment without their

---

[1]*See, e.g.,* P. APPELBAUM ET AL., INFORMED CONSENT 23 (1987); R. FADEN & T. BEAUCHAMP, A HISTORY AND THEORY OF INFORMED CONSENT 8 (1986); P. RAMSEY, THE PATIENT AS PERSON: EXPLORATIONS IN MEDICAL ETHICS 5–7 (1970) ("The principle of informed consent is the cardinal canon of loyalty joining men together in medical practice and investigation."); Bopp, Jr., *Reconciling Autonomy and the Value of Life,* 38 J. AM. GERIATRICS SOC'Y 600 (1990); Boozang, *Resuscitating Self-Determination,* 35 ARIZ. L. REV. 23, 42 (1993); Bopp, Jr. & Avila, *Invented Consent,* 42 Hastings L.J. 779, 802 (1991); Freedman, *A Moral Theory of Informed Consent,* 5 HASTINGS CTR. REP., Aug. 1975, at 32; O'Donnell, *Ethical Concepts of Consent, in* MEDICAL, MORAL AND LEGAL ISSUES IN MENTAL HEALTH CARE 1–6 (F. Ayd ed., 1974).

[2]American Hosp. Ass'n, *Statement on a Patient's Bill of Rights* 3–4 (1972), *in* W. CURRAN & E. SHAPIRO, LAW, MEDICINE AND FORENSIC SCIENCE 749–50 (3d ed. 1982); *accord* American Hosp. Ass'n, *Policy and Statement of Patients' Choices of Treatment Options* (1985), *quoted in* Bouvia v. Superior Court, 225 Cal. Rptr. 297, 303 (Ct. App. 1986). *See also* 38 U.S.C. § 4131 (1995) (informed consent requirement in Health Care Act of 1976); JOINT COMM'N ON ACCREDITATION OF HOSPITALS, ACCREDITATION MANUAL FOR HOSPITALS 65 (1990) (requiring that the medical record contain evidence of the patient's informed consent).

[3]*E.g.,* Cruzan v. Director, Mo. Dep't of Health, 497 U.S. 261, 269 (1990) ("The informed consent doctrine has become firmly entrenched in American tort law."); Cobbs v. Grant, 502 P.2d 1, 9 (Cal. 1972) ("[A] person of adult years and in sound mind has the right, in the exercise of control over his own body, to determine whether or not to submit to lawful medical treatment"); Natanson v. Kline, 350 P.2d 1093, 1100 (Kan. 1960) ("Anglo-American law starts out with the premise of thoroughgoing self-determination. It follows that each man is considered to be master of his own body, and he may, if he be of sound mind, expressly prohibit the performance of life-saving surgery, or other medical treatment. A doctor might well believe that an operation or form of treatment is desirable or necessary but the law does not permit him to substitute his own judgment for that of the patient by any form of artifice or deception."); Schloendorff v. Society of N.Y. Hosp., 105 N.E. 92, 93 (N.Y. 1914) (Cardozo, J.) ("Every human being of adult years and sound mind has a right to determine what shall be done with his own body; and a surgeon who performs an operation without his patient's consent commits an assault, for which he is liable in damages.... This is true except in cases of emergency where the patient is unconscious and where it is necessary to operate before consent can be obtained."); APPELBAUM ET AL., *supra* note 1; W. KEETON ET AL., PROSSER AND KEETON ON THE LAW OF TORTS § 9, at 39–40, § 32, at 189–92 (5th ed. 1984); Sprung & Winick, *Informed Consent in Theory and Practice: Legal and Medical Perspectives on the Informed Consent Doctrine, and a Proposed Reconceptualization,* 17 CRITICAL CARE MED. 1346 (1989); Winick, *Competency to Consent to Treatment: The Distinction Between Assent and Objection,* 28 HOUS. L. REV. 15 (1991).

[4]*Cruzan,* 497 U.S. at 270.

[5]Riggins v. Nevada, 504 U.S. 127, 133-34 (1992); *Cruzan,* 497 U.S. at 277; Washington v. Harper, 494 U.S. 210, 229 (1990).

prior informed consent and in many cases despite their express opposition.[6] This situation has begun to change in response to judicial[7] and legislative[8] recognition that mental patients

---

[6]*E.g.,* United States v. Charters, 863 F.2d 302 (4th Cir. 1988) (en banc), *cert. denied,* 494 U.S. 1064 (1990) (jail inmates awaiting trial may not refuse antipsychotic drugs); Dautremont v. Broadlawns Hosp., 827 F.2d 291, 298 (8th Cir. 1987) (hospitalized civil patients may be involuntarily treated with psychotropic drugs against their will); State *ex rel.* Jones v. Gerhardstein, 416 N.W.2d 883, 889 (Wis. 1987) ("'[T]he state and county concede that psychotropic drugs are involuntarily given to all types of patients''); A. BROOKS, LAW, PSYCHIATRY AND THE MENTAL HEALTH SYSTEM 877 (1974) ("It is widely assumed that the commitment of a person to a mental hospital, voluntary or involuntary, confers on the hospital administrators the authority to 'treat' him in whatever manner they deem appropriate.''); Goldiamond, *Toward a Constructional Approach to Social Problems: Ethical and Constitutional Issues Raised by Applied Behavior Analysis,* 2 BEHAVIORISM 1, 13 (1974) ("In practically every section of the hospital except the psychiatric ward, a patient can decline a given form of treatment, can refuse medication, and can leave the hospital AMA (against medical advice)—even when it is thought that his doing so endangers his life and limb.''); Note, *Developments in the Law—Civil Commitment of the Mentally Ill,* 87 HARV. L. REV. 1190, 1351 n.151 (1974) ("Most civil commitment statutes . . . either do not discuss a patient's right to refuse unwanted treatments . . . or allow for the overruling of a competent patient's treatment decision for all but the most intrusive types of treatment . . . .''). Indeed, some state statutes expressly authorize the treatment of hospital patients without their consent (*e.g.,* CONN. STAT. § 17a–543 (1995); LA. REV. STAT. § 40:1299.40 (1995)), and some courts have expressed the view that hospital failure to treat patients involuntarily who have sought to refuse was unprofessional and actionable. Nason v. Superintendent of Bridgewater State Hosp., 233 N.E.2d 908, 912, n.7 (Mass. 1968); Whitree v. State, 200 N.Y.S.2d 486, 501 (Ct. Cl. 1968). Although involuntary treatment without informed consent continues to be the general practice in many mental hospitals, the American Psychiatric Association has taken the position that "[a]s is the practice generally in medicine, the patient's informed consent for treatment is required except for emergency situations.'' American Psychiatric Ass'n, *Task Force on the Right to Treatment,* 134 AM. J. PSYCHIATRY 3 (1977).

[7]*See* Winick, *The Right to Refuse Psychotropic Medication: Current State of the Law and Beyond, in* THE RIGHT TO REFUSE ANTIPSYCHOTIC MEDICATION 7 (D. Rapoport & J. Parry eds., 1986). *See, e.g.,* United States v. Watson, 893 F.2d 979 (8th Cir. 1990) (psychotropic drugs); Bee v. Greaves, 744 F.2d 1387 (10th Cir. 1984), *cert. denied,* 469 U.S. 1214 (1985) (antipsychotic drugs); Lojuk v. Quandt, 706 F.2d 456 (7th Cir. 1983) (electroconvulsive therapy); Rogers v. Okin, 634 F.2d 650 (1st Cir. 1980) (en banc), *vacated and remanded sub nom.* Mills v. Rogers, 457 U.S. 291 (1982) (psychotropic drugs); Rennie v. Klein, 653 F.2d 836 (3d Cir. 1980) (en banc), *vacated and remanded,* 458 U.S. 1119 (1982) (psychotropic drugs); Knecht v. Gillman, 488 F.2d 1136 (8th Cir. 1973) (aversive conditioning); Nolen v. Peterson, 544 So.2d 863, 866–67 (Ala. 1989) (psychotropic drugs); Riese v. St. Mary's Hosp. & Med. Ctr., 243 Cal. Rptr. 241 (Ct. App. 1987), *appeal dismissed,* 774 P.2d 698 (Cal. 1989) (psychotropic drugs); People v. Medina, 705 P.2d 961 (Col. 1985) (psychotropic drugs); State v. Garcia, 658 A.2d 947 (Conn. 1995) (psychotropic drugs); *In re* Boyd, 403 A.2d 744 (D.C. Ct. App. 1979) (psychotropic drugs); *In re* Mental Commitment of M. P., 510 N.E.2d 645 (Ind. 1987) (psychotropic drugs); Clites v. State, 322 N.W.2d 917, 921-23 (Iowa Ct. App. 1982) (psychotropic drugs); Rogers v. Commissioner, 458 N.E.2d 308 (Mass. 1983) (psychotropic drugs); Kaimowitz v. Michigan Dep't of Mental Health, Civ. No. 73-19434-AW (Mich. Cir. Ct. July 10, 1973), *excerpted* at 42 U.S.L.W. 2063 (July 31, 1973), *reprinted in* BROOKS, *supra* note 6, at 902 (psychosurgery); Jarvis v. Levine, 403 N.W.2d 298 (Minn. Ct. App. 1987), *aff'd in part and rev'd in part,* 418 N.W.2d 139 (1988) (psychotropic drugs); Opinion of the Justices, 465 A.2d 484 (N.H. 1983) (psychotropic drugs); *In re* Sanders, 773 P.2d 1241 (N.M. Ct. App. 1989) (psychotropic drugs); Rivers v. Katz, 495 N.E.2d 337 (N.Y. 1986) (psychotropic drugs); *In re* K.K.B., 609 P.2d 747 (Okla. 1980) (psychotropic drugs); *In re* Boyer, 636 P.2d 1085 (Utah 1981) (psychotropic drugs); *In re* G.K., 514 A.2d 1031 (Vt. 1986) (psychotropic drugs); State *ex rel.* Jones v. Gerhardstein, 416 N.W.2d 883, 892–98 (Wis. 1987) (psychotropic drugs).

[8]Some states have enacted a statutory right to refuse treatment. *E.g.,* CAL. PENAL CODE §§ 2670–2680 (West 1995); FLA. STAT. § 394.459(3) (1995); IDAHO CODE § 66–1305 (1995); WASH. REV. CODE § 11.92.040(3) (1995); Keyhea v. Rushen, 223 Cal. Rptr. 746 (Ct. App. 1986) (enforcing statutory right of prisoners to refuse psychotropic medication); Conservatorship of Waltz, 227 Cal. Rptr. 436 (Ct. App. 1986) (enforcing statutory right of competent patients to refuse electroconvulsive treatment). *See generally* S. BRAKEL ET AL., THE MENTALLY DISABLED AND THE LAW 347 & n.242, 357–65 (table 6.2, col. 13) (3d ed. 1985) (statutory compilation); Plotkin, *Limiting the Therapeutic Orgy: Mental Patients' Right to Refuse Treatment,* 72 Nw.U.L. REV. 461, 504–25 (1977) (statutory compilation). According to a survey published in 1985, 20 states had statutory provisions relating to the administration of psychotropic medication. BRAKEL ET AL., *supra,* at 347 & n.242. According to a survey published in 1983, 45 states recognized at least a qualified right to refuse psychotropic drugs. Callahan & Longmire, *Psychiatric Patients' Right to Refuse Psychotropic Medication: A National Survey,* 7 MENTAL DISABILITY L. REP. 494, 495 (1983).

possess at least a qualified right to refuse treatment. However, in most jurisdictions and in many situations the traditional practice continues.

Although courts and legislatures have addressed the issue, the extent to which a right to refuse treatment should be recognized for those suffering from mental illness remains undecided. The United States Supreme Court dealt squarely with the issue for the first time in its 1990 decision in *Washington v. Harper*.[9] In *Harper*, which involved forcible administration of antipsychotic drugs in a state prison facility, the Court recognized that the Constitution protects a "significant liberty interest" in resisting such unwanted treatment[10] but nevertheless upheld the prison's ability to administer the drugs. *Harper* applied the deferential approach for scrutinizing constitutional claims that the Court customarily uses in the prison context.[11] Under this approach, the Court determined that the prisoner's liberty interest, although constitutionally protected, was outweighed by the state's police power interest in maintaining the security of the prison. That interest justified the state's treating the prisoner in order to protect him as well as other prisoners and correctional staff from the risk of danger he presented when not taking such drugs, a risk that had been demonstrated at an administrative hearing that the prisoner received at a correctional hospital. The Court's decision therefore provides little guidance concerning how the asserted right to refuse treatment would be dealt with outside the prison.

In the 1992 case of *Riggins v. Nevada*,[12] the Court again addressed these issues, this time in the context of the forced medication with antipsychotic drugs of a criminal defendant during his trial. *Riggins* held that due process was violated when the defendant was forced to stand trial while on a heavy dose of mellaril, an antipsychotic drug that had negatively affected his demeanor and probably also his ability to participate in the proceedings. The Court's holding was narrow, turning on the absence of sufficient findings by the trial court to justify continuing medication over the defendant's objection. However, the Court's opinion contained important dicta suggesting the standards to be applied in future cases, raising the right-to-refuse-treatment issue in the criminal trial context.

Reiterating that antipsychotic medication intrudes on a significant liberty interest,[13] the Court in *Riggins* restated the *Harper* standard as requiring that the state show both an "overriding justification" for such treatment and that it is "medically appropriate" for the

---

[9]494 U.S. 210 (1990). In a 1982 case involving the right of hospital patients to refuse psychotropic drugs, the Court had previously avoided the opportunity of addressing the constitutional issues. Mills v. Rogers, 457 U.S. 291 (1982). The Court vacated the decision of the Court of Appeals, which had recognized a federal constitutional right to refuse medication. 634 F.2d 650 (1st Cir. 1980) (en banc). The Court remanded to the lower court to consider whether an intervening decision of the Supreme Judicial Court of Massachusetts, which had recognized a right to refuse grounded in state law, rendered unnecessary the resolution of the federal constitutional question. 457 U.S. at 306. The Massachusetts case was Guardianship of Roe, 421 N.E.2d 40 (Mass. 1981). The Supreme Judicial Court of Massachusetts subsequently reiterated a right to refuse antipsychotic drugs in Rogers v. Commissioner, 458 N.E.2d 308 (Mass. 1983). The Court of Appeals thereafter approved the state procedures adopted in that case, finding them to "equal or exceed the rights provided in the federal Constitution." Rogers v. Okin, 738 F.2d 1, 9 (1st Cir. 1984).

[10]494 U.S. at 229 ("We have no doubt that . . . respondent possesses a significant liberty interest in avoiding the unwanted administration of antipsychotic drugs under the Due Process Clause of the Fourteenth Amendment.").

[11]*Id.* at 224 (applying a "standard of reasonableness"). *Harper* seems to reflect the approach of an increasingly conservative Supreme Court, disinclined to intrude into state processes and especially deferential to institutional administrators. *See, e.g.*, Thornburgh v. Abbott, 409 U.S. 401 (1989) (prisons); Turner v. Safley, 482 U.S. 78 (1987) (prisons); Regents of the University of Michigan v. Ewing, 474 U.S. 214 (1985) (state medical school's academic decisions); Youngberg v. Romeo, 457 U.S. 307 (1982) (mental/retardation facilities); Parham v. J.R., 442 U.S. 584 (1979) (mental hospitals); Ingraham v. Wright, 430 U.S. 651 (1977) (schools). It is still too early to tell whether recent appointments to the Court will affect this trend.

[12]504 U.S. 127 (1992).

[13]*Id.* at 133–34.

individual.[14] The Court identified two potential justifications for forced administration of antipsychotic medication in the criminal trial or pretrial context but found that the record in the case did not support the presence of either. First, the Court noted that the state "certainly" would have satisfied due process "if the prosecution had demonstrated and the District Court had found" that involuntary medication was "medically appropriate and, considering less intrusive alternatives, essential for the sake of *Riggins'* own safety or the safety of others."[15] Second, the Court noted that the state "might" have been able to justify "medically appropriate" involuntary medication by establishing that it could not obtain an adjudication of his criminal charges by using "less intrusive means."[16] These suggested standards were dicta, however, because the Court's holding was based on the absence in the record before it of any findings by the trial court justifying involuntary medication. As dicta, they lack binding precedential force and are open to reconsideration. Although dicta, the *Riggins* standards seem to be considerably broader than those articulated in *Harper.* Whether the Court will adhere to these broader standards in the criminal pretrial and trial context must await future determination. Moreover, whether the Court will apply these broader standards or the more narrow approach of *Harper* in other contexts—such as the administration of medication or other intrusive treatment in mental hospitals or community settings—also must await future clarification.

Thus, the Court's opinions in *Harper* and *Riggins* left the constitutional issues raised by involuntary mental health treatment substantially unresolved. Most significantly, the Court recognized that involuntary antipsychotic medication invades a "substantial liberty interest" but did not clarify whether that interest is "fundamental" and therefore deserving of strict judicial scrutiny rather than the more deferential standard applied in *Harper.* Moreover, the Court did not adequately discuss the nature of the liberty interest it found to be invaded by involuntary antipsychotic medication. A detailed analysis of the constitutional values implicated by involuntary treatment is needed for an assessment of whether the approach of *Harper* or of *Riggins* (or some other approach) will apply when other drugs and other mental health treatment techniques are sought to be administered involuntarily.

Moreover, such a detailed analysis also is needed to assess the appropriate standard when antipsychotic medication is administered involuntarily in other contexts. Both *Harper* and *Riggins* presented special considerations. In *Harper,* the right-to-refuse-treatment issue arose in the context of the need to prevent violence in a prison facility. An extraordinary degree of deference to correctional authorities in dealing with such problems of institutional violence has traditionally been applied by the courts. In *Riggins,* the issue arose in the context of the criminal trial process. Thus, the case involved the defendant's liberty interest in being free from unwanted medication coupled with his interest in having a fair trial in which he could participate with counsel in the defense. Fair process in the criminal trial has long been the subject of a special measure of judicial solicitude. Application of the right to refuse medication or other forms of mental health treatment in other contexts not raising these special concerns therefore requires further analysis and must await future judicial determination.

Thus, a detailed analysis of the constitutional questions left open by *Harper* and *Riggins* is needed in order to resolve the many issues raised by the right to refuse treatment. This book provides such an analysis. In addition to analyzing the various constitutional values affected, the book considers each of the treatment techniques and each of the contexts in which

---

[14]*Id.* at 135.
[15]*Id.*
[16]*Id.*

involuntary treatment is imposed in order to identify the appropriate standard of constitutional scrutiny that should be applied to varying right-to-refuse-treatment claims. The book then examines the various state interests asserted to justify involuntary treatment in order to analyze whether the applicable standard of constitutional scrutiny will be satisfied.

Right-to-refuse-treatment issues continue to be the subject of litigation, legislation, public discussion, and scholarly interest. Indeed, the issues have already generated a large body of commentary,[17] including a second generation of scholarly work on the empirical impact of recognizing a right to refuse treatment.[18] Yet, despite extensive public, judicial, and professional discussion, the question continues to generate substantial controversy, stimulating what has been described as "perhaps one of the most intense debates in the medicolegal world."[19] Although this controversy has continued for more than 20 years, no clear public or professional consensus about the issues has emerged.

While the controversy continues, involuntary mental health treatment persists as the general practice in many settings. In many locations, patients committed to mental hospitals are required to participate in some form of verbal psychotherapy and routinely are administered psychotropic medication without consent.[20] In addition, such patients may be

---

[17]*E.g.*, 2 M. PERLIN, MENTAL DISABILITY LAW: CIVIL AND CRIMINAL §§ 5.01–.69 (1994); THE RIGHT TO REFUSE ANTIPSYCHOTIC MEDICATION, *supra* note 7; R. SCHWITZGEBEL, LEGAL ASPECTS OF THE ENFORCED TREATMENT OF OFFENDERS (DHEW Pub. No. (ADM) 79–831, 1979); Appelbaum, *The Right to Refuse Treatment With Antipsychotic Medications: Retrospect and Prospect*, 145 AM. J. PSYCHIATRY 413 (1988); Brooks, *The Constitutional Right to Refuse Antipsychotic Medications*, 8 BULL. AM. ACAD. PSYCHIATRY & L. 179 (1980); Brooks, *The Right to Refuse Antipsychotic Medications: Law and Policy*, 39 RUTGERS L. REV. 339 (1987); Friedman, *Legal Regulation of Applied Behavior Analysis in Mental Institutions and Prisons*, 17 ARIZ. L. REV. 39, 55 (1975); Gelman, *Mental Hospital Drugs, Professionalism, and the Constitution*, 72 GEO. L.J. 1725 (1984); Gutheil, *The Right to Refuse Treatment: Paradox, Pendulum and the Quality of Care*, 4 BEHAV. SCI. & L. 265 (1986); Gutheil & Appelbaum, *"Mind Control," "Synthetic Sanity," "Artificial Competence," and Genuine Confusion: Legally Relevant Effects of Antipsychotic Medication*, 12 HOFSTRA L. REV. 77 (1983); Plotkin, *supra* note 8; Shapiro, *Legislating the Control of Behavior Control: Autonomy and the Coercive Use of Organic Therapies*, 47 S. CAL. L. REV. 237 (1974); Spece, *Conditioning and Other Technologies Used to "Treat?" "Rehabilitate?" "Demolish?" Prisoners and Mental Patients*, 45 S. CAL. L. REV. 616 (1972); Wexler, *Token and Taboo: Behavior Modification, Token Economies and the Law*, 61 CAL. L. REV. 81 (1973); Winick, *Legal Limitations on Correctional Therapy and Research*, 65 MINN. L. REV. 331 (1981) [hereinafter *Legal Limitations*]; Winick, *New Directions in the Right to Refuse Mental Health Treatment: The Implications of* Riggins v. Nevada, 2 WM. & MARY BILL OF RTS. J. 200 (1993); Winick, *The Right to Refuse Mental Health Treatment: A First Amendment Perspective*, 44 U. MIAMI L. REV. 1 (1989) [hereinafter *The Right to Refuse Mental Health Treatment*]; Winick, *supra* note 7; Comment, *Madness and Medicine: The Forcible Administration of Psychotropic Drugs*, 1980 WIS. L. REV. 497.

[18]*See, e.g.*, Appelbaum & Hoge, *Empirical Research on the Effects of Legal Policy on the Right to Refuse Treatment, in* THE RIGHT TO REFUSE ANTIPSYCHOTIC MEDICATION, *supra* note 7, at 87; Hoge et al., *The Right to Refuse Treatment Under Rogers v. Commissioner: Preliminary Empirical Findings and Comparisons*, 15 BULL. AM. ACAD. PSYCHIATRY & L. 163 (1987); Veliz & James, *Medicine Court: Rogers in Practice*, 144 AM. J. PSYCHIATRY 62 (1987); Young et al., *Treatment Refusals Among Forensic Inpatients*, 15 BULL. AM. ACAD. PSYCHIATRY & L. 5 (1987); Zito et al., *One Year Under* Rivers: *Drug Refusal in a New York State Psychiatric Facility*, 12 INT'L J.L. & PSYCHIATRY 295 (1989); Zito et al., *Clinical Characteristics of Hospitalized Psychotic Patients Who Refuse Antipsychotic Drug Therapy*, 152 AM. J. PSYCHIATRY 822 (1985). For a therapeutic jurisprudence analysis of the right suggesting areas in need of further empirical investigation, see Winick, *The Right to Refuse Treatment: A Therapeutic Jurisprudence Analysis*, 14 INT'L J.L. & PSYCHIATRY 99 (1994).

[19]Gutheil, *Legal Issues in Psychiatry, in* 2 COMPREHENSIVE TEXTBOOK OF PSYCHIATRY 2747, 2758 (H. Kaplan & B. Saddock eds., 6th ed. 1995).

[20]*See infra* chapter 3 (psychotherapy); chapter 5 (psychotropic medication. *See, e.g.*, Dautremont v. Broadlawns Hosp., 827 F.2d 291, 298 (8th Cir. 1987) (once committed to state hospital, patient may be treated with psychotropic drugs "against his wishes"); Lappe v. Lueffelholz, 815 F.2d 1173, 1176–77 (8th Cir. 1987) (once patient is hospitalized, hospital "could prescribe intramuscular injections of psychotropic medication despite [the patient's] wishes"). Until quite recently, forced medication was administered to voluntarily admitted as well as to involuntarily committed psychiatric patients. Appelbaum, *supra* note 17, at 413.

subjected involuntarily to a variety of behavior modification techniques[21] and sometimes to electroconvulsive therapy.[22] Moreover, given public attitudes toward criminals and those suffering from mental illness, it can be anticipated that the coercive application of such techniques as psychosurgery[23] and electronic stimulation of the brain[24] may seriously be advocated. Yet, unlike the treatment procedures used for most medical illnesses and conditions, a surprising lack of consensus exists within the mental health profession itself concerning the efficacy and desirability of the various techniques used to treat mental illness.[25]

Lurking in the background is the ominous specter of behavior control made possible by the coercive use of these techniques. When a society determines that an individual is mentally ill or is a criminal offender, it engages in a particularly strong form of deviance labeling. Such labeling often has the effect of depriving those so labeled of basic liberty. People determined to be mentally ill frequently are committed to psychiatric hospitals, and those convicted of crimes often are sentenced to prison. But so socially deviant are those the state labels as mentally ill and as criminals that it does not stop at labeling them and taking away their liberty. In addition, we try to change them through impositions of often intrusive treatment or "rehabilitation." For patients involuntarily institutionalized, and even more so for offenders subjected to involuntary "rehabilitation" in prison or in the community as a condition of diversion, probation, or parole, a thin line often separates treatment for mental illness from control of social deviance.[26] In the 1970s, there was growing concern that the technologies of "mind control" fictionalized in such novels as Orwell's *1984*,[27] Huxley's *A Brave New World*,[28] Burgess's *A Clockwork Orange*,[29] and Crichton's *The Terminal Man*,[30]

---

[21]*See infra* chapter 4.

[22]*See infra* chapter 6.

[23]*See infra* chapter 8.

[24]*See infra* chapter 7.

[25]*See* Ake v. Oklahoma, 470 U.S. 68, 81 (1985) ("Psychiatry is not . . . an exact science, and psychiatrists disagree widely and frequently on what constitutes mental illness, on the appropriate diagnosis to be attached to given behavior and symptoms, [and] on cure and treatment . . . ."); O'Connor v. Donaldson, 422 U.S. 563, 587 (1975) (Burger, C.J., concurring) (referring to "the wide divergence of medical opinion regarding the diagnosis of and proper therapy for mental abnormalities"); Rennie v. Klein, 462 F. Supp. 1131, 1145 (D.N.J. 1978), *modified and remanded,* 653 F.2d 836 (3d Cir. 1981) (en banc), *vacated and remanded,* 458 U.S. 1119 (1983) ("[The] lack of certainty about causation and physiopathology demonstrates the tentativeness of much psychiatric diagnosis as compared to the usual physical diagnosis. . . . [P]sychiatric diagnosis and therapy is uncertain, with great divergence of opinion in any given case."). *See generally* RESEARCH TASK FORCE OF THE NAT'L INST. OF MENTAL HEALTH, RESEARCH IN THE SERVICE OF MENTAL HEALTH (DHEW Pub. No. (ADM) 75-236, 1975) [hereinafter RESEARCH IN THE SERVICE OF MENTAL HEALTH]; J. ZISKIND, COPING WITH PSYCHIATRIC AND PSYCHOLOGICAL TESTIMONY (3d ed. 1981); Ennis & Litwack, *Psychiatry and the Presumption of Expertise: Flipping Coins in the Courtroom,* 62 CAL. L. REV. 693 (1974); Halleck, *Can We Fit the Treatment to the Patient?: Current Methodological and Theoretical Problems,* 41 BULL. MENNINGER CLINIC 303 (1977); Morse, *Crazy Behavior, Morals and Science: An Analysis of Mental Health Law,* 51 S. CAL. L. REV. 527, 558, 599, 606–07 (1978); Rosenberg, *The Crisis in Psychiatric Legitimacy: Reflections on Psychiatry, Medicine, and Public Policy, in* AMERICAN PSYCHIATRY: PAST, PRESENT, AND FUTURE 134 (G. Kriegman et al. eds., 1975); Winick, *The Right to Refuse Mental Health Treatment, supra* note 17, at 46–52.

[26]*See* G. MELTON ET AL., PSYCHOLOGICAL EVALUATIONS FOR THE COURTS: A HANDBOOK FOR MENTAL HEALTH PROFESSIONALS AND LAWYERS 35–61 (1987); WHO IS THE CLIENT? THE ETHICS OF PSYCHOLOGICAL INTERVENTION IN THE CRIMINAL JUSTICE SYSTEM (J. Monahan ed., 1980); Shestack, *Psychiatry and the Dilemmas of Dual Loyalties,* 60 A.B.A.J. 1521, 1523 (1974); Winick, *Legal Limitations, supra* note 17, at 421.

[27]G. ORWELL, 1984 (1949).

[28]A. HUXLEY, A BRAVE NEW WORLD (1931).

[29]A. BURGESS, A CLOCKWORK ORANGE (1965).

[30]M. CRICHTON, THE TERMINAL MAN (1972).

seemed nearly upon us.[31] The experience in mental hospitals and prisons in more recent years has not borne out this concern. Indeed, judicial and statutory limits on involuntary treatment[32] have significantly diminished the potential for abusive use of these techniques for social control.

Nevertheless, the concern about potential abuse continues to persist. If applied generally, the deferential approach of the Supreme Court in *Washington v. Harper*[33] could enlarge the potential for abuse. Moreover, given what seems to be an increasing shift in public attitudes against criminal offenders and those with mental illness, it is not inconceivable that social control through psychotechnology could again become a concern.

This concern should not be minimized. Advances in psychotechnology have already brought the tools of social control within the reach of government. Even though current practices may not present cause for alarm, experience has taught that the availability of tools inevitably creates a demand for their use. The psychopharmacological revolution of the past 40 years, although dramatically reducing the need for hospitalization, has made possible behavior control through medication with a potential for abuse far exceeding the "Soma" of *A Brave New World*.[34] Sophisticated application of principles of behavioral psychology and learning theory have given rise to the rapidly developing technology of behavior modification, presenting visions of state-enforced behavior control not unlike the use of reinforcement and aversive control by Big Brother in *1984* and the frightful "Ludovico Technique" by which the government "reconditioned" Alex into a model citizen in *A Clockwork Orange*.[35] Electronic stimulation of the brain, a highly experimental technique fictionalized

---

[31]*See, e.g.,* S. CHOROVER, FROM GENESIS TO GENOCIDE: THE MEANING OF HUMAN NATURE AND THE POWER OF BEHAVIOR CONTROL (1979); J. DELGADO, PHYSICAL CONTROL OF THE MIND: TOWARD A PSYCHOCIVILIZED SOCIETY (1969); P. LONDON, BEHAVIOR CONTROL (1971); NATIONAL COMMISSION FOR THE PROTECTION OF HUMAN SUBJECTS OF BIOMEDICAL AND BEHAVIORAL RESEARCH, REPORT AND RECOMMENDATIONS: PSYCHOSURGERY 65 (DHEW Pub. No. (05) 77-0001, 1977) ("Psychosurgery may be proposed [for those "involuntarily confined"] in attempts to modify behavior for social or institutional purposes not coinciding with the patient's own interests or desires."); M. PINES, THE BRAIN CHANGERS: SCIENTISTS AND THE NEW MIND CONTROL (1973); PSYCHOTECHNOLOGY: ELECTRONIC CONTROL OF MIND AND BEHAVIOR (R. Schwitzgebel ed. 1973); B. SKINNER, BEYOND FREEDOM AND DIGNITY (1971); E. VALENSTEIN, BRAIN CONTROL: A CRITICAL EXAMINATION OF BRAIN STIMULATION AND PSYCHOSURGERY (1973); STAFF OF THE SUBCOMM. ON CONSTITUTIONAL RIGHTS OF THE SENATE COMM. ON THE JUDICIARY, 93d Cong., 2d Sess., INDIVIDUAL RIGHTS AND THE FEDERAL ROLE IN BEHAVIOR MODIFICATION (1974); Chorover, *Big Brother and Psychotechnology,* PSYCHO. TODAY, Oct. 1973, at 43; Ervin, *Biological Intervention Technologies and Social Control,* 18 AM. BEHAVIOR SCI. 617 (1975); P. London, *Personal Liberty and Behavior Control Technology,* 2 HASTINGS CTR. REP., Feb. 1972, at 4; Mitford, *The Torture Cure,* HARPERS MAGAZINE, Aug. 1973, at 16; Sansweet, *Aversion Therapy: Punishing of People to Change Behavior Gains Use, Controversy,* WALL ST. J., Jan. 2, 1974, at 1.

[32]*See supra* notes 7–8.

[33]*See supra* notes 9–11 and accompanying text.

[34]Aldous Huxley wrote about "Soma," the imaginary synthetic by means of which future generations would be made both happy and docile, in his 1931 novel, BRAVE NEW WORLD. Writing in 1960, Huxley, in BRAVE NEW WORLD REVISITED, described what was then only the early stages of the modern methods of chemical persuasion, which threaten to be far more ominous than the "Soma" of BRAVE NEW WORLD. A. HUXLEY, BRAVE NEW WORLD REVISITED 89–94 (1960).

[35]*See* SKINNER, *supra* note 31; Chorover, *supra* note 31; McConnell, *Stimulus/Response: Criminals Can Be Brainwashed—Now,* PSYCHOL. TODAY 14 (Apr. 1970); Sansweet, *supra* note 31; Spece, *supra* note 17. For actual cases strikingly similar to the plight of Alex in CLOCKWISE ORANGE, see Knecht v. Gillman, 488 F.2d 1136 (8th Cir. 1973) (vomit-inducing drug in hospital aversion treatment program); Mackey v. Procunier, 477 F.2d 877 (9th Cir. 1973) (drug-inducing respiratory paralysis in prison aversion treatment program); Taylor v. Manson, No. H75137 (D. Conn., Jan. 29, 1975) (electric shocks administered to child molester's groin area while viewing slides of naked children in prison aversion treatment program). For an engaging comparison between the predictions of science fiction writers past and present and developments in the behavioral sciences, see Brodsky & Melvin, *Psy-Fi,* 5 HUMAN BEHAV. 65 (1976).

in Crichton's *The Terminal Man*, involves the implantation directly in the brain of electrical conductors that, when charged, stimulate the brain and induce the particular behavior, cognition, or sensation associated with that region of the brain.[36] Perhaps the most ominous of the technologies is psychosurgery, the controversial technique of altering behavior by destroying certain areas of the brain through direct surgical or electronic intervention.[37] Thus, a vast array of treatment technologies now exist that enable government for the first time to intrude directly and powerfully into an individual's mental processes and therefore pose a potential for abuse that cannot be ignored.

B. Populations at Risk

1. Mental Patients: In the Hospital and in the Community

Many of these treatments—the drugs, the behavioral techniques, and electroconvulsive therapy—have been shown in carefully designed clinical studies to be efficacious in the treatment of the major mental disorders. Many of these techniques have reduced patient misery and have restored millions of patients to a degree of functional normality, enabling them to resume life outside the institution. However, many of these treatments are intrusive and are experienced as distressing by patients. Most of them present a variety of unwelcome side effects, some of which are quite serious and irreversible. Moreover, some of these developing psychotechnologies are capable of altering not only specific behaviors, but the patient's personality and manner of thinking as well. Furthermore, this ominous potential will only increase: "As the knowledge of the causes and treatment of mental illness progresses, so too does the ability to treat involuntarily, to modify thoughts or behavior."[38] Thus, although these therapies may be clinically beneficial, their coercive use poses a serious threat to fundamental principles of individual autonomy and self-determination.

The potential for abuse of these techniques is at its highest for institutionalized populations. Hospitalized mental patients, particularly those committed to public institu-

---

[36]Crichton's novel describes the implantation of 40 electrodes in the brain of a violent patient for the purpose of regulating his behavior by computer. For analysis of experimentation with electronic stimulation of the brain and proposals for therapeutic applications, see DELGADO, *supra* note 31, at 171–91; PINES, *supra* note 31, at 32–54; VALENSTEIN, *supra* note 31, at 13–63, 86–114, 162–96; Heath, *Modulation of Emotion with a Brain Pacemaker,* 165 J. NERVOUS & MENTAL DISEASES 300 (1977); Ingraham & Smith, *The Use of Electronics in the Observation and Control of Human Behavior and Its Possible Use in Rehabilitation and Parole,* 7 ISSUES CRIMINOLOGY 35 (1972); Vaughan, *Psychosurgery and Brain Stimulation in Historical Perspective, in* OPERATING ON THE MIND: THE PSYCHOSURGERY CONFLICT 24, 27–29, 54–70 (W. Gaylin et al. eds., 1975).

[37]*See* V. MARK & F. ERVIN, VIOLENCE AND THE BRAIN (1970); OPERATING ON THE MIND: THE PSYCHOSURGERY CONFLICT (W. Gaylin et al., eds. 1975); S. SHUMAN, PSYCHOSURGERY AND THE MEDICAL CONTROL OF VIOLENCE: AUTONOMY AND DEVIANCE (1977); THE PSYCHOSURGERY DEBATE: SCIENTIFIC, LEGAL, AND ETHICAL PERSPECTIVES (E. Valenstein ed. 1980); VALENSTEIN, *supra* note 31, at 209–353; *Quality of Health Care—Human Experimentation: Hearings Before the Subcomm. on Health of the Senate Comm. on Labor & Pub. Welfare,* 93d Cong., 1st Sess., Pt. 2 (1973); Andy, *The Decision-Making Process in Psychosurgery,* 13 DUQ. L. REV. 783 (1975); Mark, *A Psychosurgeon's Case for Psychosurgery,* PSYCHOL. TODAY 28 (July 1974); *Symposium—Psychosurgery,* 54 B.U.L. REV. 215 (1974); Kaimowitz v. Michigan Dep't of Mental Health, Civ. No. 73-19434-AW (Mich. Cir. Ct. July 31, 1973), *excerpted at* 42 U.S.L.W. 2063 (July 31, 1973), *reprinted in* BROOKS, *supra* note 7, at 902.

[38]Roth, *The Right to Refuse Psychiatric Treatment: Law and Medicine at the Interface,* 35 EMORY L.J. 139, 140 (1986).

tions, are often poor, inarticulate, and without friends, relatives, or counsel.[39] They are vulnerable to abuse, and the abuse to which they are subjected remains relatively isolated from public scrutiny. Moreover, as a number of judicial opinions have documented, many public hospitals, understaffed and underfunded, regularly overuse and misuse psychotropic medication in flagrant disregard of the rights and welfare of their patients.[40]

The problems posed by involuntary treatment also exist for mental patients residing in the community. In the past 40 years a radical shift has occurred in the locus of mental health treatment. With the advent of psychotropic drugs, several million mental patients have been discharged from the hospital to community-based programs.[41] In 1955, 77% of all patient care episodes occurred in inpatient mental hospitals, whereas 23% were handled in outpatient settings. By 1975, the trend had reversed, with 27% of patient episodes occurring in inpatient settings, whereas 70% were dealt with through outpatient psychiatric services and 3% through day care settings.[42] The resident patient population in public mental hospitals declined from 558,922 in 1955 to 145,616 in 1979.[43] More recent estimates of the number of persons presently hospitalized on any particular day range from 100,000 to 120,000.[44] This process of deinstitutionalization has resulted in increasing numbers of former hospital patients residing and receiving treatment in nursing homes, halfway houses,

---

[39]*See* Perlin & Sadoff, *Ethical Issues in the Representation of Individuals in the Commitment Process,* 45 LAW & CONTEMP. PROBS. 161, 161 (1982).

[40]*See, e.g.,* Davis v. Hubbard, 506 F. Supp. 915, 926 (M.D. Ohio 1980) ("[T]estimony at trial established the prevalent use of drugs is countertherapeutic and can be justified only for reasons other than treatment—namely, for the convenience of staff and for punishment"); Rogers v. Okin, 478 F. Supp. 1342 (D. Mass. 1979), *aff'd in part and rev'd in part,* 634 F.2d 650 (1st Cir. 1980), *vacated sub nom.* Mills v. Rogers, 457 U.S. 291 (1982), *on remand,* 738 F.2d 1 (1st Cir. 1984); Rennie v. Klein, 476 F. Supp. 1294, 1299–1302, 1309 (D.N.J. 1979), *modified,* 653 F.2d 838 (3d Cir. 1981) (en banc), *vacated,* 458 U.S. 1119 (1982), *on remand,* 720 F.2d 266 (3d Cir. 1983). *See also* Gelman, *supra* note 17; Perlin, *Competency, Deinstitutionalization, and Homelessness: A Story of Marginalization,* 28 HOUS. L. REV. 63, 126 (1991) (referring to "public hospitals' dismal performance in the administration of antipsychotic medication").

[41]*See* Durham, *The Impact of Deinstitutionalization on the Current Treatment of the Mentally Ill,* 12 INT'L J.L. & PSYCHIATRY 117, 119–20 (1989). *See generally* L. BACHRACH, DEINSTITUTIONALIZATION: AN ANALYTICAL REVIEW AND SOCIOLOGICAL PERSPECTIVE (1976); Bassuk & Gerson, *Deinstitutionalization and Mental Health Services,* 238 SCI. AM. 46 (1978); KLERMAN, BETTER BUT NOT WELL: SOCIAL AND ETHICAL ISSUES IN THE DEINSTITUTIONALIZATION OF THE MENTALLY ILL, 3 SCHIZOPHRENIA BULL. 617 (1977). For critical perspectives on deinstitutionalization, see A. JOHNSON, OUT OF BEDLAM: THE TRUTH ABOUT DEINSTITUTIONALIZATION (1990); Arnhoff, *Social Consequences of Policy Toward Mental Illness,* 188 SCI. 1277 (1975); Durham, *supra* ; Kirk & Therrien, *Community Mental Health Myths and the Fate of Former Hospitalized Patients,* 38 PSYCHIATRY 209 (1975); Mills & Cummins, *Deinstitutionalization Reconsidered,* 5 INT'L J. L. & PSYCHIATRY 271 (1982); Perlin, *supra* note 40, at 94-112; Scull, *A New Trade in Lunacy: The Remodification of the Mental Patient,* 8 AM. BEHAV. SCI. 741 (1981); Warren, *New Forms of Social Control: The Myth of Deinstitutionalization,* 8 AM. BEHAV. SCI. 724 (1981).

[42]Klerman, *National Trends in Hospitalization,* 30 HOSP. & COMMUNITY PSYCHIATRY 110, 112 (1979). *See also* Ozarin et al., *A Quarter Century of Psychiatric Care, 1950–1974: A Statistical Review,* 27 HOSP. & COMMUNITY PSYCHIATRY 515 (1976).

[43]Shah, *Legal and Mental Health System Interactions: Major Developments and Research Needs,* 4 INT'L J. L. & PSYCHIATRY 219, 228 n.8 (1981).

[44]*See* Bachrach, *Deinstitutionalization: What Do the Numbers Mean?,* 37 HOSP. & COMMUNITY PSYCHIATRY 118 (1986) (100,000); Roth, *supra* note 38, at 142 (120,000). 1988 census data for inpatient mental hospitals from the National Institute of Mental Health showed 100,615 patients in state and county mental hospitals and 19,499 patients in Veterans Administration medical centers, CENTER FOR MENTAL HEALTH SERVICES, NAT'L INST. MENTAL HEALTH, MENTAL HEALTH, UNITED STATES 27 (table 1.5) (R. Manderscheid & M. Sonnenschein eds., 1993).

group homes, board and care facilities, and other community settings.[45] The problems raised by the involuntary application of the mental health treatment techniques therefore also exist both for these former hospital patients discharged to community treatment programs in which they are required to participate as a condition of release[46] as well as for patients who accept participation in such programs in order to avoid commitment.[47]

2. Criminal Offenders: In the Prison and in Community Programs

Involuntary treatment problems also exist for prisoners in correctional institutions as well as for offenders diverted or released to community programs, who increasingly are required to participate in rehabilitation or treatment involving these techniques. In the past 25 years, the number of community-based alternatives for the rehabilitation of offenders has

---

[45]The process of deinstitutionalization has been spurred not only by therapeutic and economic considerations, *see* Durham, *supra* note 41, at 119–20, but by constitutional requirements as well. Courts have invoked the "least restrictive alternative" principle to require the discharge of hospitalized patients to less restrictive community settings. *See, e.g.*, Lynch v. Baxley 744 F.2d 1452, 1458–59 (11th Cir. 1980); Suzuki v. Quisenberry, 411 F. Supp. 1113, 1132–33 (D. Haw. 1976); Woe v. Mathews, 408 F. Supp. 419, 429 (E.D.N.Y. 1976), *aff'd*, 562 F.2d 40 (2d Cir. 1977); Welsch v. Likens, 373 F. Supp. 487, 501–02 (D. Minn. 1974), *aff'd*, 525 F.2d 987 (8th Cir. 1975), *aff'd in part*, 550 F.2d 1182 (8th Cir. 1977), *supplemented*, 68 F.R.D. 589 (D. Minn. 1975); Wyatt v. Stickney, 344 F. Supp. 373, 379, 387, 396 (M.D. Ala. 1972), *aff'd sub nom.* Wyatt v. Aderholt, 503 F.2d 1305 (5th Cir. 1974); see O'Connor v. Donaldson, 422 U.S. 563, 575 (1975). *See generally* Chambers, *Alternatives to Civil Commitment of the Mentally Ill: Practical Guides and Constitutional Imperatives*, 70 MICH. L. REV. 1107 (1972); Hoffman & Foust, *Least Restrictive Treatment of the Mentally Ill: A Doctrine in Search of Its Senses*, 14 SAN DIEGO L. REV. 110 (1977). For analysis of the least restrictive alternative principle in the context of the right to refuse treatment, see *infra* chapter 16, part B.

[46]*See* BROOKS, *supra* note 7, at 948–51; Bursten, *Post-Hospital Mandatory Outpatient Treatment*, 143 AM. J. PSYCHIATRY 1255 (1986); Geller, *Rights, Wrongs and the Dilemma of Coerced Community Treatment*, 143 AM. J. PSYCHIATRY, 1259 (1986); *In re Richardson*, 481 A.2d 473 (D.C. App. 1989). Such mandated community treatment as a condition for release is also frequently imposed for criminal defendants hospitalized following an acquittal by reason of insanity. *E.g.*, 18 U.S.C. § 4243(f)(2)(A) & (B) (Supp. 1990) (authorizing court to order conditional discharge "under a prescribed regimen of medical, psychiatric, or psychological care or treatment"); ILL. REV. STAT. §§ 730 ILCS 5/-2-4 (1993); Bowman v. Wilson, 672 F.2d 1145, 1148 n.4 (3d Cir. 1982); Hill v. State, 358 So.2d 190, 209 (Fla. Dist. Ct. App. 1978).

[47]In many jurisdictions, as a matter of statute, commitment to a mental institution only occurs when there is no alternative treatment setting that is less restrictive and still appropriate for the patient's condition. F. HICKMAN & R. ABRAMS, PREPARATION AND TRIAL OF A CIVIL COMMITMENT CASE: PRACTICE MANUAL 34–35, 69 (1979); *e.g.*, Lynch v. Baxley, 744 F.2d 1452, 1458–59 (11th Cir. 1980); Lake v. Cameron, 364 F.2d 657 (D.C. Cir.), *cert. denied*, 382 U.S. 863 (1966); FLA. STAT. §§ 394.453, 394.459(2)(b) (1993); OHIO REV. CODE § 5122.15 (1989). Thus, the availability of a less restrictive treatment program acceptable to the patient will frequently defeat hospitalization. Moreover, courts have held that such alternatives to hospitalization must be considered at the commitment hearing under the constitutional doctrine of the "least restrictive alternative." *E.g.*, Lynch v. Baxley, 244 P.2d. at 1458–59; Covington v. Harris, 419 F.2d 617, 623 (D.C. Cir. 1969) (dicta); Stamus v. Leonhardt, 414 F. Supp. 439 (S.D. Iowa 1976); Suzuki v. Quisenberry, 411 F. Supp. 1113, 1132–33 (D. Haw. 1976); Lessard v. Schmidt, 349 F. Supp. 1078, 1103 (E.D. Wis. 1972), *vacated on other grounds*, 421 U.S. 957 (1975), *on remand*, 379 F. Supp. 1376 (E.D. Wis. 1974), *vacated on other grounds*, 421 U.S. 957 (1975), *on remand*, 413 F. Supp. 1318 (E.D. Wis. 1976); *see supra* note 45.

As a result, many patients voluntarily accept or are ordered to accept outpatient commitment in the community as a less restrictive dispositional alternative to hospitalization. *See, e.g.*, Rhode Island Dep't of Mental Health, Retardation & Hosps. v. R.B., 549 A.2d 1028 (R.I. 1988); Geller, *supra* note 46. An emerging variation on outpatient commitment is preventive commitment, in which an individual may receive outpatient commitment, often including forced medication, to prevent ultimate hospitalization, under a lesser standard than required for hospitalization. *See* Keilitz, *Empirical Studies of Involuntary Outpatient Civil Commitment: Is It Working?*, 14 MENTAL & PHYSICAL DISABILITY L. REP. 368 (1990); Stefan, *Preventive Commitment: The Concept and Its Pitfalls*, 11 MENTAL & PHYSICAL DISABILITY L. REP. 288 (1987).

increased tremendously.[48] This movement has been sparked by the failures of the existing prison system,[49] as well as by its chronic and progressive overcrowding. Moreover, there is persistent concern that prison rehabilitative efforts have not worked.[50] Increasingly, reformers have suggested smaller facilities located within the offender's home community. This suggestion is based on the hope that the offender's return can be facilitated by avoiding the isolation from the community, the severing of family ties and noncriminal associations, and the institutional culture characteristic of prison life.[51]

As a result, a system of community corrections has emerged, emphasizing the twin goals of rehabilitation and reintegration. There are expanding numbers of halfway houses, residential treatment centers, short-term and part-time custodial facilities, and other

---

[48]*See generally* ALTERNATIVES TO PRISON (G. Perlstein & T. Phelps eds., 1975); P. HAHN, COMMUNITY-BASED CORRECTIONS AND THE CRIMINAL JUSTICE SYSTEM (1975); B. MCCARTHY & B. MCCARTHY JR., COMMUNITY-BASED CORRECTIONS (1991); N. MORRIS & M. TONEY, BETWEEN PRISON AND PROBATION (1990); NEW DIRECTIONS IN THE REHABILITATION OF CRIMINAL OFFENDERS (S. Martin et al. eds., 1981); Bonta & Motiuk, *The Diversion of Incarcerated Offenders to Correctional Halfway Houses*, 24 J. CRIME & DELINQ. 302 (1987); McNew, *An Introduction to Community Corrections*, 11 HAMLINE J.L. & PUB. POL'Y 31 (1990); Petersilia, *Community Supervision: Trends and Critical Issues*, 31 CRIME & DELINQ. 339 (1985).

[49]*See, e.g.*, MCCARTHY & MCCARTHY, JR., *supra* note 48; N. MORRIS, THE FUTURE OF IMPRISONMENT 5–6 (1974); MORRIS & TONEY, *supra* note 48; W. NAGEL, THE NEW RED BARN: A CRITICAL LOOK AT AMERICAN PRISONS 138–39 (1973); PRESIDENT'S COMM'N ON LAW ENFORCEMENT & ADMINISTRATION OF JUSTICE, THE CHALLENGE OF CRIME IN A FREE SOCIETY 397 (1967) [hereinafter CHALLENGE OF CRIME]; STRUGGLE FOR JUSTICE: A REPORT ON CRIME AND PUNISHMENT IN AMERICA 23 (American Friends Service Committee 1971); Leven, *Curbing America's Addiction to Prisons*, 20 FORDHAM URB. L.J. 641, 654 (1973); Massaro, *Shame, Culture, and American Criminal Law*, 89 MICH. L. REV. 1880, 1884–88 (1990); Vitiello, *Reconsidering Rehabilitation*, 65 TUL. L. REV. 1011, 1027–29 (1991).

[50]*See* CHALLENGE OF CRIME, *supra* note 49, at 412. *See generally* D. LIPTON ET AL., THE EFFECTIVENESS OF CORRECTIONAL TREATMENT (1975); MORRIS & TONEY, *supra* note 48; Martinson, *What Works?—Questions and Answers About Prison Reform*, 35 PUB. INTEREST 22 (1974); S. REP. NO. 225, 98th Cong., 2d Sess. 51 (1984), *reprinted in* 1984 U.S.C.C.A.N. 3220, 3221 (1984); SUBCOMM. ON PENITENTIARIES AND CORRECTIONS OF THE SEN. COMM. ON THE JUDICIARY, ANNUAL REPORT, S. REP. NO. 95–909, 95th Cong., 1st Sess. (1978); Massaro, *supra* note 49, at 1884; Vitiello, *supra* note 49, at 1026; *but see* T. PALMER, CORRECTIONAL INTERVENTION AND RESEARCH 15–36 (1978). Although noting that more recent programs may show more promise, a study of offender rehabilitation performed under the auspices of the National Academy of Sciences found Lipton, Martinson, and Wilks's negative conclusions concerning the effectiveness of correctional rehabilitation "reasonably accurate and fair." *See* PANEL ON RESEARCH ON REHABILITATIVE TECHNIQUES OF THE NATIONAL RESEARCH COUNCIL, THE REHABILITATION OF CRIMINAL OFFENDERS: PROBLEMS AND PROSPECTS 5 (L. Sechrest et al. eds., 1979) [hereinafter THE REHABILITATION OF CRIMINAL OFFENDERS]. However, the study found that Palmer's "optimistic view cannot be supported." *Id.* at 31. The Panel study concluded:

> The entire body of research appears to justify only the conclusion that we do not now know of any program or method of rehabilitation that could be guaranteed to reduce the criminal activity of released offenders. Although a generous reviewer of the literature might discern some glimmers of hope, those glimmers are so few, so scattered, and so inconsistent that they do not serve as a basis for any recommendation other than continued research.

Id. at 3. For a critical analysis of the evaluation literature finding most studies inadequate for failure to measure the "strength" or intensity of the treatment or its "integrity" or consistency in administration, see Sechrest & Redner, *Strength and Integrity in Evaluation Studies, in* HOW WELL DOES IT WORK: A REVIEW OF CRIMINAL JUSTICE EVALUATION 1978 (1978).

[51]*See* MORRIS, *supra* note 49, at 384–98; E. ROTMAN, A NEW VIEW ON THE REHABILITATION OF THE CRIMINAL OFFENDER 154–60 (1990); Bonta & Gendreau, *Reexamining the Cruel and Unusual Punishment of Prison Life*, 14 LAW & HUM. BEHAV. 347, 347–48, 366 (1990); Holbert & Call, *The Perspective of State Correctional Officials on Prison Overcrowding: Causes, Court Orders, and Solutions*, 53 FED. PROB. 25, 29 (1989); Leven, *supra* note 49, at 654.

community-based placements as alternatives to total incarceration.[52] Defendants increasingly have been diverted from the criminal justice system at entry point and redirected toward a variety of community treatment settings—drug rehabilitation programs, community mental health clinics, state mental hospitals, sex offender programs, alcohol treatment programs, and day treatment centers.[53] Indeed, major portions of the criminal justice system have undergone a "process of divestment," in which whole classes of socially deviant individuals find themselves in the control of a new "therapeutic state" rather than the traditional penal process.[54] It has even been suggested that judges be permitted to sentence convicted defendants to the custody of the government for treatment and rehabilitation.[55] These developments have been accelerated by more extensive use of probation[56] and by the expansion of early or partial release programs, such as work-release, educational release, furloughs, contract parole, and other early parole programs, all of which are frequently tied to some form of community-based treatment.[57]

---

[52]*See generally* NATIONAL PRETRIAL INTERVENTION SERVICE CENTER OF THE ABA COMM'N ON CORRECTIONAL FACILITIES AND SERVICES, PRETRIAL CRIMINAL JUSTICE INTERVENTIONAL TECHNIQUES AND ACTION PROGRAMS (2d ed. 1975); R. NIMMER, DIVERSION: THE SEARCH FOR ALTERNATIVE FORMS OF PROSECUTION (1974); Carter, *The Diversion of Offenders*, 36 FED. PROB. 31 (1972); Vorenberg & Vorenberg, *Early Diversion from the Criminal Justice System, in* PRISONERS IN AMERICA 151 (L. Ohlin ed., 1973); Note, *Pretrial Diversion from the Criminal Process*, 83 YALE L.J. 827 (1974). The Federal Law Enforcement Assistance Administration has aided the movement toward early diversion by providing federal funding for the development of community corrections programs. Vorenberg & Vorenberg, *supra,* at 163.

[53]For a comprehensive bibliography concerning alternatives to institutionalization, see J. BRANTLEY, ALTERNATIVES TO INSTITUTIONALIZATION: A DEFINITIVE BIBLIOGRAPHY (1979).

[54]*See generally* N. KITTRIE, THE RIGHT TO BE DIFFERENT: DEVIANCE AND ENFORCED THERAPY (1971); *see* C. KIESLER & A. SIBULKIN, MENTAL HOSPITALIZATION: MYTHS AND FACTS ABOUT A NATIONAL CRISIS 19 (1987); Arrigo, *The Logic of Identity and the Politics of Justice: Establishing a Right to Community–Based Treatment for the Institutionalized Mentally Disabled*, 18 CRIM. & CIV. CONFINEMENT 1, 24 (1992); Weithorn, *Mental Hospitalization of Troublesome Youth: An Analysis of Skyrocketing Admission Rates*, 40 STAN. L. REV. 773 (1988); Wexler, *Therapeutic Justice*, 57 MINN. L. REV. 289 (1972). For critical perspectives on the diversion and deinstitutionalization process, see A. SCULL, DECARCERATION: COMMUNITY TREATMENT AND THE DEVIANT: A RADICAL VIEW (1977); Szasz, *Psychiatric Diversion in the Criminal Justice System, in* MENTALLY ILL OFFENDERS AND THE CRIMINAL JUSTICE SYSTEM 54 (N. Beran & B. Toomey eds., 1979). In recent years, there has been a decline in the "rehabilitative ideal" in corrections. *See generally* F. ALLEN, THE DECLINE OF THE REHABILITATIVE IDEAL: PENAL POLICY AND SOCIAL PURPOSE (1981); Burt, *Cruelty, Hypocrisy, and the Rehabilitative Ideal in Corrections,* 16 INT'L J.L. & PSYCHIATRY 359 (1993). Frustration with the failures of the rehabilitative ideal, the burgeoning of the prison population, and other social forces may already have combined to replace the "therapeutic state" with what Malcolm Feeley and Jonathan Simon have termed *the new penology*, emphasizing not the individual offender, but the actuarial consideration of aggregates. *See* Feeley & Simon, *The New Penology: Notes on the Emerging Strategy of Corrections and its Implications*, 30 CRIMINOLOGY 449 (1992).

[55]Former Chief Justice Burger has advocated a system in which "the 'guilty' defendant could be committed by the trial judge to the custody of the government for an indeterminate period for such medical treatment, psychiatric therapy, discipline, and vocational training as would help him and rehabilitate and restore him to a useful life." *See* Spece, *supra* note 17, at 617.

[56]*See* United States v. Stine, 675 F.2d 69 (3d Cir.), *cert. denied*, 458 U.S. 1110 (1982) (upholding a requirement of psychological counseling as a condition of probation); United States v. Marcado, 469 F.2d 1148, 1152–53 (2d Cir. 1972) (court may condition probation on offender's application for treatment); Moore v. United States, 387 A.2d 714, 716 (D.C. 1978) (probation conditioned on mental examination).

[57]*See, e.g.*, Washington v. Harper, 494 U.S. 210 (1990) (psychiatric treatment imposed as a condition of parole); D. CHAMPION, PROBATION AND PAROLE IN THE UNITED STATES (1990); ABA ADVISORY COMM. ON SENTENCING AND REVIEW STANDARDS RELATING TO PROBATION § 3.2(c)(v) (tentative draft 1970); ROTMAN, *supra* note 51, at 119, 155–65; SCULL, *supra* note 54, at 45–49. *See generally* L. CARNEY, PROBATION AND PAROLE: LEGAL AND SOCIAL DIMENSIONS (1977); Bonta & Motiuk, *Classification to Halfway Houses: A Quasi Experimental Evaluation*, 28 CRIMINOLOGY 497, 498 (1990); Leven, *supra* note 49, at 654.

As a result of these developments in the criminal process, an enormous potential for abuse has emerged as relatively innocuous counseling programs have been replaced, both in the prison and in the community, with increasingly more sophisticated rehabilitative programs that use medication, behavior modification, and other controversial therapies.[58] Whether these alternative programs are more effective than traditional penal incarceration is an empirical question that has received increasing attention by social scientists.[59] Although the empirical issues remain unresolved, the demand for these alternative programs accelerates and new, experimental approaches are proposed and attempted. In fact, a survey conducted in the late 1970s[60] revealed that 71% of the public favored research to develop tests that predict violent behavior, and 64% favored the coercive administration to violent offenders of a hypothetical drug presumed to prevent violence.[61] An additional 10% of the public opposed forced medication but favored the availability of such a drug as an alternative to prison.[62] Given the increasing public concern with crime, public opinion may now favor such coercive interventions by an even wider margin.

Apart from the use of the various treatment techniques for correctional rehabilitation, the risk of their use in institutional management seems likely to increase under the pressures of prison overcrowding. The risk is particularly high for psychotropic drugs, which have a tranquilizing effect and are easy to administer coercively. The Supreme Court's 1990 decision in *Washington v. Harper*[63] upheld the use of antipsychotic drugs in a state prison to treat a mentally ill inmate found dangerous to himself and others within the institution. The Court stressed that under the prison policy at issue, in addition to serving institutional needs in ensuring safety to other inmates and prison staff, the treatment authorized must also be in the prisoner's medical interests.[64] Although the Court emphasized that under the policy ''[t]he drugs may be administered for no purpose other than treatment,''[65] there is danger that this limitation will be ignored in understaffed institutions or that ''treatment'' will be

---

[58]The potential for abuse seemed especially high in the 1970s. *See* J. ABBOT, IN THE BELLY OF THE BEAST 42 (1982) (describing the use of tranquilizers for disciplinary reasons); J. MITFORD, KIND AND USUAL PUNISHMENT (1973); R. ROSS & B. MCKAY, EFFECTIVE CORRECTIONAL TREATMENT 40 (1980); ROTMAN, *supra* note 51, at 102–05; D. WEXLER, MENTAL HEALTH LAW: MAJOR ISSUES 17–18 (1981); Delgado, *Organically Induced Behavioral Change in Correctional Institutions: Release Decisions and ''New Man'' Phenomenon*, 50 S. CAL. L. REV. 215, 217–18, 223–38 (1977); Halleck, *Psychiatry and Social Control, in* MENTALLY ILL OFFENDERS AND THE CRIMINAL JUSTICE SYSTEM, *supra* note 54, at 24; Opton, *Psychiatric Violence Against Prisoners: When Therapy is Punishment*, 45 MISS. L.J. 605 (1974); D. Rothman, *Behavior Modification in Total Institutions*, 5 HASTINGS CTR. REP., Feb. 1975, at 17; Spece, *supra* note 17. Although the abuses of the 1970s seem to have subsided in recent years, the use of psychotropic medication in prison and community programs has increased dramatically and may continue to do so in the wake of the Supreme Court's decision in Washington v. Harper, 494 U.S. 210 (1990), upholding the involuntary administration of antipsychotic drugs in a state prison. *See infra* notes 63–69 and accompanying text. Moreover, the increasing shift in public attitude against offenders makes future abuses a distinct possibility.

[59]*E.g.*, P. LERMAN, COMMUNITY TREATMENT AND SOCIAL CONTROL (1975); NEW DIRECTIONS IN THE REHABILITATION OF CRIMINAL OFFENDERS, *supra* note 48.

[60]The survey was conducted through the NATIONAL COMM'N FOR THE PROTECTION OF HUMAN SUBJECTS OF BIOMEDICAL AND BEHAVIORAL RESEARCH, SPECIAL STUDY: IMPLICATIONS OF ADVANCES IN BIOMEDICAL AND BEHAVIORAL RESEARCH (1978) [hereinafter SPECIAL STUDY].

[61]Policy Research Inc. & Center for Technology Assessment, *A Comprehensive Study of the Ethical, Legal, and Social Implications of Advances in Biomedical and Behavioral Research and Technology, in* SPECIAL STUDY, *supra* note 60, at 174.

[62]*Id.*

[63]494 U.S. 210 (1990).

[64]*Id.* at 222 & n.8, 227–28. For further discussion of this ''therapeutic appropriateness principle,'' see *infra* chapter 16, part A.

[65]494 U.S. at 226.

defined expansively and inappropriately. This danger is magnified by the Court's deferential approach in the prison context. Stressing that "prison authorities are best equipped to make difficult decisions regarding prison administration"[66] and invoking "the 'policy of judicial restraint regarding prisoner complaints',"[67] the Court adopted a deferential approach for reviewing constitutional claims in the prison context. Under this approach, which the Court invoked in *Harper*, in order "[t]o ensure that courts afford appropriate deference to prison officials, . . . prison regulations alleged to infringe constitutional rights are judged under a 'reasonableness' test less restrictive than that ordinarily applied to alleged infringements of fundamental constitutional rights. . . ."[68] This language signals the lower courts not to second-guess prison authorities and insulates from effective review abuses that can be characterized as responses " 'reasonably related to legitimate penological interests.' "[69] The Court's decision in *Harper* and the deferential approach it reflects may have the effect of expanding the use of psychotropic drugs in the prison and perhaps in community programs as well, as a means of dealing with "dangerousness."

C. Questions for Analysis and a Road Map of the Project

Several important issues are raised by the involuntary administration of mental health treatment techniques to both civil patients and criminal offenders. The most fundamental issue is whether patients and offenders have a right to refuse any of the treatment techniques, and if so, which ones. This book surveys the various treatment techniques, focusing on their benefits as well as the potential for abuse they present. It then analyzes the constitutional issues raised by the general practice of involuntarily subjecting patients and offenders to these treatments.

Part II (chapters 2–8) presents an extensive description and analysis of the various mental health treatment techniques. An attempt is made to classify these techniques along a proposed continuum of intrusiveness, which I believe presents a useful means of probing the constitutional issues that are raised. The proposed continuum framework is described in chapter 2. In order to construct the continuum, chapters 3 through 8 describe, for each of the treatment techniques, the origins, methods of application, theoretical underpinnings, and effectiveness of the various therapies. These chapters also explore the extent of the coercive application of these techniques in hospital, community, and correctional settings, their potential for abuse, their primary and side effects for unwilling recipients, and their resulting degree of "intrusiveness."

The proposed continuum ranks the therapies from least to most intrusive. It starts with psychotherapy and other verbal techniques (chapter 3) and proceeds to the behavioral treatment techniques (chapter 4). It then considers psychotropic medication (chapter 5), electroconvulsive treatment (chapter 6), and finally the most intrusive of the techniques, electrical stimulation of the brain (chapter 7) and psychosurgery (chapter 8).

Part III (chapters 9–16) presents an extensive constitutional analysis of the issues raised by the involuntary application of these treatment techniques. Chapter 9 contains a brief description of the potential sources creating legal limitations on governmentally imposed therapy—statutory, regulatory, international law, and judicial. The most important of these

---

[66]*Id.* at 224 (citing Turner v. Safley, 482 U.S. 78, 84–85 (1987) and Jones v. North Carolina Prisoners' Labor Union, Inc., 433 U.S. 119, 128 (1977)).

[67]*Id.* (quoting *Turner*, 482 U.S. at 85).

[68]*Id.* (quoting O'Lone v. Estate of Shabazz, 482 U.S. 342, 349 (1987)).

[69]*Id.* at 223–24 (quoting *Turner*, 482 U.S. at 89).

sources, at least while the right to refuse treatment is still in the early stages of development, is the judiciary, and the most important source of judge-made law in this area is the federal Constitution and its state counterparts. A growing body of recent case law[70] and commentary[71] deals with the developing constitutional right of mental patients to refuse certain types of mental health treatment. Although the Supreme Court's recent decisions in *Washington v. Harper*[72] and *Riggins v. Nevada*[73] recognize that involuntary medication may implicate a constitutionally protected liberty interest, they do not explore the nature of that interest and leave unresolved many of the substantive and procedural constitutional questions raised by involuntary treatment.[74]

These open questions include the extent to which several general constitutional limits may apply: the First Amendment, which protects a right to be free from interference with mental processes; the right to privacy, personal security, and individual autonomy protected by the Due Process Clause of the Fourteenth Amendment; and the Eighth Amendment's ban on cruel and unusual punishments. Several more limited constitutional restrictions also may apply. In the case of treatment refusal on religious grounds, the First Amendment's protection of the free exercise of religion may impose limitations on governmental action. Additionally, in view of the legal right of physically ill patients to resist unwanted treatment, the general state hospital practice of involuntarily treating those diagnosed with mental illness may not survive scrutiny under the Equal Protection Clause of the Fourteenth Amendment.

This part of the book explores each of the constitutional provisions that may be invoked to restrict involuntary treatment. The origins, underlying values, conditions for applicability, and standards for reviewing asserted violations of each of these constitutional limitations are analyzed in order to determine the extent to which each may provide protection against coercive application of the various treatment techniques. As is demonstrated, the relevant constitutional rights, considered separately in chapters 10–14, differ with regard to the conditions for their application. As a result, each of the various treatment techniques requires separate analysis to determine which, if any, implicate the different constitutional provisions.

Even if one or more of these constitutional rights is burdened by a particular therapy, the question remains whether the government interests furthered by imposing treatment outweigh the individual's constitutional right to refuse it. Constitutional rights are not absolute and may be outweighed in appropriate circumstances by overriding governmental interests. Chapter 15 analyzes prior Supreme Court cases dealing with the right to refuse treatment, discussing *Harper* and *Riggins* and their implications for the many questions they leave unresolved. These cases suggest that different levels of constitutional scrutiny will be applied in the differing civil and correctional contexts in which involuntary treatment is sought to be imposed. This chapter attempts to identify the appropriate standard of scrutiny to be applied in each of these contexts.

Once the appropriate constitutional standard is identified for each treatment technique and for each context in which it is administered, the question becomes whether and when involuntary treatment will satisfy the applicable test. Chapter 15 analyzes the relevant governmental interests asserted to be furthered by involuntary treatment in each treatment

---

[70]*See supra* note 7.
[71]*See supra* notes 17–18.
[72]494 U.S. 210 (1990).
[73]504 U.S. 127 (1992).
[74]*See supra* notes 9–16 and accompanying text.

context, and the extent to which these interests can justify invasion of the applicable constitutional rights. These governmental interests may be subsumed within either the state's traditional police power or its *parens patriae* power. In the case of civil mental patients, this chapter explores the extent to which the state's police power interest in protecting other patients and hospital staff from harm can justify involuntary treatment, as well as the extent to which such treatment can be justified by the state's *parens patriae* interest in promoting the well-being of the patient.

Involuntary treatment in the correctional context raises different questions in view of the differing standards of scrutiny and differing state interests involved in rehabilitating offenders and managing prisons. Does a right to refuse treatment apply to offenders ordered to participate in prison or community treatment programs? Can judges sentence offenders to treatment in lieu of prison or as a condition of probation? Can parole boards condition parole on participation in these therapy programs? Can correctional authorities require prisoners to participate simply as part of their confinement? Does a right to refuse treatment apply to criminal defendants found incompetent to stand trial or acquitted by reason of insanity? Can the state's *parens patriae* power be invoked in the context of criminal offenders? Chapter 15 addresses these questions.

If the constitutional right burdened by involuntary treatment is ranked as "fundamental," the courts may closely scrutinize not only the state interests asserted to justify the intrusion, but also the means chosen to accomplish these interests. When is mental health treatment an impermissible means to accomplish the state's interests? Chapter 16 analyzes language in the Supreme Court's opinions in *Harper* and *Riggins* stating that antipsychotic medication may be forcibly administered only when it is medically justified. It suggests that this language reflects a newly crystallized constitutional limit on the government's mental health powers—the therapeutic appropriateness principle. Under this principle, the state may insist on involuntary treatment only when it is appropriate for the individual's condition.

Even when the treatment in question would be therapeutically appropriate, it may be impermissible if other treatment approaches or means other than treatment can accomplish the state's interests. Under traditional constitutional analysis applicable to governmental action burdening fundamental rights, courts will insist that the means used by the state be less intrusive with respect to the constitutional values at stake than alternative means that would accomplish the state's purposes. Chapter 16 also analyzes this "least intrusive alternative" principle of constitutional adjudication and its application in the context of involuntary mental health treatment.

A comprehensive constitutional analysis of all of the varying treatment techniques is attempted, using the continuum of intrusiveness framework developed in part II of the book. There are dangers in leaving development of a right to refuse treatment to *ad hoc* judicial decision making, which typically occurs in the context of cases raising especially abusive applications of the more intrusive of these techniques. Such *ad hoc* decision making may develop generalized and artificial approaches that may have the effect of skewing clinical practice. A therapist should consider several possible therapeutic approaches in the treatment of a particular patient, often in combination. In light of the current state of our knowledge concerning mental disorder and its treatment, clinicians should be flexible, eclectic, and empirical in orientation, tailoring their treatment approaches to the individual patient. Judicial or legislative limitations on some but not all of the therapies could affect clinical decision making in ways that might be countertherapeutic.[75] A comprehensive

---

[75]*See* Goldiamond, *Singling Out Behavior Modification for Legal Regulation: Some Effects on Patient Care, Psychotherapy, and Research in General*, 17 ARIZ. L. REV. 105, 111–15 (1975).

approach to these issues, considering the various alternative therapies, therefore is required. Requiring that intrusive treatment conform to the therapeutic appropriateness principle and the least intrusive means principle can help to achieve this objective.

Part III (chapters 17–20) contains an evaluation of the right to refuse treatment and an analysis of various means of implementing the right. Apart from the constitutional issues, but by no means irrelevant to their resolution, is the question of whether recognizing a right to refuse treatment would have therapeutic value. Will a patient given the right to refuse (and as a result the power to choose to accept) treatment benefit by exercising choice concerning treatment, rather than being its passive recipient? Chapter 17 conducts a therapeutic jurisprudence[76] analysis of the right to refuse treatment, concluding that if properly implemented, such a right could actually further the therapeutic objectives of mental health treatment and effect a restructuring of the therapist–patient relationship that could increase its therapeutic potential.

In analyzing issues relating to the implementation of the right to refuse treatment, it is useful to distinguish between those who assent to treatment and thereby waive whatever right they may have to refuse it (chapter 18) and those who object to treatment and invoke a right to refuse (chapter 19). Not all patients or offenders, of course, will wish to exercise a right to refuse treatment. Indeed, it can be predicted that most will accept recommended treatment, thereby waiving any right they may possess to refuse it. Chapter 18 analyzes the waiver issues presented when patients and offenders consent to treatment. What legal requirements should be applied to measure the validity of such waivers, and what procedures (if any) should be followed to assess the satisfaction of the requirements? As will be seen, these requirements for the valid waiver of rights parallel the requirements of the informed consent doctrine. Do patients and offenders have the capacity to give informed consent to treatments they may have a right to refuse? Does mental illness so impair decision-making capacity that patients should be deemed incompetent to provide informed consent to treatment? Should the consent of such patients to treatment be accepted at face value, or should an inquiry into competency be mandated? Should competence be presumed for those with mental illness? How should competence be defined in the context of individuals seeking to accept mental health treatment? What information do therapists need to provide their patients in order to permit consent to be informed? Are mental hospitals and correctional facilities so inherently coercive that the consent of their residents can never be deemed truly voluntary? Chapter 18 analyzes these issues, the requirements of the informed

---

[76]*See generally* D. WEXLER & B. WINICK, ESSAYS IN THERAPEUTIC JURISPRUDENCE (1991); B. WINICK, THERAPEUTIC JURISPRUDENCE APPLIED: ESSAYS ON MENTAL HEALTH LAW (1996); LAW IN A THERAPEUTIC KEY: DEVELOPMENTS IN THERAPEUTIC JURISPRUDENCE (D. Wexler & B. Winick eds., 1996); SYMPOSIUM—THERAPEUTIC JURISPRUDENCE: RESTRUCTURING MENTAL DISABILITY LAW, 10 N.Y.L. SCH. J. HUM. RTS. 623–926 (1993); THERAPEUTIC JURISPRUDENCE: THE LAW AS A THERAPEUTIC AGENT (D. Wexler ed., 1990); Wexler & Winick, *The Potential of Therapeutic Jurisprudence: A New Approach to Psychology and Law, in* LAW AND PSYCHOLOGY: THE BROADENING OF THE DISCIPLINE 211 (J. Ogloff ed., 1992); Wexler & Winick, *Therapeutic Jurisprudence as a New Approach to Mental Health Law Policy Analysis and Research*, 45 U. MIAMI L. REV. 979 (1991). For bibliographies of therapeutic jurisprudence work, see *Bibliography, in* LAW IN A THERAPEUTIC KEY: DEVELOPMENTS IN THERAPEUTIC JURISPRUDENCE, *supra; Bibliography of Therapeutic Jurisprudence*, 10 N.Y.L. SCH. J. HUM. RTS. 915 (1993).

consent doctrine, and the possibility for the satisfaction of these requirements in the context of mental health and correctional therapy.[77]

If instead of consenting to treatment, a patient or offender objects to it, what kind of hearing is required when the government seeks to impose treatment over objection? If patients or offenders resist treatment, what do Fifth and Fourteenth Amendment procedural due process protections require? What should be the scope and structure of a hearing in this situation? When mental patients' conditions render them incompetent to make decisions with respect to treatment, how should such decisions be made? Chapter 19 deals with procedural due process requirements for treatment refusal in these contexts, analyzing whether formal judicial adversarial hearings are required or whether more informal administrative proceedings suffice. Chapter 19 also analyzes ways of making such hearings more therapeutic for patients and suggests greater use of negotiation and mediation approaches that in many cases can be used to resolve disputes in this area without the need for more formal hearings.

Finally, a concluding chapter (chapter 20) analyzes the future of the right to refuse treatment. Can individuals facing a potential future problem with respect to involuntary treatment engage in advance planning and decision making through the use of an advance directive instrument? The popularity of the ''living will'' has produced adaptations in which individuals have increasingly executed such advance directive instruments governing their health care, and health care proxies in which a trusted relative or friend is designated as decision maker for the individual in the event of future incompetence. To what extent can such instruments be used in the context of mental health treatment? May individuals in a competent state make decisions that will be binding during a future period when mental illness may impair their competency to decide? If enforceable, may such instruments be revocable by a patient of reduced competency who now seeks to accept treatment previously refused in the instrument, or to refuse treatment previously consented to? Chapter 20 examines the use of advance directive instruments in the mental health treatment area. If enforceable, these instruments obviously will play an important role in shaping the future of the right to refuse treatment.

Right-to-refuse-treatment issues ultimately must be dealt with through ethical and professional standards governing the imposition of mental health and correctional treatment. Constitutional limits on therapy, a major focus of the book, can only mark the boundaries

---

[77]Somewhat parallel problems to those presented by the right to refuse treatment are raised by research performed with mental patients and criminal offenders. Not only are these populations subjected to involuntary treatment, but they frequently are required to participate in a variety of research programs. Mental health and correctional researchers need to perform studies with these populations, examining the efficacy of existing treatment techniques and of new experimental approaches and testing the validity of new hypotheses concerning the causes, prevention, and treatment of mental illness and criminality. Unfortunately, volunteers for such research are sometimes not available. Moreover, even when available, their consent and full knowledge could bias the sample or methodology, precluding scientifically adequate conclusions. Such research, if it is to be performed at all, must therefore frequently be conducted on an involuntary basis or with less than the full disclosure generally thought necessary for informed consent. Can research with human participants be performed on this basis? In a prior article that preliminarily addressed several of the issues in this book, I also explored the substantive constitutional limits on mental health and correctional research, analyzing whether patients and offenders have a right to resist participation in such research and the conditions for waiver of such a right. Winick, *Legal Limitations, supra* note 17. This article also analyzed the procedural due process requirements that must be met before such research may be performed. In my view, sufficient similarities between research and treatment issues exist that the continuum of intrusiveness framework developed for use in the treatment context will prove useful for resolving the constitutional issues raised by involuntary research as well. Further analysis of the constitutional limits on governmental research involving patients and offenders is beyond the scope of this book.

within which mental health and correctional personnel may operate. By their nature, such boundaries must be rather generalized and somewhat vague. Professional and ethical controls are thus important and in any event more desirable and often more effective than legal controls. Chapter 20 concludes with a preliminary analysis of professional and ethical standards in this area. It recommends that deficiencies in existing professional controls be examined by clinicians and that more detailed professional and ethical standards be developed in this area.

D. An Interdisciplinary Therapeutic Jurisprudence Approach

The issues discussed in this book are at the cutting edge of psychiatry, clinical psychology, psychopharmacology, bioethics, and law. Moreover, they reflect the traditionally differing perspectives of the principal professional disciplines involved—law, psychiatry, and psychology. Clinicians, alarmed at the early right-to-refuse-treatment cases, warned of the collapse of the public mental health system, predicting that patients who refused treatment would soon fill state hospital wards, "rotting with their rights on."[78] Lawyers, on the other hand, advocated the right as the last hope for revitalizing decaying and often detrimental state mental institutions and fulfilling the promise of appropriate treatment with dignity for their inhabitants.[79] Perhaps predictably, neither of these polar views has prevailed.[80]

The complexities of the issues can only give way when the dialogue is shorn of rhetoric. The participants must learn to speak each other's language and understand the values and perspectives of each discipline. By carefully examining both the clinical and legal issues, this book attempts an interdisciplinary therapeutic jurisprudence approach[81] to these complex questions. Moreover, because both clinicians and lawyers working in this area must have a comprehensive understanding of issues outside of their respective disciplines, the analysis is detailed and extensive footnoting is provided, allowing the reader to have access to materials that may otherwise be difficult to identify or obtain. It is hoped that this interdisciplinary approach will shape the right to refuse treatment into an instrument that will both respect patient dignity and autonomy and advance therapeutic goals.

---

[78]*See, e.g.,* Gutheil, *In Search of True Freedom: Drug Refusal, Involuntary Medication, and "Rotting with Your Rights On,"* 137 AM. J. PSYCHIATRY 327 (1980) (editorial); *see also* Gutheil, *supra* note 19, at 2178 (describing the right to refuse treatment as a "clinical issue disguised as a rights issue").

[79]*See, e.g.,* Cole, *Patients' Rights v. Doctors' Rights: Which Should Take Precedence, in* REFUSING TREATMENT IN MENTAL HEALTH INSTITUTIONS—VALUES IN CONFLICT 56–73 (A. Doudera & J. Swazey eds., 1982); Dix, *Realism and Drug Refusal: A Reply to Appelbaum and Gutheil,* 9 BULL. AM. ACAD. PSYCHIATRY & L. 180 (1981).

[80]Appelbaum, *supra* note 17, at 418.

[81]*See supra* note 76.

Part I

Mental Health
Treatment Techniques

Chapter 2
A CONTINUUM OF INTRUSIVENESS

Neither the constitutional issues raised by the involuntary application of the various mental health treatment techniques nor questions concerning the need for the regulation of these treatments can be effectively considered without a separate detailed analysis of each of the treatment modalities used in modern clinical practice. Some of the treatment refusal cases suggest the existence of a broad right to refuse treatment supported by a number of constitutional sources. However, it is neither helpful nor appropriate to conceptualize the right in such a broad fashion. The various forms of rehabilitation or treatment in question present certain common legal issues when applied coercively, but the various techniques differ markedly in ways that bear significantly on the constitutional and public policy issues presented.

In the chapters that follow in part I, each of the major techniques is examined separately. Each is described in terms of its origins, methods of application, theoretical underpinnings, and effectiveness. For each of the treatment techniques, particular attention is given to the extent to which each has been used coercively; its potential for abuse; the extent of any physical or mental intrusions accompanying its application; the nature, extent, and duration of its effects on patients; and the extent to which patients may avoid or resist such effects.

The various techniques used in the treatment of mental disorders and in the rehabilitation of criminal offenders present differing indices of what I shall call *intrusiveness*. Depending on its intrusiveness, each treatment technique merits differing legal responses. Some of the techniques, for example, may raise First Amendment issues. Some may raise constitutional privacy or substantive due process concerns. Certain techniques may implicate some but not other constitutional guarantees. Some may not present sufficient physical or mental intrusions to violate any constitutional prohibition but may nonetheless require that some kind of hearing be afforded or procedure followed before they may be applied involuntarily. For constitutional purposes, a certain threshold of intrusiveness may be posited that must be exceeded before assertion of a constitutional right requires consideration. Indeed, differing thresholds, defined by reference to the nature and effects of the technique used, may be necessary to trigger different constitutional provisions.

It is useful to attempt to construct a continuum of ''intrusiveness'' along which the various treatment methods may roughly be classified. Only at particular points on the continuum are certain of the constitutional provisions implicated. The continuum framework thus avoids singular, all-encompassing answers, reflecting instead a recognition that the balance between governmental interests and the individual rights of patients or offenders may be struck differently for particular treatment approaches.

Constitutional rights, even those ranked as ''fundamental,'' are not absolute, and inappropriate circumstances must yield to government regulation advancing compelling state interests.[1] Thus, even for those techniques that present sufficient intrusions to merit constitutional consideration, governmental interest in imposing treatment may be sufficiently strong in some instances to outweigh patients' or offenders' assertion of a

---

[1]*See infra* chapter 15.

constitutional right to resist. The inevitable balancing between government and individual interests that courts, legislatures, and administrators are called on to perform in resolving these questions will be facilitated by the continuum framework.

If a therapy invades a fundamental constitutional right, the government, in order to impose it involuntarily, may have to satisfy not only the compelling-state-interest test but also the "least restrictive alternative" principle. In the treatment context, this principle presumably would require demonstration that the particular therapy in question is generally necessary to accomplish the government's compelling interest.[2] Under this analysis, the availability of alternative therapies that are less intrusive but equally efficacious and feasible may prevent the government from imposing a more intrusive therapy. Indeed, good medical practice, and arguably medical ethics as well, would seem inconsistent with applying a more intrusive therapy when an equally efficacious, less intrusive alternative is available.[3] The proposed continuum of intrusiveness thus also is useful in applying the least restrictive alternative principle in contexts in which it is found to be constitutionally required, as well as in those in which it is deemed to be required by principles of tort law or of professional ethics.

The Supreme Court has not authoritatively decided whether the least restrictive alternative principle applies to involuntary treatment. In dicta, the Court suggested its application in the context of antipsychotic medication administered involuntarily to a criminal defendant during the pretrial and trial process.[4] However, the Court also has rejected application of the principle in the context of involuntary medication administered in prison, applying instead a less rigid balancing test.[5] Even where the least restrictive alternative principle is rejected, the continuum framework will be useful in assessing the reasonableness of government application of involuntary therapy. Indeed, even in contexts in which the courts apply a deferential "professional judgment" approach, as some lower courts have in the treatment refusal area, the continuum framework may be useful. To the extent that standards of professional practice embrace a form of the less restrictive alternative principle, the principle thereby will be at least partially absorbed into standards of constitutional review and also into principles of tort law, which impose a duty on physicians and other treatment professionals to apply the prevailing standard of care in the community.[6] Whatever the standard of judicial scrutiny, the continuum framework is therefore helpful in gauging the relative intrusiveness of the treatment method applied, and hence its reasonableness.

After analyzing the substantive aspects of the right to refuse treatment along the proposed continuum of intrusiveness, issues related to informed consent and procedural due process are also examined in light of the continuum framework. As with the substantive right-to-refuse-treatment issues, these more procedural questions are resolved differently at

---

[2]*See infra* chapter 16, part B.

[3]*See* T. BEAUCHAMP & J. CHILDRESS, PRINCIPLES OF BIOMEDICAL ETHICS 20 (2d ed. 1983) ("[W]henever there is a choice between different but equally efficacious methods of treatment, patients' benefits should be maximized and their costs and risks minimized. Any other approach would rightly be regarded as an unethical practice."); *id.* at 159 (principles of beneficence and nonmaleficence require balancing of "possible benefits against possible harms in order to maximize benefits and minimize risks of harm."). *See also infra* chapter 20, part B.

[4]Riggins v. Nevada, 504 U.S. 127, 134 (1992) (dicta).

[5]Washington v. Harper, 494 U.S. 210, 223–24 (1990) (applying a "standard of reasonableness" in evaluating the constitutionality of a prison policy authorizing involuntary medication, asking whether it is "reasonably related to legitimate penological interests."). In further elaborating on its "reasonableness" standard, the Court noted that " 'the absence of ready alternatives is evidence of the reasonableness of a prison regulation,' but this does not mean that prison officials 'have to set up and then shoot down every conceivable alternative method of accommodating the claimant's constitutional complaint.' " *Id.* at 226 (quoting Turner v. Safley, 482 U.S. 78, 90–91 (1987)).

[6]*See infra* chapter 9, part D.

different points along the continuum. In general, the more intrusive the treatment, the more procedural protections will be required before its involuntary imposition can be authorized.

In constructing the proposed continuum, the key variables for purposes of most of the relevant constitutional principles focus on the extent of any physical or mental intrusion accompanying application of the technique; the nature, extent, and duration of the treatment's effects; and the extent to which these effects may be avoided or resisted by unwilling individuals.[7] A partial but by no means exhaustive list of the therapeutic characteristics or effects that seem relevant to the inquiry—having in common perhaps no more than that, in varying degrees, reasonable patients or offenders would find them repugnant—include the extent to which the technique (a) causes pain; (b) produces harmful side effects of any kind; (c) causes irreversible organic damage; (d) invades bodily or psychological privacy; (e) involves deprivations of amenities to which the patient or offender is usually entitled; (f) involves procedures that are perceived as embarrassing or degrading; and (g) produces annoyance, frustration, anger, fear, anxiety, boredom, or other negative reactions.[8] Needless to say, some of these features are perceived as more repugnant than others, and the degree of repugnance varies with the specific nature of the technique applied, the duration of its effects, and the individual value preferences of patients or offenders. The term *intrusiveness* is thus a stipulated term intended to capture a rough weighted sum of these features and is accordingly an inherently inexact measure that varies with individual value preferences and the assessments of judges and other decision makers regarding the value preferences of ''reasonable'' patients or offenders. In this sense, comparing therapies on a scale of intrusiveness may be like comparing apples and oranges on a scale of taste. Whereas the latter may be useful in revealing only the taste preferences of the eater, I hope that the notion of intrusiveness will be a helpful, albeit inexact and oversimplified, concept for evaluating the constitutional and policy issues under discussion.

One commentator has suggested a somewhat similar continuum of ''coerciveness'' for ranking the various therapies.[9] I prefer the term *intrusiveness,* because *coerciveness* describes the manner in which a therapy is applied, not the therapy itself. Although some therapies (*e.g.,* psychosurgery) are easier to use without a patient's consent than others (*e.g.,* psychotherapy) and in this sense have a greater potential for coercive application, whether a patient is being coerced often has little to do with the ''coerciveness'' of the therapy

---

[7]*See* L. Tribe, American Constitutional Law § 15–8, at 1328–29 (2d ed. 1988); Shapiro, *Legislating the Control of Behavior Control: Autonomy and the Coercive Use of Organic Therapies,* 47 S. Cal. L. Rev. 237, 262–67 (1974) [hereinafter *Behavior Control*]; Shapiro, *Some Conceptual Tools for Appraising Psychosurgery, in* The Psychosurgery Debate: Scientific, Legal, and Ethical Perspectives 271, 276–77 (E. Valenstein ed., 1980) [hereinafter *Some Conceptual Tools*]; Spece, *Conditioning and Other Technologies Used to ''Treat?'' ''Rehabilitate?'' ''Demolish?'' Prisoners and Mental Patients,* 45 S. Cal. L. Rev. 616, 618 (1972); Winick, *Legal Limitations on Correctional Therapy and Research,* 65 Minn. L. Rev. 331, 351 (1981); Winick, *The Right to Refuse Mental Health Treatment: A First Amendment Perspective,* 44 U. Miami L. Rev. 1, 64 (1989).

[8]Shapiro has defined the concept of the intrusiveness of a therapy in terms of the following interdependent criteria:

> (i) the extent to which the effects of the therapy upon mentation are reversible; (ii) the extent to which the resulting psychic state is ''foreign,'' ''abnormal'' or ''unnatural'' for the person in question, rather than simply a restoration of his prior psychic state (that is closely related to the ''magnitude'' or ''intensity'' of the change); (iii) the rapidity with which the effects occur; (iv) the scope of the change in the total ''ecology'' of the mind's functions; (v) the extent to which one can resist *acting* in ways impelled by the psychic effects of the therapy; and (vi) the duration of the change.

Shapiro, *Behavior Control, supra* note 7, at 262. *See also* Shapiro, *Some Conceptual Tools, supra* note 7, at 276 (listing seven criteria), 277–78 (distinguishing intrusiveness from effectiveness).

[9]*See* Spece, *supra* note 7, at 618.

received. Thus, a patient may be coerced into undergoing psychotherapy but freely consent to psychosurgery; two patients may be coerced to the same degree to undergo therapies having different degrees of "coerciveness." Use of the term *intrusiveness* avoids these difficulties and focuses attention more appropriately on the nature of the therapy involved rather than on the manner of its application.

The proposed continuum of intrusiveness provides a general framework for analyzing the constitutional issues presented by involuntary administration of the various mental health and correctional therapies. Yet the continuum must be rather rough and oversimplified. Where one places any particular therapy on the continuum turns on empirical questions concerning the effects of the technique and the ability of patients or offenders to resist these effects. Many of these empirical questions remain unresolved, and some are untested and perhaps untestable. Moreover, the ranking of therapies involves inevitable value judgments concerning which effects are more or less offensive both to the relevant constitutional values and to the individual patient or offender. Individual preferences no doubt vary widely. For purposes of analyzing whether a sufficient threshold of intrusiveness is presented by a particular therapy to implicate a fundamental constitutional right, the weighing will have to be done by judges on as objective a scale as is possible under the circumstances. Once such a threshold is found to be met, however, the subjective value preferences of individual patients and offenders become significant in applying the least restrictive alternative principle in contexts where it is found to be required.[10] Although others may define points along the continuum differently than they are defined here, I hope that the framework presented will direct the inquiry away from a static, conclusory analysis and instead encourage examination of the degree of intrusiveness of the individual intervention at issue.

With these qualifications and caveats, the proposed continuum will start with psychotherapy (chapter 3) as the least intrusive of the modalities, followed in ascending order by behavior therapy (chapter 4), psychotropic medication (chapter 5), electroconvulsive therapy (chapter 6), electronic stimulation of the brain (chapter 7), and finally, psychosurgery (chapter 8). This categorization of therapies is itself problematic. Traditional categories are used for purposes of simplification, but categories may contain many components of varying degrees of intrusiveness. For example, some of the behavioral techniques (*e.g.,* aversive therapy using severe aversive conditioners) can be seen as more intrusive than some of the psychotropic medications, some (*e.g.,* modeling) as less intrusive than most if not all forms of verbal psychotherapy. Thus, the broad categories described actually overlap at points, and analysis should focus on the effects of the particular technique used, rather than, necessarily, on its place within a general therapeutic category. With this qualification, however, I hope that the general categories serve as useful tools of analysis.

For some purposes the constitutional analysis depends on the locus of the therapy, that is, whether it is administered within a prison, a hospital setting, or a community-based program. Although in general the intrusiveness of a therapy may not vary on the basis of where it is applied, the setting may be important for a number of reasons. It may be relevant, for example, to assessing the validity of informed consent. For this purpose, the setting may affect the coerciveness of a therapy, although not its intrusiveness.[11] Moreover, certain therapies (*e.g.,* behavioral techniques) may work more effectively in institutional settings than outside them, suggesting that such settings may enhance the intrusiveness of a therapy. Other therapies (*e.g.,* psychotherapy) may actually increase the length of institutionalization

---

[10]*See infra* chapter 16, part B.
[11]*See supra* note 8 and accompanying text.

if they are given in isolation (because they take so long), whereas other more intrusive therapies (*e.g.,* psychotropic medication) may diminish the length of institutionalization. The relationship between a particular therapy and the duration of confinement may thus affect substantially the recipient's assessment of intrusiveness.

In addition to these relationships between a therapy, the setting in which it is administered, and the impact on perceived intrusiveness, the right to refuse issue may also vary with the setting in which the treatment is imposed because of the differing characteristics of the setting and the differing state interests implicated. Even if the intrusiveness of a particular therapy is the same regardless of setting, some settings, because of their nature, command a greater degree of judicial deference than others in the inevitable balancing of state interests and individual rights that is a central part of constitutional adjudication. A prison environment, for example, is a uniquely dangerous place, "made up of persons with 'a demonstrated proclivity for antisocial criminal, and often violent conduct.' "[12] Mentally ill prisoners who are dangerous to themselves and others as a result of their illness thus present special problems for prison administrators, who have "not only an interest in ensuring the safety of prison staffs and administrative personnel, . . . but the duty to take reasonable measures for the prisoners' own safety."[13] As a result of these heightened state interests and the special nature of a prison environment, the Supreme Court, in order "[t]o ensure that courts afford appropriate deference to prison officials, . . . [has] determined that prison regulations alleged to infringe constitutional rights are judged under a 'reasonableness' test less restrictive than that ordinarily applied to alleged infringements of fundamental constitutional rights. . . ."[14]

Mental hospitals are environments bearing some similarities to prisons but many significant differences as well, and it is unclear to what extent the usual rules of constitutional scrutiny will be relaxed in hospitals as they have been in prisons.[15] In any case, community settings present almost none of these special problems, with the result that general constitutional standards would be applicable. Thus, the standard under which individual rights and state interests will be balanced may vary with the setting involved. Whatever the standard, of course, the balance may be struck differently for patients than for offenders in view of the varying governmental interests at stake in the different contexts. In any event, because the focus of the threshold constitutional inquiry is on the nature and effects of the various techniques themselves, the proposed continuum framework will be useful for purposes of identifying those treatments raising the need for constitutional scrutiny and for analyzing at least some of the constitutional and policy issues presented.

---

[12]Washington v. Harper, 494 U.S. 210, 224 (1990) (quoting Hudson v. Palmer, 468 U.S. 517, 526 (1984)); Jones v. North Carolina Prisoners' Labor Union, Inc., 438 U.S. 119, 132 (1977); Wolff v. McDonnell, 418 U.S. 539, 561–62 (1974).

[13]*Harper* at 225 (citing *Hudson,* 468 U.S. at 526–27; Hewitt v. Helms, 459 U.S. 460, 473 (1983)).

[14]*Id.* at 223 (quoting O'Lone v. Estate of Shabazz, 482 U.S. 342, 349 (1987)).

[15]*See infra* chapter 15.

Chapter 3
PSYCHOTHERAPY

Psychotherapy is the generic term for any form of treatment based primarily upon verbal or nonverbal communication between a therapist and a patient in a structured professional relationship.[1] It is the most basic treatment method used by mental health clinicians, either alone or in conjunction with other forms of treatment.[2] Many varieties of group and individual psychotherapy exist. There are several dozen formal psychotherapeutic systems or schools.[3] More than 400 different therapies have been reported in the professional literature, and the number and variety of new therapies grow steadily.[4] In addition, there has been a major trend toward eclecticism, with therapists integrating various psychotherapy techniques into a ''broad, comprehensive, and pragmatic approach to treatment.''[5] Millions of Americans undergo psychotherapy each year,[6] and the number of consumers continues to increase.[7] It is estimated that one-third of the American population

---

[1]AM. PSYCHIATRIC ASS'N, A PSYCHIATRIC GLOSSARY 113 (7th ed. 1994) [hereinafter PSYCHIATRIC GLOSSARY]. *See also* J. FRANK, PERSUASION AND HEALING: A COMPARATIVE STUDY OF PSYCHOTHERAPY 2–3 (rev. ed. 1974), which defines *psychotherapy* as those types of influences characterized by:

> 1. a trained, socially sanctioned healer, whose healing powers are accepted by the sufferer and by his social group or an important segment of it.

> 2. a sufferer who seeks relief from the healer.

> 3. a circumscribed, more or less structured series of contacts between the healer and the sufferer, through which the healer, often with the aid of a group, tries to produce certain changes in the sufferer's emotional state, attitudes, and behavior. All concerned believe these changes will help him. Although physical and chemical adjuncts may be used, the healing influence is primarily exercised by words, acts, and rituals in which the sufferer, healer, and—if there is one—group, participate jointly.

See generally FRANK, *supra*; L. KOLB, MODERN CLINICAL PSYCHIATRY 766–804 (1977); P. LONDON, BEHAVIOR CONTROL 47–70 (1971); RESEARCH TASK FORCE OF THE NAT'L INST. OF MENTAL HEALTH, RESEARCH IN THE SERVICE OF MENTAL HEALTH 310–25 (1975) [hereinafter RESEARCH IN MENTAL HEALTH]; Kleeman & Solomon, *Psychotherapy, in* HANDBOOK OF PSYCHIATRY 341–64 (P. Solomon & V. Patch eds., 3d ed. 1974) [hereinafter HANDBOOK OF PSYCHIATRY]; Nemiah, *Psychoanalysis and Individual Psychotherapy, in* THE AMERICAN PSYCHIATRIC ASSOCIATION COMMISSION ON PSYCHIATRIC THERAPIES, THE PSYCHIATRIC THERAPIES 321–41 (T. Karasu ed., 1984) [hereinafter PSYCHIATRIC THERAPIES].

[2]*See* G. DAVIDSON & J. NEAL, ABNORMAL PSYCHOLOGY: AN EXPERIMENTAL CLINICAL APPROACH 468 (1978) (psychoanalytically oriented therapy is the dominant force in American psychiatry and clinical psychology).

[3]LONDON, *supra* note 1, at 48. *See generally* R. HARPER, PSYCHOANALYSIS AND PSYCHOTHERAPY: 36 SYSTEMS (1959); C. PATTERSON, THEORIES OF COUNSELING AND PSYCHOTHERAPY (2d ed. 1973).

[4]Bergin & Garfield, *Introduction and Historical Overview, in* HANDBOOK OF PSYCHOTHERAPY AND BEHAVIOR CHANGE 3, 6 (A. Bergin & S. Garfield eds., 4th ed. 1994) [hereinafter HANDBOOK OF PSYCHOTHERAPY]; Freedheim & Freudenberger, *The Practice of Psychotherapy, in* HISTORY OF PSYCHOTHERAPY: A CENTURY OF CHANGE 453 (D. Freedheim ed., 1992) [hereinafter HISTORY OF PSYCHOTHERAPY]; Kazdin, *Comparative Outcome Studies of Psychotherapy: Methodological Issues and Strategies,* 54 J. CONSULTING & CLINICAL PSYCHOL. 95–105 (1986).

[5]Bergin & Lambert, *The Effectiveness of Psychotherapy, in* HANDBOOK OF PSYCHOTHERAPY, *supra* note 4, at 143; *see also* Arkowitz, *Integrative Theories of Therapy, in* HISTORY OF PSYCHOTHERAPY, *supra* note 4, at 261–93 (discussing history and current trends in psychotherapy integration); Jensen et al., *The Meaning of Eclecticism: New Survey and Analysis of Components,* 21 PROF. PSYCHOL. RES. & PRAC. 124–30 (1990) (68% of therapists claimed to be eclectic).

[6]LONDON, *supra* note 1, at 48. One estimate is that 7 million Americans receive therapy annually. M. GROSS, THE PSYCHOLOGICAL SOCIETY 8 (1978).

[7]RESEARCH IN MENTAL HEALTH, *supra* note 1, at 310; VandenBos et al., *A Century of Psychotherapy: Economic and Environmental Influences, in* HISTORY OF PSYCHOTHERAPY, *supra* note 4, at 97.

has used psychotherapy at some point in their lives.[8] Moreover, psychotherapy is practiced by the members of an expanding variety of professional and occupational categories. In addition to psychiatrists, psychologists, family therapists, social workers, and nurses, the ranks of therapists now include family doctors, members of the clergy, marital counselors, paraprofessional mental health workers, and guidance, counseling, and personnel officers in schools, colleges, and industry.[9] It is estimated that as many as 250,000 psychotherapists and counselors are performing or are available to perform psychotherapy in America today.[10]

All forms of psychotherapy attempt to ameliorate mental symptoms or control disordered behavior in the context of a patient–therapist relationship. Psychotherapy is used for an enormous range of psychogenic disturbances, including what until recently were labeled *neuroses* and *psychoses*, the personality disorders, impulse control disorders, sexual disorders, psychophysiologic disorders, and behavior problems of all kinds.[11] In its broadest sense, psychotherapy seeks to influence the attitudes of patients toward their illnesses, their own mental and physical processes, and their environment so that they may gain insight into the nature and cause of their problems.

A. Description and History

Psychotherapy has ancient origins, going back at least as far as the mystical healing rites of the priest–physicians of ancient Greece.[12] The earliest systematized method of psychotherapy was classical or Freudian psychoanalysis. In 1881 Fraulein Anna O., a hysterical young woman suffering from a variety of visual and motor disturbances, was treated by the Viennese internist, Josef Breuer. Breuer made the astonishing discovery that his patient's symptoms disappeared after she gave them verbal expression under hypnosis, a process described by Anna O. as the "talking cure." Breuer described his treatment to his friend Sigmund Freud, who was just completing his medical training, and Freud and Breuer began to work together using hypnosis for psychic catharsis in the treatment of hysteria.[13] In 1895, Breuer and Freud published *Studies on Hysteria,*[14] explaining hysteria as the result of traumatic experiences, usually sexual in nature, which the patient has repressed, and recommending treatment to enable the patient to discharge this pent-up emotion by recalling to awareness the painful experiences underlying it.

---

[8]VandenBos et al., *supra* note 7, at 97.

[9]FRANK, *supra* note 1, at 15–19, 337–38; LONDON, *supra* note 1, at 48. In 1989, the traditional "credentialed" professionals engaging in psychotherapy were estimated to include more than 30,642 psychiatrists, more than 56,000 clinical psychologists, and more than 81,000 clinical social workers. Dial et al., *Human Resources in Mental Health, in* MENTAL HEALTH, UNITED STATES 1990, 196, 208 (R. Manderscheid & A. Sonnenschein eds., 1990). A comparison to 1978 data shows the high rate of growth in each of these disciplines. *See Report of the Task Panel on Mental Health Personnel, in* II TASK PANEL REPORTS SUBMITTED TO THE PRESIDENT'S COMM'N ON MENTAL HEALTH 432, 436, 437 (1978) [hereinafter PRESIDENT'S COMM'N] (27,000 psychiatrists, more than 25,000 clinical psychologists, and more than 43,000 clinical social workers). The growing numbers of nontraditional therapists are difficult to estimate. *See id.* at 440–45.

[10]VandenBos, *supra* note 7, at 97.

[11]*See* HANDBOOK OF PSYCHIATRY, *supra* note 1, at 341–42; LONDON, *supra* note 1, at 51–53.

[12]FRANK, *supra* note 1, at 3–4; R. SLOVENKO, PSYCHIATRY AND LAW 457 (1973). For a historical review of the significant developments in the evolution of psychiatric treatment, see Overholser, *An Historical Sketch of Psychiatry, in* READINGS IN LAW AND PSYCHIATRY 3–11 (R. Allen et al. eds., 2d ed. 1975) [hereinafter READINGS].

[13]Karasu, *Psychoanalysis and Psychoanalytic Psychotherapy, in* 2 COMPREHENSIVE TEXTBOOK OF PSYCHIATRY 1442 (H. Kaplan & B. Sadock eds., 5th ed. 1989) [hereinafter TEXTBOOK OF PSYCHIATRY]; P. London, *The Future of Psychotherapy,* 3 HASTINGS CTR. REP., Feb. 1973, at 10.

[14]Breuer & Freud, *Studies on Hysteria, in* 2 STANDARD EDITION OF THE COMPLETE PSYCHOLOGICAL WORKS OF SIGMUND FREUD 3 (1964) [hereinafter COMPLETE WORKS OF FREUD]; Eagle & Wolitzky, *Psychoanalytic Theories of Psychotherapy, in* HISTORY OF PSYCHOTHERAPY, *supra* note 4, 109, 111; Karasu, *supra* note 13, at 1442–43.

By 1895, Freud began to discard the use of hypnosis and simply urged his patients to tell him all they could about themselves, thereby originating the present-day technique of free association.[15] Later, Freud developed dream interpretation and transference as a means of probing the patient's unconscious.[16] In his subsequent writings until his death in 1939, Freud developed and expanded an extensive theory of personality structure and development based on the notion that the major psychodynamic forces stem largely from the unconscious.[17] Freud's psychodynamic model proved extremely influential and dominated the development of psychoanalysis.

Classical psychoanalysis is performed by a therapist who has received psychoanalytic training[18] and usually requires three to five sessions per week lasting 45–50 minutes each over a period of 2 to 5 years.[19] Analysis is typically conducted with the patient lying on a couch and the analyst sitting outside the patient's field of vision.[20] The "fundamental rule" of psychoanalysis is that the patient must be fully candid with the analyst and verbalize whatever comes to mind.[21] Through analysis of free association and interpretation of dreams, the analyst attempts to trace the patient's emotions and behavior to the influence of repressed instinctual drives and defenses in the unconscious. At appropriate intervals the analyst offers interpretations of what the patient has revealed, designed to enable the patient to understand a particular aspect of his or her problem or behavior.[22]

The therapeutic relationship between analyst and patient is crucial to the successful psychoanalytic process.[23] One of the most important techniques used in the therapeutic relationship is *transference*, the unconscious projection onto the analyst of feelings and attitudes originally associated with important figures in the patient's early life, so as to help the patient understand his or her emotional problems and their origins.[24] The analyst, through interpretation and manipulation of the transference phenomenon, seeks to eliminate or diminish the undesirable effects of the patient's unconscious conflicts by making the patient aware of their existence, origin, and inappropriate expression in current emotions and

---

[15]*Id.* at 1443; Nemiah, *supra* note 1, at 324.

[16]Freud, *The Interpretation of Dreams, in* 4 & 5 COMPLETE WORKS OF FREUD, *supra* note 14; Karasu, *supra* note 13, at 1443; *see* Schwartz & Solomon, *Psychoanalysis, in* HANDBOOK OF PSYCHIATRY, *supra* note 1, at 489.

[17]Freud, *supra* note 14; Schwartz & Solomon, *supra* note 16, at 489.

[18]Schwartz & Solomon, *supra* note 16, at 490; *see* FRANK, *supra* note 1, at 169–79.

[19]Karasu, *supra* note 13, at 1453; Schwartz & Solomon, *supra* note 16, at 512.

[20]Karasu, *supra* note 13, at 1455–56; Schwartz & Solomon, *supra* note 16, at 513–14.

[21]Karasu, *supra* note 13, at 1456; Schwartz & Solomon, *supra* note 16, at 513; *see* Freud, *An Outline of Psychoanalysis, in* 23 COMPLETE WORKS OF FREUD, *supra* note 14, at 141:

> We pledge him to obey the fundamental rule of analysis, which is henceforward to govern his behavior toward us. He is to tell us not only what he can say intentionally and willingly, what will give him relief like a confession, but everything else as well that his self–observation yields him, everything that comes into his head, even if it is disagreeable for him to say it, even if it seems to him unimportant or actually nonsensical.

[22]LONDON, *supra* note 1, at 61–62; Karasu, *supra* note 13, at 1456; Nemiah, *supra* note 1, at 324–27.

[23]*E.g.,* S. BREHM & J. BREHM, PSYCHOLOGICAL REACTANCE: A THEORY OF FREEDOM AND CONTROL 151–55, 300–01 (1981); LONDON, *supra* note 1, at 62–63; Aaron, *The Patient's Experience of the Analyst's Subjectivity,* 1 PSYCHOANALYTIC DIALOGUE 29, 33 (1991); Adler, *Transference, Real Relationships and Alliance,* 61 INT'L J. PSYCHOANALYSIS 547 (1980); Beutler et al., *Therapist Variables in Psychotherapy Process and Outcome, in* HANDBOOK OF PSYCHOTHERAPY AND BEHAVIOR CHANGE 280–81 (S. Garfield & A. Bergin eds., 3d ed. 1986) [hereinafter HANDBOOK]; Binstock, *The Therapeutic Relationship,* 21 J. AM. PSYCHOANALYTIC ASS'N 543 (1973); Hoffman, *Discussion: Toward a Social Constructivist View of Psychoanalytic Situation,* 1 PSYCHOANALYTIC DIALOGUE 74, 75 (1991); Lambert et al., *The Effectiveness of Psychotherapy, in* HANDBOOK, *supra* at 157–211; Orlinsky & Howard, *Process and Outcome in Psychotherapy, in* HANDBOOK, *supra,* at 311.

[24]KOLB, *supra* note 1, at 772–73; LONDON, *supra* note 1, at 64–65; Adler, *supra* note 23, at 547–48; Greenson, *The Working Alliance and the Transference Neurosis,* 34 PSYCHOANALYSIS Q. 155 (1965); Karasu, *supra* note 13, at 1446–48.

behavior.[25] The different schools of psychoanalysis generally can be divided into two groups—classical or Freudian and "neo-Freudian," adhering to Freud's basic psychodynamic concepts but with several theoretical differences.[26]

B. Types of Psychotherapy

Closely related to psychoanalysis are a variety of psychoanalytical psychotherapies. Although based on the same psychodynamic model as psychoanalysis, psychoanalytic psychotherapy is less intensive, is less concerned with unconscious material, makes less use of free association and transference phenomena, and has more modest goals—the relief of symptoms and current conflicts rather than the accomplishment of basic personality change.[27] It is useful to distinguish between supportive psychotherapy and insight or depth psychotherapy.[28] The aim of supportive therapy is to reinforce the patient's existing personality structure and defense mechanisms and assisting him or her to manage current reality problems.[29] It avoids probing the patient's emotional conflicts in depth and uses such measures as inspiration, reassurance, suggestion, persuasion, counseling, and re-education.[30] Insight therapy attempts to help patients understand the roots of their problems by probing their ideas, attitudes, and feelings to uncover the unconscious motivations that may underlie their behavioral difficulties. It proceeds on the assumption that helping patients to understand why they act and feel as they do enables them to effect basic changes not only in their symptoms, but also in their underlying attitudes, reaction patterns, and life adjustment.[31] Insight therapy involves the use of a variety of techniques. These include association, to facilitate the verbalization by patients of their problems, ideas, emotions, and conflicts,[32] and interpretation, to help them gain understanding of the origin of their difficulties. As with psychoanalysis, the therapeutic relationship itself is critical to the process.

One of the most important developments in psychotherapy in the past 50 years has been the shift in emphasis from individual to group psychotherapy.[33] Group therapy applies psychotherapeutic techniques to a formally organized group of patients and seeks to

---

[25]*Id.*; Nemiah, *supra* note 1; Schwartz & Solomon, *supra* note 16, at 509–16.

[26]Schwartz & Solomon, *supra* note 16, at 489–90. The differences have been described as including

> deemphasis on the importance of sexual conflicts, increased emphasis on cultural and social forces in the personality, variations in the quantity and quality of the activity of the analyst in the treatment process, and greater stress on research, scientific principles, and the proper role of psychoanalysis as a branch of psychiatry and medicine.

Id. at 490. *See generally* R. MUNROE, SCHOOLS OF PSYCHOANALYTIC THOUGHT: AN EXPOSITION, CRITIQUE, AND ATTEMPT AT INTEGRATION (1955).

[27]Karasu, *supra* note 13, at 1442, 1457–58; Schwartz & Solomon, *Psychoanalytic Psychotherapy, in* HANDBOOK OF PSYCHIATRY, *supra* note 1, at 376–79. Other differences include the absence of a requirement that the therapist receive psychoanalytic training, the absence of the traditional couch, and a frequency of treatment of one or two visits a week for a period ranging from several months to 4 years. Karasu, *supra* note 13, at 1457–58.

[28]Karasu, *supra* note 13, at 1457–58; Kleeman & Solomon, *supra* note 1, at 353.

[29]Karasu, *supra* note 13, at 1460; Kleeman & Solomon, *supra* note 1, at 353.

[30]PSYCHIATRIC GLOSSARY, *supra* note 1, at 131; Karasu, *supra* note 13, at 1459.

[31]LONDON, *supra* note 1, at 56–58; Karasu, *supra* note 13, at 1458; Kleeman & Solomon, *supra* note 1, at 353.

[32]For a discussion of how information is obtained from the patient's unconscious through the use of free association and by examining the patient's dreams, daydreams, fantasies, parapraxias ("Freudian slips"), and peculiarities of behavior, posture, and diction, see Solomon & Sturrock, *The Psychiatric Examination, in* HANDBOOK OF PSYCHIATRY, *supra* note 1, at 26, 36–40.

[33]RESEARCH IN MENTAL HEALTH, *supra* note 1, at 312.

accomplish change in the individual's interpersonal relationships through controlled group interaction.[34] With the demonstration of its therapeutic efficacy following its widespread use during World War II as a means of allocating scarce therapeutic resources among large numbers of patients, group therapy has been adopted by therapists from all schools.[35]

An increasing number of new approaches in psychotherapy have been developed in response to changing social values; disenchantment with the slowness and expense of the traditional model of long-term, intensive psychoanalytic psychotherapy; and changing trends toward managed care in the health care delivery system.[36] These new approaches include primal therapy,[37] transactional analysis,[38] Gestalt therapy,[39] bioenergetics,[40] reality

---

[34]Everett & Solomon, *Group Therapy, in* HANDBOOK OF PSYCHIATRY, *supra* note 1, at 379. *See generally* FRANK, *supra* note 1, at 262–89; KOLB, *supra* note 1, at 793–800.

[35]RESEARCH IN MENTAL HEALTH, *supra* note 1, at 312.

[36]*See generally* Duke & Norwicki, *Theories of Personality and Psychopathology: Schools Derived From Psychology and Philosophy, in* 1 TEXTBOOK OF PSYCHIATRY, *supra* note 13, at 442; Schact & Strupp, *Recent Methods of Psychotherapy, in* 2 TEXTBOOK OF PSYCHIATRY, *supra* note 13, at 1556–57; Weiner, *Theories of Personality and Psychopathology: Other Psychodynamic Schools, in* 1 TEXTBOOK OF PSYCHIATRY, *supra* note 13, at 429. For an analysis of the factors influencing development of newer forms of the psychotherapies, see VandenBos, *supra* note 7, at 65–97.

[37]*See* A. JANOV, THE ANATOMY OF MENTAL ILLNESS: THE SCIENTIFIC BASIS OF PRIMAL THERAPY (1971); A. JANOV, THE PRIMAL REVOLUTION: TOWARD A REAL WORLD (1972); A. JANOV, THE PRIMAL SCREAM: PRIMAL THERAPY, THE CURE FOR NEUROSIS (1970). According to Janov, neurosis results from parental denial of basic infantile needs. The child's traumatic realization that his needs will never adequately be met triggers the repression of the "real" self and the emergence of an "unreal" self, which becomes the neurotic's facade. The techniques of primal therapy are designed to aid the patient to reexperience infant and early childhood experienced in their original form. "In primal therapy the release may be accompanied by violent thrashing, screaming, and convulsive behavior, an emotional release that is believed to be curative." RESEARCH IN MENTAL HEALTH, *supra* note 1, at 324.

[38]*See* E. BERNE, GAMES PEOPLE PLAY: THE PSYCHOLOGY OF HUMAN RELATIONSHIPS (1964); E. BERNE, THE STRUCTURE AND DYNAMICS OF ORGANIZATIONS AND GROUPS (1963); E. BERNE, TRANSACTIONAL ANALYSIS IN PSYCHOTHERAPY: A SYSTEMATIC INDIVIDUAL AND SOCIAL PSYCHIATRY (1961); T. HARRIS, I'M O.K.—YOU'RE O.K.: A PRACTICAL GUIDE TO TRANSACTIONAL ANALYSIS (1967). Berne subdivides the human personality into three "ego states"—parent, adult, and child—and suggests that the influence of these ego states is present in communicative exchanges ("transactions") between people. He focuses on covert meanings in interpersonal communications and on the "games" that mark interpersonal relationships—repetitive, neurotic interactions with hidden motives. Treatment includes lectures on the principles of transactional analysis, followed by individual and group sessions in which the therapist points out how the patient's interpersonal relationships reflect neurotic patterns. Weiner, *supra* note 36, at 429–30.

[39]*See* F. PERLS, GESTALT THERAPY VERBATIM (1969); F. PERLS ET AL., GESTALT THERAPY (1965). Gestalt therapy focuses on the patient's present conflicts—the "here and now" rather than on past feelings and behavior. It views self–awareness of emotional needs and individual responsibility for regulating behavior to meet such needs as essential to mental health. Repression of emotional needs is regarded as the cause of neurotic anxiety. Gestalt therapy, either individual or group, stresses sensorimotor exercises to enhance the patient's awareness of his or her physical state, and the physical expression of repressed desires. A variety of role-playing techniques are frequently used. Adlerian psychotherapy encourages patients to stop working for symbolic successes and to strive for socially useful goals. Duke & Norwicki, *supra* note 36, at 442–43. Adlerian therapists listen and observe dialectically. They ask themselves what opposites can be inferred from patients' statements and actions. *See* Weiner, *supra* note 36, at 411–413.

[40]*See* A. LOWEN, THE BETRAYAL OF THE BODY (1967). Based on the theory that blocked emotional feelings are reflected in the individuals' muscular pattern and stance, bioenergetics uses breathing and a variety of physical exercises designed to allow the patients to ventilate their feelings and thereby relieve pathological muscle tension. These and a variety of other "body" therapies can be traced to the work of Wilhelm Reich. *See* W. REICH, CHARACTER ANALYSIS (1945).

therapy,[41] rational–emotive psychotherapy,[42] logotherapy,[43] brief or short-term psychotherapy,[44] encounter and sensitivity groups,[45] transpersonal therapy,[46] transcendental medita-

---

[41]W. GLASSER, MENTAL HEALTH OR MENTAL ILLNESS? PSYCHIATRY FOR PRACTICAL ACTION (1970); W. GLAS-
SER, REALITY THERAPY (1965); W. GLASSER, SCHOOLS WITHOUT FAILURE (1969). Reality therapy stresses the
concepts of morality and responsibility, taught by the therapist, acting in a parental role, through love and discipline.
The goal of therapy is the patient's acceptance of reality and understanding that he must be responsible for his own
behavior.

[42]A. ELLIS, GROWTH THROUGH REASON: VERBATIM CASES IN RATIONAL EMOTIVE THERAPY (1971); A. ELLIS,
REASON AND EMOTION IN PSYCHOTHERAPY (1962); A. ELLIS & R. HARPER, A GUIDE TO RATIONAL LIVING IN AN
IRRATIONAL WORLD (1971); D. TOSI ET AL., THEORIES AND APPLICATIONS OF COUNSELING: SYSTEMS AND TECHNIQUES
OF COUNSELING AND PSYCHOTHERAPY (1987). Ellis's approach stresses reason, rationality, and logic as the principle
therapeutic weapons in ameliorating the patient's problems in living. The task of therapy is to isolate the patient's
irrational ideas and to replace them with more realistic and adaptive ones. This objective is accomplished by the
therapist's active and direct interventions. *See* Duke & Nowicki, *supra* note 36, at 444–45; Essig & Russell,
Analyzing Subjectivity in Therapeutic Discourse: Rogers, Perls, Ellis, and Gloria Revised, 27 PSYCHOTHERAPY 271
(1990).

[43]V. FRANKL, PSYCHOTHERAPY AND EXISTENTIALISM: SELECTED PAPERS ON LOGOTHERAPY (1967); V. FRANKL,
THE DOCTOR AND THE SOUL: FROM PSYCHOTHERAPY TO LOGOTHERAPY (1967); V. FRANKL, THE WILL TO MEANING:
FOUNDATIONS AND APPLICATION OF LOGOTHERAPY (1969). *Logotherapy* is humanistic or existential psychotherapy
directed at patients presenting problems of boredom and the inability to find meaning in life ("neogenic neurosis").
It is a supplement to psychotherapy, stressing the philosophical or spiritual dimension of human existence, and
teaching that patients must themselves discover and develop the meaning of their own lives. Logotherapy uses the
techniques of "paradoxical intention," a deliberate attempt to bring about events feared by the patient so as to
demonstrate the unrealistic nature of the patient's anxiety, and "de-reflection," a process of shifting the patient's
preoccupation with himself and his anxieties to some external goal.

[44]H. BARTEN, BRIEF THERAPIES (1971); P. SIFNEOS, SHORT-TERM PSYCHOTHERAPY AND EMOTIONAL CRISIS
(1972); Kelley, *Brief Psychotherapy, in* HANDBOOK OF PSYCHIATRY, *supra* note 1, at 366. Brief psychotherapy,
developed primarily for nonchronic patients in acute psychiatric crisis, involves a mutually agreed limit on the
number of sessions, usually 10 to 15. Techniques used in brief psychotherapy are derived from psychoanalytic
methods, but the focus is on current problems and the therapist plays a more active role. Karasu, *supra* note 13, at
1444; Kelley, *supra* at 367–76.

[45]*See* C. ROGERS, ON ENCOUNTER GROUPS (1970); R. SIROKA ET AL., SENSITIVITY TRAINING AND GROUP
ENCOUNTER (1971); Everett & Solomon, *supra* note 34, at 383.

> The term "encounter groups" encompasses a range of small groups that are characterized by face–to–face
> interactions, focusing on the here and now; intensive group experience; openness, honest interpersonal
> confrontation, and self-disclosure; and strong emotional expressions. The groups' aim is to effect
> behavioral and attitudinal change. . . . It has been estimated that 5 to 6 million people have participated in
> groups variously identified as personal growth, human relations, sensory awareness, sensitivity, self-
> awareness, etc.

RESEARCH IN MENTAL HEALTH, *supra* note 1, at 322.

[46]Transpersonal therapy "attempts to aid individuals to achieve the highest possible reaches of human nature,
including spirituality." RESEARCH IN MENTAL HEALTH, *supra* note 1, at 324. The transpersonal approach includes
such treatment forms as psychosynthesis, a psychotherapy designed "to help people develop all of their
psychological functions in harmony, as a path to the higher self," and Arica,

> an eclectic system that incorporates Middle Eastern and Oriental teachings including Yoga, Zen, Sufism,
> Kabbala, and the martial arts . . . [and offers] special diet, sensory awareness, energy–generating exercises,
> techniques for analysis of personality, interpersonal and group exercises, and various meditations. In Arica
> and related schools, a small group of trainees meets regularly as a community to help each other and to
> develop a 'group energy' that is helpful to each in attaining his highest goals of consciousness evolution.

Id.

tion,[47] psychodrama,[48] and neurolinguistic programming.[49]

As a result of the trend toward eclecticism,[50] many therapists use several of these newer approaches in combination with one another. In addition, many modern therapists use an integrative approach to treatment ''combining the behavioral and intrapsychic branches of psychotherapy into a new form of treatment,'' which has come to be known as *cognitive–behavioral therapy.*[51]

C. Effectiveness

Given the widespread use of the psychotherapies, both in private practice and in mental hospitals and other institutional settings, one would expect to find unquestioned evidence establishing their general effectiveness. Surprisingly, however, this is not the case.[52] Much of the early research performed in the 1940s and 1950s was based on retrospective individual case studies and the treating therapist's own judgments concerning the patient's progress and therefore did not meet accepted standards of scientific research.[53] More recent and carefully designed outcome studies are inconclusive, although the great majority indicate

---

[47]Transcendental meditation, a variant of Raja Yoga . . . has been tailored to habits of Westerners and does not require special postures, forced concentration, lengthy or arduous training or religious belief. Each individual is assigned a specific mantra, a euphonious syllable. Twice a day for approximately 20 minutes the practitioner relaxes and focuses his attention on the mantra. The first study of the psychological and physiological changes that accompany transcendental meditation suggests that the meditation produces a state of deep relaxation, with physiological and metabolic changes that differ from those during sleep and hypnotic trance.

RESEARCH IN MENTAL HEALTH, *supra* note 1, at 324–25.

[48]*See* D. KIPPER, PSYCHOTHERAPY THROUGH CLINICAL ROLE PLAYING 10–24 (1986) (''Psychodrama, which has sometimes been referred to as Sociodrama, is a method of group psychotherapy in which personality makeup, interpersonal relationships, conflicts, and emotional problems are explored by means of special dramatic methods.'') Sadock, *Group Psychotherapy, Combined Individual and Group Psychotherapy, and Psychodrama, in* 2 TEXTBOOK OF PSYCHIATRY, *supra* note 13, at 1531.

[49]*See* R. BANDLER & J. GRINDER, REFRAMING: NEUROLINGUISTIC PROGRAMMING AND THE TRANSFORMATION OF MEANING (1981); R. BANDLER & J. GRINDER, TRANCEFORMATIONS: NEUROLINGUISTIC PROGRAMMING AND THE STRUCTURE OF HYPNOSIS (1987). One of the most important techniques of neurolinguistic programming is reframing, which involves changing the cognitive frame in which a person perceives events. The goal of this therapy is to change the individual's understanding and appreciation of the meaning of an event, thereby changing his or her responses and behavior.

[50]See *supra* note 5 and accompanying text.

[51]Arnkoff & Glass, *Cognitive Therapy and Psychotherapy Integration, in* HISTORY OF PSYCHOTHERAPY, *supra* note 4, at 657. *See generally id.*; HOLLON & BECK, *Cognitive and Cognitive–Behavioral Therapies, in* HANDBOOK OF PSYCHOTHERAPY, *supra* note 4, at 428. Arnkoff & Glass, *supra* at 667: ''The line distinguishing behavior therapy from cognitive therapy has become blurred, to the point that *cognitive–behavioral* is a widely accepted term.'' For further discussion of cognitive–behavioral therapy, *see infra* chapter 4, notes 36–38 and accompanying text.

[52]KOLB, *supra* note 1, at 779; S. RACHMAN, THE EFFECTS OF PSYCHOTHERAPY 63 (1971); H. Blatte, *Evaluating Psychotherapies,* 3 HASTINGS CTR. REP., Sept 1973, at 4; O'Brien & Woody, *Evaluation of Psychotherapy, in* 2 TEXTBOOK OF PSYCHIATRY, *supra* note 13, at 1568–72.

[53]RESEARCH IN MENTAL HEALTH, *supra* note 1, at 313; *see* Halleck, *Can We Fit the Treatment to the Patient? Current Methodological and Theoretical Problems,* 41 BULL. MENNINGER CLINIC 303, 307 (1977).

Until two decades ago, it was difficult to find even uncontrolled follow–up studies of the results of many interventions. Before the 1950's, the major guides the clinicians used to determine treatment were his theories, his clinical experience, and the unsupported claims of other therapists as to the efficacy of various procedures.

Malan, *The Outcome Problem in Psychotherapy Research,* 29 ARCHIVES GEN. PSYCHIATRY 719 (1973).

that all the psychotherapies produce some benefits for some patients.[54] According to a report of the Research Task Force of the National Institute of Mental Health, most forms of psychotherapy are effective with about two-thirds of nonpsychotic patients.[55] However, more seriously disturbed patients, who make up the bulk of those hospitalized, do not show similar results.

One of the major difficulties in analyzing the effectiveness of psychotherapy is determining the changes that would occur in a control group of similar patients who receive no therapy. In an early influential analysis, Hans Eysenck, the noted British psychologist, surveyed 24 studies involving more than 7,000 neurotic patients who had received psychotherapy. Eysenck found that about two-thirds of the patients would have improved within 2 years of the onset of their condition even without treatment.[56] Eysenck concluded that the effectiveness of psychotherapy did not exceed this spontaneous remission rate.[57] The Eysenck study was controversial in part because of the difficulty of measuring spontaneous remission rate.[58] More recent research indicates that the spontaneous remission rate may be considerably lower than the 67% rate used by Eysenck,[59] perhaps as low as 30% to 40%.[60] Moreover, even if psychotherapy brings about improvement at no better than the spontaneous remission rate, at least some forms of psychotherapy bring earlier improvement and thus relieve patient's suffering.[61] Assuming an improvement rate of 65% for patients in therapy and a spontaneous remission rate of 40% for similar but untreated patients, then the

---

[54]Luborsky et al., *Comparative Studies of Psychotherapies: Is It True That "Everyone Has Won and All Must Have Prizes?,"* 32 ARCHIVES GEN. PSYCHIATRY 995 (1975). The reviewers found, however, that comparisons between different types of psychotherapy resulted in insignificant differences. *Id.* at 1001 (comparing individual psychotherapy with group psychotherapy, time-limited with time-unlimited psychotherapy, and client centered with other traditional psychotherapies); *accord* FRANK, *supra* note 1, at XVI; RESEARCH IN MENTAL HEALTH, *supra* note 1, at 318 ("whether or not one form of psychotherapy is superior to another has yet to be convincingly demonstrated"). The efficacy of the newer methods of psychotherapy, discussed in text accompanying *supra* notes 37–49, remains unsubstantiated. RESEARCH IN MENTAL HEALTH, *supra* note 1, at 323–24.

[55]RESEARCH IN MENTAL HEALTH, *supra* note 1, at 318; *see also* J. MELTZOFF & M. KORNREICH, RESEARCH IN PSYCHOTHERAPY 178 (1970) (review of 101 studies concluding that for both individual and group therapy, about 84% of the studies with adequate research designs showed positive effects that were statistically significant; 20% showed negative results); Bergin, *Psychotherapy Can Be Dangerous,* PSYCHOL. TODAY, Nov. 1975, at 96, 98 (concluding, based on a review of 12 carefully designed control studies involving nearly 1,000 patients, that 65% of those in therapy improved); Bergin & Lambert, *supra* note 5, at 144–48 (discussing outcome studies reporting on the effectiveness of psychotherapy for various conditions and summarizing their results in several tables); Luborsky et al., *supra* note 54, at 995 (survey of 33 studies finding that about 60% favored psychotherapy over the untreated control group, and about 40% found no significant difference between the two).

[56]Eysenck, *The Effects of Psychotherapy: An Evaluation,* 16 J. CONSULTING PSYCHOL. 319, 322 (1952).

[57]*Id.; see also* H. EYSENCK, USES AND ABUSES OF PSYCHOLOGY 195–99 (1953). A more extensive survey by Eysenck in 1965 reached essentially the same conclusion. Eysenck, *The Effects of Psychotherapy,* 1 INT'L J. PSYCHIATRY 97 (1965). For a review of criticisms of Eysenck's work and a defense of his argument, see Erwin, *Psychoanalytic Therapy: The Eysenck Argument,* 35(5) AM. PSYCHOLOGIST 435 (1980). For discussion of other studies of the spontaneous remission problem, see GROSS, *supra* note 6, at 22–23.

[58]Garfield, *Major Issues in Psychotherapy Research, in* HISTORY OF PSYCHOTHERAPY, *supra* note 4, at 345.

[59]Bergin & Lambert, *supra* note 5, at 148.

[60]RESEARCH IN MENTAL HEALTH, *supra* note 1, at 313 (estimating the median rate of spontaneous remission at close to 30%); Bergin, *The Evaluation of Therapeutic Outcomes, in* HANDBOOK *supra* note 23, at 162 (30%). In a more recent edition of their book, Bergin and Garfield essentially reach the same conclusion but no longer provide an arithmetic expression of either the rate of efficacy or spontaneous remission rate. HANDBOOK OF PSYCHOTHERAPY, *supra* note 4, at 147–49, 828 (concluding that the general effects of therapy exceeded spontaneous remission, that therapy effects were generally positive, and that therapy effects exceeded the effect of placebo control); *but see* S. RACHMAN, *supra* note 52, at 40 (65%); R. SLOANE ET AL., PSYCHOTHERAPY VERSUS BEHAVIOR THERAPY 103 (1975) (77%).

[61]Garfield, *supra* note 58, at 345.

improvement in 25% of the patients would be fairly attributable to the benefits of therapy—a clear finding of therapeutic effectiveness over nontherapy.[62]

Even though psychotherapy thus produces significant benefits, there is fairly consistent evidence that psychotherapy also produces deleterious effects.[63] Whereas only 5% of untreated patients show deterioration, 10% of treated patients suffer detrimental effects.[64] In addition to malpractice by psychotherapists,[65] there have been many reports of professional abuse of patients, including sexual abuse.[66]

Whatever benefits may exist for well-motivated nonpsychotic patients in treatment with private therapists, there are doubts regarding the effectiveness of psychotherapy for involuntarily committed patients, most of whom suffer from substantially more serious conditions than private patients and many of whom are resistant to treatment.[67] According to the Research Task Force of the National Institute of Mental Health, those who appear to benefit from psychotherapy "tend to be intelligent, highly motivated, experience acute discomfort, anticipate help, show a high degree of personality integration, are reasonably well educated, have had some social success and recognition in the past, are reflective, and can experience and express emotion."[68] Few involuntarily committed patients can be so described. Moreover, "studies have suggested that actual or assumed similarities between therapist and patient attitudes, interests, and values enhance the therapeutic relationship and the treatment outcome" and that "the middle-class white therapist has often found it difficult to be effective with patients from different cultures, races, or socio-economic levels."[69] Clearly, similarities in therapist and patient are substantially more likely to prevail in a private therapeutic relationship than in an institutional setting. These considerations

---

[62]Bergin, *supra* note 55, at 98. The 1978 Report of the Task Panel on Research of the President's Commission on Mental Health characterized the psychotherapy research as showing a detectable but modest positive effect for psychotherapy when the spontaneous remission rate is considered. PRESIDENT'S COMM'N, *supra* note 9, at 1750.

[63]Bergin & Lambert, *supra* note 5, at 176–80; *see also* GROSS, *supra* note 6, at 40–42; *Report of the Task Panel on Research, in* IV PRESIDENT'S COMM'N, *supra* note 9, at 1751; Durham & LaFond, *A Search for the Missing Premise of Involuntary Therapeutic Commitment: Effective Treatment of the Mentally Ill,* 40 RUTGERS L. REV. 303, 351–56 (1988); Halleck, *supra* note 53, at 313.

[64]RESEARCH IN MENTAL HEALTH, *supra* note 1, at 313; Bergin, *supra* note 55, at 98; *see also* Bergin & Lambert, *supra* note 5, at 176–80.

[65]*See* Smith, *Mental Health Malpractice in the 1990's,* 28 HOUS. L. REV. 209 (1991).

[66]For accounts of cases of professional abuse of patients, *see* L. FREEMAN & J. ROY, BETRAYAL (1976); W. VAN HOOSE & J. KOTTLER, ETHICAL AND LEGAL ISSUES IN COUNSELING AND PSYCHOTHERAPY 45–69 (1977); D. VISCOTT, THE MAKING OF A PSYCHIATRIST (1972); Freiberg, *The Song is Ended But the Malady Lingers On: Legal Regulation of Psychotherapy,* 22 ST. LOUIS L. J. 517 (1978); Jorgenson et al., *Therapist–Patient Sexual Exploitation and Insurance Liability,* 27 TORT & INS. L. J. 595 (1992); LeBoeuf, Note, *Psychiatric Malpractice: Exploitation of Women Patients,* 11 HARV. WOMEN'S L. J. 83 (1988); Stone, *Management of Unethical Behavior in a Psychiatric Hospital Staff,* 29 AM. J. PSYCHOTHERAPY 391 (1975); Zelen, *Sexualization of Therapeutic Relationships: The Dual Vulnerability of Patient and Therapist,* 22 PSYCHOTHERAPY 178 (1985). For cases involving such abuse, *see, e.g.,* Marlene F. v. Affiliated Psych. Med. Clinic, Inc., 257 Cal. Rptr. 98 (1989) (en banc); Roy v. Hartogs, 366 N.Y.S.2d 297 (N.Y. Civ. Ct. 1975), *modified,* 381 N.Y.S. 2d 587 (App. Div. 1976); St. Paul Fire & Marine Ins. Co. v. Downs, 247 Ill. 2d 382 (3d App. 1993); State v. Dutton, 450 N.W. 2d 189 (Minn. Ct. App. 1990); Zipkin v. Freeman, 436 S.W. 2d 753 (Mo. 1968).

[67]Durham & LaFond, *supra* note 63, at 351–56. *But see* Luborsky et al., *supra* note 54, at 1003, concluding on the basis of an initial sampling of studies that comparative outcomes between patients in therapy and untreated control groups did not vary between studies involving schizophrenic patients and those involving nonschizophrenic patients.

[68]RESEARCH IN MENTAL HEALTH, *supra* note 1, at 317; *accord Report of the Task Panel on Research, in* IV PRESIDENT'S COMM'N, *supra* note 9, at 1751.

[69]*Id.*; Sue et al., *Research on Psychotherapy With Culturally Diverse Populations, in* HANDBOOK OF PSYCHOTHERAPY, *supra* note 4, at 785.

would suggest reduced effectiveness when psychotherapy is given to patients committed to public mental hospitals, and even less for prisoners in correctional facilities. Although the evidence is far from conclusive, several literature reviews have found no persuasive evidence that coercive psychotherapy is effective in such institutional settings.[70] Unlike virtually all other mental health treatment techniques, psychotherapy thus seems to present only a limited potential for involuntary application.

D. Potential Abuse and Relative Intrusiveness

A private patient unwilling to undergo or to continue psychotherapy is not given treatment without consent.[71] Institutionalized patients, however, are occasionally subjected to individual or group psychotherapy without obtaining their informed consent, and sometimes despite their objections. Moreover, although private patients in the community may be subject to abuse and manipulation by an unscrupulous or overzealous psychotherapist, they ultimately retain the ability to discontinue therapy when they consider it to be deleterious. Institutionalized patients, however, may not have this ability and may be extremely vulnerable to therapeutic abuses.

An extended period of psychotherapy may greatly affect a patient's mental processes and can be used as a potent means of behavior control.[72] This potential for abuse is especially serious for institutionalized patients. As residents of institutions that control all aspects of their lives, they are especially vulnerable to abuse. Moreover, the "line between therapy of the pathologically deviant and control of the social deviant for non-therapeutic purposes is often a fine one."[73] In addition, not only may psychotherapy be used as a potent

---

[70]See, e.g., D. LIPTON ET AL., THE EFFECTIVENESS OF CORRECTIONAL TREATMENT (1975) (prison); PANEL ON RESEARCH ON REHABILITATIVE TECHNIQUES OF THE NATIONAL RESEARCH COUNCIL, THE REHABILITATION OF CRIMINAL OFFENDERS: PROBLEMS AND PROSPECTS 5 (L. Sechrest et al., eds., 1979) (prison); Durham & LaFond, supra note 63, at 351–56 (mental hospitals); Schwitzgebel, The Right to Effective Mental Health Treatment, 62 CAL. L. REV. 936, 946–47 (1974) (mental hospitals and prisons). See also COMMITTEE ON PSYCHIATRY AND LAW, GROUP FOR THE ADVANCEMENT OF PSYCHIATRY, PSYCHIATRY AND SEX PSYCHOPATH LEGISLATION: THE 30S TO THE 80S, at 883 (1977) [hereinafter LEGISLATION] ("Enough research already exists to indicate the high degree of uncertainty with respect to therapeutic outcomes for all [psycho]therapies."); P. MAY, TREATMENT OF SCHIZOPHRENIA 262 (1968) (psychotherapy for hospitalized schizophrenics expensive and ineffective); Anthony et al., Efficacy of Psychiatric Rehabilitation, 78 PSYCHOL. BULL. 447, 454 (1972) ("Traditional methods of treating hospitalized psychiatric patients, including individual therapy, group therapy, work therapy and drug therapy, do not affect differentially the discharged patients' community functioning as measured by recidivism and post hospital employment.") (mental hospitals, juvenile facilities, and prisons).

[71]This may not be true for an increasing number of patients coerced into therapy through the auspices of Family or Juvenile Court, Criminal Court, or departments of probation or parole. See Blatte, supra note 52, at 5.

[72]As Carl Rogers, the father of client–centered psychotherapy, has written:

Psychotherapy . . . can be one of the most subtle tools for the control of A by B. The therapist can subtly mold individuals in imitation of himself. He can cause an individual to become a submissive and conforming being. When certain therapeutic principles are used in extreme fashion, we call it brainwashing, an instance of the disintegration of the personality and a reformulation of the person along lines desired by the controlling individual. So the principles of therapy can be used as an effective means of external control of human personality and behavior.

Rogers & Skinner, Some Issues Concerning the Control of Human Behavior: A Symposium, 124 SCIENCE 1057, 1063 (1956). See also B. SKINNER, SCIENCE AND HUMAN BEHAVIOR 383 (1953) ("At certain stages in psychotherapy the therapist may gain a degree of control which is more powerful than that of many religious or governmental agents. There is always the possibility as in any controlling agency, that the control will be misused."); Blatte, supra note 52, at 5.

[73]Shestack, Psychiatry and the Dilemmas of Dual Loyalties, 60 A.B.A.J. 1521, 1523 (1974); see Breggin, Psychiatry and Psychotherapy as Political Processes, 29 AM. J. PSYCHOTHERAPY 369, 375–77 (1975).

means of behavior control, but the goals to be accomplished by its application are often set by the therapist without the participation of the patient.[74] This factor presents an especially serious potential for abuse with institutionalized patients and offenders. In the case of the private therapist, it may be reasonable to indulge the assumption that such goals are selected with the patient's values and best interest as the criteria. However, the institutional therapist has been recognized to be a "double agent," with loyalties both to the patient and to the state, which is the therapist's employer.[75] In the case of an involuntarily committed patient or sentenced prisoner, the state may well have interests quite divergent from those of the patient.

A grave potential for abuse is thus presented by involuntary psychotherapeutic techniques for institutionalized patients and offenders. There is little evidence, however, that psychotherapy has in fact been so abused in these contexts. The existence of other, more potent means of behavior control presented by the treatment methods discussed in chapters 4–8 makes it unlikely that psychotherapy would be the technique selected by a therapist determined to accomplish illegitimate ends.

Moreover, the potential for abuse is significantly diminished by the ability of patients who seek to resist the effects of psychotherapy: they may frustrate treatment by withholding cooperation.[76] The "fundamental rule" of psychotherapy requires patients to communicate openly and candidly with therapists.[77] When patients are unwilling to do this, the therapeutic process cannot even begin. Moreover, even if they cooperate with the therapists, they can effectively avoid the gradual and physically nonintrusive effects of psychotherapy with a

---

[74]As therapists, we institute certain attitudinal conditions, and the client has relatively little voice in the establishment of these conditions. We predict that if these conditions are instituted, certain behavioral consequences will ensue in the client. [T]his is largely external control, indifferent from what Skinner has described.

In Rogers & Skinner, *supra* note 72, at 1063. *See also* K. O'LEARY & G. WILSON, BEHAVIOR THERAPY: APPLICATION AND OUTCOME 29 (1975); Dalton & Hopper, *Ethical Issues in Behavior Control: A Preliminary Examination,* 2 MAN & MEDICINE 1, 6–7 (1976).

[75]*Report of the Task Panel on Legal and Ethical Issues, in* IV PRESIDENT'S COMM'N, *supra* note 9, at 1474–76; Bazelon, *Institutionalization, Deinstitutionalization and the Adversary Process,* 75 COLUM. L. REV. 897, 905–06 (1975); *Blatte, supra* note 52, at 5; *In the Service of the State: The Psychiatrist as Double Agent,* 8 HASTINGS CTR. REP. (Special Supp.) (1978); Noll, *The Psychotherapist and Informed Consent,* 133 AM. J. PSYCHIATRY 1451 (1976); Rundle, *Institution v. Ethics: The Dilemma of a Prison Doctor,* 2 HASTINGS CTR. REP. 7, Apr. 1972; Shestack, *supra* note 73.

[76]*See* Halleck, *Legal and Ethical Aspects of Behavior Control,* 131 AM. J. PSYCHIATRY 381 (1974):

The new drugs and new behavior therapy techniques make it possible to change behavior in a relatively efficient and rapid manner. Long-term psychotherapeutic techniques can, of course, also modify behavior. However, traditional psychotherapy works slowly. It gives the patient time to contemplate the meaning of behavioral change and to resist such change.

Katz, *The Right to Treatment—An Enchanting Legal Fiction?,* 36 U. CHI. L. REV. 755, 777 (1969) ("[P]sychotherapeutic techniques, to be successful, require the cooperation of the patient though the nature and quality of this cooperation is not precisely known."); Michels, *Ethical Issues of Psychological and Psychotherapeutic Means of Behavior Control: Is the Moral Contract Being Observed?,* 3 HASTINGS CTR. REP. 11, Nov. 1973:

There is a fourth and final difference [between psychotherapy] and the biological therapies. . . . Drugs or the surgeon's scalpel represent intrusive assaults against which we feel prevention is the only defense. It is different with psychotherapy; we imagine ourselves as patients to be free agents throughout the process, free to reject it and free to leave with no more scar than in any other human transaction.

Spece, *Conditioning and Other Technologies Used to "Treat?" "Rehabilitate?" "Demolish?" Prisoners and Mental Patients,* 45 S. CAL. L. REV. 616, 620 (1972).

[77]*See supra* note 21 and accompanying text.

minimal degree of mental resistance.[78] Psychotherapy thus does not have the power to transform their personality and mental attitudes, at least not without their active participation and cooperation. Requiring patients to participate in psychotherapy deprives them of the liberty to do other things and to be in other places and may expose them to statements and memories that are painful, irritating, embarrassing, and even distressing. This technique, however, cannot be used to control the mental processes of unwilling individuals, and the unpleasant effects of being required to attend psychotherapy sessions are not long-lasting. Compared with the other mental health treatment techniques discussed in succeeding chapters, psychotherapy thus is the least intrusive technique and presents the smallest degree of danger.

---

[78] *See* LEGISLATION, *supra* note 70, at 889 (''In the psychotherapy scheme one may go through treatment as a form of game playing, such as showing up for appointments and even making verbal utterances, in the absence of the type and degree of commitment required for a meaningful therapeutic relationship.'').

Chapter 4
BEHAVIOR THERAPY

A. Description and History

Behavior therapy may be defined generally as the clinical application of experimentally derived principles of psychological learning theory to teach adaptive behavior or modify maladaptive behavior by means of systematic manipulation of the patient's environment.[1] The basic principle underlying most behavior therapy techniques is that behavior is

---

[1] The term *behavior modification* is sometimes used, but I prefer the narrower term *behavior therapy*. *Behavior modification* is often defined expansively to include all treatments designed to bring about a change in behavior, including psychosurgery, electronic stimulation of the brain, electroconvulsive therapy, and psychotropic medication. *E.g.,* STAFF OF SUBCOMM. ON CONSTITUTIONAL RIGHTS OF THE SEN. COMM. ON THE JUDICIARY, 93d Cong., 2d Sess., INDIVIDUAL RIGHTS AND THE FEDERAL ROLE IN BEHAVIOR MODIFICATION 1, 11 (1974) [hereinafter INDIVIDUAL RIGHTS AND BEHAVIOR MODIFICATION]. A narrower definition, conforming to professional usage, is contained in a report prepared by the National Institute of Mental Health: "procedures that are based on the explicit and systematic application of principles and technology derived from research in experimental psychology, procedures that involve some change in the social or environmental context of a person's behavior." B. BROWN ET AL., BEHAVIOR MODIFICATION: PERSPECTIVES ON A CURRENT ISSUE 3, 75-202 (DHEW Pub. No. (ADM) 1975) [hereinafter BEHAVIOR MODIFICATION REP.]. *See also* C. FRANKS & G. WILSON, ANNUAL REVIEW OF BEHAVIOR THERAPY: THEORY AND PRACTICE 1 (1975); Alberts & Edelstein, *Training in Behavior Therapy, in* INTERNATIONAL HANDBOOK OF BEHAVIOR MODIFICATION AND THERAPY 213, 215–16 (A. Bellack et al. eds., 2d ed. 1990) [hereinafter INTERNATIONAL HANDBOOK]; Krasner, *History of Behavior Modification, in* INTERNATIONAL HANDBOOK, *supra* at 3, 8–10. *Applied behavior analysis,* a closely related but narrower term, technically applies primarily to applications of "Skinnerian" or operant conditioning. Lazarus & Fay, *Behavior Therapy, in* THE PSYCHIATRIC THERAPIES: THE AMERICAN PSYCHIATRIC ASSOCIATION COMMISSION ON PSYCHIATRIC THERAPIES 485–87 (T. Karasu ed., 1984) [hereinafter PSYCHIATRIC THERAPIES]. Goldiamond, *Singling Out Behavior Modification For Legal Regulation: Some Effects on Patient Care, Psychotherapy, and Research in General,* 17 ARIZ. L. REV. 105, 107–09 (1975); Milan, *Applied Behavior Analysis, in* INTERNATIONAL HANDBOOK, *supra* at 67. In common usage the terms *behavior therapy, behavior modification,* and *applied behavior analysis* are more or less synonymous. *See* Beck, *Behavior Therapy, in* AM. PSYCHIATRIC ASS'N COMM'N ON PSYCHIATRIC THERAPIES, THE PSYCHIATRIC THERAPIES 485, 486 (1984); Krasner, *supra* at 9. For other definitions, see H. KALISH, FROM BEHAVIORAL SCIENCE TO BEHAVIOR MODIFICATION 3 (1981); Beck, *supra* at 486–87; Friedman, *Legal Regulation of Applied Behavior Analysis in Mental Institutions and Prisons,* 17 ARIZ. L. REV. 39, 44 (1975); Krasner, *supra* at 8–10; Whitman, *Behavior Modification: Introduction and Implications,* 24 DEPAUL L. REV. 949, 952–53 (1975).

The definition of *behavior therapy* offered in the text, although widely accepted, is admittedly oversimplified. For example, techniques such as modeling, see *infra* note 30, and systematic *desensitization,* see J. WOLPE, PSYCHOTHERAPY BY RECIPROCAL INHIBITION (1958) [hereinafter RECIPROCAL INHIBITION]; Beck, *supra* at 497—both important techniques of behavior therapy—do not seem easily to meet the conditions of the definition. For a comprehensive treatment of the various techniques of behavior therapy, see A. BANDURA, PRINCIPLES OF BEHAVIOR MODIFICATION (1969); CONTEMPORARY BEHAVIOR THERAPY: CONCEPTUAL AND EMPIRICAL FOUNDATIONS (G. Wilson & C. Franks eds., 1982) [hereinafter CONTEMPORARY BEHAVIOR THERAPY]; A. KAZDIN, BEHAVIOR MODIFICATION IN APPLIED SETTINGS (3d ed. 1984); E. GAMBRILL, BEHAVIOR MODIFICATION: HANDBOOK OF ASSESSMENT, INTERVENTION AND EVALUATION (1977); M. GOLDFRIED & G. DAVISON, CLINICAL BEHAVIOR THERAPY (1976); R. RIMM & J. MASTERS, BEHAVIOR THERAPY: TECHNIQUES AND EMPIRICAL FINDINGS (2d ed. 1979); G. WILSON & F. O'LEARY, PRINCIPLES OF BEHAVIOR THERAPY (1980); J. WOLPE, THE PRACTICE OF BEHAVIOR THERAPY (1973); Beck, *supra*; Lieberman & Bedell, *Behavior Therapy, in* 2 COMPREHENSIVE TEXTBOOK OF PSYCHIATRY 1462 (H. Kaplan & B. Sadock eds. 5th ed., 1989) [hereinafter TEXTBOOK OF PSYCHIATRY]; Nathan, *Behavior Therapy, in* HANDBOOK OF PSYCHIATRY 391 (P. Solomon & V. Patch eds., 3d ed. 1974).

governed primarily by the environmental events or consequences that follow it.[2] Behavioral therapists therefore directly manipulate these consequences in order to effect an alteration of their patients' problematic behaviors. Unlike the psychodynamic model of mental illness, on which the psychotherapies are based, or the medical model in which the organic therapies are rooted, behavior therapy is derived from a psychological or learning theory model. The psychodynamic model regards patients' behavioral problems as symptomatic of an underlying personality disturbance, which becomes the focus of treatment. The medical model posits an underlying organic pathology. The learning theory model, by contrast, regards patients' behavioral symptoms as the entire problem, rather than merely manifestations of an underlying disorder.[3] Instead of attempting to cure an organic disease or to deal with the character structure or unconscious conflicts presumed to underlie the behavior, behavior therapy seeks to alter the problem behavior itself. Therapy is viewed not as an attempt to help patients reach self-understanding concerning the origins and meaning of their symptoms, but as a systematic attack on the symptoms themselves.

Behavior therapy postulates that maladaptive behaviors are learned and reinforced by the same principles of conditioning as "normal" responses and that they therefore may be altered through the systematic application of principles of learning theory validated experimentally in the animal laboratory.[4] Although principles of behavior modification were first introduced into clinical settings less than 50 years ago, the past 35 years have marked a phenomenal growth in their development and application. Behavior therapy is now a widely used treatment, particularly for managing institutional populations and children's behavior problems. Evidence of its general acceptance and increasing influence can be found in the emergence since 1963 of at least 15 new research journals devoted to behavior therapy;[5] the widespread availability of courses in behavior therapy in psychology doctoral programs,

---

[2]BEHAVIOR MODIFICATION REP., *supra* note 1, at 1; Atthowe, *Behavior Modification, Behavior Therapy and Environmental Design,* 18 AM. BEHAV. SCI. 637, 639–40 (1975); Ayllon, *Behavior Modification in Institutional Settings,* 17 ARIZ. L. REV. 3 (1975); Friedman, *supra* note 1, at 44; Klofas & Duffee, *The Change Grid and the Active Client: Challenging the Assumptions of Change Agentry in the Penal Process,* 8 CRIM. JUST. & BEHAV. 95 (1981); Lazarus & Fay, *supra* note 1, at 492.

[3]RESEARCH TASK FORCE OF THE NAT'L INST. OF MENTAL HEALTH, RESEARCH IN THE SERVICE OF MENTAL HEALTH 325 (DHEW Pub. No. (ADM) 75-236, 1975) [hereinafter RESEARCH IN MENTAL HEALTH]; Lazarus & Fay, *supra* note 1, at 492–93; Whitman, *supra* note 1, at 952.

[4]*See* RESEARCH IN MENTAL HEALTH, *supra* note 3, at 325; Agras, *Learning Theory, in* 1 TEXTBOOK OF PSYCHIATRY, *supra* note 1, at 262; Whitman, *supra* note 1, at 952. For alternative perspectives criticizing the predominant role of learning theory in human learning, see Brewer, *There Is No Convincing Evidence for Operant or Classical Conditioning in Adult Humans, in* 1 COGNITION AND THE SYMBOLIC PROCESSES 1 (1974); McKeachie, *The Decline and Fall of the Laws of Learning,* 3 EDUC. RESEARCH 7 (1974).

[5]*See, e.g.,* ADVANCES BEHAV. RES. & THERAPY (1978); BEHAV. MODIFICATION (1977); BEHAV. RES. & THERAPY (1963); BEHAV. THERAPIST (1978); BEHAV. THERAPY (1970); BEHAVIORISM (1973); BIOFEEDBACK & SELF-REG. (1973); COGNITIVE THERAPY & RES. (1977); J. APPLIED BEHAV. ANALYSIS (1966); J. BEHAV. ASSESSMENT (1979); J. BEHAV. EDUCATION (1991); J. BEHAV. MED. (1978); J. BEHAV. THERAPY & EXPERIMENTAL PSYCHIATRY (1970); J. DEVELOP. & BEHAV. PEDIATRICS (1988). In addition, accounts of behavior therapy and research have spread to the general psychiatric and psychological literature, and textbooks, monographs, and printed proceedings of meetings are appearing at an increasing rate. *See* Beck, *supra* note 1, at 485; Hoon & Lindsley, *A Comparison of Behavior and Traditional Therapy Publication Activity,* 29 AM. PSYCHOLOGIST 694 (1974); Liberman & Bedell, *supra* note 1, at 1462–63. For a graph illustrating the increase in articles about behaviorism, see Willis & Giles, *Behaviorism in the Twentieth Century: What We Have Here is a Failure to Communicate,* 9 BEHAV. THERAPY 15, 18 (1978) (using number of articles about behaviorism referenced in READERS' GUIDE TO PERIODICAL LITERATURE, 1900–74). For listings of more recent literature, see NATIONAL INSTITUTE OF MENTAL HEALTH LIBRARY JOURNAL HOLDINGS LIST (1985); BEHAVIOR MODIFICATION REP., *supra* note 1, at 25–26. Although the largest growth spurt occurred prior to 1973, "[s]ince that time the proliferation of experimental and clinical studies has continued, [and] the number of textbooks [on behavior therapy] has grown exponentially." Beck, *supra* note 1, at 485.

medical schools, and psychiatric residency programs; and the dramatic growth in govern-ment-funded research devoted to this rapidly developing field.[6]

Behavior modification techniques are now applied to virtually all types of mental illness; by practitioners ranging from psychiatrists and psychologists to parents, teachers, hospital ward attendants, and prison guards; and in settings extending from private practice to hospitals, community mental health centers, schools, prisons, and facilities for those with mental retardation.[7]

The basic principles of learning theory that underlie the diverse behavior therapy techniques can be traced to Pavlov's classic experimental work with dogs.[8] By pairing the ringing of a bell with feeding, Pavlov conditioned the dogs to salivate at the sound of the bell alone. The principles of learning that evolved from these early studies may be classified into two major learning paradigms—classical conditioning and operant conditioning.[9] Classical conditioning is based on Pavlov's work and involves respondent or reflex behavior, involuntary behavior mediated primarily by the autonomic nervous system (such as salivation) that is elicited by a preceding stimulus. A neutral (or ''conditioned'') stimulus (the bell in Pavlov's experiment), which does not normally elicit a response, is repeatedly paired with an eliciting (or ''unconditioned'') stimulus (the food powder) that normally triggers a response (salivation) until the neutral stimulus itself elicits the response, which is then called a *conditioned reflex*.[10]

B. Types of Behavior Therapy

Operant or instrumental conditioning is based on the experimental work of E.L. Thorndike[11] and B.F. Skinner[12] and involves operant behavior—''voluntary'' behavioral responses emitted by the individual, as opposed to reflexive behavior elicited by an environmental stimulus. Operant behavior is influenced by subsequent stimulation: it is

---

[6]*See* RESEARCH IN MENTAL HEALTH, *supra* note 3, at 325, 329–30. Eighty-four percent of schools providing doctoral training in psychology, sampled in a 1975 survey, offered a course in behavior modification. *Id.* at 325. Such courses are also offered in medical schools and were required in 11% of psychiatric residency programs. *Id.* Moreover, a 1973 American Psychiatric Association Task Force Report on Behavior Therapy in Psychiatry recommended that premedical education include a psychology course devoted to the experimental analysis of behavior and that training in behavioral psychiatry be made available to all psychiatric residents. *Id. See* Benassi & Lanson, *A Survey of the Teaching of Behavior Modification in Colleges and Universities,* 27 AM. PSYCHOLOGIST 1063 (1972).

[7]BEHAVIOR MODIFICATION REP., *supra* note 1, at 3; RESEARCH IN MENTAL HEALTH, *supra* note 3, at 326; Nathan, *supra* note 1, at 398; Whitman, *supra* note 1, at 953–54. Evidence of the wide-ranging application of behavior therapy in a variety of clinical settings can be found in any recent issue of the journals referred to in *supra* note 5.

[8]I. PAVLOV, WORK ON THE DIGESTIVE GLANDS (1897); I. PAVLOV, CONDITIONAL REFLEXES: AN INVESTIGATION OF THE PHYSIOLOGICAL ACTIVITY OF THE CEREBRAL CORTEX (1927). *See* RESEARCH IN MENTAL HEALTH, *supra* note 3, at 85; H. GLEITMAN, BASIC PSYCHOLOGY 71–77 (1983).

[9]GLEITMAN, *supra* note 8, at 71–90; RESEARCH IN MENTAL HEALTH, *supra* note 3, at 85–90; Whitman, *supra* note 1, at 959. A theoretical reexamination of this traditional duality is underway, and ''there is reason to hope that simplification of behavior theory through reduction to a single underlying type of behavior process is not far off.'' RESEARCH IN MENTAL HEALTH, *supra* note 3, at 4.

[10]GLEITMAN, *supra* note 8, at 72–73. For a social cognitive account of classical conditioning, see A. BANDURA, SOCIAL FOUNDATIONS OF THOUGHT AND ACTION: A SOCIAL COGNITIVE THEORY 183 (1986).

[11]E. THORNDIKE, ANIMAL INTELLIGENCE: AN EXPERIMENTAL STUDY OF THE ASSOCIATIVE PROCESS IN ANIMALS, 2 PSYCHOLOGICAL MONOGRAPHS, No. 8 (1898); E. THORNDIKE, ANIMAL INTELLIGENCE: EXPERIMENTAL STUDIES (1911); E. THORNDIKE, THE FUNDAMENTALS OF LEARNING (1932); *see* GLEITMAN, *supra* note 8, at 78–81.

[12]B. SKINNER, THE BEHAVIOR OF ORGANISMS (1938); B. SKINNER, SCIENCE AND HUMAN BEHAVIOR (1953); *see* GLEITMAN, *supra* note 8, at 84–88.

strengthened or weakened by its consequences. Skinner found that a rat in a box that contained a lever would sooner or later press the lever. If the rat received a food pellet for pressing the bar, its bar-pressing behavior increased. If no food pellet was delivered when the rat pressed the bar several times, it ceased to press the lever as frequently. Skinner called this process of increasing or decreasing the probability of future voluntary behavior through manipulation of its consequences *operant conditioning*.[13] By repeatedly presenting the individual with a rewarding or reinforcing stimulus (or a punishing or aversive stimulus), the individual learns to make (or to avoid making) specific responses.

The origins of behavior therapy have been traced to two experiments reported in the early 1920s that applied these basic principles of learning theory, originally developed in experiments with animals, to the behavior of children.[14] J.B. Watson, the founder of modern behavioral psychology, demonstrated that a fear response to a white rat could be conditioned in a young infant by presenting the rat, which previously did not elicit a fear reaction, to the child, followed immediately by a loud noise, a stimulus to which the child had previously responded with fear. After a series of such pairings, the rat itself elicited the fear response.[15] Watson suggested a number of ways to reverse the conditioned response by subsequent learning experiences, one of which was used by Mary Cover Jones to overcome a young boy's fear of rabbits by systematically bringing a rabbit closer to him while he was eating food that he liked.[16] In the 1950s these principles were applied in various clinical settings in the treatment of severely disturbed patients,[17] and they are now widely used for a variety of conditions.

Ideally, behavior therapy involves a mutual agreement between therapist and patient specifying treatment, goals, and procedures.[18] Prior to treatment, the therapist performs a

---

[13]SKINNER, SCIENCE AND HUMAN BEHAVIOR, *supra* note 12, at 62–66. Skinner's operant conditioning paradigm bears a close resemblance to Bentham's principle of utility. *See* J. BENTHAM, AN INTRODUCTION TO THE PRINCIPLES OF MORALS AND LEGISLATION 1 (1789) (''Nature has placed mankind under the governance of two sovereign masters, *pain* and *pleasure* . It is for them alone to . . . determine what we shall do.''); J. BENTHAM, THE RATIONALE OF PUNISHMENT 19 (1830) (''Pain and pleasure are the great springs of human action.''). It also relates to the model of modern economic theory that predicts behavior based on a rational calculus of costs and benefits. *See, e.g.,* J. POSNER, ECONOMIC ANALYSIS OF LAW (4th ed. 1992). For a social cognitive account of operant conditioning, see BANDURA, *supra* note 10, at 13–16, 106–14, 116, 121–22.

[14]Ferster, *Behaviorism, Behavior Modification, and Behavior Therapy, in* READINGS IN LAW AND PSYCHIATRY 107, 108 (R. Allen et al. eds., rev. ed. 1975); Whitman, *supra* note 1, at 952.

[15]Watson & Rayner, *Conditioned Emotional Reactions,* 3 J. EXPERIMENTAL PSYCHOL. 1 (1920). Watson's classic article, often referred to as the Behaviorist Manifesto, was published in 1913. Watson, *Psychology as the Behaviorist Views It,* 20 PSYCHOL. REV. 158 (1913).

[16]Jones, *A Laboratory Study Of Fear: The Case of Peter,* PEDAGOGICAL SEMINARY 308 (1924); Jones, *The Elimination of Children's Fears,* 7 J. EXPERIMENTAL PSYCHOL. 382 (1924).

[17]*E.g.,* J. WOLPE & A. LAZARUS, BEHAVIOR THERAPY TECHNIQUES: A GUIDE TO THE TREATMENT OF NEUROSES (1966); WOLPE, *supra* note 1; Ayllon & Arzin, *The Measurement and Reinforcement of Behavior of Psychotics,* 8 J. EXPERIMENTAL ANALYSIS BEHAV. 357 (1965); Ayllon & Arzin, *The Psychiatric Nurse as a Behavioral Engineer,* 2 J. EXPERIMENTAL ANALYSIS BEHAV. 323 (1959); Eysenck, *Discussion on the Role of the Psychologist in Psychoanalytic Practice: The Psychologist as Technician,* 45 PROCEEDINGS OF THE ROYAL SOC'Y OF MED. 447 (1952); Ferster & De Myer, *The Development of Performances in Autistic Children in an Automatically Controlled Environment,* 13 J. CHRONIC DISEASES 312 (1961); Lindsey & Skinner, *A Method for the Experimental Analysis of Behavior of Psychotic Patients,* 9 AM. PSYCHOLOGIST 419 (1954); *see* Beck, *supra* note 1, at 488–89.

[18]BEHAVIOR MODIFICATION REP., *supra* note 1, at 4; Freidman, *supra* note 1, at 44; Goldiamond, *supra* note 1, at 133–36; Wilson & Davison, *Behavior Therapy: A Road to Self-Control,* PSYCHOL. TODAY, Oct. 1975, at 54. Increasingly this agreement is reduced to writing. Ayllon, *supra* note 2, at 11 (''A comprehensive therapy contract is now in use which sets forth the expected behavior objectives of the treatment, the nature, methods, and duration of the treatment, and the specific criteria and social values that will be used to evaluate and measure the success of the treatment.''). For a sample form contract used by the University of Chicago Department of Psychiatry, see Goldiamond, *Toward a Constructional Approach to Social Problems. Ethical and Constitutional Issues Raised by Applied Behavior Analysis,* 2 BEHAVIOR 1, 78–80 (1974); Lazarus & Fay, *supra* note 1, at 493.

"behavioral analysis," which is a detailed description of the patient's problem behavior designed to determine the specific context and settings of daily life that distress the patient and to ascertain the environmental responses that might maintain the patient's maladaptive behaviors.[19] On the basis of this analysis, one or more of the behavior modification techniques are selected and used with the patient.

The behavior therapy techniques currently in clinical use may roughly be grouped into three major categories—positive reinforcement, aversion therapy, and systematic desensitization. Methods using positive reinforcement are based on operant conditioning; these methods reward behavioral responses sought to be strengthened ("target responses") by following their occurrence with desirable consequences ("reinforcers").[20] Such reinforcers may range from basic items like food, water, and a bed ("primary reinforcers") to grounds privileges, movies, religious services, praise, attention, gold stars, money, and tokens or points redeemable for a variety of items or privileges ("secondary reinforcers").[21]

One widely used positive reinforcement technique is known as the token economy.[22] Under this method, a quasi-economic incentive system is established within an institutional setting under which desired behavior is rewarded with tokens—"generalized" reinforcers, which may be exchanged by the patient for various items or privileges otherwise unavailable. Inappropriate behavior may result in the loss of tokens. By making the availability of reinforcers contingent on performance of the target behavior, that behavior is strengthened in the patient much as bar-pressing activity was strengthened in Skinner's rats.[23]

A variation on the token economy is the "tier system," where privileges are dependent on the patient's place in a hierarchy of tiers. In this system patients earn their way from an orientation level, in which privileges are scant or nonexistent, upward through a ranked

---

[19]RESEARCH IN MENTAL HEALTH, *supra* note 3, at 326; Lieberman & Bedell, *supra* note 1, at 1464.

[20]BANDURA, *supra* note 1, at 217–92; BEHAVIOR MODIFICATION REP., *supra* note 1, at 4–6; Lazarus & Fay, *supra* note 1, at 494–97.

[21]*E.g.*, Whitman, *supra* note 1, at 955. Sometimes the term *primary reinforcers* is used to refer to all items desired by the patient, whereas *secondary reinforcers* is used synonymously with *generalized reinforcers* to refer to tokens or points convertible by the patient to *primary reinforcers. E.g.*, Wexler, *Of Rights and Reinforcers,* 11 SAN DIEGO L. REV. 957, 958 (1974). The selection of reinforcers appropriate to the patient in question is often done through use of the "Premack Principle," which teaches that if the patient naturally engages in certain behaviors with high frequency, then the opportunity to engage in those behaviors can be used as a powerful reinforcer. *See* Premack, *Toward Empirical Behavior Laws: Positive Reinforcement,* 66 PSYCHOL. REV. 219 (1959).

[22]T. AYLLON & N. ARZIN, THE TOKEN ECONOMY: A MOTIVATIONAL SYSTEM FOR THERAPY AND REHABILITATION (1968); A. KAZDIN, THE TOKEN ECONOMY: A REVIEW AND EVALUATION (1977); BEHAVIOR MODIFICATION REP., *supra* note 1, at 5; Ayllon, *supra* note 2, at 5–6; Lazarus & Fay, *supra* note 1 at 506–07. For analysis of the legal issues raised by the token economy, see Wexler, *supra* note 21; Wexler, *Token and Taboo: Behavior Modification, Token Economies, and the Law,* 81 CAL. L. REV. 81 (1973); Bentley, *Major Legal and Ethical Issues in Behavioral Treatment: Focus on Institutionalized Mental Patients,* 5 BEHAV. SCI. & L. 359 (1987).

[23]Skinner used hungry rats and pigeons in his experiments—those "deprived of food for a certain length of time or until . . . [their] usual body-weight has been slightly reduced"—finding that "the frequency of response which results from reinforcement depends upon the degree of deprivation at the time the response is observed." SKINNER, SCIENCE AND HUMAN BEHAVIOR, *supra* note 12, at 68. Similarly, the token economy programs sometimes place the patient in a state of deprivation at the outset of therapy, providing even primary reinforcers such as meals, water, and a bed only when the patient engages in target behaviors. BEHAVIOR MODIFICATION REP., *supra* note 1, at 18–19; Wexler, *Behavior Modification Report and Legal Developments,* 18 AM. BEHAV. SCI. 679, 681–82 (1975); Wexler, *supra* note 22, at 87–88. Wexler has suggested that legal developments (such as Wyatt v. Stickney, 344 F. Supp. 373 (M.D. Ala. 1972), *aff'd sub nom.* Wyatt v. Aderholt, 503 F.2d 1305 (5th Cir. 1974), specifying minimum constitutional standards for facilities for the mentally disabled, by defining as basic rights many of the "primary" reinforcers provided only contingently in token economies) may render such reinforcers legally unavailable in token programs. Wexler, *supra* at 681–82; Wexler, *supra* note 22, at 93–95.

series of tiers with increasingly more desirable privileges and conditions.[24] The token economy has been applied in a variety of settings—closed psychiatric wards,[25] prisons,[26] facilities for delinquents,[27] and schools for normal children as well as for those with mental

---

[24]Wexler, *supra* note 22, at 88. This model was used in the controversial Federal Bureau of Prisons' Project START, conducted at the Federal Medical Center for Prisoners at Springfield, Missouri, from September 1972 until February 1974. The prisoners selected were so repeatedly disruptive as to require continual segregation. At entry level, these prisoners were denied such basic privileges as daily showers and exercise, visitors, reading material, personal property, and commissary privileges, which could be regained only by behaving in conformity with program goals. For a description of Project START, see Clonce v. Richardson, 379 F. Supp. 338 (W.D. Mo. 1974); INDIVIDUAL RIGHTS AND BEHAVIOR MODIFICATION, *supra* note 1, at 31–32, 240–72; Carlson, *Behavior Modification in the Federal Bureau of Prisons,* 1 N. ENGL. J. PRISON L. 155, 159–63 (1975). Although the controversial START project was terminated, it became a model for other prison programs. Gaylin & Blatte, *Behavior Modification in Prisons,* 13 AM. CRIM. L. REV. 11, 25 (1975). Another controversial program using a tier system was Maryland's Patuxent Institute for "defective delinquents." See *Patuxent Institution,* 5 BULL. AM. ACAD. PSYCHIATRY & L. 116–267 (1977) (symposium issue); Stanford, *A Model Clockwork-Orange Prison,* N.Y. TIMES, Sept. 12, 1972, § 6 (Magazine), at 9, 71–84. For examples of other tier programs, see Green v. Baron, 879 F.2d 305 (8th Cir. 1989) (secure medical facility); Canterino v. Wilson, 546 F. Supp. 174 (W.D. Ky. 1982) (state prison); Converse v. Nelson, No. 95-16776 (Mass. Super. Ct. [Suffolk Co.], 1995) (state hospital). *See also* Morgan v. Sproat, 432 F. Supp. 1130 (S.D. Miss. 1977) (tier program in juvenile training school). For a detailed description of the workings of a tier system used at a closed adolescent treatment center, see INDIVIDUAL RIGHTS AND BEHAVIOR MODIFICATION, *supra* note 1, at 358–71. Because the reinforcer frequently used in the tier program is the removal of unpleasant conditions, it may more aptly be termed a program of negative reinforcement. *See* Shah, *Basic Principles and Concepts, in* AM. CORRECTIONAL ASS'N COMM. ON CLASSIFICATION & TREATMENT, CORRECTIONAL CLASSIFICATION AND TREATMENT 123, 128 (1975).

[25]Teodoro Ayllon and Nathan Arzin pioneered the token economy in the early 1960s on a ward of chronically psychotic patients in an Illinois State Hospital. AYLLON & ARZIN, *supra* note 22. *See also* KAZDIN, *supra* note 1; G. PAUL & R. LENTZ, PSYCHOSOCIAL TREATMENT OF CHRONIC MENTAL PATIENTS: MILIEU VERSUS SOCIAL-LEARNING PROGRAMS (1977); Atthowe & Krasner, *Preliminary Report on the Application of Contingent Reinforcement Procedures (Token Economy) on a "Chronic" Psychiatric Ward,* 73 J. ABNORMAL PSYCHOL. 37 (1968); Beck, *supra* note 1, at 506; Boudewyns & Fry, *Token Economy Programs in V.A. Medical Centers: Where Are They Today?,* 9 BEHAV. THERAPIST 126 (1986); Kazdin & Bottzin, *The Token Economy: An Evaluative Review,* 5 J. APPLIED BEHAV. ANAL. 343 (1972); Lloyd & Abel, *Performance On a Token Economy Psychiatric Ward: A Two-Year Summary,* 8 BEHAV. RES. & THERAPY 1 (1970); Winkler, *Management of Chronic Psychiatric Patients by a Token Reinforcement System,* 3 J. APPLIED BEHAV. ANAL. 47 (1970).

[26]A survey conducted in the mid-1970s revealed that 14 states used token economy systems in their prisons. Blatte, *State Prisons and the Use of Behavior Control,* 4 HASTINGS CTR. REP., Sept. 1975, at 11. *E.g.,* M. MILAN ET AL., APPLIED BEHAVIOR ANALYSIS AND THE IMPRISONED ADULT FELON PROJECT I: THE CELL BLOCK TOKEN ECONOMY (1974); Milan & McKee, *The Cellblock Token Economy: Token Reinforcement Procedures in a Maximum Security Correctional Institution for Adult Male Felons,* 9 J. APPLIED BEHAV. ANAL. 253 (1976); Geller et al., *Behavior Modification in a Prison,* 4 CRIM. JUST. & BEHAV. 11 (1977); *see* Petrock & Walter, *Behavior Modification in Corrections: Implications for Organizational Change,* 1 N. ENGL. J. PRISON L. 203 (1974).

[27]Achievement Place, a community-based residential treatment home for court-remanded delinquent and pre-delinquent youths, established in 1967 in Lawrence, Kansas, uses a variety of behavior modification procedures, including a token economy, positive reinforcement, and fines for inappropriate behavior. Phillips, *Achievement Place: Token Reinforcement Procedures in a Home-Style Rehabilitation Setting for "Pre-Delinquent" Boys,* 1 J. APPLIED BEHAV. ANAL. 213 (1968); Phillips et al., *Achievement Place: Modification of the Behaviors of Pre-Delinquent Boys Within a Token Economy,* 4 J. APPLIED BEHAV. ANAL. 43 (1971); Phillips et al., *Achievement Place: Behavior Shaping Works for Delinquents,* PSYCHOL. TODAY 75 (June 1973). The Achievement Place model for delinquency treatment has been copied widely and many such homes are now in operation. BEHAVIOR MODIFICATION REP., *supra* note 1, at 12; *e.g.,* Denkowski & Denkowski, *Community-Based Residential Treatment of the Mentally Retarded Adolescent Offender: Phase 1, Reduction of Aggressive Behavior,* 13 J. COMMUNITY PSYCHOL. 299 (1985); Liberman et al., *Replication of the Achievement Place Model in California,* 8 J. APPLIED BEHAV. ANAL. 287 (1975).

The Federal Bureau of Prisons has used token economies in the treatment of delinquents at the National Training Center for Boys in Washington, DC, and the Robert F. Kennedy Youth Center in Morgantown, West Virginia. Carlson, *supra* note 24, at 158–59. For a description of a token economy system used in a California juvenile detention facility, see Gambrill, *The Use of Behavioral Methods in a Short-Term Detention Setting,* 3 CRIM. JUST. & BEHAV. 53 (1976). *See also* Hobbs & Holt, *The Effects of Token Reinforcement on the Behavior of Delinquents in Cottage Settings,* 9 J. APPLIED BEHAV. ANAL. 189 (1976).

retardation, hyperactivity, and emotional disturbance.[28] In addition to the token economy, other treatment techniques using positive reinforcement include shaping,[29] modeling,[30] and contingency contracting.[31]

A second major behavior therapy paradigm is aversive therapy. This approach is based on both classical and operant conditioning and consists of "an attempt to associate an undesirable behavior pattern with unpleasant stimulation or to make the unpleasant stimulation a consequence of the undesirable behavior."[32] By applying negative stimuli contingent on the occurrence of inappropriate or maladaptive behavior, aversion therapy seeks to establish a connection between the target behavior and the unpleasant stimuli and thereby induce the avoidance or suppression of the target behavior. Aversive stimuli range from frowning, disapproval, criticism, and scolding to removal of privileges, total withholding of reinforcement (*extinction*), social isolation (*time out*), fines, overcorrection, slapping, high-intensity auditory signals, lemon juice squirted into the mouth, low-level electric shock, emetic drugs, and drugs inducing respiratory paralysis.[33] Aversive methods have been used in the treatment of alcoholism, drug addiction, excessive smoking, compulsive eating,

---

[28]*E.g.*, Birnbrauer et al., *Classroom Behavior of Retarded Pupils With Token Reinforcement*, 2 J. EXPERIMENTAL CHILD PSYCHOL. 219 (1965); Broden et al., *Effects of Teacher Attention and a Token Reinforcement System in a Junior High School Class*, 36 EXCEPTIONAL CHILDREN 341 (1970); Klotz, *Development of a Behavior Management Level System: A Comprehensive School-Wide Behavior Management Program for Emotionally Disturbed Adolescents*, 31 POINTER 5 (1987); O'Leary et al., *A Token Reinforcement Program in a Public School: A Replication and Systematic Analysis*, 2 J. APPLIED BEHAV. ANAL. 277 (1969); O'Leary & Drabman, *Token Reinforcement Programs in the Classroom: A Review*, 75 PSYCHOL. BULL. 379 (1971).

[29]In shaping, "a desired behavior is broken down into successive steps that are taught one by one. Each of the steps is reinforced until it is mastered, and then the individual is moved to the next one. In this way, the new behavior is gradually learned as what the individual does becomes a closer and closer approximation of the behavioral goal." BEHAVIOR MODIFICATION REP., *supra* note 1, at 6. *See* BANDURA, *supra* note 1, at 232–34; Sidman, *Operant Techniques, in* EXPERIMENTAL FOUNDATIONS OF CLINICAL PSYCHOL. 170, 173–74 (A. Bachrach ed., 1962).

[30]Modeling involves observational learning in which a person who already knows how to perform the behavior in question demonstrates it for an observer. *See* BANDURA, *supra* note 1, at 118–216; A. BANDURA, PSYCHOLOGICAL MODELING: CONFLICTING THEORIES (1971); BANDURA, *supra* note 10, at 47–105; BEHAVIOR MODIFICATION REP., *supra* note 1, at 6; T. ROSENTHAL & B. ZIMMERMAN, SOCIAL LEARNING AND COGNITION (1978); Bandura, *Social Learning Through Imitation, in* NEBRASKA SYMPOSIUM ON MOTIVATION 211–69 (M. Jones ed., 1962); Bandura, *The Role of Imitation in Personality Development*, 18 J. NURSERY EDUC. 207 (1963); Zimmerman & Rosenthal, *Observational Learning of Rule Governed Behavior by Children*, 81 PSYCHOL. BULL. 29 (1974). For a social cognitive account of modeling, see BANDURA, *supra* note 10, at 72–78. Modeling is increasingly being used in treatment. *See* S. RACHMAN & R. HODGSON, OBSERVATIONS AND COMPULSIONS (1980); RESEARCH IN MENTAL HEALTH, *supra* note 3, at 328; Nathan, *supra* note 1, at 397. For a review of research on modeling with children, *see* Schunk, *Peer Models and Children's Behavioral Change*, 57 REV. EDUC. RES. 149 (1987).

[31]In contingency contracting (or behavioral contracting), the therapist and patient, usually working within the patient's natural environment, together choose one or more behavioral goals to be achieved and the reinforcer or aversive consequence that the patient will receive on their attainment or nonattainment. Winick, *Harnessing the Power of the Bet: Wagering with the Government as a Mechanism for Social and Individual Change*, 45 U. MIAMI L. REV. 737, 749 (1991). *See, e.g.*, D. MEICHENBAUM & D. TURK, FACILITATING TREATMENT ADHERENCE 164–84 (1987); BEHAVIOR MODIFICATION REP., *supra* note 1, at 6; D. O'BANION & D. WHALEY, BEHAVIORAL CONTRACTING: ARRANGING CONTINGENCIES OF REINFORCEMENT (1981); Kirschenbaum & Flanery, *Toward A Psychology of Behavioral Contracting*, 4 CLINICAL PSYCHOL. REV. 597 (1984). Contingency contracting has been used in marriage counseling, family therapy, and the treatment of obesity, smoking, alcoholism, drug abuse, and juvenile delinquency, and to facilitate rehabilitation of incarcerated offenders. *See* Winick, *supra* at 749–50 (citing studies).

[32]S. RACHMAN & J. TEASDALE, AVERSION THERAPY AND BEHAVIOR DISORDERS: AN ANALYSIS xii (1969); Duke & Nowicki Jr., *Theories of Personality and Psychopathology: Schools Derived From Psychology and Philosophy, in* 1 TEXTBOOK OF PSYCHIATRY, *supra* note 1, at 440; Lazarus & Fay, *supra* note 1, at 502–03. For the distinction between *aversive control*, an operant term, and *aversive conditioning*, a classical term, *see* Goldiamond, *supra* note 1, at 110 n.20. Because aversive control is a form of conditioning, I use the term *aversive conditioning* interchangeably with *aversive control* and *aversion therapy*.

[33]BEHAVIOR MODIFICATION REP., *supra* note 1, at 6–8; RACHMAN & TEASDALE, *supra* note 32, at 8–13.

sexual deviation, and compulsive shoplifting; for self-injurious behaviors in autistic children such as head banging, tongue biting, and rumination; and to alter disruptive and antisocial behavior in school children, patients hospitalized for mental illness or mental retardation, and prisoners.[34]

Another major behavior therapy approach is systematic desensitization. This technique is based on principles of classical conditioning and involves the gradual, progressive exposure of patients to anxiety-generating situations as a means of eliminating or reducing maladaptive anxiety reactions.[35] The technique has been successfully used in the treatment of phobic conditions and other psychological problems associated with emotional inhibition, such as insomnia and frigidity. In *systematic desensitization,* also known as *reciprocal inhibition,* therapists and patients construct a hierarchy of anxiety-provoking situations associated with the patients' problem. Therapists teach patients to relax deeply and then have them vividly imagine or actually experience the feared situation in graduated steps moving up the hierarchy. Patients usually do not move on to a more distressing step until they can experience the less distressing level without anxiety. In this way, by gradually pairing relaxation with the anxiety-provoking situation, patients' anxiety reaction is suppressed or counterconditioned.

Although behavioral conditioning was once understood to function under a simple stimulus–response paradigm, this traditional model neglected the all-important role of cognitive processes in human learning and behavior. In more recent years there has been a gradual shift in behavior away from the stimulus–response model to what has become

---

[34]*See generally* BANDURA, *supra* note 1, at 501–63; BEHAVIOR MODIFICATION REP., *supra* note 1, at 6–8; RACHMAN & TEASDALE, *supra* note 32; Ayllon, *supra* note 2, at 7–8; Bucher & Lovaas, *Use of Aversive Stimulation in Behavior Modification, in* MIAMI SYMPOSIUM ON THE PREDICTION OF BEHAVIOR, 1967: AVERSIVE STIMULATION 77–145 (M. Jones ed., 1968); Lazarus & Fay, *supra* note 1, at 502–03; Schwitzgebel, *Limitations on the Coercive Treatment of Offenders,* 8 CRIM. L. BULL. 267, 277–87 (1972). For clinical applications, *see, e.g.,* Arzin & Wesolowski, *Theft Reversal: An Over Correction Procedure for Eliminating Stealing by Retarded Persons,* 7 J. APPLIED BEHAV. ANALYSIS 577 (1974); Barber & Winefield, *The Influence of Stimulus Intensity and Motivational Differences on Learned Helplessness Deficits,* 8 PERSONALITY & INDIVIDUAL DIFFERENCES 25 (1987); Blatte, *supra* note 26, at 11 (reporting the use of aversion therapy in seven state prison systems); Feingold, *An Automated Technique for Aversive Conditioning in Sexual Deviations, in* PSYCHO-TECHNOLOGY: ELECTRONIC CONTROL OF MIND AND BEHAVIOR 123 (R. Schwitzgebel ed., 1973); Foreyt & Kennedy, *Treatment of Overweight by Aversion Therapy,* 9 BEHAV. RES. & THERAPY 29 (1971); Hallam & Rachman, *Some Effects of Aversion Therapy on Patients with Sexual Disorders,* 10 BEHAV. RES. & THERAPY 171 (1972); Holzinger et al., *Aversive Conditioning Treatment of Alcoholism,* 124 AM. J. PSYCHIATRY 150 (1967); Kellam, *Shoplifting Treated by Aversion to a Film,* 7 BEHAV. RES. & THERAPY 125 (1969); Lovaas et al., *Building Social Behavior in Autistic Children by Use of Electric Shock,* 1 J. EXPERIMENTAL RES. IN PERSONALITY 99 (1965); Lovibond, *Aversion Therapy for Heroin Dependence,* 2 LANCET 382 (1968); Marks & Gelder, *Transvestism and Fetishism: Clinical and Psychological Changes During Faradic Aversion,* 119 BRIT. J. PSYCHIATRY 711 (1967); Tyler & Brown, *The Use of Swift, Brief Isolation as a Group Control Device for Institutionalized Delinquents,* 5 BEHAV. RES. & THERAPY 1 (1967); Wallace et al., *Aversive Conditioning Use in Public Facilities for the Mentally Retarded,* 14 MENTAL RETARDATION 17 (1976) (aversive conditioning used in 45% of public residential facilities for those with mental retardation that responded to a survey).

[35]BANDURA, *supra* note 1, at 424–500; BEHAVIOR MODIFICATION REP., *supra* note 1, at 8–9; WOLPE & LAZARUS, *supra* note 17, at 54–101; Ayllon, *supra* note 2, at 4; Nathan, *supra* note 1, at 392–94; Nemiah & Uhde, *Phobic Disorders, in* 1 TEXTBOOK OF PSYCHIATRY, *supra* note 1, at 982. The technique was pioneered by Joseph Wolpe. *See generally* J. WOLPE, PSYCHOTHERAPY BY RECIPROCAL INHIBITION, *supra* note 1 (1958). For clinical applications, *see, e.g.,* Allen, *Effectiveness of Study Counseling and Desensitization in Alleviating Test Anxiety in College Students,* 77 J. ABNORMAL PSYCHOL. 282 (1971); Brady, *A Behavioral Approach to the Treatment of Stuttering,* 125 AM. J. PSYCHIATRY 843 (1968); Kraft, *Treatment for Sexual Perversions,* 7 BEHAV. RES. & THERAPY 215 (1969); Morganstein & Ratliff, *Systematic Desensitization as a Technique for Treating Smoking Behavior: A Preliminary Report,* 7 BEHAV. RES. & THERAPY 397 (1969); Sergeant & Yorkston, *Verbal Desensitization in the Treatment of Bronchial Asthma,* 2 LANCET 1321 (1969).

known as *cognitive behavior therapy.*[36] This new approach, "integrating behavioral and traditional approaches to psychotherapy, recognizes private events and intrapersonal factors along with the importance of environmental variables."[37] Cognitive behavior therapy regards an individual's thought processes, cognitive strategies, and beliefs as a "set of covert self-statements (private behaviors) that can be influenced by the same laws of conditioning that influence other overt behaviors."[38] As a result, the increasing number of therapists using this approach not only treat the individual's maladaptive behavior but also attempt to restructure the cognitive processes that often produce such behavior patterns.

C. Effectiveness

Behavior therapy, like psychotherapy and other treatment techniques, has proven difficult to evaluate. Clinicians using behavioral methods agree that behavior therapy is efficacious in the treatment of a wide range of problems,[39] but few systematic outcome studies comparing behavior therapy to other techniques have been performed.[40] The absence of such research was due in part to the lack of general agreement among professionals on a set of outcome measures appropriate for a comparative analysis of the various therapies. This is one of the consequences of the differing models of mental illness on which behavior therapy and psychodynamic-oriented psychotherapies are based.[41] The few comparative studies that were performed in the 1970s do not conclusively demonstrate any significant

---

[36]Arnkoff & Glass, *Cognitive Therapy and Psychotherapy Integration, in* HISTORY OF PSYCHOTHERAPY: A CENTURY OF CHANGE 657, 658 (D. Freedheim ed., 1992) [hereinafter HISTORY OF PSYCHOTHERAPY]. *See infra* notes 77–86 and accompanying text. *See generally* A. BANDURA, *supra* note 10; A. BECK, COGNITIVE THERAPY AND THE EMOTIONAL DISORDERS (1976); A. BECK & G. EMERY, ANXIETY AND PHOBIAS: A COGNITIVE PERSPECTIVE (1985); COGNITIVE-BEHAVIORAL INTERVENTIONS: THEORY, RESEARCH, AND PROCEDURES (P. KENDALL & S. HOLLON EDS., 1979); HANDBOOK OF COGNITIVE-BEHAVIORAL THERAPIES (K. Dobson ed., 1988); A. LAZARUS, BEHAVIOR THERAPY AND BEYOND (1971); M. MAHONEY, COGNITION AND BEHAVIOR MODIFICATION (1974); D. MEICHENBAUM, COGNITIVE BEHAVIOR MODIFICATION: AN INTEGRATIVE APPROACH (1977); C. THORESEN & M. MAHONEY, BEHAVIOR SELF-CONTROL (1974); D. TURK ET AL., PAIN AND BEHAVIORAL MEDICINE: A COGNITIVE BEHAVIORAL PERSPECTIVE (1983); Beck, *Cognitive Therapy: Nature and Relation to Behavior Therapy,* 1 BEHAV. THERAPY 184 (1970); Boneau, *Paradigm Regained?: Cognitive Behaviorism Restated,* 29 AM. PSYCHOL. 297 (1974); Kendall, *Cognitive Processes and Procedures in Behavior Therapy, in* REVIEW OF BEHAVIOR THERAPY: THEORY AND PRACTICE 114 (11th ed. 1987); Meichenbaum & Cameron, *Cognitive–Behavior Therapy, in* CONTEMPORARY BEHAVIOR THERAPY, *supra* note 1, at 310. A journal devoted to the field, COGNITIVE THERAPY AND RESEARCH, was founded in 1977 and edited by Michael Mahoney, a leading proponent.

[37]Arnkoff & Glass, *supra* note 36, at 658.

[38]Hollon & Beck, *Cognitive and Cognitive–Behavioral Therapies, in* HANDBOOK OF PSYCHOTHERAPY AND BEHAVIOR CHANGE, 428, 429 (A. Bergen & S. Garfield eds., 4th ed. 1994) [hereinafter HANDBOOK OF PSYCHOTHERAPY].

[39]*E.g.,* Atthowe, *supra* note 2, at 644–45; Lieberman & Bedell, *supra* note 1, at 1462–82; Nathan, *supra* note 1, at 397–98.

[40]BEHAVIOR MODIFICATION REP., *supra* note 1, at 10; Luborsky et al., *Comparative Studies of Psychotherapies: Is It True That "Everyone Has Won and All Must Have Prizes?,"* 32 ARCHIVES GEN. PSYCHIATRY 995, 1001–02 (1975).

[41]BEHAVIOR MODIFICATION REP., *supra* note 1, at 10.

difference between behavior therapy and other psychotherapies,[42] with the exception of certain phobias, some forms of compulsive behavior, and certain sexual dysfunctions, for which behavior therapy may be superior.[43] Although many systematic outcome studies were performed in the 1980s and 1990s,[44] this conclusion remains essentially the same.[45] However, recent research supports the superiority of cognitive–behavioral interventions as compared to minimal treatment and nonspecific controls and the conclusion that such interventions are equal or superior to psychosocial or pharmacological approaches and have more long-lasting effects.[46]

Although the conditioning techniques may be quite successful in effecting alterations in behavior, considerable evidence suggests that the effects of many are short-lived, restricted to the controlled clinical setting in which the conditioning occurs, and do not generalize to

---

[42]Three reviews of the comparative studies have reached essentially this conclusion. Luborsky and his colleagues reviewed 19 controlled comparisons in 12 studies (excluding comparative studies on patients with specific "habit" disturbances like bedwetting or smoking). Of these, behavior therapy was deemed superior to the other psychotherapies in 6 comparisons, but no different in 13. Finding five of the six studies favoring behavior therapy to be of relatively poor research quality, the authors concluded that the differences were insignificant. Luborsky et al., *supra* note 40, at 1001–02. Eysenck and Beech concluded that "behavior therapists have not done conspicuously better than psychotherapists and psychoanalysts in demonstrating the clinical effectiveness of their methods, as compared to other methods, or even to spontaneous remission." Eysenck & Beech, *Counter Conditioning and Related Methods, in* HANDBOOK OF PSYCHOTHERAPY AND BEHAVIOR CHANGE 543, 600 (A. Bergin & S. Garfield eds., 1971). Russell concluded: "Behavior methods appear to have almost no greater ability to change behavior than other methods previously developed . . . . After 20 years of research, there is no reliable evidence that behavior techniques are much more effective than time-honored methods of control." Russell, *The Power of Behavior Control: A Critique of Behavior Modification Methods,* 30 J. CLINICAL PSYCHOL. 111, 122 (1974). Other more recent comparative studies have reached similar results. Brand and Glenn found no statistically significant incremental efficacy of behavior group therapy over standard hospital treatment alone for clinically depressed geriatric inpatients. Brand & Glenn, *Group Behavioral Therapy with Depressed Geriatric Inpatients: An Assessment of Incremental Efficacy,* 23 BEHAV. THERAPY 475 (1992). Douglas and his colleagues found no significant group differences between groups receiving behaviorally oriented marital therapy and those receiving insight-oriented marital therapy at either termination or 6-month follow-up, but by 4-year follow-up, a significantly higher percentage of couples receiving behavioral marital therapy were divorced compared to couples receiving insight-oriented marital therapy. Douglas et al., *Long-Term Effectiveness of Behavioral Versus Insight-Oriented Marital Therapy: A 4-Year Follow-Up Study,* 59 J. CONSULTING & CLINICAL PSYCHOL. 138 (1991). Kalodner and DeLucia found that no positive change in diet occurred regardless of which type of treatment was administered. Kalodner & DeLucia, *The Individual and the Combined Effects of Cognitive Therapy and Nutrition Education as Additions to a Behavior Modification Program for Weight Loss,* 16 ADDICTIVE BEHAVIORS 255 (1991).

[43]Higgins et al., *Achieving Cocaine Abstinence with a Behavioral Approach,* 150 AM. J. PSYCHIATRY 763 (1993); Lieberman & Bedell, *supra* note 1, at 1467; Luborsky et al., *supra* note 40, at 1004. Skilled personnel in cognitive behavior therapy can permanently reduce panic and phobia by exposing patients to the symptoms of panic and feared situations. Mattick et al., *Treatment of Panic and Agoraphobia: An Integrative Review,* 178 J. NERVOUS & MENTAL DISEASE 567 (1990); *Report of the Task Panel on Research, in* IV TASK PANEL REPORTS SUBMITTED TO THE PRESIDENT'S COMM'N ON MENTAL HEALTH, 1751 (1978) [hereinafter PRESIDENT'S COMM'N TASK PANEL REPORTS]. *Contra* Russell, *supra* note 42, at 117–20.

[44]*See* Emmelkamp, *Behavior Therapy With Adults, in* HISTORY OF PSYCHOTHERAPY, *supra* note 36, at 379–417 (summarizing and analyzing comparative studies).

[45]*See* Bergin & Lambert, *The Effectiveness of Psychotherapy, in* HANDBOOK OF PSYCHOTHERAPY, *supra* note 38, at 156 ("[M]eta-analytic methods have now been extensively applied to large groups of comparative studies, and these reviews generally offer similar conclusions (i.e., little or no difference between therapies)"); *Id.* at 181 ("behavioral and cognitive methods appear to add a significant increment of efficacy with respect to a number of difficult problems (e.g., panic, phobias, and compulsion)").

[46]Hollon & Beck, *supra* note 38, at 428.

other behaviors or to "real world" settings.[47] This may be particularly true for institutionalized patients released to a community in which the contingencies of reinforcement are quite different from those within the facility where they were conditioned. Despite these difficulties and the need for additional research, it can be concluded that behavior therapies show considerable promise for the treatment of a variety of problems and are probably the treatment of choice in certain conditions. Moreover, these techniques are easily taught to nonprofessionals and therefore have a greater service delivery potential than many of the other treatment methods, can be considerably less costly, and usually require a much shorter period of time for positive results.[48]

D. Potential Abuse and Relative Intrusiveness

Although behavior therapy has undoubtedly been beneficial to many patients, some of the techniques may result in adverse effects, particularly when misapplied, a not uncommon occurrence in a field where "the procedures are generally simple enough to be used by persons lacking the training to evaluate them appropriately."[49] The aversive techniques are especially vulnerable to abuse[50] and may be seriously damaging to patients. The harmful side effects that may occur with aversion therapy include "pain, frustration, increased aggressiveness, arousal, general and specific anxieties, somatic and physiological malfunctions, and development of various unexpected and often pathological operant behaviors."[51] Moreover, although the techniques using positive reinforcement typically produce no physical side effects, the deprivations central to some of the aversive techniques may exist as well in some positive reinforcement procedures. Token economies and tier systems, for example, sometimes make meals, a bed, toilet articles, outdoor exercise, writing and reading

---

[47]BEHAVIOR MODIFICATION REP., *supra* note 1, at 7 (aversion therapy); Gruber, *Behavior Therapy: Problems in Generalization,* 2 BEHAV. THERAPY 361 (1971); Keeley et al., *Operant Chemical Intervention: Behavior Management or Beyond? Where Are the Data?,* 7 BEHAV. THERAPY 292, 302 (1976); Lieberman & Bedell, *supra* note 1, at 1464; Nathan, *supra* note 1, at 398; Russell, *supra* note 42, at 128–29 (token economies). This process may be explained in Skinnerian terms as *operant extinction,* the decrease in frequency of the conditioned response when reinforcement is no longer forthcoming. B. SKINNER, SCIENCE AND HUMAN BEHAVIOR, *supra* note 12, at 69–72.

[48]BEHAVIOR MODIFICATION REP., *supra* note 1, at 11; Nathan, *supra* note 1, at 398. The mean number of behavior therapy sessions is about 30, compared to a mean of about 600 sessions for psychoanalysis. WOLPE & LAZARUS, *supra* note 17, at 156.

[49]BEHAVIOR MODIFICATION REP., *supra* note 1, at 21. See J. MAY ET AL., GUIDELINES FOR THE USE OF BEHAVIORAL PROCEDURES IN STATE PROGRAMS FOR RETARDED PERSONS 3 (1975) ("[B]ehavioral programs have expanded so rapidly that occasions of abuses and misuses by well-intentioned but ill-informed individuals and occasionally deliberate misuses with malicious and sadistic intent have resulted.")

[50]Ayllon, *supra* note 2, at 18 n.65.

[51]S. RACHMAN & J. TEASDALE, *supra* note 32, at 90; Ayllon, *supra* note 2, at 8 (listing as side effects avoidance, escape, fear, undesirable emotional responses, and the production of inappropriate behavior, including anxiety, truancy, stealing, lying, and various nervous habits). As a result of these adverse side effects, there is consensus that aversion therapy should generally be used only as a last resort, after positive reinforcement alone has failed, and then only in conjunction with positive reinforcement so that desirable behaviors may be substituted for the problem behavior. *See* BANDURA, *supra* note 1, at 509; BEHAVIOR MODIFICATION REP., *supra* note 1, at 16; RACHMAN & J. TEASDALE, *supra* note 32, at 94; Ayllon, *supra* note 2, at 7–9, 18; Atthowe, *supra* note 2, at 640–41; Whitman, *supra* note 1, at 958.

materials, religious services, and other basic personal requirements available contingent on the patient behaving in conformity with program goals.[52]

Personnel inadequately trained in the design and implementation of behavioral programs have abused and misused these procedures.[53] The potential danger is illustrated by a scandal concerning a token economy and tier system operated at a Florida retardation training center for boys.[54] In Phase 1 of the program, the boys were able to earn tokens for appropriate behavior but, because of a defect in the program's design, they could not redeem the tokens for reinforcers until they had accumulated a sufficient number to advance to Phase

---

[52]See BEHAVIOR MODIFICATION REP., *supra* note 1, at 18; R. MARTIN, LEGAL CHALLENGES TO BEHAVIOR MODIFICATION 84 (1975); Lucero et al., *Regulating Operant Conditioning Programs,* 19 HOSP. & COMMUNITY PSYCHIATRY 53 (1968); Lieberman & Bedell, *supra* note 1, at 1463; Roth et al., *Into the Abyss: Psychiatric Reliability and Emergency Commitment Statutes,* 13 SANTA CLARA L. REV. 400, 410 (1973); Wexler, *supra* note 22, at 84–90. Programs using such fundamental privileges as reinforcers may violate patients' constitutional rights and, because they are quite unlike the natural situations prevailing outside the institution, may also be ineffective for most patients in accomplishing behavioral change that will continue outside the clinical setting. Budd & Baer, *Behavior Modification and the Law: Implications of Recent Judicial Decisions,* 4 J. PSYCHIATRY & L. 171, 190–191 (1976). Some patients, however, are so debilitated that effective treatment may require the temporary use of basic privileges as reinforcers. *Id.* at 191, 201–03.

[53]MARTIN, *supra* note 52, at 83, 107–17; MAY ET AL., *supra* note 49, at 10; Goldiamond, *supra* note 1, at 3–4; *see, e.g.,* Morgan v. Sproat, 432 F. Supp. 1130 (S.D. Miss. 1977); Morales v. Turman, 364 F. Supp. 166, 170, 175 (E.D. Tex. 1973) and 383 F. Supp. 53 (E.D. Tex. 1974), *rev'd on procedural grounds,* 535 F.2d 864 (5th Cir. 1976), *vacated and remanded,* 430 U.S. 322 (1977), *on remand,* 562 F.2d 993 (5th Cir. 1977).

[54]The following discussion is taken from an account by Wexler, a member of the Florida Division of Retardation Task Force formed to study behavior modification procedures in the wake of the retardation center scandal. Wexler, *Behavior Modification and Other Behavior Change Procedures: The Emerging Law and the Proposed Florida Guidelines,* 11 CRIM. L. BULL. 600, 609–10 (1975).

[55]Wexler, *supra* note 54, at 609. For a similar example of behavior modification abuse, also apparently due to untrained staff, see *Boy Confined: Two Teachers Fired,* MIAMI HERALD, Jan. 7, 1976, at A3, describing the use of an improvised "behavior modification" box in which retarded children were locked as a means to control violent tantrums. The 4½-by-4½-by-3-foot wooden box had no interior illumination, almost no ventilation, and only two small silver-dollar-sized holes for observation. Such "timeout" techniques are easily abused, especially in institutional settings. MARTIN, *supra* note 52, at 85–86; BEHAVIOR MODIFICATION REP., *supra* note 1, at 16; *see, e.g.,* Morgan v. Sproat, 432 F. Supp. 1130 (S.D. Miss. 1977). Additional examples of abuse caused by "breakdowns in practice" of behavior modification programs include the following:

> In one school token economy, aides would fail to record points earned by students they did not like. In one prison system the lack of administrative support resulted in no rewards being made available after points had been earned. In some programs, there are opportunities for subjective judgments in awarding points and this can lead to abuses which are difficult to detect. The verbal comments made when points are given out, not given out, or taken away can provide an opportunity for insulting remarks.

1 LAW & BEHAV. 8 (1976).

Abuses such as these could be largely dissipated by acceptance of the suggestion of the National Institute of Mental Health for

> a limitation on the decisionmaking responsibilities of program staff to those matters in which they have expertise. Persons with appropriate professional qualifications, such as a suitable level of training and

2. This delayed reinforcement rendered the tokens ineffectual to control behavior problems at precisely the time when such problems were anticipated to be most difficult. As a result, with positive reinforcement unavailable, the untrained staff were left to devise their own remedies and in frustration resorted to increasingly punitive measures:[55]

> The abuses . . . included, among many other things, forced public masturbation and forced public homosexual acts as punishment for engaging in proscribed sexual behavior; beatings with a wooden panel for running away; and washing the mouth with soap for lying, for abusive or vulgar language, or sometimes for speaking at all. Further, food, sleep, and visitation privileges were withheld as punishment; incontinence was punished by requiring residents to lie in soiled sheets and to hold soiled underwear to their noses; a resident accused of theft was addressed by staff and residents as "the thief" and was required to wear a sign so designating him; and one boy was required to walk around publicly clothed only in female underpants.

Serious abuses are presented by the involuntary application of the behavior therapies. Although leading behavior therapists[56] and professional organizations[57] consider the patient's informed consent to be an ethical prerequisite, this principle may be frequently violated in institutional settings. Coercive applications of these techniques, particularly for institutionalized populations and sometimes involving intrusive aversive methods, were

---

supervised clinical practice, are able to design and organize treatment programs, develop measurement systems, and evaluate the outcome of behavior modification programs. . . . Technicians, paraprofessionals, and other workers with only minimal training in behavior modification generally can function in the setting in which behavior is being modified but should not initiate decisions affecting the welfare of other individuals, unless those decisions are reviewed by the professional staff.
BEHAVIOR MODIFICATION REP., *supra* at 21.

[56]*E.g.,* RACHMAN & TEASDALE, *supra* note 32, at 94; Allyon, *supra* note 2, at 11–13; Bandura, *The Ethics and Social Purposes of Behavior Modification, in* 3 ANNUAL REVIEW OF BEHAVIOR THERAPY: THEORY AND PRACTICE 13 (C. Franks & G. Wilson eds., 1975) (past president of the American Psychological Association); Davison & Stuart, *Behavior Therapy and Civil Liberties,* 30 AM. PSYCHOL. 755, 760 (1975) (past presidents of the Association for Advancement of Behavior Therapy); see BEHAVIOR MODIFICATION REP., *supra* note 1, at 16, 20–21; Begelman, *Ethical and Legal Issues of Behavior Modification, in* PROGRESS IN BEHAVIOR MODIFICATION 159, 176, 184 (M. Hersen et al. eds., 1975).

[57]*E.g., Ethical Issues for Human Services,* 8 BEHAV. THERAPY 763–64 (1977) (statement of Association for Advancement of Behavior Therapy). The American Psychological Association and the American Orthopsychiatric Association, two of the leading professional organizations, were among those submitting as *amici curiae* a proposal to the district court in Wyatt v. Hardin that it adopt specific standards for the application of aversive conditioning, including a requirement that such treatment not be given without the written informed consent of the patient, or in the case of a patient incompetent to consent, without the finding of an independent review committee that such treatment is in the best interests of the patient, and the informed consent of the patient's guardian or next of kin. Proposed Revision of Standard, No. 9 relating to Bryce and Searcy Hospitals of the Court's Order of April 13, 1972, *in* Wyatt v. Stickney, 1 MENTAL DISABILITY L. REP. 55 (1976). *See also* BEHAVIOR MODIFICATION REP., *supra* note 1, at 18 ("[A]versive techniques are neither legally nor ethically acceptable when they are used . . . without the consent of the person on whom they are used, or his guardian.").

well documented in the 1970s in the literature,[58] congressional reports,[59] and cases.[60] Moreover, coercive behavior modification is not without its advocates, particularly for use

---

[58]Halleck, *Legal and Ethical Aspects of Behavior Control*, 131 Am. J. Psychiatry 381, 382 (1974):

> [A]versive therapy (with some troubling exceptions) is not regularly used with non-consenting patients. The use of operant methods with the non-consenting patient, however, is more common. Some patients are required to live in units where a token system that rewards socially approved behavior is enforced without the patient's ever having agreed to participate in such a program. Behavior-shaping programs are also used in more traditional hospital wards without his consent. In such instances the staff merely decided what type of behavior it wishes to reinforce and creates an environment that provides such reinforcement. Since there is no informed consent here the treatment can be viewed as coercive.

For examples of coercive applications of behavior therapy, see Gerber et al., *Behavior Modification in Maximum Security Settings: One Hospital's Experience*, 13 Am. Crim. L. Rev. 85 (1975) (aversive program using a drug that induces paralysis); Gambrill, *supra* note 27 (describing a token economy and tier system in juvenile detention facility); Ludwig et al., *The Control of Violent Behavior Through Faradic Shock*, 148 J. Nervous & Mental Diseases 624 (1964) (describing the use of electric shock in aversive treatment of violent patient "administered against the expressed will of the patient"); Mattocks & Jew, *Assessment of an Aversive "Contract" Program with Extreme Acting-Out Criminal Offenders*, in Experimentation With Human Beings 1016 (J. Katz ed., 1972) (describing the use of Anectine, a muscle relaxant, which when injected intravenously results in brief muscle paralysis and respiratory arrest described by the patients as a "terrible, scary experience" likened to dying or almost drowning; "five patients were included in the treatment program against their will."); Ramey, *Use of Electric Shock in the Classroom: The Remediation of Self-Abusive Behavior of a Retarded Child*, 1 Behav. Engineering 4 (No.2, Winter 1973–74) (200 volt shock to 11-year-old boy without mention of consent from child or parent), *cited in* Opton Psychiatric Violence Against Prisoners: When Therapy is Punishment, 45 Miss. L. J. 605 (No. 1, 1974); Russell, *supra* note 42, at 125 (token economies applied coercively in institutional settings); P. Steinfels, *A Clockwork Orange—Or Just a Lemon?*, 4 Hastings Ctr. Rep., Apr. 1974, at 10–11 (behavior control programs in prisons).

[59]*E.g.*, Individual Rights and Behavior Modification, *supra* note 1; Comptroller Gen'l of the U.S., Behavior Modification Programs: The Bureau of Prisons' Alternative to Long Term Segregation (Aug. 5, 1975); Report of Subcomm. on Courts, Civil Liberties, and the Administration of Justice of the House Comm. on the Judiciary, 93rd Cong., 2d Sess., Inspection of Federal Facilities of Leavenworth Penitentiary and the Medical Center for Federal Prisoners (Jan. 1974).

[60]Knecht v. Gillman, 488 F.2d 1136 (8th Cir. 1973) (vomit-inducing drug Apomorphine used in aversion treatment program at Iowa Security Medical Facility without consent); Mackey v. Procunier, 477 F.2d 877 (9th Cir. 1973) (use without consent in California prison aversion treatment program of Anectine to induce respiratory paralysis); Clonce v. Richardson, 379 F. Supp. 338 (W.D. Mo. 1974) (prisoners involuntarily placed in Project START, a tier system at the Medical Center for Federal Prisoners at Springfield, Missouri; in the "orientation" phase prisoners were barred from reading literature, religious materials, and political publications; viewing television; and listening to the radio); *see* Knight, *Child Molesters Try Shock Cure*, N.Y. Times, May 21, 1974, at 43; Wolfe & Marino, *A Program of Behavior Treatment for Incarcerated Pedophiles*, 13 Am. Crim. L. Rev. 69 (1975); Armstrong v. Bensinger, No.100, 71-2144 (N.D. Ill. 1972), *order vacated and remanded for reconsideration of relief sub nom.* United States *ex rel.* Miller v. Twomey, 479 F.2d 701 (7th Cir.), *cert. denied*, 414 U.S. 1146 (1973) (involuntary tier program at Illinois prison), *cited in* Goldberger, *Court Challenges to Prison Behavior Modification Programs: A Case Study*, 13 Am. Crim. L. Rev. 37 (1975); Swearingum v. Johnson, No. M56-73-CA, described in 2 L. & Behav. 3 (1977) (involuntary token economy program at Michigan prison).

with criminals and the socially deviant.[61] Finally, in view of the many subtle and not so subtle pressures at work in mental hospitals and prisons, consent provided by these populations may not be truly voluntary.[62]

These problems are heightened in institutional settings where the therapist not only occasionally selects treatment means without patient consultation but also may set the target goals of the procedure as well.[63] Some of the goals selected raise substantial questions. Is it appropriate to use aversive techniques to discourage masturbation,[64] to eradicate swearing,[65] or to penalize ''lack of cooperation and involvement with the individual treatment program prescribed''?[66] Should even benign positive reinforcers be used to encourage submissive sex roles in female patients,[67] to shape exceedingly docile classroom behavior in

---

[61]*See, e.g.,* McConnell, *Stimulus/Response: Criminals Can Be Brainwashed—Now,* 3 PSYCHOL. TODAY 14, 16, 74 (Apr. 1970):

> In effect, we have but two means of educating people or rats or flatworms—we can either reward them for doing the right thing or punish them for doing the wrong thing. . . . I believe that the day has come when we can combine sensory deprivation with drugs, hypnosis and astute manipulation of reward and punishment to gain almost absolute control over an individual's behavior. It should be possible then to achieve a very rapid and highly effective type of positive brainwashing that would allow us to make dramatic changes in a person's behavior and personality. . . . We should reshape our society so that we all would be trained from birth to want to do what society wants us to do. We have the techniques now to do it. Only by using them can we hope to maximize human potentiality. . . . I don't believe the Constitution of the United States gives you the right to commit a crime if you want to; therefore, the Constitution does not guarantee you the *right* to maintain inviolable the personality it forced on you in the first place—if and when the personality manifests strongly antisocial behavior. . . . Today's behavioral psychologists are the architects and engineers of the Brave New World.

See also Singer, *Psychological Studies of Punishment,* 58 CAL. L. REV. 405, 433–34, 442 (1970):

> Given the time and the resources a behavior therapy program could make a bank robber want to vomit every time he saw a bank, could make an armed robber shudder every time he saw a gun. . . . It seems reasonable that aversion therapy would most effectively suppress criminal behavior where the offender genuinely wants to reform but needs help. It should, however, also be a valuable adjunct to other forms of punishment and treatment with less cooperative subjects. While a voluntary aversion program would probably be most effective, involuntary treatment would also work. . . . [S]uccess with clinical aversion therapy indicates that its extension to the treatment of many criminal offenses would be appropriate.

A federal prison official was quoted as stating that involvement in prison behavior modification programs is ''part of the consequence of committing a crime.'' *''Behavior Mod'' Behind the Walls,* TIME, March 11, 1974, at 74.

[62]BEHAVIOR MODIFICATION REP., *supra* note 1, at 20; Freidman, *supra* note 1, at 80–87; Gaylin & Blatte, *supra* note 24, at 24 (''Although therapy is voluntary, inmates are aware that the only way to get out of Patuxent is to participate in therapy.''); Serber et al., *Behavior Modification in Maximum Security Settings: One Hospital's Experience,* 13 AM. CRIM. L. REV. 85, 88–89 (1975); *see, e.g.,* Goldsmith v. Dean, No. 2:93-CV-383 (D. Vt. filed Dec., 1993) (completion of treatment program including aversive conditioning features required as condition for sex offender release to community custody status). For a discussion of the impact of these institutional pressures on the ability of patients and prisoners to provide voluntary consent to treatment, see *infra* chapter 18.

[63]BEHAVIOR MODIFICATION REP., *supra* note 1, at 15, 17; Moya & Achtenberg, *Behavior Modification: Legal Limitations on Methods and Goals,* 50 NOTRE DAME L. REV. 230, 232 (1974); Roos, *Human Rights and Behavior Modification,* 12 MENTAL RETARDATION 3, 4, 6 (1974); Wexler, *supra* note 54, at 603; Wexler, *Behavior Modification and Legal Developments,* 18 AM. BEHAV. SCI. 679, 683 (1975).

[64]*See supra* note 55 and accompanying text.

[65]*See* Knecht v. Gillman, 488 F.2d 1136 (8th Cir. 1973) (vomit-inducing drug Apomorphine ''injected for such pieces of behavior as not getting up, for giving cigarettes against orders, for talking, for swearing, for lying'').

[66]*See* Reimringer et al., *Succinylcholine as a Modifier of Acting Out Behavior,* CLINICAL MED. July 1970, at 28–29.

[67]*See* Roth & Lerner, *Sex-Based Discrimination in the Mental Institutionalization of Women,* 62 CAL. L. REV. 789, 794–95, 801–03 (1974); Roth et al., *supra* note 52, at 410.

students,[68] to change a hospitalized patient's Southern accent into a more businesslike Midwestern accent,[69] or to encourage the performance of institutional labor by patients in hospital maintenance programs?[70] Too frequently these questions are left solely to the therapist, a practice that is especially troubling when the therapist is employed by a hospital, retardation facility, or prison with institutional interests that often conflict with the therapeutic interests of the patient.[71] One leading behavioral psychologist has questioned whether "the methods and efforts of psychologists are being used more to produce adaptable institutional residents than self-reliant individuals equipped with the personal and social resources to lead a dignified life in the larger society."[72] Moreover, although the behavior therapist is an expert in the selection of therapeutic means, the therapist has no special claim to competence in the choice of therapeutic objectives.[73] The latter involves value judgments

---

[68]*Compare* Winett & Winkler, *Current Behavior Modification in the Classroom: Be Still, Be Quiet, Be Docile,* 5 J. APPLIED BEHAV. ANALYSIS 499 (1972) *with* O'Leary, *Behavior Modification in the Classroom: A Rejoinder to Winett & Winkler,* 5 J. APPLIED BEHAV. ANALYSIS 505 (1972).

[69]*See* Goldiamond, *supra* note 1.

[70]*See* R. MARTIN, *supra* note 52, at 61; BEHAVIOR MODIFICATION REP., *supra* note 1, at 20; Kazdin & Bottzin, *supra* note 25, at 343; Wexler, *supra* note 54, at 603.

[71]Holland, Behavior Modification for Prisoners, Patients, and Other People as a Prescription for the Planned Society, Address at a meeting of the Eastern Psychological Association (Apr. 19, 1974):

> Usually the aim [of the institutional token economy programs] is to decrease assertiveness. People are "kept in their proper place." An elite stratum doles out reinforcers to a lower stratum, and the objectives are set from above, either to adapt the participant to another's goals or to exploit him for another's gain. Guards reinforce prisoners, nurses reinforce patients, and teachers reinforce students, all in order to create malleable patients, prisoners, or students. The fear of manipulative control is well founded when a professional-to-client relationship is lacking (i.e., when control is exercised by and for the benefits of persons other than those whose behavior is to be changed). They cannot choose to deal or not to deal with the professional. The behavior modifier is responsible to some third person or organization. The subject neither provides his income nor determines his promotion. The behavior modifier in prison is fundamentally and inescapably responsible to the warden or to the Bureau of Corrections, not the prisoner; in the classroom, he is responsible to the principal or Board of Education, not to the students. Simply put, today's token economies support established power structures.

See BEHAVIOR MODIFICATION REP., *supra* note 1, at 16, 21; Gambrill, *supra* note 27, at 57–58:

> most [target] behaviors which staff selected for inclusion in the [token economy] program emphasized institutional management, for example, line-ups, meal conduct, bathroom conduct, and maintenance tasks. . . . Some behaviors competed with classroom attendance. For example, most detainees would rather participate in an outside work detail than attend class and could earn more points for this than for going to class.

Ramey, *supra* note 58, at 623; Rundle, *Institution vs. Ethics: The Dilemma of Prison Doctor,* 2 HASTINGS CTR. REP., Nov. 1972, at 7.

[72]Bandura, *supra* note 56, at 16. *See also* MARTIN, *supra* note 52, at 62. For example, it has been suggested that the goal of the Federal Bureau of Prisoners' tier system for prisoners, Project START, "was clearly to make them compliant prisoners, not to rehabilitate them for a life outside the institution." 1 LAW & BEHAV. 5 (Winter 1976). Holland, *supra* note 71, at 6 ("In short, START was to make passive, non-assertive, depersonalized inmates of the total institution, to shape the institutional neurosis described in Goffman's ASYLUMS. . . . At best the aim of the program was adjustment—adjustment to the peculiar world of prisons; at worst, the program was exploitive"). *See also* BEHAVIOR MODIFICATION REP., *supra* note 1, at 16 ("Frequently, the goal of effective modification in penal institutions has been the preservation of the institution's authoritarian control. . . . [Some] programs have been directed toward making the prisoners less troublesome and easier to handle, adjusting the inmates to the needs of the institution."). Geller et al., *supra* note 26, at 32.

[73]*See* BANDURA, *supra* note 1, at 101; K. O'LEARY & G. WILSON, BEHAVIOR THERAPY: APPLICATION AND OUTCOME 27 (1975); B. SKINNER, BEYOND FREEDOM AND DIGNITY 150 (1971) ("[Behavior] technology is ethically neutral. It can be used by villain or saint. There is nothing in methodology which determines the values governing its use."). Bandura, *supra* note 56, at 17 ("There is no justification for therapists imposing their value preferences upon clients, who must bear the consequences of whatever changes they undergo. Being an expert on how to modify behavior does not entitle one to tell others how they should live their lives.").

best left to the patient when competent, or when not competent, to some substitute decision maker or decision-making process reflecting the patient's wishes or responsive solely to the patient's best interests.[74]

The behavior therapies thus present opportunities for a number of abuses, particularly when coercively applied in institutional settings. Some, notably the aversive techniques, may be quite physically intrusive and have adverse physical and emotional side effects. Some involve substantial deprivations and severe physical pain.

Do these techniques, however, present the potential for behavior control dramatically portrayed by the media and in fiction?[75] Undoubtedly many of the behavior therapies may be more difficult for a patient to resist than verbal psychotherapy. Coercive applications of potent positive or aversive stimuli may modify specific behavior even in an unwilling patient, by in effect inducing the patient's cooperation. However, there is little evidence that such behavior changes will persist, absent the patient's willingness, outside the coercive situation.[76] Thus, any behavioral changes accomplished against the patient's will are impermanent and reversible.

Although the process of conditioning was once assumed to occur automatically, it now is regarded as "cognitively mediated."[77] Behavior is no longer understood as being reflexively or mechanically conditioned by environmental stimuli.[78] Rather than automatically strengthening behavior without the conscious involvement of the individual, reinforcement functions as an "informative and motivational influence."[79] Internal cognitive processes determine how individuals experience reinforcement—how they attend to, process, and remember it—and ultimately, how it affects their present and future conduct. By experiencing reinforcement, individuals learn the instrumental or functional value of their behavior, that is, they learn to predict and to expect certain things to happen if they behave in certain ways.[80] Reinforcers thus impart information, which serves as a guide for action.[81] "Contrary to the mechanistic metaphors" of traditional behavorism, "outcomes change behavior in humans through the influence of thought."[82] Consequences or reinforcers influence action as a result of their incentive value to the individual.[83] After an individual has recognized the instrumental relation between actions and anticipated benefits or detriments, contingent reinforcers may produce behavior depending on how the individual

---

[74]*See* O'LEARY & WILSON, *supra* note 73, at 27–28; Wilson & Davison, *Behavior Therapy: A Road To Self-Control*, PSYCHOL. TODAY 52, 59–60 (1975); Roos, *supra* note 63, at 5.

[75]*E.g.,* Sansweet, *Aversion Therapy: Punishing of People to Change Behavior Gains Use, Controversy*, WALL ST. J., Jan. 2, 1974, at 1 (quoting psychiatrist as commenting that aversion therapy "smacks of Big Brother and thought control, of humans turned into automatons."); *see* Chorover, *Big Brother and Psychotechnology*, PSYCHOL. TODAY, Oct. 1973, at 43; Friedenberg, *Behavior Mod: Is the Pigeon Always Right?*, RAMPARTS, Dec. 1975, at 55. For a review of science fiction literature dealing with behavioral psychology, see Brodsky & Melvin, *Psy–Fi*, HUMAN BEHAV., Jan. 1976, at 65.

[76]Russell, *supra* note 42, at 131; *see supra* note 47 and accompanying text.

[77]Bandura, *Behavior Therapy and the Models of Man*, 29 AM. PSYCHOL. 859 (1974). *See, e.g.,* C. THORESEN & M. MAHONEY, BEHAVIORAL SELF-CONTROL (1974); Boneau, *supra* note 36, at 297.

[78]BANDURA, *supra* note 10, at 13; Bandura, *supra* note 77, at 859 ("Contrary to popular belief, the fabled reflexive conditioning in humans is largely a myth.").

[79]BANDURA, *supra* note 10, at 122; Bandura, *supra* note 77, at 860; *see also* GLEITMAN, *supra* note 8, at 96.

[80]*See* BANDURA, *supra* note 10, at 13, 42–13; GLEITMAN, *supra* note 8, at 96; B. ROTTER, SOCIAL LEARNING AND CLINICAL PSYCHOL. (1954); Bandura, *supra* note 77, at 859–60.

[81]Bandura, *supra* note 77, at 860; *see also* BANDURA, *supra* note 10, at 122 (It is "more fitting to speak of *guidance* of behavior by anticipated incentives than *reinforcement* of behavior by reinforcers.").

[82]Bandura, *supra* note 77, at 860.

[83]*Id.*

values the incentive or disincentive and the behavior itself.[84] The individual, under this account, is viewed "as a gatherer, processor, and user of information rather than as a simple reactor to external carrots, whips, and the stimuli associated with them."[85] What emerges is a reconceptualization of behavior theory that does not reject the basic insights of classical or operant conditioning, but builds on them, recasting them into a revised paradigm of cognitive behaviorism.[86]

In his presidential address before the American Psychological Association, Albert Bandura, a leading behavioral theorist, dispelled the "mechanistic metaphor" long associated with the process of conditioning:[87]

> So-called conditioned reactions are largely self-activated on the basis of learned expectations rather than automatically evoked. . . .
>
> Explanations of reinforcement originally assumed that consequences increase behavior without conscious involvement. The still prevalent notion that reinforcers can operate insidiously arouses fears that improved techniques of reinforcement will enable authorities to manipulate people without their knowledge or consent. Although the empirical issue is not yet completely resolved, there is little evidence that rewards function as automatic strengtheners of human conduct. Behavior is not much affected by its consequences without awareness of what is being reinforced. . . . After individuals discern the instrumental relationship between action and outcome, contingent rewards may produce accommodating or oppositional behavior depending on how they value the incentives, the influences and the behavior itself, and how others respond. Thus reinforcement, as it has become better understood, has changed from a mechanical strengthener of conduct to an informative and motivating influence.

It is thus helpful to regard reinforcers as "motivators" and consequences as "sources of motivation that depend heavily for their effectiveness upon the incentive preferences of those undergoing change."[88] Thus viewed, behavior therapy is not the potent instrument of social control feared by some. Changes in behavior, other than of brief duration, may not be

---

[84]See GLEITMAN, *supra* note 8, at 96; ROTTER, *supra* note 80; Bandura, *supra* note 77, at 860. This account is similar to that developed by a branch of organizational psychology known as "instrumentality theory." *See, e.g.,* F. LANDY & D. TRUMBO, PSYCHOLOGY OF WORK BEHAVIOR 293–333 (1976); V. VROOM, WORK AND MOTIVATION (1964); Galbraith & Cummings, *An Empirical Investigation of the Motivational Determinants of Task Performance: Interactive Effects Between Instrumentality-Valence and Motivation-Ability,* 2 ORGANIZATIONAL BEHAV. & HUM. PERFORMANCE 237 (1967); Peak, *Attitude and Motivation,* in NEBRASKA SYMPOSIUM ON MOTIVATION 149 (M. Jones ed., 1955).

[85]Boneau, *supra* note 36, at 308; *see also* BANDURA, *supra* note 10, at 13:

> [M]ost external influences operate through cognitive processing. During transactions with their environment, people are not merely emitting responses and experiencing outcomes. They form beliefs from observed regularities about the outcomes likely to result from actions in given situations and regulate their behavior accordingly. Contrary to claims that behavior is controlled by its immediate consequences, behavior is related to its outcomes at the level of aggregate consequences, rather than immediate effects. . . . Response consequences convey probabilistic information for forming expectancies about how outcomes relate to actions, rather than stamp in responses.

[86]See BANDURA, *supra* note 10, at 12–15; GLEITMAN, *supra* note 8, at 90–101; Bandura, *supra* note 77, at 859; Boneau, *supra* note 36, at 297; Hollon v. Beck, *supra* note 38, at 428; Mahoney, *The Cognitive Sciences and Psychotherapy: Patterns in a Developing Relationship,* in HANDBOOK OF COGNITIVE-BEHAVIORAL THERAPIES 357–60 (K. Dobson ed., 1988). *See supra* note 36 and accompanying text.

[87]Bandura, *supra* note 77, at 859, 860; *see also* BANDURA, *supra* note 1, at 99–100. A strict Skinnerian would take issue with this analysis, arguing that it is meaningless and misleading to consider the role of the "will" or the "mind." *See, e.g.,* B. SKINNER, ABOUT BEHAVIORISM 53–62, 152–70 (1974); SKINNER, *supra* note 73, at 184–66; B. SKINNER, *supra* note 12, at 87–90, 110–16, 228–29.

[88]Bandura, *supra* note 77, at 862.

accomplished by behavior therapy absent the knowledge and cooperation of the patient.[89] Aversive techniques, in particular, seem to be of limited effectiveness with uncooperative individuals.[90] As the National Institute of Mental Health concluded in a report on behavior modification:[91]

> Behavior modification is not a one-way method that can be successfully imposed on an unwilling individual. By its very nature, behavior modification will succeed only when the individual who is receiving the consequences is responsive to them and cooperates with the program. . . . Thus, in the long run, each of us retains control over his own behavior.

Compared to the psychotherapies, behavior therapy, or at least some of its techniques, may be regarded as somewhat more intrusive and perhaps potentially more hazardous. However, both treatment approaches may ultimately be resisted by unwilling patients, although the degree of resistance required may be somewhat greater for some of the behavior therapies. Although based on differing principles, some of the behavior therapy methods may be operationally identical to and have the same results as some of the techniques of psychotherapy.[92] General comparisons are difficult because of the variations within each approach. Positive conditioning using benign reinforcers, for example, may present fewer risks and be less intrusive than some of the methods of psychotherapy. This seems to be true as well for most applications of systematic desensitization, shaping, and contingency contracting, and even for aversive techniques when the negative stimulus used is mild. Modeling would seem to present the least difficulties of all the techniques. On the other hand, some aversive techniques and positive reinforcement approaches that place the patient in a state of deprivation at the outset of therapy may more seriously invade physical and mental processes and present greater hazards than almost all of the psychotherapies. Meaningful comparisons between the two approaches therefore must include careful analysis of the techniques involved and avoid broad generalizations.

[89]E. ERWIN, BEHAVIOR THERAPY: SCIENTIFIC, PHILOSOPHICAL, AND MORAL FOUNDATIONS 180–81 (1978); Marks, *The Current Status of Behavioral Psychotherapy: Theory and Practice,* 133 AM. J. PSYCHIATRY 253, 255 (1975); Russell, *supra* note 42, at 124, 131.

[90]Bandura, *supra* note 56; Note, *Aversion Therapy, Its Limited Potential for Use in the Correctional Setting,* 26 STAN. L. REV. 1327 (1974).

[91]BEHAVIOR MODIFICATION REP., *supra* note 1, at 14.

[92]Goldiamond, *supra* note 1, at 111.

Chapter 5
PSYCHOTROPIC MEDICATION

Rather than a psychodynamic[1] or a behavioral model[2] of mental illness, mental health treatment using psychotropic medication[3] tends to be rooted principally in a medical model that views mental disorders as organic diseases.[4] Like the other organic or somatic therapies to be discussed in chapters 6–8 (electroconvulsive therapy, electronic stimulation of the brain, and psychosurgery), psychotropic medication seeks to influence psychological conditions therapeutically by nonpsychological methods. Rather than using verbal or behavioral techniques, the organic therapies use chemical, electrical, hormonal, or physical interventions to "affect the brain either directly or indirectly, and thus produce or inhibit behavior and alter mood."[5] Although the "underlying etiological and pathophysiological factors of mental illness . . . remain essentially unknown,"[6] advances in research are providing increasing evidence that heredity and biochemical imbalances causing distur-

---

[1]*See* Hallec, *Treatment Planning, in* THE AMERICAN PSYCHIATRIC ASSOCIATION COMMISSION ON PSYCHIATRIC THERAPIES 9–10 (T. Karasu ed., 1984) [hereinafter PSYCHIATRIC THERAPIES]; Karasu, *Psychoanalysis and Psychoanalytic Psychotherapy, in* 2 COMPREHENSIVE TEXTBOOK OF PSYCHIATRY 1442 (H. Kaplan & B. Sadock eds., 5th ed. 1989) [hereinafter TEXTBOOK OF PSYCHIATRY]; Schwartz & Solomon, *Psychoanalysis, in* HANDBOOK OF PSYCHIATRY 489 (P. Solomon & V. Patch eds., 3d ed. 1974). *See generally supra* chapter 3.

[2]*See* A. BANDURA, PRINCIPLES OF BEHAVIOR MODIFICATION 1–3, 10–11, 16–18 (1969); RESEARCH TASK FORCE OF THE NAT'L INST. OF MENTAL HEALTH, RESEARCH IN THE SERVICE OF MENTAL HEALTH 310–25 (DHEW Pub. No. (ADM) 75-236, 1975) [hereinafter RESEARCH IN MENTAL HEALTH]; B. SKINNER, SCIENCE AND HUMAN BEHAVIOR 373 (1953); Friedman, *Legal Regulation of Applied Analysis in Mental Institutions and Prisons,* 17 ARIZ. L. REV. 39, 44 (1975); Nathan, *Behavior Therapy, in* HANDBOOK OF PSYCHIATRY, *supra* note 1, at 391. *See generally supra* chapter 4. For an attempt to integrate psychodynamic and behavioral approaches with psychotherapy, see P. WACHTEL, PSYCHOANALYSIS AND BEHAVIOR THERAPY: TOWARD AN INTEGRATION (1977).

[3]*Psychotropic* or *psychoactive* drugs are compounds that affect the mind, behavior, intellectual functions, perception, moods, and emotions. H. KAPLAN ET AL., SYNOPSIS OF PSYCHIATRY: BEHAVIORAL SCIENCES AND CLINICAL PSYCHIATRY 410 (1994); V. LONGO, NEUROPHARMACOLOGY AND BEHAVIOR 182 (1972); Klerman, *Psychotropic Drugs as Therapeutic Agents,* 2 HASTINGS CTR. REP. 81, 82 n.1 (1974); Neville, *Controlling Behavior Through Drugs: Introduction,* 2 HASTINGS CTR. STUDIES, Jan. 1974, at 65.

[4]M. GITLIN, THE PSYCHOTHERAPIST'S GUIDE TO PSYCHOPHARMACOLOGY 17 (1990). For analysis of the differing models of mental illness and their implications, see Blaney, *Implications of the Medical Model and Its Alternatives,* 132 AM. J. PSYCHIATRY 911 (1975); Zubin, *Scientific Models of Psychopathology in the 1970's, in* READINGS IN LAW AND PSYCHIATRY 82 (R. Allen et al. eds., 2d ed. 1975) [hereinafter READINGS]. For a discussion of the schism in American psychiatry between psychiatrists following the medical model and those following a psychodynamic model, see Akiskal & McKinney, *Psychiatry and Pseudopsychiatry,* 28 ARCHIVES GEN. PSYCHIATRY 367 (1973); Weiss, *The Resurgence of Biological Psychiatry: New Promise or False Hope for a Troubled Profession,* 20 PERSPECTIVES IN BIOLOGY AND MED. 573 (1977). *See also* Restak, *Psychiatry in Search of Identity,* N.Y. TIMES, Jan. 12, 1975, § 4, at 9. For a classic, although controversial, criticism of the medical model, see T. SZASZ, THE MYTH OF MENTAL ILLNESS (1961).

[5]RESEARCH IN MENTAL HEALTH, *supra* note 2, at 325. *See also* Baldessarini, *Antipsychotic Agents, in* PSYCHIATRIC THERAPIES, *supra* note 1, at 136–40 (antipsychotics); Frankel, *Electroconvulsive Therapy, in* PSYCHIATRIC THERAPIES, *supra* note 1, at 225–27; Winick, *The Right to Refuse Mental Health Treatment: A First Amendment Perspective,* 44 U. MIAMI L. REV. 1, 68, 79 (1989) (discussing the organic treatment approaches).

[6]RESEARCH IN MENTAL HEALTH, *supra* note 2, at 331. "[V]irtually all the major advances in psychopharmacology . . . have depended far more on chance than on a detailed understanding of brain chemistry that then led to the synthesis of drugs capable of correcting known abnormalities." M. GITLIN, *supra* note 4, at 17.

bances in brain function operate as contributing agents in many of the serious psychiatric disorders.[7] There is increasing acceptance of the hypothesis that one or more of the neurotransmitters—the biochemical substances that relay messages throughout the central nervous system—are implicated in the etiology of schizophrenia and the mood disorders.[8] Forty years ago only limited use was made of drugs in the treatment of mental illness, largely to facilitate psychotherapy. At that time psychotherapeutic treatment, especially psycho-analysis, was felt to be the only effective approach to treatment, and the somatic techniques were held in low esteem, particularly in the United States.[9] The evidence of the past 30 years, though, has strongly suggested that the major mental illnesses may have an organic etiol-ogy[10] and has shown that they respond to organic treatments.[11]

The introduction some 40 years ago of the antipsychotic and antidepressant drugs, and their rapid expansion in clinical practice, have revolutionized psychiatric treatment of the major mental illnesses. The Committee on Brain Sciences of the National Research Council judged chlorpromazine (Thorazine), one of the most widely used of the antipsychotic drugs, to be the outstanding single practical contribution to psychiatry in several decades.[12] First synthesized in 1950 by French chemists, chlorpromazine is a derivative of phenothiazine, a basic ingredient of methylene blue, one of the first coal tar dyes.[13] Although discovered in

---

[7]RESEARCH IN MENTAL HEALTH, *supra* note 2, at 60–84. *See also* D. GOODWIN & S. GUZE, PSYCHIATRIC DIAGNOSIS 24–26 (1989) (family studies of affective disorders); *id.* at 59–62 (family studies of schizophrenia disorders); P. JANICAK ET AL., PRINCIPLES AND PRACTICE OF PSYCHOPHARMACOLOGY 85 (1993) (schizophrenia); *id.* at 347–49 (bipolar disorder).

[8]*E.g.,* U.S. CONG., OFFICE OF TECHNOLOGY ASSESSMENT, THE BIOLOGY OF MENTAL DISORDERS: NEW DEVELOP-MENTS IN NEUROSCIENCE 77–82 (No. OTA-BA-538, 1992) [hereinafter BIOLOGY OF MENTAL DISORDERS] (dis-cussing the as yet not fully understood role of dopamine and other neurotransmitters in schizophrenia); *Id.* at 82–88 (discussing neurotransmitter imbalances and other biological factors hypothesized to play a role in mood disorders); Katz, *Hospitalization and the Mental Health Service System, in* 2 TEXTBOOK OF PSYCHIATRY, *supra* note 1, at 2083; Schildkraut et al., *Mood Disorders: Biochemical Aspects, in* 1 TEXTBOOK OF PSYCHIATRY, *supra* note 1, at 868 (discussing hypotheses that two neurotransmitters—dopamine and serotonin—are implicated in depression and bipolar mood disorders and suggesting that these disorders are characterized by reduced levels of dopamine and deficiencies in the metabolism of serotonin in the central nervous system); Wyatt et al., *Schizophrenia: Biochemical, Endocrine, and Immunological Studies, in* 1 TEXTBOOK OF PSYCHIATRY, *supra* note 1, at 717 (concluding that research supports a dopamine hypothesis for schizophrenia under which an excess of dopamine in the central nervous system—caused either by excessive production of this neurotransmitter in the brain or by deficiencies in the ability of the neurons to re-uptake it—is implicated).

[9]RESEARCH IN MENTAL HEALTH, *supra* note 2, at 331.

[10]*See supra* note 8 and accompanying text. *See also* GITLIN, *supra* note 4, at 25 ("[T]here is little doubt that disturbed biology plays a part in the vulnerability towards the major psychiatric disorders and that biological abnormalities are evident in the major disorders.").

[11]*See, e.g.,* Grebb, *Biological Therapies: Introduction and Overview, in* 2 TEXTBOOK OF PSYCHIATRY, *supra* note 1, at 1574 (overview of organic treatment techniques used for major mental illnesses). *See also* GITLIN, *supra* note 4, at 25 ("[T]he documented efficacy of medications in experiments that have controlled for the effects of expectation—double blind, placebo controlled trials—also adds to the weight of biological evidence.").

[12]RESEARCH IN MENTAL HEALTH, *supra* note 2, at 147. The Research Task Force of the National Institute of Mental Health described chlorpromazine as "one of the salient advances in the field of modern psychiatry." *Id.* at 334. *See also* R. SPIEGEL, PSYCHOPHARMACOLOGY 34 (1989); Davis et al., *Antipsychotic Drugs, in* 2 TEXTBOOK OF PSYCHIATRY, *supra* note 1, at 1591 ("therapeutic revolution initiated by chlorpromazine").

[13]The following history of the discovery of chlorpromazine is drawn from RESEARCH IN MENTAL HEALTH, *supra* note 2, at 147–48; JANICAK ET AL., *supra* note 7, at 93–94; LONGO, *supra* note 3, at 7–8; SWAZEY, CHLORPROMAZINE IN PSYCHIATRY: A STUDY OF THERAPEUTIC INNOVATION (1974); Jarvik, *Drugs Used in the Treatment of Psychiatric Disorders, in* THE PHARMACOLOGICAL BASIS OF THERAPEUTICS 151–52 (L. Goodman & A. Gilman eds., 4th ed. 1970). The discovery of chlorpromazine provides a classic illustration of the often serendipitous nature of basic scientific research. Although the use of psychotropic medication has mushroomed, the popularity of phenothiazine derivatives, like chlorpromazine, has been waning recently. L. HOLLISTER & J. CSERNANSKY, CLINICAL PHARMACOLOGY OF PSYCHOTHERAPEUTIC DRUGS 99 (3d ed. 1990).

1833, phenothiazine was first used for medical purposes in the 1930s when some of its derivatives were shown to have antihistaminic properties and a strong sedative effect. In 1952, Laborit, a French surgeon, experimented with the use of several of these derivatives in clinical anesthesia and observed that one of them, chlorpromazine, produced "artificial hibernation," a peculiar sedative effect without loss of consciousness. In the same year, Delay and Deniker tried chlorpromazine with schizophrenic patients and published a report of its therapeutic action in the treatment of several of the psychoses.

The pace of development accelerated rapidly in the next few years as dozens of studies were conducted on chlorpromazine, the other phenothiazine derivatives, and related compounds. From 1955 to 1965 more than 50 million patients were treated with chlorpromazine and over 10,000 publications described its effects.[14] By 1970, according to one estimate, 250 million people had been treated with chlorpromazine or one of the other antipsychotic medications, and these drugs had become the leading treatment technique for schizophrenia and related serious mental illnesses.[15]

A. Types of Drugs

The interest in psychoactive drugs, aroused by the successful use of chlorpromazine to treat schizophrenia, led to extensive research and clinical experimentation with related compounds. One of the drugs investigated was imipramine (Tofranil), one of the so-called tricyclic antidepressants, which was found ineffective in schizophrenia but helpful in the treatment of depression.[16] The second major class of antidepressant drugs, the monoamine oxidase inhibitors ("MAO inhibitors"), were derived from iproniazid, a compound originally developed for the treatment of tuberculosis.[17] Iproniazid was found to have unexpected side effects in tuberculosis patients, producing euphoria and hyperactivity, which led to its use in the treatment of depression, for which it proved effective.

The clinical success of these new drugs coupled with discoveries concerning the workings of the central nervous system have provided dramatic evidence of a biological basis for depression and schizophrenia, two of the most serious and prevalent of the mental illnesses. Only in this century has it been recognized that the central nervous system is composed of billions of nerve cells or neurons, connected across tiny spaces called *synapses*. Research has revealed that transmission of messages between neurons occurs through the release at nerve terminals of chemical substances, known as *neurotransmitters*. These neurotransmitters enter the synaptic space, making the membrane of the adjacent neuron more permeable and producing an electrical impulse that triggers the release of a neurotransmitter at the next synapse. The process is then rapidly repeated, enabling the transmission of electrical messages throughout the nervous system.[18]

---

[14]Jarvik, *supra* note 13, at 155.

[15]Crane, *Clinical Psychopharmacology in Its 20th Year,* 181 SCIENCE 124 (1973). *See also* P. JANICAK ET AL., *supra* note 7, at 94, 103–15; L. KOLB, MODERN CLINICAL PSYCHIATRY 829 (1977) (psychotropic drugs are "the primary therapeutic agents" in the treatment of the psychoses); R. SPIEGEL, *supra* note 12, at 34–38. Prior to the early 1950s, when the antipsychotic drugs were introduced, the mental hospital had little in the way of treatment to offer those with schizophrenia, other than essentially custodial care; however, these drugs have proven effective in treating the most distressing aspects of the condition and in allowing patients to resume life in the community. *See, e.g.,* Davis et al., *supra* note 12, at 1591–92; Katz, *supra* note 8, at 2083–84.

[16]RESEARCH IN MENTAL HEALTH, *supra* note 2, at 62; *see* JANICAK ET AL., *supra* note 7, at 227–28 (studies comparing imipramine to placebo); LONGO, *supra* note 3, at 50–51; Davis & Glassman, *Antidepressant Drugs, in* 2 TEXTBOOK OF PSYCHIATRY, *supra* note 1, at 1627–30 (efficacy studies of imipramine).

[17]RESEARCH IN MENTAL HEALTH, supra note 2, at 62; JANICAK ET AL., *supra* note 7, at 209, 233; LONGO, *supra* note 3, at 59–61.

[18]RESEARCH IN MENTAL HEALTH, *supra* note 2, at 60–62; E. VALENSTEIN, BRAIN CONTROL 116–22 (1973).

Several neurotransmitters have thus far been identified. The best known of these are serotonin, acetylcholine, and the biogenic amines, classified chemically as catecholamine—norepinephrine, the precursor of adrenaline, noradrenaline, and dopamine.[19] The action of norepinephrine is thought to be particularly significant in relation to mental disorders because its distribution is high in those regions of the limbic–hypothalamic circuit and brain stem that have been implicated in emotion.[20] Research has revealed that following the transmission of a message through the synapse and before a new message may be transmitted, the neurotransmitter must be removed from the synapse. For norepinephrine, this is done by rapid reuptake into the terminal of the transmitting neuron, where some of the norepinephrine is destroyed by the enzyme MAO.[21]

The action of the antipsychotic and antidepressant drugs on neurotransmitters has led to a theory linking serious psychiatric disorders with abnormal levels of the catecholamine neurotransmitters at brain synapses. One hypothesis—that low catecholamine levels may be related to depression—is supported by the action of two of the major classes of antidepressant drugs, both of which facilitate the effects of norepinephrine.[22] The MAO inhibitors work by inhibiting the enzyme that destroys norepinephrine; the tricyclic antidepressants, by blocking the reuptake of norepinephrine into the nerve terminals.[23] A related hypothesis—that mania may result from an oversupply of neurotransmitters[24]—is supported by the successful use of lithium to treat the manic phase of bipolar disorder. Lithium is believed to act by increasing the reuptake of norepinephrine,[25] an action opposite to that of the tricyclic antidepressants. Research has also suggested that schizophrenia may be closely related to

---

[19]"We know today which neurotransmitters act on which synapses of the peripheral nervous system, although new transmitters are continually being discovered or postulated." SPIEGEL, *supra* note 12, at 115. *See* RESEARCH IN MENTAL HEALTH, *supra* note 2, at 60–62; Baraban & Coyle, *Receptors, Monoamines, and Amino Acids, in* 1 TEXTBOOK OF PSYCHIATRY, *supra* note 1, at 48; *see also* sources cited in *supra* note 8.

[20]KOLB, *supra* note 15, at 830–32; VALENSTEIN, *supra* note 18, at 160.

[21]GITLIN, *supra* note 4, at 229–30; KOLB, *supra* note 15, at 831. *See also* RESEARCH IN MENTAL HEALTH, *supra* note 2, at 61.

[22]*See* sources cited in *supra* note 8; GITLIN, *supra* note 4, at 23; Willner, *Antidepressants and Serotoninergic Neurotransmission: An Integrative Review,* 85 PSYCHOPHARMACOLOGY 387–404 (1985). *See also* SPIEGEL, *supra* note 12, at 125–29:

> The catecholamine [norepinephrine] hypothesis brought several pharmacological findings into a satisfactory relationship, but contradicted a number of clinical observations [e.g., the serotonin hypothesis of depression and the monoamine hypotheses of depression]. . . .
>
> The serotonin hypothesis of depression . . . states that some or all depressions are due to a lack of serotonin in certain parts of the brain stem. Once again, pharmacological, clinical, biochemical and some post-mortem findings support this hypothesis. . . . [A] number of pharmacological findings can be interpreted both in favor of the catecholamine [norepinephrine] hypothesis and in defense of the serotonin hypothesis. . . . Practically speaking, antidepressants with various mechanisms of action today seem to have fairly equal therapeutic activities and differ, if at all, only with regard to their side effects. . . .
>
> [T]he monoamine hypotheses of depression have been developed emphasizing one or more aspects of the actions of clinically effective drugs in pharmacological tests. . . . [S]ince the various transmitter systems in the brain are linked by direct and indirect mechanisms and since individual transmitters do not change independently of one another, purely catecholaminergically or purely serotoninergically based depressions are unlikely. . . . [I]t is clear that the discovery of effective medication has led to hypotheses as to their mechanisms of action, and not vice versa.

[23]RESEARCH IN MENTAL HEALTH, *supra* note 2, at 62; Baraban & Coyle, *supra* note 19, at 47 ("[C]hronic administration of tricyclic antidepressants, which enhance central noradrenergic neurotransmission, results in a decrease in the number of β-adrenergic receptors in the cerebral cortex.").

[24]RESEARCH IN MENTAL HEALTH, *supra* note 2, at 181.

[25]GITLIN, *supra* note 4, at 240–49; LONGO, *supra* note 3, at 69–70; R. RYALL, MECHANISMS OF DRUG ACTION ON THE NERVOUS SYSTEM 202 (2d ed. 1989); Jefferson & Greist, *Lithium Therapy, in* 2 TEXTBOOK OF PSYCHIATRY, *supra* note 1, at 1656.

abnormal levels of dopamine, another of the neurotransmitters,[26] a theory supported by the fact that chlorpromazine and other antipsychotic drugs successfully used to treat schizophrenia block the effect of dopamine in the brain.[27]

Psychotropic drugs may be classified into four major types, on the basis of the mental disorders they are principally used to treat: (a) the antipsychotic drugs, including chlorpromazine and the other phenothiazines, as well as several other classes of drugs used in the treatment of schizophrenia and related psychoses;[28] (b) the antidepressant drugs, such as the

---

[26]RESEARCH IN MENTAL HEALTH, *supra* note 2, at 175; BIOLOGY OF MENTAL DISORDERS, *supra* note 8, at 77–82. *See* F. ANTUM ET AL., TRANSMETHYLATION PROCESS IN SCHIZOPHRENIA, BRAIN CHEMISTRY AND MENTAL DISEASES (1971); KOLB, *supra* note 15, at 384; LONGO, *supra* note 3, at 27, 43; Kety, *Recent Genetic and Biochemical Approaches to Schizophrenia, in* DRUG TREATMENT OF MENTAL DISORDERS 1, 8–10 (L. Simpson ed., 1976); Wyatt et al., *supra* note 8, at 717. Antipsychotic drugs have a normalizing effect on schizophrenia. They lessen typical schizophrenic symptoms and speed up retarded schizophrenia and slow down excited schizophrenia. Davis et al., *supra* note 12, at 1603.

[27]Gerlach, *Pharmacology and Clinical Properties of Selective Dopamine Antagonists With Focus on Substituted Benzamides, in* ANTIPSYCHOTIC DRUGS AND THEIR SIDE-EFFECTS 45–46, 59–60 (T. Barnes ed., 1993):

> The discovery of the existence of a multitude of dopamine receptors, each with partially differentiated functions, has given new vitality to research into dopamine's role in schizophrenia and has also given the hope of developing better antidopaminergic antipsychotics, with respect to efficacy and side effect potential.

> Antidopaminergic treatment is still the only significant means of producing an antipsychotic effect. The new perspective is that an antidopaminergic treatment can be selective, antagonizing specific subgroups of dopamine receptors. . . . Utilizing the different dopamine-mediated treatment principle, it should be possible to develop new antipsychotics with fewer side-effects, and hopefully also with additional therapeutic effects and negative symptoms in treatment-resistant patients.

See also RYALL, *supra* note 25, at 180–87; SPIEGEL, *supra* note 12, at 121–27; Davis et al., *supra* note 12, at 1610 ("The common denominator underlying drugs that benefit psychosis is the blockade of central dopamine receptors and the compensating increase in dopamine synthesis.").

[28]*See generally* LONGO, *supra* note 3, at 7–46; Davis & Glassman, *Antidepressant Drugs, in* 2 TEXTBOOK OF PSYCHIATRY, *supra* note 1, at 1627, 1652; Jarvik, *supra* note 13, at 155–74; Klerman, *Neuroleptics: Too Many or Too Few?, in* RATIONAL PSYCHOPHARMACOTHERAPY AND THE RIGHT TO TREATMENT 1 (F. Ayd ed., 1975) [hereinafter RATIONAL PSYCHOPHARMACOTHERAPY]; Klerman, *supra* note 3, at 83–85; Myers & Solomon, *Psychopharmacology, in* HANDBOOK OF PSYCHIATRY, *supra* note 1, at 440; Solow, *Mental Illness: Tranquilizers and Other Depressant Drugs, in* AN INTRODUCTION TO PSYCHOPHARMACOLOGY 296–306 (1971). Schizophrenia, perhaps the most disabling of the major mental illnesses, constitutes a large group of extremely serious disorders characterized by gross disturbance of thought, mood, and behavior. *See* AM. PSYCHIATRIC ASS'N, DIAGNOSTIC AND STATISTICAL MANUAL OF MENTAL DISORDERS 274–78, 285 (4th ed. 1994) (hereinafter *DSM–IV*). "In the United States the lifetime prevalence of schizophrenia has been variously reported as ranging from 1 to 1.5 percent." KAPLAN ET AL., *supra* note 3, at 458. "The incidence of schizophrenia is about 1 in 100 population and represents the most frequent single cause of severe mental illness." RYALL, *supra* note 25, at 172.

In addition to chlorpromazine, the other phenothiazines widely used are promazine (Sparine), thioridazine (Mellaril), trifluoperazine (Stelazine), fluphenazine (Prolixin), and several others. Other antipsychotic drugs widely used are chlorprothixene (Taractan), haloperidol (Haldol), chlorpromazine (Thorazine), fluphenazine (Permitil, Prolixin), loxapine (Loxitane, Paxolin), mesoridazine (Serentil), molindone (Lindone, Moban), and thiothixene (Navane). Prochlorperazine (Compazine) and primozide (Orap) are rarely used today. The terms *major tranquilizers* and *neuroleptics* are often applied to these drugs, but this usage has been criticized as confusing. GITLIN, *supra* note 4, at 295; SPIEGEL, *supra* note 12, at 4.

"The clinically useful dosages of the various antipsychotic drugs correlate best with their ability to block dopamine-2 receptors." A. SLATZBERG & J. COLE, MANUAL OF CLINICAL PSYCHOPHARMACOLOGY 84 (1991). These drugs have been shown to be more effective than placebos in the treatment of schizophrenia. *Id.* at 85.

A newer antipsychotic medication is clozapine (Clozaril). *Id.* at 127. "Clozapine is in many ways the best new development in the treatment of schizophrenia since chlorpromazine was discovered." *Id.* at 129. Clozapine is helpful for patients unable to deal with the side effects produced by standard neuroleptics. *Id.* For a discussion of the high costs and severe risk of agranulocytosis associated with clozapine, see Blackburn, *New Directions in Mental Health Advocacy? Clozapine and the Right of Medical Self-Determination,* 14 MENTAL & PHYSICAL DISABILITY L. REP. 453 (1990).

tricyclic and related tetracyclic antidepressants, the MAO inhibitors, and a number of new compounds, including fluoxetine (Prozac), used in the treatment of depression;[29] (c) the antianxiety drugs, such as diazepam (Valium), chlordiazepoxide (Librium), and meprobamate (Miltown, Equanil), used in the treatment of anxiety and tension;[30] and (d) an

---

[29]There are several classes of antidepressants. "Classic antidepressants include the tricyclic antidepressants (TCAs) and related tetracyclics as well as the monoamine oxidase inhibitors (MAOIs)." SCHATZBERG & COLE, *supra* note 28, at 31. The tricyclic drugs include imipramine (Tofranil, Janimine, Sk-Pramine), amitriptyline (Elavil, Endep), clomipramine (Anafranil), doxepin (Adapin, Sinequan), trimipramine (Surmontil), desipramine (Norpramin, Pertrofrane), nortriptyline (Pamelor, Aventyl) and protriptyline (Vivactil). The TCAs work primarily by blocking the reuptake of norepinephrine and, in some cases, of serotonin, although the pharmacologic effects of these drugs go beyond their immediate reuptake blocking effects. The effects of these drugs "include later secondary effects on pre- and postsynaptic receptors, as well as other neurotransmitter systems." SCHATZBERG & COLE, *supra* note 28, at 37. The tetracyclics include amoxapine (Asendin) and maprotiline. Amoxapine "has both norepinephrine and serotonin reuptake inhibiting properties." JANICAK ET AL., *supra* note 7, at 229. The postulated mechanism of maprotiline is that "it acts primarily by potentiation of central adrenergic synapses by blocking reuptake of norepinephrine at nerve endings." PHYSICIANS' DESK REFERENCE 874 (46th ed. 1992) [hereinafter PDR].

The MAO inhibitors include tranylcypromine (Parnate), isocarboxadid (Marplan), phenelzine (Nardil), and selegiline (Edepryl). Isocarboxadid, phenelzine, and tranylcypromine are first-generation MAO inhibitors. "[T]hey inhibit monoamine oxidase (MAO) in various organs, exerting greater effects on MAO A—for which norepinephrine and serotonin are primary substrates—than in MAO B, which acts primarily on other amines, *e.g.*, phenylethylamine." SCHATZBERG & COLE, *supra* note 28, at 235. Indeed, some patients who do not respond to tricyclics will respond dramatically to MAO inhibitors. Davis & Glassman, *supra* note 16, at 1637.

The newer agents (*e.g.*, bupropion (Wellbutrin), fluoxetine (Prozac), and trazodone (Desyrel)), introduced since the 1980s, differ from the classic antidepressants. JANICAK ET AL., *supra* note 7, at 185–292; SCHATZBERG & COLE, *supra* note 28, at 31–84. Prozac is the most popularly known of these newer agents. See JANICAK ET AL., *supra* note 7, at 492–94; P. KRAMER, LISTENING TO PROZAC (1993). Bupropion is not a norepinephrine or a serotonin reuptake blocker and does not inhibit monoamine oxidase. Although its mode of action is unclear, "it has been hypothesized to act via dopamine reuptake blockade." SCHATZBERG & COLE, *supra*, at 230. Prozac works primarily by selectively inhibiting the reuptake of serotonin. Its serotonin reuptake blocking effects are roughly 100 times those of norepinephrine or dopamine. *Id.* at 73–74. Trazodone has been "reported to be a central serotonin reuptake blocker as well as to have alpha norepinephrine receptor blocking effect." *Id.* at 66. Trazodone, however, is not as potent an inhibitor of serotonin as fluoxetine.

An additional category of drugs sometimes considered in connection with the antidepressants is the psychomotor stimulants such as methylphenidate (Ritalin) and dextroamphetamine (Dexedrin). JANICAK ET AL., *supra* note 7, at 235–36. Amphetamine and its derivatives now are thought not to be effective in the treatment of depression. *Id.* at 236. The psychomotor stimulants are frequently used in the treatment of children diagnosed as having attention-deficit hyperactivity disorder. *Id.* at 492–94.

[30]PSYCHOPATHOLOGY AND PSYCHOPHARMACOLOGY 427–39 (J. Cole et al., eds., 1973); LONGO, *supra* note 3, at 73–95; Gorman & Davis, *Antianxiety Drugs, in* 2 TEXTBOOK OF PSYCHIATRY, *supra* note 1, at 1579–91; Jarvik, *supra* note 13, at 174–80; Klerman, *supra* note 3, at 86–87; Solow, *supra* note 28, at 306–11. The antianxiety drugs include the propanediols, meprobamate (Miltown, Equanil) and tybamate (Tybatran), first introduced in 1955; the benzodiazepine compounds [chlordiazepoxide (Librium), diazepam (Valium), and oxazepam (Serax)], first introduced in 1960; and the barbiturates and the nonbarbiturate sedative hypnotics, which have been used for many years in the treatment of anxiety. The antianxiety compounds (meprobamate, chlomezanone, and buspirone), often called "minor tranquilizers," are among the most widely used of all drugs. Gorman & Davis, *supra*, at 1579 (table 31.2-2). They have been particularly useful in treating the "large spectrum of psychic disturbances called neuroses, which are characterized by anxiety, tension, mild depression, and other emotional disturbances." LONGO, *supra* note 3, at 73. *See also* SCHATZBERG & COLE, *supra* note 28, at 186.

antimanic drug, lithium, used in the treatment of bipolar disorder (formerly known as manic–depressive psychosis).[31]

The use of these drugs has burgeoned into a multimillion dollar industry. More than 178 million prescriptions for psychotropic drugs were written in 1967 in the United States alone, constituting about 17% of all American prescriptions.[32] By 1970, the number had grown to 214 million,[33] and in 1976, to 250 million. Although more current data are unavailable, the prescription of these drugs has continued to increase dramatically.[34] In 1973, about one out of every five adults used a prescription psychotropic drug.[35] Valium, probably the most frequently prescribed drug in the world, alone accounted for almost 60 million prescriptions in the United States in 1974 and was used by 1 in 10 Americans aged 18 and older.[36] Psychotropic drugs in 1975 accounted for some 25% of all American prescriptions,[37]

---

[31] Jarvik, *supra* note 13, at 193–94; Jefferson & Griest, *Lithium Therapy, in* 2 TEXTBOOK OF PSYCHIATRY, *supra* note 1, at 1655–62; Jefferson & Griest, *Therapeutic Uses of Lithium and Rubidium, in* DRUG TREATMENT OF MENTAL DISORDERS, *supra* note 26, at 193. Although frequently characterized by depression, the affective disorders sometimes involve mania, an extreme elation accompanied by hyperactivity, talkativeness, irritability, agitation, grandiosity, and accelerated thinking and speech. Lithium carbonate (Eskalith, Lithane, Lithonate) functions as a mood normalizer, preventing the severe mood swings that characterize bipolar illness, a major affective disorder in which recurring periods of mania frequently alternate with periods of depression. *DSM–IV, supra* note 28, at 350–66. First used in the treatment of mania in 1949 but not approved by the Food and Drug Administration for American use for this condition until 1970, lithium has also recently been shown to be a valuable prophylactic agent in preventing depressive episodes in patients with unipolar recurrent depression. SCHATZBERG & COLE, *supra* note 28, at 156–57; Fieve et al., *Lithium Carbonate in Affective Disorders: A Double-Blind Study of Prophylaxis in Unipolar Depression,* 32 ARCHIVES GEN. PSYCHIATRY 1541 (1975); Mendels, *Lithium in the Treatment of Depression,* 133 AM. J. PSYCHIATRY 373 (1976).

[32] GROUP FOR THE ADVANCEMENT OF PSYCHIATRY, PSYCHIATRY, PHARMACOTHERAPY, PSYCHOTHERAPY: PARA-DOXES, PROBLEMS AND PROGRESS 272–74 (1975) [hereinafter GROUP FOR THE ADVANCEMENT OF PSYCHIATRY]. Lithium has not been as successful in the treatment of schizophrenia. Davis et al., *supra* note 12, at 1613.

[33] Pekkanen, *The Impact of Promotion on Physicians' Prescribing Patterns,* 6 J. DRUG ISSUES 13, 18 (1976).

[34] *Id.* at 18. *E.g.,* in 1992, Prozac was the 17th most widely dispensed prescription product in the United States, and it was 13th in 1993. Simonsen, *Top 200 Drugs of 1993: Price of Average Rx Up Only 2.9%,* 60 PHARMACY TIMES 18, 30 (1994). In 1983, 6 types of antipsychotic drugs were among the 200 most prescribed medications in the country. Guze & Baxter, *Neuroleptic Malignant Syndrome,* 313 NEW ENG. J. MED. 163 (1985). Antipsychotic agents are widely used for conditions other than psychosis although they do not show therapeutic benefits. Beers et al., *Psychoactive Medication Use in Intermediate-Care Facility Residents,* 260 JAMA 3016, 3017 (1988). *See also* Beers, *supra,* at 3018 (the use of psychotropic drugs is prevalent in nursing homes); Fialkov & Hasley, *Psychotropic Drug Effects Contributing to Psychiatric Hospitalization of Children: A Preliminary Study,* 5 J. DEV. & BEHAV. PEDIATRICS 325 (1984) (2% of school children receive psychotropic drugs for hyperactivity, 2.3% of children in special education classes receive psychotropic drugs, 51% of institutionalized children with mental retardation receive psychotropic drugs); Gualtieri et al., *Tardive Dyskinesia and the Dilemmas of Neuroleptic Treatment,* 14 J. PSYCHIATRY & L. 187 (1987) (one-third of autistic children have been treated with antipsychotic drugs); Richardson et al., *Neuroleptic Use, Parkinsonian Symptoms, Tardive Dyskinesia, and Associated Factors in Child and Adolescent Psychiatric Patients,* 148 AM. J. PSYCHIATRY 1322 (1991) (psychotropic drugs are widely used for treating behavior problems in juveniles).

[35] Pekkanen, *supra* note 33, at 18. *See also* M. WOLFE, WORST PILLS BEST PILLS II 209 (1993) ("approximately 1.7 million people 65 and over get a prescription for an antipsychotic drug each year").

[36] Altman, *Valium, Most Prescribed Drug, Is Center of a Medical Dispute,* NEW YORK TIMES, May 19, 1974, at 1; Cant, *Valiumania,* NEW YORK TIMES MAGAZINE, Feb. 1, 1976, at 34. Waldron, *Increased Prescribing of Valium, Librium, and Other Drugs—Example of the Influence of Economic and Social Factors on the Practice of Medicine,* 7 INT'L J. HEALTH SERV. 37, 38 (1977). *But see* Simonsen, *supra* note 34, at 30 (in 1992 Valium was the 85th most widely dispensed prescription product in the United States; it was 107th in 1993).

[37] Klerman, *Psychoactive Drugs: The Medical Model and Salvation* 30, Address at Symposium on Ethical and Social Aspects of Behavior Control, Reed College, Portland, Oregon (March 5–6, 1975).

making them the most frequently prescribed class of drugs in medicine.[38] If anything, the use of these drugs has increased since then, and the psychotropic drugs have emerged as the treatment of choice for mental health and emotional problems of all kinds.

B. Effect on Mental Health Care

The antipsychotic and antidepressant medications have had a particularly profound effect on institutional psychiatry. Prior to 1955, when the phenothiazines came into widespread use, patients suffering from schizophrenia or related psychoses required long-term mental hospitalization in facilities providing primarily custodial care. Psychotic patients, often disruptive, belligerent, extremely withdrawn, delusional, and hallucinative, were largely inaccessible to psychotherapy and had a poor prognosis for return to society. The population of public mental hospitals had expanded steadily over the previous 50 years, growing by more than 10,000 patients per year for the period 1946 to 1955.[39] At that point almost half (about 559,000) of all hospital beds in the United States were occupied by mental patients, with projections for future growth at the rate of at least 10,000 beds per year.[40] Following 1955, however, this trend underwent a dramatic reversal.[41] Between 1955 and 1967, the population of public mental hospitals decreased by more than 10,000 per year to about 426,000, a level below that of 1946.[42] In 1981, the average daily number of residents in state and county mental hospitals was 138,000.[43] Recent years have witnessed an even more dramatic reduction.[44] As a result of deinstitutionalization, the locus of care has shifted dramatically from the state hospital to the community,[45] and the hospital's role has been reconceptualized. Rather than a long-term custodial facility, the hospital has become essentially a short-term medical facility designed to deal with patients in crisis, to diagnose and stabilize them on a course of medication to be continued after discharge, and then to discharge them into the community where their continued medical and social needs would be met in community-based facilities.[46]

---

[38]DiMascio, *Innovative Drug Administration Regimens and the Economics of Mental Health Care, in* RATIONAL PSYCHOPHARMACOTHERAPY, *supra* note 28, at 118.

[39]Solow, *supra* note 28, at 291; *see also* Katz, *supra* note 8, at 2083 ("At the pinnacle, one-half of all hospital beds, approximately 750,000, were for psychiatric patients. Dramatic changes in the pattern of delivery of mental health care began in the 1950s with the introduction of antipsychotic drugs and the emergence of social and community psychiatry.").

[40]Solow, *supra* note 28, at 291.

[41]Katz, *supra* note 8, at 2083; *see* BIOLOGY OF MENTAL DISORDERS, *supra* note 8, at 92–93; RESEARCH IN MENTAL HEALTH, *supra* note 2, at 331; SCHATZBERG & COLE, *supra* note 28, at 31–183; Crane, *supra* note 15, at 125; DiMascio, *supra* note 38, at 181; Jarvik, *supra* note 13, at 155; Winick, *Psychotropic Medication and Competence to Stand Trial,* 1977 AM. B. FOUND. RES. J. 769, 778–89 (1977).

[42]Solow, *supra* note 28, at 291.

[43]Goldman et al., *The Alchemy of Mental Health Policy: Homelessness and the Fourth Cycle of Reform,* 34 AM. J. PUB. HEALTH 129–32 (1983).

[44]In 1989 the population of public mental hospitals was less than 130,000. Katz, *supra* note 8, at 2083 ("Deinstitutionalization witnessed a decrease in the state psychiatric hospital population, from 560,000 in 1955 to fewer than 130,000 public state and county inpatient beds at present.").

[45]In 1955, inpatient mental hospitals accounted for 77% of all patient care episodes, whereas 23% were handled in outpatient settings. By 1975 the trend had reversed, with inpatient settings accounting for 27% of patient episodes, whereas 70% were dealt with through outpatient psychiatric services and 3% through day care settings. Klerman, *National Trends in Hospitalization,* 30 HOSP. & COMMUNITY PSYCHIATRY 110, 112 (1979). *See also* Ozarin et al., *A Quarter Century of Psychiatric Care, 1950–1974: A Statistical Review,* 27 HOSP. & COMMUNITY PSYCHIATRY 515 (1976).

[46]Katz, *supra* note 8, at 2083–86.

This massive reduction in the need for long-term hospitalization of patients in the face of increasing rates of hospital admissions[47] was made possible primarily by the phenothiazines, which permitted the control of the more deviant symptoms of psychotic illnesses. Although they do not "cure" psychotic disorders, the phenothiazines "exert a quieting effect on excited or hyperactive psychotic patients. Combativeness disappears, and relaxation and cooperativeness become prominent. Clouding of consciousness does not occur at conventional doses."[48] By reducing extreme symptoms and behavior, these drugs made patients receptive to other types of therapy and permitted many to function in the community or in less restrictive facilities on maintenance dosages of medication.[49]

The focus of treatment shifted from long-term hospitalization to inpatient treatment of short duration followed by outpatient treatment and community-based programs.[50] Perhaps more than a million patients with schizophrenia have been discharged from the hospital as a result of these drugs and function in the community on a relatively normal basis on medication, which holds in remission the extreme symptomatology and bizarre behavioral deviances of their illness.[51] Moreover, as a result of these drugs, patient interaction with hospital staff and with other patients was facilitated, and the "restrictiveness, fear, and dehumanization previously pervading the atmosphere of public mental hospitals diminished. Open wards, patient ward government, group interaction, and indeed, individual psychotherapy became possible in many, rather than in only a favored few institutions."[52]

---

[47]See Bassuk & Gerson, *Deinstitutionalization and Mental Health,* 238 SCI. AMER. 46, 47 (table) (1978).

[48]Jarvik, *supra* note 13, at 167. Spontaneous motor activity is diminished and the patient becomes indifferent to environmental stimuli. *Id.* at 158–59. These drugs "modify affective states without seriously impairing cognitive functions." KOLB, *supra* note 15, at 829.

[49]These drugs facilitate psychotherapy by making the patient "more accessible":

The pharmacological action of the drug ameliorates the presumptive CNS [central nervous system] substrate dysfunction underlying symptom formation, resulting in reduction of the patient's symptomatology, psychopathology, and/or affective discomfort. . . . This reduction of discomfort renders the patient better able to communicate and learn constructively in psychotherapy—that is, some degree of anxiety, dysphoria or symptomatology is necessary to provide a drive or motivation for psychotherapy. According to this view, high levels of tension, anxiety or symptom intensity decrease the patient's capacity to participate effectively in psychotherapy. Appropriate use of drugs is said to permit an optimum level of discomfort needed for psychotherapeutic work.

GROUP FOR THE ADVANCEMENT OF PSYCHIATRY, *supra* note 32, at 342–43. *See also* KOLB, *supra* note 15, at 429; Jarvik, *supra* note 13, at 152; Klerman, *supra* note 28, at 3.

[50]Klerman, *supra* note 28, at 3; Klerman, *supra* note 37, at 24–26.

[51]Davis, *Overview: Maintenance Therapy in Psychiatry: I. Schizophrenia,* 132 AM. J. PSYCHIATRY 1237 (1975). The effect of these drugs, like many other medications, is thus "compensatory rather than curative." L. HOLLISTER, CLINICAL USE OF PSYCHOTHERAPEUTIC DRUGS 13–14 (1973); *accord* Solow, *supra* note 28, at 294. Although able to function in the community, as a result of the typical lack of adequate rehabilitation and community-based programs, the quality of life for many of these patients may be no greater than it was in the hospital. *See* Crane, *supra* note 15, at 125:

As for the quality of the patient's adjustment after he leaves the hospital, the results of drug therapy are even less encouraging: the majority of those who live in the community continue to be unproductive and are often a burden to their families. Individuals released to foster homes or other sheltered environments may be as dependent and alienated as those confined to an institution.

[52]Myers & Solomon, *supra* note 28, at 442–43; Solow, *supra* note 28, at 291.

The antidepressant medications have made possible the relief of depression associated with the affective disorders, the most prevalent and severe of the emotional disturbances.[53] Major depression involves "a profound, unjustified sadness that can become such a burden for the affected individual that suicide becomes a possibility. At times, instead of a true sadness, the patient shows diminished affective participation in the events and situations that form his environment."[54] Before the introduction of these drugs, electroconvulsive shock was the only effective treatment for severe depression.[55] The use of antidepressant medication, which has been compared to insulin in the treatment of diabetes, has permitted effective treatment for approximately 80% of patients suffering from the major depressive illnesses.[56]

C. Effectiveness and Side Effects

Extensive evaluation in controlled double-blind studies has established the efficacy of the various psychotropic medications in the treatment of most patients, although a substantial minority do not benefit. The vast majority of these studies indicated that the antipsychotic drugs are superior to placebos and to psychotherapy or electroconvulsive

---

[53]The affective disorders

> constitute perhaps the most severe group of mental disorders in the United States in terms of prevalence, economic cost, and even mortality. Of the 20,000 suicide deaths recorded in the United States each year, more than 80 percent are believed to be precipitated by depressive illness. In this country between 3 and 8 million persons suffer from depression at any given time; roughly 15 percent of all adults have recognizable symptoms.

RESEARCH IN MENTAL HEALTH, *supra* note 2, at 179.

[54]GITLIN, *supra* note 4, at 116. LONGO, *supra* note 3, at 48; *see DSM–IV, supra* note 28, at 339–44.

[55]RESEARCH IN MENTAL HEALTH, *supra* note 2, at 62; LONGO, *supra* note 3, at 49. *See also* Davis et al., *supra* note 12, at 1595.

[56]RESEARCH IN MENTAL HEALTH, *supra* note 2, at 179–80. The MAO inhibitors work by elevating the mood of depressed patients; the tricyclic drugs work by dulling depressive ideation. W. RYALL, *supra* note 25, at 194–96. The "MAO inhibitors cause an elevation of mood in normal subjects, the tricyclic antidepressants tend to cause sedation which is accompanied by unpleasant subjective sensations. In depressed patients, imipramine causes less outright euphoria than MAO inhibitors but causes a greater attenuation of the depressive ideas." *Id.* at 196. The sedative action in normal individuals is rapid in onset with imipramine, which is the prototype of tricyclic antidepressants; however, the antidepressant action is slow to develop. *Id.* "Antidepressant activity seems to be associated with many different types of acute interaction with monoaminergic systems coupled with a down regulation of beta receptors and an up regulation of alpha receptors with chronic treatment or ECT." *Id.* at 200–01. *See* GITLIN, *supra* note 4, at 229–30. Newer antidepressants are not chemically related to the other antidepressants. The newer antidepressants include amoxapine (Asendin), bupropion hydrochloride (Wellbutrin), fluxetine hydrochloride (Prozac), maprotiline hydrochloride (Ludiomil), and trazodone hydrochloride (Desyrel). These drugs "inhibit reuptake of the neurotransmitters norepinephrine or serotonin, or both, thus restoring hyposensitive receptor sites to normal so that increased neurotransmitter concentrations can exert a therapeutic effect." C. BAER & B. WILLIAMS, CLINICAL PHARMACOLOGY AND NURSING 430 (2d ed. 1992). *See also* L. MCKENRY & E. SALERNO, PHARMACOLOGY IN NURSING 339–41 (18th ed. 1992); Giannini, *Psychotropic Drug Overdose, in* DRUG-INDUCED DYSFUNCTION IN PSYCHIATRY 41 (M. Keshavan & J. Kennedy eds., 1992). Antidepressant drugs have substantially reduced the need for hospitalization of severely depressed patients; Klerman, *supra* note 3, at 85.

therapy alone in the treatment of schizophrenia;[57] that the antidepressant drugs are superior to placebos in the treatment of the depressive psychoses;[58] that lithium is superior to

[57]*See* GROUP FOR THE ADVANCEMENT OF PSYCHIATRY, *supra* note 32, at 282, 286; JANICAK ET AL., *supra* note 7, at 154–55 (ECT less effective than antipsychotropics); Davis, *supra* note 51, at 1238 (table summarizing 24 drug placebo comparative studies); Davis et al., *supra* note 12, at 1597 (table summarizing drug–placebo comparative studies, electroconvulsive therapy, and psychotherapy); Jarvik, *supra* note 13, at 167–68; Luborsky et al., *Is It True That "Everyone Has Won and All Must Have Prizes"?*, 32 ARCHIVES GEN. PSYCHIATRY 1002 (1975) (summarizing drug–psychotherapy comparative studies); *Report of the Task Panel on Research, in* IV TASK PANEL REPORTS SUBMITTED TO THE PRESIDENT'S COMMISSION ON MENTAL HEALTH 1753–54 (1978) [hereinafter PRESIDENT'S COMMISSION TASK PANEL REPORTS]; Solow, *supra* note 28, at 298. In a highly regarded NIMH study of 400 acutely ill schizophrenic patients, 95% of those treated with phenothiazines showed improvement within 6 weeks (more than 75% showed marked or moderate improvement), compared with half of the patients treated with placebos who showed improvement (23% showed marked or moderate improvement). *National Institute of Mental Health [NIMH], Psychopharmacology Service Center Collaborative Study Group, Phenothiazine Treatment in Acute Schizophrenia,* 10 ARCHIVES GEN. PSYCHIATRY 246 (1964). However, it has been suggested that the scope of antipsychotic effect in the NIMH study may be more limited than suggested by that study. McCreadie, *Indications for Antipsychotic Drugs, in* ANTIPSYCHOTIC DRUGS AND THEIR SIDE-EFFECTS, *supra* note 27, at 159. This is based on the recent concept of positive and negative symptoms of schizophrenia. There is "no convincing evidence that antipsychotic drugs significantly improve negative symptoms." *Id*; RYALL, *supra* note 25, at 172–73. "In view of the propensity of antipsychotics to produce side-effects especially tardive dyskinesia, a recent attempt has been made, not to prescribe patients continuous antipsychotic medication as maintenance therapy, but only to prescribe such drugs when relapse appears imminent." McCreadie, *supra,* at 161. However, a recent study concluded that continuous neuroleptic prophylaxis treatment of schizophrenia was superior to brief intermittent therapy. The study found that "prolonged or frequent relapses as well as episodes of prodromal symptoms were more frequent with intermittent treatment." McCreadie, *supra,* at 161–62; *accord* Davis et al., *Maintenance Antipsychotic Medication, in* ANTIPSYCHOTIC DRUGS AND THEIR SIDE-EFFECTS, *supra,* at 190–91, 201. A recent analysis of the research on the relapse of subjects with schizophrenia concluded:

> All too frequently, the literature states that 50% of patients relapse with drugs, while 50% do not and therefore are not in need of medication. The follow-up period in most of the studies was only 4–6 months, at which time a rate of 10% per month yields about a 50% relapse rate per year. Had the period been extended to 2 years, about 87% would have relapsed. It is not known whether the curve goes into 100% relapses or not. If the observation of constant relapse is correct, the great majority of patients will relapse when switched to placebo if followed up for long enough. We think this is a reasonable observation if it is borne in mind that this applies to the type of patient being studied in these investigations, that is, patients in maintenance medication clinics. . . . [For example], reactive schizophrenic patients can have one episode and never relapse, and in these cases, long-term maintenance medication may not be necessary. . . . [The research] clearly indicates that even selected, good-risk chronic schizophrenic patients are at a high risk of relapse if not maintained on antipsychotics.

Davis et al., *supra,* at 189–91. *See also* SPIEGEL, *supra* note 12, at 205–09. Studies measuring the ability of discharged individuals with acute schizophrenia to remain in the community reveal that 60% to 70% of patients taking no drugs are rehospitalized within 1 year, whereas only 20% to 30% receiving drugs require readmission within this period. Crane, *supra* note 15, at 125; Davis, *supra* note 51, at 1244.

For an analysis of the research regarding a consistently better outcome in relapse rates for patients with maintenance antipsychotics plus psychoeducational–family therapy intervention than for patients with antipsychotics alone, see Davis et al., *supra,* at 197. *See also* SPIEGEL, *supra,* at 209–14. For criticism of the research methodology used in the drug studies, see Marholin & Phillips, *Methodological Issues in Pharmaceutical Research,* 46 AM. J. ORTHOPSYCHIATRY 477 (1976).

[58]*See* GROUP FOR THE ADVANCEMENT OF PSYCHIATRY, *supra* note 32, at 282; GITLIN, *supra* note 4, at 203–39. JANICAK ET AL., *supra* note 7, at 103–04. "[F]irst generation antidepressants such as imipramine, amitriptyline and nortriptyline can be considered effective on the basis of published data, and that there is solid evidence from placebo-controlled clinical studies for the therapeutic benefits of newer products such as chlorimipramine, maprotiline, trazodone and viloxazine." SPIEGEL, *supra* note 12, at 13, 214–15; Jarvik, *supra* note 13, at 190–92; Morris & Beck, *The Efficacy of Antidepressant Drugs,* 30 ARCHIVES GEN. PSYCHIATRY 667 (1974). The tricyclic antidepressants bring about recovery in about 70% of depressed patients, compared to a 30–40% recovery rate for patients treated with placebo. *Report of the Task Panel on Research, in* IV PRESIDENT'S COMMISSION TASK PANEL REPORTS, *supra* note 57, at 1756. However, 30% of patients show no significant response. *Id.* For certain types of depression, electroconvulsive therapy seems effective. JANICAK ET AL., *supra* note 7, at 191; *infra* chapter 6.

placebos in the treatment of bipolar disorder;[59] and that the antianxiety drugs are superior to placebos and to barbiturates in the treatment of neurotic anxiety.[60]

Although these drugs are demonstrably effective, their use is often accompanied by toxic reactions and adverse side effects, some of which are quite serious and irreversible. Most of the antipsychotic and antidepressant drugs produce a family of autonomic side effects, including blurred vision, dry mouth and throat, constipation, paralytic ileus, urinary retention, orthostatic hypotension, edema, tachycardia, palpitations, dizziness, faintness, drowsiness, fatigue, and inhibition of ejaculation.[61]

The most common side effects of the antipsychotic drugs are the extrapyramidal reactions, a family of bizarre disorders of the extrapyramidal motor system, consisting of a Parkinsonian syndrome, akathisia, dystonia, and dyskinesia.[62] The Parkinsonian syndrome, closely resembling the symptoms of Parkinson's disease, consists of muscular rigidity, fine resting tremors, a masklike face, salivation, motor retardation, a shuffling gait, and

---

[59]See Davis, *supra* note 51; Jefferson & Griest, *supra* note 31, at 1657; *Report of the Task Panel on Research, in* IV PRESIDENT'S COMMISSION TASK PANEL REPORTS, *supra* note 57, at 1757–58. For a discussion of how chlorpromazine is more effective than lithium in the treatment of some patients with bipolar disorder, see McCreadie, *supra* note 57, at 163:

> Chlorpromazine was clearly superior to lithium in treating the highly active patient. Chlorpromazine acted more quickly, produced significantly fewer dropouts, and had a lower incidence of severe side-effects. The difference between chlorpromazine and lithium was less pronounced among mildly active patients, but lithium appeared to be the better treatment. It left the patient feeling less sluggish and fatigued, and produced fewer side-effects. Further smaller studies have confirmed the two principle findings of this study, namely, that antipsychotics are more effective in the seriously disturbed manic than lithium, and that they act more quickly. No studies have clearly suggested that any one antipsychotic is more effective than any other. . . .

For a discussion of other effective drugs in the treatment of patients with bipolar disorder, see GITLIN, *supra* note 4, at 74–78.

[60]See Davis et al., *supra* note 12, at 1957 (table summarizing comparative studies); Klerman, *supra* note 3, at 86–87; *Report of the Task Panel on Research, in* IV PRESIDENT'S COMMISSION TASK PANEL REPORTS, *supra* note 57, at 1958; Roy-Bynne & Wingerson, *Pharmacotherapy of Anxiety Disorders,* 11 REVIEW OF PSYCHIATRY 260 (A. Tasman & M. Riba eds., 1992); Solow, *supra* note 28, at 308.

[61]T. DETRE & H. JARECKI, MODERN PSYCHIATRIC TREATMENT 583–84 (antipsychotic drugs), 602–05 (antidepressant drugs) (1971); JANICAK ET AL., *supra* note 7, at 164–83 (adverse effects of antipsychotics), 271–80 (adverse effects of antidepressants); Hollister, *Adverse Reactions to Psychotherapeutic Drugs, in* DRUG TREATMENT OF MENTAL DISORDERS, *supra* note 26, at 267–88; Jarvik, *supra* note 13, at 165 (antipsychotic drugs), 184–85, 189 (antidepressant drugs); Myers & Solomon, *supra* note 28, at 440–41, 446–47 (antipsychotic drugs), 453, 461 (antidepressant drugs), 460 (comparative table); Solow, *supra* note 28, at 300 (antipsychotic drugs). These symptoms are usually mild and patients develop tolerance to them. Some may be controlled by adjusting dosage. *Id.*

[62]Riggins v. Nevada, 504 U.S. 127, 133–34 (1992); Washington v. Harper, 494 U.S. 210, 229–30 (1989); DETRE & JARECKI, *supra* note 61, at 14–17; D. GOODWIN & B. GUZE, *supra* note 7, at 65–66; JANICAK ET AL., *supra* note 7, at 164–67. *See* Task Force, *Neurological Syndromes Associated With Antipsychotic Drug Use: A Special Report,* 28 ARCHIVES GEN. PSYCHIATRY 463 (1973) [hereinafter *Task Force Report*]; Myers & Solomon, *supra* note 28, at 445–46; Solow, *supra* note 28, at 299–300. The commonly accepted range of figures regarding patients on antipsychotics who will develop akathisia is 20–25%; acute dystonias, 2–5%; and the figures for parkinsonism vary widely up to 40%. *See also* Barnes & Edwards, *The Side-Effects of Antipsychotic Drugs: CNS and Neuromuscular*

pill-rolling hand movements.[63] Akathisia is a feeling of motor restlessness or of a compelling need to be in constant motion in which the patient has difficulty remaining still and is driven to pace about impatiently and tap his foot incessantly.[64] Dystonia involves bizarre muscular spasm, primarily of the muscles of the head and neck, often accompanied by facial grimacing, involuntary spasm of the tongue and mouth interfering with speech and swallowing, oculogyric crisis marked by eyes flipping to the top of the head in a painful upward gaze persisting for minutes or hours, convulsive movements of the arms and head, bizarre gaits, and difficulty in walking.[65] The dyskinesias present a broad range of bizarre tongue, face, and neck movements.[66] These extrapyramidal symptoms are subjectively quite stressful, may be incompatible with clinical improvement and with a useful life outside the hospital, and can be more unbearable than the symptoms for which the patient was originally treated.[67]

Virtually all of the extrapyramidal reactions are reversible when antipsychotic medication is discontinued. One of the dyskinesias, however, first becomes evident when antipsychotic medication is withdrawn.[68] This condition, tardive dyskinesia, is a late appearing, persistent neurological syndrome estimated to affect between 0.5% and 40% of

---

Effects, in ANTIPSYCHOTIC DRUGS AND THEIR SIDE-EFFECTS, *supra* note 27, at 217–38; Lohr, *Tardive Dyskinesia, in* DRUG-INDUCED DYSFUNCTION IN PSYCHIATRY, *supra* note 56, at 131; Steingard, *Drug-Induced Dystonias, in* DRUG-INDUCED DYSFUNCTION IN PSYCHIATRY, *supra* note 56, at 1. Because patients on antipsychotic medication are often given antiparkinson drugs to prevent or counteract extrapyramidal side effects, estimates of the use of antiparkinson drugs provide a useful index to the prevalence and risk of these side effects. It is estimated that 30% to 50% of patients on antipsychotic medication receive antiparkinson drugs. Ayd, *Treatment-Resistant Patients: A Moral, Legal and Therapeutic Challenge, in* RATIONAL PSYCHOPHARMACOTHERAPY, *supra* note 28, at 37, 55. *See* GITLIN, *supra* note 4, at 310. Even though it is often the practice to treat patients receiving high-potency dopamine blockers with antiparkinsonian agents from the start of treatment, this remains controversial because no medication is devoid of problems. Yadalam, *Drug-Induced Parkinsonism, in* DRUG-INDUCED DYSFUNCTION IN PSYCHIATRY, *supra* note 56, at 124.

    [63]This condition, like the other extrapyramidal side effects, is presumed to stem from a deficiency of dopamine caused by the action of the phenothiazines in blocking dopamine receptors, sometimes resulting in the degeneration of the dopamine neurons in the corpus striatum. Aghajanian & Rasmussen, *Basic Electrophysiology, in* 1 TEXTBOOK OF PSYCHIATRY, *supra* note 1, at 71. The Parkinson syndrome is usually treated by reduction of dosage or by the concurrent administration of antiparkinson drugs. Antiparkinson drugs, however, may be dangerous and often produce their own unwanted side effects. JANICAK ET AL., *supra* note 7, at 164–67. Moreover, they are used too often and for longer periods than necessary. Ayd, *supra* note 62, at 55; Hollister, *Polypharmacy in Psychiatry: Is it Necessary, Good or Bad?, in* RATIONAL PSYCHOPHARMACOTHERAPY, *supra* note 28, at 19, 22–23.

    [64]*See* JANICAK ET AL., *supra* note 7, at 164–65; Kendler, *A Medical Student's Experiences with Akathisia,* 133 AM. J. PSYCHIATRY 454 (1976). Antiparkinson drugs may be helpful in the treatment of this condition, but reduction in dosage of the antipsychotic drugs is frequently necessary and sedatives are also used. *Id.*

    [65]This condition is usually treated successfully with antiparkinson drugs or intramuscular medication. SCHATZBERT & COLE, *supra* note 28, at 116.

    [66]Solomon & Masdev, *Neuropsychiatry and Behavioral Neurology, in* 1 TEXTBOOK OF PSYCHIATRY, *supra* note 1, at 238.

    [67]Davis et al., *supra* note 12, at 1622–23; Van Putten, *Why Do Schizophrenic Patients Refuse to Take Their Drugs?,* 31 ARCHIVES GEN. PSYCHIATRY 67 (1974) (suggesting that the high incidence of refusal by schizophrenic outpatients to take prescribed phenothiazines is due to the extrapyramidal side effects).

    [68]JANICAK ET AL., *supra* note 7, at 167.

patients on antipsychotic medication.[69] It consists of slow, rhythmical, repetitive, involuntary movements of the mouth, lips, and tongue, sometimes accompanied by other bizarre muscular activity.[70] The most widely described symptoms constitute the "bucco–linguo masticatory" triad—sucking and smacking of the lips, protrusion of the tongue, lateral jaw movements, and blowing of the cheeks. Motor disorders in other parts of the body are frequent, including involuntary quick movements of the extremities, continuous arrhythmic wormlike movements in the distal parts of the limbs, overextension of the spine and neck, abnormal postures, shifting of weight from foot to foot, and an inability to stand or sit still. There is no known effective treatment for tardive dyskinesia, which is thought to effect permanent structural changes in the brain.[71] Another serious side effect is neuroleptic malignant syndrome, a rare but underdiagnosed condition that is fatal in 25% of cases.[72] This

[69] An American Psychiatric Association Task Force reported that 10% to 20% of patients given antipsychotic drugs for 1 year or more develop the condition. AMERICAN PSYCHIATRIC ASSOCIATION TASK FORCE ON LATE NEUROLOGICAL EFFECTS OF ANTIPSYCHOTIC DRUGS, TARDIVE DYSKINESIA 43–44 (1979) [hereinafter TARDIVE DYSKINESIA]. More recent estimates are much higher. See SCHATZBERG & COLE, supra note 28, at 327 (50% to 60%); Asnis et al., A Survey of Tardive Dyskinesia in Psychiatric Outpatients, 134 AM. J. PSYCHIATRY 12 (1977) (43.4% of psychiatric outpatients in sample studied). As the antipsychotic drugs mask the effects of tardive dyskinesia and the condition may appear only after the drugs have been discontinued or reduced, it may be that many prevalence estimates are too low. Id. Gelman, Mental Hospital Drugs, Professionalism and the Constitution, 72 GEO. L.J. 1725, 1742–43 (1984); Hollister, Antipsychotic and Antimanic Drugs (Lithium), in REVIEW OF GENERAL PSYCHIATRY 507 (H. Goldman ed., 1984) (20% to 40%); Jeste & Wyatt, Changing Epidemiology of Tardive Dyskinesia: An Overview, 138 AM. J. PSYCHIATRY 297 (1981) (25%, with prevalence progressively rising). Taub, Tardive Dsykinesia: Medical Facts and Legal Fictions, 30 ST. LOUIS U. L.J. 833, 836 (1986) ("The literature on TD cites widely varying figures for its prevalence in different patient populations, ranging from 0.5% to 65%."). The condition is "underdiagnosed at an alarming rate." Weiden et al., Clinical Non-Recognition of Neuroleptic-Induced Movement Disorders: A Cautionary Study, 144 AM. J. PSYCHIATRY 1148, 1151 (1987). One physician stated that among the mentally retarded population, there are hundred of thousands of individuals suffering from the syndrome. Lipman, Overview of Research in Psychopharmacological Treatment of the Mentally Ill/Mentally Retarded, 22 PSYCHOPHARMACOLOGY BULL. 1046, 1052 (1986). If all individuals who receive prolonged treatment with antipsychotic drugs are considered and a conservative prevalence rate of 20% is used, 1 to 2 million persons suffer from tardive dyskinesia in any given year. P. BREGGIN, PSYCHIATRIC DRUGS: HAZARDS TO THE BRAIN 108 (1983). As of yet, there is no available method of predicting who will be affected and no effective way to prevent the occurrence of tardive dyskinesia or to manage its symptoms once they are displayed. D. JESTE & R. WYATT, UNDERSTANDING AND TREATING TARDIVE DYSKINESIA 289–90 (1982); Smith & Simon, Tardive Dyskinesia Revisited, 31 MED. TRIAL TECHNIQUES Q. 342, 348 (1985).

[70] JANICAK ET AL., supra note 7, at 167; Black et al., Antipsychotic Agents: A Clinical Update, 60 MAYO CLINIC PROC. 777, 785 (1985); Crane, Persistent Dyskinesia, 122 BRIT. J. PSYCHIATRY 395 (1973); Crane, supra note 15, at 126–27; Meyers & Solomon, supra note 28, at 446; Taub, supra note 69, at 833–34.

[71] Task Force Report, supra note 62, at 463; TARDIVE DYSKINESIA, supra note 69, at 57; GITLIN, supra note 4, at 309; SCHATZBERG & COLE, supra note 28, at 100. Pathological studies indicate the presence of structural changes in the brain in patients with this condition. Christenson et al., Neuropathological Investigation of 28 Brains From Patients With Dyskinesia, 46 ACTA PSYCHIATRY SCAND. 14 (1970); Steingard, supra note 62, at 113; Taub, supra note 69, at 835 ("[I]t is generally agreed that no effective treatment has yet been discovered for TD."). See also Cichon, The Right to "Just Say No": A History and Analysis of the Right to Refuse Antipsychotic Drugs, 53 LA L. REV. 283, 304–07 (1992) (discussing effects of tardive dyskinesia).

[72] See Addonizio et al., Symptoms of Neuroleptic Malignant Syndrome on 82 Consecutive Inpatients, 143 AM. J. PSYCHIATRY 1587 (1986); Pope et al., Frequency of Presentation of Neuroleptic Malignant Syndrome in a Large Psychiatric Hospital, 143 AM. J. PSYCHIATRY 1227 (1986); see also Amicus Brief for the National Association of Protection and Advocacy Systems 14, cited in Washington v. Harper, 494 U.S. 210 (1990) (No. 88-599) (vivid description of 5 reported deaths associated with neuroleptic malignant syndrome). This syndrome typically develops swiftly, often over a 24- to 72-hour period. Cichon, supra note 71, at 308. This syndrome can last from several days to several weeks, even after antipsychotic medication is discontinued. Sternberg, Neuroleptic Malignant Syndrome: The Pendulum Swings, 143 AM. J. PSYCHIATRY 1273, 1273 (1986). Death usually occurs within 3 to 30 days after the onset of symptoms and is frequently caused by respiratory failure, cardiovascular collapse, and acute kidney failure. Cichon, supra, note 71, at 308; Sternberg, supra, at 1273.

condition is characterized by hyperthermia, severe muscular rigidity, rhythmic movements, and alterations in consciousness.[73] All antipsychotic drugs are capable of inducing neuroleptic muscular syndrome, and all patients exposed to these drugs are at risk.[74]

Even more dangerous than the extrapyramidal symptoms are the effects accompanying antipsychotic drugs resulting from hypersensitivity reactions, particularly blood dyscrasias, jaundice, and dermatological reactions.[75] Sudden death caused by ventricular fibrillation, asphyxia from regurgitated food, or convulsive seizures, although extremely rare, has been reported.[76] Also rare, and occasionally fatal, is agranulocytosis, a sudden disappearance of white blood cells that occurs with extremely high dosages; this increases the risk of infection.[77] Moreover, overmedication has been reported to be a contributing factor in the deaths of many institutionalized patients whose ability to experience symptoms of various diseases and conditions or to communicate their suffering to hospital staff is inhibited by heavy doses of antipsychotic medication.[78] Additional side effects include sedation, interference with concentration, flattening of affect, lethargy, weight gain, convulsions, metabolic and endocrinologic changes, and a variety of behavioral and emotional effects.[79]

Although tardive dyskinesia may be an irreversible condition and neuroleptic malignant syndrome and several other effects may be fatal, most of the other side effects of the drugs are short acting and disappear within hours or days of drug discontinuation. Similarly, the primary therapeutic effects of the drugs are only short acting. With the exception of Prolixin and other long-acting phenothiazines (the effects of which last for several weeks), the primary effects of the drugs may last only several hours or days. Nevertheless, many patients are continued on the drugs for lengthy periods and thus experience the effects on a continued basis. Long-term drug treatment may impair memory, reasoning ability, mental speed, learning capacity, and efficiency of mental functioning in general.[80]

Side effects accompanying use of the antidepressant and antianxiety drugs, although usually less serious than those related to the antipsychotic drugs, are not inconsiderable. The MAO inhibitors present perhaps even greater risks than the antipsychotic drugs. A variety of

---

[73]Bower, *When Antipsychotic Drugs Can Be Lethal,* 130 SCI. NEWS 260, 260 (1986); Cichon, *supra* note 71, at 308; Pope et al., *supra* note 72, at 1227;

[74]Guze & Baxter, *Neuroleptic Malignant Syndrome,* 313 NEW ENG. J. MED. 163, 163 (1985).

[75]Davis et al., *supra* note 12, at 1621; Jarvik, *supra* note 13, at 165–66; Myers & Solomon, *supra* note 28, at 445–48; Solow, *supra* note 28, at 299–301.

[76]DETRE & JARECKI, *supra* note 61, at 588–89; Lesstma & Koenig, *Sudden Death and Phenothiazene,* 18 ARCHIVES GEN. PSYCHIATRY 137 (1968); Moore & Book, *Sudden Death in Phenothiazene Therapy,* 44 PSYCHIATRY Q. 389 (1970); Myers & Solomon, *supra* note 28, at 447.

[77]JANICAK ET AL., *supra* note 7, at 177–78; Davis et al., *supra* note 12, at 1621–22; Myers & Solomon, *supra* note 28, at 448; Pisciotta, *Agranulocytosis Induced by Certain Phenothiazine Derivatives,* 208 JAMA 1862 (1969).

[78]Gupte, *Tranquilizers Held a Factor in Deaths of Mental Patients,* N.Y. TIMES, July 17, 1978, at A1 (reporting on a study by the Medical Examiner of Rockland County, New York).

[79]Brooks, *The Constitutional Right to Refuse Antipsychotic Medication,* 8 BULL. AM. ACAD. PSYCHIATRY & L. 179, 184 (1980); Sederer, *Brief Hospitalization, in* 11 REV. PSYCHIATRY 527–28 (A. Tasman & M. Riba eds., 1992); Van Putten & May, *Subjective Response as a Predictor of Outcome of Pharmacotherapy,* 35 ARCHIVES GEN. PSYCHIATRY 477, 479 (1978). One of the most troublesome of these effects is weight gain, which may amount to 1 or 2 pounds per week and may not taper off until it has reached 30 to 40 pounds. Such weight gain often has a profound effect on the patient's self-esteem and contributes to social isolation. DETRE & JARECKI, *supra* note 61, at 585.

[80]See DiMascio et al., *Behavioral Toxicity Part III: Perceptual Cognitive Functions and Part IV: Emotional (Mood) States, in* PSYCHOTROPIC DRUGS SIDE EFFECTS 132, 133 (R. Shader & A. DiMascio eds., 1977). All available antipsychotics have an approximately equal risk for causing tardive dyskinesia, except clozapine. GITLIN, *supra* note 4, at 308. Clozapine is an atypical antipsychotic that does not appear to cause tardive dyskinesia. However, clozapine is associated with a high incidence of agranulocytosis, which is potentially fatal. Lohr, *supra* note 62, at 142.

very serious toxic effects involving the liver, the brain, and the cardiovascular system as well as less serious side effects have been reported, resulting in restricted use of the MAO inhibitors.[81] The tricyclic antidepressants produce the typical autonomic effects described for the antipsychotic drugs, as well as a number of allergic and hypersensitivity reactions, cardiovascular difficulties, endocrine changes, and central nervous system effects, including persistent tremors in the upper extremities and tongue, a mild Parkinsonian syndrome, and episodes of schizophrenic excitement, confusion, or mania.[82] Acute toxicity and death may result from overdose. The newer antidepressants, however, such as fluoxetine (Prozac), produce fewer adverse reactions than tricyclic antidepressants.[83] The side effects of the antianxiety drugs are comparatively minor but can include drowsiness, vertigo, excessive appetite, nausea, headache, allergic and hematological disorders, impaired visual–motor performance and judgment, paradoxical rage reactions, hangover, drug dependence or habituation, and withdrawal symptoms.[84] Lithium, at proper therapeutic levels, rarely causes serious adverse reactions.[85]

D. Drug Administration Abuse and Relative Intrusiveness

Psychotropic drugs are much abused, particularly in institutions for the mentally disabled.[86] Such facilities commonly administer psychotropic medication on an involuntary

---

[81]GOODWIN & GUZE, *supra* note 7, at 32–33; JANICAK ET AL., *supra* note 7, at 281–85 (adverse effects of monoamine oxidase inhibitors); Davis & Glassman, *supra* note 16, at 1644–47; Jarvik, *supra* note 13, at 185–86.

[82]DETRE & JARECKI, *supra* note 61, at 602–606; GOODWIN & GUZE, *supra* note 7, at 30 ("The most common [side effects of tricyclic depressants] are dry mouth, orthostatic hypotension, and tremor."); JANICAK ET AL., *supra* note 7, at 271–80 (adverse effects of tricyclic antidepressants); Davis & Glassman, *supra* note 16, at 1645–56; Jarvik, *supra* note 13, at 189–90. Abrupt discontinuation of antidepressant drugs can lead to nausea, vomiting, increased sweating, feelings of hot and cold, insomnia, irritation, and headaches, within 5 to 7 days after withdrawal. Davis et al., *supra* note 12, at 1625. For a discussion of other antidepressants and their side effects, see *supra* notes 28–30.

[83]BAER & WILLIAMS, *supra* note 56, at 431. Seizures may occur with all of the newer antidepressants. Amoxapine and maprotiline may cause anticholinergic effects, orthostatic hypotension, and tachycardia. *Id.* Bupropion causes dose-related CNS stimulation, including anorexia, restlessness, hallucinations, seizures, insomnia, and psychotic episodes. However, the other new antidepressants commonly produce sedation. *Id.* The most common adverse reactions to fluoxetine are rashes, headaches, diarrhea, anorexia, and diaphoresis. *Id.* Trazodone may cause sedation, muscle tremors, dizziness, dry mouth, nausea, vomiting, headache, and blurred vision. MCKENRY & SALERNO, *supra* note 56, at 341.

[84]DETRE & JARECKI, *supra* note 61, at 599; JANICAK ET AL., *supra* note 7, at 432–39 (adverse effects of antianxiety drugs); Gorman & Davis, *supra* note 30, at 1647; Jarvik, *supra* note 13, at 176, 179–80; Myers & Solomon, *supra* note 28, at 436–37; Solow, *supra* note 28, at 309.

[85]GOODWIN & GUZE, *supra* note 7, at 34 ("At higher levels, disorientation, somnolence, seizures, and finally circulatory collapse may occur."). Although initial side effects may include tremor of the hands, abdominal cramps, nausea, vomiting, diarrhea, thirst, polyuria, fatigue, and weight gain, after about a week all but thirst, excessive urination, and tremor disappear. SCHATZBERG & COLE, *supra* note 28, at 158–62; Jarvik, *supra* note 13, at 194; Jefferson & Greist, *supra* note 31, at 1660–61; Myers & Solomon, *supra* note 28, at 449. These initial side effects "are usually totally reversible; they are harmless; and steps can be taken to decrease the discomfort." Brown, *Side Effects of Lithium Therapy and Their Treatment*, 21 CAN. PSYCHIATRIC ASS'N J. 13, 14 (1976). Administration of excessive amounts of lithium or failure of renal mechanisms properly to eliminate it may result in lithium toxicity, a serious condition involving central nervous system effects including confusion, impairment of consciousness, and even coma. Brown, *supra*, at 18–19; Jarvik, *supra*, at 194; Jefferson & Greist, *supra*, at 1660.

[86]Opening Statement of Sen. Bayh, Sen. Comm. on the Judiciary, Subcomm. to Investigate Juvenile Delinquency, *Hearings on the Abuse and Misuse of Controlled Drugs in Institutions*, 94th Cong., 1st Sess., vol. I, at 1–2 (1975) [hereinafter *Hearings*]; Perlin, *Competency, Deinstitutionalization, and Homelessness: A Story of Marginalization*, 28 HOUS. L. REV. 63,126 (1991) (referring to "public hospitals' dismal performance in the administration of antipsychotic medication").

basis.[87] State hospital patients, whether voluntary or involuntary, are rarely provided an explanation of the presumed benefits and potential risks of drug treatment, are seldom asked for their consent and are often forcibly injected if they resist oral medication.[88] The psychotropic drugs present a potent means for the control and modification of behavior[89] and have been widely used to change attitudes and emotions of patients.[90]

Some have even suggested the use of long-acting tranquilizers implanted beneath the skin of prisoners—a means of "chemical incapacitation" urged as an alternative to prison.[91] Moreover, these drugs have been frequently administered in institutional settings for

---

[87]A. BROOKS, LAW, PSYCHIATRY AND THE MENTAL HEALTH SYSTEM 877 (1974); Bomstein, *The Forcible Administration of Drugs to Prisoners and Mental Patients*, 9 CLEARINGHOUSE REV. 379 (1975); Gelman, *supra* note 69, at 1731–32. *See* Statement of David Ferleger, *in* Hearings, *supra* note 84, vol. II, at 168–70; Halleck, *Legal and Ethical Aspects of Behavior Control*, 131 AM. J. PSYCHIATRY 381, 382 (1974). Although for certain issues mental hospitals have witnessed "a shift from the more traditional model of staff decision-making to the sharing of decision-making power with patients," there "seems to be general agreement that . . . medication decisions are best made by trained staff members." Burstein, *Decision-Making in the Hospital Community*, 29 ARCHIVES GEN. PSYCHIATRY 732, 733 (1973). *See also* Souder v. McGuire, 423 F. Supp. 830 (M.D. Pa. 1976); Bell v. Wayne County Gen. Hosp., 384 F. Supp. 1085 (E.D. Mich. 1974); Welsch v. Likens, 373 F. Supp. 487, 503 (D. Minn. 1974), *aff'd in part and vacated in part*, 550 F.2d 1122 (8th Cir. 1977); Nelson v. Heyne, 355 F. Supp. 451 (N.D. Ind. 1972), *aff'd*, 491 F.2d 353 (7th Cir.), *cert. denied*, 417 U.S. 976 (1974); Williams v. Wilzak, 573 A.2d 809 (Md. 1990); People v. Woodall, 257 Cal. Rptr. 601 (Ct. App. 1989); Rogers v. Commissioner, 458 N.E.2d 308 (Mass. 1983); *In re* K.K.B., 609 P.2d 747 (Okla. 1980); Harmon v. McNutt, 587 P.2d 537 (Wash. 1978). *See, e.g.*, Davis v. Hubbard, 506 F. Supp. 915, 926 (M.D. Ohio 1980) ("testimony at trial established the prevalent use of drugs is counter therapeutic and can be justified only for reasons other than treatment—namely, for the convenience of staff and for punishment"); Rogers v. Okin, 478 F. Supp. 1342 (D. Mass. 1979), *aff'd in part and rev'd in part*, 634 F.2d 650 (1st Cir. 1980), *vacated sub nom.* Mills v. Rogers, 457 U.S. 291 (1982), *on remand*, 738 F.2d 1 (1st Cir. 1984); Rennie v. Klein, 476 F. Supp. 1294, 1299–1302, 1309 (D.N.J. 1979), *modified*, 653 F.2d 838 (3d Cir. 1981) (en banc), *vacated*, 458 U.S. 1119 (1982), *on remand*, 720 F.2d 266 (3d Cir. 1983).

[88]Bomstein, *supra* note 87; Ferleger, *Loosing the Chains: In-Hospital Civil Liberties of Mental Patients*, 13 SANTA CLARA L. 447, 453–54, 469–70 (1973); Gelman, *supra* note 69, at 1729; Roth et al., *Into the Abyss: Psychiatric Reliability and Emergency Commitment Statutes*, 13 SANTA CLARA L. 400, 418–19 n.70 (1973); Wexler et al., *The Administration of Psychiatric Justice: Theory and Practice in Arizona*, 13 ARIZ. L. REV. 1, 191, 204 (1971).

[89]Dorfman, *Through a Therapeutic Jurisprudence Filter: Fear and Pretextuality in Mental Disability Law*, 10 N.Y.L. SCH. J. HUM. RTS. 805, 818–19 (1993); Halleck, *supra* note 87, at 381–82; Klerman, *supra* note 3, at 3; McCarron, *The Right to Refuse Antipsychotic Drugs: Safeguarding the Mentally Incompetent Patient's Right to Procedural Due Process*, 73 MARQ. L. REV. 477, 482 n.31 (1990); P. Steinfels, *Confronting the Other Drug Problem*, 2 HASTINGS CTR. REP., Nov. 1972, at 4. *See also* Jenecks & Clauser, *Managing Behavior Problems in Nursing Homes*, 265 JAMA 502 (1991).

The potential for abusive use of psychoactive drugs for behavior control is illustrated by accounts of experimentation with Thorazine and LSD and other hallucinogens, sometimes with unaware individuals, by the Central Intelligence Agency, the Army, the Air Force, and the former U.S. Department of Health, Education and Welfare. *E.g.*, Horrock, *Drugs Tested by C.I.A. on Mental Patients*, N.Y. TIMES, Aug. 3, 1977, at A1; Szule, *The CIA's Electric Kool-Aid Acid Test*, PSYCHOL. TODAY, Nov. 1977, at 92; *Chemical and Biological Agents and the Intelligence Community*, N.Y. TIMES, April 27, 1976, at 25 (Week in Review Section); *Report Says C.I.A. Agents Picked Up Bar Patrons for L.S.D. Experiments*, N.Y. TIMES, April 29, 1976, at 25; *Mind-Drug Tests a Federal Project for Almost 25 Years*, N.Y. TIMES, Aug. 11, 1975, at 42; *Officials: Air Force Funded L.S.D. Tests*, MIAMI HERALD, July 31, 1975, at A1; *H.E.W. Reported to Have Run L.S.D. Tests on Human Subjects*, N.Y. TIMES, July 28, 1975, at 6; *G.I.'s in Test Not Aware That They Received L.S.D.*, N.Y. TIMES, July 24, 1975, at 1; *Army Seeks 1,500 to Check After-Effects of L.S.D. Test*, N.Y. TIMES, July 20, 1975, at 39.

[90]Dorfman, *supra* note 89, at 807–10; Jarvik, *supra* note 13, at 151.

[91]Lehtinen, *Technological Incapacitation: A Neglected Alternative*, 2 Q. J. CORRECTIONS 31, 35–36 (1978).

punitive, management, or control purposes unrelated to the therapeutic needs of patients.[92]
Heavy dosages of chlorpromazine are not uncommon in many state hospitals, resulting in a
"haze of drug-induced docility" in which "the patient remains generally unconcerned,
unquestioning and much easier to manage. . . ."[93] The widespread use of phenothiazines in
institutions for those with mental retardation[94] has been questioned on the basis of the
inadequacy of evaluative studies relied on to justify their use with nonpsychotic patients

---

[92]E.g., United States ex rel. Wilson v. Coughlin, 472 F.2d 100 (7th Cir. 1972) (enjoining the use of Thorazine
in a boys' training school for purposes of control or punishment); Welsch v. Likens, 373 F. Supp. 487, 503 (D. Minn.
1974), aff'd in part and vacated in part, 550 F.2d 1122 (8th Cir. 1977) (excessive use of tranquilizing drugs to
control the behavior of mentally retarded residents held cruel and unusual punishment); Nelson v. Heyne, 355 F.
Supp. 451 (N.D. Ind. 1972), aff'd, 491 F.2d 353 (7th Cir.), cert. denied, 417 U.S. 976 (1974); Wyatt v. Stickney, 344
F. Supp. 373, 380 (M.D. Ala. 1972), aff'd sub nom. Wyatt v. Aderholt, 503 F.2d 1305 (5th Cir. 1974) (enjoining the
use of medication "as punishment, for the convenience of staff, as a substitute for program, or in quantities that
interfere with the patient's treatment program"); In re Owens, No. 70J21520 (Ill. Cir. Ct., Cook County, Juv. Div.,
July 9, 1971) (Thorazine forcibly administered to residents of Illinois State School "as a behavior control device"),
rev'd on other grounds, 295 N.E.2d 455 (Ill. 1973). See S. BRACKEL & R. ROCK, THE MENTALLY DISABLED AND THE
LAW 172 (rev. ed. 1971) (referring to the "indiscriminate use of drugs on patients for the convenience of hospital
officials"); J. MITFORD, KIND AND USUAL PUNISHMENT: THE PRISON BUSINESS 129 (1973) (punitive use of drugs in
prisons); R. REDLICH & D. FREEDMAN, THE THEORY AND PRACTICE OF PSYCHIATRY 818 (1966) ("In the psychiatric
practice, we see the wholesale application of tranquilizing drugs for the benefit of the institution, that is, physicians,
nurses and administrators, and not always solely for the patients' sake."); K. WOODEN, WEEPING IN THE PLAYTIME OF
OTHERS: AMERICA'S INCARCERATED CHILDREN 140–48 (1976) (use of drugs in institutions for juveniles). See also
Opening Statement of Sen. Bayh, in Hearings, supra note 86, vol. I, at 2–3 (referring to "the indiscriminate use of
dangerous drugs for the sole purpose of controlling the conduct of institutionalized juveniles and easing the
management problems of under-staffed institutions" and to "the use of potentially harmful tranquilizers—
chemical straightjackets as it were—as a substitute for humane treatment and quality programs"); Statement of
Anthony Brandt, in Hearings, supra note 86, vol. III, at 25:

> Patients . . . told me about the use of drugs as a form of punishment or coercion; when they refused
> medication, refused to cooperate in other ways, threatened to break rules or did break them, it was common
> practice to inject three or four times their normal dose of tranquilizers, a practice psychiatrists call
> 'snowing,' to render the patient comatose and make it clear to him who's the boss.

Bomstein, supra note 87, at 383 ("Sometimes drugs are forcibly injected in order to punish or control behavior.");
Crane, supra note 15, at 125 ("Patients who present serious management problems are most likely to receive large
quantities of neuroleptics for long periods of time, although the persistence of severe psychoses would suggest that
chemotherapy is not effective in such cases."); Dorfman, supra note 89, at 807–09; McCarron, supra note 89, at
484; Opton, Psychiatric Violence Against Prisoners: When Therapy is Punishment, 45 MISS. L.J. 605, 640 (1974)
("Most drugging is for the purpose of control, for keeping prisoners quiet and docile."); Quarton, Deliberate
Efforts to Control Human Behavior and Modify Personality, 96 DAEDALUS 837, 848 (1967) ("One abuse of drugs
that occurs today in some places is the use of tranquilizers in hospitals for the mentally ill and the aged primarily to
keep troublemaking patients from annoying the staff. This use of drugs may actually prevent the life experiences
necessary for social recovery. . . ."); Rogers, The Involuntary Drugging of Juveniles in State Institutions, 10
CLEARINGHOUSE REV. 623 (1977); F. Rundle, Institution v. Ethics: The Dilemma of a Prison Doctor, 2 HASTINGS
CTR. REP., Nov. 1972, at 7, 8 (describing the use of Prolixin in the California prison system "to control unwanted
behavior"); Stefan, The Protection Racket: Rape Trauma Syndrome, Psychiatric Labeling, and Law, 88 NW. U. L.
REV. 1271, 1316 (1994).

[93]Shaffer, Introduction to Symposium: Mental Illness, the Law and Civil Liberties, 13 SANTA CLARA L. 369,
370 (1973). See, e.g., Statement of Anthony Brandt, supra note 92, at 25 ("The level of drugging was so high that
many patients slept 12 hours a day or more."); Brooks, supra note 79, at 184. Chlorpromazine, unlike some of the
other phenothiazenes, requires comparatively high dosages in order for its antipsychotic effects to be achieved. As a
result, even typical therapeutic dosages can be highly sedating. Chlorpromazine is accordingly classified as a
sedating phenothiazine, the class of phenothiazines producing the most drowsiness. DETRE & JARECKI, supra note
61, at 536–37. The sedating effects of chlorpromazine can be substantially reduced without any loss of clinical
benefits and with fewer adverse side effects, including less extrapyramidal reactions, by altering the typical hospital
practice of administering the drug on a four-times-a-day schedule to a once-a-day schedule at bedtime. HOLLISTER,
supra note 51, at 36; Blackwell, Rational Drug Use in Psychiatry, in RATIONAL PSYCHOPHARMACOTHERAPY, supra
note 28, at 187, 191–92; DiMascio, supra note 38, at 122.

[94]A 1967–1968 study found that 51% of the residents in institutions for the mentally retarded were on
psychotropic medication. Lipman, The Use of Psychopharmacological Agents in Residential Facilities for the
Retarded, in PSYCHIATRIC APPROACHES TO M.R. 387 (F. Menolasciono ed., 1970).

with mental retardation and the concern that these hazardous drugs are being used primarily to facilitate institutional management.[95] In understaffed facilities, psychotropic drugs are often administered without the supervision of a physician, and medication decisions are frequently made by nurses, given broad delegations to administer these drugs ''p.r.n.;'' such medication decisions may even be made by untrained staff.[96] Unless trained medical

[95]Statement of Gail Marker, *in Hearings, supra* note 86, at 287–352; Marker, *Phenothiazines and the Mentally Retarded: Institutional Drug Abuse?,* MENTAL HEALTH LAW PROJECT SUMMARY OF ACTIVITIES 1 (March 1975); Blonston, *Institutions Overdose Children Panel Told,* MIAMI HERALD, Aug. 1, 1975, at A20. A study of drug administration practices at one such institution, for example, revealed increased frequency of intramuscular injection of chlorpromazine prior to periods of reduced staffing, suggesting '' 'anticipatory' drug administration for 'behavioral control.' '' Thompson & Grabowski, *Ethical and Legal Guidelines for Behavior Modification, in* BEHAVIOR MODIFICATION OF THE MENTALLY RETARDED 495, 499–501 (T. Thompson & J. Grabowski eds., 2d ed. 1977).

The widespread use of these drugs in institutions for children with mental retardation and facilities for juveniles is particularly disturbing in light of increasing evidence that the phenothiazines may have adverse effects on learning ability. *See* Statement of Gail Marker, *supra* at 289 (''[A]lthough the existing evidence is not conclusive, the weight of the evidence strongly suggests that phenothiazines may slow reaction time, decrease accuracy, decrease learning performance and impair maintenance of attention to details.'' (citing R. Sprague & J. Werry, *Psychotropic Drugs and Handicapped Children, in* THE SECOND REVIEW OF SPECIAL EDUCATION 1–50 (L. Mann & D. Sabatin eds., 1974)). The Mental Health Law Project (now known as the Bazelon Center), in a petition to the Food and Drug Administration, *reprinted in Hearings, supra* note 86, vol. II, at 85–108, raised this and a number of related issues involving alleged abuses of phenothiazene drugs in institutions for the mentally retarded. Although conceding the existence of abuses, the FDA denied the petition in substance, finding that ''[w]e are not yet satisfied . . . that there is reasonable evidence associating approved use of phenothiazines with cognitive impairment in the short run. Hard data are lacking, and . . . absent altogether with regard to long-term use. . . . Until there is reasonable evidence on this point, we cannot require a warning in the labeling.'' Letter from Alexander H. Schmidt, Commissioner, Food and Drug Administration, to Dennis Lehr, Nov. 11, 1975, at 6.

[96]*E.g.,* Morales v. Turman, 383 F. Supp. 53, 104 (E.D. Tex. 1974), *rev'd on procedural grounds,* 535 F.2d 864 (5th Cir. 1976); Nelson v. Heyne, 355 F. Supp. 451, 455 (N.D. Ind. 1972), *aff'd,* 491 F.2d 353 (7th Cir.), *cert. denied,* 417 U.S. 976 (1974); *see* M. PINES, THE BRAIN CHANGERS 112 (1973); Statement of Anthony Brandt, *supra* note 92, at 25; Ferleger, *supra* note 88, at 453, 469. ''P.r.n.'' is an abbreviation for the Latin phrase ''pro re nata'' (as circumstances may require). Wexler et al., *supra* note 88, at 198, 206.

In Morales v. Turman, *supra,* the court, reviewing practices with respect to psychotropic medication at facilities for juveniles operated by the Texas Youth Council (TYC), found:

> The nurses who administer the drugs are often licensed vocational nurses rather than registered nurses, and have no expertise in the supervision of a course of powerful medication. At Mountain View, prescribed medication may be given by the nurse or by infirmary aides who have no medical training. . . .

> One of the TYC psychiatrists occasionally leaves a standing order for the nurses that, with regard to specified students, intra-muscular injections of psychotropic drugs may be given, if needed. At Mountain View, a medical doctor or psychiatrist may prescribe medication for a student ''as needed.'' The nurse, or if she is not on duty, the medically untrained infirmary aide, decides whether the medication is needed by the student. This practice extends to intramuscular injections of medication, as well as medication to be taken orally.

> At Gainesville, Thorazine and other drugs are regularly administered by the licensed vocational nurses when the registered nurse is not present. Such drugs are administered either orally or by injection. A physician's orders to administer these drugs are sometimes made to licensed vocational nurses by telephone. One licensed vocational nurse at Gainesville admitted having administered Thorazine, by injection, to a student for whom there was no prescription. The nurse explained that she understood that she was permitted to do this if a student was ''out of control.'' The nurse conceded that she had no training in the use of behavior modifying drugs and was unaware of the possible contra-indications to the use of Thorazine.

See also Nelson v. Heyne, *supra* (''Standing orders by the doctor at the Boys School permits the registered nurse on duty to prescribe dosages of specified tranquilizers upon the recommendation of the custodial staff at the Boys School.''); Statement of Dr. James Clements, *in Hearings, supra* note 86, vol. III, at 121–22:

> In all of the institutions [for the mentally retarded] that I have evaluated, not a single one required controlled drugs to be administered by a registered nurse. Untrained ward attendants generally do this. And remember, a large number of these ward attendants do not have even the equivalent of a high school diploma. Some are in fact illiterate. Some are not proficient in the English language. . . . Not only are regularly scheduled drugs given by people who may be totally unknowledgeable of dosages, contraindications, side effects, etc., but it is not unusual for P.R.N. orders to be left to their discretion. In one unit I visited recently which housed approximately 30 severely retarded non-ambulatory residents, eight of these residents had standing P.R.N. orders for drugs like Compazine, Mellaril, Valium and Vistaril.

personnel monitor the effects of these drugs on the patient, serious adverse side effects may go unnoticed and unremedied,[97] and dosage may not be individualized according to the need of the patient.[98] These problems are compounded in some hospitals by inadequate patient record-keeping practices relating to drug dosage and administration.[99]

Another possible abuse involves the use of drug concentrates rather than tablets, a practice that has dramatically increased in mental hospitals.[100] Although the use of concentrates—requiring hospital staff to measure out a patient's dose—may be appropriate for patients with swallowing difficulties or those who are known to sequester drugs in tablet form,[101] the practice presents extra risks of erroneous dosages[102] and facilitates overmedication of patients by ward staff for management purposes.[103] Because tablets are readily soluble in almost all liquids, it would appear that the use of concentrates is often unnecessary and should be restricted to the small number of cases involving unreliable or uncooperative patients who will not ingest their drugs in tablet or liquid form.

---

[97]Statement of David Ferleger, *supra* note 87, at 170:

> At Lima State Hospital . . . [b]oth licensed and unlicensed physicians prescribe medication or countersign medication orders without having seen the patient or even having knowledge of the patient's condition. On occasion, medication is prescribed without taking the patient's height and weight into account and without consideration of the amount or type of medication the patient may already be receiving. In addition, patients may go for months without seeing a doctor or having their medication changed or reviewed.

Weiden et al., *Clinical Nonrecognition of Neuroleptic Induced Movement Disorders: A Cautionary Study,* 144 AM. J. PSYCHIATRY 1148, 1150–51 (1987) (a recent study indicated a 65% nonrecognition rate of akthisia by clinical psychiatrists, which is alarming because patients with unrecognized akathisia received higher doses of antipsychotic drugs). *See* Dionne, *Reports a Misuse of Drugs by Three State Mental Hospitals,* N.Y. TIMES, July 11, 1978, at 9 (report by New York State Comptroller that patients at three state hospitals studied were not routinely tested to determine whether the drugs in their system had reached toxic levels). The problem of inadequate monitoring of drug effects is particularly serious where antipsychotic drugs are being administered in view of the risks of tardive dyskinesia. Early detection is the key factor in the probability of early remission of the effects of tardive dyskinesia, and patients receiving antipsychotic drugs for a period in excess of 3 months should be periodically examined to determine the presence of early signs. *See also* Lohr, *supra* note 62, at 141–43. Such examination should be performed by skilled and experienced diagnosticians, as tardive dyskinesia is often confused with the lesser movement disorders such as dystonia and akathisia. A patient treated for these latter conditions with an antiparkinson drug who actually suffers from tardive dyskinesia may experience a worsening of this condition and a decrease in the chances of eventual remission. *See also* RYALL, *supra* note 25, at 187–88. Experienced diagnosticians would be alerted to the fact that being older in age, being female, and having a mood disorder are all risk factors to be considered in the diagnosis of tardive dyskinesia. GITLIN, *supra* note 4, at 308–09; Lohr, *supra,* at 131–32.

[98]Statement of James W. Ellis, *in Hearings, supra* note 86, at 280; *see* Nelson v. Heyne, 491 F.2d 353, 357 nn.10 & 11 (7th Cir.), *cert. denied,* 417 U.S. 976 (1974). In many institutions for the mentally disabled, even when drug administration is supervised by physicians, these physicians, many of whom are not licensed to practice medicine outside of the institutions, are often insufficiently trained in psychopharmacology. Statement of James W. Ellis, *supra,* at 280.

[99]*See* Dionne, *supra* note 97 (audit found documentation at least partly lacking in 57% of patient records studied at three state hospitals).

[100]DiMascio, *supra* note 38, at 124.

[101]KOLB, *supra* note 15, at 835; DiMascio, *supra* note 38, at 125.

[102]DiMascio, *supra* note 38, at 125.

[103]DiMascio, doubting that the sudden increase in use of concentrates is due to an increase in the number of patients who are unreliable drug takers, expresses the view that the growing popularity of concentrates was puzzling. *Id.* A possible explanation can be found in the admission by an employee of South Florida State Hospital, in a candid conversation with staff counsel to the American Civil Liberties Union of Florida, that concentrates facilitate the overmedication of patient troublemakers by ward staff who sometimes add extra concentrate to the patient's dosage. Personal communication from Terry DeMeo, staff counsel to the American Civil Liberties Union of Florida, Aug. 31, 1976.

Current psychiatric practice with respect to the prescription of psychotropic medication is questionable in a number of important respects. In general, there appears to be a tendency to overprescribe these drugs, to use them inappropriately, and to make medication decisions before a proper diagnosis has been made.[104] Many physicians, including psychiatrists, dispense antipsychotic drugs "in a non-specific palliative fashion for any and all complaints with an emotional cast" and use antianxiety medication for "[s]uch ubiquitous symptoms as insomnia, irritability, etc. . . . without any attempt made to establish a definitive diagnosis."[105] Antipsychotic drugs are sometimes used by uninformed practitioners to treat anxiety in patients for whom antianxiety drugs have not produced the desired symptomatic relief.[106] This practice is based on the mistaken belief that because the antipsychotics are often called "major tranquilizers," they must be more effective than the antianxiety drugs or "minor tranquilizers," in the treatment of anxiety; in fact, these drugs are actually ineffective for this condition and may cause detrimental side effects, making matters even worse for such patients.[107] The antipsychotic drugs are prescribed automatically by many psychiatrists for all patients diagnosed with schizophrenia, a practice that has been criticized as an inappropriate "knee-jerk response."[108] Moreover, these drugs are often continued for patients with schizophrenia, even when they have proved ineffective following use in adequate dosage and duration.[109] Wide variations in the dosage of antipsychotic drugs exist

---

[104]Klein, *Who Should Not Be Treated With Neuroleptics, But Often Are, in* RATIONAL PSYCHOPHARMACOTHERAPY, *supra* note 28, at 29. *See supra* notes 34, 93 and accompanying text. *See also* DiMascio, *supra* note 38, at 119:

> Psychotropic drugs are prescribed in a manner that has been characterized as "legitimatized drug abuse"; that is, the drugs are overused, underused, used inappropriately, and used in a way that may not be in the best interest of the patient. Further, they are prescribed in a way that is not consistent with their pharmacology, with the latest research findings, nor in the most cost-efficient manner.

The Food and Drug Administration has recognized the existence of these abuses:

> In treatment of mentally retarded patients with phenothiazenes and related drugs, proper diagnosis may be lacking; dosages employed may be larger than needed to achieve a justifiable therapeutic effect; administration may frequently be continued for unnecessarily long periods; and monitoring of patients may be generally inadequate. These problems are related to other difficulties experienced in institutions for the mentally disabled, such as overcrowding, custodial approaches to therapy, insufficient availability of high quality medical and professional personnel, and outdated facilities. . . . This continuing excessive and poorly supervised use of phenothiazenes and related drugs demands that the public, and particularly those directly involved in the health, training, and maintenance of the mentally retarded, be informed of the limitations on use of these drugs, so that usage may be based on correct and current information.

Letter from Alexander M. Schmidt, *supra* note 95, at 3.

[105]Klein, *supra* note 104, at 29. *See also* Waldron, *supra* note 36, at 39: "Much of the prescribing of Valium and Librium is for diagnosed somatic conditions, even though only a very few controlled studies have found that Valium or Librium is effective in relieving anxiety associated with somatic illness. . . ."

[106]Klein, *supra* note 104, at 30.

[107]*Id.*; Klein, *Diagnosis of Anxiety and Differential Use of Antianxiety Drugs, in* DRUG TREATMENT OF MENTAL DISORDERS, *supra* note 26, at 62–63. Although the antipsychotic drugs are prescribed by some physicians for a variety of mental disorders, claims that such drugs are indicated for the treatment of mental conditions other than schizophrenia and related diseases remain unconfirmed. Crane, *supra* note 15, at 124.

[108]Klein, *supra* note 104, at 34.

[109]*Id.* at 31. *See also* Ayd, *supra* note 62, at 49:

> Some patients have been given the same drug for as long as a decade or more with little or no further benefit after the initial improvement. Furthermore, an unknown but substantial number of these chronically ill patients are being given neuroleptics that either they do not need or in doses in excess of what they truly require.

even within reasonably homogeneous classes of patients, and dosages far exceeding those recommended by the manufacturers are not uncommon.[110]

A widespread abuse with uncooperative hospital patients is the administration of antipsychotic drugs within hours of admission and before a diagnosis can properly be made.[111] This presents the risk of permanently obscuring a proper diagnosis.[112] The practice often stems from inadequate hospital staffing and appears highly inappropriate because, in the view of a leading psychopharmacologist, "any reasonably well-staffed, closed psychiatric ward can maintain a patient under observation for 48 hours regardless of how psychotic he is. This allows sufficient time to gather diagnostic material and to observe the waning of any toxic episodes or hysterical outbursts."[113] The often standard practice of heavily sedating newly admitted hospital patients is particularly questionable because it may render patients unable to contest effectively their commitment at a hearing[114] and "has the undisputed effect of depriving the patient of initiative and the will to resist."[115] Another apparently widespread misuse of psychotropic medication is the common practice of treating patients with a combination of drugs.[116] This practice is often unnecessary, may exacerbate the adverse side effects of these drugs, and in some cases may be quite hazard-

---

[110]Crane, *supra* note 15, at 125; Dionne, *supra* note 97. In general, psychotropic drugs should be administered at the lowest effective dose. JANICAK ET AL., *supra* note 7, at 108; Shader, *On Guidelines for Maximum Dosage*, 135 AM. J. PSYCHIATRY 489 (1978). Dosage-related abuses may be especially common in hospitals for criminal offenders, where dosages of chlorpromazine tend to be larger than in civil hospitals, suggesting the abuse of this drug for control and punitive purposes. *See* BROOKS, *supra* note 87, at 878. In other contexts, physicians have been held liable for drug administration practices that deviate from the manufacturer's recommendations in package inserts. *E.g.*, Mulder v. Parke Davis & Co., 181 N.W.2d 882 (Minn. 1970); Koury v. Follo, 158 S.E. 548 (N.C. 1968).

[111]Klein, *supra* note 104, at 30. This may occur even for cooperative voluntary patients. *See, e.g.*, Statement of Anthony Brandt, *supra* note 92, vol. III, at 25 (report by researcher who committed himself to a mental hospital and was given, shortly after admission, a large dose of phenothiazene "without any but the most superficial psychiatric diagnosis having been made. It was therefore unspecific to my presumed 'illness'....").

[112]Klein, *supra* note 104, at 31.

[113]*Id.* at 38.

[114]Lessard v. Schmidt, 349 F. Supp. 1078, 1092 (E.D. Wis. 1972), *vacated on procedural grounds,* 414 U.S. 473 (1974), *reinstated on remand,* 379 F. Supp. 1376 (E.D. Wis. 1974), *vacated on procedural grounds,* 421 U.S. 957 (1975), *reinstated on remand,* 413 F. Supp. 1318 (E.D. Wis. 1976) ("[D]ue process is not accorded by an ex parte hearing in which the individual has no meaningful opportunity to be heard . . . because of incapacity caused by medication. . . ."); *accord* Dorsey v. Solomon, 435 F. Supp. 725 (D. Md. 1977), *aff'd in part and remanded,* 604 F.2d 271 (4th Cir. 1979) (upholding a defendant's right to refuse medication "which will adversely impair his ability to participate at the hearing" to determine whether he should be committed following his acquittal by reason of insanity); Suzuki v. Quisinberry, 411 F. Supp. 1113, 1129 (D. Hawaii 1976), *declaratory relief granted,* 438 F. Supp. 1106 (D. Hawaii 1977), *modified,* 617 F.2d 173 (9th Cir. 1980); Doremus v. Farrell, 407 F. Supp. 509, 515 (D. Neb. 1975); Lynch v. Baxley, 386 F. Supp. 378, 389 (M.D. Ala. 1974), *rev'd and remanded,* 651 F.2d 387 (5th Cir. 1981), *dismissed on motion for summary judgment in an unpublished decision, rev'd and remanded,* 744 F.2d 1452 (11th Cir. 1984); Bell v. Wayne Co. Hosp., 384 F. Supp. 1085, 1110 (E.D. Mich. 1974); Roth et al., *supra* note 86, at 418–19; Wexler et al., *supra* note 88, at 66–69. This problem is particularly difficult with antipsychotic drugs which are highly sedating during the initial days of administration when the patient has not as yet become tolerant to their effects. Jarvik, *supra* note 13, at 156.

[115]Ennis, *Civil Liberties and Mental Illness*, 7 CRIM. L. BULL. 101, 116 (1971). *See* United States v. Christensen, 18 F.3d 822, 825–26 (9th Cir. 1994) (mental or emotional instability of a defendant should have provoked suspicion that waiver of right to a jury trial may not have been knowingly, voluntarily, and intelligently tendered, particularly when a prisoner was taking powerful psychotropic drugs).

[116]Hollister, *supra* note 61; Kapur & Kambhampati, *Drug Interactions in Psychopharmacology, in* DRUG-INDUCED DYSFUNCTION IN PSYCHIATRY, *supra* note 56, at 21.

ous.[117] Although in certain patients such polypharmacy is indicated, the practice is used "far more often than experimental evidence or common sense dictates."[118]

Current practices of administering psychoactive drugs present unacceptably high risks, particularly in view of the serious toxic reactions and adverse side effects often accompanying their use. The neurological side effects of the antipsychotic drugs, particularly tardive dyskinesia, call for a reexamination of the widespread use of these drugs and a careful balancing in individual cases of the risks associated with their long-term use against anticipated benefits. These side effects have prompted criticism in the medical journals of the "sometimes senseless ritualization of drug therapy, the continuation of medications for persons who are unimproved or even asymptomatic for many months or even years."[119] Commentators who have called for "a reexamination of the evidence in favor of prolonged maintenance antipsychotic therapy"[120] have suggested that the "indiscriminate and excessive use of potentially dangerous drugs for all schizophrenic patients (and for nonpsychotic subjects) is certainly not justified medically . . ." and have advocated "[p]eriodic assessments of therapeutic and unwanted effects" and more selectivity in the prescribing of these drugs.[121] Certainly more care should be taken to minimize unnecessary use of psychoactive medication. These drugs should never be prescribed until an appropriate diagnosis has been made.[122] Patients on these drugs should be closely monitored by a physician and dosages carefully regulated.[123] The widespread practice of administering combinations of drugs should be scrutinized.[124] In view of estimates that perhaps 50% of outpatients diagnosed with schizophrenia might not be worse off if their medications were withdrawn, consideration should be given to taking patients off antipsychotic drugs periodically for "drug-free

---

[117]Ayd, *supra* note 62; DiMascio, *supra* note 38, at 125; Hollister, *supra* note 61, at 267. Kapur & Kambhampati, *supra* note 116, at 21–34; Kaufman, *Drug Interactions Involving Psychotherapeutic Agents, in* DRUG TREATMENT OF MENTAL DISORDERS, *supra* note 26, at 289–309.

[118]Hollister, *supra* note 61, at 27. *See* Dionne, *supra* note 97 (25% of patients studied at three state hospitals were being treated with two or more drugs even though State Department of Mental Hygiene guidelines cautioned against this practice). "The magnitude of this problem may be estimated from one survey of intermediate care facilities where the patients received an average of 8.1 medicines." Kapur & Kambhampati, *supra* note 116, at 21.

[119]Baldessarini & Lipinski, *Risks Versus Benefits of Antipsychotic Drugs,* 289 N. ENGL. J. MED. 427 (1973). *See* Statement of Anthony Brandt, *supra* note 92, at 25 ("[E]very patient on my ward was receiving drugs, even those who had been there twenty or thirty years and had no apparent symptomatology whatever."); Lohr, *supra* note 62, at 134–36; Steingard, *supra* note 62, at 108–11.

[120]Gardos & Cole, *Maintenance Antipsychotic Therapy: Is the Cure Worse than the Disease?,* 133 AM. J. PSYCHIATRY 32 (1976).

[121]Crane, *supra* note 15, at 127; *accord Task Force Report, supra* note 62, at 466; Freedman, *Editorial Comment,* 28 ARCHIVES GEN. PSYCHIATRY 466 (1973).

[122]GITLIN, *supra* note 4, at 11–13; Kapur & Kambhampati, *supra* note 116, at 34; Keshavan, *Principles of Drug Therapy in Psychiatry, in* DRUG-INDUCED DYSFUNCTION IN PSYCHIATRY, *supra* note 56, at 34; Klein, *supra* note 104, at 30. *But see* Sederer, *supra* note 79, at 527 ("Acute hallucinations, delusions, and agitation are responsive to neuroleptics regardless of whether the patient has a schizophrenic disorder, an affective psychosis, or an organic psychosis.").

[123]Baldessarini & Lipinski, *supra* note 119, at 428; Solow, *supra* note 28, at 305. In order to minimize the risk of tardive dyskinesia "every effort should be made to use the lowest effective dose in the hospital situation." Davis, *supra* note 51, at 1243.

[124]*See supra* notes 116–18 and accompanying text.

holidays'' to determine the feasibility of drug discontinuation.[125] In any event, it would seem inappropriate to leave the difficult choice of whether the benefits of psychotropic medication outweigh its risks for a particular patient to the uncontrolled discretion of the treating psychiatrist. In view of the potentially grave consequences, the patient, if competent, should participate fully in the treatment decision. If the patient is incompetent to so participate, the decision should be made by a substitute decision maker responsive solely to the patient's best interest, which for an institutionalized patient should not necessarily be the treating psychiatrist.

Much of the abuse and misuse of the psychoactive drugs stems from a lack of sufficient expertise in the proper prescription of these medications.[126] It has been suggested that the excessive use of these drugs is attributable to the lack of adequate training of most physicians in psychopharmacology and to the promotional impact of the pharmaceutical industry.[127] According to one estimate, only 17% of prescriptions for psychoactive drugs are written by psychiatrists and neurologists.[128] A 1976 study found that the drug companies spent from $3,000 to $5,000 annually on each physician in advertising and promotions.[129] Advertising, personal visits by drug industry salespersons, and the *PDR* (written by the drug companies themselves and distributed free to all physicians) constitute major influences on doctors' prescribing habits. Studies show that a majority of doctors feel their prescribing behavior is ''markedly'' influenced by information from drug industry sources.[130] Moreover, these sources are often misleading. A study of evaluations of Valium and Librium demonstrated that industry-sponsored sources—advertisements and the *PDR*—recommended these drugs for substantially more uses than had independent medical journal articles.[131] These industry-controlled sources of drug information are not adequately monitored by the Food and Drug Administration.[132] The typical physician, always pressed for time, is especially susceptible

---

[125]Gardos & Cole, *supra* note 120, at 34–36; *accord Task Force Report, supra* note 62, at 465; Ayd, *supra* note 62, at 49–50; Baldessarini & Lipinski, *supra* note 119, at 428; Davis, *supra* note 51, at 1242–43; Crane & Sheets, *Tardive Dyskinesia and Drug Therapy In Geriatric Patients,* 30 ARCHIVES GEN. PSYCHIATRY 343 (1974); Prien & Klett, *An Appraisal of the Long-Term Use of Tranquilizing Medication with Hospitalized Chronic Schizophrenics: A Review of the Drug Discontinuation Literature,* 5 SCHIZOPHRENIA BULL. 64 (1972). Such drug-free trials are widely recommended as a means of early detection of tardive dyskinesia and prevention of the hazards of long-term drug administration. Crane, *Prevention and Management of Tardive Dyskinesia,* 129 AM. J. PSYCHIATRY 126 (1972); Slovenko, *On the Legal Aspects of Tardive Dyskinesia,* 7 J. PSYCHIATRY & L. 295, 300 (1979). More recent research, however, has questioned the wisdom of periodic drug-free holidays. *See also* GITLIN, *supra* note 4, at 308 (''Short ''drug holidays'' from antipsychotic drugs do not decrease the risk of Tardive Dyskinesia; if anything, this rapid on/off dopamine blockage may increase the risk by accelerating receptor supersensitivity which may be the mechanism for TD.''); Davis et al., *supra* note 12, at 1609 (noting absence of controlled studies supporting proposals for drug-free holidays and suggesting that some clinical observations hint at an opposite conclusion); Tanner & Klawans, *Tardive Dynskinesia: Prevention and Treatment,* 9 CLINICAL NEUROPHARMACOLOGY S-76, S-77 (Supp. 2 1986) (''Although drug-free periods during neuroleptic regimens have been proposed by some as a means of reducing the risk of developing tardive dyskinesia, others have reported an increase in tardive in patients having frequent drug-free periods.'').

[126]DiMascio, *supra* note 38, at 118–19; Mason, *Basic Principles in the Use of Antipsychotic Agents,* 24 HOSP. & COMMUNITY PSYCHIATRY 825 (1973); Taylor, *Preface, in* RATIONAL PSYCHOPHARMACOTHERAPY, *supra* note 28, at IX, X. Antipsychotic drugs are widely used in patients with mental retardation. Davis et al., *supra* note 12, at 1597. *See supra* notes 34, 95, and accompanying text.

[127]DiMascio, *supra* note 38, at 118; Pekkanen, *The Impact of Promotion on Physicians' Prescribing Patterns,* 6 J. DRUG ISSUES 13 (1976); Waldron, *supra* note 36, at 38. *See* M. Pines, The Brain Changers 108–09 (1973).

[128]Waldron, *supra* note 36, at 39.

[129]Pekkanen, *supra* note 127, at 14.

[130]Waldron, *supra* note 36, at 44.

[131]*Id.* at 44–48.

[132]Pekkanen, *supra* note 127, at 14–20. The drug companies are reported to invest considerable resources in fighting federal regulation. Waldron, *supra* note 36, at 49, 56.

to these promotions because psychopharmacology still receives insufficient attention in medical schools—from 3 to 6 hours of formal class training at most[133]—and is still such a rapidly developing field, having evolved after many current physicians had graduated from medical school.[134] Abuses in the administration of psychoactive drugs are thus hardly surprising.

The psychotropic drugs, although efficacious in the treatment of many mental patients, thus present serious abuses and risks, particularly when involuntarily administered to institutionalized patients. The primary and side effects of these drugs are both physically and mentally intrusive, occur rapidly, and cannot be resisted by unwilling patients. Moreover, although the primary effects of the drugs may last only several hours, side effects may be quite long lasting and in some cases irreversible and even fatal.[135] Patients frequently experience these side effects as highly unpleasant, painful, and debilitating.

Compared to the psychotherapies (chapter 3) and the behavior therapies (chapter 4), psychotropic medication is therefore the most intrusive and hazardous of the treatment techniques thus far considered. Moreover, it presents perhaps a greater potential for misuse and abuse than even the more intrusive and hazardous organic treatment methods to be considered hereafter—electroconvulsive therapy (chapter 6), electronic stimulation of the brain (chapter 7), and psychosurgery (chapter 8). Unlike these techniques, which are difficult and costly to administer and are generally regarded with suspicion and concern, drugs are inexpensive, may be administered easily, and their use has become so pervasive in our society that they are deceptively ''palatable.''[136] As Gerald Klerman, former administrator of the Alcohol, Drug Abuse, and Mental Health Administration and a leading psychopharmacologist, has warned, psychoactive drugs are ''sufficiently dangerous, if misused, to merit fear and concern, as well as respect.''[137]

---

[133]Pekkanen, *supra* note 127, at 16; Tietz, *Informed Consent in the Prescription Drug Context: The Special Case*, 61 WASH. L. REV. 367, 390–91 (1986); *see also* Laizure, *The Pharmacist's Duty to Warn When Dispensing Prescription Drugs: Recent Tennessee Developments*, 22 MEM. ST. U. L. REV. 517 (1992). A 1972 survey revealed that fewer than 20% of American medical schools offered a formal course in clinical psychopharmacology. DiMascio, *supra* note 38, at 119. Moreover, fewer than 25% of psychiatric hospitals offering psychiatric residency programs in 1971 provided more than 4 hours of formalized instruction in this area. *Id.* In 1988, the American College of Physicians acknowledged that the pharmacology training for physicians was lacking. Cowen, *Changing Relationship Between Pharmacists and Physicians*, AM. J. HOSP. PHARMACY, Nov. 1992, at 2717–18. Today, it is still possible that doctors receive little formal classroom training in pharmacology because medical school accreditation merely requires that the curriculum include the content of the discipline traditionally titled pharmacology and therapeutics; the standards for accreditation do not specify how that content should be taught. Liaison Committee on Medical Education, *Standards for Accreditation for Medical Education Programs Leading to the M.D. Degree, in* FUNCTIONS AND STRUCTURE OF A MEDICAL SCHOOL 13 (1993).

[134]Pekkanen, *supra* note 127, at 19. Tardive dyskinesia was first reported in 1957, and more than 100 papers reporting on over 2,000 cases were published in the next 15 years. Crane, *supra* note 15, at 127. Nonetheless, it was reported that in 1972 many physicians were still unaware of this problem or seemed to be completely unconcerned about it. *Id.* Perhaps it is not surprising that 1972 was the first year in which any of the manufacturers of the antipsychotic drugs included in their package inserts a reference to tardive dyskinesia. *Id.*

[135]Although the primary effects of most of the psychoactive drugs last no longer than from several hours to one day, one class of drugs, the long-acting phenothiazines, last from 2 to 3 weeks and sometimes as long as 8 weeks when injected intramuscularly. *See* Ayd, *The Depot Fluphenazines: A Reappraisal After 10 Years Clinical Experience*, 132 AM. J. PSYCHIATRY 491 (1975); Groves & Mandell, *The Long-Acting Phenothiazines*, 32 ARCHIVES GEN. PSYCHIATRY 893 (1975).

[136]*See* Klerman, *Better But Not Well: Social and Ethical Issues in the Deinstitutionalization of the Mentally Ill*, 3 SCHIZOPHRENIA BULL. 617, 619 (1977).

[137]*Id.*

Chapter 6
ELECTROCONVULSIVE THERAPY

A. Description and History

Electroconvulsive therapy (ECT), another of the organic treatment techniques, consists of the passage of electrical current through the brain by means of electrodes applied to the patient's temples in order to produce convulsions resembling the grand mal seizure in epilepsy.[1] Originally named *electroshock* therapy[2] (a misnomer because the patient's reaction is not comparable to surgical shock and he or she actually feels no electrical shock), ECT continues to be controversial.[3] Although its use has been relegated to a secondary role,[4] ECT remains an accepted treatment modality.[5] The promise of psychopharmacology in the treatment of depression and continued controversy and fear about ECT fostered by a vocal

---

[1] *See generally* T. DETRE & H. JARECKI, MODERN PSYCHIATRIC TREATMENT 635–55 (1971); P. JANICAK ET AL., PRINCIPLES AND PRACTICE OF PSYCHOPHARMACOTHERAPY 293 (1993); L. KALINOWSKY & P. HOCH, SOMATIC TREATMENTS IN PSYCHIATRY 128–207 (1961); PSYCHOBIOLOGY OF CONVULSIVE THERAPY (M. Fink et al. eds., 1974) [hereinafter CONVULSIVE THERAPY]; Frankel, *Electroconvulsive Therapy, in* AMERICAN PSYCHIATRIC ASSOCIATION COMMISSION ON PSYCHIATRIC THERAPIES, THE PSYCHIATRIC THERAPIES 291 (T. Karasu ed., 1984); Lebensohn, *The Place of Electroshock Therapy (EST) in Present-Day Psychiatry, in* READINGS IN LAW AND PSYCHIATRY 91 (R. Allen et al. eds., 2d ed. 1975) [hereinafter READINGS]; Patch & Solomon, *Electroconvulsive Therapy & Other Somatic Therapies, in* HANDBOOK OF PSYCHIATRY 464 (P. Solomon & V. Patch eds., 3d ed. 1974); Weiner, *Electroconvulsive Therapy, in* 2 COMPREHENSIVE TEXTBOOK OF PSYCHIATRY 1670 (H. Kaplan & B. Sadock eds., 5th ed. 1989) [hereinafter TEXTBOOK OF PSYCHIATRY].

[2] Weiner, *supra* note 1, at 1671.

[3] "Probably no other widely-used form of treatment has caused as much controversy. . . ." F. MILLER ET AL., THE MENTAL HEALTH PROCESS 60 (2d ed. 1976) [hereinafter MENTAL HEALTH PROCESS]. Controversy surrounding ECT exists within the psychiatric profession. DETRE & JARECKI, *supra* note 1, at 636 ("Those who administer ECT are likely to be derogated as 'psychiatric electricians' and relegated to the lowest rung on the profession's status ladder."); Lebensohn, *supra* note 1, at 92 ("The attitude toward ECT is often one of smug condescension. The psychiatrist who still administers ECT is often regarded with the kind of disdain that gynecologists used to reserve for colleagues who performed 'therapeutic' abortions."). The general public also frowns on ECT, as demonstrated by the withdrawal of Senator Eagleton as the 1972 Democratic candidate for the vice-presidency following the revelation of his previous ECT treatment. A survey conducted by a task force of the American Psychiatric Association of a sample of the Association's membership revealed that 32% opposed the use of ECT (2% were "totally opposed"; 22% "generally opposed"; and 8% "tend to be more opposed than favorable"); 1% were ambivalent; and 67% favored it (7% were "decidedly favorable"; 54% "generally favorable"; and 6% "tend to be more favorable than opposed"). ELECTROCONVULSIVE THERAPY (1978), *noted in* 3 MENTAL DISABILITY L. REP. 144 (1979); Fink, *Impact of the Antipsychiatric Movement on the Revival of Electroconvulsive Therapy in the United States,* 14 PSYCHIATRIC CLINICS OF NORTH AMERICA 793, 793 (1991).

[4] AMERICAN PSYCHIATRIC ASS'N TASK FORCE REPORT, THE PRACTICE OF ELECTROCONVULSIVE THERAPY: RECOMMENDATIONS FOR TREATMENT, TRAINING, AND PRIVILEGING 50 (1990) [hereinafter APA TASK FORCE REP.] ("ECT is most often used in patients when other treatments have failed."); JANICAK ET AL., *supra* note 1, at 293.

[5] ELECTROCONVULSIVE THERAPY, *supra* note 3, at 310; *see also* Lebensohn, *supra* note 1, at 92; Sederer, *Brief Hospitalization, in* AMERICAN PSYCHIATRIC PRESS, II REVIEW OF PSYCHIATRY 530 (A. Tasman & M. Riba eds., 1992) ("For severely ill, affectively disordered patients, especially those with psychotic symptoms or the elderly, electroconvulsive therapy (ECT) is highly effective and markedly underutilized. In response to a history (now very dated) of overuse and indiscriminate use, ECT has been disparaged and undertaught for 30 years."); Weiner, *supra* note 1, at 1671.

antipsychiatric movement led to decreased use of ECT in the 1970s and 1980s.[6] However, the continued lack of response of some patients to medication and increasing financial pressure to limit the length of hospital stays have combined to produce a recent resurgence in the use of ECT.[7] An estimated 100,000 people undergo ECT annually in the United States.[8]

The convulsive therapies originated with the mistaken belief that epilepsy and schizophrenia never occurred in the same patient and with the observation that some mental patients suddenly lost their symptoms following a spontaneous convulsion.[9] As a result, efforts were made in the 1930s to induce convulsions as a method of treatment. Manfred Sakel, an Austrian psychiatrist, used insulin to induce a hyperglycemic coma to treat individuals with schizophrenia.[10] Ladislaus von Meduna of Hungary experimented with convulsions induced by intramuscular injections of camphor in oil, and later, of Metrazol, a soluble synthetic camphor preparation.[11] In 1938, the Italian psychiatrist Ugo Cerletti introduced electricity as a means of inducing convulsions. ECT proved easier to administer and more predictable in its effects than the pharmacological convulsive agents; it induced immediate loss of consciousness, sparing the patient much discomfort, and unlike the drugs, did not provoke a preconvulsive panic.[12] As a result, ECT soon replaced these other convulsive methods.[13]

As usually administered, ECT requires patients to lie on their backs on a table with electrodes placed on the anterior portion of both temples.[14] A gauze-covered tongue depressor or other gag is placed in the mouth to prevent tongue or lip biting during the convulsion. Between 70 and 130 volts of alternating current are administered for one-tenth to one-half second. (The voltage and duration may vary depending on patients' seizure thresholds.) In the traditional unmodified technique, the electrical current immediately renders patients unconscious, followed by a tight contraction of the muscles lasting about 10 seconds, producing a rigid extension of the body (the "tonic phase"). After this, patients have a 30- to 40-second series of spasmodic muscular contractions alternating with relaxation, which produces flailing movements of the arms and legs (the "clonic phase"). Today, muscle-relaxing drugs are used to prevent the violent spasms that in the past had often resulted in fractures. A general anesthetic is administered to prevent patients from consciously experiencing the suffocationlike effects of the muscle relaxants on breathing, and oxygen is given to prevent anoxia. Patients regain consciousness several minutes after

---

[6]Abrams, *The Treatment That Will Not Die: Electroconvulsive Therapy,* 17 PSYCHIATRIC CLINICS OF NORTH AMERICA 525, 529 (1994); Fink, *supra* note 3, at 794–96.

[7]Abrams, *supra* note 6, at 529; Fink, *supra* note 3, at 794.

[8]Frank, *Electroshock: Death, Brain Damage, Memory Loss and Brainwashing,* 11 J. MIND & BEHAV. 489, 493 (1990); Sackheim, *The Cognitive Effects of Electroconvulsive Therapy, in* COGNITIVE DISORDERS, PATHOPHYSIOLOGY AND TREATMENT 183 (L. Thal et al. eds., 1992).

[9]Patch & Solomon, *supra* note 1, at 465; Weiner, *supra* note 1, at 1670.

[10]Lebensohn, *supra* note 1, at 92; Weiner, *supra* note 1, at 1670.

[11]DETRE & JARECKI, *supra* note 1, at 635; Abrams, *supra* note 6, at 526–27; Lebensohn, *supra* note 1, at 92; Weiner, *supra* note 1, at 1670.

[12]DETRE & JARECKI, *supra* note 1, at 635; JANICAK, *supra* note 1, at 293 ("The use of electrical stimulation to induce therapeutic seizures is the safest and most efficient form of convulsive therapy (i.e., versus pharmacoconvulsive therapy)."); KALINOWSKY & P. HOCH, *supra* note 1, at 124–26, 128.

[13]Insulin coma therapy is now rarely used. L. KOLB, MODERN CLINICAL PSYCHIATRY 865 (1977) (limited to schizophrenia); Patch & Solomon, *supra* note 1, at 464; Weiner, *supra* note 1, at 1687. ECT has replaced the use of camphor and Metrazol. DETRE & JARECKI, *supra* note 1, at 635. The anesthetic hexafluorodiethyl ether (Indoklon), generally administered by inhalation, is no longer in use. Weiner, *supra* note 1, at 1671.

[14]The following discussion of the techniques of administering ECT is drawn from APA TASK FORCE REP., *supra* note 4, at 22–34; DETRE & JARECKI, *supra* note 1, at 636–44; Frank, *supra* note 8, at 495–96; Lebensohn, *supra* note 1, at 92–93; Patch & Solomon, *supra* note 1, at 465–66; Weiner, *supra* note 1, at 1671, 1672.

the convulsion but remain in a state of confusion and disorientation for another 15 to 30 minutes, at times accompanied by excitement and combativeness. Headache and nausea sometimes occur. Patients do not consciously experience the electrical current and have no memory of the treatment when they awaken.[15] The number and frequency of treatments vary; for depressive illness, 4 to 12 treatments spaced 2 days apart are usual, and for schizophrenia, 18 to 25 are used. After several treatments, periods of disorientation and confusion lasting several days at a time occur and recent memory is disturbed. Following treatment, a 1- to 2-week convalescent period is necessary during which patients must be closely supervised.

B. Effectiveness

Although originally used to treat schizophrenia, ECT has proven much more effective in treating the depressive disorders. There is general, although not universal, agreement that ECT is the most rapid and for many patients the most effective treatment for the symptoms of major depression and the depressed stages of bipolar disorder, and it is also helpful for other disorders accompanied by severe depression.[16] Opinion is divided concerning the role of ECT in the treatment of schizophrenia. The use of antipsychotic medication has largely

---

[15] *Contra* Friedberg, *Electroshock Therapy: Let's Stop Blasting the Brain*, PSYCHOL. TODAY, Aug. 1975, at 98:

While barbituates do produce sleep, they do not bring a complete loss of feeling. Among former ECT patients I interviewed many could recall the instant of shock itself, even though unable to recall surrounding events. One young man reported: That pain went right through your head. All you're aware of is this jolting pain going through your mind like an electric crowbar.

[16] APA TASK FORCE REP., *supra* note 4, at 6–8; RESEARCH TASK FORCE OF THE NAT'L INST. OF MENTAL HEALTH, DHEW Pub. No. (ADM) 75-236, RESEARCH IN THE SERVICE OF MENTAL HEALTH 337 (1978) [hereinafter RESEARCH IN MENTAL HEALTH]; *accord* DETRE & JARECKI, *supra* note 1, at 644 (ECT effective in 77% to 94% of depressed patients, compared to an effective rate of 66% for drugs; differences, however, disappear 6 to 12 months after treatment); JANICAK ET AL., *supra* note 1, at 293, 299 (extrapolation of data from studies analyzing ECT's efficacy versus other drug treatments); KOLB, *supra* note 13, at 860–61 ("full or social recovery" in 80% or more of cases; ECT saves many patients who would otherwise commit suicide); SCHATZBERG & COLE, MANUAL OF CLINICAL PSYCHOPHARMACOLOGY 108 (1991) (referring to ECT as "undeniably effective in psychotic depression"); Hurwitz, *Electroconvulsive Therapy: A Review,* 15 PSYCHIATRY 303, 306 (1974) (table summarizing ECT/antidepressant drug comparative studies); Lebensohn, *supra* note 1, at 93, 94; Patch & Solomon, *supra* note 1, at 465–66; TASK FORCE TO STUDY AND RECOMMEND STANDARDS FOR THE ADMINISTRATION OF ELECTROCONVULSIVE THERAPY, *Electro-Convulsive Therapy in Massachusetts: A Task Force Report, in* MENTAL HEALTH PROCESS, *supra* note 3, at 62, 68–70 [hereinafter *Mass. ECT Task Force Rep.*]; Weiner, *supra* note 1, at 1676–77. *Contra* Costello, *Electroconvulsive Therapy: Is Further Investigation Necessary?,* 21 CAN. PSYCHIATRY ASS'N J. 61 (1976) (claims about ECT's effectiveness remain unproven); Friedberg, *supra* note 15 ("Despite all the studies, the effectiveness of ECT remains unproven, and cannot be proved, because controlled study is impossible. Since the damaging effects of ECT are so striking, there is no way to create a double-blind study in which the evaluators could not know which patients had received ECT."); Friedberg, *ECT as a Neurological Injury,* 14 PSYCHIATRIC OPINION 16, 18 (1977); Giamartino, *Electroconvulsive Therapy and the Illusion of Treatment,* 35 PSYCHOL. REP. 1127, 1128 (1974) (citing conflicting studies, characterizing the empirical evidence in support of the beneficial effects of ECT as "not convincing," and concluding that ECT "has not achieved a universal acceptance among psychiatrists"); Grimm, *Convulsions as Therapy: The Outer Shadows,* 15 PSYCHIATRIC OPINION 30, 45–46 (1978) (suggesting that favorable results may be due to the Hawthorne effect). For a summary of the conflicting results of comparative studies, see MILLER ET AL., *supra* note 3, at 74–76. ECT is also claimed to be of value in the treatment of mania. McCabe, *ECT in the Treatment of Mania: A Controlled Study,* 133 AM. J. PSYCHIATRY 688 (1976).

supplanted ECT for this condition.[17] ECT is not effective in the treatment of the character disorders and anxiety disorders.[18] Like many of the psychotropic drugs, ECT is not a curative procedure. It offers symptomatic relief and can hasten the progress of a depressive episode to shorten its duration, and it may help patients to reestablish control, thereby making them accessible to psychotherapy.[19] Although there are many theories purporting to explain the therapeutic effects of ECT,[20] recent evidence points to a neurochemical basis— that ECT increases the rate at which the brain synthesizes the neurotransmitter, norepinephrine[21]—similar to the effects of the antidepressant drugs.[22]

C. Side Effects

The risks and complications accompanying ECT have been greatly reduced by the use of muscle-relaxing drugs, which prevent the violent muscular contractions that frequently led to bone fractures and dislocations in unmodified ECT in the past.[23] ECT using muscle relaxants also presents some risk. Some patients experience apnea, a temporary cessation of

---

[17]JANICAK ET AL., *supra* note 1, at 154 ("Antipsychotics have long since replaced insulin shock and ECT for the treatment of schizophrenia."); *Mass. ECT Task Force Rep., supra* note 16, at 63–70; Weiner, *supra* note 1, at 1677. For claims that ECT is effective in the treatment of schizophrenia, see May et al., *Schizophrenia—A Follow-Up Study of Results of Treatment. II. Hospital Stay Over Two To Five Years,* 33 ARCHIVES GEN. PSYCHIATRY 481 (1976); Sullivan, *Treatment of Acute Schizophrenia: The Place of ECT,* 35 DISEASES OF THE NERVOUS SYSTEM 467–69 (1974); Wells, *Electroconvulsive Treatment for Schizophrenia: A Ten-Year Survey in a University Hospital Psychiatric Department,* 14 COMP. PSYCHIATRY 291 (1973). Approximately 10% to 20% of patients receiving ECT suffer from schizophrenia. In chronic schizophrenia, only 5%–10% of patients given ECT have been reported to show a major improvement. These data are largely based on drug nonresponders. Weiner, *supra* note 1, at 1677. *But see* D. GOODWIN & S. GUZE, PSYCHIATRIC DIAGNOSIS 65 (1989) ("Occasionally, the combination of antipsychotics and electroconvulsive treatments may produce better results than antipsychotics alone."); Weiner & Coffey, *Electroconvulsive Therapy in the United States,* 27 PSYCHOPHARMACOLOGY BULL. 9, 12 (1991) (ECT has substantial efficacy in carefully selected schizophrenic population).

[18]*Mass. ECT Task Force Rep., supra* note 16, at 62, 70; Patch & Solomon, *supra* note 1, at 465. *But see* APA TASK FORCE REP., *supra* note 4, at 56 (reports of favorable outcome for severe obsessive–compulsive disorder); Jenike, *New Developments in Treatment of Obsessive–Compulsive Disorder, in* II REVIEW OF PSYCHIATRY, *supra* note 5, at 334.

[19]*Mass. ECT Task Force Rep., supra* note 16, at 68. *But see* DETRE & JARECKI, *supra* note 1, at 178 (expressing concern regarding the effects of ECT on the patient's self-image and future collaboration).

[20]JANICAK ET AL., *supra* note 1, at 295–96; Lebensohn, *supra* note 1, at 93; Miller, *Psychological Theories of E.C.T.: A Review,* 113 BRIT. J. PSYCHIATRY 301 (1967); Watts, *ECT: How Does It Work?,* WORLD MEDICINE, Jan. 28, 1976, at 27; Weiner, *supra* note 1, at 1675.

[21]JANICAK ET AL., *supra* note 1, at 295; RESEARCH IN MENTAL HEALTH, *supra* note 16, at 62–63, 337; Hofstatter & Girgis, *Neurotransmitter Mechanisms Underlying Psychiatric Surgery, Electroconvulsive Therapy and Antidepressive Drug Therapy, in* MODERN CONCEPTS IN PSYCHIATRIC SURGERY 3, 8–9 (E. Hitchcock et al. eds., 1979) [hereinafter PSYCHIATRIC SURGERY]; Kety, *Biochemical and Neurochemical Effects of Electroconvulsive Shock, in* CONVULSIVE THERAPY, *supra* note 1, at 285; Kety, *Effects of Repeated Electroconvulsive Shock on Brain Catecholamines, in* CONVULSIVE THERAPY, *supra* note 1, at 231; Schildkraut & Draskoczy, *Effects of Electroconvulsive Shock on Norepinephrine Turnover and Metabolism: Basic and Clinical Studies, in* CONVULSIVE THERAPY, *supra* note 1 at 143.

[22]JANICAK ET AL., *supra* note 1, at 295. *See supra* chapter 5.

[23]DETRE & JARECKI, *supra* note 1, at 640–41; JANICAK ET AL., *supra* note 1, at 313; Hurwitz, *supra* note 14, at 305; Kahn et al., *Electroconvulsive Therapy,* 16 PSYCHIATRIC CLINICS OF NORTH AMERICA 497, 499 (1993); Lebensohn, *supra* note 1, at 93; Weiner, *supra* note 1, at 1677. Notwithstanding the availability of muscle relaxants, it still has been considered acceptable medical practice to administer ECT without them. *See* Pettis v. State Dep't of Hosp., 336 So.2d 521, 528 (Fla. 1976). Other complications of unmodified ECT include soft-tissue tears, apnea, aspiration of foreign substances into the lungs, pulmonary embolism, cardiac failure or arrhythmias (or both), increased intracranial pressure, rupture of internal organs, hemorrhages, kidney damage, dental injuries, and postconvulsion excitement or delirium.

the breathing impulse, chest wall spasm, coughing, spasms of the larynx or the windpipe, aspiration of foreign matter into the lungs, cardiac irregularities, or even allergic responses to the medication.[24] These complications occur in only 1 out of every 2,600 treatments and are usually relatively benign, resulting in fatality in about 1 out of every 28,000 applications.[25] An additional risk is the development of psychotic symptoms, particularly for patients with schizoid- or schizophrenic-disposing factors.[26]

The most serious and disturbing side effects, confusion and loss of memory, occur in virtually all cases.[27] The brief loss of identity experienced upon awakening from treatment, in which patients do not know who or where they are, is subjectively quite unpleasant and has been cited as the source of the fear many patients have of ECT.[28] Brief confusion follows even the first treatment, but the disorientation becomes longer and more severe the more treatments the patients receive. After several treatments, patients' confused state may persist for days at a time and may continue until several weeks after the completion of ECT. During this convalescent period, they must be closely supervised and should not drive, transact business, or resume employment. Left unattended, they may wander off and become lost. Amnesia during the period of treatment and for events occurring close before ("retrograde amnesia") is common. The more treatments a patient receives, "the further back his memory disturbance extends and the more globally disoriented he becomes."[29] Events of the past may be forgotten, and following 12 to 15 treatments, patients are unable to remember the names or faces of those around them, and, in extreme cases, "will not even remember his own occupation."[30] ECT also affects memory for events experienced after treatment ("anterograde amnesia").[31] The grossest symptoms of confusion and memory loss usually recede within several weeks of the final treatment, although the more ECT

---

[24]JANICAK ET AL., *supra* note 1, at 316. *Hurwitz, supra* note 16, at 305.

[25]APA TASK FORCE REPORT, *supra* note 4, at 59 (mortality rate approximately 1 in 10,000); DETRE & JARECKI, *supra* note 1, at 640. *See Hurwitz supra* note 16, at 306 (table summarizing mortality studies).

[26]Elmore & Sugarman, *Precipitation of Psychosis During Electroshock Therapy,* 36 DISEASES NERVOUS SYS. 115 (1975).

[27]The following discussion is drawn from DETRE & JARECKI, *supra* note 1, at 641–44; Dornbush & Williams, *Memory and ECT, in* CONVULSIVE THERAPY, *supra* note 1, at 199; Frank, *supra* note 8, at 502–04; Harper & Wiens, *Electroconvulsive Therapy and Memory,* 161 J. NERVOUS MENTAL DISEASE 245 (1975); Lebensohn, *Problems in Obtaining Informed Consent for Electroshock Therapy, in* READINGS, *supra* note 1, at 386–89; Weiner, *supra* note 1, at 1677–78.

[28]Weiner, *supra* note 1, at 1677. For a literary description of this experience, see K. KESEY, ONE FLEW OVER THE CUCKOO'S NEST 242 (1962):

> There had been times when I'd wandered around in a daze for as long as two weeks after a shock treatment, living in that foggy, jumbled blur which is a whole lot like the ragged edge of sleep, that gray zone between light and dark, or between sleeping and waking or living and dying, where you know you're not unconscious any more but don't know yet what day it is or who you are or what's the use of coming back at all—for two weeks.

For a patient's account of ECT, see Frank, *supra* note 8, at 489–91.

[29]DETRE & JARECKI, *supra* note 1, at 642. Retrograde amnesia is attributed to the effects of ECT on the consolidation process in memory, the transition from impermanence to permanence of the memory trace. Before consolidation is complete, the memory trace is vulnerable to disruption. The trauma of ECT, much like a serious head injury, may result in memory loss to the extent that the trace is still impermanent. Dornbush & Williams, *supra* note 25, at 203; McGaugh & Williams, *Neurophysiological and Behavioral Effects of Convulsive Phenomena, in* CONVULSIVE THERAPY, *supra* note 1, at 279, 280. *See generally* Sackheim, *supra* note 8, at 206 (summarizing and analyzing studies on the effect of cumulative numbers of ECT treatments).

[30]DETRE & JARECKI, *supra* note 1, at 642.

[31]JANICAK ET AL., *supra* note 1, at 315; McGaugh & Williams, *supra* note 29, at 282. Studies concentrating on the anterograde effects of ECT have shown "that ECT affects retention and not learning . . . and that long term memory is more affected than short term memory." Dornbush & Williams, *supra* note 27 at 201.

treatments patients have had and the older they are, the longer symptom recession will take.[32] Whether brain damage and permanent memory loss result from ECT is the subject of dispute.[33] Many commentators claim that memory impairment disappears within weeks or months of the completion of treatment.[34] Others assert that ''some memory gaps and difficulty in retaining new material may persist for six months or longer; a few details may not be recalled for as long as 12 to 18 months; and some memories, especially of events that took place during the weeks of treatment, may be lost altogether. . . .''[35] No systematic, long-term studies support the claim of ECT advocates that memory loss is always reversible,[36] and ''almost every experienced clinician knows of a number of patients whose memory functions have in some measure remained impaired indefinitely.''[37]

Because ECT traditionally has been so controversial, the National Institutes of Health, in conjunction with the National Institutes of Mental Health, convened a Consensus

---

[32]DETRE & JARECKI, *supra* note 1, at 642–43; Khan et al., *supra* note 23, at 504.

[33]APA TASK FORCE REP., *supra* note 4, at 61; P. BREGGIN, TOXIC PSYCHIATRY 197–98 (1991); RESEARCH IN MENTAL HEALTH, *supra* note 16, at 337; Frank, *supra* note 8, at 500–02; Giamartino, *supra* note 16, at 1128–29; *Mass. ECT Task Force Rep., supra* note 16, at 63–64; *Report of the Task Panel on Research, in* IV TASK PANEL REPORTS SUBMITTED TO THE PRESIDENT'S COMM'N ON MENTAL HEALTH 1761–62 (1978) [hereinafter PRESIDENT'S COMM'N]. *Compare, e.g.,* Friedberg, *supra* note 15, at 98–99 *with* Blachly, *Attitudes, Data and Technological Promise of ECT,* 14 PSYCHIATRIC OPINION 9, 11 (1977) *and* Weiner, *supra* note 1, at 1677–78.

[34]*E.g.,* APA TASK FORCE REP., *supra* note 4, at 61. Squire & Chase, *Memory Functions Six to Nine Months After Electroconvulsive Therapy,* 32 ARCHIVES GEN. PSYCHIATRY 1557 (1975); Weiner, *supra* note 1, at 1677.

[35]APA TASK FORCE REP., *supra* note 4, at 61; DETRE & JARECKI, *supra* note 1, at 643.

[36]APA TASK FORCE REP., *supra* note 4, at 61; DETRE & JARECKI, *supra* note 1, at 643; Dornbush & Williams, *supra* note 27, at 203. Moreover, existing means of testing memory loss may not be sufficiently sensitive to detect the small, intermittent, or subtle changes in memory or its processes that patients experience as devastating. Grimm, *supra* note 16, at 31.

[37]APA TASK FORCE REP., *supra* note 4, at 61 (''A small minority of patients, however, report persistent deficits''). DETRE & JARECKI, *supra* note 1, at 643. For an anecdotal account of a patient who experienced permanent memory impairment affecting her occupational skills as a government economist, see Roueche, *Annals of Medicine: As Empty as Eve,* THE NEW YORKER, Sept. 1974, at 84, 95–96:

> I came from the office that first day feeling panicky. I didn't know where to turn. I didn't know what to do. I was terrified . . . all my beloved knowledge, everything I had learned in my field during twenty years or more, was gone. I'd lost the body of knowledge that constituted my professional skill. I'd lost everything that professionals take for granted. I'd lost my experience, my knowing. But it was worse than that. I felt that I'd lost my self . . .

> . . . I went back to the office determined to try . . . It was like learning to walk—I started out taking little baby steps . . . Every now and then, I'd get a little glimmer. But mostly it was discouraging. There weren't just gaps in my memory. There were oceans and oceans of blankness . . . I couldn't seem to retain. I couldn't hang on to my relearning. Or only a part of it. The rest kept sliding away again.

For an account of permanent memory impairment by a practicing psychiatrist who underwent ECT, see Anonymous, *The Experience of Electro-Convulsive Therapy,* 111 BRIT. J. PSYCHIATRY 365 (1965):

> I have always had a good topographical sense and have been able to memorize maps and, for example, find my way with ease around the Underground system of London, from schemata in my head without recourse to maps. With the second course of ECT, though not the first, my topographic schemata have become totally disorganized. I must look at a map in order to visualize the route from A to B, and I have forgotten completely the patterns that previously have been almost second nature to me. It was with considerable effort that I am learning them again. Similarly, I have considerable difficulty in finding my way about my filing system which previously was familiar to me through years of use, but now seems strange so that I am at a loss to know where to start searching.

See also A. HOTCHNER, PAPA HEMINGWAY: A PERSONAL MEMOIR 328 (1966) (report of memory loss following ECT treatment of Ernest Hemingway).

Development Conference on ECT in 1985.[38] After hearing reports from experts, health professionals, and former patients, a consensus panel representing psychiatry, psychology, neurology, psychopharmacology, epidemiology, law, and the general public issued a consensus statement. The panel concluded that it was "well established" that ECT produces deficits in memory function "which have been demonstrated objectively and repeatedly, [and which] persist after termination of a normal course of ECT."[39] The consensus statement also concluded that the "ability to learn and retain new information is adversely affected" for several weeks following the administration of ECT.[40] Although "objective evidence based on neuropsychological testing" was found to demonstrate loss of memory for several weeks, such "objective tests have not firmly established persistent or permanent deficits for a more extensive period. . . ."[41] Nevertheless, research conducted as long as 3 years after treatment found that many patients report continued impairment of memory.[42] Some patients were found to perceive ECT as a "terrifying experience," "an abusive invasion of personal autonomy," and the cause of "extreme distress from persistent memory deficits."[43] These patients' perceptions must be weighed heavily in determining the relative intrusiveness of ECT compared to other treatment modalities.

D. Abuse of ECT and Relative Intrusiveness

Abuses in the administration of ECT have been reported. Some psychiatrists "enthusiastically recommend ECT in almost all psychiatric conditions, believing, with only their personal clinical experience to support their opinions, in the relative omnipotence of ECT."[44] ECT is used sparingly in many hospitals, yet frequently in certain proprietary hospitals, a disparity perhaps caused more by economic than by therapeutic factors.[45] ECT has allegedly been used by some state hospitals without administration of a prior physical and neurological examination[46] and without warning patients of the risks of memory loss

---

[38]5 NATIONAL INSTITUTE OF HEALTH & NATIONAL INSTITUTE OF MENTAL HEALTH, ELECTROCONVULSIVE THERAPY: CONSENSUS DEVELOPMENT CONFERENCE STATEMENT, No. 11 (1985), *reprinted in* R. SPRING ET AL., PATIENTS, PSYCHIATRISTS AND LAWYERS: LAW AND THE MENTAL HEALTH SYSTEM 129 (1989).

[39]*Id.* at 132.

[40]*Id.*

[41]*Id.*

[42]*Id.*

[43]*Id. See also* Fox, *Patients' Fear Of and Objections to Electroconvulsive Therapy,* 44 HOSP. & COMMUNITY PSYCHIATRY 357, 358 (1993) (14% of patients reported reluctance to be treated again; 29% indicated that ECT was a frightening treatment to have).]

[44]*Mass. ECT Task Force Rep., supra* note 16, at 64. *See also Hurwitz, supra* note 16 (reporting the use of ECT "in almost every diagnostic category of the standard nomenclature"); Robitscher, *Psychosurgery and Other Somatic Means of Altering Behavior,* 2 BULL. AM. ACAD. PSYCHIATRY & L. 7, 12 (1974) (reporting the use of ECT for schizophrenia, neurotic depression, sociopathic behavior, alcoholism, and for a "teenager hospitalized for smoking marijuana!").

[45]Robitscher, *supra* note 44, at 12. *See* D. VISCOTT, THE MAKING OF A PSYCHIATRIST 356 (1972) ("Finding that the patient has insurance seemed like the most common indication for giving electroshock."); Giamartino, *supra* note 16, at 1331 (suggesting that financial and other "motives other than the welfare of the patient have influenced the choice" of ECT).

[46]Nelson v. Hudspeth, 9 CLEARINGHOUSE REV. 352 (S.D. Miss. July 24, 1975 (complaint filed); *see* Wyatt v. Hardin, [1976], 1 MENTAL DISABILITY L. REP. 55, 57 (M.D. Ala. Feb. 28, 1975, *modified* July 1, 1975) (ordering a state hospital to perform a complete physical and neurological examination within 10 days prior to the commencement of each series of ECT treatments). Administration of ECT without adequate prior diagnosis may have serious adverse effects for the patient. For example, an undiagnosed benign brain tumor or scar from previous brain injury may cause behavior changes that are worsened by ECT but would be curable by neurosurgery. Beresford, *Judicial Review of Medical Treatment Programs,* 12 CAL. W.L. REV. 331, 346 (1976).

and other adverse side effects.[47] In many facilities staff are inadequately trained in the procedure and administer it improperly.[48] One highly questionable experimental practice is known as "regressive" or "depatterning" ECT.[49] This technique involves a large number of shock treatments administered at frequent intervals—four to six per day for a number of weeks—in an attempt to regress the patient to a point of complete confusion. Patients develop a reversible organic psychosis, becoming incontinent, unable to feed themselves, grossly disoriented, mute, oblivious to their surroundings, and totally dependent. It is thought that a fresh start from this totally regressed state will be effective. However, the value of this technique remains unproved,[50] and its use in clinical practice is therefore highly questionable.[51]

As with the other treatment techniques discussed, ECT is frequently administered to nonconsenting patients[52] and has been used in state hospitals and prisons for punitive or disciplinary purposes.[53] Moreover, ECT, like psychotropic medication, is used by some

---

[47]J. FRIEDBERG, SHOCK TREATMENT IS NOT GOOD FOR YOUR BRAIN 13, 42 (1976); R. SLOVENKO, PSYCHIATRY AND LAW 410–11 (1973). For a form used by one practitioner to obtain patient consent to ECT, describing possible risks and complications, see Lebensohn, *supra* note 1, at 387–89.

[48]JANICAK ET AL., *supra* note 1, at 293.

[49]DETRE & JARECKI, *supra* note 1, at 147–48, 650; KALINOWSKY & HOCH, *supra* note 1, at 151; Abrams, *Multiple ECT: What Have We Learned, in* CONVULSIVE THERAPY, *supra* note 1, at 79; Frankel, *supra* note 1, at 291; *Mass. ECT Task Force Rep., supra* note 16, at 67, 72.

[50]Abrams, *supra* note 49, at 79; *Mass. ECT Task Force Report, supra* note 16, at 72–73.

[51]*See* Wyatt v. Hardin, [1976] 1 MENTAL DISABILITY L. REP. 55, 57 (M.D. Ala. Feb. 28, 1975, *modified* July 1, 1975) ("Regressive, multiple or depatterning electroconvulsive techniques shall not be utilized.").

[52]SLOVENKO, *supra* note 47, at 545–50; Beresford, *Legal Issues Related to Electroconvulsive Therapy*, 25 ARCHIVES GEN. PSYCHIATRY 100 (1971); Halleck, *Legal and Ethical Aspects of Behavior Control*, 131 AM. J. PSYCHIATRY 382 (1974); J. Robitscher, *Informed Consent: When Can It Be Withdrawn?*, 2 HASTINGS CTR. REP., June 1972, at 10, 11. For cases challenging involuntary use of ECT, see Lojuk v. Quandt, 706 F.2d 1456 (7th Cir. 1983); Nelson v. Hudspeth, 11 CLEARINGHOUSE REV. 505 (S.D. Miss. May 17, 1977) (denying defendants' motion for summary judgment in class action challenging state hospital's administration of ECT without patient consent); Bell v. Wayne County Gen. Hosp., 384 F. Supp. 1085 (E.D. Mich. 1974) (invalidating Michigan statute insofar as it permits involuntary ECT during prehearing detention); Price v. Sheppard, 239 N.W.2d 905 (Minn. 1976) (upholding state hospital administration of ECT to minor child against parent's express wishes, but prescribing procedures for future use of ECT); Doe v. Klein, 2 MENTAL DISABILITY L. REP. 475, 476 (N.J. Super. Ct. App. Div. 1976) (consent order prohibiting state hospital administration of ECT without informed consent); New York City Health & Hosp. Corp. v. Stein, 335 N.Y.S.2d 461 (Sup. Ct. 1972) (refusing to permit hospital to administer ECT to nonconsenting patient, even with consent of patient's mother). Anonymous v. State, 236 N.Y.S.2d 88 (Sup. Ct. 1963) (upholding administration of insulin shock to 34-year-old state hospital patient with consent of parent).

[53]S. BRACKEL & R. ROCK, THE MENTALLY DISABLED AND THE LAW 163 (rev. ed. 1971) ("Some attendants reportedly make threats of electroshock treatment in order to keep peace and quiet in the ward or to control those patients who do not satisfy the attendant's standards of behavior. One attendant, for example, admitted having put a patient on the 'shock list' in order to give himself and the ward some rest from a particularly boring story."); N. KITTRIE, THE RIGHT TO BE DIFFERENT: DEVIANCE AND ENFORCED THERAPY 307 (1971) ("Sometimes shock treatments are administered in view of other patients, perhaps as a general deterrent."); SLOVENKO, *supra* note 47, at 124; K. WOODEN, WEEPING IN THE PLAYTIME OF OTHERS: AMERICA'S INCARCERATED CHILDREN 147 (1976) (describing punitive use of ECT on a 17-year-old in a California prison); Dispoldo, *Arizona's 'Clockwork Orange' Bill*, N.Y. TIMES, June 20, 1974, at 39 (description by Arizona prisoner of "shock treatments—called 'Edison Medicine' by prisoners—used as punishment to reduce the vigor and vitality of jailhouse lawyers and inmates considered 'political radicals' by prison officials."); Robitscher, *supra* note 44, at 12–13 (ECT has been "given to enforce hospital discipline—an investigation of the Lima (Ohio) State Hospital revealed that patients were kept in line by the administration of and by the threat of shock. . . . Sometimes ECT is used for punitive purposes. It is a way of showing the patient who causes commotion 'who is boss' and, in addition to reducing the patient to the point where he cannot effectively protest or assert legal rights, also to 'teach him a lesson'."); Roth & Lerner, *Sex-Based Discrimination in the Mental Institutionalization of Women*, 62 CAL. L. REV. 804 (1974) (woman in city hospital given ECT for "sexually acting out" with male patients). *Cf.* KESEY, *supra* note 28 (fictional account).

hospitals for the convenience of the staff "since the effect of successive shock treatments is to render the patient more and more confused, regressed, non-combative, pliable, and above all, forgetful."[54]

Existing clinical practices involving ECT must be reexamined. Although it is efficacious in the treatment of depression, the hazardous character of ECT and its physically and mentally intrusive effects should limit its application (with a few exceptions) to cases where an attempt to treat the patient with antidepressant medication has been unsuccessful.[55] The traditional techniques of administering ECT, involving placement of electrodes on both temples and the use of diphasic sinusoidal electrical current, should be carefully considered by clinicians and used more sparingly in patients showing signs of severe cognitive deficits.[56] Some innovative procedures—including unilateral placement on the nondominant cerebral hemisphere and the use of "pulse current" and the delivery of brief pulses of electrical current of short duration resulting in a smaller amount of current passing through the patient's brain—appear at least as efficacious as traditional techniques and cause less memory disturbance.[57] These newer techniques therefore should be considered for more widespread adoption in an attempt to reduce posttreatment side effects.

ECT is hazardous and physically and mentally intrusive. It induces unconsciousness and confusion. ECT involves side effects that are distressing and, at least in some cases, memory impairment that is irreversible. Moreover, it may not be resisted by unwilling patients. As a result, ECT plainly is more intrusive than psychotherapy and behavior therapy. Comparison of ECT with the psychotropic drugs is more difficult. It is clearly more problematic than many of the medications, particularly the antianxiety drugs, lithium, and some of the antidepressant drugs. Yet, ECT may be less hazardous and less subject to abuse than some of the antipsychotic and antidepressant drugs, although the highly intrusive and degrading character of the treatment as well as its impact on mental processes may make it subjectively more distressing in the minds of patients. Significant in this regard is the response of the American Psychiatric Association, as *amicus curiae,* to a request by the United States District Court in *Wyatt v. Hardin* for its views concerning a proposed revision of standards previously issued by the court for the imposition of ECT and other hazardous

---

[54]Robitscher, *supra* note 44, at 12.

[55]DETRE & JARECKI, *supra* note 1, at 647–48:

> other considerations being equal, shock therapy is indicated only after an attempt to treat the patient with drugs has failed. However, ECT should be the physician's initial preference when
>
> 1. previous episodes of the same illness have not responded to drug treatment;
>
> 2. the patient's medical condition (first trimester of pregnancy, history of multiple drug idiosyncrasies) make drug use inadvisable;
>
> 3. the patient's illness is severe and progressing so rapidly that no time is available for even a brief trial on drugs; or
>
> 4. the available treatment facilities are inadequate or the responsible family members cannot be relied on to supervise his medication.

See also id. at 178–80.

[56]*See* APA TASK FORCE REPORT, *supra* note 4, at 62.

[57]*See* ELECTROCONVULSIVE THERAPY, *supra* note 3; F. MILLER ET AL., *supra* note 3, at 61–62; RESEARCH IN MENTAL HEALTH, *supra* note 16, at 337; Blachly, *supra* note 33, at 10-11; Cohen et al., *Antidepressant Effects of Unilateral Electric Convulsive Shock Therapy,* 31 ARCHIVES GEN. PSYCHIATRY 673 (1974); Fink, *Clinical Progress in Convulsive Therapy, in* CONVULSIVE THERAPY, *supra* note 1, at 271, 273; McGaugh & Williams, *supra* note 29, at 282-83; *Report of the Task Panel on Research, in* PRESIDENT'S COMM'N, *supra* note 33, at 1762; Robertson & Inglis, *The Effects of Electroconvulsive Therapy on Human Learning and Memory,* 18 CAN. PSYCH. REV. 285 (1977).

treatment procedures at Alabama hospitals.[58] The American Psychiatric Association's submission distinguished between ECT and psychotropic drugs, urging that the court adopt special procedures for determining informed consent to the former but not to the latter.[59] ECT therefore should be considered the most intrusive of the treatment techniques thus far considered.

---

[58]Wyatt v. Hardin, *supra* note 46. The standard at issue, Standard 9 of the court's order of April 13, 1972, provided that "Patients have a right not to be subjected to treatment procedures such as lobotomy, electroconvulsive treatment, aversive reinforcement conditioning or other unusual or hazardous treatment procedures without their express and informed consent after consultation with counsel or interested party of the patient's choice." Wyatt v. Stickney, 344 F. Supp. 373, 380 (M.D. Ala. 1972), *aff'd in part, remanded in part, and rev'd in part sub nom.* Wyatt v. Aderholt, 503 F.2d 1305 (5th Cir. 1974). In September 1974, defendants and the Human Rights Committee of one of the hospitals sought a modification of Standard 9 to permit greater flexibility in administration of ECT. On Oct. 1, 1974, the court requested proposed revisions from *amici,* one of which was the American Psychiatric Association.

[59]Brief of *Amicus Curiae,* American Psychiatric Ass'n, at 7–8, Wyatt v. Hardin, [1976], 1 MENTAL DISABILITY L. REP. 55, 57 (M.D. Ala., Feb. 28, 1975, *modified* July 1, 1975) (No. 3195-N) (addressing the question of suggested amendments to Standard 9). For special procedures for ECT adopted by the court, *see id .* at 56–57. For further discussion of informed consent to ECT, see APA TASK FORCE REP., *supra* note 4, at 11–14, 64–71, 155–58; Frankel, *supra* note 1, at 239–41; Levine et al., *Informed Consent in the Treatment of Geriatric Patients,* 19 BULL. AM. ACAD. PSYCHIATRY & L. 395 (1991).

Chapter 7
ELECTRONIC STIMULATION OF THE BRAIN

A. Description and History

Electronic stimulation of the brain (ESB) has thus far received only limited clinical application.[1] Still a highly experimental technique, it involves the surgical implantation of minute electrodes directly into certain subcortical regions of the brain associated with particular behavior patterns or mental states. When charged, these electrodes stimulate these regions, inducing desired or inhibiting unwanted behaviors or sensations.

---

[1] *See generally* H. CLARK, ALTERING BEHAVIOR: THE ETHICS OF CONTROLLED EXPERIENCE 14 (1986); J. DELGADO, PHYSICAL CONTROL OF THE MIND: TOWARD A PSYCHOCIVILIZED SOCIETY (1969); P. LONDON, BEHAVIOR CONTROL 177–91 (1969); M. PINES, THE BRAIN CHANGERS: SCIENTISTS AND THE NEW MIND CONTROL 32–54 (1973); E. VALENSTEIN, BRAIN CONTROL: A CRITICAL EVALUATION OF BRAIN STIMULATION AND PSYCHOSURGERY 13–63, 86–114, 162–96 (1973); Gorney, *The New Biology and the Future of Man,* 15 U.C.L.A. L. REV. 273, 338–41 (1968); Heath, *Modulation of Emotion With a Brain Pacemaker,* 165 J. NERVOUS & MENTAL DIS. 300 (1977); Ingraham & Smith, *The Use of Electronics in the Observation and Control of Human Behavior and Its Possible Use in Rehabilitation and Parole,* 7 ISSUES IN CRIMINOLOGY 35 (1972); *Physical Manipulation of the Brain,* HASTINGS CTR. REP. (Special Supp.) (1973) [hereinafter *Physical Manipulation of the Brain*]; Vaughan, *Psychosurgery and Brain Stimulation in Historical Perspective, in* OPERATING ON THE MIND: THE PSYCHOSURGERY CONFLICT 24 (W. Gaylin et al. eds., 1975) [hereinafter OPERATING ON THE MIND]; Winick, *Legal Limitations on Correctional Therapy and Research,* 65 MINN. L. REV. 331, 370–71 (1981).

According to Jose Delgado, perhaps the leading proponent of ESB, the working hypotheses underlying this technique are as follows:

(1) There are basic mechanisms in the brain responsible for all mental activities, including perceptions, emotions, abstract thought, social relations, and the most refined artistic creations. (2) These mechanisms may be detected, analyzed, influenced, and sometimes substituted for by means of physical and chemical technology. . . . (3) Predictable behavior and mental responses may be induced by direct manipulation of the brain. (4) We can substitute intelligent and purposeful determination of neuronal functions for blind, automatic responses.

DELGADO, *supra,* at 68.

The leading proponent of its use in the treatment of mental disorders, Robert G. Heath, postulates that psychosis is "a consequence of a disruption of the physiological mechanism for emotional expression [in] brain sites where activity correlates with pleasurable emotion and levels of awareness." Heath, *supra,* at 302–03. According to Heath, the rationale for the therapeutic use of ESB is as follows:

Delivery of a stimulus capable of continuously modulating the physiological circuitry for emotion so as to activate the septal region while concomitantly inhibiting activity of the hippocampus, should override the dysrhythmia demonstrated in psychotic patients (including schizophrenics) and abolishing the dysrhythmia should eliminate the symptoms arising from the defects in pleasure and lowered awareness that are responsible for disorders of thought.

Id. at 303.

Although electrical stimulation is the most common method of physically manipulating the brain, chemical stimulation has also been used experimentally. CLARK, *supra,* at 32–35; LONDON, *supra,* at 178; VALENSTEIN, *supra,* at 114–22; Vaughan, *supra,* at 58–59. For a discussion of intracerebral radio stimulation of the brain by use of an instrument known as the *stimoceiver,* see CLARK, *supra,* at 29; Delgado, *Intracerebral Radio Stimulation and Recording in Completely Free Patients, in* PSYCHOTECHNOLOGY: ELECTRONIC CONTROL OF MIND AND BEHAVIOR 184 (R. Schwitzgebel ed., 1973). For a description of the use of "an implantable receiver, permitting brain stimulation (without existing wires) at selected parameters for an indefinite time," see Heath, *supra,* at 302.

The origins of ESB can be traced to studies in the 1800s demonstrating that electrical stimulation of the brains of animals produced movement of various muscles, thereby enabling the mapping of motor areas of the brain.[2] The first attempt at electrical stimulation of a human brain apparently occurred when a Cincinnati surgeon inserted insulated needles connected to a double cell battery into a cancerous opening in the skull of his feeble-minded patient. The current elicited a variety of sensations from different parts of the patient's body, and when its strength was increased, her face contorted, she began to cry, and she went into convulsions, which apparently resulted in her death.

Electrical stimulation was used experimentally in the early 1900s in neurosurgery, as a means of localizing brain functions, thus enabling mapping of the human cortex and avoidance of unnecessary removal of critical tissue in brain surgery. The development of stereotaxic instruments, which position the skull in a fixed plane, allowing the accurate placing of small electrodes into almost any sector of the brain with the aid of three-dimensional anatomical maps, as well as developments in synthetics, microminiature electronic equipment, and telemetry, enabled sophisticated experimentation revealing the role of subcortical regions of the brain—notably the hypothalamus and portions of the limbic system—in controlling emotion.

Experiments in the 1950s demonstrated that stimulation of these subcortical regions produces an aversive emotional state motivating an animal to avoid repetition of behavior, and that the brain contains certain "pleasure centers," areas which when stimulated produce pleasurable reactions of such high intensity that such stimulation serves as a much more powerful reinforcer than food or sex.[3] Indeed, so apparently pleasurable is such stimulation that if an electrode is implanted into the pleasure center of an animal and connected to a device enabling electrical self-stimulation when the animal presses a bar, the animal, allowed free choice between food and electrical self-stimulation, will self-stimulate until it starves to death.[4] Animal experiments have demonstrated the use of ESB in manipulating a great variety of behaviors and emotions, ranging from simple movements to eating, drinking, hoarding, maternal behavior, withdrawal, and sexual behavior.[5]

Although the relevance of animal implant studies to human beings is uncertain,[6] ESB has been used in patients for a variety of diagnostic and therapeutic purposes:

> in connection with [brain] surgery, . . . for changing speech patterns, relieving epileptic seizures, diagnosing and treating intractable pain, controlling some involuntary movements, and inducing and blocking hostile, aggressive impulses and an assortment of thought patterns, hallucinations, laughter, memories, sexual expressions, and pleasant shifts of moods—as well as physiological functions like heart rate, urination, muscle contraction, hearing, and blood pressure.[7]

---

[2]The following discussion of the origins of ESB is drawn from VALENSTEIN, *supra* note 1, at 18–40; Vaughan, *supra* note 1, at 55–57. For a historical discussion of ESB, see Thomas & Young, *A Note on the Early History of Electrical Stimulation of the Brain,* 120 J. GEN. PSYCHOL. 73 (1993).

[3]*Report of the Task Panel on Research, in* IV TASK PANEL REPORTS SUBMITTED TO THE PRESIDENT'S COMM'N ON MENTAL HEALTH 1662 (1978) [hereinafter PRESIDENT'S COMM'N].

[4]*Id.* The power of ESB is also illustrated by experiments in which stimulation induced an attentive rhesus monkey with a strong maternal instinct to ignore her baby. A dramatic demonstration involved the ability of remote control ESB to abruptly halt a charging brave bull at the press of a button. DELGADO, *supra* note 1, at 168–72.

[5]VALENSTEIN, *supra* note 1, at 44–46; LONDON, *supra* note 1, at 179–83; Vaughan, *supra* note 1, at 56–57.

[6]LONDON, *supra* note 1, at 183; VALENSTEIN, *supra* note 1, at 104–06.

[7]LONDON, *supra* note 1, at 184. *See also* DELGADO, *supra* note 1, at 196–200. Brain stimulation for pain control has received considerable attention. *See* Duncan et al., *Deep Brain Stimulation: A Review of Basic Research and Clinical Studies,* 45 PAIN 49 (1991); Young & Rinaldi, *Brain Stimulation for Relief of Chronic Pain, in* TEXTBOOK OF PAIN 1225–27 (P. Wall & R. Melzack eds., 3d ed. 1994).

ESB has thus far received only limited application in the treatment of mental patients, but there are reports of its therapeutic use for neurotic behavior,[8] phobias, compulsive obsessions,[9] schizophrenia,[10] depression,[11] to change the sexual orientation of a homosexual by positive conditioning,[12] and in the treatment of uncontrollable violent–aggressive behavior.[13] Clinical application in cases of mental illness has been so minimal, however, that ESB must be regarded as a highly experimental treatment method.[14]

B. Potential Abuse of ESB and Relative Intrusiveness

The potential for abuse centers primarily on the apparent potency of ESB as a conditioning device.[15] Unlike traditional reinforcers, which are thought to function as motivators that patients are capable of resisting, ESB operates with a "peculiar directness of

---

[8]DELGADO, *supra* note 1, at 87–88; Heath, *supra* note 1, at 312–13.

[9]DELGADO, *supra* note 1, at 133–34; Dieckman, *Chronic Mediothalmic Stimulation for Control of Phobias, in* MODERN CONCEPTS IN PSYCHIATRIC SURGERY (E. Hitchcock et al. eds., 1979) [hereinafter PSYCHIATRIC SURGERY].

[10]DELGADO, *supra* note 1, at 143; PINES, *supra* note 1, at 50; Heath, *supra* note 1, at 308–12; Heath et al., *Brain Mechanisms in Psychiatric Illness: Rationale for and Results of Treatment with Cerebellar Stimulation, in* PSYCHIATRIC SURGERY, *supra* note 9, at 77; Vaughan, *supra* note 1, at 57.

[11]Heath et al., *supra* note 10.

[12]CLARK, *supra* note 1, at 102; Robinson, *Therapies: a Clear and Present Danger,* 28 AM. PSYCHOLOGIST 129, 132 (1973); Vaughan, *supra* note 1, at 60.

[13]V. MARK & F. ERVIN, VIOLENCE AND THE BRAIN 92–97 (1970); PINES, *supra* note 1, at 201–02; Heath, *supra* note 1, at 306–07; Heath et al., *supra* note 10; Heath, *Correlation of Brain Activity With Emotion: A Basis for Developing Treatment of Violent–Aggressive Behavior,* 20 J. AM. ACAD. PSYCHOANALYSIS 335, 342 (1992); Vaughan, *supra* note 1, at 62–63. Thomas R., the patient involved, is cited by his physicians, the authors of VIOLENCE AND THE BRAIN, as evidence in support of their controversial view that a causal connection exists between brain damage and violence. For critical analysis, see Chorover, *The Pacification of the Brain,* PSYCHOL. TODAY, May 1974, at 59; Hodson, *Reflections Concerning Violence and the Brain,* 9 CRIM. L. BULL. 684 (1973); Wexler, *Book Review,* 85 HARV. L. REV. 1489 (1972). Thomas R. appears to be the model for Harry Benson, the patient in Michael Crichton's fictional account of ESB, THE TERMINAL MAN (1972).

[14]DELGADO, *supra* note 1, at 209; VALENSTEIN, *supra* note 1, at 341; *see* R. MARTIN, LEGAL CHALLENGES TO BEHAVIOR MODIFICATION 129 (1975) (calling for legislation to control ESB experimentation). The experimental nature of ESB is indicated by the fact that the leading textbook on psychiatric treatment methods does not deal with this technique. *E.g.,* COMPREHENSIVE TEXTBOOK OF PSYCHIATRY (H. Kaplan & B. Sadock eds., 5th ed. 1989). Even the leading proponent of the therapeutic use of ESB in the treatment of mental disorders, Robert G. Heath, who reported on its successful use on 10 of 11 patients with previously intractable psychiatric illness, describes the technique as "experimental" and urges its consideration only for patients who have not responded in adequate trials with conventional therapy. Heath, *supra* note 1, at 395, 315. Valenstein finds "no reason to believe that brain stimulation will have wide application in the treatment of psychiatric disorders." Valenstein, *Science Fiction Fantasy and the Brain,* 12 PSYCHOL. TODAY, July 1978, at 29, 31.

[15]*See* LONDON, *supra* note 1, at 189–90:

[S]maller and smaller instruments, better and better materials, more and more powerful batteries—all are in the works, and surely other things not yet envisioned here. No one needs to know what the limits of surgical control will be to know without a doubt, upon examining the work to date, that it will be possible someday to control very refined behavior by both chemical and electrical means.

See also Vaughan, *supra* note 1, at 28:

If fear or pleasure are systematically elicited by ESB in association with specific situations, behavioral responses can be achieved in accordance with well-established principles of learning. These changes could be under the control of a therapist, the person himself, or any operator who controls the stimulation apparatus. The obvious possibilities for misuse of these potential techniques has led some to question the desirability of further experimentation in this area and to doubt the wisdom of any therapeutic application of ESB or chemostimulation.

Even its proponents recognize that without adequate safeguards, ESB "could be ... a ... subtle and dangerous weapon...." DELGADO, *supra* note 1, at 248–49.

effect which removes it from the subject's monitoring or control."[16] Another potential danger is the use of ESB to immobilize or incapacitate criminals or mental patients. It has been suggested, for example, that ESB be used in conjunction with radio telemetry devices surgically implanted in criminal offenders. As an alternative to incarceration, the offender would be released from prison, subject to electronic monitoring of certain physiological data that presumably would enable the prediction of dangerous behavior and its control through ESB administered by an internal telemetry receiver.[17] However, the present lack of predictability in the responses produced by ESB,[18] the expense of the procedure,[19] and the limited number of neurosurgeons skilled in this technique[20] make it unlikely that the potential for widespread abuse will be realized in the near future.

The effects of ESB are essentially reversible.[21] Apparently no permanent anatomical change in the brain results beyond the minimal damage caused by the destruction of a few cells during implantation of the electrodes[22] (although there is some risk that scar tissue around the electrodes might produce epileptic seizures[23]). Because brain tissue is insensitive, the electrodes do not cause any discomfort.[24] ESB must, however, be regarded as a hazardous, unpredictable, experimental procedure that is extremely intrusive.[25] By rapidly

---

[16]Vaughan, *supra* note 1, at 24. *See also* DELGADO, *supra* note 1, at 214:

> [With traditional techniques the individual] . . . always had the privilege of deciding his own fate. New neurological technology, however, has a refined efficiency. The individual is defenseless against direct manipulation of the brain because he is deprived of his most intimate mechanisms of biological reactivity. In experiments, electrical stimulation of appropriate intensity always prevailed over free will, and, for example, flexion of the hand evoked by stimulation of the motor cortex cannot be voluntarily avoided.

See also DELGADO, *supra* note 1, at 114 ("When the patient was warned of the oncoming stimulation and was asked to try to keep his fingers extended, he could not prevent the evoked movement and commented, 'I guess, Doctor, that your electricity is stronger than my will.' ").

[17]Lehtinen, *Technological Incapacitation: A Neglected Alternative,* 2 Q. J. CORRECTIONS 31, 35 (1978).

[18]PINES, *supra* note 1, at 49, 52 (quoting James Olds, the scientist whose research was instrumental in the discovery of the "pleasure center"); VALENSTEIN, *supra* note 1, at 113–14; Ingraham & Smith, *supra* note 1, at 41; Valenstein, *Firing Line: Discussion of Psychosurgery and Brain Control, in* READINGS IN LAW AND PSYCHIATRY 100, 104 (R. Allen et al. eds., 2d ed. 1975).

[19]Young & Rinaldi, *supra* note 7, at 1231 (cost of implanting two electrodes about $60,000).

[20]CLARK, *supra* note 1, at 51, 156; Robitscher, *Psychosurgery and Other Somatic Means of Altering Behavior,* 2 BULL. AM. ACAD. PSYCHIATRY & L. 7, 30 (1974); Vaughan, *supra* note 1, at 24, 60–62.

[21]*Hearings on S.971, S.878, & S.J. Res. 871 Before the Subcomm. on Health, Sen. Comm. on Labor & Public Welfare,* 93d Cong., 1st Sess., pt. 2, at 342 (1973) (testimony of Dr. Bertram Brown, former Director of NIMH); PINES, *supra* note 1, at 231; Physical Manipulation of the Brain, *supra* note 1, at 8 (comments of E.A. Bering, Jr., of the National Institute of Neurological Diseases and Stroke); Robitscher, *supra* note 20, at 30; Vaughan, *supra* note 1, at 27.

[22]DELGADO, *supra* note 1, at 84–85:

> It is true that implantation of electrodes destroys neurons along the path of penetration, breaking up capillary vessels and later producing a local reaction involving the formation of a thin fibrotic capsule along the implantation tract. It has been proven, however, that local hemorrhage is negligible and that because of the well-known functional redundancy of neural tissue with abundance of duplication in its circuits, the destruction of a relatively small group of neurons does not produce any detectable deficit.

See also VALENSTEIN, *supra* note 1, at 105; Vaughan, *supra* note 1, at 60.

[23]PINES, *supra* note 1, at 216.

[24]LONDON, *supra* note 1, at 177.

[25]*Id.* at 185:

> [T]hinking has been blocked by ESB, so that people oriented in time and space and able to follow the doctor's instructions in other ways could not answer questions or pronounce a single word. "I could not coordinate my thoughts," one explained. "My head felt as if I had drunk a lot of beer." And another said, "I don't know why, but I could not speak."

and directly modifying the state of the brain itself in a manner the patient is incapable of resisting, ESB affects the personal identity and autonomy of the patient more than any other treatment technique with the exception of psychosurgery[26] and should therefore be classified as the most intrusive procedure thus far considered.[27]

---

[26]Neville, *Zalmoxis or the Morals of ESB and Psychosurgery, in* OPERATING ON THE MIND, *supra* note 1, at 87, 89, 93–95. Psychosurgery is discussed in *infra* chapter 8.

[27]*Physical Manipulation of the Brain, supra* note 1, at 16 (placing ESB after psychotherapy and drugs but before psychosurgery in a ranking of treatment methods ''according to reversibility and least potential damage to the psychological structure of the individual.'') (comments of Vaughan).

Chapter 8
PSYCHOSURGERY

A. Description and History

The most radical and controversial of the psychotechnologies, *psychosurgery* may be defined as the "surgical removal or destruction of brain tissue or the cutting of brain tissue to disconnect one part of the brain from another, with the intent of altering behavior, even though there may be no direct evidence of structural disease or damage in the brain."[1] Probably originating in the early notion that mental illness stems from structural abnormalities in the brain,[2] this procedure can be traced to the ancient Roman practice of inflicting sword wounds to the head of the insane to relieve suffering.[3]

Brain surgery for the treatment of mental illness was apparently first attempted in 1891 by Gottlieb Burckhardt, a Swiss physician, who removed parts of the cerebral cortex to quiet patients experiencing hallucinations, and in 1910 by Ludwig Puusepp, a Russian neurosurgeon, who cut the fibers between the parietal and frontal cortex on one side of the brain

---

[1]*Hearings on S.971, S.878, & S.J. Res. 871 Before the Subcomm. on Health, Sen. Comm. on Labor & Public Welfare*, 93d Cong., 1st Sess., pt. 2, at 399 (1973) (testimony of Dr. Bertram Brown, former Director of NIMH) [hereinafter *Hearings*]. *See* B. Brown et al., Psychosurgery: Perspective on a Current Issue 1 (DHEW Pub. No. (HSM) 73-9119, 1973) [hereinafter Psychosurgery]; Merskey, *Ethical Aspects of the Physical Manipulation of the Brain, in* Psychiatric Ethics 131 (S. Bloch & P. Chodoff eds., 1981) (defining *psychosurgery* as the "selective surgical removal or destruction" of "nerve pathways with a view to influencing behavior"); National Research Service Award Act of 1974, § 202(c), 42 U.S.C. § 2891 (1974) (repealed) (creating a National Commission for the Protection of Human Subjects of Biomedical and Behavioral Research [hereinafter Nat'l Comm'n] and requiring the Commission to study, among other subjects, psychosurgery, and defining *psychosurgery* as

> brain surgery on (1) normal brain tissue of an individual, who does not suffer from any physical disease, for the purpose of changing or controlling the behavior or emotions of such individual, or (2) diseased brain tissue of an individual, if the sole object of the performance of such surgery is to control, change or affect any behavioral or emotional disturbance of such individual. Such term does not include brain surgery designed to cure or ameliorate the effects of epilepsy and electric shock treatments.

Valenstein, *Historical Perspective, in* The Psychosurgery Debate: Scientific Legal, and Ethical Perspectives 12 (1980) [hereinafter Psychosurgery Debate]. *See also* Bolwig, *Biological Treatments Other Than Drugs (Electroconvulsive Therapy, Brain Surgery, Insulin Therapy, and Phototherapy), in* Treatment of Mental Disorders: A Review of Effectiveness 112 (N. Sartorius et al. eds., 1993); Yap, *Psychosurgery: Its definition,* 1 Am. J. Forensic Psychiatry 83 (1979). The surgical treatment of epilepsy as well as any other neurosurgical treatment to repair or remove damaged brain tissue or to remove brain tumors is usually excluded from the definition of psychosurgery. B. Brown et al., *supra,* at 1. For a critical examination of the various definitions of psychosurgery, see S. Shuman, Psychosurgery and the Medical Control of Violence: Autonomy and Deviance 24–47 (1977).

[2]E. Valenstein, Brain Control: A Critical Evaluation of Brain Stimulation and Psychosurgery 264 (1973); Valenstein, *supra* note 1, at 14; Vaughan, *Psychosurgery and Brain Stimulation in Historical Perspective, in* Operating on the Mind: The Psychosurgery Conflict 29–39 (W. Gaylin et al. eds., 3d ed. 1975) [hereinafter Operating on the Mind].

[3]Restak, *The Promise and Peril of Psychosurgery,* Sat. Rev. World, Sept. 25, 1973, at 54, 55.

in manic–depressive patients.[4] However, it was not until the frontal lobe surgery performed by the Portuguese neurologist Egas Moniz in 1935 that the modern practice of psychosurgery began. While attending a conference, Moniz heard the report of two brain researchers describing the striking behavioral changes occurring in an agitated chimpanzee following surgical destruction of the prefrontal area of its cerebral cortex. When he returned to Portugal, Moniz attempted this procedure on mental patients who had not responded to other treatment methods and published his results, claiming that the patients were either cured or rendered calm and easier to manage. Moniz's optimistic reports were soon confirmed by Walter Freeman and James Watts in the United States, and frontal lobe surgery, or lobotomy, gained in popularity over the next 15 years, with operations being performed on more than 100,000 patients worldwide, ranging from those with chronic schizophrenia to nonhospitalized individuals suffering various neuroses.[5]

The "standard" lobotomy involved surgical opening of the skull and the cutting or removal of subcortical tissue. Freeman, who was a professor of neurology but not a surgeon, introduced the transorbital technique or "icepick" lobotomy, requiring no surgical opening of the skull but simply the insertion of a leukotome (a sharp instrument shaped like an icepick) into the orbit between the eyeball and the upper eyelid, where the skull is particularly thin, followed by manipulation of the instrument to sever the fiber connections between the base of the frontal lobes and the remainder of the brain.[6] A gross procedure done without direct observation, this simplified technique facilitated the performance of lobotomies by general physicians in nonhospital settings, which, coupled with mounting pressure to deal with the thousands of returning World War II veterans who were psychiatrically disabled, resulted in rapid growth in the use of the prefrontal lobotomy.[7] Perhaps as many as 40,000 patients in America alone were operated on during the postwar period.[8]

The rapid expansion in the use of lobotomy in the late 1940s, following retrospective reports by individual psychosurgeons of favorable results (including hospital discharges of institutionalized patients with chronic schizophrenia), occurred before its therapeutic effects

---

[4]The following historical account is drawn from E. VALENSTEIN, *supra* note 2, at 53–56, 266–69; E. VALENSTEIN, GREAT AND DESPERATE CURES: THE RISE AND DECLINE OF PSYCHOSURGERY AND OTHER RADICAL TREATMENTS FOR MENTAL ILLNESS (1986); Chorover, *Psychosurgery: A Neuropsychological Perspective*, 54 B.U. L. REV. 231, 332–34 (1974); Ette, *From Theory to Practice: The Unconventional Contribution of Gottlieb Burckhardt to Psychosurgery*, 45 BRAIN & LANGUAGE 578–85 (1993); Henn, *Psychosurgery, in* 2 COMPREHENSIVE TEXTBOOK OF PSYCHIATRY 1679 (H. Kaplan & B. Sadock eds., 5th ed. 1989); Merskey, *supra* note 1, at 140–41; Valenstein, *supra* note 1, at 19–23; Vaughan, *supra* note 2, at 39–41.

[5]In 1949, Moniz was awarded the Nobel Prize in Medicine for his work in lobotomy. H. KAPLAN ET AL., KAPLAN AND SADOCK'S SYNOPSIS OF PSYCHIATRY: BEHAVIORAL SCIENCES CLINICAL PSYCHIATRY 1013 (7th ed. 1994); Henn, *supra* note 4, at 1679.

[6]In addition to the leukotome, psychosurgeons have destroyed brain tissue by a variety of methods, including

injecting alcohol (Moniz's original method), uroselectane, phenol, procaine, Myodil, and olive oil; by suction, freezing (cryocautery), diathermy, and ultrasonic beams; by beaming gamma and beta rays through the skull; by implanting radium and Yttrium seeds; by electrolysis, electrocoagulation, and electrocautery.

Older, *Psychosurgery: Ethical Issues and a Proposal for Control*, 44 AM. J. ORTHOPSYCHIATRY 661–62 (1974). *See also* E. VALENSTEIN, *supra* note 4, at 284–85.

[7]Of the 632,000 men discharged from the armed forces during World War II for psychiatric reasons, few could be admitted to the already crowded mental hospitals. Faced with an insufficient number of psychiatrists and pressure from relatives for rapid treatment, the Veterans Administration accepted the early optimistic reports on lobotomy and encouraged its use. E. VALENSTEIN, *supra* note 2, at 55 & 390 n.7; E. VALENSTEIN, *supra* note 4, at 177–78.

[8]NAT'L COMM'N, REPORT AND RECOMMENDATIONS: PSYCHOSURGERY (DHEW Pub. No. (OS) 77-0001 (1977)) [hereinafter NAT'L COMM'N PSYCHOSURGERY REPORT]. *See* E. VALENSTEIN, *supra* note 4, at 178 ("After the Second World War, psychosurgery increased in virtually every country where there were neurosurgeons.").

were adequately studied. The subsequent publication of reports of undesirable side effects, as well as the introduction of the psychoactive drugs in the early 1950s, resulted in a sharp decline in psychosurgery.[9] Although lobotomy rendered patients calm, it also resulted in intellectual deterioration and personality changes, including apathetic, irresponsible, and asocial behavior, as well as a general blunting of emotional responsiveness and impairment of judgment, initiative, and creativity.[10] Moreover, a variety of additional side effects, including irritability, epileptic seizures, disturbance of sleep or appetite, thirst, and sexuality and other manifestations of neurological trauma were not uncommon. With the realization that the "cure" was often worse than the disease, lobotomy fell into disfavor, and "no responsible scientist today would condone a classical lobotomy operation."[11]

Although the lobotomy was abandoned, some neurosurgeons continued to experiment with new psychosurgical techniques and, with the realization that many patients were unresponsive to the newer drug therapies and ECT, psychosurgery underwent a resurgence.[12] The newer procedures were considerably more selective and sophisticated than lobotomy and, with advances in the knowledge of neuroanatomy, brain areas other than the frontal lobes are now targeted. Stereotaxic methods allow pinpoint placement of miniature electrodes in precise locations of the brain using geometric coordinates and X-ray inspection.[13] The passage of current through the electrode, in an amount greater than that used in ESB, results in the destruction of tissue at the electrode tip. These techniques have made structures deep within the brain accessible for destruction, and the major focus of psychosurgery shifted from the frontal lobes to the limbic system. The intermediate brain

[9]*See* E. VALENSTEIN, *supra* note 4, at 3; Donnelly, *Psychosurgery, in* THE PSYCHIATRIC THERAPIES 257 (Am. Psychiatric Ass'n Comm'n on Psychiatric Therapies) (T. Karasu ed., 1984); Schwartz & Africa, *Schizophrenic Disorders, in* REVIEW OF GENERAL PSYCHIATRY 311 (H. Goldman ed., 2d ed. 1988) ("[Psychosurgery] has fallen from favor now that the efficacy of antipsychotic medications has been established.").

[10]*Hearings, supra* note 1, at 340; P. BREGGIN, TOXIC PSYCHIATRY 54 (1991) ("emotionality fades" and there is a "weakening of initiative"); E. VALENSTEIN, *supra* note 2, at 55–56, 298–307; E. VALENSTEIN, *supra* note 4, at 255–56 (study finding significant decrement in IQ following lobotomy); Chorover, *supra* note 4, at 234; Robitscher, *Psychosurgery and Other Somatic Means of Altering Behavior,* 2 BULL. AM. ACAD. PSYCHIATRY & L. 7, 16 (1974); Vaughan, *supra* note 2, at 41–42. Walter Freeman, the dean of American lobotomy, who himself performed more than 4,000 such operations, later acknowledged these side effects: "What the investigator misses most in the more highly intelligent individuals is their ability to introspect, to speculate, to philosophize, especially in regard to one's self. . . . [O]n the whole psychosurgery reduces creativity, sometimes to the vanishing point." Freeman, *Psychosurgery, in* 2 AMERICAN HANDBOOK OF PSYCHIATRY 1524, 1526–35 (S. Arieti ed., 1959).

[11]*Hearings, supra* note 1, at 340 (testimony of Bertram Brown, former director of NIMH). *See* E. VALENSTEIN, *supra* note 4, at 284; Bolwig, *supra* note 1, at 112 ("frontal leukotomy is now viewed with clinical revulsion").

[12]H. CLARK, ALTERING BEHAVIOR: THE ETHICS OF CONTROLLED EXPERIENCE 93 (1986); E. VALENSTEIN, *supra* note 2, at 316–26; Breggin, *The Return of Lobotomy and Psychosurgery,* 118 CONG. REC. E1602 (daily ed. Feb. 24, 1972); Chorover, *supra* note 4, at 235; Older, *supra* note 6, at 661–62.

[13]V. MARK & F. ERVIN, VIOLENCE AND THE BRAIN 71–85 (1970); E. VALENSTEIN, *supra* note 4, at 284–85; Chorover, *supra* note 4, at 235–37; Goldman, *Introduction to Psychiatric Treatment, in* REVIEW OF GENERAL PSYCHIATRY, *supra* note 9, at 504. Stereotaxic methods have been regarded as an effective treatment for intractable affective disorders. *See* Honig et al., *The Stalemate Position,* 33 INT'L J. SOC. PSYCHIATRY 195 (1987). For a discussion of stereotaxic techniques, see BOSCH, STEREOTAXIC TECHNIQUES IN CLINICAL NEUROSURGERY 130–44 (1986).

area is thought to play a critical role in mediating emotional reactions.[14] Between 400 and 500 psychosurgical operations per year were performed in the early 1970s in the United States[15] by less than 150 neurosurgeons.[16] The numbers declined rapidly thereafter,[17] and

---

[14]The term "limbus" refers to a border or a margin, and, in the mammalian brain, the limbic system is comprised of a number of regions that collectively form a border around certain phylogenetically old or "lower" brain regions that are found in reptiles as well as in mammals. In traditional anatomical terms, the limbic system is comprised of certain "primitive" portions of the cerebral cortex—including the hippocampus, hippocampal gyrus and cingulate gyrus—and a number of deeper-lying structures with which the limbic cortex has primary connections—including the amygdala, septal nuclei, anterior thalamic nuclei and hypothalamus. Overlying the limbic system, especially in the primates, is the enormous mushrooming neocortex with which are usually associated various "higher cognitive functions" such as the development of written and spoken languages. From a schematic standpoint, then, the limbic system occupies an intermediate position between what may loosely be called the "lower" and the "higher" systems of the brain. It therefore seems ideally situated to receive, transform and transmit signals passing between phylogenetically old brain structures involved in stereotyped behavior patterns and visceral and glandular responses, on the one hand, and phylogenetically newer brain regions involved in sensation, perception, thought, language and other complex social acts, on the other hand. . . .

In summary, the limbic system appears to derive information from many sources and to operate in terms of the diverse emotional feelings that ultimately guide behavior required for self-preservation and the preservation of the species. In human beings, limbic mechanisms appear to underlie the entire range of affective functions from which we derive our sense of individuality and those concepts of reality that are fundamental to our beliefs concerning what is true and important.

Chorover, *supra* note 4, at 237. *See also* V. MARK & F. ERVIN, *supra* note 13, at 13–24; E. VALENSTEIN, *supra* note 2, at 47–50, 274–77. The theory underlying surgical intervention into the limbic system has been described and questioned by Restak:

According to limbic-system theory, disturbed emotional patterns (violence, deep depressions, suicidal tendencies, etc.) are partly the results of a form of "short circuitry" between the limbic system and the rest of the brain. Cutting of the amygdala or cingulum is intended to interrupt these faulty "connections" in the hope that new connections will develop or that the interruption will abolish the disturbed behavior patterns. In actuality, the correlation between behavior patterns and limbic structures is at best disputable.

Restak, *supra* note 3, at 56. In his report prepared for the National Commission, Valenstein, reviewing the purported physiological rationale for psychosurgery, concluded that "[m]any of the arguments have to be viewed as 'pseudophysiological' in that the rationale is supported by analogies that imply some physiological process, but do not actually provide any specific explanatory mechanisms." Valenstein, *The Practice of Psychosurgery: A Survey of the Literature (1971–1976), in* APPENDIX: PSYCHOSURGERY I–10 (DHEW Pub. No. (OS) 77-0002 (1977)) [hereinafter APPENDIX: PSYCHOSURGERY]. A survey of some leading psychosurgeons conducted by Valenstein "in order to obtain their views on the specificity of brain targets in psychosurgery," found "such strong and significant disagreement among those who practice psychosurgery, [that] it cannot be convincingly argued that our understanding of the physiological basis of psychosurgery has advanced very far." *Id.* at I-16-17. For a neurophysiological explanation of the therapeutic effects of psychosurgery, suggesting that the procedure works by restoring normal neurotransmitter equilibrium in limbic structures, see Corkin et al., *Safety and Efficacy of Cingulotomy for Pain and Psychiatric Disorder, in* MODERN CONCEPTS OF PSYCHIATRIC SURGERY 253, 268 (E. Hitchcock et al. eds., 1979) [hereinafter MODERN CONCEPTS IN PSYCHIATRIC SURGERY]; Hofstatter & Girgis, *Neurotransmitter Mechanisms Underlying Psychiatric Surgery, Electroconvulsive Therapy and Antidepressive Drug Therapy, in* MODERN CONCEPTS OF PSYCHIATRIC SURGERY, *supra,* at 3, 8–9.

[15]Valenstein, *supra* note 14, at I-26-27 (400–500 annually). It is difficult to estimate the extent of psychosurgery because much of it is performed by private practitioners and the government compiles no data. B. BROWN ET AL., *supra* note 1, at 3. The 500 per-year estimate for the period of the early 1970s represented an increase over the previous 15 years. *Id.* Estimates of the extent of psychosurgery performed annually in the 1970s in other countries included between 200 and 250 operations in England, 83 in Australia, 29 in Canada, 30 in India, 15–25 in Japan, 40–53 in Czechoslovakia, and 10–25 in Mexico. Valenstein, *supra,* at I-26, I-31-34. At that time, psychosurgery was also known to be performed regularly in Spain, Argentina, Poland, France, Germany, Holland, Denmark, Sweden, and Finland, but not in the Soviet Union, where it was outlawed in the early 1950s. *Id.* at I–34.

following a critical report by a national commission in 1977, use of the procedure has become rare.[18] There is still interest in psychosurgery around the world, but "the existence of alternative treatments and the opposition to psychosurgery make it unlikely that there will be any substantial increase in psychosurgery."[19] Thus, "psychosurgery is rarely used at present and has been clouded with myriad ethical and legal issues."[20]

B. Effectiveness and Hazards

Although the newer psychosurgical techniques reduce adverse side effects, the therapeutic effects appear to be similar to lobotomy. The procedure is less a cure than a pacifier. Psychiatric symptoms are not removed; rather, patients' emotional responses to their symptoms are reduced.[21] Their reaction to unpleasant sensations is diminished, and they are no longer concerned with the previously disturbing manifestations of their illness.[22] This diminished reaction and emotional responsiveness also explains the unwanted personality changes that appear to persist in some patients with the newer techniques, although to a considerably lesser extent than with lobotomy. The newer procedures have been reported to cause intellectual deterioration, emotional blunting, and undesirable behavioral responses and social adjustment.[23] However, "the risk of permanent adverse intellectual, emotional, and physical side effects [has been] reported as minimal."[24] In a well-publicized 1973 case,

---

[16]A 1976 estimate of 500 procedures per year prepared by an American Psychiatric Association Task Force was arrived at following a mailing to all members of the American Association of Neurological Surgeons and the Congress of Neurological Surgeons (1,902 individuals). *See* Schmeck, *Decline Reported in Psychosurgery,* N.Y. TIMES, June 12, 1976, at 20. Of the 1,481 responding (78%), 110 American neurosurgeons reported that they perform psychosurgery. Valenstein, *supra* note 14, at I-24-25. If the percentage of those responding who perform psychosurgery (7.5%) remains the same for those not responding, the total of American psychosurgeons would be 141. *Id.* at I–26. *See also* E. VALENSTEIN, *supra* note 4, at 284 ("In 1971, over seventy neurosurgeons in the United States had performed some psychosurgery.").

[17]*See* Donnelly, *supra* note 9, at 256 ("[P]sychosurgery procedures per year has dropped rapidly in recent years."); Schwartz & Africa, *supra* note 9, at 311 ("[F]ewer than 400 such surgeries were performed in the USA in 1977, and psychosurgery is now rarely used in the USA."); Valenstein, *supra* note 14, at I-27.

[18]NAT'L COMM'N PSYCHOSURGERY REPORT, *supra* note 8, at 22. Simon, *Somatic Therapies and the Law, in* 1 REVIEW OF CLINICAL PSYCHIATRY AND THE LAW 63 (R. Simon ed., 1990). Boston's Massachusetts General Hospital is one of the world's only hospitals with regular psychosurgery practices, and only 15 to 20 psychosurgeries are performed there per year. The psychosurgical procedure performed at Massachusetts General Hospital is a pinpoint procedure called *cingulotomy,* and it is only used in the most desperate cases. Miller, WALL ST. J., Dec. 1, 1994, at 1, 12.

[19]VALENSTEIN, *supra* note 4, at 290.

[20]Simon, *supra* note 18, at 63. *See also* R. SIMON, CLINICAL PSYCHIATRY AND THE LAW 252–53 (2d ed. 1992).

[21]Breggin, *New Information in the Debate Over Psychosurgery, in Hearings, supra* note 1, at 437, 441–49 (reviewing studies and reports).

[22]*Id.*

[23]A paranoid patient who is tortured by hallucinations and delusions may still hear the threatening voices after the operation, but he is less concerned about them. Likewise, after the operation, a severe obsessive-compulsive patient is able to overcome his phobias or compulsive urges because their emotional impact is reduced.

Id.

[24]Henn, *supra* note 4, at 1680.

Kaimowitz v. Department of Mental Health, a three-judge Michigan court concluded, based on extensive expert testimony, that adverse effects of psychosurgery are as follows:[25]

> Psychosurgery flattens emotional responses, leads to lack of abstract reasoning ability, leads to a lack of capacity for new learning and causes general sedation and apathy. It can lead to impairment of memory and in some instances unexpected responses to psychosurgery are observed. It has been found, for example, that heightened rage reaction can follow surgical intervention on the amygdala, just as placidity can.

However, in its 1977 report on psychosurgery, the National Commission for the Protection of Human Subjects of Biomedical and Behavioral Research considered data unavailable to the Michigan court and found the court's conclusions concerning the hazards of the newer procedures to be overstated.[26] The emotional and intellectual side effects are often difficult to assess in view of the lack of objective tests reported on in the evaluative literature and the unavailability of such tests to measure intellectual changes following psychosurgery.[27] However, the most extensive review of the literature ever conducted, prepared for the National Commission by Elliot Valenstein, a leading psychosurgery scholar, concluded that "there is little justification for the frequent claim that there is no intellectual change following surgery. . . ."[28] On the other hand, the same review concluded that personality changes following psychosurgery "are relatively infrequent and characterized as 'mild' and 'transient,' "[29] and that "[t]he risk of permanent adverse intellectual, emotional, and physical side effects is reported as minimal . . . in sharp contrast to the results from the older lobotomy operations. . . ."[30] Of course, a substantial number of cases are not reported in the literature—at most 27% of practicing psychosurgeons were found to publish their results[31]—and the large number of psychosurgeons who perform three or fewer procedures per year, a number probably too small to permit the development or maintenance of an adequate level of professional skill, suggests the possibility that reports in the literature, on which the National Commission's conclusions were heavily based, may not adequately reflect the extent of adverse effects suffered by patients.[32]

---

[25]Civ. No. 73-19434-AW, Slip op. at 17 (Cir. Ct. Wayne County [Mich.] July 10, 1973), *excerpted at* 42 U.S.L.W. 2063 (July 31, 1973). *See* Chorover, *supra* note 4, at 247; Donnelly, *supra* note 9, at 260–62; Older, *supra* note 6, at 663, 669. Valenstein, reviewing all published reports of physical and emotional complications of psychosurgical procedures performed after 1965, lists the following claimed adverse effects:

> the physical complications . . . [include] seizures, weight changes, paralysis, dyskinesias, loss of smell, bladder or bowel incontinence and endocrine changes. . . .

> Emotional and behavioral complications are described primarily by such terms as lethargy (loss of motivation and/or affect), generalized or specific disinhibition (volubility, lowered personal standards, carelessness, immature behavior, shoplifting, extravagant behavior, irritability, aggression), increases or decreases in sexuality, and inability to work.

Valenstein, *supra* note 14, at I–80.

[26]NAT'L COMM'N PSYCHOSURGERY REPORT, *supra* note 8, at 22.

[27]*Id.*

[28]Valenstein, *supra* note 14, at I–51.

[29]*Id.* at I–89.

[30]*Id.* at I–96.

[31]*Id.* at I–29. For discussion of the "publication effect," see Russell, *The Power of Behavior Control: A Critique of Behavior Modification Methods,* 30 J. CLINICAL PSYCHOL. 111, 113–14 (1974); Grundner et al., Behavior Modification: An Empirical Analysis of the "State of the Art" 14, 16 (Oct. 1974) (unpublished paper) (suggesting the need for a behavioral "Journal of Negative Results").

[32]Valenstein and the National Commission both acknowledge that "a considerable amount of experience with psychosurgery does not become part of the scientific literature." NAT'L COMM'N PSYCHOSURGERY REPORT, *supra* note 8, at 28; Valenstein, *supra* note 14, at I–29.

Despite lack of knowledge and agreement concerning the extent and duration of adverse effects accompanying the newer procedures, psychosurgery may continue to be used, although rarely, to relieve the symptoms of patients suffering from a variety of conditions when other treatment methods have proved unavailing. Although not used in schizophrenia,[33] psychosurgery sometimes is used as a treatment of last resort for chronically and severely disturbed neurotic individuals, particularly of the obsessive–compulsive type, and for chronically depressed patients.[34] In addition, it has been used to treat pedophilia, frigidity, nymphomania, alcoholism, drug addiction, compulsive stealing, compulsive gambling, obesity, childhood hyperkinesis,[35] homosexuality, and (in its most controversial application) violent and aggressive behavior.[36] Proponents of psychosurgery have cited impressive rates of patient improvement which, it is claimed, more than offset the adverse effects of surgery.[37] However, virtually all studies of psychosurgery have been retrospective

---

[33]H. KAPLAN ET AL., *supra* note 5, at 483 ("Although sophisticated approaches to psychosurgery for schizophrenia may eventually be developed, psychosurgery is no longer considered an appropriate treatment of schizophrenia, but is being used on a limited experimental basis."); Donnelly, *supra* note 9, at 260 ("consensus in U.S. that psychosurgery is not effective in schizophrenia."). *But see* Valenstein, *supra* note 14, at I-169-70 (letter from Robert G. Sheppard), I-171-72 (letter from M. Hunter Brown).

[34]P. BREGGIN, *supra* note 10, at 261–62; P. JANICAK ET AL., PRINCIPLES AND PRACTICE OF PSYCHOPHAR-MACOTHERAPY 472 (1993); Bolwig, *supra* note 1, at 114 ("best results seem to come in the treatment of chronic depression and obsessive-compulsive disorders."); Goldman, *Introduction to Psychiatric Treatment, in* REVIEW OF GENERAL PSYCHIATRY, *supra* note 9, at 504; Nagy, *Anxiety Disorders, in* CLINICAL PSYCHIATRY FOR MEDICAL STUDENTS 259 (A. Stoudemire ed., 2d. ed. 1994) ("In severe, debilitating cases that have failed all attempts at more conservative treatment, psychosurgical techniques . . . can be beneficial."). *See* E. VALENSTEIN, *supra* note 2, at 317; Valenstein, *supra* note 14, at I-37. Patients who indicate overlapping of severe depressive symptoms, including vegetative symptoms, obsession, compulsion, and chronic high levels of anxiety, are most likely to benefit from psychosurgical procedure. Henn, *supra* note 4, at 1679.

[35]J. KLEINIG, ETHICAL ISSUES IN PSYCHOSURGERY 34–35 (1985); Dieckmann et al., *Long-Term Results of Hypothalamotomy in Sexual Offenses, in* MODERN CONCEPTS IN PSYCHIATRIC SURGERY, *supra* note 14, at 187; Older, *supra* note 6, at 662; Valenstein, *supra* note 14, at I-42-43, I-45-46 (tables summarizing data on different diagnostic categories for which psychosurgery was used in the 1970s).

[36]J. KLEINIG, *supra* note 35, at 32-34; E. VALENSTEIN, *supra* note 2, at 209–63; Mayanagi & Sano, *Long-Term Follow-Up Results of the Posterodeial Hypothalamotomy, in* MODERN CONCEPTS IN PSYCHIATRIC SURGERY, *supra* note 13, at 197; Schvarcz, *Results of Separate Versus Combined Amygdalotomy and Hypothalomotomy for Behavior Disorders, in* MODERN CONCEPTS IN PSYCHIATRIC SURGERY, *supra,* at 205; Valenstein, *supra* note 1, at 43–44; Vaughan, *supra* note 2, at 47–54. The leading American proponents of this use of psychosurgery are Vernon Mark, a neurosurgeon, and Frank Ervin, a psychiatrist. *See* V. MARK & F. ERVIN, *supra* note 13, at 92–97; Mark, *A Psychosurgeon's Case for Psychosurgery,* PSYCHOL. TODAY, July 1974, at 28; V. Mark, *Brain Surgery in Aggressive Epileptics,* 3 HASTINGS CTR. REP., Feb. 1973, at 1. A leading proponent of psychosurgery for hyperkinetic children is O.J. Andy, former head of the Department of Neurosurgery of the University of Mississippi. *See Hearings, supra* note 1, at 348 (testimony of Andy). Andy, *The Decision-Making Process in Psychosurgery,* 13 DUQUESNE L. REV. 783 (1975). The use of psychosurgery for controlling violence has been heavily criticized. The leading critic is Peter Breggin, a psychiatrist. *See, e.g.,* Breggin, *Psychosurgery for Political Purposes,* 13 DUQUESNE L. REV. 841 (1975). Ayub Ommaya, then director of the research section of the National Institute of Neurological Diseases and Stroke, testified in the *Kaimowitz* case that "[t]he role of psychosurgery . . . has little, if any, applicability for violent behavior." Restak, *supra* note 3, at 57.

[37]H. KAPLAN ET AL., *supra* note 5, at 1013 ("When patients are carefully selected, between 50 and 70 percent have significant therapeutic improvement with psychosurgery. Fewer than 3 percent become worse."); Valenstein, *supra* note 14, at I–77. *See, e.g.,* Baily et al., *The Control of Affective Illness by Cingulotractomy: A Review of 150 Cases,* 2 MED. J. AUSTL. 366 (1973) (up to 94% of patients improved); Bernstein et al., *Lobotomy in Private Practice: Long-Term Follow-up,* 32 ARCHIVES GEN. PSYCHIATRY 1041 (1975); Bridges, *Psychosurgery Today: Psychiatric Aspects,* 65 PROCEEDINGS ROYAL SOC'Y MED. 1104 (1972); Bridges et al., *A Comparative Review of Patients with Obsessional Neurosis and with Depression Treated by Psychosurgery,* 123 BRIT. J. PSYCHIATRY 663 (1973); Knight, *Neurosurgical Aspects of Psychosurgery,* 65 PROCEEDINGS ROYAL SOC'Y MED. 1099 (1972); Older, *supra* note 6, at 663 (citing studies); Strom-Olsen & Carlisle, *Bi-Frontal Stereotactic Tractotomy,* 118 BRIT. J. PSYCHIATRY 141 (1971); Sweet, *Treatment of Medically Intractable Mental Disease by Limited Frontal Leukotomy—Justifiable?,* 289 N. ENGL. J. MED. 1117 (1973).

anecdotal reports by proponents of the technique, rather than prospective control studies; therefore, the result is that the evaluative literature in this area is seriously flawed.[38] Using a standard rating scale of scientific merit in which ratings are assigned on a 6-point scale from 1 to 6 (with 1 representing the best scientific design and use of data and 6 representing only descriptive information and lacking comparison groups), almost 90% of the American psychosurgery evaluative literature received a rating of 4 or higher—a rating of such low scientific value that it is unlikely "that an animal study with such a low rating would be accepted for publication by the editors of a respected experimental journal"—and 41% received a rating of 6.[39] In view of the inadequacies of the existing evaluative literature, it must be concluded that "the current state of knowledge is insufficient to permit a clearcut comparison of the potential benefits and possible risks of psychosurgery."[40]

As part of its congressionally mandated review of psychosurgery, and in view of the lack of adequate existing studies, the National Commission for the Protection of Human Subjects of Biomedical and Behavioral Research commissioned two largely retrospective studies performed by independent teams of scientists and clinicians of separate groups of

---

[38]According to the National Commission:

> The ideal study to evaluate the efficacy of psychosurgery would be a prospective one, in which patients undergoing psychosurgery would be matched with controls who had been recommended for surgery but did not undergo the procedure, or with patients for whom alternative therapies, i.e., drugs and psychotherapies had been administered. It would define specific surgical interventions, including adequate and consistent pre-operative evaluation of all patients using a selected battery of tests, and would permit follow-up according to a specified protocol over an established time period.

NAT'L COMM'N, Psychosurgery, 5 (June 20, 1975) (unpublished preliminary paper). However, "[i]nadequacy of pre- and post-operative behavioral and psychological testing, lack of long-term follow-up of patients, and general inadequacies of clinical and behavioral reporting characterize much of the published literature." *Psychosurgery Report of the Nat'l Institute of Mental Health*, Jan. 21, 1974, in INDIVIDUAL RIGHTS AND THE FEDERAL ROLE IN BEHAVIOR MODIFICATION, 93d Cong., 2d Sess., 142, 144 (1974) [hereinafter NIMH REPORT]. In addition, "most of the data are uncontrolled and presented in terms of improvement on vaguely defined scales." E. VALENSTEIN, *supra* note 4, at 321; *see also* Bolwig, *supra* note 1, at 112 ("controlled studies are impossible to perform."). "In general, insufficient details are provided [and] these reports have customarily been presented by those doing the surgery. . . ." *Id.* at 318; *accord* Vaughan, *supra* note 2, at 43–44. "Because many of the judgments are based on subjective impressions, often from limited samples of the patient's behavior, and from information obtained from people who may not want to offend the physician, there are any number of ways the results may reflect unconscious bias." Valenstein, *supra* note 14, at I–59. The existing literature may also be seriously incomplete since, according to one study, at most only 27% of psychosurgeons publish their results. NAT'L COMM'N PSYCHOSURGERY REPORT, *supra* note 8, at 28; Valenstein, *supra*, at I–29. Studies reporting positive results have also taken inadequate account of the probably strong placebo effect in psychosurgery. Annas & Glantz, *Psychosurgery: The Law's Response*, 54 B.U. L. REV. 249, 259–60 (1974); Corkin et al., *supra* note 14, at 266, 268; Valenstein, *supra*, at I-63-65. Moreover, "[a] growing body of evidence now suggests that the new wave of American psychosurgeons have also engaged in the practice of exaggerating good results, ignoring side effects, and even distorting the outcomes of treatment." Older, *supra* note 6, at 664. The controversy surrounding favorable retrospective reports by proponents of psychosurgery can be illustrated by comparing the favorable reports by Mark and Ervin concerning two of their celebrated patients, Thomas R. and Julia S. *See* V. MARK & F. ERVIN, *supra* note 13, at 93–108, with contradictory reports by Breggin, *supra* note 36, at 844 and 846, and Chorover, *supra* note 4, at 240–45.

[39]NAT'L COMM'N PSYCHOSURGERY REPORT, *supra* note 8, at 29.

[40]Valenstein, *supra* note 14, at I–60. A review of the literature revealed only 10 reasonably well-controlled studies and found that "[m]ost, possibly all, of these investigations seem to have serious methodological limitations." Templer, *The Efficacy of Psychosurgery*, 9 BIOLOGICAL PSYCHIATRY 205, 208 (1974). The study found that "the main support for the efficacy of psychosurgery rests upon clinical impression . . ." and concluded that "if the scrupulously objective observer is asked whether psychosurgery is effective, he must say that he is not certain." *Id.*

patients who had undergone psychosurgery.[41] The two teams evaluated a total of 61 patients receiving four different psychosurgical procedures performed by four different surgeons between 1965 and 1975, as well as control groups.[42] Following a series of psychological, neurological, and electroencephalographic examinations designed to measure intelligence, attention, memory, visual–spatial abilities, verbal and nonverbal fluency, ability to shift sets in categorization, and motor functions, as well as interviews with the patients and their families,[43] the studies found ''evidence that (1) more than half of the patients improved significantly following psychosurgery, although a few were worse and some unchanged, and (2) none of the patients experienced significant neurological or psychological impairment attributable to the surgery.''[44] Moreover, with some exceptions, both reports found no significant cognitive deficits attributable to psychosurgery.[45] Although recognizing that both reports suffer from the inherent limitations of retrospective studies[46] and the possibility that the relationship between the particularly concerned and attentive surgeons involved in the studies and their devoted patients may have played a central role in achieving favorable results, the Commission concluded that ''[t]hese studies appear to rebut any presumption that all forms of psychosurgery are unsafe and ineffective.''[47] Finding ''that certain psychosurgical procedures are less hazardous than previously thought and potentially of significant therapeutic value,''[48] the Commission encouraged the former United States Department of Health, Education, and Welfare to support further research, subject to institutional review board approval such as generally precedes research involving human subjects and limited to consenting patients, to evaluate the safety and efficacy of psy-

---

[41]Mirsky & Orzack, *Final Report on Psychosurgery Pilot Study, in* APPENDIX: PSYCHOSURGERY, *supra* note 14, at 11–1; Teuber et al., *A Study of Cingulotomy in Man, in* APPENDIX: PSYCHOSURGERY, *supra,* at 111–1. The Teuber study examined 18 of 34 patients preoperatively as well as postoperatively; the Mirsky & Orzack study was exclusively retrospective.

[42]NAT'L COMM'N PSYCHOSURGERY REPORT, *supra* note 8, at 32.

[43]*Id.* at 32–33, 58.

[44]*Id.* at 58. A continuation study of one of the two groups subsequently reported similar results. Corkin et al., *supra* note 14, at 253.

[45]NAT'L COMM'N PSYCHOSURGERY REPORT, *supra* note 8, at 37. The Mirsky and Orzack study found impairment in some patients on the Wisconsin card-sorting task, a test of the patient's ability to shift from one category to another. *Id.*; Mirsky & Orzack, *supra* note 41, at II–37. The Teuber study found impairment in learning the tactical stylus maze. NAT'L COMM'N PSYCHOSURGERY REPORT, *supra,* at 36–37; Teuber et al., *supra* note 41, at III–68. Mirsky & Orzack hypothesized ''that recovery from the severe and crippling psychiatric illnesses from which these patients suffer may in some cases be made at a price—the loss of certain cognitive capacities.'' Mirsky & Orzack, *supra,* at II–38. For a subsequent study finding no significant lasting deterioration of cognitive functions in a group of 37 patients who had undergone psychosurgery, see Vasko & Kullberg, *Results of Psychological Testing of Cognitive Functions in Patients Undergoing Stereotactic Surgery, in* MODERN CONCEPTS IN PSYCHIATRIC SURGERY, *supra* note 14, at 303.

[46]THE NAT'L COMM'N PSYCHOSURGERY REPORT, *supra* note 8, at 26, referred to

the acknowledged limitations of a retrospective study: that there would be no preoperative evaluation of the patients, performed by the same team, against which to measure gains or losses of function clearly attributable to the surgical intervention. Such preoperative data as would exist might be uneven both in quantity and in quality, since the data would be obtainable only through medical records provided by psychiatrists and surgeons directly responsible for the patients' care.

See also Mirsky & Orzack, *supra* note 41, at II-38-40.

[47]NAT'L COMM'N PSYCHOSURGERY REPORT, *supra* note 8, at 37–38.

[48]*Id.*

chosurgery.[49] Even though the studies prepared for the Commission suggest that certain of the procedures may be less experimental than had been thought, psychosurgery must still be regarded as a strictly experimental procedure in view of the unpredictability of outcome and because its effectiveness and safety have not yet been established by recognized methods of clinical evaluation.[50]

C. Abuse of Psychosurgery and Relative Intrusiveness

In addition to the widespread and premature experimentation with lobotomy in the 1940s, abuses in the use of psychosurgery have included its use on children as young as 4 years of age,[51] its unregulated use by surgeons without prior review or approval by a third

---

[49]*Id.* at 57–61, 70–72. The federal government prohibits funded research on psychosurgery. NIMH REPORT, *supra* note 39, at 26. One Commission member dissented from this recommendation. NAT'L COMM'N PSY-CHOSURGERY REPORT, *supra* note 8, at 73–76. For criticism of the Commission's conclusions as unsupported by its evidence, see Annas, *Psychosurgery: Procedural Safeguards,* 7 HASTINGS CTR. REP. 11–12 (April 1977). Annas contends that eliminating from the 61 patients studied those whose surgery was designed to relieve emotional responses to pain—cases that arguably should not be deemed psychosurgery—reduces the success rate to about 43%. Moreover, almost half of the remaining patients encountered success only after prior surgery had not succeeded. Had these prior attempts been counted as failures, the overall success rate in the nonpain group would have dropped to less than 30%, less than the placebo effect identified for surgery. Professor Annas argues that "given the built-in bias in the selection process, the very limited sampling, and problems in testing and comparability, . . . no conclusions about psychosurgery in general can be drawn from the Commission's data." *Id.* at 12.

[50]NAT'L COMM'N PSYCHOSURGERY REPORT, *supra* note 8, at 10, 59 (safety and efficacy not yet demonstrated to the degree that psychosurgical procedures may be deemed "accepted practice"), 70–72; *Id.* at 55 (statement of Nat'l Ass'n for Mental Health, Inc.); NIMH REPORT, *supra* note 38, at 144; PSYCHIATRY AND SEX PSYCHOPATH LEGISLATION, supra note 27, at 916; Memorandum of *Amicus Curiae,* American Psychiatric Ass'n, Human Rights Committee of one of the hospitals sought a modification of Standard 9 to permit greater flexibility in administration of ECT. On Oct. 1, 1974, the court requested proposed revisions from *amici,* one of which was the American Psychiatric Association. Brief of *Amicus Curiae,* American Psychiatric Ass'n, Wyatt v. Hardin, [1976] 1 MENTAL DISABILITY L. REP. 55 (M.D. Ala., Feb. 28, 1975, *modified* July 1, 1975) (No. 3195-N) (addressing the question of suggested amendments to Standard 9). The American Psychiatric Association, founded in 1844, is the largest association of physicians specializing in psychiatry, containing a high percentage of the psychiatrists in America. Memorandum in Support of Motion of American Psychiatric Ass'n for Leave to Participate as *Amicus Curiae,* Wyatt v. Hardin, *supra.* The special procedures for ECT adopted by the court are set forth in 1 MENTAL DISABILITY L. REP. at 56–57 (1976); Chorover, *supra* note 4, at 247; Meister, *The Need for Policy, in* OPERATING ON THE MIND, *supra* note 2, at 169, 176–78; Vaughan, *supra* note 2, at 68; Restak, *supra* note 3, at 57; *contra Hearings, supra* note 1, at 350 (testimony of O.J. Andy); NAT'L COMM'N PSYCHOSURGERY REPORT, *supra* note 8, at 48 (statement of Charles A. Fager, of Am. Ass'n of Neurological Surgeons and the Cong. of Neurological Surgeons), 53 (statement of M. Hunter Brown).

[51]Older, *supra* note 6, at 669–70; Valenstein, *supra* note 14, at I-89-91. After describing the use of psychosurgery on young children, Older criticized the practice on the following grounds:

> One is that children often simply outgrow disorders of childhood. Many hard-to-manage children become productive adults, but no one ever grows a new amygdala. A second is that the justification for these operations on children is often tenuous in the extreme. Hyperkinesis is a category of disorder that is often used as a basis for surgery. Yet hyperkinesis, like minimal brain damage, is seen by many as a dumping ground for cases that do not readily fit other diagnostic categories. Young children have undergone psychosurgery on grounds as vague as "hyperoral tendencies," "wandering tendencies," and being "destructive." Aside from the vagueness of these descriptions, there is no apparent awareness on the part of the surgeon that wandering and destructive behaviors may be appropriate responses to certain situations.

Older, *supra,* at 670. *See also* NAT'L COMM'N PSYCHOSURGERY REPORT, *supra* note 8, at 47 (statement of Kenneth Heilman of the Int'l Neuropsychological Soc'y); *Id.* at 53–54 (statement of Ernest A. Bates). The Nat'l Comm'n recommended imposing stringent conditions on the performance of psychosurgery on children. *Id.* at 67–70.

party[52] and without adequate exploration of alternative treatments,[53] its performance by neurosurgeons who operate so infrequently that it may not be possible "to maintain adequate skill of competence,"[54] and its administration pursuant to procedures that do not conform to requirements for experimental techniques.[55] Moreover, as with the other treatment modalities, psychosurgery has been used for nonconsenting patients and for institutionalized patients who may be incapable of giving informed consent.[56] Psychosurgery presents the disturbing potential of use for social control purposes, particularly

---

[52]*Hearings, supra* note 1, at 354 (testimony of O.J. Andy as to lack of peer or other review concerning the decision to use psychosurgery); M. PINES, THE BRAIN CHANGERS: SCIENTISTS AND THE NEW MIND CONTROL 226–27 (1973); Annas & Glantz, *supra* note 38, at 260 ("Dr. Thomas Ballentine of the Massachusetts General Hospital regularly performs cingulotomies for depression, anxiety states, obsessional neurosis, and intractable pain without independent review of either his surgical protocols or his consent procedures."). These practices are inconsistent with what has been described as "a growing consensus that there should be some form of advance review mechanism for weighing proposals relating to psychosurgery." Beresford, *Judicial Review of Medical Treatment Programs,* 12 CAL. W. L. REV. 356 (1976). Although a number of states have enacted legislation regulating psychosurgery, *e.g.,* FLA. STAT. § 458.325 (1995), "the practice of psychosurgery, despite its potential for medical harm, is largely unregulated and unreviewed." Knowles, *Beyond the "Cuckoo's Nest": A Proposal for Federal Regulation of Psychosurgery,* 12 HARV. J. LEG. 610, 626 (1975).

[53]E. VALENSTEIN, *supra* note 4, at 316; *See also* NIMH REPORT, *supra* note 38, at 143 ("Psychosurgery critics claim, often correctly, that confinement in an institution does not guarantee adequate attempts at therapeutic measures short of psychosurgery, and that psychosurgery is frequently performed before other alternatives are tried to an adequate extent"); Bolwig, *supra* note 1, at 114 ("The indiscriminate use of this type of therapy is a major factor that has lead to disquiet, so that the procedure has been abandoned or made illegal in many parts of the world."); Salpukas, *Psychosurgery Case in Middle West Poses Complex Questions in Medicine and Law,* N.Y. TIMES, April 2, 1973, at 19 (quoting Ayub Ommaya of NIMH as stating that of the many patients referred to him for psychosurgery with the evaluation that all other treatments had been unsuccessfully attempted, "in the majority of cases we find that this is not really true, that what is commonly available or practically available has not been done."); *Valenstein, supra* note 14, at I-85-86 (psychosurgery frequently performed on obsessive–compulsive and phobic patients without exploration of behavior therapy techniques indicating considerable success for these conditions). For purposes of exploring treatment alternatives to psychosurgery, hospitalization alone should not constitute treatment. Older, *supra* note 6, at 672. For proposed criteria of exploration of alternative therapies, see Lehman & Ostrow, *Quizzing the Expert: Clinical Criteria for Psychosurgery,* 9 HOSP. PHYSICIAN 24 (1973).

[54]NAT'L COMM'N PSYCHOSURGERY REPORT, *supra* note 8, at 28; *Valenstein, supra* note 14, at I-27-28 (25% of operations are performed by surgeons doing three or fewer operations per year; 70–80% of psychosurgeons perform less than three operations per year and many perform only one per year).

[55]Annas & Glantz, *supra* note 38, at 260. The National Institute of Mental Health made the following recommendation in this regard:

> Psychosurgery should be regarded as an experimental therapy at the present time—as such, it should not be considered to be a form of therapy which can be made generally available to the public because of the peculiar nature of the procedure and of the problems with which it deals. Special constraints that apply to any experimental therapeutic procedure are required and the procedure should only be undertaken in those circumstances where there is special competence and experience and in institutional environments where appropriate safeguards are documented to be available.
>
> The designation of psychosurgery as an experimental therapy imposes a number of stringent but essential constraints on practice: comprehensive research protocols must be developed whenever psychosurgery is undertaken in order to assure that the maximum scientific value and information is obtained; psychosurgery should be conducted only in hospitals with strong and intimate affiliation with, and commitment to, academic sciences; it is absolutely essential that informed consent procedures be given primary consideration; every effort must be made to insure that all reasonable alternative therapies, based on our present state of knowledge, are attempted to an adequate extent before resorting to psychosurgery.

NIMH REPORT, *supra* note 38, at 144–45.

[56]Halleck, *Legal and Ethical Aspects of Behavior Control,* 131 AM. J. PSYCHIATRY 382 (1974); Heldman, *Behavior Modification and Other Legal Imbroglios of Human Experimentation,* 52 J. URBAN L. 155, 164 n.40 (1974). *See* NIMH REPORT, *supra* note 38, at 40–41 (quoting a letter from an official of the Veterans Administration indicating that in V.A. hospitals where the patient's "capacity to form sound judgements for himself is seriously impaired" a variety of treatments, including psychosurgery, may at times be "insisted upon despite the patient's temporary objections"). For judicial challenges to non-consensual psychosurgery, see Mackey v. Procunier, No.73-2203 (9th Cir., Sept. 5, 1973), 2 PRISON L. RPTR. 486 (1973); Chickensky v. Providence Hosp., Civ. No.74-000422-GC (Cir. Ct. Wayne County, Mich., *complaint filed,* Jan. 1974), *cited in* Heldman, *supra,* at 164 n.40. For a description of three cases challenging the validity of proxy consent to psychosurgery, see *Three Court Test for Psychosurgery,* MED. WORLD NEWS, Oct. 18, 1976 at 27.

for confined patients and prisoners,[57] and because of its calming effects, probably has been

---

[57]*See* NIMH REPORT, *supra* note 38, at 144 (''No psychosurgery should be performed on involuntarily confined persons or persons incapable of giving consent, either by reason of age or mental condition.''); M. PINES, *supra* note 54, at 227–28. When a patient is unable to consent to treatment the question of proxy arises.

The answer to this has given rise to a number of proposals for different solutions, to each of which cogent objections have been raised. In some states, legislatures have already enacted statutes either prohibiting psychosurgery outright or creating procedures to be followed in order for legally valid informed consent to be obtained, usually removing control of clinical decisions from the hands of physicians.

Donnelly, *supra* note 9, at 267. In Kaimowitz v. Department of Mental Health, Civ. No.73-19434-AW, *slip op.* at 25–29, (Cir. Ct. Wayne County [Mich.] July 10, 1973), *excerpted* at 42 U.S.L.W. 2063 (July 31, 1973), the court, in a case involving an involuntarily confined mental patient who had previously consented to psychosurgery, held that involuntary patients are incompetent as a matter of law to give informed consent to experimental psychosurgery:

Although an involuntarily detained mental patient may have a sufficient I.Q. to intellectually comprehend his circumstances ... the very nature of his incarceration diminishes the capacity to consent to psychosurgery. He is particularly vulnerable as a result of his mental condition, the deprivation stemming from involuntary confinement, and the effects of the phenomenon of ''institutionalization. . . .''

Institutionalization tends to strip the individual of the support which permits him to maintain his sense of self-worth and the value of his own physical and mental integrity. An involuntarily confined mental patient clearly has diminished capacity for making a decision about irreversible experimental psychosurgery. . . .

The second element of an informed consent is knowledge of the risk involved and the procedures to be undertaken. It was obvious from the record made in this case that the facts surrounding experimental brain surgery are profoundly uncertain, and the lack of knowledge on the subject makes a knowledgeable consent to psychosurgery literally impossible.

We turn now to the third element of an informed consent, that of voluntariness. It is obvious that the most important thing to a large number of involuntarily detained mental patients incarcerated for an unknown length of time, is freedom.

The Nuremberg standards require that the experimental subjects be so situated as to exercise free power of choice without the intervention of any element of force, fraud, deceit, duress, overreaching, or other ulterior form of constraint or coercion. It is impossible for an involuntarily detained mental patient to be free of ulterior forms of restraint or coercion when his very release from the institution may depend upon his cooperating with the institutional authorities and giving consent to experimental surgery.

The privileges of an involuntarily detained patient and the rights he exercises in the institution are within the control of the institutional authorities. . . .

The involuntarily detained mental patient is in an inherently coercive atmosphere even though no direct pressures may be placed upon him. He finds himself stripped of customary amenities and defenses. Free movement is restricted. He becomes a part of communal living subject to the control of the institutional authorities.

Involuntarily confined mental patients live in an inherently coercive institutional environment. Indirect and subtle psychological coercion has profound effect upon the patient population. Involuntarily confined patients cannot reason as equals with the doctors and administrators over whether they should undergo psychosurgery. They are not able to voluntarily give informed consent because of the inherent inequality in their position.

Although on the facts of *Kaimowitz,* the court may have reached the right result, see Burt, *Why We Should Keep Prisoners from the Doctors,* 5 HASTINGS CENTER REP. 25, Feb. 1975, its reasoning is unsatisfactory and its seemingly broad holding concerning the effects of institutionalization on the ability of patients to give informed consent would give rise to absurd and constitutionally dubious results. *See* NAT'L COMM'N PSYCHOSURGERY REPORT, *supra* note 8, at 19; Murphy, *Total Institutions and the Possibility of Consent to Organic Therapies,* 5 HUMAN RIGHTS 25 (1975); Wexler, *Mental Health Law and the Movement Toward Voluntary Treatment,* 62 CAL. L. REV. 671, 677–81 (1974); Winick, *Legal Limitations on Correctional Therapy and Research,* 65 MINN. L. REV. 331, 383–92 (1981); *infra* chapter 18.

Although *Kaimowitz* may deal too broadly with the impact of institutionalization on the ability of patients to give informed consent to psychosurgery, the voluntariness problem is a complex and troubling one. At least, the consent of vulnerable populations, such as confined patients and prisoners, should be scrutinized to prevent violation of the informed consent rule. NAT'L COMM'N PSYCHOSURGERY REPORT, *supra,* at 64–67 (recommending imposing extensive review and stringent conditions on the performance of psychosurgery on involuntarily confined mental patients and prisoners). An example of abuse in this area is the report of psychosurgery having been performed on three prisoners in a California prison hospital ''to control violent, aggressive spasms. . . .'' Aarons, *Brain Surgery Tested on 3 California Convicts,* WASHINGTON POST, Feb. 25, 1972, A1, *quoted in* Shapiro, *Legislating the Control of Behavior Control: Autonomy and the Coercive Use of Organic Therapies,* 47 So. CAL. L. REV. 237, 247 n.16 (1974). Although the prisoners gave consent to the operations, *id.,* it is reported that ''the consent form . . . explicitly stated that the prisoner would be released from solitary confinement in return for his 'consent' to treatment.'' Breggin, *supra* note 21, at 393.

used in some understaffed facilities for management and custodial purposes.[58]

Psychosurgery is thus a highly experimental treatment technique, the efficacy of which is yet to be demonstrated in scientifically adequate clinical studies. It is potentially hazardous and can severely impair the patient's intellectual and emotional capacities, although the incidence and duration of these serious effects may be considerably less than is commonly supposed. The most physically and mentally intrusive of all mental health treatment techniques, psychosurgery is irreversible, both in the perhaps trivial sense that destroyed brain tissue does not regenerate[59] and in the sense that it may result, at least in some cases, in permanent alteration in personality.[60] By directly modifying the patient's brain, psychosurgery produces major but largely unpredictable effects that cannot be resisted and that alter the individual's thoughts, feelings, behavior, and perhaps identity.[61] For these reasons psychosurgery, although deserving of further research subject to appropriate safeguards, must be considered the most intrusive of all mental health treatment techniques.[62]

---

[58]*Hearings, supra* note 1, at 347 (testimony of Brown); NAT'L COMM'N PSYCHOSURGERY REPORT, *supra* note 8, at 45–46 (statement of Congressman Louis Stokes); P. BREGGIN, *supra* note 12, at 261; J. KLEINIG, *supra* note 35, at 53–54, 124; E. VALENSTEIN, *supra* note 4, at 287; Annas, *supra* note 49, at 11; Breggin, *supra* note 21; Mearns, *Law and the Physical Control of the Mind: Experimentation in Psychosurgery,* 25 CASE W. L. REV. 565, 582–85, 601 (1975); Older, *supra* note 6, at 670–72; Ricketts, *Editorial: The New Psychosurgery,* 226 J. AM. MED. ASS'N 779 (1973) ("[T]he psychosurgery of today [for violent patients] can be more than therapy; it can be looked upon as manipulation of selected individuals for the protection of society."). For an allegation that psychosurgery is used more frequently with women than with men in order to keep women submissive and domesticated, see Roth & Lerner, *Sex-Based Discrimination in the Mental Institutionalization of Women,* 62 CAL. L. REV. 805–806 (1974). *But see* Valenstein, *supra* note 14, at I-88–89, finding that although 56% of psychosurgical procedures described in the literature were female, "[t]hese results do not differ significantly from the sex ratio distribution in [diagnostic categories for which psychosurgery is performed] . . . and therefore do not support the belief that females are being preferentially selected for psychosurgery." For allegations that psychosurgery is used as a tool of racist oppression against Blacks, see Mason, *Brain Surgery to Control Behavior,* EBONY, Feb. 1973, at 62. *Compare* E. VALENSTEIN, *supra* note 14, at I-87–88 (finding that minority group members account for very few of the patients given psychosurgery). The present potential for use of psychosurgery on a large scale for purposes of social control seems remote in view of the complexity and expense of the modern methods and the small number of neurosurgeons qualified in these techniques. Edgar, *Regulating Psychosurgery: Issues of Public Policy and Law, in* OPERATING ON THE MIND, *supra* note 2, at 117, 137; Older, *supra* note 6, at 671.

[59]*See* M. PINES, *supra* note 52, at 228; Breggin, *The Return of Lobotomy and Psychosurgery, reprinted in Hearings, supra* note 1, at 455, 475 ("[A] major function of state hospital lobotomy is to make it easier and economically cheaper to keep the patients institutionalized."); *Hearings, supra,* at 351 (testimony of O. J. Andy, proposing psychosurgery "for custodial purposes when patient requires constant attention, supervision, and an inordinate amount of institutional care."); Mearns, *supra* note 58, at 583, 601; Older, *supra* note 6, at 665; Schwartz, *In the Name of Treatment: Autonomy, Civil Commitment, and Right to Refuse Treatment,* 50 NOTRE DAME L. REV. 808, 816 (1975).

[60]*Physical Manipulation of the Brain,* HASTINGS CTR. REP. (Special Supp., 1973) (comments of E. Berings, Jr., of the National Institute of Neurological Diseases and Stroke: "a surgical lesion destroys part of the brain and is an irreversible, permanent anatomical change. If you don't like the result you're stuck with it and it can only be changed by making the lesion larger or another somewhere else."); Vaughan, *supra* note 2, at 27.

[61]Restak, *supra* note 3, at 54. For a critical analysis of the notion of "irreversible" in the context of psychosurgery and a suggestion that discussion should focus not on reversibility but on the desirability of the changes provided, *see* Shuman, *The Emotional, Medical and Legal Reasons for the Special Concern About Psychosurgery, in* MEDICAL, MORAL AND LEGAL ISSUES IN MENTAL HEALTH CARE 48, 55–58 (F. Ayd ed., 1974). *But see* H. KAPLAN ET AL., *supra* note 5 at 1013 "([U]ndesired changes in personality have not been noted with the modern limited procedures."); Donnelly, *supra* note 9, at 265.

[62]*See* Simon, *supra* note 18, at 63 ("Without a doubt, the most intrusive of all psychiatric treatments is psychosurgery.").

Part II

Constitutional Limitations on Involuntary Mental Health and Correctional Treatment

Chapter 9
THE CONSTITUTION AND OTHER SOURCES OF LEGAL LIMITATION ON GOVERNMENTALLY IMPOSED THERAPY

The focus of this book is constitutional limitations on involuntary mental health and correctional treatment. In addition to the Constitution, however, other potential legal limitations on treatment deserve at least brief analysis. These limitations derive from several sources—statutes, regulations, international law, and nonconstitutional judicial decisions. Before analyzing the constitutional issues, however, it seems appropriate to provide a brief description of these other potential legal restrictions on treatment.[1]

A. Statutory Limits

An increasing number of states place statutory limits on coercive treatment of mental patients, and a few of these statutes apply to prisoners as well.[2] California has been the forerunner in adopting statutory limits on therapy and has the most extensive statutory approach to these problems. A pioneering statute limits the use of "organic therapies" on mental patients and prisoners by declaring that all persons "have a fundamental right against enforced interference with their thought process, states of mind, and patterns of mentation."[3] The statute guarantees that, with certain exceptions, competent persons may refuse "organic therapies," including "the use of any drugs, electric shocks, electronic stimulation of the brain, or infliction of physical pain when used as an aversive or reinforcing stimulus in a program of aversive, classical, or operant conditioning."[4] Psychosurgery is prohibited for persons lacking the capacity for informed consent.[5] To administer any other organic therapy to a person not capable of consenting,[6] the state must first obtain a court order[7] after demonstrating that the proposed therapy will be beneficial, its administration is supported by a compelling state interest, no less onerous alternative therapies are available,

---

[1]For a more detailed description of these legal limitations, see Winick, *Legal Limitations on Correctional Therapy and Research,* 65 MINN. L. REV. 331, 336–44 (1981).

[2]*See* S. BRAKEL ET AL., THE MENTALLY DISABLED AND THE LAW 347 & n.242, 357–65 (table 6.2, col. 13) (3d ed. 1985) (20 states with statutory provisions relating to administration of medication in facilities for the mentally disabled); Callahan & Longmire, *Psychiatric Patients' Right to Refuse Psychotropic Medication: A National Survey,* 7 MENTAL DISABILITY L. REP. 494, 499 (1983) (15 states with statutory provisions establishing at least a qualified right to refuse medication); Plotkin, *Limiting the Therapeutic Orgy: Mental Patients' Right to Refuse Treatment,* 72 Nw. U. L. REV. 461, 504–25 (1977) (statutory compilation); *see, e.g.,* CAL. PENAL CODE §§ 2670–2680 (West 1995); FLA. STAT. § 394.459(3) (1995); IDAHO CODE § 66–1305 (1995); WASH. REV. CODE § 11.92.040(3) (1995); Keyhea v. Rushen, 223 Cal. Rptr. 746 (Ct. App. 1986) (enforcing statutory right of prisoners to refuse psychotropic medication); Conservatorship of Waltz, 225 Cal. Rptr. 664 (Ct. App. 1986) (enforcing statutory right of competent patients to refuse electroconvulsive therapy [ECT]).

[3]CAL. PENAL CODE §§ 2670–2680 (West 1995). *See generally* Shapiro, *Legislating the Control of Behavior Control: Autonomy and the Coercive Use of Organic Therapies,* 47 S. CAL. L. REV. 237 (1974).

[4]CAL. PENAL CODE § 2670.5(c)(3).

[5]*Id.* § 3507.

[6]*Id.* § 2670.5(b).

[7]*Id.* § 2675(a).

and the therapy is in accordance with medical–psychiatric practice.[8] Other provisions of the California statute place special limits on the use of psychotropic medication and behavioral techniques on prisoners.[9] Psychotropic drugs may be used in the treatment of prisoners only when they are a part of the prisoners' conventional medical treatment and are carefully monitored and evaluated.[10] Behavioral techniques may be used only if they are "medically and socially acceptable" and do not inflict permanent physical or psychological injury.[11]

Another legislative right-to-refuse-treatment model is illustrated by the Florida statute.[12] In general, the statute requires "express and informed consent" for treatment.[13] Such consent must be voluntarily given in writing after "sufficient explanation and disclosure of the subject matter involved to enable the person . . . to make a knowing and willful decision without any element of force, fraud, deceit, duress, or other form of constraint or coercion."[14] A voluntary patient who refuses to consent to treatment or revokes consent must be discharged within 3 days thereof; in the event the patient meets the criteria for involuntary commitment, commitment proceedings must be instituted within 3 days.[15] If any patient (voluntarily or involuntarily) refuses treatment and is not discharged, "emergency treatment" may be administered "in the least restrictive manner," provided that a physician determines in writing that such treatment "is necessary for the safety of the patient or others."[16]

Apart from such an emergency situation, involuntary treatment may also be authorized if "essential to appropriate care" for a patient found to be incompetent.[17] To invoke this exception, the hospital administrator must petition the court for a hearing to determine the patient's *competency to consent to treatment,* which the statute defines as whether the patient's "judgment is so affected by his mental illness that he lacks the capacity to make a well-reasoned, willful, and knowing decision concerning treatment."[18] If the court finds the patient to be incompetent to consent to treatment, it must appoint a "guardian advocate," who may consent to treatment on behalf of the patient as a surrogate decision maker.[19] In the case of ECT or surgical procedures requiring general anesthesia, advance written permission must be obtained from the patient if competent, or if incompetent, from the patient's guardian.[20] Thus, although a physician may authorize emergency treatment with psychotropic medication if necessary for the safety of the patient or others, involuntary treatment with surgery or ECT may be administered only if the patient has been judicially determined to be incompetent and the guardian consents.

Other than on the most intrusive therapies,[21] state or local statutory limits on treatment are still somewhat rare. According to a 1985 survey, 20 states have statutory provisions

---

[8]*Id.* § 2679(b).

[9]*Id.* § 3507.

[10]*Id.* An additional limitation exists for the use of such drugs in research. Research use of these drugs is restricted to testing the pharmacological or chemical properties of the drugs when there is no serious risk to the individual's mental or physical well-being. *Id.*

[11]*Id.* § 3508.

[12]FLA. STAT. § 394.459(3)(a) (1995).

[13]*Id.*

[14]*Id.* § 394.455(19).

[15]*Id.* § 394.459(3)(a).

[16]*Id.*

[17]*Id.*

[18]*Id.*

[19]*Id.*

[20]*Id.* § 394.459(3)(b).

[21]BRAKEL ET AL., *supra* note 2, at 357–65 (table 6.2, col. 3).

placing limits on the administration of psychotropic medication in facilities for the mentally disabled.[22] Despite legislative reports, hearings, and proposals in this area, no federal statutes presently govern these matters.[23] As the trend toward therapeutic intervention grows, there will undoubtedly be more state and federal legislative approaches to these issues.

B. Regulatory Limits

Another source of legal control over mental health and correctional treatment is regulatory law—rules adopted by a federal, state, or local mental health, corrections agency, or other administrative unit to regulate the provision of treatment. According to a 1983 survey, 19 states had such regulatory limits on the use of psychotropic medication in mental hospitals.[24] Administrative agencies or departments, acting pursuant to statutory delegation of authority from the legislature, may impose substantive limits on the application of the various treatment techniques, as well as procedures designed to prevent abuses. Increased administrative regulation in this area can be anticipated.

C. International Law Limits

International customary or common law and treaties to which the United States is a party may also place restrictions on the imposition of mental health and correctional treatment. Although international law primarily governs relations between countries and traditionally has been thought not to deal with claims by individuals against their own nations, customary international law and international agreements have created obligations for countries in relation to individuals, including their own nationals.[25] Indeed, in recent years a customary international law of human rights has emerged.[26]

An important source of international human rights is the Universal Declaration of Human Rights, adopted by the United Nations General Assembly in 1948.[27] The rights recognized in the Universal Declaration include freedom of thought, conscience, and religion, as well as freedom of opinion and expression. These rights are violated by coercive mind control through use of mental health treatment techniques. The clearest case for violation of these provisions occurs when a nation uses such techniques to deal with political or religious dissidents, as happened in the former Soviet Union. However, even in conventional treatment contexts, at least some of these techniques can be conceived to violate the Universal Declaration. The United States has frequently reiterated its acceptance

---

[22]*Id.* at 357–65 (table 6.2, col. 13).

[23]*See* Winick, *supra* note 1, at 339–40.

[24]Callahan & Longmire, *supra* note 2, at 499; *see, e.g.,* Rules of the Fla. Dep't of Health and Rehabilitative Services, ch. 10E-5.034, FLA. ADMIN. CODE (1986); N.J. Div. of Mental Health and Hospitals Administrative Bulletin 78-3 (1978), *reprinted in* Rennie v. Klein, 462 F. Supp. 1131, 1148–51 (D.N.J. 1978); N.Y.C.R.R. §§ 27.8–.9, *discussed in* Project Release v. Prevost, 722 F.2d 960, 979–81 (2d Cir. 1983).

[25]AMERICAN LAW INSTITUTE, RESTATEMENT OF THE LAW, FOREIGN RELATIONS LAW OF THE UNITED STATES (1987) [hereinafter AMERICAN LAW INSTITUTE].

[26]D'Amato, *The Concept of Human Rights in International Law,* 82 COLUM. L. REV. 1110, 1128–29 (1982); Gostin, *Human Rights in Mental Health, in* PSYCHIATRY, HUMAN RIGHTS AND THE LAW 148 (M. Roth & R. Bluglass eds., 1985).

[27]United Nations General Assembly Res. 217, 3 GAOR (A/810) at 71, Dec. 10, 1948. *See also American Declaration on the Rights and Duties of Men, Pan American Union Final Act of the Ninth Conference of American States* 38 (1948), *reprinted in* L. SOHN & T. BUERGENTHAL, BASIC DOCUMENTS ON INTERNATIONAL PROTECTION OF HUMAN RIGHTS 187 (1973).

of the Universal Declaration, but its status as an independently binding source of law that is enforceable in domestic courts is uncertain.[28]

Although neither a treaty nor a part of customary law, a resolution of the United Nations General Assembly adopted in 1991 contains a detailed provision recognizing the patient's right to refuse mental health treatment. This resolution, the *Principles for the Protection of Persons with Mental Illness,*[29] is the most detailed and comprehensive codification of mental disability rights under international law.[30] *Principle 11,* dealing specifically with the right to refuse treatment, provides that no patient may be subject to treatment without informed consent.[31] The consent requirement, a "centerpiece" of the *Principles,* seeks to assure that consent is "a product of participation in decision-making."[32] Under the *Principles,* such consent can be obtained only after "appropriate disclosure"[33] and must be "obtained freely, without threats or improper inducements."[34] "Appropriate disclosure" involves four basic components: the patient must be told about (a) the diagnostic assessment; (b) the purpose, method, likely duration, and expected benefit of the proposed treatment; (c) alternative modes of treatment, including those less intrusive; and (d) possible pain or discomfort, risks, and side-effects of the proposed treatment.[35] The informed consent requirement, however, may be overridden in certain circumstances. An involuntary patient[36] may be treated without consent if an "independent authority"[37] determines that the patient lacks the mental capacity to give or withhold informed consent and that the treatment is in the patient's best interests.[38] In addition, the "independent authority" may authorize involuntary medication, even if the patient is competent, if permitted by domestic law, when it determines that, "having regard to the patient's own safety or the safety of others,"[39] the patient unreasonably withholds consent for medication and medication is "in the best interest of the patient's health needs."[40] The *Principles* also permit involuntary medication to be administered on an emergency basis "in order to prevent immediate imminent harm to the patient or to other persons."[41] Any treatment imposed must also conform to the least restrictive alternative principle. The *Principles* require that the patient be treated "with the least restrictive or intrusive treatment appropriate to the patient's health needs."[42] Even when treatment is

---

[28]AMERICAN LAW INSTITUTE, *supra* note 25, at 140–41, 146. *See generally* Lillich, *Invoking International Rights in Domestic Courts,* 54 U. CIN. L. REV. 367 (1985).

[29]*Principles for the Protection of Persons with Mental Illness and for the Improvement of Mental Health Care,* G.A. Res. 119, U.N. GAOR, 46th Sess., Supp. No. 49, Annex, at 188–92, U.N. Doc. A/46/49 (1991) [hereinafter *Principles*], *reproduced in* Rosenthal & Rubenstein, *International Human Rights Advocacy under the "Principles for the Protection of Persons with Mental Illness,"* 16 INT'L. J.L. & PSYCHIATRY 259, 291–300 (Appendix A) (1993).

[30]Rosenthal & Rubenstein, *supra* note 29, at 259.

[31]*Principles, supra* note 29.

[32]Rosenthal & Rubenstein, *supra* note 29, at 264. Principle 9(2), for example, requires the treatment plan to be discussed with the patient. Principle 12(1) requires that patients be informed of their rights and how to exercise them.

[33]*Id.*

[34]*Principles, supra* note 29, at Principle 11(1).

[35]*Id.* at Principle 11(2).

[36]*Id.* at Principle 11(6)(a).

[37]*Independent authority* is defined as "a competent and independent authority prescribed by domestic law." *Id.* at 292.

[38]*Id.* at Principle 11(6)(b) & (c).

[39]*Id.* at Principle 11(6)(b).

[40]*Id.* at Principle 11(6)(c).

[41]*Id.* at Principle 11(8).

[42]*Id.* at Principle 9(1).

authorized in the absence of the patient's informed consent, *Principle 11(9)* requires "every effort" to be made to keep the patient informed about and involved in the course of treatment.[43]

The *Principles* place particular emphasis on seeking to protect patients from harm. Every patient "shall be protected from harm, including unjustified medication" and other abuses.[44] Certain practices are absolutely forbidden, including involuntary sterilization,[45] involuntary administration of psychosurgery or other intrusive and irreversible treatments,[46] and experimental treatment without informed consent.[47]

Principle 11(16) provides for an appeal process for any patient subjected to treatment without consent. This appeal is an independent and impartial review body, which may be judicial in nature.[48] The review body must include at least one mental health practitioner, whose advice it must take into account.[49]

Another arguably relevant source of international law is the Nuremberg Code.[50] The Code provides a comprehensive statement of the requirements of informed consent to human experimentation and broadly asserts that the consent of the subject is "absolutely essential." To the extent that any of the treatment techniques administered to mental patients or criminal offenders can be considered experimental (such as psychosurgery[51] and electronic stimulation of the brain[52]) or are applied in an experimental manner, the Code could be considered a source of international customary law that would place limits on governmental use of such therapies.[53] The Code specifies that informed consent to human experimentation must be competent, voluntary, informed, and understanding.[54]

Although it reflects widely shared views of medical ethics, it remains unclear whether the Nuremberg Code, which is assertedly based on "the principles of the law of nations,"[55] has the force of international law.[56] As an international law of human rights develops, the principles of the Code probably will be absorbed into customary international law; indeed,

---

[43]*Id.* at Principle 11(9).

[44]*Id.* at Principle 8(2).

[45]*Id.* at Principle 11(12).

[46]*Id.* at Principle 11(14).

[47]*Id.* at Principle 11(15).

[48]*Id.* at Principle 12(16).

[49]*Id.* at Principle 17(1). The values scope and limitations of the *Principles* are described further in *Rosenthal & Rubenstein, supra* note 29, at 260.

[50]The "Code" is actually the 10 principles on human experimentation set forth in the judgment of the Nuremberg Military Tribunal in the case of United States v. Karl Brandt. *See The Medical Case, in* I & II Trials of War Criminals Before the Nuremberg Military Tribunals (1949) [hereinafter Nuremberg Trials], *reprinted in* J. Katz, Experimentation With Human Beings 292 (1972). The principles set forth in the *Brandt* case—the trial of 23 German physicians for war crimes involving experiments with prisoners of war and civilians—have come to be known as the "Nuremberg Code." *See* II Nuremberg Trials, *supra* at 181–82, *reprinted in* Katz, *supra* at 305–06.

[51]*See supra* chapter 8.

[52]*See supra* chapter 7.

[53]Although it speaks broadly of all human experimentation, the Code was adopted in the context of nontherapeutic medical experimentation. Its application outside this area—to therapeutic medical research—is therefore uncertain.

[54]*See* II Nuremberg Trials, *supra* note 50, at 181-82, *in* J. Katz, *supra* note 50, at 305–06. Article 7 of the *International Covenant on Civilian Political Rights* contains a parallel provision that "no one shall be subjected without his free consent to medical or scientific experimentation," *quoted in* American Law Institute, *supra* note 25, at 165.

[55]*See* II Nuremberg Trials, *supra* note 50, at 183, *reprinted in* Katz, *supra* note 50, at 306.

[56]*See* Jonnes, *The Nuremberg Lawyers,* Nat'l L. J., Jan. 7, 1980, at 1 (disagreement among former Nuremberg prosecutors as to the status of the Nuremberg principles in international law).

some commentators already regard the Code and its progeny, the Declaration of Helsinki,[57] as a part of international customary law.[58] Moreover, a developing consensus views at least some of the provisions of the Universal Declaration as having been so absorbed.[59] To the extent that these principles are or become absorbed in the customary law of human rights, they will be part of the law of the United States, to be applied as such by state as well as federal courts.[60]

In any event, the Nuremberg Code and the Declaration of Helsinki have been and will continue to be influential in the formulation of policy and law in this area. For example, regulations of the U.S. Department of Health and Human Services and other federal agencies on the protection of individuals are derived from the Code.[61] A Michigan trial court adopted the Code's requirements for informed consent in *Kaimowitz v. Michigan Department of Mental Health,*[62] an influential opinion restricting the use of psychosurgery. Furthermore, because the Nuremberg Code and the Declaration of Helsinki may be regarded as formal expressions of agreed-upon medical ethics in the conduct of experimentation, their principles may be absorbed into tort law standards governing medical malpractice.

[57]*Reprinted in* NATIONAL COMM'N FOR THE PROTECTION OF HUMAN SUBJECTS OF BIOMEDICAL AND BEHAVIORAL RESEARCH, RESEARCH INVOLVING PRISONERS 21–1 to 21–6 app. (1976). The Declaration was adopted by the Eighteenth World Medical Assembly in Helsinki, Finland, in 1964, and was revised by the Twenty-Ninth World Medical Assembly in Tokyo, Japan, in 1975. *See* CONTEMPORARY ISSUES IN BIOETHICS 4–5 (T. Beauchamp & L. Walters eds., 1978).

[58]*See* G. ANNAS ET AL., INFORMED CONSENT TO HUMAN EXPERIMENTATION: THE SUBJECT'S DILEMMA 8 (1977); R. WOETZEL, THE NUREMBERG TRIAL IN INTERNATIONAL LAW 239 (1962).

[59]*See* AMERICAN LAW INSTITUTE, *supra* note 25, at 140–41; *see, e.g.,* Wyatt v. Stickney, 344 F. Supp. 387, 390 n.6 (M.D. Ala. 1972), *aff'd sub. nom.* Wyatt v. Aderholt, 503 F.2d 1305 (5th Cir. 1974) (recognizing a constitutional right to habilitation and citing to Article 2, U.N. Declaration of the Rights of Mentally Retarded Persons); Herr, *Rights of Disabled Persons: International Principles and American Experiences,* 12 COLUM. HUM. RTS. L. REV. 1, 9–11 (1980); Lillich, *The Role of Domestic Courts in Promoting International Human Rights Norms,* 24 N.Y.L. SCH. L. REV. 153 (1978) (analyzing New York state and federal court cases in which litigants invoked international human rights norms).

[60]AMERICAN LAW INSTITUTE, *supra* note 25, at 158; *see* The Paquete Habana, 175 U.S. 677, 700 (1898); Doe v. Plyler, 628 F.2d 448 (5th Cir. 1980), *aff'd on other grounds,* 457 U.S. 202 (1982) (article 45 of Protocol of Buenos Aires, Feb. 27, 1967, 21 U.S.T. 607, T.I.A.S. No. 6847, cited in support of requiring provision of education for alien children); Filartiga v. Pena-Irala, 630 F.2d 876 (2d Cir. 1980) (deliberate torture perpetrated under color of official authority held to be a violation of customary law supporting the jurisdiction of the district courts of the United States "of a civil action by an alien for a tort only, committed in violation of the law of nations," 28 U.S.C. § 1350, brought against a former official of Paraguay); Rodriguez-Fernandez v. Wilkinson, 505 F. Supp. 787 (D. Kan. 1980) (United States may not indefinitely detain an excludable alien because arbitrary detention is prohibited by customary international law; even though such detention does not violate U.S. constitutional or statutory law, "it is judicially remediable as a violation of international law"), *aff'd on other grounds,* 654 F.2d 1382 (10th Cir. 1981) (international law principles taken into account in construing statute not to authorize such detention in the circumstances); Sterling v. Cupp, 625 P.2d 123, 131 (Or. 1982) (referring to international standards for treatment of prisoners; *but see* Lillich, *The Proper Role of Domestic Courts in the International Legal Order,* 11 VA. J. INT'L L. 9 (1970) (customary international law is merely a source of domestic law; rather than being independently binding, such law, although persuasive, has validity in U.S. courts only insofar as its principles are adopted by such courts).

[61]*See* Veatch, *Ethical Principles in Medical Experimentation, in* ETHICAL AND LEGAL ISSUES OF SOCIAL EXPERIMENTATION 32–33 (A. Rivlin & P. Timpane eds., 1975).

[62]No. 73-19434-AW (Wayne [Mich.] Cir. Ct. July 10, 1973), *reprinted in* A. BROOKS, LAW, PSYCHIATRY, AND THE MENTAL HEALTH SYSTEM 902, 913–14 (1974).

D. Tort Law Limits

Judicial action based on other than constitutional principles may also provide a source of legal limitation on unwanted therapy. Tort law, developed over time through court decision, for example, may authorize the award of damages against governmental or private therapists to compensate patients or offenders subjected to abusive practices. Common law doctrines of trespass and battery provide a remedy in damages for deliberate touching or other invasions of bodily integrity that are not legally privileged or to which the victim has not consented.[63] Thus, any medical procedure performed without first obtaining the informed consent of the patient is, with few exceptions, an actionable tort.[64] As Justice Cardozo stated in his classic formulation of the principle: "Every human being of adult years and sound mind has a right to determine what shall be done with his own body; and a surgeon who performs an operation without his patient's consent commits an assault, for which he is liable in damages."[65] Although traditionally this principle has not been thought to be applicable in mental hospitals,[66] the courts are beginning to apply it to mental patients[67] and prisoners[68] subjected to intrusive treatment without consent.

Other tort theories may also apply. Any treatment performed in a negligent fashion and causing injury, for example, would be actionable malpractice even if consent had been

---

[63]*See* PROSSER AND KEETON ON THE LAW OF TORTS 39–40 (W. Keeton ed., 1984); Stone, *The Right to Refuse Treatment: Why Psychiatrists Should and Can Make It Work,* 38 ARCHIVES GEN. PSYCHIATRY 358 (1981); *see, e.g.,* Davis v. Hubbard, 506 F. Supp. 915, 930 (N.D. Ohio 1980).

[64]PROSSER AND KEETON ON THE LAW OF TORTS, *supra* note 63, at 39–40. If consent was not obtained, the patient may recover damages even if the procedure did not result in harm. *Id.; see* Goldstein, *For Harold Lasswell: Some Reflections on Human Dignity, Entrapment, Informed Consent, and the Plea Bargain,* 84 YALE L.J. 683, 691 (1975).

[65]Schloendorff v. Society of N.Y. Hosp., 105 N.E. 92, 93 (N.Y. 1914).

[66]*E.g.,* Rogers v. Okin, 478 F. Supp. 1342, 1383–84 (D. Mass. 1979) (law of malpractice more appropriate than intentional tort theories in deciding claims arising at mental hospitals, including right-to-refuse-treatment claims), *aff'd in part and rev'd in part on other grounds,* 634 F.2d 650 (1st Cir. 1980) (en banc), *vacated and remanded,* 457 U.S. 291 (1982), *on remand,* 738 F.2d 1 (1st Cir. 1983); Winters v. Miller, 306 F. Supp. 1158 (E.D.N.Y. 1969) (rejecting battery claim based on involuntary administration of psychotropic drugs), *rev'd on other grounds,* 446 F.2d 65 (2d Cir.), *cert. denied,* 404 U.S. 985 (1971); Belger v. Arnot, 183 N.E.2d 866 (Mass. 1962) (rejecting battery claim based on involuntary electroconvulsive therapy); Anonymous v. State, 236 N.Y.S.2d 88 (App. Div. 1963) (assault and battery claim dismissed where father of adult mental patient had consented to ECT).

[67]*E.g.,* Lojuk v. Quandt, 706 F.2d 1456, 1460 (7th Cir. 1983) (nonconsensual ECT applied to patient incompetent to make treatment decisions constitutes tortious battery); Goedecke v. State, 603 P.2d 123, 125 (Colo. 1979) (en banc) ("[A] patient's common law right to decline medical treatment" is "preserved intact in the absence of some finding reached by a competent tribunal, that the patient's illness has so impaired his judgment that he is incapable of participating in decisions affecting his health") (psychotropic drugs); Stowers v. Ardmore Acres Hosp., 172 N.W.2d 497 (Ct. App. 1969), *aff'd,* 191 N.W.2d 355 (Mich. 1971) (assault and battery for private mental hospital to inject patient, who had not been found incompetent, with psychotropic drugs over her objection); New York City Health & Hosp. Corp. v. Stein, 335 N.Y.S.2d 461 (Sup. Ct. 1972) (ECT could not be administered to nonconsenting patient, even though patient's mother had consented); *see* BRAKEL ET AL., *supra* note 2, at 347; Note, *A Common Law Remedy for Forcible Medication of the Institutionalized Mentally Ill,* 82 COLUM. L. REV. 1720 (1982).

[68]*E.g.,* Irwin v. Arrendale, 159 S.E.2d 719, 725 (Ga. Ct. App. 1967) (X-ray procedure performed on prisoner without consent constituted a battery).

obtained.[69] Failure to divulge the potential risks of a particular treatment, thereby effectively preventing a fully informed consent, may also constitute malpractice.[70] Other traditional torts, such as invasion of privacy and intentional or negligent infliction of severe emotional distress, might also provide grounds for a claim.[71]

The question remains whether policies favoring treatment of the mentally ill and rehabilitation of offenders renders privileged treatment that would otherwise be tortious. These issues have rarely been litigated in the hospital and prison context, and even less so in noninstitutional settings. Patients and prisoners generally lack the resources to press damage actions against their keepers, and tort lawyers rarely take such cases on a contingent fee basis. Moreover, mental hospital and correctional officials are clothed with immunity from liability for tortious conduct occurring in good faith.[72] For these and other institutional reasons, slowly developing tort law is not likely to provide an adequate source of limitation

---

[69]PROSSER AND KEETON ON THE LAW OF TORTS, *supra* note 63, at 189–93; *see, e.g.,* Rogers v. Okin, 478 F. Supp. 1392, 1384–88 (D. Mass. 1979) (rejecting malpractice claim based on forced administration of psychotropic drugs at state mental hospital), *aff'd in part and rev'd in part on other grounds,* 634 F.2d 650 (1st Cir. 1980) (en banc), *vacated and remanded on other grounds,* 457 U.S. 291 (1982), *on remand,* 738 F.2d 1 (1st Cir. 1984); Cox v. Hecker, 218 F. Supp. 749 (E.D. Pa. 1963) (same), *aff'd per curiam,* 350 F.2d 958 (3d Cir.), *cert. denied,* 379 U.S. 823 (1964). *See generally* R. COHEN, MALPRACTICE: A GUIDE FOR MENTAL HEALTH PRACTITIONERS (1979); D. DAWIDOFF, THE MALPRACTICE OF PSYCHIATRISTS: MALPRACTICE IN PSYCHOANALYSIS, PSYCHOTHERAPY AND PSYCHIATRY (1973); B. FURROW, MALPRACTICE IN PSYCHOTHERAPY (1980); S. HALLECK, LAW IN THE PRACTICE OF PSYCHIATRY: A HANDBOOK FOR CLINICIANS 11–107 (1980); D. HOGAN, THE REGULATION OF PSYCHOTHERAPISTS, VOL. III: A REVIEW OF MALPRACTICE SUITS IN THE UNITED STATES (1979); J. KING, THE LAW OF MEDICAL MALPRACTICE IN A NUTSHELL 130–80 (1986); D. LOUISELL & H. WILLIAMS, MEDICAL MALPRACTICE §§ 23.01–3.22 (1977); R. SADOFF, LEGAL ISSUES IN THE CARE OF PSYCHIATRIC PATIENTS: A GUIDE FOR THE MENTAL HEALTH PROFESSIONAL 62–70 (1982); Bromberg, *The Perils of Psychiatry,* 13 PSYCHIATRIC ANNALS 219 (1983).

[70]Rogers v. Okin, 478 F. Supp. 1342, 1386–88 (D. Mass. 1979) (recognizing possibility of such a claim by mental patients who were not advised of potential risks of psychotropic medication, but rejecting claim on basis that during the relevant period (1973–1975) such failure would not "have been considered sub-standard medical practice"), *aff'd in part and rev'd in part on other grounds,* 634 F.2d 650 (1st Cir. 1980), *vacated and remanded on other grounds,* 457 U.S. 291 (1982), *on remand,* 738 F.2d 1 (1st Cir. 1984); Davis v. Hubbard, 506 F. Supp. 915, 931–32 (N.D. Ga. 1980); Woods v. Brumlop, 377 P.2d 520 (N.M. 1962) (failure to warn patient about the risks of ECT); *see* Canterbury v. Spence, 464 F.2d 772 (D.C. Cir.), *cert. denied,* 409 U.S. 1064 (1972) (physician may not fail to divulge information on ground that patient might, as a result, forgo therapy); HALLECK, *supra* note 69, at 89–98.

[71]*See* Friedman, *Legal Regulation of Applied Behavior Analysis in Mental Institutions and Prisons,* 17 ARIZ. L. REV. 39, 55 (1975). *See generally* PROSSER AND KEETON ON THE LAW OF TORTS, *supra* note 63, at 55–66 (intentional infliction of emotional distress); *id.* at 359 (negligent infliction of emotional distress); *id.* at 849–58 (invasion of privacy). For an argument (never accepted) that psychotherapy should be subjected to strict liability, see Comment, *Injuries Precipitated by Psychotherapy: Liability Without Fault as a Basis for Recovery,* 20 SAN DIEGO L. REV. 401 (1975).

[72]*See, e.g.,* Youngberg v. Romeo, 457 U.S. 307, 323 (1982) (mental retardation facility staff); Procunier v. Navarette, 434 U.S. 555, 561–62 (1978) (prison officials); O'Connor v. Donaldson, 422 U.S. 563, 577 (1975) (mental hospital administrators and clinicians); Rogers v. Okin, 478 F. Supp. 1342, 1381–83 (D. Mass. 1979) (mental hospital administrators and clinicians), *aff'd in part and rev'd in part on other grounds,* 634 F.2d 650 (1st Cir. 1980) (en banc), *vacated and remanded,* 457 U.S. 291 (1982), *on remand,* 738 F.2d 1 (1st Cir. 1984).

on mental health and correctional therapy, at least absent constitutional recognition of a right to refuse treatment.[73]

E. Constitutional Limits

The above-mentioned sources of legal restriction on involuntary treatment are potentially significant and will be increasingly important. However, by far the most important basis for limiting involuntary therapy is the U.S. Constitution, and, to varying degrees, state constitutions.[74] If a constitutional basis for a right to refuse treatment is recognized by the courts, then legislatures will respond with statutory enactments safeguarding the right and administrative agencies will fill in the details with rules and regulations. Moreover, as violations of the Constitution[75] and noncompliance with statutory or regulatory duties[76] give rise to actions in tort, the recognition of a constitutional right in this area inevitably will result in the expansion of tort law remedies to secure and protect a right to refuse. If, on the other hand, courts reject a constitutional basis for a right to refuse, the availability of such a right will depend largely on the response of the political process. If the public perceives that abuses of these therapies are widespread, legislatures and agencies will respond with statutory and regulatory limits. Mental patients and offenders are at an obvious disadvantage in the political process, however. On the whole, the members of these groups are indigent, inarticulate, and unorganized. The mounting public concern with crime and the fear that most people have of mental patients will make rehabilitative approaches attractive, and legislatures and their agents—the correctional and mental health departments—will not be inclined to impose restrictions that clinicians view as unwarranted.

If a right to refuse treatment is to be recognized by the law, the development of constitutional doctrine in this area thus seems crucial. Although the Burger Court was undoubtedly less activist than its predecessor, the Warren Court—a trend that has continued

---

[73]If a constitutional right to refuse treatment is recognized, then violation of the right gives rise to an implied action in tort. *See* Carlson v. Green, 446 U.S. 14 (1980); Davis v. Passman, 442 U.S. 228 (1979); Bivens v. Six Unknown Agents of the Federal Bureau of Narcotics, 405 U.S. 388 (1971); *see, e.g.,* Lojuk v. Quandt, 706 F.2d 1456, 1467–70 (7th Cir. 1983). Moreover, such a constitutional tort committed by state officials would be subject to redress in federal court under the Civil Rights Act of 1871, 42 U.S.C. § 1983 (1994). *E.g.,* Zinermon v. Burch, 494 U.S. 113 (1990) (Section 1983 action against state hospital for admitting patient to mental hospital without ascertaining patient's consent or competence to consent to voluntary admission). *See generally* T. EISENBERG, FEDERAL CIVIL RIGHTS LEGISLATION 380–86 (3d ed. 1991); Note, *Developments in the Law—Section 1983 and Federalism,* 90 HARV. L. REV. 1133 (1977). Not only is this generally a more favorable forum for the vindication of constitutional rights than the state courts, *see* Neuborne, *The Myth of Parity,* 90 HARV. L. REV. 1105 (1977), but unlike in the typical state court tort case, attorneys fees are available for prevailing parties under the Civil Rights Attorney's Fees Award Act of 1976, 42 U.S.C. § 1988 (1994); *see, e.g.,* Hensley v. Eckerhart, 461 U.S. 424 (1983); Hutto v. Finney, 437 U.S. 678 (1978). This in turn should encourage more attorneys to undertake such suits even for indigent clients.

[74]*See* Brennan, *State Constitutions and the Protection of Individual Rights,* 90 HARV. L. REV. 489 (1977); Perlin, *State Constitutions and Statutes as Sources of Rights for the Mentally Disabled: The Last Frontier?,* 20 LOY. L.A. L. REV. 1249, 1250–51 (1987).

[75]*See* cases cited in *supra* note 73. The Supreme Court of Minnesota, after finding that involuntary administration of ECT implicated constitutional privacy and fashioning rules for the imposition of intrusive treatments, explicitly warned that "[i]n the future, of course, institutional doctors must warned that "[i]n the future, of course, institutional doctors must comply with the new procedures set forth in this opinion for authorizing more severe forms of therapy, *e.g.,* electroshock therapy, in order to remain protected by . . . [a good faith] privilege from tort liability." Price v. Sheppard, 239 N.W.2d 905, 912 n.9 (Minn. 1976).

[76]*See, e.g.,* Ross v. Hartman, 139 F.2d 14 (D.C. Cir. 1943); Martin v. Herzog, 126 N.E. 814 (N.Y. 1920); Morris, *The Role of Administrative Safety Measures in Negligence Actions,* 28 TEX. L. REV. 143 (1949); Thayer, *Public Wrongs and Private Action,* 27 HARV. L. REV. 317 (1914).

under the Rehnquist Court—the Supreme Court has continued to expand constitutional doctrine to deal with the increasingly complex problems of modern society. Moreover, although as recently as 35 years ago, most courts applied a "hands-off" policy with respect to mental patients and prisoners seeking judicial remedies against hospital and prison authorities,[77] a virtual revolution has since occurred in the areas of prisoners' rights and the rights of mental patients.[78] In view of the deferential approach that federal courts took (until recently) to these institutions, it could accurately be stated that prisoners and mental patients "lacked full citizenship rights; they existed as a lower legal caste."[79] With the extension of constitutional rights to racial minorities, the poor, criminal defendants, illegitimates, aliens, and women, commencing in the post-World War II era and accelerating in the 1960s, it was perhaps inevitable that the Constitution would begin to penetrate these closed institutions. Sophisticated litigation strategies to extend the rights of these populations emerged as a result of the rise of public interest lawyers and law firms, the expansion of the litigation program of such traditional civil rights organizations as the American Civil Liberties Union and the Legal Defense and Education Fund of the NAACP, Inc., and the appearance of such new organizations as the Mental Health Law Project (now renamed the Bazelon Center).[80] At the same time, procedural barriers to bringing such suits in federal courts generally were eased, particularly with expanding judicial constructions of the Civil Rights Act of 1871.[81]

The legal onslaught took as its first target the prisons. Starting in the 1960s, prisoners have filed increasing numbers of civil rights actions challenging the constitutionality of prison conditions and restrictions. In response, courts increasingly extended constitutional protections to state and federal prisoners and fashioned judicial remedies for the violation of

---

[77]*See, e.g.,* Ross v. Hartman, 139 F.2d 14 (D.C. Cir. 1943); Martin v. Herzog, 126 N.E. 814 (N.Y. 1920); Morris, *supra* note 76; Thayer, *supra* note 76.

[78]Haas, *Judicial Politics and Correctional Reform: An Analysis of the Decline of the "Hands Off Doctrine,"* 1977 DET. U. L. REV. 795; Note, *Decency and Fairness: An Emerging Judicial Role in Prison Reform,* 57 VA. L. REV. 841 (1971).

[79]With respect to prisoners, the prevailing attitude was that they were "slave[s] of the state" with no rights. Ruffin v. Commonwealth, 62 Va. 790, 796 (1871).

[80]*See* Wald & Friedman, *The Politics of Mental Health Advocacy in the United States,* 1 INT'L J.L. & PSYCHIATRY 137, 147 (1978).

[81]A critical decision was Monroe v. Pape, 365 U.S. 167 (1961), which resurrected the then rarely used Civil Rights Act of 1871, 42 U.S.C. § 1983, and, together with other decisions, turned it into a potent weapon for lawyers seeking damages and injunctions against state abuses of individual rights. *See generally* T. EISENBERG, *supra* note 73; Chayes, *The Supreme Court, 1981 Term—Forward: Public Law Litigation and the Burger Court,* 96 HARV. L. REV. 4 (1982); Note, *supra* note 73. An additional development of significance was a series of cases recognizing and expanding a due process right of access to courts for prisoners, in the process opening the door to prison litigants. Johnson v. Avery, 393 U.S. 483 (1969), held that unless the state provided some alternate form of legal assistance to prisoners, it could not ban jailhouse lawyering. *Johnson* and a later case, Wolff v. McDonnell, 418 U.S. 539 (1974), applying *Johnson* to civil rights actions as well as habeas corpus petitions, greatly increased the access of prisoners to fellow inmates with some legal experience willing to help in the preparation of court papers. *See also* Procunier v. Martinez, 416 U.S. 396 (1974) (invalidating a rule preventing law students from entering prisons to assist lawyers in case investigations). Haines v. Kerner, 404 U.S. 519 (1972), and Hughes v. Rowe, 449 U.S. 5 (1980), made it clear that the liberal rules of pleading applied to complaints prepared by prisoners, rendering them even less subject to summary dismissal for inartful pleading than are those of nonprisoner litigants. Bounds v. Smith, 430 U.S. 817 (1977), further encouraged jailhouse lawyering by holding that states could not deny prisoners access to adequate law libraries or other legal assistance to prepare constitutional claims. Although the Supreme Court and the lower federal courts more recently have made access to the federal courts somewhat more difficult, litigation by mental patients and prisoners of constitutional claims in the federal courts remains largely available.

constitutional rights,[82] exhibiting a degree of activism approved by the Burger Court: "The deplorable conditions and draconian restrictions of some of our nation's prisons are too well known to require recounting here, and the federal courts rightly have condemned the sordid aspects of our prison system."[83] It is now generally recognized that prisoners "retain all of their constitutional rights except for those which must be impinged upon for security or rehabilitative purposes."[84] The Supreme Court has repeatedly reiterated that "convicted prisoners do not forfeit all constitutional protections by reason of their conviction and confinement in prison."[85] The Court had noted that "there is no iron curtain drawn between the Constitution and the prisons of this country."[86] The Supreme Court has recognized that due process protections applied to prisoners subjected to additional deprivations of liberty or property,[87] that prisoners generally enjoy freedom of speech and religion under the First Amendment,[88] and that they are protected against both invidious racial discrimination under the Equal Protection Clause[89] and cruel and unusual punishment under the Eighth Amendment.[90]

These developments in the prisoners' rights context were soon cited by the champions of the mentally ill. The courts were quick to recognize that neither the prison gate nor the mental hospital door could shut out the Constitution. Indeed, the Supreme Court recognized that "[p]ersons who have been involuntarily committed are entitled to more considerate treatment and conditions of confinement than criminals whose conditions of confinement are designed to punish."[91] As one federal circuit court of appeals has noted, in rejecting the state's contention that involuntary commitment takes away all aspects of a patient's constitutional liberty, "the patient's liberty is diminished [by commitment] only to the

---

[82]*See generally* J. GEBERT & N. COHEN, RIGHTS OF PRISONERS (1981); S. KRANTZ, THE LAW OF CORRECTIONS AND PRISONERS' RIGHTS (3D ED. 1986); LEGAL RIGHTS OF PRISONERS (G. ALPERT ED., 1980); PRISONERS' RIGHTS SOURCEBOOK: THEORY, LITIGATION, PRACTICE (M. HERMAN & M. HAFT EDS., 1973); II PRISONERS' RIGHTS SOURCEBOOK: THEORY, LITIGATION, PRACTICE (I. Robbins ed., 1980); Turner, *When Prisoners Sue: A Study of Prisoner Section 1983 Suits in the Federal Courts,* 92 HARV. L. REV. 610 (1979).

[83]Bell v. Wolfish, 441 U.S. 520, 562 (1979).

[84]Jones v. Wittenberg, 323 F. Supp. 93, 98 (N.D. Ohio 1971), *enforced,* 330 F. Supp. 707 (N.D. Ohio 1971), *aff'd sub nom.* Jones v. Metzger, 456 F.2d 854 (6th Cir. 1972).

[85]*Bell,* 441 U.S. at 545–46.

[86]Wolff v. McDonnell, 418 U.S. 539, 555–56 (1976).

[87]*See, e.g.,* Vitek v. Jones, 445 U.S. 480, 488–91 (1980) (due process hearing required for prison–hospital transfers); Bounds v. Smith, 430 U.S. 817, 817–18 (1977) (due process right of access to the courts); Wolff v. McDonnell, 418 U.S. 539, 555–56 (1974) (minimal due process proceedings required for certain prison disciplinary proceedings).

[88]*See, e.g.,* Pell v. Procunier, 417 U.S. 817, 822 (1974) (speech); Cruz v. Beto, 405 U.S. 319, 322 (1972) (religion).

[89]*See, e.g.,* Lee v. Washington, 390 U.S. 333, 333 (1968).

[90]*See, e.g.,* Carlson v. Green, 446 U.S. 14 (1980); Hutto v. Finney, 437 U.S. 678, 685 (1978); Estelle v. Gamble, 429 U.S. 97, 102–05 (1976). *See also* Bell v. Wolfish, 441 U.S. 520, 535 & n.16 (1979) (punishment of pretrial detainees would violate substantive due process).

[91]Youngberg v. Romeo, 457 U.S. 307, 321–22 (1982). The Court held that commitment under proper procedure does not deprive the patient of all substantive liberty interests protected by the Constitution, *id.* at 316, and explicitly recognized that patients have a constitutional right to personal security, to reasonably safe conditions of confinement, to freedom from unreasonable bodily restraint, and to such minimally adequate habilitation or training as may reasonably be required to ensure safety and freedom from undue restraint. *Id.* at 316–19. For general discussions of the rights of patients, see G. ANNAS, THE RIGHTS OF HOSPITAL PATIENTS (1975); BRAKEL ET AL., *supra* note 2; B. ENNIS & R. EMERY, THE RIGHTS OF MENTAL PATIENTS (rev. ed. 1978); P. FREIDMAN, THE RIGHTS OF MENTALLY RETARDED PERSONS (1976).

extent necessary to allow for confinement by the state so as to prevent him from being a danger to himself or to others.''[92]

Thus, a dramatic transformation has occurred in the law pertaining to mental patients and prisoners. In the past 20 years, the battleground has shifted to litigation on behalf of these groups asserting various provisions of the Constitution as restrictions on unwanted imposition of treatment. The Constitution contains a variety of broad and vaguely worded limitations on governmental action. The Fourteenth Amendment, for example, expressly limits the states' power to deprive any person of life, liberty, or property without due process and guarantees to all citizens the equal protection of the laws. Although by their terms these general clauses do not refer to the problems raised by involuntary treatment, these constitutional restrictions, as well as a number of more specific ones (e.g., those dealing with freedom of speech, freedom from cruel and unusual punishment, and the guarantee of the free exercise of religion), are capable of being construed to impose limitations on governmental imposition of unwanted therapy. The following chapters examine each of these constitutional provisions in detail to determine the extent to which they can serve as a basis for a constitutional right to refuse treatment.

---

[92]Rennie v. Klein, 653 F.2d 838, 843 (3d Cir. 1981) (en banc), *vacated and remanded on other grounds,* 458 U.S. 1119 (1982), *on remand,* 720 F.2d 266 (3d Cir. 1983) (en banc).

Chapter 10
THE FIRST AMENDMENT AND
MENTAL HEALTH TREATMENT:
Constitutional Protection Against Interference
With Mental Processes

A. Origins and Scope of the First Amendment

The First Amendment to the United States Constitution provides: "Congress shall make no law . . . abridging the freedom of speech. . . ."[1] Can this language apply to involuntary mental health treatment? Does it limit the activities of state hospitals or prisons? The First Amendment restricts only the exercise of federal power; it does not purport to apply to the states.[2] As a preliminary matter, one might consider whether the principles of the First Amendment can serve as limitations on state and local mental health and correctional institutions.

The First Amendment is one of a group of amendments to the Constitution, collectively known as the Bill of Rights. These amendments were passed by the First Congress and ratified by the states in 1791 in order to protect individual liberties against the new national government.[3] During the debates on ratification of the Constitution in the 13 colonies, opponents of ratification suggested that the absence of a Bill of Rights guaranteeing individual liberty created a grave potential for tyranny by the new federal government. Five of the 11 colonies that ratified the Constitution by early 1789 proposed amendments guaranteeing individual liberty against federal government encroachment.[4] In response to these concerns, the Bill of Rights was adopted to limit federal authority.

Except for several relatively minor limitations imposed on state legislatures,[5] the original Constitution did not place direct restrictions on the authority of the states to abridge personal rights until the adoption of the post-Civil War amendments: the Thirteenth, Fourteenth, and Fifteenth Amendments. The Fourteenth Amendment was ratified on July 28, 1868. It effected a fundamental reordering of the American constitutional system, providing considerably greater protection for individual liberties than was contained

---

[1] U.S. CONST. amend. I.

[2] E.g., Baron v. Baltimore, 32 U.S. (7 Pet.) 243 (1833); Permoli v. Municipality No. 1 of New Orleans, 44 U.S. (3 How.) 589, 609 (1845); see Warren, The New "Liberty" Under the Fourteenth Amendment, 39 HARV. L. REV. 431, 433–36 (1926). Moreover, the First Amendment does not restrict the actions of private persons. E.g., Public Utils. Comm'n v. Pollak, 343 U.S. 451, 461 (1952).

[3] G. GUNTHER, CONSTITUTIONAL LAW 406 (12th ed. 1991); M. NIMMER, NIMMER ON FREEDOM OF SPEECH § 1.01, at 1–2 to 1–3 (1984); J. NOWAK & R. ROTUNDA, CONSTITUTIONAL LAW (4th ed. 1991); L. TRIBE, AMERICAN CONSTITUTIONAL LAW § 1–2, at 3–4 (2d ed. 1988); Levy, Bill of Rights, in ESSAYS ON THE MAKING OF THE CONSTITUTION 258, 260, 266–67, 277 (L. Levy ed., 2d ed. 1987).

[4] See 1 J. ELLIOTT, DEBATES ON THE FEDERAL CONSTITUTION 328, 334 (1891); 3 Id. at 659; 4 Id. at 244. See generally B. SCHWARTZ, THE GREAT RIGHTS OF MANKIND 119–59 (1977).

[5] E.g., U.S. CONST. art. I, § 10, cl. 1 (banning any Bill of Attainder, ex post facto law, or law impairing the obligation of contracts); Id. at art. IV, § 1 (Full Faith and Credit Clause); Id. at art. IV, § 2 (Privileges and Immunities Clause); see NOWAK & ROTUNDA, supra note 3, at 331–32.

originally in the Constitution.[6] The Fourteenth Amendment prohibits states from depriving "any person of life, liberty, or property, without due process of law" and from denying "to any person within its jurisdiction the equal protection of the laws."[7] These broad and general provisions embody an evolving concept of liberty subject to constitutional protection against state encroachment.[8] The Supreme Court has read the Due Process Clause of the Fourteenth Amendment broadly, construing it to incorporate, on a selective basis, various protections of the Bill of Rights, thereby making these fundamental guarantees applicable to the states.[9] Although the Court in 1922 stated that the Fourteenth Amendment did not impose "any restrictions about 'freedom of speech' "[10] on the states, in 1925 it recognized that the First Amendment applied to the states through the Fourteenth Amendment.[11] Since then, the Court has repeatedly reiterated the First Amendment's limitations on state authority.[12]

The First Amendment thus serves as a limitation on governmental action at all levels—federal, state, and local.[13] The critical question is whether it can be construed to apply in the context of involuntary mental health treatment. Does the First Amendment restrict the government when it seeks to treat mental patients or rehabilitate offenders?

B. Construing "Freedom of Speech": Does the First Amendment Protect Mental Processes?

1. The Supreme Court's Methodology: Deriving Corollary Rights From Freedom of Speech

Aside from the protection of the free exercise of religion, discussed in chapter 13, the only right mentioned in the First Amendment that could conceivably apply to involuntary mental health treatment is freedom of speech, a right that at most seems to be only indirectly affected. Like other constitutional provisions, however, the protection of freedom of speech,

---

[6]*See* R. CORTNER, THE SUPREME COURT AND THE SECOND BILL OF RIGHTS 11 (1981); Kaczorowski, *To Begin the Nation Anew: Congress, Citizenship and Civil Rights After the Civil War,* 92 AMERICAN HIST. REV. 45 (1981). *See generally* W. NELSON, THE FOURTEENTH AMENDMENT: FROM POLITICAL PRINCIPLE TO JUDICIAL DOCTRINE (1988).

[7]U.S. CONST. amend. XIV, § 1.

[8]Duncan v. Louisiana, 391 U.S. 145, 175 (1968) (Harlan, J., dissenting).

[9]NOWAK & ROTUNDA, *supra* note 3, at 332–35, 380–94, 360–72; TRIBE, *supra* note 3, § 11–2, at 772–74; *see, e.g.,* Benton v. Maryland, 395 U.S. 784 (1969) (Fifth Amendment right against double jeopardy); Duncan v. Louisiana, 391 U.S. 145 (1968) (Sixth Amendment right to jury trial). DeJonge v. Oregon, 299 U.S. 353 (1937) (First Amendment right to petition); Near v. Minnesota, 283 U.S. 697 (1931) (First Amendment right to freedom of press); Fiske v. Kansas, 274 U.S. 380 (1927) (First Amendment right to freedom of speech); Chicago, B. & Q. R.R. v. Chicago, 166 U.S. 226 (1897) (Fifth Amendment right to just compensation).

[10]Prudential Ins. Co. v. Cheek, 259 U.S. 530, 543 (1922).

[11]Gitlow v. New York, 268 U.S. 652, 666 (1925) (dicta). For a discussion of the inclusion of the First Amendment within the liberty protected by the Due Process Clause of the Fourteenth Amendment, see Warren, *supra* note 2, at 455–59. The Court first used the First Amendment to invalidate a state abridgement of free speech in Fiske v. Kansas, 274 U.S. 380 (1927).

[12]*E.g.,* Wallace v. Jaffree, 472 U.S. 38, 49–50 (1985) (plurality opinion).

[13]Although the Fourteenth Amendment restricts the actions of the states, its coverage extends to all state action, including that taken by local agencies. *E.g.,* West Va. State Bd. of Educ. v. Barnette, 319 U.S. 624, 637–38 (1943) ("The Fourteenth Amendment, as now applied to the States, protects the citizen against the State itself and all of its creatures. . . . There are village tyrants as well as village Hampdens, but none who acts under color of law is beyond reach of the Constitution.").

one of the "majestic generalities of the Bill of Rights,"[14] is an ambiguous and open-ended concept that can be construed broadly to realize the basic purposes the provision was designed to accomplish. Although the First Amendment "literally forbids the abridgement only of 'speech,' " the Supreme Court has long recognized that its protection "does not end at the spoken or written word."[15] Thus, the First Amendment protects conduct that is communicative in nature[16] and even music (as a form of expression[17]). Similarly, in a variety of other contexts the Court has derived from freedom of speech a number of corollary rights deemed essential to the purposes of the First Amendment.

Illustrations of this methodology are useful in analyzing whether the First Amendment can be read to limit involuntary mental health treatment. A leading example is freedom of association. The Supreme Court has recognized "a right to associate for the purpose of engaging in those activities protected by the First Amendment—speech, assembly, petition for the redress of grievances, and the exercise of religion."[18] The Court has deemed freedom of association to be guaranteed by the Constitution because it is "an indispensable means of preserving" these enumerated liberties.[19] These explicitly guaranteed freedoms "could not be vigorously protected . . . unless a correlative freedom to engage in group effort toward those ends were not also guaranteed."[20] Thus, the Court has long found "implicit in the right to engage in activities protected by the First Amendment a corresponding right to associate with others" in pursuit of these activities.[21] Although freedom of association "is not expressly included in the First Amendment, its existence is necessary in making the express guarantees fully meaningful."[22] Without protection for association and other "peripheral rights the specific rights would be less secure."[23]

---

[14]*Barnette,* 319 U.S. at 639; *see also* Globe Newspaper Co. v. Superior Court, 457 U.S. 596, 604 (1982) ("[W]e have long eschewed any "narrow, literal conception' of the [First] Amendment's terms, . . . for the Framers were concerned with broad principles. . . ."); Gompers v. United States, 233 U.S. 604, 610 (1914) (Holmes, J.):

> [T]he provisions of the Constitution are not mathematical formulas having their essence in their form; they are organic living institutions transplanted from English soil. Their significance is vital not formal; it is to be gathered not simply by taking the words and a dictionary, but by considering their origin and the line of their growth.

Fiss, *The Supreme Court, 1978 Term—Foreword: The Forms of Justice,* 93 HARV. L. REV. 1, 1, 11 (1979).

[15]Texas v. Johnson, 491 U.S. 397, 404 (1989).

[16]In recognizing that flag burning for expressive purposes is within the protection of the First Amendment, the Court in *Johnson* followed a long line of cases that found various kinds of conduct to be "sufficiently imbued with elements of communication to fall within the scope of the First and Fourteenth Amendments." *Id.* (quoting Spence v. Washington, 418 U.S. 405, 409 (1974)); *see, e.g.,* United States v. Grace, 461 U.S. 171, 176 (1983) (picketing); *Spence,* 418 U.S. at 409–10 (attaching a peace sign to a flag); Schacht v. United States, 398 U.S. 58 (1970) (wearing of American military uniform in a dramatic presentation criticizing Vietnam War); Tinker v. Des Moines Indep. Community School Dist., 393 U.S. 503, 505–06 (1969) (wearing of black arm bands to protest Vietnam War); Amalgamated Food Employees Union Local 590 v. Logan Valley Plaza, Inc., 391 U.S. 308, 313–14 (1968) (picketing); Brown v. Louisiana, 383 U.S. 131, 141–42 (1966) (sit-in demonstration); *Barnette,* 319 U.S. at 632 (refusing to salute the flag); Stromberg v. California, 283 U.S. 359, 368–69 (1931) (displaying a red flag).

[17]Ward v. Rock Against Racism, 491 U.S. 781, 790 (1989).

[18]Roberts v. United States Jaycees, 468 U.S. 609, 618 (1984); *see, e.g.,* NAACP v. Clairborne Hardware Co., 458 U.S. 886 (1982); Citizens Against Rent Control v. City of Berkeley, 454 U.S. 290 (1981); Abood v. Detroit Bd. of Educ., 431 U.S. 209, 233 (1977); Elrod v. Burns, 427 U.S. 347, 355–57 (1976) (plurality opinion); Cousins v. Wigoda, 419 U.S. 477, 487 (1975) (right to choose political party); Healy v. James, 408 U.S. 169, 181 (1972); United States v. Robel, 389 U.S. 258, 263 n.7 (1967); NAACP v. Button, 371 U.S. 415 (1963) (group legal practice); NAACP v. Alabama *ex rei.* Patterson, 357 U.S. 449, 460-61 (1958). *See generally* TRIBE, *supra* note 3, § 12–23, at 977–86.

[19]*Roberts,* 468 U.S. at 618.

[20]*Id.* at 622.

[21]*Id.*

[22]Griswold v. Connecticut, 381 U.S. 479, 483 (1965).

[23]*Id.*

Not only is freedom of association a derivative safeguard of the liberties explicitly guaranteed by the First Amendment, but other rights have in turn been derived from the freedom to associate. These include, for example, the right to make financial contributions to an organization for the purpose of spreading a political message.[24] Because making such a contribution "enables like-minded persons to pool their resources in furtherance of common political goals,"[25] the Court has reasoned that limitations on the freedom to contribute "implicate fundamental First Amendment interests."[26] Moreover, the Court has held that the First Amendment protects not only the right of an individual to associate with others in an organization and to contribute to that organization, but also a right not to be compelled by the government to join an organization[27] or to contribute financially to the support of an organization's efforts to advance an ideological cause the individual may oppose.[28] "Freedom of association . . . plainly presupposes a freedom not to associate."[29]

Another First Amendment right derived from the freedom of association is the right to "privacy in one's associations"—the right to be free of compelled disclosure of membership in an association.[30] Because of the "vital relationship" between this right and the freedom to associate, the Court has deemed privacy in group association to be "indispensable to [the] preservation of freedom of association. . . ."[31]

Similarly, the Court has construed the First Amendment to protect not only the right to speak freely but also "the right to refrain from speaking at all."[32] The Court reasoned that "[a] system which secures the right to proselytize religious, political, and ideological causes must also guarantee the concomitant right to decline to foster such concepts."[33] The right to speak and the right to refrain from speaking are, in the Court's words, "complementary components" and are thus both within the protection of the First Amendment.[34]

In a 1982 case, the Court used this methodology to recognize a "right to receive information and ideas" as "an inherent corollary of the right of free speech and press that are explicitly guaranteed" by the First Amendment.[35] The Court stressed that effective speech

---

[24]Citizens Against Rent Control v. City of Berkeley, 454 U.S. 290 (1981); First Nat'l Bank v. Bellotti, 435 U.S. 765 (1978); Buckley v. Valeo, 424 U.S. 1 (1976).

[25]*Buckley,* 424 U.S. at 22.

[26]*Id.* at 23.

[27]Elrod v. Burns, 427 U.S. 347, 363–64 & n.17 (1976) (city prohibited from compelling individual to associate with a political party as a condition of retaining public employment).

[28]Abood v. Detroit Bd. of Educ., 431 U.S. 209, 235 (1977) (Public school teachers could not be required, as a condition of employment, to contribute union dues to be used for union's expenditures for ideological causes not germane to collective bargaining.).

[29]Roberts v. United States Jaycees, 468 U.S. 609, 623 (1984).

[30]NAACP v. Alabama *ex rel.* Patterson, 357 U.S. 449, 462 (1958).

[31]*Id.*

[32]Wooley v. Maynard, 430 U.S. 705, 714 (1977) (state could not require motor vehicles to bear license plates embossed with the state motto—"Live Free or Die"—over objection of Jehovah's Witnesses who viewed the motto as repugnant to their moral, religious, and political beliefs). See also West Va. State Bd. of Educ. v. Barnette, 319 U.S. 624, 633–34 (1943) (public school students could not be required to participate in compulsory flag salute).

[33]*Wooley,* 430 U.S. at 714. *See also* Pacific Gas & Elec. Co. v. Public Utils. Comm'n, 475 U.S. 1, 8 (1986) (plurality opinion) ("a concomitant freedom *not* to speak publicly") (quoting Harper & Row Publishers, Inc. v. Nation Enterprises, 471 U.S. 539, 559 (1985)).

[34]*Wooley,* 430 U.S. at 714.

[35]Board of Educ. v. Pico, 457 U.S. 853, 867 (1982) (plurality opinion) (Constitution prohibited school board from removing disagreeable books from school library). The plurality opinion, authored by Justice Brennan, cited prior cases recognizing a "right to receive information and ideas." *Id.; see* First Nat'l Bank v. Bellotti, 435 U.S. 765, 783 (1978); Lamont v. Postmaster Gen., 381 U.S. 301, 308 (1965) (Brennan, J., concurring); Martin v. City of Struthers, 319 U.S. 141, 143 (1943). *See also Pacific Gas,* 475 U.S. at 8 (plurality opinion) ("[T]he First Amendment protects the public's interest in receiving information") ; Thornhill v. Alabama, 310 U.S. 88, 102 (1940); *infra* notes 118–26 and accompanying text.

requires listeners[36] and that recognition of a right to receive information was thus necessary to give meaning to the First Amendment rights of speakers. Furthermore, the Court found that the right to receive ideas and information was a "necessary predicate to the recipient's meaningful exercise of his own rights of speech, press, and political freedom."[37]

Thus, by stressing that the right of freedom of speech "has broad scope,"[38] the Court in a number of contexts has construed freedom of speech to protect other rights that it found to be "corollary" rights, "complementary components" of the right, "concomitant rights," "corresponding rights," "peripheral rights," or rights that are "implicit in," "presupposed" by, "indispensable to," or "a necessary predicate" to the exercise of the right of freedom of speech.[39] In these cases the Court viewed these derivative rights as necessary to protect the purposes underlying the First Amendment and did not hesitate to read "freedom of speech" expansively to cover them as well.[40]

2. Supreme Court Protection for "Freedom of Thought," "Freedom of Mind," and "Freedom of Belief"

The Supreme Court has applied this same approach in differing contexts to protect "freedom of belief," "freedom of mind," or "freedom of thought." Although the Court has never considered the application of the First Amendment in the context of involuntary treatment of mental patients or criminal offenders, these cases provide ample support for construing the First Amendment to place limits on at least the more intrusive therapies. Indeed, a number of state and lower federal court decisions have applied the language in these Supreme Court cases to extend First Amendment protection against such intrusive therapies as psychosurgery,[41] electroconvulsive therapy,[42] and psychotropic medication.[43]

Perhaps the Court's first reference to First Amendment protection for mental processes came in Justice Brandeis's concurring opinion in *Whitney v. California*.[44] Brandeis referred to the ultimate end of the state as making people "free to develop their faculties" and stressed that "freedom to think as you will" is "indispensable to the discovery and spread of

---

[36]*Pico*, 457 U.S. at 867.

[37]*Id.*

[38]*E.g., Martin*, 319 U.S. at 143; Bridges v. California, 314 U.S. 252, 263 (1941) (The First Amendment "must be taken as a command of the broadest scope that explicit language, read in the context of a liberty-loving society, will allow.").

[39]*See supra* notes 14–37 and accompanying text.

[40]*See* Globe Newspaper Co. v. Superior Court, 457 U.S. 596, 604 (1982) ("The First Amendment is thus broad enough to encompass those rights that, while not unambiguously enumerated in the very terms of the Amendment, are nonetheless necessary to the enjoyment of other First Amendment rights."); Lamont v. Postmaster Gen., 381 U.S. 301, 308 (1965) (Brennan, J., concurring) ("It is true that the First Amendment contains no specific guarantee of access to publications. However, the protection of the Bill of Rights goes beyond the specific guarantees to protect from congressional abridgment those equally fundamental personal rights necessary to make the express guarantees fully meaningful.").

[41]Kaimowitz v. Michigan Dep't of Mental Health, Civ. No. 73-19434-AW (Mich. Cir. Ct. July 10, 1973), *reprinted in* A. BROOKS, LAW, PSYCHIATRY AND THE MENTAL HEALTH SYSTEM, at 902, 916–19 (1974).

[42]Lojuk v. Quandt, 706 F.2d 1456 (7th Cir. 1983).

[43]Bee v. Greaves, 744 F.2d 1387, 1393–94 (10th Cir. 1984), *cert. denied*, 469 U.S. 1214 (1985); Scott v. Plante, 532 F.2d 939, 946 (3d Cir. 1976), *vacated and remanded*, 458 U.S. 1101 (1982); Davis v. Hubbard, 506 F. Supp. 915, 933 (N.D. Ohio 1980); Rogers v. Okin, 478 F. Supp. 1342, 1366–67 (D. Mass. 1979), *aff'd in part and rev'd in part on other grounds*, 634 F.2d 650 (1st Cir. 1980), *vacated and remanded sub nom.* Mills v. Rogers, 457 U.S. 291 (1982), *on remand sub nom.* Rogers v. Okin, 738 F.2d 1 (1st Cir. 1984); *see also* Mackey v. Procunier, 477 F.2d 877, 878 (9th Cir. 1973) (The involuntary use of succinylcholine as part of an aversive conditioning program would raise serious constitutional questions concerning "impermissible tinkering with the mental processes.").

[44]274 U.S. 357 (1927).

political truth.''[45] The Court again treated the First Amendment as providing protection for ''freedom of thought'' in Justice Cardozo's opinion in *Palko v. Connecticut.*[46] Together with freedom of speech, Cardozo referred to freedom of thought as ''the matrix, the indispensable condition, of nearly every other form of freedom.''[47] In *Griswold v. Connecticut,* Justice Douglas also listed ''freedom of thought'' as one of the rights comprehended by freedom of speech.[48] In addition, the Court in several contexts has referred to the First Amendment as protecting ''freedom of mind.''[49]

In a number of Supreme Court cases that distinguish between the government's power to regulate conduct and its power to regulate thought or belief, the Court has recognized a First Amendment freedom to believe. For example, in *Cantwell v. Connecticut,*[50] the Court distinguished ''freedom to believe'' from freedom to act.[51] ''The first,'' the Court noted, ''is absolute but, in the nature of things, the second cannot be.''[52]

In these cases distinguishing belief from conduct, the question was whether the regulation of certain kinds of conduct diminish impermissibly the freedom of individuals to think and believe as they wish. Even when upholding governmental regulation, the Court recognized that freedom of thought and belief are immune from governmental control. Assuming the viability of a distinction between thoughts and beliefs on the one hand and conduct on the other, it would seem that most mental health interventions affect both. Although all of these treatment techniques undoubtedly affect behavior, all except the behavioral techniques seek to bring about a change in mental processes—to affect attitudes, emotions, thoughts, and beliefs.

Of course, not every attempt by government to change attitudes or beliefs raises First Amendment problems. Government in America has enormous power to disseminate ideas and information. It seeks to inculcate values in public school students, to warn consumers about health and safety hazards, and to persuade the public to give its approval to a variety of policies and programs.[53] Indeed, government is the largest communicator in American society.[54] Much of what government does undoubtedly has the effect of changing attitudes and beliefs, but it is sensible to distinguish between methods that individuals are free to resist and the more systematic and intrusive methods of mental health treatment, which unwilling individuals may not resist. Although not all of these treatments intrude sufficiently on mental processes to trigger First Amendment inquiry, the more intrusive of the treatment techniques do seem to implicate the First Amendment values reflected in the Supreme Court cases.

---

[45]*Id.* at 375–76.

[46]302 U.S. 319 (1937).

[47]*Id.* at 326–27.

[48]381 U.S. 479, 481 (1965).

[49]*E.g.,* Wooley v. Maynard, 430 U.S. 705, 715 (1977); Thomas v. Collins, 323 U.S. 516, 531 (1945); Prince v. Massachusetts, 321 U.S. 158, 164 (1944); West Va. State Bd. of Educ. v. Barnette, 319 U.S. 624, 637 (1943); *Palko,* 302 U.S. at 326–27.

[50]310 U.S. 296 (1940).

[51]*Id.* at 303–04.

[52]*Id.; accord* American Communications Ass'n v. Douds, 339 U.S. 382 (1950) (plurality opinion).

[53]*See* Meese v. Keene, 481 U.S. 465 (1987) (Department of Justice designation of foreign films as ''political propaganda'' held not to violate First Amendment); Block v. Meese, 793 F.2d 1303, 1312–14 (D.C. Cir. 1986) (Scalia, J.) (discussing government speech designed to influence decisionmaking). *See generally* J. TUSSMAN, GOVERNMENT AND THE MIND (1977).

[54]*See generally* M. YUDOF, WHEN GOVERNMENT SPEAKS: POLITICS, LAW, AND GOVERNMENT EXPRESSION IN AMERICA (1983); Ingber, *The Marketplace of Ideas: A Legitimizing Myth,* 1984 DUKE L.J. 1, 27–30; Shiffrin, *Government Speech,* 27 UCLA L. REV. 565 (1980); Ziegler, *Government Speech and the Constitution: The Limits of Official Partisanship,* 21 B.C. L. REV. 578 (1980).

3. When Government Attempts To Impose Orthodoxy of Belief

Another area of First Amendment jurisprudence that suggests constitutional protection for thought and belief arose in response to various governmental attempts to impose orthodoxy of belief. In the seminal case *West Virginia State Board of Education v. Barnette,*[55] the Supreme Court considered a challenge to a school requirement that all teachers and pupils participate in a flag salute ceremony involving a "stiff-arm" salute and the repeating of the Pledge of Allegiance. Jehovah's Witnesses challenged the compulsory ceremony as inconsistent with their religious beliefs, asserting what the Court characterized as "a right of self-determination in matters that touch individual opinion and personal attitude."[56] The Court distinguished between instruction concerning the meaning of the flag, which would not offend the Constitution, and "a compulsion of students to declare a belief."[57] The Court considered a requirement that the individual "communicate by word and sign his acceptance of the political ideas . . . [the flag] bespeaks"[58] to be an "affirmation of a belief and an attitude of mind."[59] Furthermore, the Court noted that determining whether the First Amendment permitted the government to order observance of such a ritual did not depend on the Court's assessment of the value of the exercise[60] or on whether the objection to participation in the compulsory ceremony was religious in nature.[61] Finally, the Court rejected the notion that the benevolent motives of the school authorities would save the constitutionality of the requirement.[62] In emphatic language, the Court invalidated the compelled flag salute as an unconstitutional invasion of "the sphere of intellect and spirit which it is the purpose of the First Amendment to our Constitution to reserve from official control."[63] "If there is any fixed star in our constitutional constellation," the Court declared, "it is that no official, high or petty, can prescribe what shall be orthodox in politics, nationalism, religion, or other matters of opinion or force citizens to confess by word or act their faith therein."[64] According to the Court, the First Amendment erects a constitutional preference for "individual freedom of mind" over "officially disciplined uniformity for which history indicates a disappointing and disastrous end."[65] Central to our American freedoms is the "freedom to be intellectually and spiritually diverse."[66] "We can have intellectual individualism and the rich cultural diversities that we owe to exceptional

---

[55]319 U.S. 624 (1943).

[56]*Id.* at 631.

[57]*Id.*

[58]*Id.* at 633.

[59]*Id.*

[60][V]alidity of the asserted power to force an American citizen publicly to profess any statement of belief or to engage in any ceremony of assent to one, presents questions of power that must be considered independently of any idea we may have as to the utility of the ceremony in question.
Id. at 634. The Court held that the students' liberty of conscience could not be infringed in the name of "national unity" or "patriotism." *Id.* at 640–41.

[61]*Id.* at 634–35.

[62]*Id.* at 640.

[63]*Id.* at 642.

[64]*Id. See also* Torcaso v. Watkins, 367 U.S. 488, 495–96 (1961) (finding a state constitutional requirement that a notary public declare his belief in God in order to receive his appointment to be an unconstitutional invasion of the freedom of belief and religion).

[65]*Barnette,* 319 U.S. at 637.

[66]*Id.* at 641.

minds,'' noted the Court, ''only at the price of occasional eccentricity and abnormal attitudes.''[67]

The Court has followed the *Barnette* doctrine in other contexts, both within and without the school. In *Tinker v. Des Moines Independent Community School District*[68] the Court relied on *Barnette* in concluding that the First Amendment prohibited the suspension of students who refused to remove black arm bands worn to protest the Vietnam War.[69] The Court also reiterated its earlier repudiation of the principle that a state could conduct its public schools so as to ''foster a homogeneous people.''[70] ''In our system,'' the Court warned, ''students may not be regarded as closed-circuit recipients of only that which the State chooses to communicate.''[71]

The Court also relied on *Barnette*'s ban on government attempts to impose orthodoxy of belief in *Elrod v. Burns*,[72] holding unconstitutional the discharge of Republican employees of a sheriff's department solely because of their political party affiliation.[73] The Court explicitly recognized freedom of belief as a First Amendment guarantee, stating that ''freedom of belief and association constitute the core of those activities protected by the First Amendment.''[74] The Court reaffirmed *Burns* and *Barnette* in subsequent patronage hiring[75] and dismissal cases,[76] holding that the First Amendment protects public employees from being denied employment or being discharged on the basis of what they believe.

The Court again invoked the principle of *Barnette* in two 1977 cases. In *Wooley v. Maynard*,[77] the Court considered a state statutory requirement that noncommercial motor vehicles bear license plates embossed with the state motto, ''Live Free or Die.'' Two Jehovah's Witnesses attacked the requirement as repugnant to their moral, religious, and political beliefs. The Court invalidated the statute as inconsistent with ''the right of freedom of thought protected by the First Amendment,'' which the Court found to include both the ''right to speak freely and the right to refrain from speaking at all.''[78] The Court considered the right to speak and the right to refrain from speaking to be ''complementary components of the broader concept of 'individual freedom of mind.' ''[79] As in *Barnette*, the statutory requirement in *Wooley* was a ''state measure which forces an individual . . . to be an instrument for fostering public adherence to an ideological point of view he finds unacceptable.''[80] The Court found this to invade ''the sphere of intellect and spirit which it is the purpose of the First Amendment to our Constitution to reserve from all official control.''[81]

---

[67]*Id.* at 641–42.

[68]393 U.S. 503 (1969).

[69]*Id.* at 507, 514.

[70]*Id.* at 511 (quoting Meyer v. Nebraska, 262 U.S. 390, 402 (1923)).

[71]*Id.*

[72]427 U.S. 347 (1976).

[73]*Id.* at 356.

[74]*Id.*

[75]Rutan v. Republican Party of Illinois, 497 U.S. 62, 79 (1990).

[76]Branti v. Finkel, 445 U.S. 507, 515 (1980).

[77]430 U.S. 705 (1977).

[78]*Id.* at 714; *accord* Harper & Row Publishers, Inc. v. Nation Enters., 471 U.S. 539 (1985) (''Freedom of thought and expression 'includes both the right to speak freely and the right to refrain from speaking at all.' '') (quoting *Wooley*, 430 U.S. at 714).

[79]430 U.S. at 714 (quoting West Va. State Bd. of Educ. v. Barnette, 319 U.S. 624, 637 (1943)).

[80]*Id.* at 715.

[81]*Id.* (quoting *Barnette*, 319 U.S. at 642).

"The First Amendment," the Court noted, "protects the right of individuals to hold a point of view different from the majority. . . ."[82]

In *Abood v. Detroit Board of Education*,[83] the Court considered a state statute that conditioned employment of public school teachers, whether or not union members, on their paying the union a service charge equal to union dues. The union used a portion of the revenue to advance various political and ideological activities. The Court held that this requirement violated the First Amendment rights of teachers who objected to compulsory financial support for an ideological message with which they disagreed. The Court found that "at the heart of the First Amendment is the notion that an individual should be free to believe as he will, and that in a free society one's beliefs should be shaped by his mind and his conscience rather than coerced by the State."[84] Moreover, the Court noted, this "freedom of belief is no incidental or secondary aspect of the First Amendment's protections."[85]

Wooley and *Abood* thus extend the *Barnette* principle to recognize a negative speech right—the right of individuals to refrain from speaking or being compelled to associate with ideological views with which they disagree.[86] The Court expanded the concept of negative speech rights in *Pacific Gas & Electric Co. v. Public Utilities Commission*,[87] in which it held that an order of the Public Utilities Commission granting a consumer group access to the utility billing envelopes of a power company violated the company's First Amendment rights. This "forced association with potentially hostile views burdens the expression of views different from" those of the consumer group and "risks forcing [the utility company] to speak where it would prefer to remain silent."[88] "[T]he choice to speak," the Court affirmed, "includes within it the choice of what not to say."[89]

Barnette and its progeny thus recognize a broad constitutional interest in "freedom of conscience"[90] and "freedom of mind."[91] These cases provide further support for a First Amendment right to be free of the invasions of mental processes brought about by at least the more intrusive of the mental health treatment techniques. If there is a "sphere of intellect and spirit" reserved from official control,[92] then that protected sphere must include the individual's basic personality, emotions, attitudes, and beliefs. Again, not every government interference constitutes "official control"; governmental attempts to influence attitudes, emotions, and beliefs will rarely rise to this level. However, intrusive mental health treatment techniques, like psychosurgery, that effect massive changes in the individual's

---

[82]*Id.*

[83]431 U.S. 209 (1977).

[84]*Id.* at 234–35. *See also* First Nat'l Bank v. Bellotti, 435 U.S. 765, 816 (1978) (White, J., dissenting, joined by Brennan & Marshall, J.J.) (individuals have First Amendment "right to adhere to [their] own beliefs and to refuse to support the . . . views of others"); Elrod v. Burns, 427 U.S. 347, 372 (1976) (First Amendment recognizes the rights of every citizen "to believe as he will and to act and associate according to his beliefs"); Prince v. Massachusetts, 321 U.S. 158, 164 (1944) ("freedom of the mind").

[85]*Abood*, 431 U.S. at 235.

[86]This principle had earlier been applied in Miami Herald Publishing Co. v. Tornillo, 416 U.S. 241 (1974), which invalidated a statutory requirement that newspapers provide a right of reply to candidates whose character or record they had criticized. The right-to-reply statute was unconstitutional because it required the newspaper to disseminate a message with which it disagreed. *Id.* at 258.

[87]475 U.S. 1 (1986) (plurality opinion).

[88]*Id.* at 18.

[89]*Id.* at 16.

[90]*Id.* at 32 (Rehnquist, J., dissenting, joined by White & Stevens, J.J.).

[91]*Id.* (quoting Wooley v. Maynard, 430 U.S. 705, 714 (1977)). *See also* West Va. State Bd. of Educ. v. Barnette, 319 U.S. 624, 637 (1943).

[92]*Barnette*, 319 U.S. at 642, *quoted in Wooley*, 430 U.S. at 715.

personality, mental processes, and emotional responsiveness that the individual is unable to resist, clearly constitute a direct and serious invasion of "individual freedom of mind."[93] If "at the heart of the First Amendment is the notion that . . . one's beliefs should be shaped by his mind and his conscience rather than coerced by the State,"[94] then treatment techniques that coerce beliefs, attitudes, and mental processes certainly implicate the values protected by the First Amendment. Just as a public school may not require its students to affirm "a belief and an attitude of mind"[95] or "to confess by word or act their faith" in some official orthodoxy,[96] the state may not subject mental patients and offenders to treatment that requires them to discard particular attitudes or beliefs and affirm attitudes and beliefs prescribed by state rehabilitators. Like car owners,[97] newspapers,[98] and power companies,[99] mental patients and offenders may not be subjected to "forced association"[100] with particular views. Moreover, *Barnette* teaches that the state may not justify coerced orthodoxy by the high value it places on the objectives it seeks to achieve or by the benevolent motives of governmental officials.[101]

4. First Amendment Protection of Private Thoughts

The 1969 Supreme Court case of *Stanley v. Georgia*[102] provides an additional and significant source of support for the existence of a First Amendment right to be free of interference with mental processes. *Stanley* involved a prosecution for the private possession of obscene materials in the home. The defendant asserted a constitutional "right to satisfy his intellectual and emotional needs in the privacy of his own home" and a "right to be free from state inquiry into the contents of his library."[103] In broad language, the Court stated that "[o]ur whole constitutional heritage rebels at the thought of giving government the power to control men's minds."[104] The Court concluded that the state "cannot constitutionally premise legislation on the desirability of controlling a person's private thoughts."[105] So sweeping is this language that Tribe has suggested it may place "the activities actually going on within the head" absolutely beyond government control.[106]

Significantly, the *Stanley* Court rejected Georgia's argument that just as it could protect the bodies of its citizens by prohibiting the possession of things thought detrimental to their welfare, it also could protect their minds from the effects of obscenity.[107] This contention, the Court found, amounts to a state's assertion of the authority "to control the moral content

---

[93]*Wooley,* 430 U.S. at 714 (quoting *Barnette,* 319 U.S. at 637).

[94]Abood v. Detroit Bd. of Educ., 431 U.S. 209, 234–35 (1977).

[95]*Barnette,* 319 U.S. at 633.

[96]*Id.* at 642.

[97]*See, e.g.,* Wooley v. Maynard, 430 U.S. 705 (1977).

[98]*See, e.g.,* Miami Herald Publishing Co. v. Tornillo, 418 U.S. 241 (1974).

[99]*See, e.g.,* Pacific Gas & Elec. Co. v. Pub. Utils. Comm'n, 475 U.S. 1 (1986).

[100]*Id.* at 18 (plurality opinion).

[101]*See supra* text accompanying notes 60 & 62.

[102] 394 U.S. 557 (1969).

[103]*Id.* at 565.

[104]*Id.*.

[105]*Id.* at 566.

[106]TRIBE, *supra* note 3, § 15–5, at 1315.

[107]*Stanley,* 394 U.S. at 560, 565.

of a person's thoughts.''[108] The Court rejected this assertion as ''wholly inconsistent with the philosophy of the First Amendment.''[109]

Although in subsequent cases the Court narrowed *Stanley* to the private possession of obscenity in the home and refused to extend it to prohibit state control over the public display or distribution of obscene material,[110] the Court has continued to recognize the validity of the principle *Stanley* had announced. In these cases the state was not attempting ''to control the minds or thoughts'' of those who patronized the theaters in question; the prevention of distribution of obscenity ''is distinct from a control of reason and the intellect.''[111] *Stanley* thus provides First Amendment protection for the possession and use of material that itself is unprotected by the Constitution; although the state may make criminal the importation, mailing, or display of such material or its sale to a willing buyer, it may not punish its private possession. The state's action was not unconstitutional merely because some human '' 'thoughts' may be incidentally affected'' by the restrictions imposed.[112] The Court saw an analogy in the government's power to regulate the sale of drugs even though ''[t]he fantasies of a drug addict are his own and beyond the reach of government. . . .''[113] Justice Harlan, concurring in *United States v. Reidel*,[114] described the constitutional interest protected in *Stanley* as ''the First Amendment right of the individual to be free from governmental programs of thought control, however such programs might be justified in terms of permissible state objectives''[115] and the ''freedom from governmental manipulation of the content of a man's mind. . . .''[116]

If government lacks the ''power to control men's minds''[117] by regulating the content of their libraries, then surely it also must lack the power to do so more directly by imposing powerful therapies that regulate the content of the mind itself. Again, governmental programs or even imposed therapies that only incidentally affect thoughts and beliefs will not implicate the First Amendment. Intrusive therapies that ''control'' the mind, on the other hand, would appear to raise First Amendment problems. And, as *Stanley* teaches, the government's desire to protect the patient's welfare by rehabilitating his mind, however legitimate this motive may be, cuts strongly against the grain of First Amendment jurisprudence.

5. The First Amendment Right To Receive Information and Ideas

An additional line of Supreme Court cases that supports First Amendment protection of mental processes deals with the developing First Amendment ''right to receive information

---

[108]*Id.* at 565.

[109]*Id.* at 565–66.

[110]*See* United States v. Orito, 413 U.S. 139 (1973); United States v. Twelve 200-Foot Reels, 413 U.S. 123 (1973); Paris Adult Theater I v. Slaton, 413 U.S. 49 (1973); United States v. Reidel, 402 U.S. 351 (1971).

[111]*Paris Adult Theater,* 413 U.S. at 67. *See also Reidel,* 402 U.S. at 356 (''freedom of mind and thought'' protected by *Stanley* does not require recognition of a right to distribute or sell obscene materials).

[112]*Paris Adult Theater,* 413 U.S. at 67.

[113]*Id.*

[114]402 U.S. 351 (1971).

[115]*Id.* at 359 (Harlan, J., concurring).

[116]*Id.*

[117]Stanley v. Georgia, 394 U.S. 557, 565 (1969).

and ideas.''[118] The Court has found this right, like freedom of association, to be an ''inherent corollary'' of the First Amendment.[119] Thus, in *Board of Education v. Pico*,[120] the Court invoked the right to receive information in preventing the removal of unpopular books from a school library.[121] The Court expressed concern that a contrary ruling would encourage the kind of ''officially prescribed orthodoxy'' that the First Amendment condemns.[122] ''Our Constitution,'' the Court stressed, ''does not permit the official suppression of *ideas*.''[123]

If the First Amendment forbids government suppression of ideas through removal of certain books from the school library, then it clearly should forbid government suppression of ideas through the more direct methods of psychotechnology. If anything, the prospect of ''officially prescribed orthodoxy'' imposed surgically or pharmacologically is more ominous than the orthodoxy that could be brought about by controlling the contents of the school library. Indeed, as Justice Rehnquist noted in a dissenting opinion in *Pico*, ''the denial of access to ideas inhibits one's own acquisition of knowledge only when that denial is relatively complete.''[124] Because ''the removed books are readily available to students and non-students alike at the corner bookstore or the public library,''[125] in Justice Rehnquist's view the removal of books from the school library did not materially deny access to ideas in violation of the First Amendment. Moreover, as the dissent pointed out, official action that impedes access to ideas is inherently different from official suppression of the ideas themselves.[126]

Compared to the control of books in the school library, intrusive mental health therapy presents a much greater potential for suppression of ideas and the imposition of an ''officially prescribed orthodoxy.'' Moreover, unlike censorship in the library, mental patients and offenders cannot resist such therapy or even mitigate its effects through exposure to competing ideas. To the extent that intrusive mental health treatment techniques can effectively suppress ideas and substitute new ones, the First Amendment values protected by the Court in the school library case would be at much greater risk. If the Constitution protects ''the right to receive information and ideas'' as an ''inherent corollary'' of the right of free speech, then it would seem even more necessary that it protect the right to hold information and ideas—to maintain beliefs, attitudes, and emotions free of direct and irresistible government manipulation of mental processes.

---

[118]Board of Educ. v. Pico, 457 U.S. 853, 867 (1982) (plurality opinion). *See also* Pacific Gas & Elec. Co. v. Public Utils. Comm'n, 475 U.S. 1, 7 (1986) (plurality opinion); Globe Newspaper Co., Inc. v. Superior Court, 457 U.S. 596 (1982); Richmond Newspapers, Inc. v. Virginia, 448 U.S. 555 (1980) (plurality opinion); Virginia State Bd. of Pharmacy v. Virginia Citizens Consumer Council, Inc., 425 U.S. 748, 756–57 (1976); Procunier v. Martinez, 416 U.S. 396, 408 (1974); Kleindienst v. Mandel, 408 U.S. 753, 762–63 (1972); *Stanley*, 394 U.S. at 564; Lamont v. Postmaster Gen., 381 U.S. 301, 308 (1965) (Brennan, J., concurring); Griswold v. Connecticut, 381 U.S. 479, 482 (1965); Martin v. City of Struthers, 319 U.S. 141 (1943); Thornhill v. Alabama, 310 U.S. 88, 102 (1940). *See generally* Emerson, *Legal Foundations of the Right to Know*, 1976 WASH. U. L.Q., no. 1 at 1 (1976).

[119]*Pico*, 457 U.S. at 867.

[120]457 U.S. 853 (1982) (plurality opinion).

[121]*Id*. at 871–72.

[122]*Id*. at 871.

[123]*Id*.

[124]*Id*. at 913 (Rehnquist, J., dissenting).

[125]*Id*.

[126]*Id*. at 916.

6. Freedom From Intrusion Into Mental Processes as an Indispensable Condition for Freedom of Expression

Several different strands of First Amendment theory thus converge to support the existence of a First Amendment right to be free of at least serious and irresistible intrusions on mental processes. The principles of "freedom of the mind," "freedom of belief," and "freedom of thought" apply in the context of coerced mental health treatment. "The core of freedom of belief" concerns the right of individuals "to form and hold ideas and opinions which are not communicated to others."[127] This freedom must be a prerequisite to freedom of speech; without protection for freedom of the mind, freedom to speak would be meaningless. In fact, the "inward activities" of thought, belief, and emotion are the very essence of speech, "for speech has meaning and value only insofar as it reflects these [inward] activities."[128] Thus, although thoughts and beliefs are not literally speech, they are so interdependent with speech that a system of freedom of expression is inconceivable without protection for the integrity of mental processes.[129] A Supreme Court faithful to the principle that freedom "to believe" lies "at the heart of the First Amendment"[130] should have little difficulty extending First Amendment protection to the inward activities of the mind.

A right to hold ideas and opinions free of government coercion "makes it possible for citizens generally to exercise their rights of free speech and press in a meaningful manner . . ."[131] even more than the freedom to associate with others or the right of access to ideas. In the context of government imposition of mental health treatment, courts[132] and commentators[133] have recognized this necessary connection between freedom from intrusion into mental processes and freedom of expression. Freedom of expression would be illusory if government could intrude directly into mental processes to alter the very thoughts,

---

[127]T. EMERSON, TOWARD A GENERAL THEORY OF THE FIRST AMENDMENT 64 (Random House ed. 1966).

[128]Note, *Content Regulation and the Dimensions of Free Expression,* 96 HARV. L. REV. 1854, 1862 (1983).

[129]EMERSON, *supra* note 127, at 64. *See also* T. EMERSON, THE SYSTEM OF FREEDOM OF EXPRESSION 21–22 (1970). Emerson commented:

> Belief . . . is not strictly "expression." Forming or holding a belief occurs prior to expression. But it is the first stage in the process of expression, and it tends to progress into expression. Hence safeguarding the right to form and hold beliefs is essential in maintaining a system of freedom of expression. Freedom of belief, therefore, must be held included within the protection of the First Amendment.

Id..

[130]*Abood,* 431 U.S. 209, 234–35 (1977). *See also* Wallace v. Jaffree, 472 U.S. 38, 49 (1985) (plurality opinion) ("[T]he First Amendment was adopted to curtail the power of Congress to interfere with the individual's freedom to believe. . . .").

[131]*Pico,* 457 U.S. 853, 868 (1982) (plurality opinion).

[132]*E.g.,* Rogers v. Okin, 478 F. Supp. 1342, 1367 (D. Mass. 1979), *aff'd in part and rev'd in part,* 634 F.2d 650 (1st Cir. 1980), *vacated and remanded sub nom.* Mills v. Rogers, 457 U.S. 291 (1982) (First Amendment protection for the communication of ideas "presupposes a capacity to produce ideas," which therefore "is entitled to comparable constitutional protection"); Kaimowitz v. Michigan Dep't of Mental Health, Civ. No. 73-19434-AW (Mich. Cir. Ct. July 10, 1973), *reprinted in* BROOKS, *supra* note 41, at 902, 917 ("To the extent that the First Amendment protects the dissemination of ideas and the expression of thoughts, it equally must protect the individual's right to generate ideas.").

[133]*E.g.,* TRIBE, *supra* note 3, § 15–7, at 1322 ("The guarantee of free expression is inextricably linked to the protection and preservation of open and unfettered mental activity. . . ."); Shapiro, *Legislating the Control of Behavior Control: Autonomy and the Coercive Use of Organic Therapies,* 47 S. CAL. L. REV. 237, 255–57 (1974) (If the First Amendment protects communication, it must also protect "mentation"—"a person's power to generate thought, ideas and mental activity.").

beliefs, or attitudes that would be expressed.[134] Indeed, if the First Amendment protected communication of ideas but allowed government manipulation of mental processes, "totalitarianism and freedom of expression could be characteristics of the same society."[135]

The right to hold ideas and opinions must be accorded special protection, because it is a predicate to the exercise of other First Amendment protected rights. Whatever limited power government may have to interfere with freedom to express ideas, it must enjoy even less power to interfere with the holding of ideas. When the government attempts to coerce beliefs, it "[i]nvades the innermost privacy of the individual and cuts off the right of expression at its source."[136] Thus, government interference with thought processes and beliefs functions as a form of prior restraint on expression.[137] Like a prior restraint, such coercive intrusion into mental processes has "an immediate and irreversible" impact that irretrievably prevents exercise of the right of expression.[138] Like other prior restraints, such intrusions should be subject to a strong presumption of unconstitutionality.[139] Indeed, Emerson has argued that "the holding of a belief" should be "afforded complete protection from state coercion."[140] The arguments of Emerson and other First Amendment theorists[141] for absolute protection have not, however, been judicially accepted, at least in other First Amendment contexts. Although the First Amendment clearly states that "Congress shall

---

[134]One commentator stated:

> [T]he notion of a right of freedom of speech presupposes that the beliefs, opinions, and viewpoints expressed are not the products of deliberate governmental efforts to shape and condition those beliefs. The First Amendment could serve no meaningful function in a society in which government preconditioned the speaker. Such a society could dispense with the right of freedom of speech as an irrelevancy.

van Geel, *The Search for Constitutional Limits on Government Authority to Inculcate Youth*, 62 TEX. L. REV. 197 (1983).

[135]Arons & Lawrence, *The Manipulation of Consciousness: A First Amendment Critique of Schooling*, 15 HARV. C.R.-C.L. L. REV. 309, 312 (1980); *see also id.* at 313 ("Today, the opportunity to manipulate consciousness precedes and may do away with the need to manipulate expression.").

[136]EMERSON, *supra* note 127, at 64. *See also id.* at 6–7; *Barnette*, 319 U.S. 624, 637 (1943) (school may not "strangle the free mind at its source").

[137]For applications of the prior restraint doctrine, see Fort Wayne Books, Inc. v. Indiana, 489 U.S. 46 (1989); City of Lakewood v. Plain Dealer Publishing Co., 486 U.S. 750 (1988); Nebraska Press Ass'n v. Stuart, 427 U.S. 539 (1976); New York Times Co. v. United States, 403 U.S. 713 (1971); Freedman v. Maryland, 380 U.S. 51 (1965); Kunz v. New York, 340 U.S. 290 (1951); Saia v. New York, 334 U.S. 558 (1948); Lovell v. City of Griffin, 303 U.S. 444 (1938); Near v. Minnesota, 283 U.S. 697 (1931). *See generally* NOWAK & ROTUNDA, *supra* note 3, at 969–78; M. REDISH, FREEDOM OF EXPRESSION: A CRITICAL ANALYSIS 127–71 (1984); Blasi, *Toward a Theory of Prior Restraint: The Central Linkage*, 66 MINN. L. REV. 11 (1981); Emerson, *The Doctrine of Prior Restraint*, 20 LAW & CONTEMP. PROBS. 648 (1955); Jeffries, *Rethinking Prior Restraint*, 92 YALE L.J. 409 (1983); Mayton, *Toward a Theory of First Amendment Process: Injunctions of Speech, Subsequent Punishment, and the Costs of the Prior Restraint Doctrine*, 67 CORNELL L. REV. 245 (1982); Redish, *The Proper Role of the Prior Restraint Doctrine in First Amendment Theory*, 70 VA. L. REV. 53 (1984). The prevention of prior restraints on expression "may have been the main purpose" of the First Amendment. Schenck v. United States, 249 U.S. 47, 51–52 (1919); *see* Patterson v. Colorado, 205 U.S. 454, 462 (1907); GUNTHER, *supra* note 3, at 1202.

[138]*Nebraska Press Ass'n*, 427 U.S. at 559.

[139]"Any prior restraint on expression comes to . . . [the] Court with a "heavy presumption' against its constitutional validity." Organization for a Better Austin v. Keefe, 402 U.S. 415, 419 (1971) (quoting Bantam Books, Inc. v. Sullivan, 372 U.S. 58, 70 (1963)).

[140]EMERSON, *supra* note 127, at 64.

[141]*See, e.g.*, Meiklejohn, *The First Amendment is an Absolute*, 1961 SUP. CT. REV. 245, 257–58:

> A citizen may be told when and where and in what manner he may or may not speak, write, assemble, and so on. On the other hand, he may not be told what he shall or shall not believe. In that realm, each citizen is sovereign. He exercises powers that the body politic reserves for its own members.

make no law ... abridging the freedom of speech''[142] and commentators have debated whether First Amendment rights are ''absolute,''[143] the Supreme Court has never accepted this view.[144] Rather, the Court's approach gives ''nearly absolute'' protection to certain expression, requiring that government demonstrate that any abridgment be justified as necessary to further a ''compelling state interest.''[145] Because the Court uses this approach for restriction of protected expression, governmental efforts to intrude on private thoughts and ideas should receive scrutiny at least as exacting. Thus, at a minimum, mental processes should be presumptively protected by the First Amendment against intrusive interference by the state, and the presumption should be strong. Unless the government can demonstrate a compelling necessity to justify such interference, a person's private thoughts and mental processes should remain undisturbed.

C. Mental Processes and the Values of the First Amendment

Reading the First Amendment to protect mental processes from the kind of direct governmental intrusion presented by at least some of the mental health treatment techniques thus is supported by the language of various Supreme Court cases and by the logical and factual connection between such protection and freedom of expression. In addition, recognition of such protection is essential to the values underlying the First Amendment. The Framers of the First Amendment ''were concerned above all else with spiritual liberty: freedom to think, to believe, and to worship.''[146] In wording the Amendment, they therefore placed freedom of conscience first in their enumeration of rights, moving only then to freedom of speech and press, and then to the political rights of assembly and petition for the redress of grievances.[147] Although the Framers considered these political rights to be critical, they recognized that such rights depended on the more basic freedoms to think and to believe. Jefferson, Madison, and the other makers of the U.S. Constitution were children of the Enlightenment:[148]

> They believed above all else in the power of reason, in the search for truth, in progress and the ultimate perfectibility of man. Freedom of inquiry and liberty of expression were deemed essential to the discovery and spread of truth, for only by the endless testing of debate could error be exposed, truth emerge, and men enjoy the opportunities for human progress.[149]

---

[142]U.S. CONST. amend. I.

[143]See, e.g., NOWAK & ROTUNDA, supra note 3, at 942–43; TRIBE, supra note 3, § 12–2, at 791–93; Frantz, The First Amendment in the Balance, 71 YALE L.J. 1424 (1962); Mendelson, On the Meaning of the First Amendment: Absolutes in the Balance, 50 CAL. L. REV. 821 (1962).

[144]See Konigsberg v. State Bar, 366 U.S. 36 (1961) (Harlan, J.); id. at 56–80 (Black, J., dissenting); Chaplinsky v. New Hampshire, 315 U.S. 568, 571–72 (1942); Schenck v. United States, 249 U.S. 47 (1919). Even the vigorous protection against prior restraints is not absolute. E.g., Nebraska Press Ass'n v. Stuart, 427 U.S. 539 (1976).

[145]See TRIBE, supra note 3, § 12–8, at 832–36.

[146]Cox, The Supreme Court, 1979 Term—Forward: Freedom of Expression in the Burger Court, 94 HARV. L. REV. 1, 1 (1980).

[147]Id.

[148]See B. BAILYN, THE IDEOLOGICAL ORIGINS OF THE AMERICAN REVOLUTION 26–30 (1967). See generally H. MAY, THE ENLIGHTENMENT IN AMERICA (1976); G. WILLS, INVENTING AMERICA (1978); G. WOOD, THE CREATION OF THE AMERICAN REPUBLIC, 1776–1787 (1969); Cox, supra note 146, at 1–2; Smith, The Constitution and Autonomy, 60 TEX. L. REV. 175, 176–81 (1982).

[149]Cox, supra note 146, at 2.

The First Amendment serves a number of values central to our constitutional scheme. Emerson, a leading First Amendment scholar, provided a frequently cited cataloguing of these basic values:[150]

> First, freedom of expression is essential as a means of assuring individual self-fulfillment. . . . Second, freedom of expression is an essential process for advancing knowledge and discovering truth. . . . Third, freedom of expression is essential to provide for participation in decisionmaking by all members of society. . . . Finally, freedom of expression is . . . an essential mechanism for maintaining the balance between stability and change.

Each of these values would be served by affording constitutional protection for mental processes. Emerson derived the value of individual self-fulfillment "from the widely accepted premise of Western thought that the proper end of man is the realization of his character and potentialities as a human being."[151] This widely shared premise shapes much of our constitutional heritage, for as Justice Brandeis has noted, "[t]hose who won our independence believed that the final end of the State was to make men free to develop their faculties. . . ."[152] Brandeis's emphasis on "freedom to think"[153] makes it clear that he was referring to our mental faculties. Mental faculties distinguish humans from other species that lack such unique cognitive and communicative capacities.[154] Suppression of belief is thus "an affront to the dignity of man, a negation of man's essential nature."[155]

---

[150]T. EMERSON, THE SYSTEM OF FREEDOM OF EXPRESSION, *supra* note 129, at 6. *See also* EMERSON, *supra* note 127, at 3; REDISH, *supra* note 137, at 9 (citing Emerson and describing him as "probably the leading modern theorist of free speech"); Bork, *Neutral Principles and Some First Amendment Problems,* 47 IND. L.J. 1, 24–25 (1971).

[151]EMERSON, *supra* note 127, at 4. *See also* First Nat'l Bank v. Bellotti, 435 U.S. 765, 804–05 (1978) (White, J., dissenting, joined by Brennan & Marshall, J.J.) ("'[S]ome have considered . . . the principal function of the First Amendment [to be] the use of communication as a means of self-expression, self-realization and self-fulfillment. . . .'") (citing EMERSON, *supra* note 127, at 4–7); *id.* at 777 n.12 (opinion of the Court) (citing EMERSON, *supra* note 129, at 6); Doe v. Bolton, 410 U.S. 179, 211 (1973) (Douglas, J., concurring) (referring to "the autonomous control over the development and expression of one's intellect, interests, tastes, and personality" as "rights protected by the First Amendment") (emphasis omitted); Police Dep't v. Mosley, 408 U.S. 92, 95–96 (1972) (recognizing the assurance of "self-fulfillment for each individual" as an important goal of the First Amendment); GUNTHER, *supra* note 3, at 1001–02; NIMMER, *supra* note 3, § 1.03, at 1–49 to 1–52; F. SCHAUER, FREE SPEECH: A PHILOSOPHICAL ENQUIRY 47–59 (1982); TRIBE, *supra* note 3, § 12–1, at 787–89; Redish, *The Value of Free Speech,* 130 U. PA. L. REV. 591, 593–94 (1982) (emphasizing the value of "individual self-realization"); Richards, *Free Speech and Obscenity Law: Toward a Moral Theory of the First Amendment,* 123 U. PA. L. REV. 45 (1974); Scanlon, *A Theory of Freedom of Expression,* 1 PHIL. & PUB. AFF. 204 (1972) (emphasizing the value of personal autonomy); Stone, *Content Regulation and the First Amendment,* 25 WM. & MARY L. REV. 189, 193 (1983) ("individual self-fulfillment").

[152]Whitney v. California, 274 U.S. 357, 375 (1927) (Brandeis, J., concurring, joined by Holmes, J.).

[153]*Id.* (referring to "the deliberative forces" and "freedom to think as you will"). *See also* Olmstead v. United States, 277 U.S. 438, 478 (1928) (Brandeis, J., dissenting).

[154]*See* EMERSON, *supra* note 127, at 4; REDISH, *supra* note 137, at 18 (First Amendment viewed as a "recognition of the overriding importance of developing the uniquely human abilities to think, reason and appreciate"); Blasi, *The Checking Value in First Amendment Theory,* 1977 AM. B. FOUND. RES. J. 521, 545.

[155]EMERSON, *supra* note 127, at 5; *see also* ARISTOTLE, NICHOMACHEAN ETHICS X.7 (J. Thomson trans. 1953) (the intellect is the "true self of the individual"; intellectual activity is the "best and pleasantest for man, because the intellectual more than anything else *is* the man"); TRIBE, *supra* note 3, § 12–1, at 785–87; Blasi, *supra* note 154, at 544–45; Cox, *supra* note 146, at 1.

Development of the mind and the process of conscious thought—including the ability to think in abstract terms, to imagine, and to have and communicate emotions and thoughts—is essential to the identification and achievement of self-fulfillment goals. Indeed, these mental processes are central to the development of individual identity itself. Both man's individual and social nature depend on intellectual activities of thought, belief, and emotion. Therefore, a constitutional scheme valuing individual self-fulfillment must protect a right to form and hold beliefs and opinions, indeed must protect the right of each individual to develop his own unique personality.[156] The makers of the Constitution recognized that individual self-fulfillment and the development of what Justice Brandeis characterized as "man's spiritual nature, of his feelings and of his intellect"[157] are essential to the pursuit of happiness. To achieve these values the First Amendment must protect not only outward manifestations of expression but also mental processes, those "inward activities" that are the essence of expression.[158]

Thus, both freedom of mind and freedom of expression are central to our constitutional scheme and worthy of protection because of their intrinsic and not merely instrumental value.[159] Of course, both serve significant instrumental values as well,[160] and these also support the argument for constitutional protection of freedom of mind and belief. Both freedoms are important social goods and together constitute "the best process for advancing knowledge and discovering truth."[161] Brandeis defended "freedom to think as you will and to speak as you think" as "means indispensable to the discovery and spread of political truth."[162] The classic invocation of these values as justifications for freedom of expression came in a World War I era opinion authored by Justice Holmes. Holmes spoke of the marketplace of ideas in a celebrated dissenting opinion:[163]

> [W]hen men have realized that time has upset many fighting faiths, they may come to believe even more than they believe the very foundations of their own conduct that the ultimate good desired is better reached by free trade in ideas—that the best test of truth is the power of the thought to get itself accepted in the competition of the market, and that truth is the only ground upon which their wishes safely can be carried out.

---

[156]EMERSON, *supra* note 127, at 4–5.

[157]Olmstead v. United States, 277 U.S. 438, 478 (1928) (Brandeis, J., dissenting).

[158]*See* Note, *supra* note 128, at 1862–63.

[159]TRIBE, *supra* note 3, § 12–1, at 786–89; Blasi, *supra* note 154, at 545. *See also* ARISTOTLE, *supra* note 155, at X.7 ("[T]he activity of contemplation is the only one that is praised on its own account").

[160]"The constitutional guarantee of free speech 'serves significant societal interests' wholly apart from the speaker's interest in self-expression." Pacific Gas & Elec. Co. v. Public Utils. Comm'n, 475 U.S. 1, 7 (1986) (plurality opinion) (quoting First Nat'l Bank v. Bellotti, 435 U.S. 765, 776 (1978)).

[161]EMERSON, *supra* note 127, at 7.

[162]Whitney v. California, 274 U.S. 357, 375 (1927) (Brandeis, J., concurring, joined by Holmes, J.).

[163]Abrams v. United States, 250 U.S. 616, 630 (1919) (Holmes, J., dissenting, joined by Brandeis, J.). *See also Whitney*, 274 U.S. at 375 (defending "freedom to think as you will and to speak as you think" as "means indispensable to the discovery and spread of political truth"). *See generally* J. MILL, ON LIBERTY 19–67 (Liberal Arts Press ed. 1956) (Chapter II: Of the Liberty of Thought and Discussion); J. MILTON, AREOPAGITICA 51–52 (J. Hales rev. ed. 1949) (1st ed. 1644) ("Let . . . [Truth] and Fals[e]hood grapple; who ever knew Truth put to the wors[e], in a free and open encounter?").

The marketplace of ideas metaphor has emerged as a dominant motif in First Amendment jurisprudence.[164] This model admits all beliefs and opinions to the marketplace, for "the usefulness of an opinion is itself [a] matter of opinion."[165] Just as the attainment of truth suffers when opinions are excluded from the marketplace because they are deemed to be incorrect, the exclusion of the ideas of those regarded as insane or criminal will also frustrate this goal. Differentiating the sane from the insane may be no easier than distinguishing true from false opinions;[166] indeed, similar assumptions of infallibility are involved.[167] Chafee, an eminent First Amendment scholar, warned against "entrusting to fallible human beings a power over the minds of others."[168] Benjamin Franklin, Chaffee reminds us, acknowledged the desirability of stamping out evil thought but questioned "whether any human being is good and wise enough" to be entrusted with such power.[169]

If sophisticated treatment techniques are used to suppress what the government considers to be the disordered thoughts of mental patients and offenders, the competition of the marketplace of ideas will be reduced, inevitably decreasing the potential for truth to emerge. The First Amendment does not permit the state to "contract the spectrum of available knowledge."[170]

The additional values Emerson invokes to justify our system of free expression are to some degree interrelated. The First Amendment permits public participation in decision making through a process of open discussion available to all members of society. This is particularly significant for political decisions; indeed, the First Amendment is "indispens-

---

[164]*E.g.,* Texas v. Johnson, 491 U.S. 397, 416 (1989); Pacific Gas & Elec. Co. v. Public Utils. Comm'n, 475 U.S. 1 (1986) (plurality opinion); Zauderer v. Office of Disciplinary Counsel, 471 U.S. 626, 642 (1985); Board of Educ. v. Pico, 457 U.S. 853, 867 (1982) (plurality opinion); Widmar v. Vincent, 454 U.S. 263, 267 n.5 (1981); Citizens Against Rent Control v. City of Berkeley, 454 U.S. 290, 295 (1981) (First Amendment protects "a marketplace for the clash of different views and conflicting ideas"); Consolidated Edison Co. v. Pub. Serv. Comm'n, 447 U.S. 530, 537–38 (1980); FCC v. Pacifica Found., 438 U.S. 726, 745–46 (1978); Virginia State Bd. of Pharmacy v. Virginia Citizens Consumer Council, Inc., 425 U.S. 748, 760 (1976); Bigelow v. Virginia, 421 U.S. 809, 826 (1975); Miami Herald Publishing Co. v. Tornillo, 418 U.S. 241, 248 (1974); Red Lion Broadcasting Co. v. FCC, 395 U.S. 367, 390 (1969); Keyishian v. Board of Regents, 385 U.S. 589, 603 (1967); Time, Inc. v. Hill, 385 U.S. 374, 382 (1966); Dennis v. United States, 341 U.S. 494, 503 (1951); Z. CHAFEE, FREE SPEECH IN THE UNITED STATES 136–38, 298 (1948); A. MEIKLEJOHN, FREE SPEECH AND ITS RELATION TO SELF-GOVERNMENT 82–89 (1948); SCHAUER, *supra* note 151, at 15–34; TRIBE, *supra* note 3, § 12–1, at 785. *See also Johnson,* 491 U.S. at 416 ("the joust of principles protected by the First Amendment"). *See generally* Baker, *Scope of the First Amendment Freedom of Speech,* 25 UCLA L. REV. 964, 967–81 (1978); Cole, *Agon at Agora: Creative Misreadings in the First Amendment Tradition,* 95 YALE L.J. 857 (1986); Winter, *Transcendental Nonsense, Metaphoric Reasoning and the Cognitive Stakes for Law,* 137 U. PA. L. REV. 1105, 1188–95 (1989).

[165]MILL, *supra* note 163, at 27.

[166]*See* Rosenhan, *On Being Sane in Insane Places,* 179 SCIENCE 250 (1973); *infra* notes 217–69 and accompanying text. *See also* MILL, *supra* note 163, at 83–84. *See generally* T. SCHEFF, BEING MENTALLY ILL (1966).

[167]*See* CHAFEE, *supra* note 164, at 520; J. MILL, *supra* note 163, at 21–22; NIMMER, *supra* note 3, § 1.02[A], at 1–8 to 1–9.

[168]CHAFFEE, *supra* note 164, at 520.

[169]*Id. See also* American Communications Ass'n v. Douds, 339 U.S. 382, 442–43 (1950) (Jackson, J., concurring & dissenting) ("It is not the function of our Government to keep the citizen from falling into error; it is the function of the citizen to keep the Government from falling into error. We could justify any censorship only when the censors are better shielded against error than the censored.").

[170]Griswold v. Connecticut, 381 U.S. 479, 482 (1965).

able to decisionmaking in a democracy."[171] In a related sense, the system of free expression is essential to maintaining the balance between stability and change in the community, helping to legitimize the political process and to foster greater cohesion in society.[172]

If freedom of expression is critical to securing these values, then freedom of mind and of belief, necessary predicates to any meaningful freedom of expression, are also essential. The Supreme Court has described the central meaning of the First Amendment as the "profound national commitment to the principle that debate on public issues should be uninhibited, robust, and wide-open."[173] Fostering such debate serves a "central purpose" of the Amendment, "to protect the free discussion of governmental affairs."[174] The Court has more recently reiterated that the "primary aim" of the First Amendment "is the full protection of speech upon issues of public concern."[175]

Mental patients and criminal offenders may not be excluded from the public debate on governmental affairs. "[C]onditions in jails and prison," as well as in mental hospitals, "'are clearly matters of great public importance,'"[176] and "with greater information, the public can more intelligently form opinions about" these public issues.[177] Indeed, in view of the high potential for abuse within the closed institutions of the prison and mental hospital, it is particularly important to encourage these groups to participate in political dialogue in order to serve what Blasi has described as the "checking value" of the First Amendment— the value that free speech can serve in limiting the abuse of power by public officials.[178] The writings of institutionalized mental patients from the asylum have historically played an

[171]First Nat'l Bank v. Bellotti, 435 U.S. 765, 777 (1978); see Globe Newspaper Co. v. Superior Court, 457 U.S. 596, 604 (1982); Mills v. Alabama, 384 U.S. 214, 218 (1966); Stromberg v. California, 283 U.S. 359, 369 (1931); EMERSON, supra note 127, at 10. See generally MEIKLEJOHN, supra note 164; A. MEIKLEJOHN, POLITICAL FREEDOM (1965); SCHAUER, supra note 151, at 35–46; Bork, supra note 150, at 26–28; Brennan, The Supreme Court and the Meiklejohn Interpretation of the First Amendment, 79 HARV. L. REV. 1, 14–20 (1965); Stone, supra note 151, at 193.

[172]EMERSON, supra note 127, at 11–12; Emerson, First Amendment Doctrine and the Burger Court, 68 CAL. L. REV. 422, 428 (1980); see also NIMMER, supra note 3, at § 1.04 (the "safety valve function"); Bork, supra note 150, at 25 ("safety valve for society").

[173]New York Times Co. v. Sullivan, 376 U.S. 254, 270 (1964); see Kalven, The New York Times Case: A Note on "The Central Meaning of the First Amendment," 1964 SUP. CT. REV. 191, 204–10.

[174]Abood v. Detroit Bd. of Educ., 431 U.S. 209, 231 (1977) (citing Abood, 431 U.S. at 259) (Powell, J., concurring) (quoting Mills v. Alabama, 384 U.S. 214, 218 (1966); Buckley v. Valeo, 424 U.S. 1, 14 (1976)); accord Globe Newspaper, 457 U.S. at 604; Bellotti, 435 U.S. at 776–77; Mills, 384 U.S. at 218.

[175]Connick v. Myers, 461 U.S. 138, 154 (1983). See also Dun & Bradstreet, Inc. v. Greenmoss Builders, Inc., 472 U.S. 749, 759 (1985) ("[S]peech on public issues occupies the 'highest rung of the hierarchy of First Amendment values.' ") (quoting NAACP v. Clairborne Hardware Co., 458 U.S. 886, 913 (1982); Carey v. Brown, 447 U.S. 455, 467 (1980)); id. at 759 (" '[S]peech concerning public affairs is more than self-expression; it is the essence of self-government.' ") (quoting Connick, 461 U.S. at 145; Garrison v. Louisiana, 379 U.S. 64, 74–75 (1964)).

[176]Houchins v. KQED, 438 U.S. 1, 8 (1978) (quoting Pell v. Procunier, 417 U.S. 817, 830 n.7 (1974)).
[177]Houchins, 438 U.S. at 8.
[178]Blasi, supra note 154, at 523; e.g., Nebraska Press Ass'n v. Stuart, 427 U.S. 539, 560 (1976); see J. GOBERT & N. COHEN, RIGHTS OF PRISONERS § 4.01, at 101 (1981).

important role in reforming the mental health system.[179] Courts have recognized that even convicted prisoners have a First Amendment right to communicate outside the institution.[180] Moreover, the public enjoys First Amendment protection against unjustified governmental interference with communications from prisoners and patients.[181] Although the Supreme Court has upheld restrictions on the direct access of the news media to prison facilities, it did so in view of "[a] number of alternatives [that] are available to prevent problems in penal facilities from escaping public attention."[182] In addition, prisoners[183] and mental patients[184] are accorded a right of relatively unrestricted communication with attorneys, courts, and other public officials, not only to effectuate their right to contest the legality of their confinement but also to ensure that institutional abuses may be brought to public attention and redressed. The rights of prisoners and patients to communicate to those outside the institution—to assert legal rights, to criticize officials, to report on conditions, or for other purposes—as well as the reciprocal right of the public to receive such communications would be meaningless if institutional authorities could materially alter the mental processes

---

[179]See R. PORTER, A SOCIAL HISTORY OF MADNESS: THE WORLD THROUGH THE EYES OF THE INSANE 126–35, 167–209, 248–50 (1987) (discussing the work of a number of patient–reformers, including John Perceval, founder of the Alleged Lunatics' Friend Society, a pressure group to protect the interests of the improperly confined in mid-19th-century England, and Clifford Beers, the leading figure in the National Committee for Mental Hygiene and the evangelist of the influential Mental Hygiene Movement in early 20th-century America). Perceval's protests against the institutions in which he was confined were published in J. PERCEVAL, A NARRATIVE OF THE TREATMENT RECEIVED BY A GENTLEMAN, DURING A STATE OF MENTAL DERANGEMENT, contained in two volumes printed in 1838 and 1840 and reprinted as PERCEVAL'S NARRATIVE: A PATIENT'S ACCOUNT OF HIS PSYCHOSIS (G. Bateson ed., 1961). See R. PORTER, supra at 248. Beers's book, A MIND THAT FOUND ITSELF, originally published in 1908, went through 22 editions in the next 25 years. See R. PORTER at 249.

[180]E.g., Pell v. Procunier, 417 U.S. 817, 824 (1974) (rejecting claims of news media to conduct interviews with prisoners and of prisoners to participate in such interviews in order to inform the public about prison conditions in light of right of prisoners to write letters to the media); Procunier v. Martinez, 416 U.S. 396 (1974) (right of inmates to send written communications outside the prison), overruled in part on other grounds, Thornburgh v. Abbott, 490 U.S. 401 (1989); see GOBERT & COHEN, supra note 178, §§ 4.00–4.07. Mental hospital patients also have a First Amendment right to communicate outside the hospital. See, e.g., Brown v. Schubert, 347 F. Supp. 1232, 1234 (E.D. Wis. 1972), supplemented, 389 F. Supp. 281, 283–84 (E.D. Wis. 1975); Wyatt v. Stickney, 344 F. Supp. 373, 379–80 (M.D. Ala. 1972), aff'd in part and rev'd in part sub nom. Wyatt v. Aderholt, 503 F.2d 1305 (5th Cir. 1974); Stowers v. Wolodzko, 191 N.W.2d 355 (Mich. 1971) (statutory right). See generally Gostin, Freedom of Expression and the Mentally Disordered: Philosophical and Constitutional Perspectives, 50 NOTRE DAME L. REV. 419 (1975); Note, The Committed Mentally Ill and Their Right to Communicate, 7 WAKE FOREST L. REV. 297 (1971).

[181]Procunier v. Martinez, 416 U.S. at 412–13.

[182]Houchins v. KQED, Inc., 438 U.S. 1, 12 (1978); see Saxbe v. Washington Post Co., 417 U.S. 843 (1974); Pell, 417 U.S. at 824–28.

[183]See, e.g., Bounds v. Smith, 430 U.S. 817 (1977) (due process right of access to courts); Wolff v. McDonnell, 418 U.S. 539, 576–80 (1974) (due process right of access to courts, First Amendment right of correspondence with attorneys); Ex parte Hull, 312 U.S. 546 (1941) (due process right of access to courts); Taylor v. Sterrett, 532 F.2d 462 (5th Cir. 1976) (outgoing mail to courts and judicial officials may not be opened); Craig v. Hocker, 405 F. Supp. 656 (D. Nev. 1975) (outgoing mail to attorneys may not be censored or confiscated). See generally GOBERT & COHEN, supra note 178, §§ 2.00–2.14.

[184]See, e.g., Ward v. Kort, 762 F.2d 856, 858 (10th Cir. 1985) (constitutional right of access to the courts); Johnson v. Brelje, 701 F.2d 1201, 1207 (7th Cir. 1983) (same); Coe v. Maryland, No. K-83–4248 (D. Md. April 4, 1985) (consent decree funding legal assistance program to secure constitutional right of access to courts); Wyatt, 344 F. Supp. at 379–80 (unrestricted right to send and receive sealed mail from attorneys, private physicians, courts, and public officials); N.J. STAT. ANN. § 30.4–24.2g(1) (West 1981) (statutory right to communicate with lawyers); WIS. STAT. ANN. § 51.61(1)(c) (West 1987) (statutory right to communicate with officials, committing court, and mental health agency); Garvey, Freedom and Choice in Constitutional Law, 94 HARV. L. REV. 1756, 1772–73 (1981); Note, supra note 180, at 307–11.

of their charges through involuntary treatment techniques or modify the content of such communication or the individual's desire to engage in it.

The essential values justifying the First Amendment thus would be substantially undermined if speech were to remain unimpaired but mental processes could be controlled. Governmental attempts to intrude directly into mental processes to effect changes in thoughts, beliefs, opinions, and emotions must therefore be regarded as hostile to First Amendment principles.

D. Arguments Against First Amendment Protection for Mental Processes

1. Does the First Amendment Protect Insane or Disordered Thoughts?

Even if the First Amendment must generally be read to protect thoughts, should it be read to protect insane or disordered thoughts?[185] A contention that it should not is arguably supported by several Supreme Court cases holding that certain types of speech are totally unprotected by the First Amendment. This approach was first articulated in the Court's 1942 opinion in *Chaplinsky v. New Hampshire.*[186] The Court noted several narrow "classes of speech" that are outside the protection of the Constitution.[187] These include "the lewd and obscene, the profane, the libelous, and the insulting or 'fighting words'."[188] These utterances, the Court observed, "are no essential part of any exposition of ideas, and are of such slight social value as a step to truth that any benefit that may be derived from them is clearly outweighed by the social interest in order and morality."[189] This dictum has led to a two-level theory of the First Amendment. Although the Court has fully protected most kinds of speech against government abridgement absent compelling necessity, certain limited categories of expression have been treated as being so worthless that they are beyond the Amendment's protection.[190] In addition to "fighting words," the Court has excluded libelous utterances[191] and obscenity[192] from constitutional protection.

---

[185]*See* Rennie v. Klein, 462 F. Supp. 1131, 1144 (D.N.J. 1978) ("The court need not reach the question of whether insane or disordered thought is within the scope of First Amendment protection."), *aff'd in part, modified in part, and remanded,* 653 F.2d 836 (3d Cir. 1981) (en banc), *vacated and remanded,* 458 U.S. 1119 (1982), *on remand,* 720 F.2d 266 (3d Cir. 1983) (en banc).

[186]315 U.S. 568 (1942).

[187]*Id.* at 571–72.

[188]*Id.*

[189]*Id.*

[190]*See* Tribe, *supra* note 3, § 12–18.

[191]Beauharnais v. Illinois, 343 U.S. 250 (1952). *But see* New York Times Co. v. Sullivan, 376 U.S. 254, 269 (1964) (some libelous statements concerning public officials protected by First Amendment); Gertz v. Robert Welch, Inc., 418 U.S. 323, 341 (1974) (The First Amendment protects defamatory statements in the absence of fault even for defendants who are not public figures.); Curtis Publishing Co. v. Butts, 388 U.S. 130 (1967) (extending *New York Times* to public figures). Although undercut, *Beauharnais* continues to be cited for the proposition that libelous utterances are not protected by the First Amendment. Bose Corp. v. Consumers Union, 466 U.S. 485, 504 (1984).

[192]Sable Communications, Inc. v. FCC, 492 U.S. 115, 124–25 (1989); Miller v. California, 413 U.S. 15 (1973); Roth v. United States, 354 U.S. 476 (1957). *But see* Stanley v. Georgia, 394 U.S. 561 (1969) (private possession and use of obscenity protected by First Amendment). In *Miller,* the Court adopted a three-part test for defining obscenity: It must "appeal to the prurient interest"; it must portray specifically defined sexual conduct in a "patently offensive way"; and it must lack "serious literary, artistic, political or scientific value" when viewed as a whole. *Miller,* 413 U.S. at 24.

Although the Court had appeared to be moving away from this dichotomy between protected and unprotected speech,[193] its modern opinions continue to cite the distinction.[194] In fact, in the 1982 case of *New York v. Ferber,* the Court seemed to define distribution of child pornography as a new category of unprotected speech.[195] Although nonobscene, this material visually depicts sexual conduct by children. However, *Ferber* may not signal a return to the *Chaplinsky* doctrine of noncovered expression. Whether the Court will actually treat child pornography as outside the coverage of the First Amendment is an open question: The *Ferber* Court cited *Chaplinsky* and other unprotected speech cases, but it did not determine that child pornography was totally devoid of First Amendment value.[196] Further-more, the Court's discussion of the strong state interest in the regulation of child pornography[197] would have been unnecessary had this category of expression been treated as altogether beyond the ambit of the First Amendment. Citations to *Chaplinsky* and its progeny notwithstanding, the technique used in *Ferber* thus does not seem to be one of noncoverage.[198]

To whatever extent the *Chaplinsky* doctrine survives, and it appears to have vitality at least in the obscenity area,[199] it constitutes a recognition that at least some limited categories of unprotected speech are removed altogether from First Amendment review, even though they involve regulation of the content of expression—for which exacting scrutiny is usually reserved. Rather than requiring a showing that the government restriction is necessary to

---

[193]*Chaplinsky* has been substantially eviscerated in the "fighting words" context. *See, e.g.,* Brown v. Oklahoma, 408 U.S. 914 (1972); Lewis v. New Orleans, 408 U.S. 913 (1972); Rosenfeld v. New Jersey, 408 U.S. 901 (1972); Gooding v. Wilson, 405 U.S. 518 (1972); Cohen v. California, 403 U.S. 15 (1971). In Texas v. Johnson, the flag-burning case, the Court rejected an argument that the burning of a flag was within the "fighting words" exception of *Chaplinsky* and stated that "[n]o reasonable onlooker would have regarded Johnson's generalized expression of dissatisfaction with the policies of the Federal Government as a direct personal insult or an invitation to exchange fisticuffs." Texas v. Johnson, 491 U.S. 397, 409 (1989). *See also* Madsen v. Women's Health Center, 114 S. Ct. 2516, 2520 (1994).

Beauharnais, the libelous utterances case, has been eclipsed by Brandenburg v. Ohio, 395 U.S. 444 (1969) (per curiam), Garrison v. Louisiana, 379 U.S. 64 (1964), and New York Times Co. v. Sullivan, 376 U.S. 254 (1964).

Commercial advertising, once in the unprotected category, Valentine v. Chrestensen, 316 U.S. 52 (1942), is now deemed protected. City of Cincinnati v. Discovery Network, Inc., 507 U.S. 410 (1993); Board of Trustees v. Fox, 492 U.S. 469 (1989); Posadas de Puerto Rico Assoc. v. Tourism Co., 478 U.S. 328 (1986); Zauderer v. Office of Disciplinary Counsel, 471 U.S. 626 (1985); *In re* R.M.J., 455 U.S. 191 (1982); Central Hudson Gas & Elec. Corp. v. Public Serv. Comm'n, 447 U.S. 557 (1980); Friedman v. Rogers, 440 U.S. 1 (1979); Ohralik v. Ohio State Bar Ass'n, 436 U.S. 447 (1978); Linmark Assocs., Inc. v. Township of Willingboro, 431 U.S. 85 (1977); Virginia State Bd. of Pharmacy v. Virginia Citizens Consumer Council, Inc., 425 U.S. 748 (1976). For the approach used by the Court in commercial speech cases, see *infra* notes 213–15 and accompanying text.

Perhaps only the obscenity category of noncovered speech survives today. *See* Schauer, *Codifying The First Amendment: New York v. Ferber,* 1982 Sup. Ct. Rev. 285, 303; *see, e.g., Sable Communications,* 492 U.S. at 124–25; Miller, *supra* note 192. *But see* Stanley v. Georgia, 394 U.S. 561 (1969) (private possession and use of pornography protected by First Amendment). *See generally* Schauer, *supra* at 302–04.

[194]Dun & Bradstreet, Inc. v. Greenmoss Builders, Inc., 472 U.S. 749, 758 & n.5 (1985) (obscene speech and "fighting words" accorded no protection); Bose Corp. v. Consumers Union, 466 U.S. 485, 504 & n.22 (1984) (obscenity and libel considered unprotected); New York v. Ferber, 458 U.S. 747, 764 (1982) (child pornography unprotected).

[195]*Ferber,* 458 U.S. at 764 ("[C]hild pornography . . ., like obscenity, is unprotected by the First Amendment."); *accord* Osborne v. Ohio, 495 U.S. 103 (1990).

[196]*Ferber,* 458 U.S. at 763–64.

[197]The Court described the state interest as both "compelling" and "of surpassing importance." *Ferber,* 458 U.S. at 757. *See also Osborne,* 495 U.S. at 112 (stressing the "importance of the state's interest in protecting the victims of child pornography").

[198]Schauer, *supra* note 193, at 303–04.

[199]*See supra* notes 192–94.

further a "compelling state interest"—the usual standard for justifying abridgement of First Amendment rights[200]—the government will be permitted to regulate these types of expression "subject only to the barest due process scrutiny."[201]

In a related doctrinal development, the Court or several members of it have begun to treat certain categories of speech as having a "lower value" than, for example, political speech.[202] Restrictions on such "lower value" speech are then scrutinized under a standard that places a lesser burden of justification on government than would be applied to speech within the core values of the First Amendment. A plurality of the Court in *Young v. American Mini Theatres, Inc.,* suggested that nonobscene but sexually explicit speech deserves less constitutional protection than other types of protected speech.[203] The Court upheld a zoning ordinance restricting the location of theaters showing sexually explicit "adult" movies, finding that the societal interest in protecting the free flow of sexually explicit materials was of "a wholly different, and lesser, magnitude" than the interest in protecting other kinds of expression.[204] The Court applied a balancing test, finding that the city's desire to protect its neighborhoods was sufficiently compelling to justify the ordinance.[205]

Another plurality of the Court used a similar balancing approach in *FCC v. Pacifica Foundation,*[206] upholding the authority of the Federal Communications Commission to regulate radio broadcasts that the Court considered indecent although not obscene.[207] In a somewhat ambiguous 1986 opinion, a Court majority may have embraced for the first time the notion that nonobscene sexually explicit speech deserves less protection than other kinds of protected speech. In *City of Renton v. Playtime Theatres, Inc.,*[208] the Court upheld a zoning ordinance that restricted the location of adult theaters, quoting in a footnote language from the *American Mini Theatres* plurality opinion that suggested that such sexually explicit speech is of a "wholly different, and lesser, magnitude than the interest of untrammelled political debate."[209]

This approach, however, may be limited to zoning restrictions and to radio or television broadcasting during times of the day when children are exposed to it. A unanimous Supreme Court more recently distinguished *Pacifica* on this basis from indecent but nonobscene sexually oriented private commercial telephone communications, known as "dial-a-porn." In *Sable Communications, Inc. v. FCC,*[210] the Court invalidated a total ban on such

---

[200]*See infra* notes 476–83 and accompanying text.

[201]TRIBE, *supra* note 3, § 12–8, at 832, 837.

[202]*See* GUNTHER, *supra* note 3, at 1138 & n.4, 1146–47; L. TRIBE, *supra* note 3, § 12–18, at 928–34.

[203]427 U.S. 50, 70 (1976) (plurality opinion).

[204]*Id.* Only four Justices joined that part of the Court's opinion that suggested lesser First Amendment protection for sexually explicit speech. Justice Stevens wrote the opinion for the Court, and this portion of it was joined by Chief Justice Burger and Justices White and Rehnquist. Justice Powell concurred but did not join Justice Stevens's opinion on this point. *Id.* at 73.

[205]*Id.* at 71–73.

[206]438 U.S. 726 (1978) (plurality opinion).

[207]In this respect, Justice Stevens's opinion was joined only by Chief Justice Burger and Justice Rehnquist. *Id.* at 729. Justice Powell, in a concurring opinion joined by Justice Blackmun, refused to agree that offensive although nonobscene speech deserves less protection than other types of speech:

> I do not subscribe to the theory that the Justices of this Court are free generally to decide on the basis of its content which speech protected by the First Amendment is most "valuable" and hence deserving of the most protection and which is less "valuable" and hence deserving of less protection.

Id. at 761 (Powell, J., concurring).

[208]475 U.S. 41 (1986).

[209]*Id.* at 49 n.2 (quoting Young v. American Mini Theatres, Inc., 427 U.S. 50, 70 (1976)).

[210]492 U.S. 115 (1989).

communications, finding *Pacifica* to involve merely a partial ban on broadcasting and to be limited to contexts involving the "captive audience" problem presented there.[211] Applying traditional strict scrutiny, the Court found that the total ban on such telephone communications "far exceeds that which is necessary to limit the access of minors to such messages"[212] and was therefore unconstitutional. The Court thus treated the sexually explicit speech before it as entitled to full First Amendment protection, although it acknowledged that at least in certain circumstances sexually explicit speech would be scrutinized under a lesser standard.

In addition to nonobscene sexually explicit speech, the Court has accorded "lesser value" to certain kinds of commercial speech under the First Amendment. In *Central Hudson Gas & Electric Co. v. Public Service Commission,*[213] the Court explicitly recognized that "[t]he Constitution . . . accords a lesser protection to commercial speech than to other constitutionally guaranteed expression."[214] For commercial speech the Court uses a form of intermediate scrutiny, permitting restrictions only if they directly advance substantial government interests and are narrowly tailored to achieve them.[215]

These cases, involving what the Court or some members of it have regarded as "less valuable" speech, have not used the approach of *Chaplinsky,* under which such communication would be excluded altogether from First Amendment coverage. Rather, the Court has accorded these kinds of speech some constitutional protection, applying a balancing approach or a form of intermediate scrutiny rather than the strict scrutiny usually applicable to intrusions on First Amendment protected speech.

An argument could be framed on the basis of *Chaplinsky* and its progeny (or on the more recent cases suggesting that certain "lesser value" speech be accorded lesser constitutional protection) that insane or disordered thought is without value and therefore outside the ambit of First Amendment protection, or of lower value, and therefore deserving only of lesser scrutiny.[216] This argument is unconvincing, however, for a number of reasons. First, the distinction between sane and disordered thought is elusive,[217] particularly in view of the imprecision of the diagnostic categories used in defining mental illness and clinicians' lack

---

[211]*Id.* at 127–28.

[212]*Id.* at 131.

[213]447 U.S. 557 (1980).

[214]*Id.* at 562–63; *accord* Board of Trustees v. Fox, 492 U.S. 469, 477 (1989) (referring to the "subordinate position [of commercial speech] in the scale of First Amendment values"); Dun & Bradstreet, Inc. v. Greenmoss Builders, Inc., 472 U.S. 749, 758–59 (1985) (plurality opinion) ("not all speech is of equal First Amendment importance"; distinguishing speech "on matters of public concern" from speech "on matters of purely private concern," the latter being "of less First Amendment concern").

[215]*Fox,* 492 U.S. at 477; Posadas de Puerto Rico Assoc. v. Tourism Co., 478 U.S. 328, 339 (1986) (applying these tests somewhat deferentially); Zauderer v. Office of Disciplinary Counsel, 471 U.S. 626, 628 (1985); Central Hudson Gas & Elec. Corp. v. Public Serv. Comm'n, 447 U.S. 557, 562–63 (1980). The Court in *Fox* clarified that the narrow tailoring standard is not as demanding as the "least restrictive means" requirement. 492 U.S. at 475–82. For other commercial speech cases, see *supra* note 193.

[216]*See supra* note 185; Appelbaum & Gutheil, *"Rotting With Their Rights On": Constitutional Theory and Clinical Reality in Drug Refusal by Psychiatric Patients,* 7 BULL. AM. ACAD. PSYCHIATRY & L. 306, 312–13 (1979); Shapiro, *supra* note 133, at 270–71.

[217]*See* Shapiro, *supra* note 133, at 270; Morse, *A Preference for Liberty: The Case Against Involuntary Commitment of the Mentally Disordered,* 70 CAL. L. REV. 54, 64–65 (1982); Morse, *Crazy Behavior, Morals, and Science: An Analysis of Mental Health Law,* 51 S. CAL. L. REV. 527, 540, 572–74, 632–35 (1978); Winick, *Restructuring Competency to Stand Trial,* 32 UCLA L. REV. 921, 970–71 (1985); *supra* notes 166–67 and accompanying text.

of consistency in applying them.[218] The diagnostic criteria for mental illness have become progressively more specific in recent years,[219] particularly with the 1980 adoption (*DSM–III*)[220] and 1987 revision (*DSM–III–R*)[221] of the third edition of the *Diagnostic and Statistical Manual for Mental Disorder* and the 1994 publication of the fourth edition (*DSM–IV*).[222] However, the criteria remain imprecise and value laden. The various editions of the *DSM*, developed by the American Psychiatric Association, are the official specifications of diagnostic criteria widely used by mental health clinicians in America. The approach of the *DSM* is animated by a strong commitment to Baconian empiricism in the definition of the diagnostic criteria,[223] which the drafters characterize as " 'descriptive' in that the definitions of the disorders are generally limited to descriptions of the clinical features of the disorders."[224] A diagnosis of mental abnormality calls for a clinician's interpretation of "behavioral signs or symptoms."[225] Although this may appear to be an exercise in description, it inevitably involves "subjective cultural judgments about what is abnormal."[226]

The goal of strict empiricism has not and cannot be achieved because the label *mental disorder* contains an inherently evaluative component. Under *DSM–III, DSM–II–R, and DSM–IV, mental disorders* are defined through use of the concepts of "distress" and "impairment" in "important areas of functioning."[227] The concept of mental disorder presupposes a standard of normality against which unusual behavior is measured. Consider the following hypothetical: Lawyers (and their spouses) understand well the aphorism, "Law is a jealous mistress." The work is demanding and frequently involves long hours. Some law firms expect their attorneys to bill 3,200 hours per year or even more. Indeed, some lawyers work so hard that their work interferes with their ability to function effectively in other aspects of their lives. Their roles as spouses, parents, or friends may suffer; they lack the time to enjoy nature, read literature, listen to music, contemplate philosophy, or even to engage in physical exercise. Their family and friends complain that they lack balance in their lives and have become "workaholics." Some lawyers experience distress as a result of their professional choice. Yet others love the law, including the long hours, citing their pleasure in

---

[218]*See* Ake v. Oklahoma, 470 U.S. 68, 81 (1985) ("Psychiatry is not, however, an exact science, and psychiatrists disagree widely and frequently on what constitutes mental illness, on the appropriate diagnosis to be attached to given behavior and symptoms, on cure and treatment. . . ."); Addington v. Texas, 441 U.S. 418, 432 (1979) (recognizing "the uncertainties of psychiatric diagnosis"); O'Connor v. Donaldson, 422 U.S. 563, 587 (1975) (Burger, C.J., concurring) (referring to the "wide divergence of medical opinion regarding the diagnosis of and proper therapy for mental abnormalities"). *See generally* J. ZISKIN, COPING WITH PSYCHIATRIC AND PSYCHOLOGICAL TESTIMONY (3d ed. 1981); Ennis & Litwack, *Psychiatry and the Presumption of Expertise: Flipping Coins in the Courtroom*, 62 CAL. L. REV. 693 (1974); Morse, *Crazy Behavior, Morals, and Science: An Analysis of Mental Health Law, supra* note 217, at 542–60.

[219]Westermeyer, *Psychiatric Diagnosis Across Cultural Boundaries*, 142 AM. J. PSYCHIATRY 798, 799 (1985).

[220]AMERICAN PSYCHIATRIC ASSOCIATION, DIAGNOSTIC AND STATISTICAL MANUAL OF MENTAL DISORDERS (3d ed. 1980) [hereinafter *DSM–III*].

[221]AMERICAN PSYCHIATRIC ASSOCIATION, DIAGNOSTIC AND STATISTICAL MANUAL OF MENTAL DISORDERS (3d ed. rev. 1987) [hereinafter *DSM–III–R*].

[222]AMERICAN PSYCHIATRIC ASSOCIATION, DIAGNOSTIC AND STATISTICAL MANUAL OF MENTAL DISORDERS (4th ed. 1994) [hereinafter *DSM–IV*].

[223]*See* Faust & Miner, *The Empiricist and His New Clothes: DSM–III in Perspective*, 143 AM. J. PSYCHIATRY 962, 962 (1986).

[224]*DSM–III–R, supra* note 221, at xxiii; *see also DSM–III, supra* note 220, at 7.

[225]*DSM–III–R, supra* note 221, at xxiii.

[226]Johnson, *Contributions of Anthropology to Psychiatry, in* REVIEW OF GENERAL PSYCHIATRY 180, 184 (H. Goldman ed., 1984).

[227]*DSM–III, supra* note 220, at 6; *DSM–III–R, supra* note 221, at xxii; *DSM–IV, supra* note 222, at xxi.

the craft of the work, or the economic rewards, or other reasons. For some, this behavior may have its roots in childhood conflicts; for some it may constitute a form of addiction to the adrenalin that the stress of the work stimulates.[228] Suppose the American Psychiatric Association Board of Trustees were to add "workaholism" to the categories of mental disorder and that a new medication were developed to treat this condition.[229] Would these developments render the First Amendment inapplicable to the involuntary administration of such treatment to lawyers diagnosed as "workaholics"?[230]

A leading architect of the three most recent versions of the *DSM* concedes that "[t]he concept of 'disorder' always involves a value judgment."[231] People are diagnosed as mentally ill on the basis of a judgment that their behavior is abnormal. The criteria of "distress" and "impairment" in important areas of functioning "are permeated by dominant social values and are shaped, in part, by the preference for a statistical definition of normality and abnormality."[232] "Attitudinal, political, historical, and perhaps even economic factors" can influence both the definition of diagnostic criteria and their application.[233] An illustration of the impact of social and moral values on the definition of diagnostic criteria is the classification of homosexuality as a mental disorder.[234] Prior to 1973, homosexuality per se was defined as a disorder, but in that year the American Psychiatric Association Board of Trustees, following heated debate, removed it from this category and substituted a new classification, "Sexual Orientation Disturbance," restricted to homosexu-

---

[228]*See* Lyons, *Stress Addiction: "Life in the Fast Lane' May Have Its Benefits,* N.Y. TIMES, July 26, 1983, C1 at 1, col. 1 ("The Type A individual has perhaps become addicted to his own adrenaline and unconsciously seeks ways to get those little surges"); *cf.* Roy et al., *Extraversion in Pathological Gamblers: Correlates With Indexes of Noradrenergic Function,* 46 ARCHIVES GEN. PSYCHIATRY 679 (1989) (reporting on research suggesting that gamblers may have an abnormality of the adrenergic system and may engage in gambling behavior to increase the levels of certain brain chemicals).

[229]*See* Machlowitz, *A New Take on Type A,* N.Y. TIMES, May 3, 1987, § 6 (Magazine), at 40 (predicting a pharmacological approach to treatment of "Type A" behavior).

[230]An example drawn from history provides an additional illustration of the inherent manipulability of categories like "disordered" or "mentally ill" based on political or social considerations masquerading as medical judgments. In the ante-bellum South, a Louisiana doctor, Samuel W. Cartwright, attributed the behavior patterns of some slaves that overseers "erroneously" called "rascality," to a disease, peculiar to Blacks, which he termed *Dysaethesia aethiopica.* K. STAMPP, THE PECULIAR INSTITUTION: SLAVERY IN THE ANTE-BELLUM SOUTH 102 (1968). The symptoms of this condition, which Cartwright attributed entirely to "the stupidness of mind and insensibility of the nerves induced by the disease," were described by the doctor as follows:

> An African who suffered from this exotic affliction was "apt to do much mischief" which appeared "as if intentional." He destroyed or wasted everything he touched, abused the livestock, and injured the crops. When he was driven to his labor he performed his tasks "in a headlong, careless manner, treading down with his feet or cutting with his hoe the plants" he was supposed to cultivate, breaking his tools, and "spoiling everything."

Id. According to Cartwright, slaves who absconded from their masters suffered from a second "disease of the mind" that was unique to Blacks, termed *Drapetomania,* "the disease causing negroes to run away." *Id.* at 109. Most southern doctors rejected Cartwright's theories, and the *Charleston Medical Journal* criticized Cartwright's "mixture of medicine and politics." *Id.* at 309. However, had the treatments of modern psychiatry then been available, it is easily conceivable that their involuntary use for slaves afflicted with these "diseases of the mind" could have been defended by the same principles of benevolence and social utility advanced by Cartwright.

[231]Spitzer, *The Diagnostic Status of Homosexuality in DSM–III: A Reformulation of the Issues,* 138 AM. J. PSYCHIATRY 210, 214 (1981). Dr. Spitzer was chair of the American Psychiatric Association committees that developed both *DSM–III* and *DSM–III–R* and was also a member and a special adviser to the committee that developed *DSM–IV.*

[232]Faust & Miner, *supra* note 223, at 963.

[233]Westermeyer, *supra* note 219, at 799.

[234]*See* Spitzer, *supra* note 231.

als disturbed by their sexual orientation or wishing to change it.[235] *DSM–III* further modified the definition of this category and renamed it "Ego-dystonic Homosexuality."[236] The category was subsequently deleted in *DSM–III–R* and *DSM–IV*, which merely listed "persistent and marked distress about one's sexual orientation" as an example of "Sexual Disorders Not Otherwise Specified."[237]

In light of the focus in the definition of mental disorders in *DSM–III, DSM–III–R*, and *DSM–IV* on the concepts of "distress" and "impairment" in "important areas of functioning,"[238] homosexuals who do not experience distress as a result of their sexual orientation could nonetheless be considered disordered because of impairment in one or more important areas of functioning.[239] The individual's occupational life would undoubtedly be considered one such area of functioning. Consider the case of a well-adjusted homosexual whose revelation of his sexual orientation impairs his occupational functioning because of the negative attitudes of his employer or co-workers. In this case, if such occupational impairment is deemed to justify considering the individual's homosexuality a mental disorder, the social and moral values of these others would constitute the determinative factor. Another area of functioning that might be considered impaired is the homosexual's sexuality itself. However, whether sexual functioning should be deemed "an important area of functioning" and whether heterosexual functioning should be used as the norm both turn on value judgments, not empirical determinations.[240]

Even for conditions that by wide or even universal agreement produce distress and interfere in important areas of social and occupational functioning—schizophrenia, for example—and that, therefore, should be considered mental disorders, the clinical determination of who suffers from the disorder raises similar problems. Diagnostic reliability—the probability that two clinicians will agree with each other's diagnosis—may be only 50% to 60% for schizophrenia and 30% to 40% for depression and affective disorder.[241] Within psychiatry there remains wide disagreement concerning the nature and causes of schizophrenia and many of the other mental illnesses.[242] There simply is no "litmus test" available for the diagnosis of these conditions.[243] Unlike physical illnesses, for which objective investigatory procedures are usually available for making and confirming diagnoses, the assessment of mental illness depends almost exclusively on subjective clinical judgment.[244] The lack of theoretical consensus among clinicians concerning schizophrenia and other conditions inevitably produces varying application of diagnostic criteria. The various editions of the *DSM* seek to address this problem by claiming a "generally atheoretical

---

[235]*Id.* at 210.

[236]*Id.* at 210–11.

[237]*DSM–III–R, supra* note 221, at 296; *DSM–IV, supra* note 222, at 538.

[238]*See supra* note 222.

[239]*See* Spitzer, *supra* note 231, at 212.

[240]*Id.*

[241]Westermeyer, *supra* note 219, at 801. *See generally* Ennis & Litwack, *supra* note 218, at 697–708, 729–32.

[242]*See, e.g.,* D. MECHANIC, MENTAL HEALTH AND SOCIAL POLICY 14–17 (1969). Winick, *Ambiguities in the Legal Meaning and Significance of Mental Illness,* 1 PSYCHOL. PUB. POL'Y & L., 534 (1995).

[243]Cancro, *Introduction to Etiologic Studies of the Schizophrenic Disorders, in* PSYCHIATRY 1982 ANNUAL REVIEW 91 (L. Grinspoon ed., 1982) ("There is no independent test to confirm or to reject the diagnosis of schizophrenia. There is no tissue or body fluid which can be sent to the laboratory to ascertain which individuals are false positives or false negatives.").

[244]MECHANIC, *supra* note 242, at 17.

approach'' to etiology,[245] one which focuses on the consequences of a condition rather than its causes.[246] This claim reinforces the notion that clinicians applying the diagnostic criteria are merely observing and describing ''facts.'' Facts, however, are not theory neutral. Diverse work in philosophy of science has repeatedly demonstrated that the observation and reporting of facts are inevitably theory driven.[247] Medical diagnoses are by their nature ''hypotheses based on some underlying theory or set of assumptions.''[248] Given the lack of consensus concerning the etiology of these conditions and the imprecision of their symptoms,[249] divergence in the clinical application of the criteria used to define them is not surprising.[250] Moreover, although the more recent editions of the *DSM* narrow the definition of schizophrenia and deemphasize the role of such inherently subjective criteria as dysfunction in personal relationships,[251] many clinicians may continue to apply a broader notion of schizophrenia.[252]

The problem of subjectivity in the application of psychiatric diagnostic criteria is exacerbated when White, middle-class, and overwhelmingly male clinicians are called on to interpret the signs and symptoms of culturally foreign patients—a scenario that frequently occurs in urban communities and in mental hospitals and prisons generally.[253] This problem produces erroneous commitment and unnecessary harmful intrusive treatment not only of

---

[245]This excerpt is illustrative:

> For most of the *DSM–III–R* disorders . . . the etiology is unknown. Many theories have been advanced and buttressed by evidence—not always convincing—attempting to explain how these disorders come about. The approach taken in *DSM–III–R* with regard to etiology is that the inclusion of etiologic theories would be an obstacle to use of the manual by clinicians of varying theoretical orientations, since it would not be possible to present all reasonable etiologic theories for each disorder.

DSM–III–R, supra note 221, at xxiii.

[246]Spitzer, *supra* note 231, at 211–13.

[247]*See, e.g.,* W. GOODMAN, WAYS OF WORLDMAKING 2–3 (1978); R. HARE, THE PHILOSOPHIES OF SCIENCE 11 (1972); T. KUHN, THE STRUCTURE OF SCIENTIFIC REVOLUTIONS 66 (2d ed. 1970); K. POPPER, THE LOGIC OF SCIENTIFIC DISCOVERY 94–95 (1959); H. PUTNAM, REASON, TRUTH AND HISTORY 54 (1981); N. RESCHER, EMPIRICAL INQUIRY 18, 70–72 (1982); M. TURNER, PSYCHOLOGY AND THE PHILOSOPHY OF SCIENCE 14–15 (1967); W. WEIMER, NOTES ON THE METHODOLOGY OF SCIENTIFIC RESEARCH 20–26 (1979); Faust & Miner, *supra* note 223, at 964–65; *see also* Winter, *supra* note 164, at 1131.

[248]MECHANIC, *supra* note 242, at 18.

[249]The introduction to *DSM–III–R* itself concedes that the manual's classification of mental disorders provides no ''precise boundaries'' or ''sharp boundaries'' for differentiating one disorder from another or from no disorder at all. *DSM–III–R, supra* note 221, at xxii–iii.

[250]Cancro, *supra* note 243, at 91 (''Diagnosis remains a clinical activity based on arbitrarily selected clinical phenomena. The limitation of the diagnostic method guarantees heterogeneity in the sample and in part accounts for the fact that all studies of the schizophrenic syndrome are less reliable than is desirable.'').

[251]*Id.* at 85–86, 90.

[252]Many of the divergent diagnoses of John Hinckley offered by the numerous psychiatrists who testified at his celebrated trial were not contained in the *DSM* and thus illustrate that even expert psychiatric witnesses ''do not feel bound by the *DSM–III* diagnostic categories.'' A. STONE, LAW, PSYCHIATRY, AND MORALITY 84–85, 91 (1984). The tendency of clinicians not to feel bound by the *DSM* may be augmented by criticism of the DSM's artificial clarity and abbreviated character and the suggestion that clinicians ''go on to a broad-based assessment of other characteristics of the person, including his or her social functioning, distortions of meaning, psychological conflicts, and coping mechanisms.'' Strauss, *The Clinical Pictures and Diagnosis of the Schizophrenic Disorders, in* PSYCHIATRY 1982 ANNUAL REVIEW, *supra* note 243, at 87, 90–91.

[253]*See* Johnson, *supra* note 226, at 184. Indeed, both *DSM–III–R* and *DSM–IV* specifically caution clinicians concerning this problem. *DSM–III–R, supra* note 221, at xxvi–vii; *DSM–IV, supra* note 222, at xxiv–xxv (ethnic and cultural considerations).

ethnic and racial minorities,[254] but also of immigrant populations. Many immigrants cannot communicate effectively in English, with the result that their symptoms are easily misunderstood by clinicians whose cultural distance from these individuals is compounded by a language barrier. In an ironic variation of this problem, many institution psychiatrists, accepting employment in state hospitals or prisons where full licensure often is not required, are foreign born and foreign trained, frequently with an even greater cultural and language distance from their patients.[255]

Thus, for several reasons, the *DSM*'s "appearance of objectivity is largely illusory."[256] Although mental illness is not a myth,[257] the criteria used to define it are subjective and imprecise and their application inevitably involves value judgments, often beyond the professional competence of clinicians. Indeed, except in the clearest of cases, determining who is mentally ill is a social and moral judgment as much as a clinical one.[258]

As a result, allowing application of the First Amendment to turn upon this distinction is dangerous.[259] The most familiar example is psychiatric practice in the former Soviet Union, where there was no equivalent of the First Amendment. Dissident political beliefs were defined as disordered and their proponents declared mentally ill, committed to hospitals, and subjected to intrusive mental health treatment to change their beliefs.[260] Surely many of the Soviet psychiatrists who participated in these practices in the pre-Perestroika era did so out of what they considered to be benevolent motives.[261] In the social and political context

[254]National statistics on admissions to state and county psychiatric hospitals reveal that Black men are hospitalized at a rate 2.8 times greater than White men, and Black women at a rate 2.5 times greater than white women. Rosenthal & Carty, *Impediments to Services for Black and Hispanic People with Mental Illness* 3 (June 1988) (unpublished manuscript, prepared, by Mental Health Law Project under contract with National Institute of Mental Health [NIMH]) (citing 1987 NIMH statistics). While 48.9% of Whites were hospitalized involuntarily, 56.6% of non-Whites were so hospitalized. *Id.* Moreover, these statistics show that Black inpatients were diagnosed with schizophrenia at almost twice the rate of White inpatients, and this disparity is even greater for Black women compared to White women. *Id.* at 4. Hispanic inpatients are diagnosed as schizophrenic at a rate 1.4 times that of White inpatients. *Id.* There is a growing concern that these disparities, rather than reflecting some inherent racial susceptibility to psychopathology, are the result of misdiagnosis caused by the sociocultural distance between clinicians and these minority group patients. *See* Adebimpe, *Overview: White Norms and Psychiatric Diagnosis of Black Psychiatric Patients,* 138 Am. J. Psychiatry 279, 279, 281–83 (1981); Jones & Gray, *Problems of Diagnosing Schizophrenia and Affective Disorders Among Blacks,* 37 Hosp. & Community Psychiatry 61, 61–65 (1986); Rosenthal & Carty, *supra* at 4–7. "Language not understood is often considered evidence of thought disorder; styles of relating are sometimes misinterpreted as disturbances in affect; and unfamiliar mannerisms are considered bizarre." Jones & Gray, *supra* at 33.

[255]*See* Rosenthal & Carty, *supra* note 254, at 6; Solomon, *Racial Factors in Mental Health Service Utilization,* 11 Psychosocial Rehabilitation J. 3, 10 (1988).

[256]Faust & Miner, *supra* note 223, at 963.

[257]In his many writings, psychiatrist Thomas Szasz argues that mental illness is a myth and a metaphor. *See, e.g.,* T. Szasz, The Manufacture of Madness (1970); T. Szasz, The Myth of Mental Illness (1961). Many of Szasz's criticisms of how the law treats mental illness are valid. *Compare, e.g.,* Winick, *supra* note 217 *with* T. Szasz, Psychiatric Justice (1965). However, Szasz's basic analysis is flawed. *See, e.g.,* Mechanic, *supra* note 242, at 17–19; Moore, *Some Myths About "Mental Illness,"* 32 Archives Gen. Psychiatry 1483 (1975); Reiss, *A Critique of Thomas S. Szasz's "Myth of Mental Illness,"* 128 Am. J. Psychiatry 1081 (1972).

[258]*See* H. Fingarette, The Meaning of Criminal Insanity 37 (1972); Morse, *A Preference for Liberty: The Case Against Involuntary Commitment of the Mentally Disordered, supra* note 236, at 559–60; Shapiro, *supra* note 133, at 270; Winick, *supra* note 217, at 966–67.

[259]*See supra* notes 165–69 and accompanying text.

[260]*See* S. Bloch & P. Reddaway, Psychiatric Terror: How Soviet Psychiatry is Used to Suppress Dissent (1977); H. Fireside, Soviet Psychoprisons (1979); Chalidze, *A Comparison of Norms—Rights of the Mentally Ill and Allegedly Mentally Ill,* 1 N.Y.L. Sch. Hum. Rts. Ann. 75, 85–86 (1983); Clarity, *A Freed Dissident Says Soviet Doctors Sought to Break His Political Beliefs,* N.Y. Times, Feb. 4, 1976, at A1, 8.

[261]*See* Stone, *supra* note 252, at 6; Wing, *Psychiatry in the Soviet Union,* Brit. Med. J. 433 (1974).

within which these psychiatrists lived and worked, political dissidents could be considered disordered, if only because they were so obviously self-destructive.[262] In any event, treatment could be justified as better for such individuals than the alternative treatment they would receive at the hands of the KGB.[263] Such "benevolence" is not unknown among American psychiatrists. In the American criminal justice system, for example, many psychiatrists have traditionally overdiagnosed incompetency to stand trial on the basis of the often mistaken belief that incompetency commitment would be better for the defendant than the criminal process.[264] This has frequently resulted in lengthy commitment of defendants to substandard forensic hospitals. When fundamental constitutional values are at stake, close judicial scrutiny of governmental action is appropriate even (and perhaps especially) when that action is justified by benevolent motives.[265] Especially when First Amendment values are at risk, courts have traditionally been concerned with leaving unstructured discretion in the hands of enforcement officials.[266] Society can no more trust the "good psychiatrist" than it can the "good cop."

The First Amendment plays a central role in American society; in many ways it is one of the most important defining characteristics of the American political system. A society often defines itself reactively by renouncing alternative visions; we characterize ourselves by disavowing what we are not. This approach is reflected in Justice Kennedy's opinion for the Court in *Ward v. Rock Against Racism*.[267] In analyzing why music (although not speech) is protected by the First Amendment, Justice Kennedy compared U.S. society to totalitarian regimes in which certain kinds of music have been suppressed as threatening the interests of the state.[268] The First Amendment, Justice Kennedy affirmed, "prohibits any like attempts in our own legal order."[269] The First Amendment similarly demands strict scrutiny of intrusive treatments of the kind used to treat "disordered" thought in the former Soviet Union and of any similar attempts here.

Even if the potential for abusive application of categories like "mentally ill" or "disordered" is considered small in the U.S. system,[270] accepting the legitimacy of these categories as a basis for avoiding First Amendment scrutiny threatens basic First Amendment values. Even those who are clearly and seriously mentally ill—suffering from a severe case of schizophrenia, for example, a condition manifested by gross disturbances in thinking

---

[262]*See* STONE, *supra* note 252, at 21.

[263]*See id.* at 6.

[264]*See* R. ROESCH & S. GOLDING, COMPETENCY TO STAND TRIAL 48–49 (1980); A. STONE, MENTAL HEALTH AND LAW: A SYSTEM IN TRANSITION 205–06 (DHEW Pub. No. (ADM) 76–176, 1975); Hess & Thomas, *Incompetency to Stand Trial: Procedures, Results and Problems,* 119 AM. J. PSYCHIATRY 713 (1963); Winick, *supra* note 217, at 983.

[265]*See* City of Richmond v. J.A. Croson Co., 448 U.S. 469, 499 (1989); *In re* Gault, 387 U.S. 1, 18 (1967).

[266]*See, e.g.,* City of Lakewood v. Plain Dealer Publishing Co., 486 U.S. 1310, 756 (1988); Shuttlesworth v. City of Birmingham, 394 U.S. 147, 150–51 (1969).

[267]491 U.S. 781.

[268]*Id.* at 2753 (citing 2 DIALOGUES OF PLATO, REPUBLIC, bk. III, at 231, 245–48 (B. Jowett trans., 4th ed. 1953); *Musical Freedom and Why Dictators Fear It,* N.Y. TIMES, Aug. 23, 1981, B1; *Soviet Schizophrenia Toward Stravinsky,* N.Y. TIMES, June 26, 1982, A25; *Symphonic Voice from China Is Heard Again,* N.Y. TIMES, Oct. 11, 1987, B27).

[269]*Ward,* 491 U.S. at 790.

[270]*But see* STONE, *supra* note 252, at 3–36 (discussing the political misuse of psychiatry in the cases of Soviet general Petro Grigorenko and American general Edwin Walker).

and perception[271]—have fluctuating periods of relatively undisturbed thought.[272] Many individuals with schizophrenia engage in such creative activity as art and poetry.[273] Although schizophrenia is undeniably a painful and distressing condition, it includes aspects that lead some psychiatrists to regard it as a great growth experience, a voyage of discovery.[274] "[S]ome schizophrenic experiences . . . can be definitely seen as an enlargement and enrichment of human life."[275] Certain aspects of schizophrenic thinking "permit an enlargement of the human experience, can open new horizons and lead to new paths of feeling and understanding."[276] Indeed, some psychiatrists, although in a distinct minority, interpret the condition "as a positive development that reveals truths to fellow men and opens new paths toward greater moral values."[277] Society may have much to learn from individuals with schizophrenia: "From [their] protestations we may learn many sociological truths, generally hidden from the average citizen, and we may learn to recognize every day hypocrisies which we meekly accept as ineluctable facts of life."[278] As the poet Emily Dickinson put it: "Much madness is divinest Sense—To a discerning Eye. . . ."[279] In a

---

[271]J. Grebb & R. Cancro, *Schizophrenia: Clinical Features, in* 1 COMPREHENSIVE TEXTBOOK OF PSYCHIATRY 761–62 (H. Kaplan & B. Sadock eds., 5th ed. 1989); *infra* note 366 and accompanying text.

[272]Morse, *Crazy Behavior, Morals, and Science: An Analysis of Mental Health Law, supra* note 217, at 573, 588 (mentally ill people have a significant capacity for normal and rational behavior); Winick, *supra* note 217, at 970–71. The fluctuating nature of mental illness is also revealed by empirical studies demonstrating that competency of mental patients is intermittent. C. LIDZ ET AL., INFORMED CONSENT: A STUDY OF DECISIONMAKING IN PSYCHIATRY 198–99 (1984); *see also* Appelbaum & Roth, *Clinical Issues in the Assessment of Competency,* 138 AM. J. PSYCHIATRY 1462, 1465 (1981) (competency fluctuates over time).

[273]*See* S. ARIETI, INTERPRETATION OF SCHIZOPHRENIA 351–74 (2d ed. 1974). *See generally* PORTER, *supra* note 179 (examining autobiographical writings of the mentally ill).

[274]Gregory Bateson, in his introduction to John Perceval's NARRATIVE, invokes this metaphor, characterizing schizophrenia as a "voyage of discovery" from which the patient "comes back with insights different from those of the inhabitants who never embarked on such a voyage." Bateson, *Introduction* to J. PERCEVAL, A NARRATIVE OF THE TREATMENT EXPERIENCED BY A GENTLEMAN, DURING A STATE OF MENTAL DERANGEMENT at v, xiii–xiv (G. Bateson rev. ed. 1961) (1840). Similarly, R.D. Laing portrays schizophrenia as a "journey" by the patient "to explore the inner space and time of consciousness." R. LAING, THE POLITICS OF EXPERIENCE 126–27 (1967). Laing suggests that in the future, people will come to see "that what we call "schizophrenia' was one of the forms in which, often through quite ordinary people, the light began to break through the cracks in the all-too-closed minds." *Id.* at 129.

[275]ARIETI, *supra* note 273, at 378–79.

[276]*Id.* at 379.

[277]*Id.* at 125.

[278]*Id.* at 379. Social historian Roy Porter's analysis of the autobiographies of the insane led him to conclude:

> The writings of the mad can be read not just as symptoms of diseases or syndromes, but as coherent communications in their own right. . . .
>   . . . [T]heir testaments plainly echo, albeit often in an unconventional or distorted idiom, the ideas, values, aspirations, hopes and fears of their contemporaries. They use the language of their age, though often in ways which are highly unorthodox. When we read the writings of the mad, we gain an enhanced insight into the sheer range of what could be thought and felt, at the margins. We might compare the way historians of popular culture have told us to listen sympathetically to the popular idiom of graffiti, to riddles, to the lore and language of schoolchildren, or to the cosmologies of heretics arraigned before the Inquisition.

PORTER, *supra* note 179, at 2.

[279]THE POEMS OF EMILY DICKINSON 337 (T. Johnson ed. 1955).

sense, the mentally ill hold up a mirror to the rest of society, which looks away only at its peril.[280]

Unlike "fighting words" and obscenity, which by definition are "utterly without redeeming social importance,"[281] the mentation and expressive conduct of the mentally ill may well have social and intrinsic value. Moreover, both of these are within the core values protected by the First Amendment.[282] Under the *Chaplinsky* doctrine, the category of unprotected expression is limited only to expression that is deemed totally unrelated to the purposes of the First Amendment.[283] Expression implicating First Amendment values, however, even if of limited or no social utility, is within the protection of the Constitution. The Supreme Court has recognized the "right to receive information and ideas, regardless of their social worth."[284] It has reiterated that First Amendment protection does not turn upon the "social utility of the ideas and beliefs which are offered."[285] Even ideas deemed "offensive,"[286] "loathsome,"[287] "noxious,"[288] and "immoral"[289] may be protected. Thoughts deemed "disordered" would seem no less entitled to First Amendment protection. Furthermore, because the mentation and expressive conduct of the mentally ill serve values within the core of those traditionally protected by the First Amendment,[290] the reduced scrutiny approach that has emerged from cases involving what some members of the

---

[280]*See* PORTER, *supra* note 179, at 3:

> [W]hat the mad say is illuminating because it presents a world through the looking-glass, or indeed holds up the mirror to the logic (and psycho-logic) of sane society. It focuses and puts to the test the nature and limits of the rationality, humanity and "understanding" of the normal. In that sense, the late French philosopher Michel Foucault was quite right to insist that the history of unreason must be coterminous with the history of reason. They are doubles.
>
> Furthermore, examined in this light, the consciousness of the mad confronts that of the sane to constitute a kind of hall of mirrors. When we juxtapose the mind of the insane with that of reason, society and culture, we see two facets, two expressions, two faces, and each puts the question to the other. If normality condemns madness as irrational, subhuman, perverse, madness typically replies in kind, has its own *tu quoque*. Rather like children playing at being adults, the mad highlight the hypocrisies, double standards and sheer callous obliviousness of sane society. The writings of the mad challenge the discourse of the normal, challenge its right to be the objective mouthpiece of the times. The assumption that there exist definitive and unitary standards of truth and falsehood, reality and delusion, is put to the test.

[281]Roth v. United States, 354 U.S. 476, 484 (1957).

[282]*See supra* notes 150–84 and accompanying text.

[283]Schauer, *supra* note 193, at 303–04.

[284]Stanley v. Georgia, 394 U.S. 557, 564 (1969); *see also* Winters v. New York, 333 U.S. 507, 510 (1948) ("Though we can see nothing of any possible value to society in these magazines, they are as much entitled to the protection of free speech as the best of literature.").

[285]New York Times Co. v. Sullivan, 376 U.S. 254, 271 (1964) (quoting NAACP v. Button, 371 U.S. 415, 445 (1963)). *See also* Gertz v. Robert Welch, Inc., 418 U.S. 323, 339–41 (1974) (false assertions of fact are protected by the First Amendment even though they do not contribute to the search for truth and hence have no constitutional value).

[286]Texas v. Johnson, 491 U.S. 397, 414 (1989) (citing cases).

[287]*See* Abrams v. United States, 250 U.S. 616, 630 (1919) (Holmes, J., dissenting). Thus, although loathsome, the ideas of the Nazi party are protected by the First Amendment. *See* Collin v. Smith, 578 F.2d 1197 (7th Cir.), *cert. denied,* 439 U.S. 916 (1978); Village of Skokie v. National Socialist Party of Am., 69 Ill. 2d 605, 373 N.E.2d 21 (1978). *See generally* A. NEIER, DEFENDING MY ENEMY: AMERICAN NAZIS, THE SKOKIE CASE, AND THE RISKS OF FREEDOM (1979).

[288]Whitney v. California, 274 U.S. 357, 375 (1927) (Brandeis & Holmes, J.J., concurring).

[289]Stanley v. Georgia, 394 U.S. 557, 565 n.8 (1969) (quoting Henkins, *Morals and the Constitution: The Sin of Obscenity,* 63 COLUM. L. REV. 391, 395 (1963)); *see also* Kingsley Int'l Pictures Corp. v. Regents of the Univ. of N.Y., 360 U.S. 684, 689 (1959) (invalidating statute prohibiting exhibition of motion pictures portraying adultery favorably as inconsistent with the First Amendment, which "is not confined to the expression of ideas that are conventional or shared by a majority").

[290]*See supra* notes 150–84 and accompanying text.

Court regard as ''lesser value'' speech—the sexually explicit speech presented in *American Mini Theaters, Pacifica,* and *Playtime Theaters,*[291] and some forms of commercial speech[292]—would also seem inapplicable.

Stanley v. Georgia,[293] which involved the right to possess obscenity in the privacy of the home, seems especially relevant to the question of First Amendment protection for ''disordered'' thought and expression. In *Stanley,* the Court rejected as inconsistent with the First Amendment the state's assertion of the right ''to protect the individual's mind from the effects of obscenity.''[294] Many would undoubtedly label as ''disordered'' the thoughts and emotions of the individual observing obscene films. Thus, the Court's rejection of the state's argument as little more than an ''assertion that the State has the right to control the moral content of a person's thoughts''[295] should preclude a similar argument that the state may intervene into mental processes to protect the individual's mind from ''disordered'' thoughts.

Stanley can be reconciled with the cases holding that obscenity is outside the ambit of the First Amendment by drawing a distinction between the public display or distribution of obscenity and its private possession for personal use in the home.[296] Although the government may prohibit the former, the First Amendment insulates from government control ''a person's private thoughts,''[297] even if they are regarded as disordered. The Court in *Stanley* endorsed the views expressed in Justice Brandeis's celebrated dissenting opinion in *Olmstead v. United States.*[298] Brandeis, writing in the 1928 wire-tapping case, had warned against future advances in science and technology that could provide ''means of exploring unexpressed beliefs, thoughts and emotions.''[299] The Constitution, Brandeis affirmed, protects against such intrusions:

> The makers of our Constitution undertook to secure conditions favorable to the pursuit of happiness. They recognized the significance of man's spiritual nature, of his feelings and of his intellect. . . . They sought to protect Americans in their beliefs, their thoughts, their emotions and their sensations. They conferred as against the Government, the right to be let alone—the most comprehensive of rights and the right most valued by civilized men.[300]

Justice Brandeis's eloquent language has frequently been quoted. On one such occasion, former Chief Justice Burger, while a judge on the United States Court of Appeals for the District of Columbia Circuit, invoked Brandeis's words to reject the notion that the exercise of constitutional rights may turn on a judgment concerning the wisdom or propriety of an individual's choices:

---

[291]*See supra* notes 202–13 and accompanying text.

[292]*See supra* notes 214–15 and accompanying text. For an analysis concluding that commercial speech does not serve the core values of the First Amendment, see Jackson & Jeffries, *Commercial Speech: Economic Due Process and the First Amendment,* 65 VA. L. REV. 1 (1979).

[293]394 U.S. 557 (1969).

[294]*Id.* at 565. When the state's interest, however, is the protection of others rather than merely of the individual consumer of obscene materials, the state's regulatory interest is considerably stronger. *See* Osborne v. Ohio, 495 U.S. 103, 109 (1990) (upholding child pornography statute, distinguishing *Stanley* as involving merely a ''paternalistic interest in regulating'' the consumer's mind, and stressing the state's interest in protecting the child victims of such pornography).

[295]*Stanley,* 394 U.S. at 565.

[296]*See supra* notes 111–13 and accompanying text.

[297]*Stanley,* 394 U.S. at 566.

[298]*Id.* at 564 (quoting Olmstead v. United States, 277 U.S. 438, 478 (1928) (Brandeis, J., dissenting)).

[299]*Olmstead,* 277 U.S. at 474.

[300]*Id.* at 478.

Nothing in this utterance suggests that Justice Brandeis thought an individual possessed these rights only as to *sensible* beliefs, *valid* thoughts, *reasonable* emotions, or *well-founded* sensations. I suggest he intended to include a great many foolish, unreasonable and even absurd ideas which do not conform, such as refusing medical treatment even at great risk.[301]

Full First Amendment protection should therefore extend to all thoughts and mental processes, even those labeled *insane* or *disordered.*

2. Is the First Amendment Implicated by Treatment That Restores Mental Processes to a "Normal" or "Healthy" State?

The above analysis also meets the related contention that mental health treatment cannot raise First Amendment problems because, rather than interfering with mental processes, such treatment enhances the patient's capacity to think and liberates the mind by freeing it from mental illness.[302] It is true that when properly used, many of these treatments—the psychotropic drugs, for example—are "normative in their mechanism of action, that is, they restore existing imbalance toward the balanced norm."[303] The fact remains, however, that although these treatments may be beneficial and clinically desirable, they nonetheless constitute government alteration of thought processes. Distinguishing "normal" from "abnormal" mental states may be no easier and no less dangerous than distinguishing "sane" from "disordered" thought.[304] Moreover, treatment designed to restore the thought processes of a patient or offender to a "normal" state of functioning seems analogous to governmental efforts to inculcate patriotic values in school children by use of the compulsory flag salute invalidated in *West Virginia State Board of Education v. Barnette*[305] or to protect the minds of citizens from the effects of obscenity by the methods condemned in *Stanley v. Georgia.*[306] In both *Barnette* and *Stanley,* the governmental intrusions into mental privacy can be defended as attempts to bring about a state of normality. The analogy is particularly strong in *Stanley* because the prohibition on private possession and use of obscenity involved there could be defended as an attempt to enhance the citizen's capacity to think normally and liberate his mind by freeing it from invasion by material that tends "to deprave and corrupt those whose minds are open to such immoral influences."[307]

Mental processes must remain presumptively immune from governmental control in a system committed to the values of the First Amendment. Government alteration of mental processes, even if designed to restore the individual to some prior or "normal" mental state

---

[301]*In re* President of Georgetown College, Inc., 331 F.2d 1010, 1017 (D.C. Cir. 1964) (separate statement of Burger, J., respecting denial of rehearing en banc).

[302]*See* Appelbaum & Gutheil, *supra* note 216, at 311–12; Cole, *Patients' Rights vs. Doctors' Rights: Which Should Take Precedence?, in* REFUSING TREATMENT IN MENTAL HEALTH INSTITUTIONS—VALUES IN CONFLICT 56, 69 (A. Doudera & J. Swazey eds., 1982); Gutheil, *In Search of True Freedom: Drug Refusal, Involuntary Medication, and "Rotting With Your Rights On,"* 137 AM. J. PSYCHIATRY 327, 327 (1980).

[303]Appelbaum & Gutheil, *supra* note 216, at 308; *see also* Gutheil & Appelbaum, *"Mind Control," "Synthetic Sanity," "Artificial Competence," and Genuine Confusion: Legally Relevant Effects of Antipsychotic Medication,* 12 HOFSTRA L. REV. 77, 101 (1983) (the "acknowledged normalizing effects of the antipsychotic medications"); *id.* at 118 (referring to the "normalizing effects" of the drugs; the drugs facilitate "the re-emergence of normal patterns of cognition"; "their effect is to alter mental functioning in the direction of normality").

[304]*See supra* notes 217–60 and accompanying text.

[305]319 U.S. 624 (1943); *see supra* notes 55–67 and accompanying text.

[306]394 U.S. 557 (1969); *see supra* notes 102–06 and accompanying text.

[307]This was the test for obscenity put forth by Lord Chief Justice Cockburn in Regina v. Hicklin, 3 L.R.-Q.B. 360, 368 (1868), a test that was widely adopted by American courts. *See* TRIBE, *supra* note 3, § 12–16, at 906.

or to accomplish other beneficial results, should be subject to scrutiny under the First Amendment. In a related context, a California appellate court applied First Amendment scrutiny to statutory requirements that imposed procedural impediments on a patient's choice of undergoing psychosurgery and electroconvulsive therapy (ECT).[308] These regulations, designed to protect patients from what the legislature viewed as intrusive and hazardous treatments, mandated special consent and record-keeping procedures and a review of the patient's capacity to consent by three appointed physicians.[309] The court recognized that these were plainly not attempts by the state "to control . . . what is thought by mental patients, nor how they think. . . ."[310] Rather, they were exercises of the state's police power designed to protect patient safety.[311] Nonetheless, the court found that "despite the lack of any showing the state has attempted to regulate freedom of thought, this legislation may diminish this right."[312] These statutory impediments on patient access to therapies that "touch upon thought processes in significant ways" accordingly required strict constitutional scrutiny.[313]

Subjecting the imposition of mental health treatment to First Amendment scrutiny does not necessarily condemn the mentally ill to their psychoses, so that they may enjoy merely the dubious freedom to "rot with their rights on," as some commentators have suggested.[314] Rather, it erects a presumption against forced governmental intrusion into the mind, one that may be overcome only on a showing of compelling necessity, thus requiring careful scrutiny both of the ends sought by intrusive treatment and the means selected to accomplish those ends. In this sense the contention that the First Amendment should not be implicated by mental health treatment designed to restore individuals' control over their own minds by liberating it from the effects of their illness misses the mark. Although this argument may be relevant (and indeed perhaps even persuasive on the question of whether an individual's First Amendment right to resist unwanted mental intrusions may be outweighed in particular circumstances), it must be rejected as an argument against First Amendment consideration of these issues.[315]

E. Judicial Recognition of a First Amendment Right To Refuse Treatment: The Lower Court Decisions

Although the Supreme Court has never considered the question, some state and lower federal court decisions have recognized a First Amendment basis for patient refusal of treatment. Without extensive analysis, these courts concluded that government alteration of mental processes through at least certain forms of mental health treatment is subject to First Amendment scrutiny. As the First Amendment protects freedom of expression, these courts reasoned, then it also must protect the more basic right to generate and to hold ideas.

The first such case to apply the First Amendment in this context was *Kaimowitz v. Michigan Department of Mental Health*,[316] a 1973 state court decision involving psy-

---

[308]Aden v. Younger, 129 Cal. Rptr. 535 (Ct. App. 1976).

[309]*Id.* at 539.

[310]*Id.* at 546.

[311]*Id.* at 545–46.

[312]*Id.* at 546.

[313]*Id.*

[314]Appelbaum & Gutheil, *supra* note 216; Gutheil, *supra* note 302.

[315]*Id.*

[316]Civ. No. 73–19434–AW (Mich. Cir. Ct. July 10, 1973), *reprinted in* Brooks, *supra* note 41, at 902.

chosurgery, the most intrusive of the mental health treatment techniques.[317] *Kaimowitz* involved a criminal defendant charged with murder and rape who was held in a state mental hospital under the Michigan sexual psychopath law. The defendant was transferred to a state facility that used experimental psychosurgery for the treatment of uncontrollable aggression; the facility was conducting a study that involved an experimental design comparing the effects of surgery on the amygdaloid portion of the limbic system of the brain with the effects of a drug on male hormone flow. Although he had signed an ''informed consent'' form to participate in the study and although the procedure was approved by both a scientific review committee and a human rights committee, a public interest lawyer learned of the experiment and filed suit to enjoin it. Finding psychosurgery to be clearly experimental and posing substantial and in some cases unknown dangers to research participants, the court ruled that its imposition on an involuntarily detained patient would violate the First Amendment.[318] The court held that the First Amendment protects the individual's ''mental processes, the communication of ideas, and the generation of ideas,''[319] reasoning that to the extent that the amendment protects the dissemination and expression of ideas, ''it equally must protect the individual's right to generate ideas.''[320] Finding that psychosurgery seriously and irreversibly impairs ''the power to generate ideas,'' the court held that its imposition would be unconstitutional.[321] The First Amendment, the court found, prevents government from attempting ''to control men's minds, thoughts, and expressions'' through the surgical intervention at issue.[322]

The first federal court opinion to suggest that the First Amendment might limit involuntary treatment was *Mackey v. Procunier*.[323] That case involved the involuntary use of the drug succinylcholine in an aversive conditioning program at a state prison medical facility. The drug, characterized as a ''breath-stopping and paralyzing ''fright drug,'' resulted in the prisoner–study participant regularly suffering ''nightmares in which he relives the frightening experience and awakens unable to breathe.''[324] These allegations of mental intrusion and effect were sufficient for the United States Court of Appeals for the Ninth Circuit to rule that the prisoner's complaint raised serious constitutional questions of ''impermissible tinkering with the mental processes.''[325]

The First Amendment has also been invoked in cases involving the involuntary administration of antipsychotic medication to state mental hospital patients and pretrial detainees. In *Scott v. Plante*,[326] the United States Court of Appeals for the Third Circuit reversed the dismissal for failure to state a claim of a complaint filed by a patient at a state mental hospital that attacked the involuntary administration of antipsychotic medication. The court held that ''the involuntary administration of drugs which affect mental processes, if it occurred, could amount, under an appropriate set of facts, to an interference with Scott's

---

[317]*See infra* notes 342–46 and accompanying text.

[318]Kaimowitz v. Michigan Dep't of Mental Health, Civ. No. 73–19434–AW (Mich. Cir. Ct. July 10, 1973), *reprinted in* BROOKS, *supra* note 41, at 918–19.

[319]*Id., reprinted in* BROOKS, *supra* note 41, at 917.

[320]*Id.*

[321]*Id.*, at 918. *See also* Aden v. Younger, 129 Cal. Rptr. 535, 546 (Cal. Ct. App. 1976) (statutory procedures impeding patient access to psychosurgery and electroconvulsive therapy implicate First Amendment freedom of thought).

[322]Kaimowitz v. Michigan Dep't of Mental Health, Civ. No. 73–19434–AW (Mich. Cir. Ct. July 10, 1973), *reprinted in* BROOKS, *supra* note 41, at 918–19.

[323]477 F.2d 877 (9th Cir. 1973).

[324]*Id.* at 877.

[325]*Id.* at 878.

[326]532 F.2d 939 (3d Cir. 1976), *vacated and remanded,* 458 U.S. 1101 (1982).

rights under the First Amendment.''[327] Because of the procedural posture of the case, the appellate court did not determine what would be an appropriate set of facts sufficient to violate the First Amendment but merely decided that Scott's complaint should not have been dismissed because it was possible that the evidence would show a First Amendment violation.

In *Bee v. Greaves,*[328] pretrial detainees challenged the involuntary administration of antipsychotic drugs. Finding that the drugs can affect the "ability to think and communicate,''[329] the U.S. Court of Appeals for the Tenth Circuit recognized a right to refuse them protected by the First Amendment, which the court held implicitly protects "the capacity to produce ideas.''[330] The district court in *Rogers v. Okin,*[331] the Boston State Hospital case, also found a First Amendment basis for a right to refuse psychotropic drugs, which the court concluded have "the potential to affect and change a patient's mood, attitude and capacity to think.''[332] The court found the "right to produce a thought or refuse to do so'' to be protected by the First Amendment.[333] "Without the capacity to think, we merely exist, not function,'' the court reasoned.[334] "Realistically, the capacity to think and decide is a fundamental element of freedom.''[335] The court derived the "right to produce a thought'' from the First Amendment's protection of the communication of ideas which, in the court's view, "presupposes a capacity to produce ideas.''[336] "Whatever powers the Constitution has granted our government,'' the court concluded, "involuntary mind control is not one of them, absent extraordinary circumstances.''[337]

The U.S. Court of Appeals for the Seventh Circuit applied this approach to the imposition of unwanted ECT in a tort suit brought by a voluntary patient in a Veteran's Administration hospital.[338] Noting that "compulsory treatment with mind-altering drugs may invade a patient's First Amendment interests in being able to think and communicate freely,'' the court found the same interests to be implicated by compulsory ECT.[339]

---

[327]532 F.2d at 946 (citing *Mackey* and *Kaimowitz*).

[328]744 F.2d 1387, 1394 (10th Cir. 1984), *cert. denied,* 469 U.S. 1214 (1985); *rev'd & remanded* 669 F. Supp. 372 (D.Utah 1987).

[329]*Id.* at 1394.

[330]*Id.; accord* Girouard v. O'Brien, No. 83–3316–0, 1988 U.S. Dist. LEXIS 4342 (D. Kan. April 4, 1988).

[331]478 F. Supp. 1342 (D. Mass. 1979), *aff'd in part and rev'd in part on other grounds,* 634 F.2d 650 (1st Cir. 1980), *vacated and remanded sub nom.* Mills v. Rogers, 457 U.S. 291 (1982), *on remand,* 738 F.2d 1 (1st Cir. 1984).

[332]478 F. Supp. at 1366.

[333]*Id.* at 1367.

[334]*Id.*

[335]*Id.*

[336]*Id.*

[337]*Id.* On appeal, the United States Court of Appeals for the First Circuit affirmed on the basis of constitutional privacy grounds and found it unnecessary to address the First Amendment issue. Rogers v. Okin, 634 F.2d 650, 653, 654 n.2 (1st Cir. 1980); *see also* Davis v. Hubbard, 506 F. Supp. 915, 933 (N.D. Ohio 1980), discussing the First Amendment but grounding a right to refuse psychotropic medication on constitutional privacy. The court noted that the forced administration of these drugs "implicates a person's interest in being able to think and to communicate freely.'' 506 F. Supp. at 933. At another point, the court, mentioning the "serious, long term, if not permanent, side effects'' of the drugs, stated that they "deaden the patient's ability to think.'' *Id.* at 936. Referring to the state's "attempts to use treatment as a means of controlling thought, either by inhibiting an inmate's ability to think or by coercing acceptance of particular thoughts and beliefs,'' the court suggested that "government action which directly affects the mental processes would be unconstitutional under the First Amendment.'' *Id.* at 933 (dicta).

[338]Lojuk v. Quandt, 706 F.2d 1456 (7th Cir. 1983).

[339]*Id.* at 1465. *See also* Aden v. Younger, 129 Cal. Rptr. 535, 546 (Cal. Ct. App. 1976) (statutory procedures impeding patient access to psychosurgery and ECT implicate First Amendment freedom of thought).

F. Mental Health Treatment Techniques and the First Amendment: An Application of the Continuum of Intrusiveness

Although these lower court cases do not analyze the issues in detail, their determination—that the First Amendment limits the imposition of intrusive therapies—seems essentially correct. However, to conclude that the First Amendment protects mental processes against certain kinds of governmental intrusions does not mean that all mental health treatment techniques will raise First Amendment questions. As previously noted, government in America has broad power to communicate ideas and take other actions that undoubtedly have enormous effects on the mental processes of at least some individuals.[340] Surely such effects alone do not render the governmental conduct in question suspect under the First Amendment. American society is complex, and government plays a significant role; governmental attempts to educate, to persuade, and to induce a variety of actions are essential to any meaningful exercise of governmental power. It is only when these government activities pass a certain threshold of intrusiveness—imposing particular beliefs or thoughts, or displacing others, by means that may not be avoided or resisted, and when the duration of these effects is sufficiently long-lasting as not to fall within a *de minimis* category—that the First Amendment will be implicated.[341] Rather than concluding that all involuntary mental health treatment automatically triggers First Amendment scrutiny, it therefore seems essential to examine separately each of the various treatment techniques on the continuum of intrusiveness framework previously developed.[342] The critical question is whether the nature, extent, and duration of the particular technique's effects intrudes sufficiently on mental processes to raise First Amendment concerns.

1. Psychosurgery

Psychosurgery presents the strongest case for First Amendment scrutiny. It is difficult to imagine a more intrusive invasion of mental processes than this procedure, which consists of the surgical removal or destruction of brain tissues performed with the intent of altering emotions and behavior.[343] The procedure (now rarely used) typically has a massive impact on intellectual functioning. In addition to a number of substantial physical risks, psychosurgery frequently results in intellectual deterioration and emotional blunting.[344] The *Kaimowitz* court, which found that involuntary psychosurgery would violate the First Amendment, premised its conclusion on extensive expert testimony concerning the serious adverse affects of the procedure on mental processes. The court stated: "Psychosurgery flattens emotional responses, leads to lack of abstract reasoning ability, leads to a loss of capacity for new learning, and causes general sedation and apathy. It can lead to impairment

---

[340]*See supra* note 54 and accompanying text.

[341]*See* TRIBE, *supra* note 3, § 15–8, at 1328–29; Shapiro, *Legislating the Control of Behavior Control: Autonomy and the Coercive Use of Organic Therapies,* 47 S. CAL. L. REV. 237, 262–67 (1974); Winick, *Legal Limitations on Correctional Therapy and Research,* 65 MINN. L. REV. 331, 351 (1981).

[342]*See supra* chapters 2–8.

[343]*See supra* chapter 8.

[344]*See* Chorover, *Psychosurgery: A Neuropsychological Perspective,* 54 B.U. L. REV. 231, 247 (1974); Valenstein, *The Practice of Psychosurgery: A Survey of the Literature (1971–1976), in* NATIONAL COMMISSION FOR THE PROTECTION OF HUMAN SUBJECTS OF BIOMEDICAL AND BEHAVIORAL RESEARCH, *Appendix to* PSYCHOSURGERY I– 56, I–80 (1977).

of memory, and in some instances unexpected responses to psychosurgery are observed."[345] The National Commission for the Protection of Human Subjects of Biomedical and Behavioral Research reviewed psychosurgery and found the *Kaimowitz* court's conclusions concerning the hazards of the newer psychosurgical procedures to be somewhat over-stated,[346] but it did not seriously question the conclusion that intellectual change frequently occurs. Indeed, Valenstein reviewed the literature for the National Commission and rejected the claim that psychosurgery does not result in intellectual change.[347] Although the empirical evidence concerning the effects of the newer procedures is incomplete, there appears to be little doubt that what might be characterized as unwanted personality changes following the surgery do occur, as does some amount of intellectual deterioration.

Clearly, any impairment of intellectual and emotional capacities brought about by psychosurgery would implicate First Amendment concerns, even if the incidence and duration of these serious effects occur less frequently than is commonly supposed. Moreover, psychosurgery is irreversible, at least in the sense that destroyed brain tissue does not regenerate, and perhaps also in the sense that permanent alteration in personality may result in at least some cases. Psychosurgery is a direct intervention into the brain itself, it cannot be resisted by patients, and it surgically alters their thoughts, feelings, behavior, and perhaps their very identities. Because of the substantial risks of psychosurgery, and at least until new research can demonstrate that the newer, more refined procedures do not have these effects, courts will agree with the basic conclusion of *Kaimowitz,* the only case to consider the issue, that psychosurgery imposed on an involuntary basis at least presumptively violates the First Amendment.

2. Electronic Stimulation of the Brain

Although somewhat less threatening to First Amendment values than psychosurgery, electronic stimulation of the brain (ESB)[348] is another surgical intervention into the brain itself that should also trigger First Amendment scrutiny. In this procedure, electrodes are planted directly into certain regions of the brain and stimulated electrically, inducing or inhibiting behaviors and sensations. ESB has been used for "inducing and blocking . . . an assortment of thought patterns, hallucinations [sic], laughter, memories, sexual expressions, and pleasant shifts of moods. . . ."[349] It can be used directly to interfere with thought and communication:[350]

> [T]hinking has been blocked by ESB, so that people oriented in time and space and able to follow the doctor's instructions in other ways, could not answer questions or pronounce a single word. "I could not coordinate my thoughts," one explained. "My head felt as if I had drunk a lot of beer." Another said, "I don't know why, but I could not speak."

---

[345]Kaimowitz v. Michigan Dep't of Mental Health, Civ. No. 73–19434–AW (Mich. Cir. Ct. July 10, 1973), *reprinted in* BROOKS, *supra* note 41, at 909.

[346]NATIONAL COMMISSION FOR THE PROTECTION OF HUMAN SUBJECTS OF BIOMEDICAL AND BEHAVIORAL RESEARCH, PSYCHOSURGERY 22 (1977).

[347]Valenstein, *supra* note 344, at I–58. Dr. Valenstein did conclude, however, that personality changes are "relatively infrequent and characterized as "mild' and "transient,' " *id.* at I–89, and that "[t]he risk of permanent adverse intellectual, emotional, and physical side effects is reported as minimal . . . in sharp contrast to the results from the older lobotomy operations." *Id.* at I–96.

[348]*See supra* chapter 7.

[349]P. LONDON, BEHAVIOR CONTROL 146 (1969).

[350]*Id.* at 147.

ESB operates with a "peculiar directness of effect which removes it from the subject's monitoring or control."[351] In general, the effects of ESB seem to be short-lived.[352] Even if only of short duration, however—and there is virtually no empirical evidence concerning the long-term effects of this highly experimental procedure—the ability of ESB to block thoughts and communication by directly modifying the state of the brain itself in a manner the patient is incapable of resisting raises fundamental First Amendment concerns. Like psychosurgery, ESB's direct interference with mental processes must be regarded as presumptively invalid under the First Amendment.

3. ECT

ECT[353] also directly affects the brain. Electrical current is passed directly through the brain, inducing convulsions and unconsciousness (unless unconsciousness has previously been induced through general anesthesia). Although the period of unconsciousness lasts only several minutes, patients remain in a state of confusion and disorientation for 15 to 30 minutes, and some patients claim persisting confusion and loss of memory. After several treatments, patients experience periods of disorientation and confusion lasting several days.

The mental confusion and loss of memory that occurs in virtually all cases[354] directly implicate First Amendment concerns. The more ECT treatments administered, and the older the patient, the longer such confusion and memory loss continue.[355] Although there is considerable controversy concerning whether ECT results in brain damage and permanent memory loss, many patients claim permanent memory impairment.[356] Because ECT traditionally has been so controversial, the National Institutes of Health in conjunction with the National Institute of Mental Health convened a Consensus Development Conference on ECT in 1985.[357] After hearing reports from experts, health professionals, and former patients, a consensus panel representing psychiatry, psychology, neurology, psychopharmacology, epidemiology, law, and the general public issued a consensus statement. It concluded that it was "well established" that ECT produces deficits in memory function "which have been demonstrated objectively and repeatedly, [and which] persist after termination of a normal course of ECT."[358] The consensus statement also concluded that the "ability to learn and retain new information is adversely affected" for several weeks following the administration of ECT.[359] Although "objective evidence based on neuropsychological testing" was found to demonstrate loss of memory for several weeks, such "objective tests have not firmly established persistent or permanent deficits for a more

[351]Vaughan, *Psychosurgery and Brain Stimulation in Historical Perspective* 24, *in* OPERATING ON THE MIND: THE PSYCHOSURGERY CONFLICT (W. Gaylin et al. eds., 1975).

[352]E. VALENSTEIN, BRAIN CONTROL: A CRITICAL EXAMINATION OF BRAIN STIMULATION AND PSYCHOSURGERY 105 (1973); Vaughan, *supra* note 351, at 60.

[353]*See supra* chapter 6.

[354]T. DETRE & H. JARECKI, MODERN PSYCHIATRIC TREATMENT 641–44 (1971); Dornbush & Williams, *Memory and ECT,* 194 *in* PSYCHOBIOLOGY OF CONVULSIVE THERAPY (M. Fink et al. eds., 1974); Harper & Wiens, *Electroconvulsive Therapy and Memory,* 161 J. NERVOUS & MENTAL DISEASES 245 (1975).

[355]DETRE & JARECKI, *supra* note 354, at 642–43.

[356]*Id.* at 643.

[357]5 NATIONAL INSTITUTES OF HEALTH & NATIONAL INSTITUTE OF MENTAL HEALTH, ELECTROCONVULSIVE THERAPY: CONSENSUS DEVELOPMENT CONFERENCE STATEMENT, No. 11 (1985), *reprinted in* R. SPRING ET AL., PATIENTS, PSYCHIATRISTS AND LAWYERS: LAW AND THE MENTAL HEALTH SYSTEM 129 (1989) [hereinafter PATIENTS, PSYCHIATRISTS AND LAWYERS].

[358]*Id.* at 132.

[359]*Id.*

extensive period. . . .''[360] Nevertheless, research conducted as long as 3 years after treatment found that many patients report continued memory impairment.[361] Some patients perceived ECT as a ''terrifying experience,'' ''an abusive invasion of personal autonomy,'' and the cause of ''extreme distress from persistent memory deficits.''[362]

Because it induces unconsciousness, mental confusion, and memory loss, ECT certainly raises First Amendment problems. Furthermore, the effects of the procedure cannot be resisted and, at least in some cases, ECT may result in irreversible memory impairment. As the U.S. Court of Appeals for the Seventh Circuit found in *Lojuk v. Quandt*,[363] the effects of ECT on mental processes, and particularly on memory, clearly implicate First Amendment concerns.[364]

4. Psychotropic Medication

By definition, psychotropic drugs are compounds that affect the mind, intellectual functions, perception, moods, and emotions.[365] Indeed, the Supreme Court in *Mills v. Rogers* acknowledged that these drugs are '' 'mind-altering.' Their effectiveness resides in their capacity to achieve such effects.''[366] They directly intrude on mental processes and cannot be resisted. Moreover, their primary effects alter mental processes (usually in a clinically beneficial way, although a change nonetheless), and the toxic reactions and adverse side effects accompanying most of the drugs also frequently have a debilitating effect on mental processes. Because the differing classes of drugs present somewhat different effects, they are analyzed separately.

(a) Antipsychotic Drugs

Antipsychotic drugs have a dramatic effect on mental processes, often in a beneficial direction, by promoting thought coherence and reducing thought disorder in those suffering from schizophrenia. Schizophrenia is typically marked by disturbances in content of thought, such as bizarre delusions; form of thought, such as loosening of associations, in which ideas shift from one subject to an unrelated one; perception, such as auditory or visual hallucinations; and affect, such as blunting, flattening, or inappropriateness of emotional response.[367] Antipsychotic drugs reduce these and other symptoms of schizophrenia,[368] altering mental functioning in the direction of normality,[369] but altering it nonetheless.

---

[360]*Id.*

[361]*Id.*

[362]*Id.*

[363]706 F.2d 1456 (7th Cir. 1983); *see supra* notes 338–39 and accompanying text.

[364]*Lojuk,* 706 F.2d at 1465.

[365]V. LONGO, NEUROPHARMACOLOGY AND BEHAVIOR 182 (1972); Klerman, *Psychotropic Drugs as Therapeutic Agents,* 2 HASTINGS CTR. REP., Jan. 1974, at 82 n.1; *see* Winick, *Psychotropic Medication and Competence to Stand Trial,* 1977 AM. B. FOUND. RES. J. 769.

[366]457 U.S. 291, 293 n.1 (1982); *accord* Riggins v. Nevada, 504 U.S. 127, 137 (1992) (''sedation-like effect [of antipsychotic medication] may be severe enough (akinesia) to affect thought processes''); *id.* at 1819 (''The side effects of antipsychotic drugs may alter demeanor in a way that will prejudice all facets of the defense.'') (Kennedy, J., concurring); Washington v. Harper, 494 U.S. 210, 230 (1989) (''Other side effects of [antipsychotics] include akathesia (motor restlessness, often characterized by an inability to sit still); neuroleptic malignant syndrome (a relatively rare condition that can lead to death from cardiac dysfunction); and tardive dyskinesia, perhaps the most discussed side effect of antipsychotic drugs.'').

[367]*DSM–IV, supra* note 222, at 273, 285.

[368]Gutheil & Appelbaum, *supra* note 303, at 100–01 (*citing* studies).

[369]*Id.* at 118.

In a 1983 article Gutheil and Appelbaum conducted a review of the literature concerning the effects of antipsychotic medication on mentation[370] in order to challenge the conclusion reached in several right-to-refuse-medication cases that these drugs affect thought processes in ways that can be described as "mind control."[371] Three of four studies testing the effects of the drugs on memory concluded that there was no effect, although one study showed a significant decrease in the ability of patients to recall digits.[372] Most experimental studies of the effects of the drugs on psychomotor functioning showed no effect, although earlier studies found some impairment. Furthermore, considerable clinical experience documented in the literature revealed that impaired motor function was often one of the side effects of the drugs.[373] Studies of the effects of the drugs on attention and perception showed mixed results, with roughly equal numbers of studies showing impairment in function, improvement in function, or no change.[374] Most studies of the effects on complex cognitive functions indicated that the drugs improve functioning, although a few studies demonstrated negative effects.[375] Gutheil and Appelbaum concluded that the available evidence suggests "that antipsychotic medications lack the subtle, deleterious effects on mental functioning" attributed to them in judicial opinions.[376] In their view, the evidence was inconsistent with a conception of the drugs as "mind-altering, thought inhibiting, or destructive of personality in a negative sense."[377] Although the specter of "mind control" brought about by these drugs may thus be misleading, the studies examined by Gutheil and Appelbaum demonstrate that the drugs do affect mental processes. The effect on mental functioning is usually positive, but some studies did show impairment in functioning. Moreover, Gutheil and Appelbaum conceded that some of the side effects of the drugs, particularly akinesia and akathisia, often affect mentation adversely.[378]

The side effects of antipsychotic drugs[379] cannot be ignored in analyzing the First Amendment question. Indeed, it seems misleading to call them *side effects,* a label that denigrates their impact on patients. Although these side effects are unintended, they are intrinsic to the drugs' benevolent properties and should not be trivialized, particularly because patients frequently experience them to be distressing enough to outweigh the drugs' positive clinical effects. All of the antipsychotic drugs are sedating, particularly the low-potency phenothiazines.[380] In early periods of drug administration, the patient often

---

[370]*Id.* at 101–17.

[371]*See, e.g.,* Davis v. Hubbard, 506 F. Supp. 915, 933 (N.D. Ohio 1980) ("controlling thought"); Rogers v. Okin, 478 F. Supp. 1342, 1367 (D. Mass. 1979) ("involuntary mind control"), *aff'd in part and rev'd in part on other grounds,* 634 F.2d 650 (1st Cir. 1980), *vacated and remanded sub nom.* Mills v. Rogers, 457 U.S. 291 (1982), *on remand,* 738 F.2d 1 (1st Cir. 1984).

[372]Gutheil & Appelbaum, *supra* note 303, at 104–05.

[373]*Id.* at 104–09.

[374]*Id.* at 110–13.

[375]*Id.* at 113–17.

[376]*Id.* at 119.

[377]*Id.*

[378]*Id.* at 106–09, 119.

[379]For a summary of these side effects, see Winick, *The Right to Refuse Psychotropic Medication, in* THE RIGHT TO REFUSE ANTIPSYCHOTIC MEDICATION 7 (D. Rapaport & J. Parry eds., 1986), Winick, *supra* note 365, at 782–83 (citing authorities).

[380]AMERICAN MEDICAL ASSOCIATION, DRUG EVALUATIONS 111–50 (6th ed. 1986), *reprinted in* R. SPRING ET AL., PATIENTS, PSYCHIATRISTS AND LAWYERS, *supra* note 357, at 104, 109–10.

experiences heavy sedation, clouded consciousness, and impaired judgment.[381] The sedation itself has a dramatic effect on mental processes, frequently interfering with the ability to think and almost always curtailing concentration.[382] Although many patients become habituated to the drugs over time, with the result that after several days or weeks cognitive functions are little affected and sedation is minimal, some patients never get used to the effects of the drugs.[383]

Many of the physical side effects accompanying these drugs, although not directly affecting mental processes, are so distressing that they frequently interfere with a patient's power of concentration and ability to think clearly. Autonomic side effects of these drugs such as dizziness, faintness, drowsiness, and fatigue all interfere with concentration. Hypotension, resulting in decreased blood flow to the brain, leaves patients feeling light-headed and interferes with concentration. The extrapyramidal reactions to these drugs, although again primarily physical in effect, also often are so distressing that concentration is affected. Akathisia, in particular, presents this problem. The patient experiences a constant motor restlessness and fidgeting and is driven to pace about impatiently and tap his foot incessantly. Dystonia, which involves bizarre muscular spasms accompanied by facial grimacing and involuntary spasms of the tongue, can interfere with communicative ability. Similarly, the dyskinesias produce a broad range of bizarre tongue, face, and neck movements, which substantially limit both verbal and nonverbal communication and often impair concentration. Tardive dyskinesia, a persistent neurological syndrome affecting a substantial percentage of patients subjected to long-term antipsychotic drug treatment,[384] is often experienced as extremely distressing, to the extent that concentration is impaired. No effective treatment for the condition is available, and it is thought to cause permanent structural changes in the brain.[385] Another serious side effect is neuroleptic malignant syndrome, a rare but underdiagnosed condition that is fatal in 25% percent of cases.[386] This

---

[381] See Jarvik, *Drugs Used in the Treatment of Psychiatric Disorders, in* THE PHARMACOLOGICAL BASIS OF THERAPEUTICS 151, 167 (L. Goodman & A. Gilman eds., 1970); Winick, *Psychotropic Medication in the Criminal Trial Process: The Constitutional and Therapeutic Implications of* Riggins v. Nevada, 10 N.Y.L. SCH. J. HUM. RTS. 637, 665–66 (1993); Winick, *supra* note 365, at 778, 789 (describing the history, functioning, and side effects of antipsychotic drugs and other types of medication used to treat defendants found incompetent to stand trial).

[382] Appelbaum, *Can Mental Patients Say No to Drugs?*, N.Y. TIMES, March 21, 1982, § 6 (Magazine), at 46, 51 ("The drugs' sedative effects may lead to drowsiness or, in the extreme, a spaced-out state in which thinking itself becomes difficult."); Winick, *supra* note 365, at 665, 781–84.

[383] See Solow, *Drug Therapy of Mental Illness: Tranquilizers and Other Depressant Drugs, in* AN INTRODUCTION TO PSYCHOPHARMACOLOGY 289, 307 (R. Rech & K. Moore eds., 1971).

[384] An American Psychiatric Association Task Force reported that 10% to 20% of patients given antipsychotic drugs for one year or more develop the condition. AMERICAN PSYCHIATRIC ASSOCIATION TASK FORCE ON LATE NEUROLOGICAL EFFECTS OF ANTIPSYCHOTIC DRUGS, TARDIVE DYSKINESIA 43–44 (1979) [hereinafter TARDIVE DYSKINESIA]. More recent estimates are much higher. *See* A. SCHATZBERG & J. COLE, MANUAL OF CLINICAL PSYCHOPHARMACOLOGY 122 (1991) (50% to 60%); Hollister, *Antipsychotic and Antimanic Drugs* (Lithium), *in* REVIEW OF GENERAL PSYCHIATRY 507 (H. Goldman ed., 1984) (20% to 40%); Jeste & Wyatt, *Changing Epidemiology of Tardive Dyskinesia: An Overview*, 138 AM. J. PSYCHIATRY 297 (1981) (25%, with prevalence progressively rising). Moreover, the condition is "underdiagnosed at an alarming rate." Weiden et al., *Clinical Nonrecognition of Neuroleptic-Induced Movement Disorders: A Cautionary Study*, 144 AM. J. PSYCHIATRY 1148, 1151 (1987).

[385] TARDIVE DYSKINESIA, *supra* note 384, at 57; SCHATZBERG & COLE, *supra* note 384, at 100; Christensen, Moller & Faurbye, *Neuropathological Investigation of 28 Brains from Patients with Dyskinesia*, 46 ACTA PSYCHIATRY SCAND. 14 (1970).

[386] See Addonizio et al., *Symptoms of Neuroleptic Malignant Syndrome in 82 Consecutive Inpatients*, 143 AM. J. PSYCHIATRY 1587 (1986); Pope et al., *Frequency of Presentation of Neuroleptic Malignant Syndrome in a Large Psychiatric Hospital*, 143 AM. J. PSYCHIATRY 1227 (1986).

condition is characterized by muscular rigidity, rhythmic movements, and alterations in consciousness.

Brooks has summarized the "cognitive side effects" of the antipsychotic drugs as follows: "Some patients cannot concentrate or think straight because of their medications. Reading or talking becomes impossible, and the patient retreats into an intellectual vacuum. For a patient who has even modest intellectual interests, cognitive side effects can be extremely distressing."[387] Moreover, the antipsychotic drugs have similarly dramatic emotional side effects. All of them produce a depression of mood.[388] Patients experience the typical "flattening" of emotional affect as boredom, lethargy, docility, listlessness, apathy, and purposelessness.[389] Patients frequently complain of this effect when they describe the drugs as placing them in a "chemical straight-jacket" or inducing "zombiism."[390]

Although tardive dyskinesia may be irreversible, other side effects of the drugs are short-acting and disappear within hours or days of drug discontinuation. Similarly, the primary therapeutic effects of the drugs are only short-acting. With the exception of Prolixin and other long-acting phenothiazines, the effects of which last for several weeks, the primary effects of the drugs may last only several hours or days. Nevertheless, many patients are continued on the drugs for lengthy periods and thus experience the effects on a continued basis. Long-term drug treatment may impair memory, reasoning ability, mental speed, learning capacity, and efficiency of mental functioning in general.[391] These results directly implicate basic First Amendment values.

It must be acknowledged that the primary effects of antipsychotic drugs are normalizing or restorative; they reduce the level of grossly distorted thinking characteristic of schizophrenia.[392] The drugs "are generally incapable of creating thoughts, views, ideas, or opinions de novo or of permanently inhibiting the process of thought generation."[393] In view of the beneficial effects of the drugs on mental processes, it may seem paradoxical to regard them as intrusions on mental processes that trigger First Amendment scrutiny. Nonetheless, they are undeniably "mind-altering,"[394] even if not "mind-controlling." Moreover, the drugs do restore most patients' ability to concentrate that had been so impaired by the psychosis, but some patients experience the drugs themselves as interfering with concentration, particularly in view of their serious side effects.

Antipsychotic drugs thus have both positive and negative effects on mental processes. These effects have led virtually all courts that have considered the question to conclude that

---

[387]Brooks, *The Constitutional Right to Refuse Antipsychotic Medication,* 8 BULL. AM. ACAD. PSYCHIATRY & L. 179, 184 (1980). A prisoner who was given the drugs described the mental effects as follows: "Your thoughts are broken, incoherent; you can't hold a train of thought for even a minute. Your mind is like a slot machine, every wheel spinning a different thought. . . ." Opton, *Psychiatric Violence Against Prisoners: When Therapy is Punishment,* 45 MISS. L.J. 605, 641 (1974).

[388]PATIENTS, PSYCHIATRISTS AND LAWYERS, *supra* note 357, at 109.

[389]Van Putten & May, *Subjective Response as a Predictor of Outcome of Pharmacotherapy,* 35 ARCHIVES GEN. PSYCHIATRY 477, 479 (1978).

[390]*See* Brooks, *supra* note 387, at 184.

[391]*See* DiMascio et al., *Behavioral Toxicity Part III: Perceptual–Cognitive Functions and Part IV: Emotional (Mood) States, in* PSYCHOTROPIC DRUGS SIDE EFFECTS 132, 133 (R. Shader & A. DiMascio eds., 1977).

[392]Davis et al., *Antipsychotic Drugs, in* 2 COMPREHENSIVE TEXTBOOK OF PSYCHIATRY, *supra* note 271, at 1595, 1597.

[393]Appelbaum & Gutheil, *supra* note 216, at 308.

[394]Mills v. Rogers, 457 U.S. 291, 293 n.1 (1982); Rogers v. Okin, 478 F. Supp. 1342, 1360 (D. Mass. 1979), *aff'd in part and rev'd in part on other grounds,* 634 F.2d 650 (1st Cir. 1980), *vacated and remanded sub nom.* Mills v. Rogers, 457 U.S. 291 (1982), *on remand,* 738 F.2d 1 (1st Cir. 1984).

the First Amendment provides a basis for a right to refuse antipsychotic drug treatment.[395] One court, however, has expressly rejected a First Amendment theory, finding instead a right to refuse treatment grounded in constitutional privacy.[396] Although accepting the premise that the First Amendment protects against certain kinds of interferences with mental processes, the district court in *Rennie v. Klein* declined to apply the First Amendment to the facts before it.[397] Because the plaintiff, a mental patient, had asserted a desire to be cured (and indeed had claimed a right to treatment), the *Rennie* court in effect found that he had waived any First Amendment right he might have raised in objection to the hospital's efforts to treat his thought disorder with medication. Moreover, the court based its decision on the evidence that the patient's ability to perform on intelligence tests was not impaired and that the drugs' side effects were "temporary and expected to last only a few days or a couple of weeks."[398] In the court's view, these effects on "mentation" differed sharply from the effects involved in the *Kaimowitz* psychosurgery case.[399] The court concluded that "if forced medication is otherwise proper"—a conclusion that it thereafter questioned on privacy grounds—"the temporary dulling of the senses accompanying it does not rise to the level of the First Amendment violations found in *Kaimowitz*."[400]

Every other court to have considered a First Amendment contention in the context of antipsychotic drugs has found a First Amendment basis for drug refusal, and in light of the *Rennie* court's acceptance of a constitutional privacy basis for such a right, its rejection of the contention must be considered dicta. In *Bee v. Greaves,*[401] the U.S. Court of Appeals for the Tenth Circuit found that the First Amendment implicitly protects "the capacity to produce ideas."[402] Finding that "[a]ntipsychotic drugs have the capacity to severely and even permanently affect an individual's ability to think and communicate,"[403] the court recognized a First Amendment right of pretrial detainees to resist the drugs.[404] The district court in *Rogers v. Okin* found a First Amendment violation on the basis of evidence showing that "psychotropic medication has the potential to affect and change a patient's mood, attitude and capacity to think."[405] Although conceding that such effects may be considered "positive steps on the road to recovery,"[406] the court noted that "the validity of psychotropic drugs as a reasonable course of medical treatment is not the core issue

---

[395]*See supra* note 43 (cases); *supra* notes 325–36 and accompanying text. The First Amendment issue was not presented in Washington v. Harper, 494 U.S. at 258 n.32.

[396]Rennie v. Klein, 462 F. Supp. 1131 (D.N.J. 1978), *aff'd in part, modified in part, and remanded,* 653 F.2d 836 (3d Cir. 1981) (en banc), *vacated and remanded,* 458 U.S. 1119 (1982), *on remand,* 720 F.2d 266 (3d Cir. 1983) (en banc).

[397]*Id.,* 458 U.S. at 1144.

[398]*Id.*

[399]*Id.*

[400]*Id.*

[401]744 F.2d 1387 (10th Cir. 1984), *cert. denied,* 469 U.S. 1214 (1985).

[402]*Id.* at 1394.

[403]*Id.*

[404]*Id.*

[405]478 F. Supp. 1342, 1366 (D. Mass. 1979), *aff'd in part and rev'd in part on other grounds,* 634 F.2d 650 (1st Cir. 1980), *vacated and remanded sub nom.* Mills v. Rogers, 457 U.S. 291 (1982), *on remand,* 738 F.2d 1 (1st Cir. 1984).

[406]*Id.,* 478 F. Supp. at 1366–67.

here."[407] Rather, the court found the fundamental question to be whether the state may impose on the patient "by forcibly injecting mind-altering drugs into his system in a non-emergency situation."[408]

The courts in *Bee* and *Rogers* both correctly concluded that antipsychotic drugs can affect the patient's ability to think and communicate. Administered in sufficiently high dosages and for long periods, these drugs undeniably have serious effects on mentation and communication and should accordingly receive First Amendment scrutiny. However, the *Rennie* dicta suggests that future application of the First Amendment to psychotropic medication may turn on the evidentiary showing concerning the effects of the drug in question on the particular patient involved. Some of the antipsychotic drugs intrude more on mental processes than others, and the length of drug administration and perhaps even the dosage used is also relevant to the First Amendment question. Thus, brief administration of one of the milder drugs or administration in a moderate dosage that is not heavily sedating may be thought of as not intruding sufficiently on First Amendment values. The courts may also draw a distinction between a brief course of emergency treatment to stabilize an acute patient and long-term drug administration for a chronic patient where the risk of serious and lingering side effects is greater.[409]

On the other hand, all of these drugs affect mental processes even when administered briefly. When the side effects interfere with concentration and the ability to think and to communicate, First Amendment values are plainly implicated. Although there may well be a de minimis level of intrusion below which the courts will not apply First Amendment scrutiny,[410] a typical course of treatment with medication for hospitalized patients passes any such threshold. The conclusion that involuntary treatment with these drugs generally requires scrutiny under the First Amendment thus seems correct.

(b) Antidepressant Drugs

Antidepressant drugs act largely on mood or emotion, rather than on thoughts, but, of course, emotions and thoughts are closely interrelated. Indeed, emotion and emotional expression are essential elements of any definition of personality. People's emotions and how they express them vitally affect both the content and the form and style of communication.

Moreover, the physical side effects accompanying the use of most of the antidepressant drugs, albeit not usually as serious as those related to the antipsychotic drugs, are essentially similar for all but some of the lower classes of antidepressants.[411] Like the antipsychotic drugs, the antidepressants are often highly sedating and therefore interfere with concentration. Antidepressants occasionally result in confusion, memory impairment, disorientation, and episodes of schizophrenic excitement or mania, although these symptoms usually

---

[407]*Id.* at 1367.

[408]*Id.*

[409]*See infra* notes 410–33 and accompanying text.

[410]*See* City of Dallas v. Stanglin, 490 U.S. 19, 26 (1989) ("It is possible to find some kernel of expression in almost every activity a person undertakes—for example, walking down the street, or meeting one's friends at a shopping mall—but such a kernel is not sufficient to bring the activity within the protection of the First Amendment.") (rejecting First Amendment freedom of association claim against licensing of dance halls in which admission was restricted to persons between the ages of 14 and 18 on the ground that coming together to engage in recreational dancing is not protected by the First Amendment).

[411]*See supra* chapter 5; Winick, *supra* note 379, at 786–89.

subside within 1 to 2 days after withdrawal of the drug.[412] In general, the antidepressant drugs restore the ability to concentrate, but some patients report the opposite effect. Although considerably less serious than the effects of the antipsychotic drugs, the effects of the antidepressants on mental processes also appear to be sufficiently intrusive to trigger First Amendment scrutiny.

(c) Antianxiety Drugs

Although the antianxiety drugs are rarely administered on an involuntary basis, their occasional coercive use merits constitutional consideration. The side effects of these drugs are relatively minor compared to those of the antipsychotics and antidepressants. The drugs do not cause extrapyramidal or autonomic effects. They do, however, depress the central nervous system, which causes their most common side effects, sedation and drowsiness.[413] In some patients, particularly the elderly, visual–motor performance and judgment may be impaired.[414] Because these effects are short-acting, the antianxiety drugs, particularly at low dosages, may not be sufficient to trigger First Amendment scrutiny. On the other hand, at dosages that produce sedation and concentration impairment, the effects on mental processes are arguably sufficient to implicate the First Amendment.

(d) Antimanic Drugs

Lithium and other antimanic drugs function as mood normalizers, preventing the severe mood swings that characterize bipolar (formerly known as manic–depressive) illness, a major affective disorder in which recurring periods of mania alternate with periods of depression. Lithium, the most widely used of these drugs, stabilizes the patient's mood within a more clinically acceptable range. At proper therapeutic levels, lithium rarely causes adverse reactions;[415] however, excessive amounts of lithium or failure of renal mechanisms properly to eliminate the drug may result in lithium toxicity, a serious condition involving the central nervous system that may cause confusion, impairment of consciousness, and even coma.[416] Because therapeutic and toxic levels of the drug are so close, toxicity is a constant risk and must be closely monitored.[417] At therapeutic levels, none of the relatively mild side effects of the drug interfere with mental processes. Unlike the other psychotropic drugs, lithium has no general sedating properties.[418]

The most troubling First Amendment issue concerning the use of lithium relates to its effect on creativity. Mood swings and creativity are definitely associated. In fact, many of the world's great artists—the composers Handel, Rossini, and Schumann, the novelists Balzac, Hemingway, Melville, and Virginia Woolf, the poets Byron, Coleridge, and Tennyson, the artists Van Gogh and Jackson Pollock, and theatrical director Joshua Logan,

---

[412]Davis, *Antidepressant Drugs, in* 2 COMPREHENSIVE TEXTBOOK OF PSYCHIATRY, *supra* note 271, at 2290, 2299.

[413]Gorman & Davis, *Antianxiety Drugs, in* 2 COMPREHENSIVE TEXTBOOK OF PSYCHIATRY, *supra* note 271, at 1581, 1583; DETRE & JARECKI, *supra* note 354, at 599; Jarvik, *supra* note 381, at 176; Meyers & Solomon, *Psychopharmacology, in* HANDBOOK OF PSYCHIATRY 427, 436–37 (P. Solomon & V. Patch eds., 2d ed. 1974).

[414]Meyers & Solomon, *supra* note 413, at 436–37.

[415]Brown, *Side Effects of Lithium Therapy and Their Treatment*, 21 CAN. PSYCHIATRY ASS'N J. 13 (1976).

[416]Brown, *supra* note 415, at 18–19; Fieve, *Lithium Therapy, in* 2 COMPREHENSIVE TEXTBOOK OF PSYCHIATRY, *supra* note 271, at 2350.

[417]Fieve, *supra* note 416, at 2351.

[418]Jarvik, *supra* note 381, at 193; Meyers & Solomon, *supra* note 413, at 448.

to name a few—have had either mania or bipolar disorder.[419] Periods of great creativity frequently coincide with the manic phase of the condition.[420] "There is a fine and at times invisible line between mania and creativity."[421] Fieve, one of the pioneers in the use of lithium, concedes that treatment with lithium may interfere with creativity. Because many artists fear that such treatment will deprive them of their talent, the drug's effects on creativity present difficult questions for psychiatrists.[422] In a study of 24 artists treated with lithium, 6 thought that the treatment lowered their creativity, and 4 stopped treatment for this reason.[423] Six artists reported no change in creativity, and 12 reported positive effects— greater quantity and quality and more artistic discipline. Plainly, at least for some artists, their mood inspires and enhances their creativity. The mood and emotion expressed in the work of certain artists, composers, and writers are what an audience responds to so strongly. Indeed, that expression is precisely what has led to the classification of the work of some such artists—Van Gogh and Jackson Pollock, for example—as expressionists.

Fieve concludes that moods, energy states, and creativity are inextricably linked but that when creative artists experience abnormally low or high moods, their creative work suffers.[424] Lithium may therefore assist many creative patients. Although Fieve concludes that overall creative output becomes more consistent with lithium and that the drug does not interfere with the quality of the work, he concedes that the potential effect on creativity may make lithium treatment inadvisable when symptoms of mood swing are not debilitating or destructive.[425] In Fieve's view, each patient should be considered on an individual basis. "Some artists become so accommodated to their mild highs and lows that they consider these episodes as basic facets of their personalities and really want no change in their way of life. These patients should be left alone."[426]

---

[419]R. FIEVE, MOODSWING: THE THIRD REVOLUTION IN PSYCHIATRY 55–59 (Morrow Book ed., 1975); K. JAMISON, TOUCHED WITH FIRE: MANIC–DEPRESSIVE ILLNESS AND THE ARTISTIC TEMPERAMENT 5 (1993) ("Recent research strongly suggests that, compared with the general population, writers, and artists show a vastly disproportionate rate of manic–depressive or depressive illness."); id. at 88 ("Many lines of evidence point to a strong relationship between mood disorders and achievement, especially artistic achievement."); id. at 89 (discussing findings from other studies pointing to "a strong association between mood disorders and creativity"); id. at 240 (discussing "strong scientific and biographical evidence linking manic-depressive illness and its related temperaments to artistic imagination and expression"); E. KRAEPELIN, MANIC-DEPRESSIVE INSANITY & PARANOIA 17 (1976) (linking increased artistic productively to manic–depressive illness); Ludwig, Creative Achievement and Psychopathology: Comparisons Among Professions, 46 AM. J. PSYCHOTHERAPY 330 (1992) (study of individuals whose biographies had been reviewed in the New York Times Book Review section from 1960 to 1990 showing highest rate of mania, psychosis, and psychiatric hospitalizations among poets and other creative artists); see JAMISON, supra at 149–237 (discussing various artists, writers, poets, and composers); DeLong & Aldershof, Association of Special Abilities With Juvenile Manic-Depressive Illness, 14 ANN. NEUROLOGY 362 (1983) (documenting an unusually high incidence of special abilities, including artistic, language, and mathematical abilities, in a sample of children with manic-depressive illness). Although some have suggested that Jackson Pollock suffered from schizophrenia, this diagnosis is in dispute, and his symptoms strongly suggest the possibility of bipolar disorder. See B. FRIEDMAN, JACKSON POLLOCK: ENERGY MADE VISIBLE 42, 47 (1972) ("depressive mania," "overintensity").

[420]FIEVE, supra note 419, at 55; JAMISON, supra note 419, at 105–06.

[421]FIEVE, supra note 419, at 60.

[422]Id.

[423]Shou, Artistic Productivity and Lithium Prophylaxis in Manic Depressive Illness, 135 BRIT. J. PSYCHIATRY 97 (1979).

[424]FIEVE, supra note 419, at 69. See also JAMISON, supra note 419, at 7–8 (Some writers and artists discontinue lithium "because they feel that drug side effects interfere with the clarity and rapidity of their thought or diminish their levels of enthusiasm, emotion, and energy.").

[425]Id.

[426]Id. at 69–70.

Although lithium is undeniably helpful in the treatment of bipolar or manic–depressive illness, some patients complain that it "controls" them (by controlling their mood).[427] Clearly the possibility that lithium may blunt creative processes or capacity raises grave First Amendment concerns for patients who wish to resist this treatment. Lithium treatment to control a patient's emotional tone or mood by keeping it within some government official's notion of acceptable levels may be compared to and distinguished from governmental regulation of sound levels at concerts in the park, upheld by the Supreme Court against a First Amendment challenge. In *Ward v. Rock Against Racism*,[428] the Court considered city guidelines for concerts held at the park. In order to control excessive volume at such concerts in the interests of other users of the park and residents of nearby areas, the guidelines required use of sound equipment furnished by the city and administered by an independent professional sound technician. During musical performances, the city's sound technicians controlled the sound and volume, but they gave sponsors of the events autonomy with respect to sound mix and balance.[429] Conceding that "[m]usic, as a form of expression and communication, is protected under the First Amendment,"[430] the Court found the regulations at issue to be content neutral—justified without regard to the artistic content of the performance.[431] The Court conceded, however, that any attempt by government to interfere with sound mix for aesthetic purposes "would raise serious First Amendment concerns."[432]

Regulating a patient's mood within governmentally approved levels would seem more like government interference in artistic judgment, such as by controlling the sound mix or balance at a concert, than the reasonable restrictions on time, place, and manner that the Court found the volume regulations in *Ward* to be. Mood is an inherent and significant component of personality itself. The content and expression of ideas are heavily influenced by mood. In this sense, regulation of mood inevitably regulates the content of expression. In addition, apart from its impact on mood, lithium also has cognitive side effects producing mental slowing, impaired concentration, and detrimental effects on associational processing.[433] For these reasons, involuntary imposition of lithium should trigger First Amendment scrutiny.

Psychotropic drugs in general thus present primary and side effects that are mentally intrusive, occur rapidly, and cannot be resisted by unwilling patients. Although the primary effects of the drugs may last only several hours, the side effects of many may be long-lasting or even irreversible. Not surprisingly, patients frequently consider the side effects of some of these drugs to be highly unpleasant, painful, and debilitating. Frequently, the effects are so distressing that they interfere with the ability to concentrate and to communicate. Because of their direct effect on mental processes and intellectual functioning, involuntary use of

---

[427]JAMISON, *supra* note 419 at 241–42; *see* Fieve, *Patient Rejection of Lithium,* 218 JAMA 864 (1971) (anecdotal report of patients on lithium describing patient complaints that lithium acted as a "brake" on creativity and diminished expression, drive, and incentive).

[428]491 U.S. 781 (1989).

[429]*Id.* at 788.

[430]*Id.* at 790.

[431]*Id.* at 792.

[432]*Id.* at 793.

[433]JAMISON, *supra* note 419, at 243, 246; SHAW, EFFECTS OF LITHIUM ON ASSOCIATIVE PRODUCTIVITY (1986); Christodoulou et al., *Side Effects of Lithium,* 77 ACTA PSYCHIATRICA BELG. 260–66 (1977).

psychotropic medication, as several lower courts have concluded, should raise First Amendment questions.

5. Behavior Therapy

Behavior therapy focuses not on mental processes but on behavior.[434] Unlike even the verbal techniques, which focus on changing thought processes and perceptions as a means to change behavior, the behavioral techniques ignore mental processes[435] and focus exclusively on changing the external environment. Both in theory and usually in practice, therefore, the behavioral techniques are the least intrusive on mental processes.[436] These techniques may well raise constitutional privacy concerns. Some aversive conditioning techniques—using drugs, electric shocks, and other physically intrusive stimuli—may infringe on a liberty interest in personal security and bodily integrity. With extremely few exceptions, however, these techniques do not appear to present sufficiently serious effects on mental processes to trigger First Amendment scrutiny.

Not only do these techniques not change mental processes, but evidence suggests that they bring about behavioral changes only in cooperative patients. For treatment to be successful, it cannot be forced on patients against their will.[437] Reinforcers do not work in a mechanical fashion to induce behavior changes automatically without the cooperation of individuals; rather, they function as "motivators," depending for their success on the "incentive preferences of those undergoing change."[438]

(a) Positive Reinforcement Techniques

The positive reinforcement techniques seem to raise few First Amendment concerns. Surely the use of certain reinforcers may prove too tantalizing for at least some patients and offenders to resist—cable TV, air conditioning, better physical conditions, more appetizing food, monetary rewards, or the approval of the parole board or hospital release committee, for example. However, even these strong inducements to change do not seem to alter mental processes in any way sufficient to trigger constitutional scrutiny. Indeed, society outside of prisons and hospitals is pervaded by governmental incentives designed to induce a variety of behaviors and attitudes. Businesses are offered various tax credits. Students are given "A's" if they perform well in school. Army recruits are given bonuses and other incentives to enlist. Moreover, variable reinforcers, such as the chance to hit the financial jackpot in the lottery, are powerful inducers of gambling behavior. Even within the prison, inmates are granted "good time" credit toward parole eligibility for good conduct and participation in rehabilitative programs as "a tangible reward for positive efforts made during incarceration."[439] In each case the government provides rewards for the explicit purpose of inducing

---

[434]*See supra* chapter 4.

[435]*Id.*

[436]*Id.*

[437]*See* ERWIN, BEHAVIOR THERAPY: SCIENTIFIC, PHILOSOPHICAL AND MORAL FOUNDATIONS 180–81 (1978) (citing Marks, *The Current Status of Behavioral Psychotherapy: Theory and Practice,* 133 AM. J. PSYCHIATRY 253, 255 (1976)); Winick, *supra* note 341, at 360.

[438]Bandura, *Behavior Therapy and the Models of Man,* 29 AM. PSYCHOLOGIST 859, 862 (1974); Winick, *Harnessing the Power of the Bet: Wagering with the Government as a Mechanism for Social and Individual Change,* 45 U. MIAMI L. REV. 737, 740–72 (1991); Winick, note 341, at 360–61.

[439]N.Y. COMP. CODES R. & REGS. tit. 7, § 260.1(a) (1983).

or reinforcing certain behavior. However, few would contend that these positive reinforcements implicate First Amendment freedom of thought.[440]

Although the use of reinforcers in a structured behavior modification program in a hospital or prison may induce behavior change more effectively than outside such an environment, it is difficult to see how patients or offenders who decide to alter their behavior in order to obtain cable TV or some other reward could argue that First Amendment rights have thereby been violated.[441] Whatever effects positive reinforcement may have, considerable evidence suggests that these effects are short-lived and perhaps restricted to the controlled clinical setting in which conditioning occurs.[442] Moreover, these techniques do not appear to work in such a direct and intrusive fashion that they deprive individuals of effective control over their own behavior, as do the organic therapies. In view of the temporary nature of the effects of positive reinforcement and individuals' ability to resist behavioral changes facilitated by this technique, it seems unlikely that application of these techniques without consent will be found to violate the First Amendment.

(b) Aversive Therapy

The aversive techniques could present differing problems, depending on the aversive stimulus that is used. For example, the court in *Mackey v. Procunier* found that the use of the drug succinylcholine in a prison mental hospital aversive conditioning program raised serious First Amendment concerns.[443] So distressing were the effects of this drug, which paralyzed the diaphragm, producing sensations of suffocation and drowning, that the court concluded that the prisoner's allegations of mental intrusion and effect were sufficient to raise constitutional questions of "impermissible tinkering with the mental processes."[444] Aside from the use of negative stimuli that either directly or indirectly affect mental processes, however, the aversive techniques do not seem to raise First Amendment concerns. Like other behavioral approaches, they are ineffective with uncooperative individuals.[445] Any behavioral changes accomplished against the individual's will are impermanent and reversible. In this respect, even the aversive approaches are substantially distinct from the more direct, mentally intrusive organic techniques, which do not depend for their effects on the individual's cooperation.

(c) Other Behavioral Treatment Techniques

Other behavioral techniques, such as systematic desensitization, shaping, contingency contracting, and cognitive behavior therapy, are also purely dependent on the individual's

---

[440]*See* Maher v. Roe, 432 U.S. 464, 475–76 (1977):

> There is a basic difference between direct state interference with a protected activity and state encouragement of an alternative activity consonant with legislative policy . . . [w]hen the State attempts to impose its will by force of law; the State's power to encourage actions deemed to be in the public interest is necessarily far broader. [footnote omitted]

Accord Webster v. Reproductive Health Servs., 492 U.S. 490, 506 (1989).

[441]Winick, *supra* note 341, at 361–62.

[442]*See* B. BROWN ET AL., BEHAVIOR MODIFICATION: PERSPECTIVES ON A CURRENT ISSUE 14 (1975); Gruber, *Behavior Therapy: Problems in Generalization,* 2 BEHAV. THERAPY 361, 361–68 (1971).

[443]477 F.2d 877 (9th Cir. 1973); *see supra* notes 323–25 and accompanying text.

[444]*Mackey,* 477 F.2d at 878.

[445]*See* Bandura, *The Ethical and Social Purposes of Behavior Modification, in* ANNUAL REVIEW OF BEHAVIOR THERAPY: THEORY AND PRACTICE 16 (C. Franks & G. Wilson eds. 1975); Note, *Aversion Therapy: Its Limited Potential for Use in a Correctional Setting,* 26 STAN. L. REV. 1327 (1974).

willing cooperation and do not seem to involve any mental intrusions. Modeling presents the fewest difficulties of any technique considered and would certainly raise no First Amendment concerns. In general, although some of the behavioral techniques may raise other constitutional problems, the First Amendment does not seem implicated by these approaches.

6. Psychotherapy and Other Verbal Techniques

At the lower end of the intrusiveness continuum are the verbal techniques—psychoanalysis, psychotherapy, counseling, group therapy, and educational programs.[446] Unlike the behavioral therapies, these verbal techniques usually focus on changing thought processes, emotions, and perceptions. Moreover, when successful, they can have a massive effect on attitudes, beliefs, and personality. Nevertheless, the verbal techniques work in essentially a nonintrusive fashion. Those compelled to participate in a verbal therapy program who seek to resist attitudinal or personality change are readily able to frustrate these approaches and avoid their effects simply by withholding cooperation.

(a) Psychotherapy

Psychotherapy works slowly, affording the patients time to contemplate the meaning of behavior change and to accept or resist such change.[447] Unlike with the organic therapies, which cannot be resisted, the patient retains a veto over the ability of the verbal techniques to effect changes in attitudes and behavior. "[W]e imagine ourselves as patients to be free agents throughout the process, free to reject it and free to leave with no more scar than in any other human transaction."[448] A patient who seeks to resist the effects of psychotherapy can thus totally frustrate treatment by withholding cooperation. The "fundamental rule" of psychotherapy requires the patient to communicate openly and candidly with the therapist.[449] If the patient is unwilling to play this role, the therapeutic process cannot even begin. Trust is an indispensable condition for successful therapy. Moreover, even if patients cooperate in at least the surface rituals of the therapeutic process, they can effectively avoid the gradual and nonintrusive effects of psychotherapy with a minimal degree of mental resistance. Patients may undergo psychotherapy "as a form of game playing, such as showing up for appointments and even making verbal utterances, in the absence of the type

---

[446]See supra chapter 3.

[447]See Halleck, Legal and Ethical Aspects of Behavior Control, 131 AM. J. PSYCHIATRY 381, 381 (1974); Katz, The Rights to Treatment—An Enchanting Legal Fiction?, 36 U. CHI. L. REV. 755, 777 (1969). In this sense psychotherapy should be distinguished from the more concentrated application of techniques that have come to be known as "brainwashing" or "coercive persuasion." See generally Peterson v. Sorlien, 299 N.W.2d 123, 126 (Minn. 1980), cert. denied, 450 U.S. 1031 (1981); R. LIFTON, THOUGHT REFORM AND THE PSYCHOLOGY OF TOTALISM (1961); E. SCHEIN, COERCIVE PERSUASION (1961); Delgado, Ascription of Criminal States of Mind: Toward a Defense Theory for the Coercively Persuaded ("Brainwashed") Defendant, 63 MINN. L. REV. 1 (1978).

[448]Michels, Ethical Issues of Psychological and Psychotherapeutic Means of Behavior Control: Is the Moral Contract Being Observed?, 3 HASTINGS CTR REP., APR. 1973, AT 11, 11.

[449]See S. FREUD, AN OUTLINE OF PSYCHOANALYSIS, in 23 STANDARD EDITION OF THE COMPLETE PSYCHOLOGICAL WORKS OF SIGMUND FREUD 141 (1964); Stewart, Psychoanalysis and Psychoanalytical Psychotherapy, in 2 COMPREHENSIVE TEXTBOOK OF PSYCHIATRY, supra note 271, at 2113, 2117; Schwartz & Solomon, Psychoanalysis, in HANDBOOK OF PSYCHIATRY 489, 513 (P. Solomon & V. Patch eds., 2d ed. 1974).

and degree of commitment required for a meaningful therapeutic relationship."[450] One who is resistant to therapy can avoid its effects even if compelled to play the role of patient.

(b) Counseling Programs for Offenders

If a patient in psychotherapy can resist or avoid the effects of this technique at will, an offender can even more easily avoid the intrusions of the "counseling" provided by counselors in prison and community programs (who generally lack the professional abilities of psychotherapists). This conclusion is supported by a review of 13 studies of correctional psychotherapy in institutional and community settings, which found such therapy is more likely to be effective, if at all, "when the subjects are amenable to treatment rather than nonamenable."[451]

Educational and vocational programs, which prisoners and offenders in the community are frequently required to attend, are no more effective or intrusive than counseling for those disinterested in learning. Students in primary and secondary schools, in their "most formative and impressionable years,"[452] may be vulnerable to the socialization process that occurs in our educational systems whether or not they are willing participants, although all students no doubt share the common experience of having been able to "tune out" the efforts of their teachers. In any event, prisoners and even adolescents adjudged juvenile delinquents (who are long past their formative years) generally have the power to resist unwanted education. Even the strong verbal exhortation of prison inmates, bordering on threats of physical abuse and typical of direct confrontation-style programs, such as the Juvenile Awareness Project at Rahway State Prison portrayed in the film "Scared Straight," are within the power of the listener to accept or reject.[453]

Although these programs apparently effected no significant changes in individuals, prison confinement itself—which such programs are designed to scare future offenders into avoiding—may produce profound changes in attitude and behavior. Indeed, this is one of the main purposes of prison confinement.[454] The prison, particularly its correctional therapy and educational programs, had long been dominated by the attempt to indoctrinate inmates in traditional middle-class values.[455] Nevertheless, confinement alone, whatever its effects on mental processes, is not thought to violate the First Amendment,[456] in part for reasons that apply as well to verbal rehabilitative approaches: Any changes in attitude and behavior they produce are gradual and can be resisted. Despite the great potential for indoctrination within "total institutions" such as prisons and hospitals,[457] there is little evidence that these

---

[450]COMMITTEE ON PSYCHIATRY & LAW OF THE GROUP FOR THE ADVANCEMENT OF PSYCHIATRY, PSYCHIATRY AND SEX PSYCHOPATH LEGISLATION: THE 30s TO THE 80s, at 889 (1977).

[451]D. LIPTON ET AL., THE EFFECTIVENESS OF CORRECTIONAL TREATMENT 213 (1975).

[452]Board of Educ. v. Pico, 457 U.S. 853, 894 (1982) (Powell, J., dissenting).

[453]Rutgers University School of Criminal Justice completed two evaluations of the Juvenile Awareness Project that confirm this observation. J. Finckenhauer & J. Storti, Juvenile Awareness Project Help: Evaluation Report No. 1 (1979) (unpublished); J. Finckenhauer, Juvenile Awareness Project Evaluation Report No. 2 (April 18, 1979) (unpublished). The evaluations compared attitude and behavior changes in a group of juveniles that had attended the project with a control group that had not. The results were mixed, with no significant changes in attitude or behavior shown conclusively to be due to participation in the project. Thus, it would seem that the participants were able to accept or reject what the program offered.

[454]See Wolff v. McDonnell, 418 U.S. 539, 562–63 (1974).

[455]AMERICAN FRIENDS SERVICE COMMITTEE, STRUGGLE FOR JUSTICE: A REPORT ON CRIME AND PUNISHMENT IN AMERICA 43 (1971) [hereinafter STRUGGLE FOR JUSTICE].

[456]See TRIBE, supra note 3, § 15–8, at 1327; Shapiro, supra note 133, at 261.

[457]See generally E. GOFFMAN, ASYLUMS (1961).

attempts have succeeded in instilling attitudinal or behavioral change in unwilling inmates. We speak of prisoners who "take advantage" of these rehabilitative programs, implying that the choice is largely voluntary.

Prison and parole systems place a premium on participation in rehabilitative programs, and most prisoners are well aware of this. In fact, much inmate participation in educational programs may be motivated by little more than the desire to increase their chances for parole.[458] Even if this motivation is considered to coerce participation in such programs, participation in verbal rehabilitative efforts does not ensure accomplishment of program goals, particularly for the many prisoners for whom participation is little more than a facade.[459] Even if inmate participation is coerced by the potential rewards, prisoners remain free to reject any substantial intrusion or permanent change in mental processes. In any event, education programs and treatment efforts in general are constitutionally limited by the principle expressed in *West Virginia State Board of Education v. Barnette,*[460] the compulsory flag salute case, that the state may not attempt to impose orthodoxy of belief.[461] Neither patients nor offenders, therefore, may be required by such programs to affirm their belief in any officially held view on a matter of religion, politics, or opinion.[462]

Only two reported decisions have involved challenges to the involuntary application of purely verbal techniques. Both suits arose from compulsory attendance at prison education classes in Arkansas. In *Rutherford v. Hutto,*[463] the prisoner, classified as illiterate although possessing some slight ability to read and write, was forced to attend classes at the prison pursuant to an Arkansas statute. He claimed that such compulsory attendance violated his First Amendment rights as well as other constitutional provisions. The prison school required 8 hours of attendance one day a week; classes were ungraded, and students were permitted to move along at their own pace. The court noted that "no particular pressure [is] put on any student to achieve or to achieve at any particular rate. No sanctions are imposed if a student performs poorly."[464] Although it noted that an inmate "cannot be forced to learn," the court concluded that the state may "lead the horse to water even though it knows that the horse cannot be made to drink."[465] In view of the state's authority to compel the performance of uncompensated labor, the court could find nothing constitutionally objectionable in compelling participation in the school program. Declaring there is no "constitutional right to be ignorant" or "to remain uneducated," the court rejected the prisoner's constitutional challenge.[466]

In the second Arkansas prison education case, *Jackson v. McLemore,*[467] a prisoner, forced to attend an education program, was placed in segregated confinement for refusing his teacher's order to spell certain words. The district court dismissed the complaint, which had

---

[458]STRUGGLE FOR JUSTICE, *supra* note 455, at 97–98.

[459]*Id.*

[460]319 U.S. 624, 642 (1943).

[461]*See* Abood v. Detroit Bd. of Educ., 431 U.S. 209, 234–35 (1977); Wooley v. Maynard, 430 U.S. 705, 714–15 (1977); Epperson v. Arkansas, 393 U.S. 97, 104–05 (1968); Keyishian v. Board of Regents, 385 U.S. 589, 603 (First Amendment "does not tolerate laws that cast a pall of orthodoxy over the classroom"); Abington School Dist. v. Schempp, 374 U.S. 203, 222–24 (1963); Engel v. Vitale, 370 U.S. 421, 425, 435 (1962); *Barnette,* 319 U.S. at 642; *supra* notes 55–85 and accompanying text.

[462]*Barnette,* 319 U.S. at 642.

[463]377 F. Supp. 268 (E.D. Ark. 1974).

[464]*Id.* at 271.

[465]*Id.* at 272–73.

[466]*Id.* at 272.

[467]523 F.2d 838 (8th Cir. 1975).

asserted a "constitutional right to be let alone,"[468] and the court of appeals affirmed.[469] Expressing agreement with the approach taken in *Rutherford,* the circuit court stressed that "[i]t would defeat the purpose of rehabilitation if access to [rehabilitative] programs could be at the option of the prisoner."[470] The court, however, limited its holding to the type of rehabilitative program before it, finding that no showing had been made that the program was "being purposefully used to infringe upon protected constitutional rights."[471] Moreover, the court indicated that although a prisoner may be required to participate in the school program, he "may not be punished simply because he failed to learn, either through inability or lack of motivation."[472]

A 1952 Supreme Court case, involving a captive audience of a quite different kind, also suggests that unwanted verbal exhortation may not create constitutional difficulties.[473] Public buses had been equipped with FM radios, which broadcast commercial advertising. Two passengers brought suit, but the Supreme Court rejected their claim that, as captive auditors, their First Amendment or Fifth Amendment privacy rights had been violated.[474] Although public buses and public prisons and hospitals have little in common, the effects of mandatory "verbal programming," in terms of the listener's ability to resist, are nonetheless substantially similar.

Even the subtle kind of persuasion that marks much of psychotherapy, including sophisticated manipulation of transference and countertransference phenomena, occurs so gradually and is so dependent on the willingness of individuals to participate meaningfully and to seek change that it should not be deemed to intrude sufficiently on mental processes to trigger First Amendment scrutiny. Because patients and offenders can resist the effects of these essentially verbal interventions, they may readily be distinguished from the more coercive treatment methods found to violate the First Amendment in cases involving psychosurgery, ECT, or psychotropic medication. In this sense, the verbal techniques are similar to the behavioral therapies; both can effectively change attitudes and behavior, but both ultimately depend on the individual's cooperation and willingness to change. Accordingly, neither of these treatment approaches should be deemed to require First Amendment scrutiny.

G. The Burden Imposed on Government To Justify Abridgments of First Amendment Rights

Some types of mental health treatment raise First Amendment issues whereas others do not. Although the First Amendment should be construed to protect mental processes against the kinds of intrusions characterized by the organic therapies, this conclusion does not mean that such protection is absolute.[475] Constitutional rights are not absolute, and even

---

[468]*Id.* at 839.

[469]*Id.* at 840.

[470]*Id.* at 839.

[471]*Id.*

[472]*Id.*

[473]Public Utils. Comm'n v. Pollak, 343 U.S. 451 (1952).

[474]*Id.* at 461–63; *see also* Redrup v. New York, 386 U.S. 767, 769 (1967) (reversing obscenity convictions on the basis that there was no "assault upon individual privacy by publication in a manner so obtrusive as to make it impossible for an unwilling individual to avoid exposure to it.").

[475]*See supra* note 38 and accompanying text.

fundamental rights, such as those protected by the First Amendment, must yield to government restriction when necessary to advance a compelling governmental interest.[476]

What standard of review is applied to measure the constitutionality of treatment approaches raising First Amendment concerns? In other First Amendment contexts, the Supreme Court has subjected to "the most exacting scrutiny"[477] state attempts to abridge protected interests. The Court has indicated that in balancing individual interests against governmental interests, "the State may prevail only upon showing a subordinating interest which is compelling."[478] The governmental interest advanced "must be paramount, one of vital importance, and the burden is on the government to show the existence of such an interest."[479] "To characterize the quality of the governmental interest which must appear, the Court has employed a variety of descriptive terms: compelling; substantial; subordinating; paramount; cogent; strong."[480]

Even when this heavy burden is carried, the government is required to use means "narrowly tailored"[481] or "closely drawn to avoid unnecessary abridgment"[482] of the First Amendment interest in question. The "limitation of First Amendment freedoms" must be "no greater than is necessary or essential to the protection of the particular governmental interest involved."[483] To justify an infringement on First Amendment rights, it must be found that the state interest "cannot be achieved through means significantly less restrictive" of the right involved.[484]

This "exacting scrutiny"—insisting on compelling governmental interests and least restrictive means to accomplish them in order to justify infringement of First Amendment protected activity—is applied generally in First Amendment cases, but not in certain contexts. As previously discussed,[485] in certain limited areas the Supreme Court has used less stringent standards of review—for example, in cases dealing with sexually explicit

---

[476]E.g., Roberts v. United States Jaycees, 468 U.S. 609, 623 (1984) ("The right to associate for expressive purposes is not, however, absolute.").

[477]Texas v. Johnson, 491 U.S. 397, 412 (1989); Boos v. Barry, 485 U.S. 312, 321 (1988); First Nat'l Bank v. Bellotti, 435 U.S. 765, 786 (1978); Elrod v. Burns, 427 U.S. 347, 362 (1976).

[478]Bellotti, 435 U.S. at 786; Bates v. City of Little Rock, 361 U.S. 516 (1960).

[479]Elrod, 427 U.S. at 362; see Bellotti, 435 U.S. at 786; Brandenburg v. Ohio, 395 U.S. 444, 447 (1969).

[480]Barnes v. Glen Theatre, Inc., 501 U.S. 560, 567 (1991); United States v. O'Brien, 391 U.S. 367, 376–77 (1968) (footnote omitted); see also Florida Star v. B.J.F., 491 U.S. 524, 541 (1989) ("a state interest of the highest order").

[481]Florida Star, 491 U.S. at 541; Boos, 485 U.S. at 329; Pacific Gas & Elec. Co. v. Public Utils. Comm'n, 475 U.S. 1, 19 (1986) (plurality opinion); Globe Newspaper Co. v. Superior Court, 457 U.S. 596, 610 (1982); Consolidated Edison Co. v. Public Serv. Comm'n, 447 U.S. 530, 535 (1980).

[482]E.g., Buckley v. Valeo, 424 U.S. 1, 25 (1976); Brown v. Hartlage, 456 U.S. 45, 53–54 (1982); Bellotti, 435 U.S. at 786; see NAACP v. Button, 371 U.S. 415, 438 (1963); Shelton v. Tucker, 364 U.S. 479, 488 (1960); Martin v. City of Struthers, 319 U.S. 141, 149 (1943); Schneider v. State, 308 U.S. 147, 164 (1939); TRIBE, supra note 3, § 12–8, at 833:

> The Court also requires an especially close nexus between ends and means. A statute must be narrowly drawn so that a challenged act of government is clearly an efficacious means to achieve permissible objectives of government and is narrowly aimed at those permissible objectives so as not unnecessarily to reach expressive conduct protected by the First Amendment.

E.g., Sable Communications, Inc. v. FCC, 492 U.S. 115, 126 (1989) ("narrowly drawn regulations designed to serve those interests without unnecessarily interfering with First Amendment freedoms").

[483]Seattle Times Co. v. Rhinehart, 467 U.S. 20, 32 (1984) (quoting Procunier v. Martinez, 416 U.S. 396, 413 (1974)).

[484]Roberts v. United States Jaycees, 468 U.S. 609, 623 (1984); see Brown v. Socialist Workers '74 Campaign Comm., 459 U.S. 87, 91–92 (1982); Democratic Party v. Wisconsin, 450 U.S. 107, 124 (1981); Elrod v. Burns, 427 U.S. 347, 363 (1976); Buckley, 424 U.S. at 25; Button, 371 U.S. at 438; Shelton, 364 U.S. at 488.

[485]See supra notes 195–98 & 202–15 and accompanying text.

speech,[486] child pornography,[487] and commercial speech.[488] Unlike these activities, however, the mentation and expressive conduct of the mentally ill serve important values within the core of those traditionally protected by the First Amendment.[489] As a result, this lesser scrutiny applied in cases involving what some members of the Court regard as "lower value" speech should be inapplicable in the context of forced treatment of the mentally ill. Because freedom of mental processes is a predicate for the exercise of all First Amendment protected rights,[490] it generally should be entitled to full First Amendment protection, including the "exacting scrutiny" typically applied in the First Amendment context.

The Supreme Court also has applied lesser scrutiny to "content-neutral" restrictions on First Amendment activity.[491] For example, laws prohibiting speech near hospitals, banning billboards in residential communities, imposing license fees for demonstrations, or forbidding the distribution of leaflets in public places[492] are content-neutral restrictions that limit communication without regard to the message conveyed.[493] By contrast, "content-based" restrictions, which are subject to exacting scrutiny, limit communication because of the message conveyed.[494] Content-neutral restrictions are subjected to lesser scrutiny, under which the Court uses a balancing test considering the extent to which the restriction limits communication, whether it is "narrowly tailored to serve a significant governmental interest," and whether it "leave[s] open ample alternative channels of communication."[495] Unlike content-based restrictions, which are presumed to violate the First Amendment, " 'content-neutral' time, place and manner regulations are acceptable so long as they are designed to serve a substantial governmental interest and do not unreasonably limit alternative avenues of communication."[496]

Is involuntary mental health treatment content based or content neutral within this dichotomy? The distinction seems awkward in the context of mental health treatment, which is directed not primarily at communication, but rather at mental processes. However, mental health treatment restricts thoughts, beliefs, and mental attitudes precisely because they are

---

[486]City of Renton v. Playtime Theatres, Inc., 475 U.S. 41 (1986); FCC v. Pacifica Found., 438 U.S. 726 (1978) (plurality opinion); Young v. American Mini Theatres, Inc., 427 U.S. 50 (1976) (plurality opinion); see supra notes 202–09 and accompanying text.

[487]Ferber v. New York, 458 U.S. 747 (1982); see supra notes 195–98 and accompanying text.

[488]See, e.g., Posadas de Puerto Rico Assoc. v. Tourism Co., 478 U.S. 328 (1986); Central Hudson Gas & Elec. Co. v. Public Serv. Comm'n, 447 U.S. 557 (1980); Virginia State Bd. of Pharmacy v. Virginia Citizens Consumer Council, Inc., 425 U.S. 748 (1976); supra notes 213–15 and accompanying text.

[489]See supra notes 217–92 and accompanying text.

[490]See supra notes 127–35 and accompanying text.

[491]See, e.g., Ward v. Rock Against Racism, 491 U.S. 781 (1989); Frisby v. Schultz, 487 U.S. 474 (1988); City of Renton v. Playtime Theatres, Inc., 475 U.S. 41 (1986); Clark v. Community for Creative Non-Violence, 468 U.S. 288 (1984); Heffron v. International Soc'y for Krishna Consciousness, Inc., 452 U.S. 640 (1981). See also Stephan, The First Amendment and Content Discrimination, 68 VA. L. REV. 203 (1982); Stone, Content Regulation and the First Amendment, 25 WM. & MARY L. REV. 189 (1983).

[492]Stone, supra note 491, at 189–90.

[493]See Ward, 487 U.S. at 791; Stone, supra note 491, at 189.

[494]See e.g., City of Cincinnati v. Discovery Network, Inc., 113 S. Ct. 1505 (1993); City of Lakewood v. Plain Dealer Publishing Co., 486 U.S. 750 (1988); Boos v. Barry, 485 U.S. 312 (1988); Regan v. Time, Inc., 468 U.S. 641 (1984); Carey v. Brown, 447 U.S. 455 (1980); Erznoznik v. City of Jacksonville, 422 U.S. 205 (1975); Police Dep't v. Mosley, 408 U.S. 92 (1972); Stone, supra note 491, at 190.

[495]Ward, 487 U.S. at 791; Frisby, 487 U.S. at 481 (quoting Perry Educ. Ass'n v. Perry Local Educator's Ass'n, 460 U.S. 37, 45 (1983)). To be "narrowly tailored" to serve the government's interest does not in this context require that it be "the least-restrictive or least-intrusive means of doing so." Ward, 487 U.S. at 798.

[496]City of Renton v. Playtime Theatres, Inc., 475 U.S. 41, 47 (1986); accord Frisby, 487 U.S. 479; Perry, 460 U.S. at 45.

deemed disordered, that is, because of their content. It simply cannot be said that the justification for such treatment "ha[s] nothing to do with content."[497] Moreover, such treatment would seem content based because it restricts the opportunity for the expression itself—the very ability to maintain the thoughts, beliefs, and mental attitudes that themselves are the precursors to expression—not merely a particular means of expression. Such treatment therefore does not merely restrict the time, place, and manner of expression or of the exercise of mental processes; it directly changes mental processes. Nothing could be a greater threat to First Amendment values. Because mental processes unimpaired by government are a predicate to the exercise of all other First Amendment protected interests, intrusive treatment designed to change such processes should generally be subjected to the exacting scrutiny usually applied in the First Amendment area, rather than the balancing approach applied to content-neutral restrictions.

Whether and in what circumstances these "exacting" standards of First Amendment scrutiny can be satisfied in the context of involuntary mental health treatment for either mental patients or criminal offenders is analyzed in chapters 15 and 16. First Amendment and indeed all constitutional protections have been applied differently to those in prisons and other special environments than to those in the community. In some circumstances the Supreme Court has relaxed these "exacting" standards in such special environments, and chapter 15 examines the extent to which such reduced constitutional scrutiny is appropriate in prisons and mental hospitals.

---

[497]*Ward,* 491 U.S. at 792 (quoting *Boos,* 485 U.S. at 320).

Chapter 11
SUBSTANTIVE DUE PROCESS AND MENTAL HEALTH TREATMENT:
Constitutional Protection for Bodily Integrity, Mental Privacy, and Individual Autonomy

A. The Evolution of Due Process: From Procedure to Substance

The Due Process Clauses of the Fifth Amendment (applicable to the federal government) and of the Fourteenth Amendment (applicable to the states) prohibit government from depriving any person of life, liberty, or property without due process of law.[1] An analysis of whether these provisions place constitutional limits on involuntary mental health treatment must begin with a historical examination of their original meaning and subsequent transformation. The amendments were ratified in 1791 and 1868, respectively. Under the original understanding, these clauses were rather limited in scope. Neither their language nor their history suggests that they imposed substantive limitations on governmental authority; rather, they appeared "to focus only on the processes by which life, liberty, or property is taken . . . ."[2] Although the language of the Due Process Clause suggests that the focus was

---

[1] U.S. CONST. amends. V, XIV, § 1.

[2] *See* Bowers v. Hardwick, 478 U.S. 186, 191 (1986) (noting that "despite the language of the Due Process clauses of the Fifth and Fourteenth Amendments," these clauses have been interpreted to have a substantive content"); Moore v. City of E. Cleveland, 431 U.S. 494, 537 (1977) (White, J., dissenting) (noting that "the substantive content of the Clause is suggested neither by its language nor by preconstitutional history."); *see also* E. CORWIN, THE TWILIGHT OF THE SUPREME COURT: A HISTORY OF OUR CONSTITUTIONAL THEORY 95 (1934) (stating that "no one . . . had ever suggested that the term 'due process of law' had any other than its anciently established and self-evident meaning of correct procedure"); J. ELY, DEMOCRACY AND DISTRUST 15–18 (1980) (observing that "there is simply no avoiding the fact that the word that follows 'due' is 'process' "); L. HAND, THE BILL OF RIGHTS 35–36 (1958) (noting that when the Due Process Clause first appeared in chapter III of 28th of Edward III, it "was regarded as the equivalent of the phrase '*per legem terrae*,' which meant no more than customary legal procedure"); R. MCCLOSKEY, THE AMERICAN SUPREME COURT 116 (1960) (stating that "the due process clause . . . had usually been interpreted as having only a procedural meaning"); J. NOWAK & R. ROTUNDA, CONSTITUTIONAL LAW (355 4th ed. 1991) (noting that "the early American legal theorists' idea of due process focused on the procedural feature of the concept"); B. TWISS, LAWYERS AND THE CONSTITUTION: HOW LAISSEZ-FAIRE CAME TO THE SUPREME COURT 26 (1942) (noting the Due Process Clause was almost "universally" considered as "only a procedural guarantee"); Easterbrook, *Substance and Due Process,* 1982 SUP. CT. REV. 85, 95–102 (discussing antecedents of constitutional right to substantive due process); Haines, *Judicial Review of Legislation in the United States and the Doctrine of Vested Rights and of Implied Limitations on Legislatures,* 3 TEX. L. REV. 1, 1 (1924) (examining early interpretations of right to due process of law); Hamilton, *The Path of Due Process of Law, in* AMERICAN CONSTITUTIONAL LAW: HISTORICAL ESSAYS 129, 132–33 (L. Levy ed., 1966) (same); Henkin, *Privacy and Autonomy,* 74 COLUM. L. REV. 1410, 1412 (concluding that neither the text nor the history of the Due Process Clause suggests a substantive component); Hough, *Due Process of Law—Today,* 32 HARV. L. REV. 218, 223–24 (1919) (interpreting due process rights as they existed prior to Civil War); Perry, *Abortion, the Public Morals, and the Police Power: The Ethical Function of Substantive Due Process,* 23 UCLA L. REV. 689, 695 (1976) (concluding that it is "received wisdom" that original meaning of due process was solely procedural); Stevens, *The Third Branch of Liberty,* 41 U. MIAMI L. REV. 277, 278 (1986) (observing that "the plain language of the due process clause seems to speak only of procedure").

on ''process,''[3] the use of the phrase ''of law'' following the phrase ''due process'' provides a textual basis for a wider reading.[4] However, in the pre-Civil War era due process was viewed predominantly as procedural, and the Due Process Clause of the Fifth Amendment was of little significance as a substantive limitation on governmental action.[5]

That due process was not used substantively during the pre-Civil War period was not surprising.[6] In the early years of the republic the Supreme Court was not eager to invalidate acts of the federal government. To the contrary, the Court was dominated by the Federalists during this period, and it attempted to expand the power of the federal government.[7] Moreover, this was not a period in which the federal government was active in ways that limited the liberty or property of individuals; restrictions on the use of property during this era came from the states, which were beyond the reach of the Fifth Amendment.[8]

Although application of the Due Process Clause to impose substantive restrictions on government was extremely limited in this early period, the clause gradually became associated in the judicial and popular mind with the notion that arbitrary exercises of governmental power serving no public good were not binding law.[9] This view of due process was furthered by the abolitionist debates of the mid-19th century, which drew heavily on natural rights concepts.[10] Acceptance of this conception of due process was accelerated by the influence of state judiciaries, which at the time were beginning to constitutionalize this kind of natural rights thinking.[11] In the pre-Civil War period, these forces began to be reflected in judicial decisions suggesting that due process might impose substantive limits on legislation, thereby serving as the vehicle for the infusion of natural rights notions into our

---

[3]See, e.g., Whitney v. California, 271 U.S. 357, 373 (1927) (Brandeis, J., concurring); ELY, supra note 2, at 18; Stevens, supra note 2, at 278.

[4]Tribe, The Puzzling Persistence of Process-Based Constitutional Theories, 89 YALE L.J. 1063, 1066 n.9 (1980) (''[T]he words that follow 'due process' are 'of law,' seems to have been the textual point of departure for substantive due process.''); see, e.g., Hurtado v. California, 110 U.S. 516, 535–36 (1884) (An arbitrary exercise of legislative power, even though in the form of legislation, is not law. ''It is not every act, legislative in form, that is law. Law is something more than mere will exerted as an act of power.'').

[5]TWISS, supra note 2, at 26; Haines, supra note 2, at 1; Hough, supra note 2, at 223–24. For criticism of the accuracy of this prevalent view, see Graham, Procedure to Substance—Extra-Judicial Rise of Due Process, 1830–1860, 40 CAL. L. REV. 483 (1952); Strong, The Economic Philosophy of Lochner: Emergence Embrasure and Emasculation, 15 ARIZ. L. REV. 419, 420 & n.2 (1973).

[6]NOWAK & ROTUNDA, supra note 2, at 351–52.

[7]Id. Indeed, in the pre–Civil War period the Court invalidated only two federal statutes. Marbury v. Madison, 5 U.S. (1 Cranch) 137 (1803); Scott v. Sandford, 60 U.S. (19 How.) 393 (1857).

[8]NOWAK & ROTUNDA, supra note 2, at 352. Because the only Due Process Clause existing at this time was contained in the Fifth Amendment, which does not restrict the states (see Baron v. Baltimore, 32 U.S. (7 Pet.) 243 (1833); supra chapter 10, note 2, and accompanying text), it would have been unthinkable to apply due process to such state restrictions on property.

[9]See A. HOWARD, THE ROAD FROM RUNNYMEDE: MAGNA CARTA AND CONSTITUTIONALISM IN AMERICA 305–07 (1968); Corwin, The Doctrine of Due Process of Law Before the Civil War, 24 HARV. L. REV. 366, 373–74 (1911); Perry, supra note 2, at 698–99; Williams, ''Liberty'' in the Due Process Clauses of the Fifth and Fourteenth Amendments: The Framers' Intentions, 53 U. COLO. L. REV. 117, 118 (1981).

[10]See generally J. TENBROECK, THE ANTISLAVERY ORIGINS OF THE FOURTEENTH AMENDMENT (1951); Nelson, The Impact of the Antislavery Movement Upon Styles of Judicial Reasoning in Nineteenth Century America, 87 HARV. L. REV. 513, 525–66 (1974); Perry, supra note 2, at 698–99.

[11]Grey, Do We Have an Unwritten Constitution?, 27 STAN. L. REV. 703, 716 (1975); Mendelson, A Missing Link in the Evolution of Due Process, 10 VAND. L. REV. 125 (1956); Perry, supra note 2, at 699 n.50.

written Constitution.[12] Chief Justice Taney's opinion in the controversial *Dred Scott* decision—holding that Congress' attempt to bar slavery in certain territories constituted a deprivation of the property rights of slaveholders and that the Missouri Compromise was therefore unconstitutional—ironically represented one of the earliest expansions of due process and the first time the Supreme Court had invoked the clause in a substantive sense.[13] *Dred Scott* was viewed as a judicial endorsement of slavery, and it provoked violent reaction.[14] Ultimately, its holding that slaves were not "citizens" was overruled by the Civil War Amendments. In light of this reaction, the Court after the war relied on other more specific constitutional provisions to control state and federal legislation, rather than the Due Process Clause.[15]

The Fourteenth Amendment was ratified in 1868 after the Civil War. Although the amendment's Due Process Clause, as well as its other clauses, were designed to impose constitutional limits on state authority, it was far from clear what those limits were intended to be.[16] Indeed, not only was the precise meaning of the Due Process Clause unclear when the Fourteenth Amendment was adopted, but considerable evidence suggests that its meaning was intentionally left undefined.[17]

The notion that the Due Process Clauses imposed substantive and not merely procedural limits on government began to emerge more rapidly after adoption of the Fourteenth Amendment. This was the period of the American industrial revolution, and the growth of capital and corporate industry led to increased economic regulation by the states. Such regulation in turn led to a corresponding increase in activity by attorneys for the railroads and other regulated industries, who increasingly asserted substantive due process claims.[18]

These arguments were resisted in the *Slaughter-House Cases* in 1873, which not only gave a restrictive reading to the Privileges and Immunities Clause of the Fourteenth Amendment but also read the Due Process Clause narrowly to guarantee only procedural due process. The Court rejected the argument of the dissenters, which had attempted to infuse natural rights ideology into the Due Process Clause and use it as a substantive restraint on

---

[12]*See* E. CORWIN, LIBERTY AGAINST GOVERNMENT 92–109 (1948); G. GUNTHER, CONSTITUTIONAL LAW 436 (12th ed. 1991). Perhaps the best known state case in this period using a state constitutional due process clause in a substantive way was Wynehamer v. People, 13 N.Y. 378 (1856), which invalidated a liquor prohibition law applied to liquor owned before passage of the statute on the basis that it violated the vested property rights of owners. *See* CORWIN, *supra* at 102 (describing this case as "a new starting point in the history of due process of law"); *id.* at 101–09.

[13]Scott v. Sandford, 60 U.S. (19 How.) 393, 450 (1857):

> [A]n act of Congress which deprives a citizen of the United States of his liberty or property, merely because he came himself or brought his property into a particular Territory of the United States, and who had committed no offense against the laws, could hardly be dignified with the name of due process of law.

See CORWIN, *supra* note 12, at 110–14; GUNTHER, *supra* note 12, at 436; Corwin, *supra* note 9, at 460.

[14]NOWAK & ROTUNDA, *supra* note 2, at 356; Nelson, *supra* note 10, at 545, 548–49. Before becoming president, Abraham Lincoln criticized the decision in the Lincoln–Douglas senatorial campaign debates of 1858. 2 THE COLLECTED WORKS OF ABRAHAM LINCOLN 494 (R. Basler ed., 1953); 3 *id.* at 255.

[15]NOWAK & ROTUNDA, *supra* note 2, at 356–57.

[16]McCLOSKEY, *supra* note 2, at 115–17; NOWAK & ROTUNDA, *supra* note 2, at 357–58; Kaczorowski, *Revolutionary Constitutionalism in the Era of the Civil War and Reconstruction,* 61 N.Y.U. L. REV. 863, 922–23 (1986); Perry, *supra* note 2, at 699.

[17]A. BICKEL, THE LEAST DANGEROUS BRANCH 104 (1962); McCLOSKEY, *supra* note 2, at 117–18; Bickel, *The Original Understanding and the Segregation Decision,* 69 HARV. L. REV. 1, 61–65 (1955); Kaczorowski, *supra* note 16, at 926–28; Perry, *supra* note 2, at 699.

[18]GUNTHER, *supra* note 12, at 436–37; NOWAK & ROTUNDA, *supra* note 2, at 359–60; TWISS, *supra* note 2, at 42–173; Monaghan, *Of "Liberty" and "Property,"* 62 CORNELL L. REV. 405, 412 (1977); Perry, *supra* note 2, at 700.

state legislation.[19] Substantive due process arguments continued to be made, however, in both contemporary legal literature[20] and litigation resisting economic regulation, and these arguments prevailed in some state courts during this period.[21] In the late 1870s and the 1880s, Supreme Court opinions began to suggest substantive due process limits on legislative powers, including their use only to accomplish a public purpose.[22] Finally, in the 1887 case of *Mugler v. Kansas,* the Court, although sustaining a law prohibiting intoxicating beverages, stated that it would scrutinize the substantive reasonableness of state legislation:[23]

> If . . . a statute purporting to have been enacted to protect the public health, the public morals, or the public safety, has no real or substantial relation to those objects, or is a palpable invasion of rights secured by the fundamental law, it is the duty of Courts to so adjudge, and thereby give effect to the Constitution.

Ten years later, in *Allgeyer v. Louisiana,* the Court for the first time invalidated a state statute on the basis of substantive due process, finding that a statutory regulation of the conduct of insurance business violated liberty of contract.[24]

The Court embarked on a new regime of substantive due process in the 1905 case of *Lochner v. New York.*[25] In *Lochner,* the Court invalidated a law prohibiting the employment of bakers for more than 10 hours a day or 60 hours a week on the ground that it violated liberty of contract between employer and employee, a liberty interest protected by due process. *Lochner* came to symbolize the era that was to prevail for the next 30 years of judicial intervention into economic regulation. Under *Lochner,* the justices freely substituted their laissez-faire economic philosophy for the economic and social choices made by Congress and the state legislatures.[26] The *Lochner* doctrine and particularly its laissez-faire application were criticized by Justice Holmes, who charged that the Fourteenth Amendment "does not enact Mr. Herbert Spencer's Social Statics."[27] However, the doctrine was to prevail and during the *Lochner* era the Court frequently used substantive due process to

---

[19]Slaughter-House Cases, 83 U.S. (16 Wall.) 36 (1873); *see id.* at 122 (Bradley, J., dissenting).

[20]The most influential authority was Thomas M. Cooley. *See, e.g.,* T. COOLEY, CONSTITUTIONAL LIMITATIONS 354–56 (1st ed. 1868); *id.* at 438–41 (4th ed. 1878); T. COOLEY, THE GENERAL PRINCIPLES OF CONSTITUTIONAL LAW IN THE UNITED STATES OF AMERICA 222–24 (1978 reprint of 1880 ed.) [hereinafter GENERAL PRINCIPLES]; *see* CORWIN, *supra* note 12, at 116 (describing CONSTITUTIONAL LIMITATIONS as "the most influential treatise ever published on American constitutional law"); MCCLOSKEY, *supra* note 2, at 131; TWISS, *supra* note 2, at 25–30; Pious, *introduction to* COOLEY, GENERAL PRINCIPLES, *supra* at unnumbered p.1 (describing Cooley as "the most influential and most cited authority on American constitutional law in the post–Civil War period"); *id.* at p.2 (CONSTITUTIONAL LIMITATIONS "established the idea of a 'substantive due process' standard that federal courts could apply under the Fourteenth Amendment to strike down state legislation that trespassed the limits set on police powers.").

[21]*See, e.g., In re* Jacobs, 98 N.Y. 98 (1885) (invalidating under state due process clause statute prohibiting the manufacture of cigars in tenement houses); *see* CORWIN, *supra* note 12, at 136–38; GUNTHER, *supra* note 12, at 446 & n.6; NOWAK & ROTUNDA, *supra* note 2, at 360.

[22]*See* Loan Association v. Topeka, 87 U.S. (20 Wall.) 655 (1874); Munn v. Illinois, 94 U.S. 113 (1877); The Railroad Commission Cases, 116 U.S. 307 (1886); CORWIN, *supra* note 12, at 128–36, 179; GUNTHER, *supra* note 12, at 437–38; NOWAK & ROTUNDA, *supra* note 2, at 360–61; L. TRIBE, AMERICAN CONSTITUTIONAL LAW § 8–1, at 563–67 (2d ed. 1988); Perry, *supra* note 2, at 701.

[23]123 U.S. 623, 661 (1887) (dicta); *see* CORWIN, *supra* note 12, at 143–44.

[24]165 U.S. 578 (1897); *see* CORWIN, *supra* note 12, at 146.

[25]198 U.S. 45 (1905).

[26]*See* GUNTHER, *supra* note 12, at 432; TRIBE, *supra* note 22, § 8–2, at 434–35; Hamilton, *supra* note 2; Strong, *supra* note 5, at 436–49.

[27]198 U.S. at 75–76.

invalidate economic regulation, particularly legislation regulating prices, labor relations, and business activities.[28]

The retreat from *Lochner* began in the mid-1930s,[29] and the use of substantive due process to champion economic and property rights against economic legislation has now been rejected by the Court.[30] But although *Lochner* is dead in the area of the protection of economic and property rights, the doctrine of substantive due process continues to live in the area of noneconomic rights.[31]

Griswold v. Connecticut,[32] the 1965 Connecticut birth control case, marked the modern reemergence of substantive due process doctrine in the noneconomic area. Haunted by the ghost of *Lochner*, the Court in *Griswold* invoked a constitutional ''right of privacy,'' which it found in the ''penumbras, formed by emanations'' from various specific guarantees in the Bill of Rights.[33] This right, rather than substantive due process, was applied to invalidate the statutory ban in the use of contraceptives. The Court specifically declined the invitation to invoke *Lochner*,[34] rejecting a role as ''super-legislature to determine the wisdom, need, and propriety of laws that touch economic problems, business affairs, or social conditions.''[35] The Court found that the law in question, however, ''operates directly on an intimate relation of husband and wife'' protected by a constitutional right of privacy.[36] The subterfuge of ''penumbras,'' however, merely masked the fact that the right of privacy recognized by the Court was an aspect of liberty protected by substantive due process.[37] Although Justice Douglas's opinion for the *Griswold* Court never mentioned due process, the Connecticut birth control statute could have been held unconstitutional only under the Due Process Clause of the Fourteenth Amendment. A right of privacy derived from the penumbras of the Bill of Rights presumably could protect against federal action only. To protect against state

---

[28]GUNTHER, *supra* note 12, at 432, 444–45; Strong, *supra* note 5, at 436–49.

[29]*See, e.g.,* West Coast Hotel Co. v. Parrish, 300 U.S. 379 (1937); Nebbia v. New York, 291 U.S. 502 (1934).

[30]*E.g.,* Ferguson v. Skrupa, 372 U.S. 726 (1963); Williamson v. Lee Optical Co., 348 U.S. 483 (1955); Day–Bright Lighting, Inc. v. Missouri, 342 U.S. 421 (1952); Lincoln Fed. Labor Union v. Northwestern Iron & Metal Co., 335 U.S. 525 (1949); *see* Strong, *supra* note 5, at 449–54.

[31]GUNTHER, *supra* note 12, at 432, 446; Garfield, *Privacy, Abortion, and Judicial Review: Haunted by the Ghost of Lochner,* 61 WASH. L. REV. 293, 352–54 (1986); Henkin, *supra* note 2, at 1427; Perry, *supra* note 2, at 704–06. Even the staunchest judicial critics of *Lochner*—Justices Holmes, Brandeis, and Douglas—accepted the notion that the Due Process Clause ''applies to matters of substantive law as well as to matters of procedure.'' Whitney v. California, 274 U.S. 357, 373 (1927) (Brandeis, J., dissenting); Adkins v. Children's Hosp., 261 U.S. 525, 567 (1923) (Holmes, J., dissenting); Lochner v. New York, 198 U.S. 45, 75–76 (1905) (Holmes, J., dissenting); Poe v. Ullman, 367 U.S. 497, 517–18 (1961) (Douglas, J., dissenting).

[32]381 U.S. 479 (1965).

[33]*Id.* at 484.

[34]*Id.* at 481–82.

[35]*Id.* at 482.

[36]*Id.* at 482, 485.

[37]*See* Roe v. Wade, 410 U.S. 113, 168 (1973) (Stewart, J., concurring) (*Griswold* can be understood only as a substantive due process case); G. HUGHS, THE CONSCIENCE OF THE COURTS 72 (1975) (''There can be no doubt that [the specter of *Lochner*] accounts for the circuitous reasoning of *Griswold*. Terrified by history to talk openly in terms of substantive liberty rights under the Fourteenth Amendment, the justices talked instead in fragile and convoluted reasoning of privacy rights swirling around in ectoplasmic emanations.''); Garfield, *supra* note 31, at 306 & n.82 (substantive due process rationale of *Griswold* not made explicit, ''probably in a studied effort to avoid the stigma of *Lochner*.''); Henkin, *supra* note 2, at 1428 (''Perhaps it was too difficult for most of the justices candidly to rehabilitate substantive due process at one blow after decades of silence and obloquy and within the fearful memories of New Deal survivors.''); Perry, *supra* note 2, at 705 (''The modern Supreme Court, still reeling from the political shell-shock incurred in the 'old substantive due process' battles through the 1930's, has been reluctant to call a spade a spade.'').

action, this right of privacy would have had to be an aspect of liberty protected by the Due Process Clause of the Fourteenth Amendment.[38]

More recently, the Court has explicitly recognized that the right of privacy is grounded in substantive due process. In *Roe v. Wade,* the 1973 abortion case, the Court invalidated a state statute restricting abortion as inconsistent with the woman's fundamental right of privacy, "founded in the Fourteenth Amendment's concept of personal liberty and restrictions upon state action."[39] The modern Court has expressly recognized that "the due process clause of the Fourteenth Amendment not only accords procedural safeguards to protected interests, but likewise protects substantive aspects of liberty against impermissible governmental restrictions."[40] In a more recent treatment of these issues, the Court rejected the claim that due process protects a right to engage in consensual homosexual conduct, but it explicitly acknowledged that

> despite the language of the Due Process Clauses of the Fifth and Fourteenth Amendments, which appears to focus only on the processes by which life, liberty, or property is taken, the cases are legion in which those Clauses have been interpreted to have substantive content, subsuming rights that to a great extent are immune from federal or state regulation or proscription.[41]

The Due Process Clauses thus impose substantive limits on governmental action. Unless sufficient justification is found for a violation of the rights protected by the Due Process Clauses—rights to life, liberty, and property—these rights may not be transgressed. For our purposes, the question thus becomes whether the mental health treatment techniques can be considered to infringe "liberty" or other interests protected by the Due Process Clauses.

B. The Expanding Conception of "Liberty" Within the Meaning of the Due Process Clauses

Historical accounts of the original understanding of the term *liberty* in the Due Process Clause of the Fifth Amendment suggest a narrow view of liberty, restricted to freedom from incarceration or similar physical restraint of the person.[42] English antecedents of the Due Process Clause stem from the thirty-ninth article of the Magna Carta of 1215, which reads: "No free man shall be taken or imprisoned or dispossessed, or outlawed, or banished, or any way destroyed, nor will we go upon him, nor send upon him, except by the legal judgment of his peers or by the law of the land."[43] After several variations, the concept was refined in the

---

[38]Garfield, *supra* note 31, at 306 & n.82. *See also* Emerson, *Nine Justices in Search of a Doctrine,* 64 MICH. L. REV. 219 (1965); Henkin, *supra* note 2, at 1428; Kauper, *Penumbras, Peripheries, Emanations, Things Fundamental and Things Forgotten,* 64 MICH. L. REV. 235 (1965).

[39]410 U.S. 113, 153 (1973); *accord* Whalen v. Roe, 429 U.S. 589, 599 n.23 (1977); Moore v. City of E. Cleveland, 431 U.S. 494, 502 (1977) ([T]he history of substantive due process "counsels caution and restraint. But it does not counsel abandonment . . . .").

[40]Harrah Ind. School Dist. v. Martin, 440 U.S. 194, 197 (1979); Kelley v. Johnson, 425 U.S. 238, 244 (1976).

[41]Bowers v. Hardwick, 472 U.S. 578 (1986).

[42]Hough, *supra* note 2, at 222–23; Shattuck, *The True Meaning of the Term "Liberty" in Those Clauses in the Federal and State Constitutions Which Protect "Life, Liberty and Property,"* 4 HARV. L. REV. 365 (1891); Warren, *The New "Liberty" Under the Fourteenth Amendment,* 39 HARV. L. REV. 431, 440 (1926); Williams, *supra* note 9, at 120–27.

[43]SOURCES OF OUR LIBERTIES 17 (R. Perry ed., 1959); *see id.* at xi, 428; Corwin, *supra* note 9, at 368; McIlwain, *Due Process of Law in Magna Carta,* 14 COLUM. L. REV. 27 (1914); Shattuck, *supra* note 42, at 372; Williams, *supra* note 9, at 120.

statute of 28 Edward III: "No man, of whatever estate or condition he be, shall be put out of land or tenement, nor taken nor imprisoned, nor disinherited, nor put to death, without being brought in answer by due process of law."[44] This apparently was the first appearance of the phrase "due process of law"[45] and supports a narrow reading of the clause as being limited to the absence of incarceration or similar physical restraint.

None of the English antecedents of the Due Process Clause, however, used the word *liberty*, and it is thus possible that the Framers of the Fifth Amendment, by using the words "life, liberty or property," intended to broaden the interests protected.[46] Contrary evidence, however, is provided by the Due Process Clauses of the state constitutions that were in effect at the time the Fifth Amendment was adopted. These state constitutions provide a bridge between the English antecedents and the federal constitutional provision and suggest that the Framers intended no such broadening.[47] These provisions linked "liberty" to criminal trials and can be construed as encompassing only freedom from incarceration or similar physical restraint.[48] The legislative history of the Fifth Amendment also supports this conclusion,[49] as does the relationship between the Fifth Amendment and the language of the other first 10 amendments.[50] This narrow view of the concept of "liberty" is also reflected in the pre-Civil War judicial treatment of the Fifth Amendment's Due Process Clause and its state counterparts.[51]

Was the Due Process Clause contained in Section 1 of the Fourteenth Amendment intended to have a broader meaning? The Amendment was designed to provide a constitutional foundation for the Civil Rights Act of 1866, adopted over President Andrew Johnson's veto grounded on concerns about the constitutionality of the Act. It also was adopted to ensure federal protection for the newly freed slaves whose efforts to earn a living were hampered by the "black codes" of the Southern states.[52] The post-Civil War Thirteenth Amendment, ratified in 1865, had constitutionalized President Lincoln's Emancipation Proclamation abolishing slavery. Yet the statutes adopted in several of the states frustrated this purpose. Justice Miller's opinion for the Supreme Court in the *Slaughter-House Cases* reflect virtually a contemporaneous view of the historical background of the post-Civil War Amendments. In Miller's words, these state statutes "imposed upon the colored race onerous disabilities and burdens, and curtailed their rights in the pursuit of life,

---

[44]28 EDW. III, c.3 (1354); *see* CORWIN, *supra* note 12, at 91; Corwin, *supra* note 9, at 368; Shattuck, *supra* note 42, at 372–73; Williams, *supra* note 9, at 120–21.

[45]*Id.* at 121.

[46]*Id.*

[47]*Id.; see id.* at 121–24 (reviewing the Due Process Clauses of the constitutions of Maryland, Massachusetts, New Hampshire, New Jersey, North Carolina, Pennsylvania, South Carolina, Vermont, and Virginia). Some form of due process clause is contained in all the state declarations of rights adopted prior to the United States Constitution. SOURCES OF OUR LIBERTIES, *supra* note 43, at 429.

[48]Williams, *supra* note 9, at 121–24.

[49]*Id.* at 124–26.

[50]Warren, *supra* note 42, at 127.

[51]*Id.*

[52]Slaughter-House Cases, 83 U.S. (16 Wall.) 36 (1873); GUNTHER, *supra* note 12, at 400; NOWAK & ROTUNDA, *supra* note 2, at 357; Kaczorowski, *supra* note 16, at 910–13; Faczorowski, *To Begin the Nation Anew: Congress, Citizenship, and Civil Rights After the Civil War,* 92 AMERICAN HIST. REV. 45, 51–55 (1987); Williams, *supra* note 9, at 117–18, 128–31.

liberty, and property to such an extent that their freedom was of little value. . . ."[53] These state statutes, although restricting the civil rights of Blacks in social and occupational contexts, did not impose physical restraints. As a result, Miller's reference to "liberty" would seem to have a wider meaning than the common law conception of that term. As a consequence of the effects of the "black codes" to perpetuate a form of slavery, the perception grew that "the conditions of the slave race would, without further protection of the Federal government, be almost as bad as it was before," and that "something more was necessary in the way of constitutional protection. . . ."[54] The Fourteenth Amendment was the result.

These historical antecedents of the Fourteenth Amendment support the argument that "liberty" in the Due Process Clause of the Fourteenth Amendment was designed to extend beyond freedom from incarceration to protect occupational liberty as well, and perhaps even freedom from other governmental restraints.[55] However, it was probably the Privileges and Immunities Clause of the Fourteenth Amendment, rather than the Due Process Clause, that was designed to accomplish these purposes.[56] But the legislative history of the Fourteenth Amendment is far from clear,[57] and there is respectable authority for the proposition that at the time of the adoption of the Fourteenth Amendment, the precise content of that clause was intended to be left to future generations to answer in the light of developing experience.[58]

Like other constitutional provisions, the Due Process Clause contains ambiguous and open-ended language than can be construed broadly to effectuate its purposes as they may be conceived and reconceived over time in light of the experiences and exigencies of succeeding generations. The vague provisions of the Constitution, as Justice Frankfurter has stated, "are *purposely* left to gather meaning from experience."[59] The provisions of the Constitution, as Justice Holmes described them, are "organic living institutions transplanted from English soil. Their significance is vital not formal; it is to be gathered not simply by taking the words in a dictionary, but by considering their origin and the line of their growth."[60] This "organic" view of the Constitution is widely supported by constitutional

---

[53]Slaughter-House Cases, 83 U.S. at 71. *See generally* T. WILSON, THE BLACK CODES OF THE SOUTH (1965).

[54]83 U.S. at 70.

[55]Williams, *supra* note 9, at 118.

[56]CORWIN, *supra* note 12, at 118; ELY, *supra* note 2, at 22–24; Williams, *supra* note 9, at 118, 131–33.

[57]ELY, *supra* note 2, at 25–27; R. MCCLOSKEY, *supra* note 2, at 116–17; Kaczorowski, *supra* note 16, at 922–23; Perry, *supra* note 2, at 699; Williams, *supra* note 9, at 117–18, 133.

> When referring to the rights that supporters of the Civil Rights Act of 1866 and the fourteenth amendment intended to secure, congressmen and senators used interchangeably terms such as 'civil rights,' 'privileges and immunities,' 'rights to life, liberty, and property,' 'Bill of Rights,' 'fundamental rights,' 'rights of person and property,' and 'rights of citizens.'

Kaczorowski, *supra* note 16, at 922 n.288.

[58]BICKEL, *supra* note 17, at 104; MCCLOSKEY, *supra* note 2, at 118; Bickel, *supra* note 17, at 61–65; Kaczorowski, *supra* note 16, at 926–28; Perry, *supra* note 2, at 699, 706, 713–19.

[59]National Mut. Ins. Co. v. Tidewater Transfer Co., 337 U.S. 582, 646 (1949) (Frankfurter, J., dissenting). In this sense the Constitution, as Chief Justice Marshall stated, is "intended to endure for ages to come, and consequently, to be adapted to the various crises of human affairs." McCulloch v. Maryland, 17 U.S. (4 Wheat.) 316, 415 (1819) (emphasis in original). Perhaps the most explicit recognition of this principle of constitutional jurisprudence is the Court's construction of the Eighth Amendment's prohibition of cruel and unusual punishments as reflecting society's "evolving standards of decency." *See, e.g.,* Trop v. Dulles, 356 U.S. 86, 101 (1958) (plurality opinion); Weems v. United States, 217 U.S. 349, 371, 373, 378 (1910).

[60]Gompers v. United States, 233 U.S. 604, 610 (1914).

scholars[61] and has special application to the open-textured language chosen for the Amendment—"liberty," "property," "due process of law," and "privileges and immunities." As the second Justice Harlan has stated:

> [t]he very breadth and generality of the [Fourteenth] Amendment's provisions suggested that its authors did not suppose that the Nation would always be limited to mid-19th century conceptions of "liberty" and "due process of law" but that the increasing experience and evolving conscience of the American people would add new "intermediate premises."[62]

If the purpose of the Privileges and Immunities Clause of the Fourteenth Amendment was to protect occupational liberty and other liberties of the newly freed slaves, that purpose was soon frustrated by the Supreme Court's evisceration of the clause in the *Slaughter-House Cases* of 1873.[63] The plaintiffs in the *Slaughter-House Cases* had relied not only on the Privileges and Immunities Clause but also contended that the Louisiana statute there involved, creating a butcher's monopoly, had deprived them of liberty and property without due process of law. The majority did not even address the "liberty" contention but expressly rejected the property argument.[64] In dissent, Justice Bradley not only relied on the Privileges and Immunities Clause but also contended that the state statute violated the due process liberty interest of plaintiffs. In his view, "a law that prohibits a large class of citizens from adopting a lawful employment, or from following a lawful employment previously adopted, does deprive them of liberty as well as property, without due process of law. Their right of choice is a portion of the liberty; their occupation is their property."[65] This broadened definition of *liberty* beyond freedom from external restraint to include freedom of occupational choice would have used the Due Process Clause to effectuate the purposes of the Privileges and Immunities Clause. Although the Court rejected this vision of the Due Process Clause in the *Slaughter-House Cases,* it was soon to change its view.

Barely 4 years after the *Slaughter-House Cases,* in 1877, the Court without analysis expanded the notion of "liberty" within the Due Process Clause to include the right of a

---

[61]*See, e.g.,* BICKEL, *supra* note 17, at 102–09; A. COX, THE ROLE OF THE SUPREME COURT IN AMERICAN GOVERNMENT 63 (1976); McCLOSKEY, *supra* note 2, at 15 (The Constitution was "[c]onceived in ambiguity," the Framers intending that it mean "whatever the circumstances of the future will allow it to mean."); M. PERRY, THE CONSTITUTION, THE COURTS, AND HUMAN RIGHTS: AN INQUIRY INTO THE LEGITIMACY OF CONSTITUTIONAL POLICYMAKING BY THE JUDICIARY 33–34 (1982); TRIBE, *supra* note 22 § 10–7, at 670; Brest, *The Misconceived Quest for the Original Understanding,* 60 B.U. L. REV. 204 (1980); Black, *The Unfinished Business of the Warren Court,* 46 WASH. L. REV. 1, 31–45 (1970); Fiss, *The Supreme Court, 1978 Term—Forward: The Forms of Justice,* 93 HARV. L. REV. 1, 1, 11 (1979); Grey, *supra* note 11; Levy, *Introduction in* AMERICAN CONSTITUTIONAL LAW: HISTORICAL ESSAYS, *supra* note 2, at 2 ("The framers also had a genius for studied imprecision or calculated ambiguity. . . . [T]he Constitution thereby permitted, even encouraged, nay necessitated, continuous reinterpretation and adaptation. . . . The principles themselves, not their framers' understanding and application of them, are meant to endure."); Perry, *supra* note 2, at 713–19; Perry, *Noninterpretive Review in Human Rights Cases: A Functional Justification,* 56 N.Y.U. L. REV. 278 (1981); Stevens, *Judicial Restraint,* 22 SAN DIEGO L. REV. 437, 451 n.35 (1985) ("[T]he vast open spaces in the text" of the Constitution indicated that its authors "implicitly delegated the power to fill those spaces to future generations of lawmakers."). It is not without its critics, however, among both judges and scholars. *See, e.g.,* Harper v. Virginia Bd. of Elections, 383 U.S. 663, 670 (1966) (Black, J., dissenting); R. BERGER, GOVERNMENT BY JUDICIARY: THE TRANSFORMATION OF THE FOURTEENTH AMENDMENT (1977); ELY, *supra* note 2 (criticizing "noninterpretive" review in the area of substantive due process but praising it in the First Amendment and Equal Protection contexts); Bork, *Neutral Principles and Some First Amendment Problems,* 47 IND. L.J. 1 (1971); Rehnquist, *The Notion of a Living Constitution,* 54 TEX. L. REV. 693 (1976).

[62]Duncan v. Louisiana, 391 U.S. 145, 175 (1968) (Harlan, J., dissenting).

[63]83 U.S. (16 Wall.) 36 (1873).

[64]*Id.* at 80.

[65]*Id.* at 122 (Bradley, J., dissenting).

nonresident defendant to be free of the determination of his personal rights by a court lacking jurisdiction over his person.[66] Although the Court did not expressly define this as a "liberty" interest within the meaning of the Due Process Clause, that is plainly what it was, and the modern Court has more recently made this explicit.[67]

Seven years later, in 1884, the Court again considered the same Louisiana monopoly statute involved in the *Slaughter-House Cases* and again rejected an attack based on both the Privileges and Immunities Clause and the Due Process Clause.[68] Justice Bradley again dissented, urging an expanded definition of *liberty,* in an opinion joined by Justice Field and by the new Justices, Holland and Woods. The pursuit of "his chosen calling," according to the dissent, is "a material part of the liberty of the citizen. . . . The right to follow any of the common occupations of life is . . . a large ingredient in the civil liberty of the citizens."[69]

In a decision 4 years later, in 1888, upholding a state oleomargarine statute, Justice Harlan, in dictum, accepted the proposition urged by the defendant that "the privilege of pursuing an ordinary calling or trade" is a liberty guaranteed by the Fourteenth Amendment.[70] In a dissenting opinion, Justice Field argued for a broad definition of *liberty* as meaning

> something more than freedom from physical restraint or imprisonment. It means freedom not merely to go where one may choose, but to do such acts as he may judge for his best interests, not inconsistent with the equal rights of others; that is, to follow such pursuits as may be best adapted to his faculties, and which will give him the highest enjoyment.[71]

Finally, in 1897, the Supreme Court adopted the broad meaning of the term *liberty* that had been urged in the dissenting opinions of Justices Bradley and Field. In *Allgeyer v. Louisiana,* the Court stated:[72]

> The liberty mentioned in that Amendment means, not only the right of the citizen to be free from the mere physical restraint of his person, as by incarceration, but the term is deemed to embrace the right of the citizen to be free in the enjoyment of all his faculties; to be free to use them in all lawful ways; to live and work where he will; to earn his livelihood by any lawful calling; to pursue any livelihood or avocation, and for that purpose to enter into all contracts which may be proper, necessary and essential to his carrying out to a successful conclusion the purposes above mentioned.

---

[66]Pennoyer v. Neff, 95 U.S. 714, 733 (1877) ("Since the adoption of the Fourteenth Amendment . . . proceedings in a court of jurisdiction to determine the personal rights and obligations of parties over whom that court has no jurisdiction do not constitute due process of law."). In so doing, the Court subsumed common law jurisdiction notions within the Due Process Clause. *See* Hazzard, *A General Theory of State Court Jurisdiction,* 1965 SUP. CT. REV. 241.

[67]Insurance Corp. of Ireland v. Compagnie Des Bauxites, 456 U.S. 694, 702 (1982) ("The requirement that a court have personal jurisdiction flows . . . from the Due Process Clause. The personal jurisdiction requirement recognizes and protects an individual liberty interest."); *id.* at 702 n.10 ("the individual liberty interest preserved by the Due Process Clause"). *See also* May v. Anderson, 345 U.S. 528, 533 (1953) (mother's right to custody of her child is a "personal right" protected by due process that cannot be taken away absent jurisdiction *in personam*).

[68]Butchers' Union v. Crescent City Co., 111 U.S. 746 (1884).

[69]*Id.* at 765, 762 (dissenting opinion). By this time contemporary legal literature had already adopted the view that "liberty within the Due Process Clauses extended considerably beyond freedom from external restraint, and included the right of the individual "to choose his own employment . . . .'" T. COOLEY, GENERAL PRINCIPLES, *supra* note 20, at 231; *id.* at 225 ("The comprehensive word is liberty; and by this is meant not merely freedom to move about unrestrained, but such liberty of conduct, choice, and action as the law gives and protects.").

[70]Powell v. Pennsylvania, 127 U.S. 678, 684 (1888).

[71]*Id.*

[72]165 U.S. 578, 589 (1897).

This opinion marked a substantial departure from the understanding of *liberty* that had prevailed in 1791 and that had been applied by the state courts prior to 1868.[73] Thereafter, the term *liberty* was given a gradually expanding meaning and application. In 1900, the Court stated that *liberty* included "the right of locomotion, the right to move from one place to another, according to inclination. . . ."[74] In 1905, the Court upheld a compulsory vaccination statute against a challenge that it violated the liberty of every person "to care for his own body and health in such way as to him seems best. . . ."[75] The Court found the compulsory vaccination scheme to be a proper exercise of the police power, but noted that "[t]here is, of course, a sphere within which the individual may assert the supremacy of his own will, and rightfully dispute the authority of any human government—especially of any free government existing under a written constitution, to interfere with the exercise of that will."[76]

A particularly broad statement of the meaning of *liberty* within the cognizance of the Fourteenth Amendment, and one that has frequently been cited by the modern Court,[77] came in *Meyer v. Nebraska* in 1923.[78] The Court invalidated a state statute forbidding the teaching in school of any language other than English and offered the following expansive definition of *liberty*:[79]

> While this Court has not attempted to define with exactness the liberty thus guaranteed, the term has received much consideration and some of the included things have been definitely stated. Without doubt, it denotes not merely freedom from bodily restraint but also the right of the individual to contract, to engage in any of the common occupations of life, to acquire useful knowledge, to marry, establish a home and bring up children, to worship God according to the dictates of his own conscience, and generally to enjoy those privileges long recognized at common law as essential to the orderly pursuit of happiness by free men.

In more recent years, the Court has continued to expand the definition of *liberty* within the meaning of the Due Process Clauses. In *Bolling v. Sharpe* (1954), the Court held that the right to equal protection of the laws, explicitly protected against state intrusion by the Fourteenth Amendment, was a liberty interest protected against federal infringement by the

---

[73]Warren, *supra* note 42, at 449.

[74]Williams v. Fears, 179 U.S. 270, 274 (1900).

[75]Jacobson v. Massachusetts, 197 U.S. 11, 26 (1905).

[76]*Id.* at 29.

[77]*See, e.g.,* Moore v. City of E. Cleveland, 431 U.S. 494, 499 (1977) (Powell, J.); *id.* at 536 (Stewart & Rehnquist, J.J., dissenting); *id.* at 545 (White, J., dissenting); Ingraham v. Wright, 430 U.S. 651, 673 (1977); Board of Regents v. Roth, 408 U.S. 564, 572 (1972).

[78]262 U.S. 390 (1923).

[79]*Id.* at 399. Much of this statement is dicta as the liberty interest found infringed was the teacher's right "to teach" and "the right of parents to engage in suitable instruction of their children. . . ." *Id.* at 400. *See also* Pierce v. Society of Sisters, 268 U.S. 510, 534 (1925) ("liberty of parents and guardians to direct the upbringing and education of children under their control"); Gitlow v. New York, 266 U.S. 652, 666 (1925) (Freedom of speech and of the press protected by the First Amendment are "liberties" protected by the Due Process Clause of the Fourteenth Amendment from impairment by the states); Wolff Packing Co. v. Court of Industrial Relations, 262 U.S. 522, 540 (1923) ("the freedom of contract and of labor secured by the Fourteenth Amendment"); Butler v. Perry, 240 U.S. 328, 333 (1916) (Fourteenth Amendment "liberty" was "intended to preserve and protect fundamental rights long recognized under the common law system."); Truax v. Raich, 239 U.S. 33, 41 (1915) ("the right to work for a living in the common occupations of the community" held a liberty interest); Chicago B. & Q. R.R. v. McGuire, 219 U.S. 549, 567 (1911) (freedom of contract); Berea College v. Kentucky, 211 U.S. 45, 67 (1908) (Harlan, J., dissenting) ("the right to impart and receive instruction not harmful to the public"); Williams v. Fears, 179 U.S. 270, 274 (1900) ("the right of locomotion, the right to remove from one place to another according to inclination, is an attribute of personal liberty").

Fifth Amendment Due Process Clause.[80] The Court noted that "liberty" is not "confined to mere freedom from bodily restraint" but "extends to the full range of conduct which the individual is free to pursue, and it cannot be restricted except for a proper governmental objective."[81] The modern Court has also held that the right to travel is a liberty interest within the meaning of the Due Process Clause.[82] It also has found that the "right to personal security," which is a "historic liberty interest" protected by due process, is implicated when the state administers school paddling,[83] subjects residents of mental retardation facilities to unsafe conditions,[84] subjects pretrial detainees to punishment prior to an adjudication of guilt,[85] and transfers prisoners to mental hospitals where they would receive "[c]ompelled treatment in the form of mandatory behavior modification programs."[86] In addition, the Court has found that the right to freedom from bodily restraint, "the core of the liberty protected by the due process clause," is implicated by subjecting residents of retardation facilities to physical restraints.[87] Furthermore, the Court has recognized that "freedom of personal choice in matters of marriage and family life" is a liberty interest[88] implicated by statutory prohibitions and restrictions on the sale or distribution of contraceptives,[89] on abortion,[90] and on the right to marry,[91] and by zoning limits on family living arrangements.[92]

The Due Process Clauses have thus been given a gradually expanding construction by the Supreme Court. They are now read to impose substantive and not merely procedural limitations on governmental actions intruding on liberty or property interests. Moreover, the Court has expanded the concept of liberty protected by due process considerably beyond its historic origins of freedom from bodily restraint. It now includes the full range of privileges regarded both at common law and as essential to the pursuit of happiness. The Court has construed the Due Process Clause of the Fourteenth Amendment not only to incorporate virtually all of the specific provisions of the Bill of Rights,[93] but also to protect liberty interests not specifically enumerated in the Constitution, expressing the view that the

---

[80]347 U.S. 497, 499–500 (1954).

[81]*Id.* at 499–500.

[82]Aptheker v. Secretary of State, 378 U.S. 506, 505–06 (1964); Kent v. Dulles, 357 U.S. 116, 125–26 (1958) (dicta).

[83]Ingraham v. Wright, 430 U.S. 651, 673–74 (1977).

[84]Youngberg v. Romeo, 457 U.S. 307, 315–16 (1982).

[85]Bell v. Wolfish, 441 U.S. 520, 535 & n.16 (1979).

[86]Vitek v. Jones, 445 U.S. 480, 492 (1980).

[87]Youngberg v. Romeo, 457

[88]Zablocki v. Redhail, 434 U.S. 374, 384–85 & n.10 (1978) (concluding that right of privacy protects individual's decision whether or not to marry); Smith v. Organization of Foster Families for Equality & Reform, 431 U.S. 816, 842 (1977) (concluding that right of privacy exists with respect to family life); Moore v. City of E. Cleveland, 431 U.S. 494, 499 (1977) (same); Cleveland Board of Educ. v. LaFleur, 414 U.S. 632, 639–40 (1974). *See also* Kelley v. Johnson, 425 U.S. 238, 244 (1976) (concluding that there is "freedom of choice with respect to certain basic matters of procreation, marriage, and family life").

[89]Carey v. Population Servs. Int'l, 431 U.S. 678 (1977); Eisenstadt v. Baird, 405 U.S. 438 (1972); Griswold v. Connecticut, 381 U.S. 479 (1965).

[90]Planned Parenthood v. Casey, 505 US. 833 (1992); Thornburgh v. American College of Obstetricians & Gynecologists, 476 U.S. 747 (1986); City of Akron v. Akron Center for Reproductive Health, 462 U.S. 416 (1983); Planned Parenthood v. Danforth, 428 U.S. 52 (1976); Roe v. Wade, 410 U.S. 113 (1973).

[91]Turner v. Safley, 482 U.S. 78 (1978); Zablocki v. Redhail, 434 U.S. 374 (1978); *see* Loving v. Virginia, 388 U.S. 1 (1967).

[92]Moore v. City of E. Cleveland, 431 U.S. 494 (1977).

[93]*See* GUNTHER, *supra* note 12, at 419–20; TRIBE, *supra* note 22, § 11–2, at 567–69; *see, e.g.,* Duncan v. Louisiana, 391 U.S. 145, 148 (1968).

Framers believed that "the full scope of the liberty guaranteed by the Due Process Clause cannot be found in or limited by the precise terms of the specific guarantee elsewhere provided in the Constitution."[94] As the Court has indicated, "[i]n a constitution for free people, there can be no doubt that the meaning of "liberty" must be broad indeed."[95]

For the purposes of this discussion, the question then becomes whether the mental health treatment techniques to which patients and some offenders are subjected involuntarily intrude on any of these protected "liberty" interests. As chapter 1 mentions, the Supreme Court in two cases decided in the 1990s—*Washington v. Harper* and *Riggins v. Nevada*—determined that involuntary administration of antipsychotic medication involves a serious intrusion on the individual's "significant liberty interest" protected by due process.[96] Yet the Court did not explain precisely what liberty interest was implicated or analyze the standard of constitutional scrutiny that should be applied. Do these drugs (and other intrusive mental health treatment approaches) invade a "fundamental" liberty interest, requiring strict scrutiny? By failing to clarify the nature of the liberty interest it found to be involved in *Harper* and *Riggins*, the court left this question substantially open. A detailed analysis of the differing types of liberty that might be implicated by involuntary treatment is therefore necessary.

C. Liberty Interests Implicated by Involuntary Mental Health Treatment

Three liberty interests are arguably implicated when government imposes unwanted mental health treatment. These are related although somewhat distinct interests often associated with the constitutional right of privacy—the liberty interests in bodily integrity, in mental privacy, and in individual autonomy. Each is analyzed separately.

1. The Liberty Interest in Bodily Integrity

The common law traditionally has accorded special protection to freedom from unwarranted personal contact. English law dating back at least to the mid-13th century provided a tort remedy—the writ of trespass *viet armis*—for unauthorized contacts with the person.[97] This gradually evolved into the modern tort of battery, which is premised on

---

[94]Moore v. City of E. Cleveland, 431 U.S. 494, 502 (1977) (quoting Poe v. Ullman, 367 U.S. 497, 543 (1961) (Harlan, J., dissenting)). *See* 3 J. STORY, COMMENTARIES ON THE CONSTITUTION OF THE UNITED STATES 715–16 (1833) ([T]he "Bill of Rights presumes the existence of a substantial body of rights not specifically enumerated but easily perceived in the broad concept of liberty and so numerous and so obvious as to preclude listing them."); TRIBE, *supra* note 22, § 11–3, at 569–70. This broad conception of due process as extending to the protection of unenumerated rights is also supported by the text of the Ninth Amendment, *see* U.S. CONST. amend. IX ("The enumeration in the Constitution of certain rights, shall not be construed to deny or disparage others retained by the people."), and by the debates on ratification of the Constitution. *See* ELY, *supra* note 2, at 34–41; Levy, *The Bill of Rights, in* ESSAYS ON THE MAKING OF THE CONSTITUTION 258, 282 (L. Levy ed., 2d ed. 1987); Richards, *Constitutional Legitimacy and Constitutional Privacy*, 61 N.Y.U. L. REV. 800, 840–42 (1986).

[95]Board of Regents v. Roth, 408 U.S. 564, 572 (1972).

[96]Riggins v. Nevada, 504 U.S. 127, 133–34 (1992); Washington v. Harper, 494 U.S. 210, 221 (1990).

[97]F. MAITLAND, THE FORMS OF ACTION AT COMMON LAW 40, 43, 53 (1971 ed.). *See generally* Dreiser, *The Development of Principle in Trespass*, 27 YALE L.J. 220 (1917); Woodbine, *The Origins of the Action of Trespass*, 33 YALE L.J. 799 (1924).

protection of the individual's interest in bodily integrity and physical security.[98] Recognition of this interest in bodily integrity was not limited, however, to the law of torts. The thirty-ninth article of Magna Carta provided that an individual could not be deprived of personal security "except by the legal judgment of his peers or by the law of the land."[99] Moreover, Blackstone identified "the right of personal security" as one of the three elements of "liberty" guaranteed to all English citizens.[100]

This interest in personal security and bodily integrity received early recognition in American constitutional history. In *Union Pacific Railway Co. v. Botsford*,[101] decided in 1891, the Supreme Court held that plaintiffs in civil injury suits may not be forced to submit to surgical examination concerning the extent of injuries sustained and stated that "[n]o right is held more sacred or is more carefully guarded by the common law, than the right of every individual to the possession and control of his own person, free from all restraint or interference of others, unless by clear and unquestionable authority of the law."[102] Although the *Botsford* Court did not purport to announce a constitutional right,[103] it referred broadly to the "inviolability of the person," the invasion of which was "an indignity, an assault, and a trespass. . . ."[104] In an 1894 case, the Court quoted a prior lower court opinion by Justice Field, stating that "of all the rights of the citizen, few are of greater importance or more essential to his peace and happiness than the right of personal security. . . [which] involves . . . protection of his person from assault. . . ."[105] In *Jacobson v. Massachusetts*,[106] the 1905 compulsory vaccination case discussed earlier, the Court found that although there exists "a sphere within which the individual may assert the supremacy of his own will" against interference by the state, the police power interest in protecting the public health from epidemics justifies reasonable regulations that impinge on the "control of one's body."[107]

Language in several Fourth Amendment cases dealing with body searches also supports constitutional protection for bodily integrity.[108] "The overriding function of the Fourth Amendment," the Court has noted, "is to protect personal privacy and dignity against

---

[98]*See* RESTATEMENT OF TORTS §§ 13, 18 (1934); RESTATEMENT (SECOND) OF TORTS §§ 13, 18, 19 (1965).

[99]*See* Shattuck, *supra* note 42, at 372–73 (*quoted in* Ingraham v. Wright, 430 U. S. 651, 637 n.41 (1977)).

[100]1 W. BLACKSTONE, COMMENTARIES 134; Shattuck, *supra* note 42, at 373. The right to personal security was also included by Chancellor Kent in his definition of the "inalienable rights" of citizens. 2 J. KENT, COMMENTARIES ON AMERICAN LAW 1–13, 32–39 (O. Holmes ed. 12th ed. 1873).

[101]141 U.S. 250 (1891).

[102]*Id.* at 252.

[103]*See* Sibbach v. Wilson & Co., 312 U.S. 1, 11 (1941); Schlagenhauf v. Holder, 379 U.S. 104, 112–14 (1964); *but see Sibbach,* 312 U.S. at 17–18 (Frankfurter, J., dissenting) (although *Botsford* has "no constitutional sanction," it expresses strong historical concern for the inviolability of the body).

[104]141 U.S. at 252.

[105]Interstate Commerce Commission v. Brimson, 154 U.S. 447, 479 (1894) (quoting *In re* Pacific Ry. Comm'n, 32 Fed. Rep. 241, 250 (1887)).

[106]197 U.S. 11 (1905).

[107]*Id.* at 29.

[108]Fourth Amendment cases were cited by Justice Douglas in his opinion for the Court in Griswold v. Connecticut, 381 U.S. 479, 484–85 (1965), recognizing a constitutional right of privacy in the "penumbras" of various Bill of Rights protections. One of these opinions—Boyd v. United States, 116 U.S. 616, 630 (1886) (Bradley, J., dissenting)—had quoted Lord Camden's opinion in Entick v. Carrington, 19 Howell's St. Tr. 1029

unwarranted intrusion by the State.''[109] In a leading Fourth Amendment case the Court cited *Botsford* in referring to the ''inestimable right of personal security.''[110] In *Breithaupt v. Abram,* the Court upheld the taking of a blood test to establish that a driver was intoxicated, finding that

> [a]s against the right of an individual that his person be held inviolable, even against so slight an intrusion as is involved in applying a blood test of the kind to which millions of Americans submit as a matter of course nearly every day, must be weighed the interests of society in the scientific determination of intoxication, one of the great causes of the mortal hazards of the road.[111]

Reaffirming this decision in *Schmerber v. California,*[112] the Court noted that ''[t]he integrity of an individual's person is a cherished value of our society'' and cautioned that ''more substantial intrusions, or intrusions under other conditions'' might well be treated differently than the ''minor intrusions . . . under stringent limited conditions'' involved in the blood test at issue.[113] Significantly, the *Schmerber* Court noted that ''searches involving intrusions beyond the body's surface'' could not be justified ''on the mere chance that desired evidence might be obtained'' but would required ''a clear indication that in fact such evidence will be found. . . .''[114] The Court also distinguished these blood test cases from its prior decision in *Rochin v. California,*[115] which had found a degrading and unhygienic body search to violate due process. In *Rochin,* drugs swallowed by the defendant were extracted by a stomach pump, a method found to ''shock the conscience'' in violation of due process.

   In more recent cases, the Court has explicitly recognized that ''[a]mong the historic liberties'' protected by the Due Process Clauses ''was a right to be free from and to obtain judicial relief for, unjustified intrusions on personal security.''[116] Although recognizing a ''*de minimus* level of imposition with which the Constitution is not concerned,'' the Court in

---

(1765), referring to the ''indefeasible right of personal security. . . .'' For Fourth Amendment cases dealing with body searches, see Schmerber v. California, 384 U.S. 757, 771 (1966) (finding compulsory blood test of suspected intoxicated driver to be ''routine'' and to involve ''virtually no risk, trauma, or pain'' and thus upholding compulsory blood test against Fourth Amendment attack); Winston v. Lee, 470 U.S. 753, 761, 765–66 (finding surgical removal of bullet from criminal suspect's body for use as evidence to be ''severe'' intrusion presenting disputed ''medical risks'' and thus holding that such procedure would violate Fourth Amendment).

[109]Schmerber v. California, 384 U.S. 757, 767 (1966).

[110]Terry v. Ohio, 392 U.S. 1, 8–9 (1968). *See also id.* at 109 ('' '[T]he Fourth Amendment protects people, not places,' and wherever an individual may harbor a 'reasonable expectation of privacy,' he is entitled to be free from unreasonable governmental intrusion.'') (quoting Katz v. United States, 398 U.S. 347, 351 (1968)), and *id.* at 361 (Harlan, J., concurring).

[111]352 U.S. 432, 439 (1957).

[112]384 U.S. 757, 772 (1966).

[113]*Id.* at 772.

[114]*Id.* at 769–70.

[115]342 U.S. 165 (1952).

[116]Ingraham v. Wright, 430 U.S. 651, 673 (1977); *accord,* Youngberg v. Romeo, 457 U.S. 307, 315 (1982); Vitek v. Jones, 445 U.S. 480, 492 (1980).

Ingraham v. Wright found that school paddling involving "restraining the child and inflicting appreciable physical pain" implicated this liberty interest.[117] In a subsequent case that is significant to the right-to-refuse-treatment question, the Supreme Court quoted the language from the school paddling case concerning constitutional protection against "unjustified intrusions on personal security" in concluding that due process required a hearing prior to involuntary transfer of a prisoner to a mental hospital.[118] The Court found that "[c]ompelled treatment in the form of mandatory behavior modification programs" as a treatment for mental illness implicated this liberty interest protected by the Constitution.[119] In a subsequent case involving a resident of a mental retardation facility, the Court held that the due process liberty interest in "personal security" supports a constitutional right to reasonably safe conditions of confinement and freedom from unreasonable bodily restraints, both of which survive involuntary commitment.[120]

Lower courts have treated these Supreme Court cases as providing support for constitutional protection of bodily privacy against forced treatment that is intrusive and more than *de minimus* in its effects. For example, in a Ninth Circuit Court of Appeals case the right to bodily privacy was applied in the prison context to permit a damage action under the Civil Rights Act for a state prisoner subjected to hemorrhoid surgery without his consent and over his expressed objections.[121] The court found "a constitutionally protected right to be secure in the privacy in one's own body against invasions by the state except where necessary to support a compelling state interest."[122] In a case decided by the Seventh Circuit Court of Appeals, the court found that compulsory electroconvulsive therapy implicated the constitutional privacy interest in "bodily integrity, personal security and personal dignity."[123] This constitutional interest in "bodily integrity, personal security and personal dignity" has been consistently recognized by state and lower federal courts in cases decided prior to *Harper* and *Riggins* involving involuntary administration of psychotropic medication.[124]

These lower court decisions, finding the liberty interest in bodily integrity and personal security to be implicated by intrusive organic therapies such as electroconvulsive therapy

---

[117]Ingraham v. Wright, 430 U.S. at 674. Although the Court in *Ingraham* rejected the contention that school paddling constituted cruel and unusual punishment, finding the Eighth Amendment inapplicable in the schools, 430 U.S. at 674, the Court did not consider whether such corporal punishment violated substantive due process, because the grant of certiorari was limited so as to exclude this question. *Id.* at 673 & n.12.

[118]Vitek v. Jones, 445 U.S. 480, 492 (1980).

[119]*Id.*

[120]Youngberg v. Romeo, 457 U.S. 308, 315–16 (1982).

[121]Runnels v. Rosendale, 489 F.2d 733 (9th Cir. 1974).

[122]*Id.* at 735.

[123]Lojuk v. Quandt, 706 F.2d 1456, 1465 (7th Cir. 1983).

[124]Bee v. Greaves, 744 F.2d 1387, 1393 (10th Cir. 1984), *cert. denied,* 469 U.S. 1214 (1985) (constitutional "liberty interest in freedom from physical and mental restraint of the kind potentially imposed by antipsychotic drugs"); Johnson v. Silvers, 742 F.2d 823, 825 (4th Cir. 1984) ("the forcible administration of antipsychotic drugs present a sufficiently analogous intrusion upon bodily security [to the bodily restraints involved in *Youngberg*] to give rise to such a protected liberty interest"); Rogers v. Okin, 634 F.2d 650, 653 (1st Cir. 1980) (constitutional right "in being left free by the state to decide . . . whether to submit to the serious and potentially harmful medical

and psychotropic medication, seem plainly correct and provide at least a partial doctrinal foundation for the Supreme Court's ambiguous substantive due process holdings in *Washington v. Harper* and *Riggins v. Nevada*. In both cases, the Court stressed the intrusive physical effects of antipsychotic medication and its side effects. However, the Court never clarified the nature of the liberty interest it found to be implicated. By emphasizing the physical intrusions, however, the Court at least implied that the liberty interest in bodily integrity and personal security was involved.

---

treatment that is represented by the administration of antipsychotic drugs'' derived from ''the penumbral right to privacy, bodily integrity or personal security''), *vacated and remanded sub nom.* Mills v. Rogers, 457 U.S. 291 (1982), *on remand*, 738 F.2d 1 (1st Cir. 1984); Osgood v. District of Columbia, 567 F. Supp. 1026, 1032 (D.D.C. 1983) (same); Scott v. Plante, 532 F.2d 939, 946 n.9 (3d Cir. 1976) (''right to bodily privacy''); Project Release v. Prevost, 551 F. Supp. 1298, 1309 (E.D.N.Y. 1982), *aff'd*, 722 F.2d 960 (2d Cir. 1983) (''[f]orceable medication to alter mental processes and limit physical movement . . . analogous to bodily restraint''); Davis v. Hubbard, 506 F. Supp. 915, 930 (N.D. Ohio 1980) (''bodily integrity'' and ''personal dignity''); Rennie v. Klein, 462 F. Supp. 1131, 1144 (D.N.J. 1978) (''the right of privacy is broad enough to include the right to protect one's mental processes from governmental interference'' and the ''individual's autonomy over his own body''), *aff'd in part, modified in part, and remanded*, 653 F.2d 836 (3d Cir. 1980) (en banc), *vacated and remanded*, 458 U.S. 1119 (1982), *on remand*, 720 F.2d 266 (3d Cir. 1983) (en banc); Large v. Superior Court, 714 P.2d 399, 406 (Ariz. 1986) (en banc) (psychotropic medication imposed for controlling behavior violates due process right to freedom from bodily restraint); Anderson v. Arizona, 633 P.2d 570, 574 (Ariz. Ct. App. 1982) (due process liberty interest in freedom from bodily restraint ''[t]o the extent that medication is administered forceably and/or for the purpose of accomplishing bodily restraint''); Rogers v. Commissioner, 458 N.E.2d 308, 314 (Mass. 1983) (right to refuse psychotropic medication ''has constitutional and common law origins . . . which protect each person's 'strong interest in being free from non–consensual invasion of his bodily integrity' ''); Opinion of the Justices, 465 A.2d 484, 488 (N.H. 1983) (state constitution affords mentally ill persons ''a right to be free from unjustified intrusion upon their personal security''); *In re* K.K.B., 609 P.2d 747, 749 (Okla. 1980) (psychotropic drugs ''are intrusive in nature and an invasion of the body'' in violation of constitutional right to privacy).

Several years ago it appeared likely that the Supreme Court would resolve the question whether involuntary treatment with psychotropic drugs implicates a liberty interest protected by due process. The Court had granted certiorari in the Boston State Hospital case, in which the lower courts had recognized such a liberty interest. Rogers v. Okin, *supra*. In the Supreme Court, the parties agreed that the Constitution ''recognizes a liberty interest in avoiding the unwarranted administration of antipsychotic drugs,'' Mills v. Rogers, 457 U.S. 291, 299 (1982), and the Court ''assume[d] for purposes of [its] decision that involuntarily committed mental patients do retain liberty interests protected directly by the Constitution, . . . and that these interests are implicated by the involuntary administration of antipsychotic drugs.'' *Id.* at 299 n.16. However, the Court declined to resolve the issue in light of an intervening decision by the Supreme Judicial Court of Massachusetts recognizing a right to refuse psychotropic drugs as a matter of state law in a related context. *See* Guardianship of Roe, III, 521 N.E.2d 74 (Mass. 1981). The Court thus vacated the judgment in *Rogers* and remanded for consideration by the lower courts of whether the state court decision had rendered unnecessary resolution of the federal constitutional question. *See* Rogers v. Okin, 738 F.2d 1 (1st Cir. 1984) (on remand). Although the Supreme Court in *Rogers* thus avoided deciding whether the Constitution protects such a liberty interest, its opinion ''appears to indicate that there is such an interest.'' Project Release v. Prevost, 722 F.2d 960, 979 (2d Cir. 1983); *accord* S. Brakel et al., The Mentally Disabled and the Law 345 (3d ed. 1985). *See also* Vitek v. Jones, 445 U.S. 480 (1980) (liberty interest implicated by transfer of prisoner to mental hospital for psychiatric treatment, including psychotropic drugs, given the stigma of mental hospitalization).

The intrusive treatment techniques, such as electroconvulsive therapy and psychotropic medication, as well as the most intrusive treatments on the continuum of intrusiveness—the surgical interventions of psychosurgery[125] and electronic stimulation of the brain[126]—are characterized by direct physical interventions into the body and by effects that cannot be resisted.[127] Both psychosurgery and electronic stimulation of the brain are highly experimental techniques involving brain surgery, a profound intrusion of bodily integrity. Electroconvulsive therapy involves the passage of an electrical current through the brain by the means of electrodes applied to the patient's temples.[128] Muscle-relaxing drugs and anesthesia are administered, and the patient loses consciousness and then experiences electrically induced convulsions. This technique is thus both hazardous and extremely intrusive physically. Psychotropic drugs also involve intrusion into the body, with physical side effects and toxic reactions that are sometimes quite serious and irreversible.[129]

The conclusion that involuntary administration of the surgical and organic treatment techniques implicate a constitutional right of privacy protecting bodily integrity also is supported by the Supreme Court's decision in *Winston v. Lee*.[130] In that case, the Court affirmed an injunction against an involuntary surgical operation to remove a bullet from the chest of a suspect charged with attempted robbery. Although it applied the Fourth Amendment's ban on unreasonable searches and seizures, rather than the substantive due process, the *Winston* Court noted that the Fourth Amendment "protects 'expectations of privacy,' . . . the individual's expectations that in certain places and at certain times he has 'the right to be let alone—the most comprehensive of rights and the one most valued by civilized men.' "[131] The Court found that a compelled surgical intrusion into an individual's body for evidence "implicates expectations of privacy and security of such magnitude that the intrusion may be 'unreasonable' even if likely to produce evidence of a crime."[132] The

---

[125]*See supra* chapter 8.

[126]*See supra* chapter 7.

[127]*See* Katz, *The Right to Treatment—An Enchanting Legal Fiction?*, 36 U. CHI. L. REV. 755, 776–77 (1969); Shapiro, *Legislating the Control of Behavior Control: Autonomy and the Coercive Use of Organic Therapies*, 47 S. CAL. L. REV. 237, 240–44 (1974); Winick, *Legal Limitations on Correctional Therapy and Research*, 65 MINN. L. REV. 331, 365–73 (1981).

[128]*See supra* chapter 6; THE PSYCHIATRIC THERAPIES: THE AMERICAN PSYCHIATRIC ASSOCIATION COMM'N ON PSYCHIATRIC THERAPIES 218–25 (T. Karasu ed., 1984) [hereinafter PSYCHIATRIC THERAPIES]; T. DETRE & H. JARECKI, MODERN PSYCHIATRIC TREATMENT 635–55 (1971); L. KALINOWSKY & P. HOCH, SOMATIC TREATMENTS IN PSYCHIATRY 128–207 (1977); PSYCHOBIOLOGY OF CONVULSIVE THERAPY (M. Fink et al. eds., 1974).

[129]*See supra* chapter 5; DETRE & JARECKI, *supra* note 128, at 579–84 (antipsychotics), 602–06 (antidepressants); J. JANICAK ET AL., PRINCIPLES AND PRACTICE OF PSYCHOPHARMACOTHERAPY 164–83 (adverse effects of antipsychotics), 271–80 (adverse effects of antidepressants) (1993); A. SCHATZBERG & J. COLE, MANUAL OF CLINICAL PSYCHOPHARMOCOLOGY 57–63 (antidepressants), 110–27 (antipsychotics) (1991); American College of Neuropsychopharmacology—Food and Drug Administration Task Force, *Neurological Syndromes Associated with Antipsychotic Drug Use: A Special Report*, 28 ARCHIVES GEN. PSYCHIATRY 463 (1973); Arrigo, *Paternalism, Civil Commitment and Illness Politics: Assessing the Current Debate and Outlining Future Direction*, 7 J. L. & HEALTH 131, 148 (1992–93); Cichon, *The Right to "Just Say No": A History and Analysis of the Right to Refuse Antipsychotic Drugs*, 93 LA. L. REV. 283, 297–310 (1992); Davis & Glassman, *Antidepressant Drugs, in* 2 COMPREHENSIVE TEXTBOOK OF PSYCHIATRY 1627, 1644–48 (H. Kaplan & B. Sadock eds., 5th ed. 1989); Davis et al., *Antipsychotic Drugs, id.* at 1591, 1620 (table 31.3–20); Jarvik, *Drugs Used in the Treatment of Psychiatric Disorders, in* THE PHARMACOLOGICAL NATURE OF THERAPEUTICS 165 (antipsychotics), 174–86 (antidepressants) (L. Goodman & A. Gilman eds., 1970); Winick, *Psychotropic Medication and Competence to Stand Trial*, 1977 AM. B. FOUND. RES. J. 769, 782 (antipsychotics), 786–89 (antidepressants).

[130]470 U.S. 753 (1985).

[131]*Id.* at 1616 (quoting Olmstead v. United States, 277 U.S. 438, 478 (1928) (Brandeis, J., dissenting)).

[132]*Id.* at 759.

Court distinguished its prior decision in *Schmerber v. California*,[133] upholding against Fourth Amendment attack a compelled blood test of a suspected intoxicated driver. A blood test, even though it involved piercing the individual's skin, constituted merely a minimal intrusion on bodily privacy, the Court held, in view of its "routine" nature in everyday life and the fact that it "involves virtually no risk, trauma, or pain."[134] By contrast, the surgery at issue in *Winston v. Lee* involved an attempt by the state to "take control of respondent's body, and since it involved general anesthesia, to 'drug him' with narcotics and barbiturates into a state of unconsciousness...."[135] Moreover, the proposed operation entailed a "severe" intrusion on privacy interests "with medical risks ... [which] although apparently not extremely severe, are a subject of considerable dispute...."[136] The "extent of intrusion upon the individual's dignitary interests in personal privacy and bodily integrity" brought about by the operation far exceeded that of the blood test in *Schmerber* and produced far more "damage [to] the individual's sense of personal privacy and security...."[137]

In view of their effects on a patient's consciousness, the considerable risk of serious bodily side effects, and their impact on the patient's sense of personal privacy and security, the surgical and organic treatment techniques seem more analogous to the surgical operation in *Winston v. Lee* than to the routine blood test in *Schmerber v. California*. Thus, with the exception of bodily intrusions that are merely *de minimus*, involuntary surgical and organic interventions for patients and offenders should be deemed to intrude on the due process liberty interest in bodily integrity and personal security, requiring substantive justification by the government.

The verbal and most of the behavioral techniques, however, would not seem to implicate the liberty interest in bodily integrity. Verbal therapies involve verbal or nonverbal communication between patient and therapist but no bodily invasion.[138] Although the sound waves emitted by therapists may intrude into the ears of patients, this intrusion would seem within the *de minimus* exception.[139]

Some of the behavioral techniques, particularly the aversive programs using electric shocks or drugs that cause nausea or apnea, involve direct physical intrusions and would therefore implicate a liberty interest in bodily integrity.[140] Other techniques used in aversive programs, however, such as forfeiture of privileges, verbal disapproval, or isolated confinements, are not at all physically intrusive.[141] Nor are the techniques using positive reinforce-

---

[133]384 U.S. 757 (1966).

[134]384 U.S. at 771.

[135]Winston v. Lee, 470 U.S. at 765.

[136]*Id.* at 766.

[137]*Id.* at 761–62.

[138]*See supra* chapter 3.

[139]*See* Public Utils. Comm'n. v. Pollak, 343 U.S. 451 (1952) (transit company regulated by federal agency broadcasting radio advertisements in buses and streetcars held not to violate Fifth Amendment privacy rights).

[140]*See supra* chapter 4.

[141]Although these techniques do not implicate the liberty interest in bodily integrity, they may implicate other liberty or property interests protected by due process, requiring substantive justification by the state. For loss of privilege, for example, if the privilege forfeited is one to which the individual has a legitimate claim of entitlement under state law, it will be deemed a property interest. *See* Goss v. Lopez, 419 U.S. 565, 574 (1975); Board of Regents v. Roth, 408 U.S. 564, 577 (1972); Goldberg v. Kelly, 397 U.S. 254, 262–63 (1970); Winick, *supra* note 127, at 393. Moreover, the privilege forfeited may be a liberty interest protected either by state law or by the Constitution. *E.g.,* Mills v. Rogers, 457 U.S. 291, 301 (1982); Vitek v. Jones, 445 U.S. 480, 488–91 (1980); Wolff v. McDonnell, 410 U.S. 539, 557–78 (1974); Morrissey v. Brewer, 408 U.S. 471, 480–82 (1972). Similarly, isolated confinement also implicates a separate liberty interest in being free of external restraint. *E.g.,* Wolff v. McDonnell, *supra*; Enomoto v. Wright, 462 F. Supp. 397, 402–03 (N.D. Cal. 1976), *aff'd,* 434 U.S. 1052 (1978); *see* Youngberg v. Romeo, 430 U.S. 307, 316 (1982).

ment—the provision of rewards and reinforcements on the occurrence of behavioral responses sought to be established or strengthened.[142] Positive reinforcement procedures involving substantial entry-level deprivations may merit different treatment, however. Token economies and tier systems, for example, sometimes make basic personal requirements available contingent on behavior that conforms with program goals.[143] Decisions recognizing that the Constitution requires minimum conditions and standards for prisoners[144] and institutionalized mental patients[145] severely limit the use of these basic rights and privileges as reinforcers in positive reinforcement programs. Because the Supreme Court in *Youngberg v. Romeo* has held that the liberty interest in "personal security" supports a constitutional right on the part of residents of mental retardation facilities to reasonably safe conditions of confinement,[146] both prisoners and patients should be able to assert a similar liberty interest to attack positive reinforcement programs that involve entry-level deprivations falling below these minimum conditions and standards. Moreover, administrative regulations, such as those of the Federal Bureau of Prisons specifying minimum conditions and privileges for prisoners,[147] may also limit the use of such reinforcers in token or tier programs. With limited exceptions, then, the behavioral techniques do not intrude on the liberty interest in bodily integrity and personal security.

What level of judicial scrutiny is applied to the surgical and organic techniques that intrude on the liberty interest in bodily integrity? Although the Supreme Court in *Riggins* used the language of strict scrutiny in discussing the standards that would apply to consider the constitutionality of involuntary administration of antipsychotic drugs to a criminal defendant during trial, the Court's language was dicta and the serious impact of the medication on the defendant's trial rights leaves unclear whether these standards would apply in nontrial contexts.[148] Whether the level of justification required is the higher standard applied to the surgical intrusion in *Winston v. Lee* or the somewhat lesser standard applied to the routine blood test in *Schmerber* and *Breithaupt*[149] will depend on the nature of the intrusion involved and the seriousness and duration of its effects. Even lesser intrusions, if they go "beyond the body's surface,"[150] require more than minimal scrutiny.[151] That at least an intermediate level of scrutiny is required by such bodily invasions is indicated by the Court's statement in *Schmerber* that even so minor an intrusion as the routine blood test must

---

[142]*See supra* chapter 4.

[143]*See* Wexler, *Token and Taboo: Behavior Modification, Token Economies, and the Law*, 61 CAL. L. REV. 81, 84–90 (1973).

[144]*See, e.g.,* James v. Wallace, 533 F.2d 963 (5th Cir. 1976); *see* Winick, *supra* note 127, at 362.

[145]*See, e.g.,* Wyatt v. Stickney, 344 F. Supp. 373 (N.D. Ala. 1972), *aff'd sub nom.* Wyatt v. Aderholt, 503 F.2d 1305 (5th Cir. 1974); *see* Wexler, *supra* note 143, at 93–95.

[146]457 U.S. 308, 315–16 (1982); *see supra* note 120 and accompanying text.

[147]*See* 28 C.F.R. §§ 540–551 (1986). Regulations such as this give rise to both liberty and property interests, created not by the Constitution, but by positive law. *See supra* note 141.

[148]*See infra* chapter 15.

[149]Breithaupt v. Abram, 352 U.S. 432, 439 (1959).

[150]Schmerber v. California, 384. U.S. 757, 769 (1966).

[151]TRIBE, *supra* note 22, § 15–9, at 914–15:

Although compulsory vaccination, compelled blood tests, extractions of contraband narcotics from the rectal cavity, and even surgical removal of a bullet, have sometimes been upheld on a showing of clear necessity, procedural regularity, and minimal pain, in each case the matter has been taken with enough seriousness to warrant a conclusion that an aspect of personhood was at stake, and that government's burden was to provide more than minimal justification for its action.

be justified by more than just some chance that evidence will be found; it requires "a clear indication" that evidence will be obtained.[152]

The Court's earlier treatment of compulsory vaccination in *Jacobson v. Massachusetts*[153] also supports the application of at least intermediate scrutiny. Clearly, vaccination to "stamp out the disease of smallpox"[154] and to prevent its spread is a public health measure at the heart of the state's police power, a compelling end by any measure. Significantly, however, the *Jacobson* Court also scrutinized the means used by the state to accomplish these compelling ends. The Court noted that[155]

> it might be that an acknowledged power of a local community to protect itself against an epidemic threatening the safety of all might be exercised in particular circumstances and in reference to particular persons in such an arbitrary, unreasonable manner, or might go far beyond what was reasonably required for the safety of the public, as to authorize or compel the courts to interfere for the protection of such persons.

The "methods employed" in *Jacobson*, however, survived this scrutiny, the Court finding that they could not be said to have "no real or substantial relation to the protection of the public health and the public safety."[156] Moreover, the petitioner had not asserted that the vaccination presented any threat to his health, although the Court was careful to note that the result might be otherwise if he was "not at the time a fit subject of the vaccination," or if it "would seriously impair his health, or probably cause his death."[157] This analysis of the means used by the state suggests that the intrusion into bodily integrity presented by even a routine and nondangerous vaccination required considerably more than the minimal scrutiny of the rational relationship test.

Intrusions beyond the body's surface will thus implicate due process, requiring some governmental justification, the precise level of which will depend on the seriousness of the intrusion involved and the resulting impact on personal security and individual dignity.

---

[152]384 U.S. at 773.

[153]197 U.S. 11 (1905).

[154]*Id.* at 31.

[155]*Id.* at 28.

[156]*Id.* at 31.

[157]*Id.* at 39. The Court's decision in Buck v. Bell, 274 U.S. 200 (1927), upholding compulsory sterilization of an institutionalized "mentally defective" woman, also bears analysis. In an opinion by Justice Holmes, the Court found that the plaintiff was a "feebleminded" woman who was the daughter of a "feebleminded mother in the same institution, and the mother of an illegitimate feebleminded child." *Id.* at 205. The procedure used—salpingectomy—was described by the Court as "without serious pain or substantial danger to life . . . ." *Id.* The Court proceeded on the assumption that "heredity plays an important part in the transmission of insanity, imbecility . . . ." *Id.* at 206. Given these assumptions, the procedure was upheld as an exercise of the state's police power, "in order to prevent our being swamped with incompetence." *Id.* at 207. "Three generations of imbeciles," Holmes concluded, "are enough." *Id.* This opinion, of course, is much criticized, *see, e.g.,* Lombardo, *Three Generations, No Imbeciles: A New Light on* Buck v. Bell, 60 N.Y.U. L. REV. 30 (1985), and the assumptions about heredity upon which it was based are false. *See, e.g., id.* Moreover, the case's constitutional premises have been seriously undercut by an intervening decision characterizing the right to procreate as "one of the basic civil rights of men . . . . fundamental to the very existence and survival of the race." Skinner v. Oklahoma *ex rel.* Williamson, 316 U.S. 535, 541 (1942). In any case, given the Court's assumptions and the unavailability in 1927 of other reasonable methods of preventing pregnancy, such as the birth control pill, its approach may not be inconsistent with the analysis in text that intrusions "beyond the body's surface" should merit at least an intermediate level of scrutiny.

2. Mental Privacy

The constitutional right of privacy invoked in *Griswold v. Connecticut*,[158] and now properly seen as an aspect of the liberty protected by the Due Process Clauses,[159] is sometimes traced to Justice Brandeis's celebrated dissenting opinion in *Olmstead v. United States,* an early wiretapping case.[160] Dissenting from the Court's refusal to treat wiretapping as an invasion of the Fourth Amendment, Brandeis stated:[161]

> The makers of our Constitution undertook to secure conditions favorable to the pursuit of happiness. They recognized the significance of man's spiritual nature, of his feelings and of his intellect. They knew that only a part of his pain, pleasure and satisfactions of life are to be found in material things. They sought to protect Americans in their beliefs, their thoughts, their emotions and their sensations. They conferred, as against the Government, the right to be let alone—the most comprehensive of rights and the right most valued by civilized men.

To the extent that constitutional liberty protects a zone of privacy within which the individual has a "right to be let alone," it must encompass mental privacy. Indeed, Justice Douglas, the author of the *Griswold* Court opinion, probed this theme in an earlier dissenting opinion in *Public Utilities Commission v. Pollak,* the case involving the First and Fifth Amendment Due Process challenge to radio programming broadcast in streetcars and buses in the District of Columbia.[162] The *Pollak* Court spoke of a constitutional right of privacy[163] but rejected the contention that such a right in a public streetcar was equal to the privacy to which individuals are entitled in their own homes.[164] In dissent, Justice Douglas argued that "liberty" within the meaning of the Due Process Clause of the Fifth Amendment includes privacy, the "right to be let alone," which is the "beginning of all freedom."[165] "To think as one chooses, to believe what one wishes are important aspects of the Constitutional right to be let alone," Douglas stated.[166] "The right of privacy," he concluded, "is a powerful deterrent to any one who would control men's minds."[167]

The notion that constitutional privacy protects beliefs, thoughts, emotions, and sensations—in short, mental privacy—received substantial support in *Stanley v. Georgia,* the case discussed in the preceding chapter dealing with the possession of obscenity in the privacy of the home.[168] The *Stanley* Court quoted Brandeis's *Olmstead* dissent as a source for a fundamental "right to be free, except in very limited circumstances, from unwanted governmental intrusions into ones privacy."[169] In a prosecution for possession of obscene materials, the defendant asserted a constitutional right "to satisfy his intellectual and emotional needs in the privacy of his own home" and "to be free from state inquiry into the contents of his library."[170] In eloquent language, the Court stated that "[o]ur whole constitutional heritage rebels at the thought of giving government the power to control men's

---

[158]381 U.S. 479 (1965); *see supra* notes 32–38 and accompanying text.

[159]*See supra* notes 39–41 and accompanying text.

[160]277 U.S. 438, 478 (1928) (Brandeis, J., dissenting).

[161]*Id.*

[162]343 U.S. 451, 467–69 (1952) (Douglas, J., dissenting); *see supra* note 139 and accompanying text.

[163]343 U.S. at 463–64.

[164]*Id.* at 464.

[165]*Id.* at 467 (Douglas, J., dissenting).

[166]*Id.* at 468.

[167]*Id.* at 469.

[168]394 U.S. 557 (1969); *see supra* chapter 10.

[169]394 U.S. at 564.

[170]*Id.* at 565.

minds."[171] Government, the Court found, "cannot constitutionally premise legislation on the desirability of controlling a person's private thoughts."[172]

Although *Stanley* arose at the intersection of the First Amendment and the privacy of the home, it provides substantial support for the proposition that constitutional liberty protects mental privacy and limits governmental "power to control men's minds." Plainly, if government lacks the power to control the mind by regulating the content of an individual's library, it may not do so through mental health treatment interventions that regulate the mind more directly. Therapies intruding directly on mental processes in significant ways that are incapable of being resisted should thus be deemed to implicate this liberty interest in mental privacy.

Some state and lower federal court opinions have reached this conclusion in the context of intrusive therapies such as psychosurgery, psychotropic medication, and aversive conditioning. In *Mackey v. Procunier,* the Ninth Circuit Court of Appeals indicated that the use of the paralyzing drug succinycholine in a prison aversive conditioning program would "raise serious constitutional questions respecting . . . impermissible tinkering with the mental processes."[173] The *Kaimowitz* psychosurgery case also recognized a constitutional right of privacy extending to mental processes in holding involuntary psychosurgery to be unconstitutional:[174]

> There is no privacy more deserving of constitutional protection than that of one's mind. . . . Intrusion into one's intellect, when one is involuntarily detained and subject to the control of institutional authorities, is an intrusion into one's constitutionally protected right of privacy. If one is not protected in his thoughts, behavior, personality and identity, then the right of privacy becomes meaningless.

In *Souder v. McGuire,* the district court found that involuntary administration of psychotropic medication "amounts to an unwarranted governmental intrusion into the patient's thought processes in violation of his constitutional right to privacy."[175] The same conclusion concerning psychotropic drugs and mental privacy has been reached by several other federal courts.[176]

For reasons set out in detail in the preceding chapter dealing with the First Amendment, these decisions seem clearly correct and provide an additional doctrinal foundation for the Supreme Court's conclusion in *Washington v. Harper* and *Riggins v. Nevada* that intrusive treatments like antipsychotic medication implicate a liberty interest protected by due process. The intrusive surgical procedures—psychosurgery[177] and electronic stimulation of the brain[178]—intrude directly on mental processes with substantial effects, modifying the state of the brain itself in a way beyond the control of the patient. Not only does

---

[171]*Id.*

[172]*Id.* at 566.

[173]477 F.2d 877, 878 (9th Cir. 1973).

[174]Kaimowitz v. Michigan Dep't of Mental Health, No. 73-19434-AW (Mich. Cir. Ct. July 10, 1973).

[175]423 F. Supp. 830, 832 (E.D. Pa. 1976).

[176]*See, e.g.,* Bee v. Greaves, 744 F.2d 1387, 1392–93 (10th Cir. 1984), *cert. denied,* 469 U.S. 1214 (1985) (constitutional "liberty interest in freedom from physical and mental restraint"); Davis v. Hubbard, 506 F. Supp. 915, 933 (N.D. Ohio 1980) ("[T]he power to control men's minds" is inconsistent "with almost any concept of liberty."); Rennie v. Klein, 462 F. Supp. 1131, 1144 (D.N.J. 1978) ("[T]he right of privacy is broad enough to include the right to protect one's mental processes from governmental interference."), *aff'd in part, modified in part, and remanded,* 653 F.2d 836 (3d Cir. 1980) (en banc), *vacated and remanded,* 458 U.S. 1119 (1982), *on remand,* 720 F.2d 266 (3d Cir. 1983) (en banc).

[177]*See supra* chapter 8.

[178]*See supra* chapter 7.

electroconvulsive therapy render patients unconscious, but after regaining consciousness they remain in a state of confusion and disorientation for a period, and some patients experience persisting confusion and loss of memory.[179] In view of the impact of electroconvulsive therapy on mental processes and particularly on memory, this intrusion would clearly implicate the liberty interest in mental privacy.

Psychotropic medication by its very nature affects mental processes, both in its primary effects and in some of its side effects.[180] As the Supreme Court recognized in both *Harper* and *Riggins,* these drugs "alter the chemical balance in a patient's brain," producing "changes . . . in his or her cognitive processes."[181] Moreover, as Justice Kennedy noted in his concurring opinion in *Riggins,* these drugs are sedating, may interfere with concentration in ways that impede individuals' abilities to understand and follow trials in which they are involved, and may directly affect verbal and nonverbal communication, including speech itself.[182] As a result, these drugs should be deemed to implicate mental privacy.

With very few exceptions, such as the use of the drugs as aversive conditioners involved in *Mackey v. Procunier,*[183] the behavioral techniques do not interfere with mental processes in any irresistible, pervasive, or permanent fashion. Because psychotherapy and the other verbal techniques tend to work slowly, affording the patient the opportunity to accept or reject change, these techniques should not be deemed to implicate constitutional privacy. Although these techniques may have a massive impact on mental processes when the patient cooperates and desires change, these effects remain in the patient's control. Thus, only the surgical and organic treatment techniques should be deemed to implicate the liberty interest in mental privacy.

Intrusions on mental processes that are sufficiently serious to implicate the liberty interest in mental privacy would seem also to implicate the First Amendment.[184] These two separate constitutional protections thus converge to insulate mental processes from unjustified governmental interference. Because of the substantial overlap of these protections, the heightened level of judicial scrutiny applied in the First Amendment context—requiring compelling governmental ends and least restrictive means[185]—would appear appropriate here as well.

3. Privacy–Autonomy: Constitutional Protection for Personal Choice in Matters Vitally Affecting the Individual

Another branch of privacy doctrine that supports a constitutional right to refuse treatment is that recognizing a liberty interest "in independence in making certain kinds of important decisions."[186] Respect for individual autonomy is deeply rooted in American constitutional history and tradition, which were heavily influenced by Enlightenment views

---

[179]*See supra* chapter 6. Some confusion and loss of memory occurs in virtually all cases. *See* PSYCHIATRIC THERAPIES *supra* note 128, at 230; DETRE & JARECKI, *supra* note 128, at 641–44; Dornbush & Williams, *Memory and ECT, in* PSYCHOBIOLOGY OF CONVULSIVE THERAPY, *supra* note 128, at 199. *See generally* Harper & Wiens, *Electroconvulsive Therapy and Memory,* 161 J. NERVOUS & MENTAL DISEASES 245 (1975).

[180]*See supra* chapter 5.

[181]*Riggins,* 504 U.S. at 134; *Harper,* 494 U.S. at 229–30.

[182]*Riggins,* 504 U.S. at 142–43 (Kennedy, J., concurring).

[183]477 F.2d 877 (9th Cir. 1973); *see supra* note 173 and accompanying text.

[184]*See supra* chapter 10.

[185]*See id.*

[186]Whalen v. Roe, 429 U.S. 589, 599–600 (1977); *see generally* Winick, *On Autonomy: Legal and Psychological Perspectives,* 37 VILL. L. REV. 1705 (1992).

of popular sovereignty and limited government.[187] A central principle in the thinking of John Locke, the ideological father of the American Revolution,[188] was that[189]

> there ought to exist a certain minimum area of personal freedom which must on no account be violated; for if it is overstepped, the individual will find himself in an area too narrow for even that minimum development of his natural facilities which alone makes it possible to pursue, and even to conceive, the various ends which men hold good or right or sacred.

Jefferson regarded human rights as an indissoluble birthright, given by the Creator and therefore inalienable. When Jefferson emphasized the rights to "life, liberty, and the pursuit of happiness"[190] among those "inalienable rights"[191] with which all persons are endowed, he referred to a right that individuals had against the government to pursue their own ends in their own ways. Jefferson reiterated this ideal in his first Inaugural Address, calling for a "wise and frugal Government, which shall restrain men from injuring one another, [but] shall leave them otherwise free to regulate their own pursuits of industry and improvement."[192] To secure this right of personal autonomy, among other "blessings of liberty," the colonists ordained and established the Constitution.[193] The autonomy principle was absorbed into American legal theory and ultimately constitutionalized in the doctrine of substantive due process.[194]

Early recognition that substantive due process protects individual self-determination regarding important decisions came in Justice Bradley's dissent in the *Slaughter-House*

---

[187]*See* M. ADLER, WE HOLD THESE TRUTHS: UNDERSTANDING THE IDEAS AND IDEALS OF THE CONSTITUTION (1987); B. BAILYN, THE IDEOLOGICAL ORIGINS OF THE AMERICAN REVOLUTION 26–27 (1967) (concluding that Enlightenment theories were "directly influential in shaping the thought of the Revolutionary generation"); C. BECKER, THE DECLARATION OF INDEPENDENCE: A STUDY IN THE HISTORY OF POLITICAL IDEAS 24–79 (1942) (discussing pervasive influence of various Enlightenment theorists on Jefferson and others); Henkin, *supra* note 2, at 1412–13 (noting that Constitution blended concepts of popular sovereignty with limited government); Smith, *The Constitution and Autonomy*, 60 TEX. L. REV. 175, 176–80 (1982) (discussing theories of various Enlightenment theorists and their effect on early American political thought); Winick, *supra* note 186, at 1707–15 (analyzing philosophical foundations at autonomy in American political theory).

[188]*See* D. FARBER & S. SHERRY, A HISTORY OF THE AMERICAN CONSTITUTION 5–6, 9–12, 39, 259 (1990). *See also* J. ROCHE, COURTS AND RIGHTS 9–10 (1961) (noting Locke's "enormous impact" on colonial political thought); G. WOOD, THE CREATION OF THE AMERICAN REPUBLIC 1776–87, at 14, 283–84 (1969) (noting that Locke's social compact concept became increasingly significant after 1776). The ideological origins of the American Revolution also included the Scottish "moral sense" philosophers, whose thinking was fully consistent with the liberalism of Locke. *See* G. WILLS, INVENTING AMERICA (1978) (discussing the relationship between Locke's ideology and moral sense philosophy and concluding that Locke's ideology influenced moral sense philosophers).

[189]I. BERLIN, FOUR ESSAYS ON LIBERTY 124 (1977). The principle of autonomy is also reflected in two major traditions in modern Western philosophy—consequentialist theories, such as the utilitarianism of John Stuart Mill, and ontological theories, such as those of Immanuel Kant and, more recently, John Rawls. *See* I. KANT, FOUNDATIONS OF THE METAPHYSICS OF MORALS (L. Beck trans., 1949); J. MILL, ON LIBERTY (C. Shields ed., 1956); J. RAWLS, A THEORY OF JUSTICE (1971). *See also* J. FEINBERG, RIGHTS, JUSTICE, AND THE BOUNDS OF LIBERTY: ESSAYS IN SOCIAL PHILOSOPHY 110–29 (1980); Dworkin, *Paternalism, in* MORALITY AND THE LAW 107 (R. Wasserstrom ed., 1971); Morris, *Persons and Punishment,* 52 THE MONIST 475 (1968).

[190]THE DECLARATION OF INDEPENDENCE para. 2 (U.S. 1776)

[191]*Id.*

[192]Thomas Jefferson, First Inaugural Address (Mar. 4, 1801) *in* INAUGURAL ADDRESSES OF THE PRESIDENTS OF THE UNITED STATES 13, 15 (Bicentennial ed. 1989).

[193] *See* U.S. CONST. pmbl.

[194]*See* Winick, *supra* note 186, at 1715–43.

Cases of 1873, endorsing the right of occupational choice.[195] The Supreme Court ultimately adopted the principle that liberty includes occupational choice in the *Allgeyer* case in 1897.[196] In the 1905 compulsory vaccination case, *Jacobson v. Massachusetts,* the Court recognized the existence of "a sphere within which the individual may assert the supremacy of his own will" against government interference.[197] In *Meyer v. Nebraska*[198] and *Pierce v. Society of Sisters,*[199] the forerunners of modern privacy doctrine, the Court recognized that this "sphere" includes the liberty of parents "to direct the upbringing and education of [their] children."[200]

A significant application of the constitutional notion of privacy–autonomy occurred in *Griswold v. Connecticut,* in which the Court, striking down a state statutory ban on contraceptives, found a right of privacy inhering in the marital relationship.[201] By holding that the decision whether to use contraceptives was best left to those affected by that decision—the married couple—the Court recognized the autonomy of the individual in an important personal area of life. Moreover, the Court strictly scrutinized the statutory intrusion on this right of marital privacy. Quoting a First Amendment freedom of association case, the Court applied what it called the "familiar principle" that governmental purposes "may not be achieved by means which sweep unnecessarily broadly and thereby invade the area of protected freedoms."[202] That the Court's holding in *Griswold* involved individual autonomy rather than merely deference to the marital relationship was demonstrated in *Eisenstadt v. Baird,* in which a statute permitting distribution of contraceptives to married

---

[195]83 U.S. (16 Wall.) 36, 122 (1873); *see also* Butcher's Union v. Crescent City Co., 111 U.S. 746, 762 (1884) (Bradley, J., concurring) ("The right to follow any of the common occupations of life . . . is a large ingredient in the civil liberty of the citizen."). By this time, Judge Cooley, the most influential constitutional scholar of the period, had written that "the liberty protected by due process included the right of the individual to choose his own employment." COOLEY, *supra* note 20, at 231.

[196]165 U.S. 578 (1897). Recognition of a liberty interest in occupational choice does not mean that the state may not regulate the occupations. In a variety of cases, however, the Court has recognized that conditions or other qualifications imposed by occupational licensing schemes must as a matter of substantive due process bear a reasonable relationship to the competency of the individual to engage in the occupation in question. *See, e.g.,* Schware v. Board of Bar Examiners, 353 U.S. 232, 239 (1957); Douglas v. Noble, 261 U.S. 156, 168 (1923); Dent v. West Virginia, 129 U.S. 114, 123–24 (1889).

[197]197 U.S. 11, 29 (1905).

[198]262 U.S. 390 (1923). In *Meyer,* a parochial school teacher challenged a Nebraska statute that made it unlawful to teach foreign languages to students who had not yet passed the eighth grade. *Id.* at 396–97. The teacher had been convicted for teaching German to a 10-year-old child. *Id.* at 396. The Court determined that the Nebraska statute violated the Fourteenth Amendment. *Id.* at 402. In its analysis, the Court noted that the "liberty" guaranteed by the Fourteenth Amendment encompassed the teacher's right to teach and the parents' right to engage a foreign language instructor for their children. *Id.* at 400. Accordingly, the Court found that the state had impermissibly interfered with those protected rights. *Id.* at 402.

[199]268 U.S. 510 (1925). *Pierce* involved a challenge to Oregon's Compulsory Education Act, which required every person having custody of a school-age child to send the child "to a public school for the period of time a public school shall be held" during the year. *Id.* at 530. A parochial school challenged the Act, asserting that the Act interfered with "the rights of parents to choose schools," "the right of the child to influence the parent's choice," and the right of teachers to engage in their profession. *Id.* at 532. The Court held that the Act impermissibly interfered with "the liberty of parents and guardians to direct the upbringing and education of children under their control." *Id.* at 534–35.

[200]*Pierce,* 268 U.S. at 534. *See also* Parham v. J.R., 442 U.S. 584, 602 (1979).

[201]381 U.S. 479 (1965); *see supra* notes 32–38 and accompanying text.

[202]*Griswold,* 381 U.S. at 485 (quoting NAACP v. Alabama, 377 U.S. 288, 307 (1964)). Under the *Griswold* standard, the government must use the least restrictive means to accomplish its end. *See id.* Moreover, the end must be "compelling." *See id.* The Court also had previously applied such a stringent standard in Aptheker v. Secretary of State, 378 U.S. 500, 508 (1964) (right to travel).

but not unmarried persons was found unconstitutional.[203] The Court held that "[i]f the right of privacy means anything, it is the right of the *individual*, married or single, to be free from unwarranted governmental intrusion into matters so fundamentally affecting a person as the decision whether to bear or beget a child."[204]

One of the most significant expositions of the right to privacy–autonomy is the Supreme Court's 1973 opinion in *Roe v. Wade*, declaring that a woman's decision to have an abortion is within the protected zone of constitutional privacy.[205] This right of privacy, which the Court found protected by the Due Process Clause of the Fourteenth Amendment, was deemed "broad enough to encompass a woman's decision whether or not to terminate her pregnancy."[206] The Court stressed the serious detrimental consequences that would result from denying this choice to the pregnant woman:[207]

> Specific and direct harm medically diagnosable even in early pregnancy may be involved. Maternity, or additional offspring, may force upon the woman a distressful life and future. Psychological harm may be imminent. Mental and physical health may be taxed by child care. There is also the distress, for all concerned, associated with the unwanted child, and there is the problem of bringing a child into a family already unable, psychologically and otherwise, to care for it.

Although these considerations led the Court to find that the right of privacy concerning the abortion decision was "fundamental," the Court declined to treat it as an "absolute" right; rather, like other constitutional rights, it must yield to government regulation in appropriate circumstances.[208] As in *Griswold*, however, the Court used strict scrutiny, insisting that to predominate, any regulation of the abortion decision during the first two trimesters of pregnancy must advance a "compelling state interest," and "must be narrowly drawn to express only the legitimate state interest at stake."[209]

In subsequent decisions dealing with the abortion controversy, the Court reendorsed the principle of privacy–autonomy, stating that "the Constitution embodies a promise that a certain private sphere of individual liberty will be kept largely beyond the reach of government."[210] In *Thornburgh v. American College of Obstetricians & Gynecologists*, which broadly reaffirmed *Roe*, the Court explained the importance of the abortion decision to the woman involved and noted:[211]

---

[203]405 U.S. 438, 453–54 (1972); *see also* Carey v. Population Servs. Int'l, 431 U.S. 678 (1977) (applying *Griswold* to invalidate ban on sale of contraceptives to minors).

[204]405 U.S. at 453.

[205]410 U.S. 113 (1973). *Roe* involved a class action challenge to a Texas abortion law that criminalized abortions unless the abortions were performed to save the mother's life. *Id.* at 117–18. The Court held that the Texas statute impermissibly infringed on a woman's "right of privacy." *Id.* at 153.

[206]*Id.* at 153.

[207]*Id.*

[208]*Id.* at 155.

[209]*Id.* at 155–56. In the Court's view, the fetus is not viable, and thus is not a "person" during the first trimester of pregnancy. *See id.* at 163. Further, during the first trimester, the medical risks of abortion to women are no greater than those of childbirth. *See id.* On the basis of these premises, the Court concluded that the state interest cannot outweigh the woman's interest, and she therefore is free to make the abortion decision without state interference. *Id.* at 164. During the second trimester, when the medical risks of abortion increase, the state's interest in maternal health justifies some regulation of the abortion process, but the woman must still be left free to make the decision. *See id.* Finally, in the third trimester, when the child can live outside the mother's womb and thus becomes a "person" in the constitutional sense, the state's interest in the life of the child becomes sufficiently compelling to justify prohibiting abortion. *See id.* at 164–65.

[210]Thornburgh v. American College of Obstetricians & Gynecologists, 476 U.S. 747, 772 (1986).

[211]*Id.*

> Few decisions are more personal and intimate, more properly private, or more basic to individual dignity and autonomy than a woman's decision . . . whether to end her pregnancy. A woman's right to make that choice freely is fundamental. Any other result, in our view, would protect inadequately a central part of the sphere of liberty that our law guarantees equally to all.

In a concurring opinion, Justice Stevens described the importance of the decision faced by the pregnant woman as "a difficult choice having serious and personal consequences of major importance to her own future."[212] In a ringing endorsement of autonomy values, Stevens noted that *Roe* stands for the presumption "that it is far better to permit some individuals to make incorrect decisions than to deny all individuals the right to make decisions that have a profound affect upon their destiny."[213]

In its most recent treatment of the abortion issue, a more conservative Supreme Court in *Planned Parenthood v. Casey* modified *Roe*'s trimester approach, adopting instead a test that inquires whether a state regulation unduly burdens the woman's decision.[214] Nonetheless, a majority of the Court broadly reaffirmed *Roe*'s central holding. The Court made it clear that, at bottom, *Roe*'s result is dictated by our Constitution's commitment to the autonomy principle. In the view of a majority of the Justices, matters involving "the most intimate and personal choices a person may make in a lifetime, choices central to personal dignity and autonomy, are central to the liberty protected by the Fourteenth Amendment."[215] In language that has broad implications for the constitutional protection of autonomy, these Justices affirmed: "At the heart of liberty is the right to define one's own concept of existence, of meaning, of the universe, and of the mystery of human life. Beliefs about these matters could not define the attributes of personhood were they formed under compulsion of the State."[216]

By invoking either the rubric of "privacy" or the concept of "liberty," the Supreme Court has recognized in a number of areas that due process protects a zone of autonomous decision making in matters that are personal, intimate, and of extreme importance to the individual—those matters dealing with marriage, procreation, contraception, abortion, family relationships, child rearing and education, occupation, residence, and travel. How far does this sphere of personal autonomy extend? Clearly it cannot cover all individual choices, or for that matter, all choices regarded by the individual as important ones. Otherwise, given the burdens of strict scrutiny, a wide variety of governmental regulations would be subject to invalidation, and the law would return to the discredited doctrine of *Lochner*.[217] This role for the Court as "super-legislature" was expressly rejected in *Griswold,* the case introducing modern privacy doctrine.[218] Under modern constitutional theory, to receive recognition as

---

[212]*Id.* at 781 (Stevens, J., concurring).

[213]*Id.* The Court has also invoked autonomy values in a variety of cases in the criminal context. *See, e.g.,* Faretta v. California, 422 U.S. 806, 834 (1975) (defendant has constitutional right to waive counsel and represent himself; the decision of the individual "who will bear the personal consequences of a conviction" should be respected; his choice should be honored out of "that respect for the individual which is the lifeblood of the law."); *id.* at 833–34 ("[T]hose who wrote the Bill of Rights . . . understood the inestimable worth of free choice."); Winick, *supra* note 186, at 1747–53 (analyzing cases reflecting deference to the autonomy of the defendant in the criminal process).

[214]505 U.S. 833, 876–78 (1992) (joint opinion of O'Connor, J., Kennedy, J., & Souter, J.).

[215]*Id.* at 851. *See also id.* at 912 (Stevens, J., concurring in part and dissenting in part); *id.* at 922 (Blackmun, J., concurring in part, concurring in judgment, and dissenting in part).

[216]*Id.* at 851.

[217]*See supra* notes 25–30 and accompanying text.

[218]*See supra* note 35 and accompanying text.

an aspect of the right to privacy, intrusions on which must meet strict scrutiny, the area of decisional choice involved must directly affect a "fundamental right."[219]

What rights are fundamental? In holding a prohibition on distributing contraceptives to minors offensive to the constitutional right of privacy, the Court in *Carey v. Population Services International* noted:[220]

> While the outer limits of [the right of personal privacy] have not been marked by the Court, it is clear that among the decisions that an individual may make without unjustified government interference are personal decisions "relating to marriage, . . . procreation, . . . contraception, . . . family relationships, . . . and child rearing and education. . . .

What do these categories have in common? Some commentators have criticized the Court for offering "little assistance to one's understanding of what it is that makes all this a unit."[221] As Justice Stevens has noted, they all deal "with the individual's right to make certain unusually important decisions that will affect his own, or his family's destiny. The Court has referred to such decisions as implicating 'basic values,' as being 'fundamental,' and as being dignified by history and tradition."[222] They are all "personal and intimate,"[223] having "serious and personal consequences of major importance. . . ."[224] However, it is not enough that these decisions are central to an individual's life. The Court has held that the "personal and intimate" choice of sexual identity, at least where that choice is homosexual, is not protected by constitutional privacy.[225] In rejecting this claim, the Court characterized those fundamental rights protected by constitutional privacy as " 'implicit in the concept of ordered liberty' " or " 'deeply rooted in this Nation's history and tradition.' "[226] If the asserted right in question fails to meet this standard, it is not a "fundamental" right and will not merit heightened scrutiny. Although the right in question may be a liberty interest within the meaning of the Due Process Clause, if it is not "fundamental," the substantive protection afforded by that clause is limited. Governmental intrusions on such nonfundamental liberties will be subjected only to minimal judicial scrutiny, under which the Court will apply a deferential rational basis test.[227]

---

[219]*E.g.*, Bowers v. Hardwick, 472 U.S. 577 (1986) (rejecting constitutional privacy claim for consensual homosexual conduct, on the basis that there is no fundamental right to engage in such conduct).

[220]431 U.S. 678, 684 (1977). In other contexts the Court has referred to the "freedom of personal choice in matters of marriage and family life . . . ." Zablocki v. Redhail, 434 U.S. 374, 385 (1978); Smith v. Organization of Foster Families for Equality & Reform, 431 U.S. 816, 842 (1977); Moore v. City of E. Cleveland, 431 U.S. 494, 499 (1977); Cleveland Board of Educ. v. LaFleur, 414 U.S. 632, 639–40 (1974); *see* Kelley v. Johnson, 425 U.S. 238, 244 (1976) (freedom of choice with respect to certain basic matters of procreation, marriage, and family life.").

[221]Ely, *The Supreme Court, 1977 Term—Forward: On Discovering Fundamental Values*, 92 HARV. L. REV. 5, 11 n.40 (1978).

[222]*Thornburgh*, 476 U.S. at 781 n.11 (Stevens, J., concurring) (*quoting* Fitzgerald v. Porter Mem. Hosp., 523 F.2d 716, 719–20 (7th Cir. 1975) (Stevens, J.), *cert. denied*, 425 U.S. 916 (1976)).

[223]Thornburgh v. American College of Obstetricians & Gynecologists, 476 U.S. at 772.

[224]*Id.* at 781 (Stevens, J., concurring).

[225]Bowers v. Hardwick, 478 U.S. 186 (1986).

[226]*Id.* (quoting Palko v. Connecticut, 302 U.S. 319, 325 (1937); and Moore v. City of E. Cleveland, 431 U.S. 494, 503 (1977)).

[227]*See, e.g.*, Bowers v. Hardwick, 478 U.S. 186 (1986) (right to engage in consensual homosexual conduct); Kelley v. Johnson, 425 U.S. 238 (1976) (right of policeman to determine hair length); Village of Belle Terre v. Boraas, 416 U.S. 1 (1974) (right of unrelated persons to reside together); *see also* Thornburgh v. American College of Obstetricians & Gynecologists, 476 U.S. 747, 790 (White, J., dissenting) (arguing that the freedom to choose to have an abortion, although a liberty interest protected by the Due Process Clause, is not a "fundamental" one, and therefore should receive only minimal scrutiny).

Is the decision whether to accept treatment with the various mental health interventions as personal, intimate, and serious as those involving marriage, procreation, contraception, family relationships, and child rearing and education? Is individual decision making in matters of personal health as fundamental and as dignified by our history and traditions as are choices in these areas?

The Supreme Court has only recently recognized that substantive due process protects the right to make personal health decisions.[228] Like other constitutionally protected autonomy rights, the right to self-determination in matters of personal health is deeply rooted in constitutional traditions. The right is an outgrowth of the "historic liberty interest" in "personal security" and bodily integrity.[229] In the 1905 case *Jacobson v. Massachusetts,* the Court upheld compulsory vaccination for smallpox against a claim that such vaccination violated the liberty of every person "to care for his own body and health in such way as to him seems best."[230] However, the Court treated the claim seriously. The Court considered the vaccination to be routine and noted that no claim had been made that it presented any risk to the petitioner's health.[231] Absent any evidence that the individual's health would be adversely affected by the vaccination, the state's police power interest in protecting the public health from the spread of a highly contagious disease justified interference in what otherwise would be an area preserved by the Constitution for individual self-determination.

The common law origins of this right of the individual to exercise control over health care have been recognized frequently. More than 80 years ago, Justice Cardozo, then a judge serving on the New York Court of Appeals, memorialized the right to make personal health decisions in language that has been quoted often: "Every human being of adult years and sound mind has a right to determine what shall be done with his own body; and a surgeon who performs an operation without his patient's consent commits an assault for which he is liable in damages."[232] Case law developing the informed consent doctrine as a device to

---

[228] *See* Riggins v. Nevada, 504 U.S. 127 (1992) (concluding that Due Process Clause protects criminal defendant's interest in avoiding involuntary administration of antipsychotic drugs); Washington v. Harper, 494 U.S. 210, 221–22 (1990) (acknowledging that criminal defendant possessed "a significant liberty interest in avoiding the unwanted administration of antipsychotic drugs under the Due Process Clause of the Fourteenth Amendment"); Cruzan v. Director, Missouri Dep't of Health, 497 U.S. 261, 279 (1990) (concluding that competent person has constitutionally protected interest in refusing unwanted medical treatment). Similarly, in *Doe v. Bolton,* a companion case to *Roe,* Justice Douglas referred to "the freedom to care for one's health and person" as being a fundamental right protected by the Due Process Clause of the Fourteenth Amendment. Doe v. Bolton, 410 U.S. 179, 192 (1973) (Douglas, J., concurring).

[229] *See supra* notes 97–105 and accompanying text.

[230] 197 U.S. 11, 26 (1905).

[231] *Jacobson,* 197 U.S. at 29. *Compare* Schmerber v. California, 384 U.S. 757, 771 (1966) (finding compulsory blood test of suspected intoxicated driver to be "routine" and to involve "virtually no risk, trauma, or pain" and thus upholding compulsory blood test against Fourth Amendment attack) *with Winston v. Lee,* 470 U.S. at 761, 765–66 (finding surgical removal of bullet from criminal suspect's body for use as evidence to be "severe" intrusion presenting disputed "medical risks" and thus holding that such procedure would violate Fourth Amendment).

[232] Schloendorff v. Soc'y of N.Y. Hosp., 105 N.E. 92, 93 (N.Y. 1914). In *Schloendorff,* a surgeon was held liable for assault when the surgeon removed a fibroid tumor from the patient while the patient was unconscious. *Id.* In another state court opinion from this period, the Oklahoma Supreme Court referred to "the free citizen's first and greatest right . . . the right to the inviolability of his person," and therefore forbade a physician "to violate without permission the bodily integrity of his patient." Rolater v. Strain, 137 P. 96, 97 (Okla. 1913).

protect the patient's right to refuse treatment has grounded the right in the common law's deference to individual autonomy:[233]

> Anglo-American law starts with the premise of thorough-going self-determination. It follows that each man is considered to be master of his own body and he may, if he be of sound mind, expressly prohibit the performance of life saving surgery, or other medical treatment. A doctor might well believe that an operation or form of treatment is desirable or necessary but the law does not permit him to substitute his own judgment for that of the patient.

The principles of tort law have embraced the principle of informed consent in order to vindicate patients' control over decisions affecting their own health.[234] Absent an emergency or incompetency, the individual must voluntarily consent before medical treatment may be administered, and the physician is required to provide sufficient information so that the choice is informed. "[T]rue consent to what happens to one's self is the informed exercise of a choice, and that entails an opportunity to evaluate knowledgeably the options available and the risks attendant upon each."[235] The "root premise" of the informed consent doctrine is the "concept, fundamental in American jurisprudence, that the individual may control what shall be done with his own body."[236] Unless incompetent, the patient's medical decisions must be respected, no matter how foolish these decisions are thought to be.[237]

---

[233]Natanson v. Kline, 350 P.2d, 1093, 1104 (Kan. 1960). *See also* Ericson v. Dilgard, 252 N.Y.S.2d 705, 706 (Sup. Ct. 1962) ("[I]t is the individual who is the subject of a medical decision who has the final say and . . . this must necessarily be so in a system of government which gives the greatest possible protection to the individual in furtherance of his own desires.").

[234]*See, e.g.,* Cruzan v. Director, Missouri Dep't of Health, 497 U.S. 261, 269 (1990); P. APPELBAUM ET AL., INFORMED CONSENT: LEGAL THEORY AND CLINICAL PRACTICE (1981); W. KEETON ET AL., PROSSER AND KEETON ON THE LAW OF TORTS §§ 9, 32 (5th ed. 1984); Sprung & Winick, *Informed Consent in Theory and Practice: Legal and Medical Perspectives on the Informed Consent Doctrine, and a Proposed Reconceptualization,* 17 CRITICAL CARE MED. 1346 (1989); Winick, *Competency to Consent to Treatment: The Distinction Between Assent and Objection,* 28 HOUS. L. REV. 15, 27 (1991); Note, *Developments in the Law–Medical Technology and the Law,* 103 HARV. L. REV. 1519, 1661 (1990); *infra* chapter 18.

[235]Canterbury v. Spence, 464 F.2d 772, 780 (D.C. Cir. 1972), *cert. denied,* 409 U.S. 1064 (1972).
[236]*Id.*

[237]*See* Tune v. Walter Reed Army Medical Hosp., 602 F. Supp. 1452, 1455 (D.D.C. 1985) (holding that competent adult has right to have life–support system removed even though death will likely result); Bouvia v. Superior Court, 225 Cal. Rptr. 297, 301 (Dist. Ct. App. 1986) (holding that mentally competent patient has right to refuse nasogastric tube); *In re* Estate of Brooks, 205 N.E.2d 435, 442 (Ill. 1965) (concluding that, absent a clear and present danger, patient's refusal to take blood transfusion must be respected even if unwise); Lane v. Candura, 376 N.E.2d 1232, 1235–36 (Mass. Ct. App. 1978) (concluding that irrationality of patient's decision does not justify conclusion that patient is legally incompetent); Downer v. Veilleux, 322 A.2d 82, 91 (Me. 1974) (acknowledging competent adult's right to refuse treatment or cure, however unwise adult's sense of values may be to others); *In re* Conroy, 486 A.2d 1209, 1225 (N.J. 1985) (noting that patient's right to informed consent must be respected even when it conflicts with values of medical profession as whole); *In re* Quackenbush, 383 A.2d 785, 789 (Morris County [N.J.] Ct. 1978) (holding that mentally competent individual has right to refuse operation involving extensive bodily invasion even absent dim prognosis); New York City Health & Hosps. Corp. v. Stein, 335 N.Y.S.2d 461, 465 (Sup. Ct. 1972) (concluding that patient not adjudicated incompetent may refuse recommended ECT treatment); *In re* Yetter, 62 Pa. D. & C.2d 619, 623 (1973) (concluding that constitutional right of privacy includes right of mature, competent adult to refuse to accept medical recommendations that may prolong individual's life). *See also* S. BRAKEL ET AL., THE MENTALLY DISABLED AND THE LAW 340 (3d ed. 1985); PRESIDENT'S COMM'N FOR THE STUDY OF ETHICAL PROBS. IN MED. & BIOMED. & BEHAV. RES., DECIDING TO FORGO LIFE SUSTAINING TREATMENT: ETHICAL, MEDICAL AND LEGAL ISSUES IN TREATMENT DECISIONS 40 (1983) [hereinafter DECIDING TO FORGO LIFE SUSTAINING TREATMENT]; Perry, *A Problem With Refusing Certain Forms of Psychiatric Treatment,* 20 SOC. SCI. MED. 645, 646 (1985).

An application of the right to make personal health decisions that has received much recent attention is what has become known as the "right to die." In *In re Quinlan,*[238] the New Jersey Supreme Court approved the appointment of a parent as guardian for a comatose adult subsisting in a chronic vegetative state and recognized the parent's ability to discontinue life-sustaining treatment for the patient. The court relied on *Roe v. Wade* to support a constitutional right of privacy extending to personal health decisions, including the decision to discontinue life-support systems. The court reasoned that in *Roe,* the Constitution was read to "interdict judicial intrusion into many aspects of personal decision."[239] In *Quinlan,* the right of privacy was found to be "broad enough to encompass a patient's decision to decline medical treatment under certain circumstances, in much the same way as it is broad enough to encompass a woman's decision to terminate pregnancy under certain conditions."[240] Even though the patient in *Quinlan* was "grossly incompetent,"[241] the court found that the Constitution protected her "independent right of choice,"[242] which her father as guardian could exercise on her behalf during her incompetency.

Quinlan has been widely followed in cases recognizing a constitutional right to refuse treatment, including life-sustaining treatment, on the part of both competent and incompetent patients.[243] Citing state court decisions that upheld the right of the individual to make personal medical decisions, the Supreme Court, in a 1990 decision, *Cruzan v. Director, Missouri Department of Health,*[244] expressed its "assumption" that "a competent person

---

[238]355 A.2d 647 (N.J.), *cert. denied,* 429 U.S. 922 (1976).

[239] *Id.* at 663.

[240]*Id.*

[241]*Id.* at 664. The patient, Karen Quinlan, was in an unresponsive comatose condition with no cognitive function. *Id.*

[242]*Id.*

[243]*See, e.g.,* Rasmussen v. Fleming, 741 P.2d 674 (Ariz. 1987); Donaldson v. Van de Kamp, 4 Cal. Rptr. 2d 59 (Ct. App. 1992); Bouvia v. Superior Court, 225 Cal. Rptr. 297 (Ct. App. 1986); Bartling v. Superior Court, 209 Cal. Rptr. 220 (Ct. App. 1984); Foody v. Manchester Memorial Hosp., 482 A.2d 713 (Conn. Super. Ct. 1984); Severns v. Wilmington Medical Ctr., Inc., 421 A.2d 1334 (Del. 1980); Satz v. Pearlmutter, 379 So. 2d 359 (Fla. 1980); Guardianship of Barry, 445 So. 2d 365 (Fla. Dist. Ct. App. 1984); Guardianship of Roe, III, 421 N.E.2d 40 (Mass. 1981); *In re* Spring, 405 N.E.2d 115 (Mass. 1980); Superintendent of Belchertown Sch. v. Saikewicz, 370 N.E.2d 417 (Mass. 1977); *In re* Torres, 357 N.W.2d 332 (Minn. 1984); McKay v. Bergstedt, 801 P.2d 617 (Nev. 1990); *In re* Conroy, 486 A.2d 1209 (N.J. 1985); *In re* Quackenbush, 383 A.2d 785 (Morris County [N.J.] Ct. 1978); Leach v. Akron Gen. Med. Ctr., 426 N.E.2d 809 (Ohio 1980); Guardianship of Ingram, 689 P.2d 1363 (Wash. 1984); *In re* Colyer, 660 P.2d 738 (Wash. 1983), *modified by In re* Hamlin, 689 P.2d 1372 (Wash. 1984). *See also* AMERICAN MEDICAL ASS'N COUNCIL ON ETHICAL AND JUDICIAL AFFAIRS, WITHHOLDING OR WITHDRAWING LIFE PROLONGING MEDICAL TREATMENT (1986); DECIDING TO FORGO LIFE SUSTAINING TREATMENT, *supra* note 237, at 5 (1983); AMERICAN HOSP. ASS'N, POLICY AND STATEMENT OF PATIENT'S CHOICES OF TREATMENT OPTIONS (1985); Annas & Densberger, *Competence to Refuse Medical Treatment: Autonomy vs. Paternalism,* 15 U. TOL. L. REV. 561 (1984); Byrn, *Compulsory Lifesaving Treatment for the Competent Adult,* 44 FORDHAM L. REV. 1 (1975); Cantor, *A Patient's Decision to Discontinue Life-Sustaining Medical Treatment: Bodily Integrity vs. the Preservation of Life,* 26 RUTGERS L. REV. 228 (1973); Capron, *Informed Consent in Catastrophic Disease Research and Treatment,* 123 U. PA. L. REV. 340 (1975); Ronzetti, *Constituting Family and Death Through the Struggle with State Power:* Cruzan v. Director, Missouri Department of Health, 46 U. MIAMI L. REV. 149 (1991); Swartz, *The Patient Who Refuses Medical Treatment: Dilemma for Hospitals and Physicians,* 11 AM. J.L. & MED. 147 (1985); Note, *Developments in the Law—Medical Technology and the Law,* 103 HARV. L. REV. 1519, 1661 (1990).

[244]497 U.S. 261 (1990). In *Cruzan,* the Court determined that it was constitutionally permissible for a state to require "clear and convincing evidence" of a patient's desires before terminating life-sustaining medical treatment. *Id.* at 283. The Missouri Supreme Court had rejected the request of parents of a comatose accident victim to withdraw artificial feeding and hydration because "there was no clear and convincing evidence of [the patient's] desire to have life-sustaining treatment withdrawn under such circumstances." *Id.* at 263. The U.S. Supreme Court determined that the Missouri Supreme Court's "clear and convincing evidence" requirement furthered the state's interest in preservation of human life and did not violate the patient's due process rights. *Id.* at 281.

has a liberty interest under the Due Process Clause in refusing medical treatment.''[245] The *Cruzan* Court recognized that this liberty interest could be exercised by surrogate decision makers, acting on the patient's behalf during a period of incompetency, and could be invoked even to discontinue life-sustaining procedures or nutrition, as long as the individual, while competent, clearly expressed a wish that this be done.[246] In a concurring opinion, Justice O'Connor noted that ''our notions of liberty are inextricably entwined with our idea of physical freedom and self-determination.''[247]

Thus, the right to make personal medical decisions, including the right to refuse even life-sustaining treatments, is a liberty interest protected by due process. This right, particularly where the consequences are significant to the individual, is firmly rooted in our traditions. Moreover, it is as personal and intimate as other decisions recognized by the Court as protected by the fundamental right of privacy—those dealing with marriage, procreation, contraception, family relationships, and child rearing and education. ''The constitutional right to privacy,'' as stated by the Supreme Judicial Court of Massachusetts, ''is an expression of the sanctity of individual free choice and self-determination as fundamental constituents of life. The value of life as so perceived is lessened not by a decision to refuse treatment, but by the failure to allow a competent human being the right of choice.''[248]

This principle that constitutional privacy protects a right of patients to control the course of their medical treatment should apply as well in the context of mental health treatment imposed on patients and offenders. Mental health treatment is as intimate and personal as any medical intervention, and in most cases even more so. Such treatment, affecting the individual's mental processes and personality itself, can vitally affect the individual's sense of dignity and personhood and the ''ability to define one's own concept of existence . . . .''[249] Moreover, allowing individual choice in the matter of mental health treatment, as opposed to permitting state coercion, can have a dramatic effect on the success of treatment.[250] Personal autonomy in mental health treatment decision making is thus of vital importance to the individual.

Some state and lower federal court decisions have invoked the autonomy branch of the privacy doctrine to support a right to refuse intrusive mental health treatment, finding that the fundamental liberty interest in independence in making certain important decisions extends to the administration of psychotropic drugs[251] and electroconvulsive therapy.[252] These decisions provide a third doctrinal foundation for the Supreme Court's unexplained

---

[245]*Id.* at 278–79.

[246]*See id.* at 282.

[247]*Id.* at 287 (O'Connor, J., concurring).

[248]Superintendent of Belchertown School v. Saikewicz, 370 N.E.2d 417, 426 (Mass. 1977).

[249]Planned Parenthood v. Casey, 505 U.S. 833, 851 (1992) (joint opinion of O'Connor, J., Kennedy, J., and Souter, J.).

[250]*See infra* chapter 17 (analyzing the therapeutic benefits of patient choice and antitherapeutic consequences of coerced treatment); Winick, *The Right to Refuse Mental Health Treatment: A Therapeutic Jurisprudence Analysis*, 17 INT'L J.L. & PSYCHIATRY 99 (1994).

[251]Bee v. Greaves, 744 F.2d 1387, 1392–93 (10th Cir. 1984), *cert. denied,* 469 U.S. 1214 (1985); Rogers v. Okin, 634 F.2d 650, 653 (1st Cir. 1980), *aff'g in part, rev'g in part and vacating and remanding,* 478 F. Supp. 1342, 1366 (D. Mass. 1979), *vacated and remanded sub nom.* Mills v. Rogers, 457 U.S. 291 (1982), *on remand,* 738 F.2d 1 (1st Cir. 1984); Davis v. Hubbard, 506 F. Supp. 915, 930–32 (N.D. Ohio 1980); Rennie v. Klein, 462 F. Supp. 1131, 1144 (D.N.J. 1978), *aff'd in part, modified in part, and remanded,* 653 F.2d 836 (3d Cir. 1980) (en banc), *vacated and remanded,* 458 U.S. 1119 (1982), *on remand,* 720 F.2d 266 (3d Cir. 1983) (en banc); Guardianship of Roe, III, 421 N.E.2d 40, 51 n.9 (Mass. 1981); Rivers v. Katz, 67 N.Y.2d 485, 504 N.Y.S.2d 74, 78 (1986); *In re* K.K.B., 609 P.2d 747, 750–52 (Okla. 1980).

[252]Lojuk v. Quandt, 706 F.2d 1456, 1465 (7th Cir. 1983); Price v. Sheppard, 239 N.W.2d 905, 910 (Minn. 1976).

determination in *Washington v. Harper* and *Riggins v. Nevada* that involuntary administration of antipsychotic medication implicates a liberty interest protected by due process. Because these organic treatment techniques, as well as the more intrusive surgical techniques of psychosurgery and electronic stimulation of the brain, cannot be resisted by the unwilling patient and pose serious adverse health consequences, they intrude substantially on the right of privacy–autonomy. These intrusions are so serious and long-lasting that the liberty interest invaded by these treatments should be considered "fundamental," requiring heightened judicial scrutiny when sought to be imposed coercively. In the case of the verbal and behavior techniques, on the other hand, the patient is able to resist treatment effects by withholding cooperation. Moreover, these techniques rarely present serious risks to health. As a result, these less intrusive treatments do not seem to intrude sufficiently on individual self-determination to trigger the heightened scrutiny of constitutional privacy–autonomy protection.[253]

Three separate although somewhat related liberty interests protected by the Due Process Clauses thus converge to support a right of mental patients and offenders to refuse intrusive mental health treatment—the interests in bodily integrity, in mental privacy, and in individual autonomy in matters vitally affecting the individual. The surgical and organic techniques present sufficient intrusions on bodily and mental integrity to justify constitutional scrutiny. The primary and side effects of these therapies, many of which are experienced as distressing and debilitating by patients, are sufficiently serious that the decision to submit to them is one for which personal autonomy should be respected. The verbal and most of the behavioral techniques either do not implicate these aspects of constitutional liberty or do so only in ways meriting deferential minimal judicial scrutiny. However, the intrusive techniques should receive at least intermediate and in most cases strict judicial scrutiny, requiring significant if not compelling governmental interests and means chosen to accomplish those interests that are carefully tailored to bring them about. Whether these standards are satisfied for mental health treatment imposed on patients and offenders is considered in chapters 15 and 16.

---

[253]*See supra* chapters 3, 4, and 10.

Chapter 12
TREATMENT AS PUNISHMENT:
Eighth Amendment Limits on Mental Health Interventions

The Eighth Amendment to the Constitution, applicable to the states through the Due Process Clause of the Fourteenth Amendment,[1] prohibits the infliction of "cruel and unusual punishments."[2] Does this prohibition apply to the involuntary administration of mental health treatment to patients and offenders? To the extent that at least some of the more intrusive treatment techniques are experienced as painful and distressing, they may be regarded as "punishments" by their recipients. Indeed, aversive conditioning, one of the behavioral treatment techniques, involves the systematic administration of painful stimuli— such as electric shocks or drugs that cause nausea or apnea—in an effort to extinguish or reduce the frequency of inappropriate or maladaptive behavior.[3] Can these treatments, however, be considered "punishments" within the meaning of the Constitution? If so, are they "cruel and unusual"? If the Eighth Amendment applies to treatment administered in prisons, does it also apply to treatment administered in mental hospitals? Does the Eighth Amendment apply when the government's purpose is to rehabilitate offenders rather than to inflict retribution by subjecting them to painful stimuli or conditions designed to make them suffer for their offenses? Should the use of forced treatment administered for the purpose of institutional discipline in the prison or the hospital implicate the Eighth Amendment? Should the Eighth Amendment be read to limit the expanding array of behavior modification techniques—increasingly used in clinical practice—when used in correctional contexts?

A. The Evolving Meaning of Cruel and Unusual Punishment

The Cruel and Unusual Punishment Clause, which originated in the English Bill of Rights,[4] initially was interpreted to require a showing that the punishment in question would have been regarded as cruel and unusual by the Framers in 1791.[5] In 1910, however, the

---

[1] *E.g.*, Ford v. Wainwright, 477 U.S. 399 (1986); Estelle v. Gamble, 429 U.S. 97 (1976); Robinson v. California, 370 U.S. 660 (1962).

[2] U.S. CONST. amend. VIII.

[3] *See* B. BROWN ET AL., BEHAVIOR MODIFICATION: PERSPECTIVES ON A CURRENT ISSUE 6–8 (1975); S. RACHMAN & J. TEASDALE, AVERSIVE THERAPY AND BEHAVIOR DISORDERS: AN ANALYSIS, at xii, 13 (1969); Note, *Aversive Therapy: Punishment as Treatment and Treatment as Cruel and Unusual Punishment*, 49 S. CAL. L. REV. 880 (1976); *supra* chapter 4. For a discussion of the similarities between aversive conditioning and penal sanctions, see Singer, *Psychological Studies of Punishment*, 58 CAL. L. REV. 405 (1970).

[4] Bill of Rights, 1 W. & M. Sess. 2, ch. 2 (1689); *see* Ingraham v. Wright, 430 U.S. 651, 664 (1977); Furman v. Georgia, 408 U.S. 238, 243 n.3 (1972) (Douglas, J., concurring); Trop v. Dulles, 356 U.S. 86, 100 (1958) (plurality opinion); Granucci, *"Nor Cruel and Unusual Punishments Inflicted:" The Original Meaning*, 57 CAL. L. REV. 839, 852–53 (1969). Although the English version apparently was designed to prohibit unauthorized punishments and those beyond the authority of the sentencing court, *see* Gregg v. Georgia, 428 U.S. 153, 169 (1976); Granucci, *supra*, at 859–60, the Framers of the American version were mainly concerned with outlawing tortures and other "barbarous" forms of punishment. *Gregg*, 428 U.S. at 170; Granucci, *supra*, at 842.

[5] *See* Furman v. Georgia, 408 U.S. 238, 265 (1972) (Brennan, J., concurring); Goldberg & Dershowitz, *Declaring the Death Penalty Unconstitutional*, 83 HARV. L. REV. 1773, 1785–86 (1970).

Supreme Court rejected this strictly historical approach, recognizing instead the "expansive and vital character" of the clause.[6] The Court found that the prohibition "is not fastened to the obsolete but may acquire meaning as public opinion becomes enlightened by a humane justice."[7] Although the clause initially was construed to prohibit only outright torture and physical cruelty,[8] under this evolving standard it was soon read to ban excessive or disproportionate penalties,[9] as well as those which, although not physically barbarous, "involve the unnecessary and wanton infliction of pain. . . ."[10] Capital punishment, a common criminal sanction in 1791,[11] is now considered to be cruel and unusual if imposed for certain crimes[12] or pursuant to statutes making it mandatory on conviction[13] or if administered in an arbitrary way[14] or under unfair procedures.[15]

Under the approach applied by the modern Court, the Eighth Amendment is interpreted in a "flexible and dynamic manner"[16] and read to "draw its meaning from the evolving

---

[6]Weems v. United States, 217 U.S. 349, 376–77 (1910).

[7]Id. at 378.

[8]See In re Kemmler, 136 U.S. 436, 446–48 (1890) (electrocution found constitutional); Wilkerson v. Utah, 99 U.S. 130, 135–36 (1879) (execution by firing squad held constitutional); Granucci, supra note 4, at 842; Note, The Cruel and Unusual Punishment Clause and the Substantive Criminal Law, 79 HARV. L. REV. 635, 637 (1966). Punishments condemned as cruel and unusual at the time of the adoption of the Constitution included burning at the stake, the iron boot, disemboweling, crucifixion, breaking at the wheel, pillorying, decapitation, the rack, the thumbscrew, and other tortures producing a lingering death. See Furman v. Georgia, 408 U.S. 238, 264–65 (1972) (Brennan, J., concurring); Robinson v. California, 370 U.S. 600, 675 (1962); Weems v. United States, 217 U.S. 349, 399–400 (1910); In re Kemmler, 136 U.S. at 447; Wilkerson, 99 U.S. at 135–36. The view of the Framers of the Eighth Amendment—that the cruel and unusual punishments clause was limited to the prohibition of barbarous methods of punishment—appears to have been based on a misinterpretation of the intent of the drafters of the English Bill of Rights. See Granucci, supra note 4.

[9]See Weems v. United States, 217 U.S. 249 (1910) (15 years of hard labor in chains for forgery held unconstitutional). This view of the clause had earlier been articulated by Justice Field in his dissenting opinion in O'Neil v. Vermont, 144 U.S. 323, 338–40 (1892). For modern applications of this aspect of the Eighth Amendment, see Solem v. Helm, 463 U.S. 277 (1983); Enmund v. Florida, 458 U.S. 782 (1982); Coker v. Georgia, 433 U.S. 584, 592 (1977) (plurality opinion).

[10]Whitley v. Albers, 475 U.S. 312, 319 (1986); Rhodes v. Chapman, 452 U.S. 337, 346 (1981); Ingraham v. Wright, 430 U.S. 651, 670 (1977); Estelle v. Gamble, 429 U.S. 97, 103 (1976); Gregg v. Georgia, 428 U.S. 153, 173 (1976) (plurality opinion). "Among 'unnecessary and wanton' inflictions of pain are those that are 'totally without penological justification.' " Rhodes, 452 U.S. at 346 (quoting Gregg, 428 U.S. at 183, and Gamble, 429 U.S. at 103).

[11]Gregg, 428 U.S. at 177.

[12]See Enmund v. Florida, 458 U.S. 782 (1982) (unconstitutional for felony murder when defendant neither committed the murder himself, attempted to do so, nor intended to take life); Coker v. Georgia, 433 U.S. 584, 599–600 (1977) (plurality opinion) (unconstitutional for rape).

[13]See Sumner v. Shuman, 483 U.S. 66 (1987); Roberts v. Louisiana, 431 U.S. 633 (1977) (per curiam); Woodson v. North Carolina, 428 U.S. 280 (1976) (plurality opinion); Roberts v. Louisiana, 428 U.S. 325 (1976) (plurality opinion).

[14]See Furman v. Georgia, 408 U.S. 238 (1972).

[15]Gilmore v. Taylor, 509 U.S. 333, 341 (1993) ("[T]he Eighth Amendment requires a greater degree of accuracy and fact finding [in a capital case] than would be due in a noncapital case."); see, e.g., Booth v. Maryland, 482 U.S. 496 (1987); Gray v. Mississippi, 481 U.S. 648 (1987); Hitchcock v. Dugger, 481 U.S. 393 (1987); Turner v. Murray, 476 U.S. 28 (1986); Skipper v. South Carolina, 476 U.S. 1 (1986); Caldwell v. Mississippi, 472 U.S. 320 (1985); Ake v. Oklahoma, 470 U.S. 68 (1985); Eddings v. Oklahoma, 455 U.S. 104 (1982); Bullington v. Missouri, 451 U.S. 430 (1981); Estelle v. Smith, 451 U.S. 454 (1981); Adams v. Texas, 448 U.S. 38 (1980); Beck v. Alabama, 447 U.S. 625 (1980); Green v. Georgia, 442 U.S. 95 (1979) (per curiam); Lockett v. Ohio, 438 U.S. 586 (1978) (plurality opinion); Gardner v. Florida, 430 U.S. 349 (1977); Witherspoon v. Illinois, 391 U.S. 510 (1968). The Court, however, has rejected the contention that the death penalty is inherently cruel and unusual punishment. E.g., Gregg v. Georgia, 428 U.S. 153 (1976). In so doing, the Court found that capital punishment did not violate contemporary values as measured by "objective indicia" derived from history and the actions of state legislatures and capital juries. Coker v. Georgia, 433 U.S. 584, 593–96 (1977); Gregg, 428 U.S. at 176–87.

[16]Rhodes v. Chapman, 452 U.S. 337, 345 (1981); Gregg, 428 U.S. at 171.

standards of decency that mark the progress of a maturing society."[17] At its core, the Eighth Amendment prohibits "the infliction of uncivilized and inhuman punishments. The State, even as it punishes, must treat its members with respect for their intrinsic worth as human beings. A punishment is 'cruel and unusual' therefore, if it does not comport with human dignity."[18]

The Eighth Amendment was originally regarded as a limitation on criminal sentences. However, it now is read to apply as well to the treatment received by offenders in correctional facilities and to the general conditions of their confinement.[19] The Supreme Court recently reiterated such broadened Eighth Amendment protection over the vigorous dissents of Justice Thomas, who argued that the prohibition should be limited to criminal sentences and should not apply to conditions of confinement.[20]

B. The Eighth Amendment in Mental Hospitals

Several of the early right-to-refuse-treatment cases applied the Eighth Amendment to involuntary treatment. These cases involved challenges to the use of drugs in hospital and prison aversive conditioning programs[21] and the involuntary administration of psychotropic medication in state hospitals and juvenile facilities.[22] More recent cases, however, have rejected an Eighth Amendment basis for a right to refuse treatment.[23]

Two threshold problems arise when applying the Eighth Amendment to the right-to-refuse-treatment question, at least when it arises in the hospital rather than the prison context. First, does the Eighth Amendment apply to a mental hospital that is not part of a prison?

---

[17]*Rhodes*, 452 U.S. at 346; Estelle v. Gamble, 429 U.S. 97, 102 (1976); Trop v. Dulles, 356 U.S. 86, 101 (1958) (plurality opinion).

[18]Furman v. Georgia, 408 U.S. 238, 270 (Brennan, J., concurring). *See also* Hutto v. Finney, 437 U.S. 678, 685 (1978) (Eighth Amendment prohibits penalties that "transgress today's 'broad and idealistic concepts of dignity, critical standards, humanity, and decency'. "); Estelle v. Gamble, 429 U.S. 97, 102 (1976) (same); Trop v. Dulles, 356 U.S. 86, 100 (1958) (plurality opinion) ("The basic concept underlying the Eighth Amendment is nothing less than the dignity of man. While the State has the power to punish, the Amendment stands to assure that this power be exercised within the limits of civilized standards.").

[19]*See, e.g.*, Farmer v. Brennan, 511 U.S. 825, 833 (1994) (holding that prison officials may be held liable under the Eighth Amendment for prison conditions when they disregarded substantive risk of serious harm to inmates); Helling v. McKinney, 509 U.S. 25, 31 (1993) ("It is undisputed that the treatment a prisoner receives in prison and the conditions under which he is confined are subject to scrutiny under the Eighth Amendment."); Hudson v. McMillan, 503 U.S. 1 (1992) (excessive physical force against prisoner); Wilson v. Seiter, 501 U.S. 294, 300 (1991) ("The thread common to all [Eighth Amendment prison cases] is that 'punishment' has been deliberately administered for a penal or disciplinary purpose.") (quoting Johnson v. Glick, 481 F.2d 1028, 1032 (2d Cir. 1973)) (Friendly, J.); Rhodes v. Chapman, 452 U.S. 337 (1981) (conditions of confinement such as double-celling considered under Eighth Amendment); *id.* at 347 ("Conditions must not involve the wanton and unnecessary infliction of pain, nor may they be grossly disproportionate to the severity of the crime warranting imprisonment."); Hutto v. Finney, 437 U.S. 678 (1978) (punitive isolation held to violate Eighth Amendment); Estelle v. Gamble, 429 U.S. 97 (1976) (denial of needed medical care held to violate Eighth Amendment); Gutterman, *The Contours of Eighth Amendment Prison Jurisprudence: Conditions of Confinement*, 48 SMU L. REV. 373 (1995).

[20]Helling v. McKinney, 113 S. Ct. 2475, 2484 (1993) (Thomas, J., joined by Scalia, J., dissenting); Hudson v. McMillan, 504 U.S. 1, 17 (1992) (Thomas, J., joined by Scalia, J., dissenting).

[21]Knecht v. Gillman, 488 F.2d 1136 (8th Cir. 1973); Mackey v. Procunier, 477 F.2d 877 (9th Cir. 1973).

[22]Scott v. Plante, 532 F.2d 939, 946–47 (3d Cir. 1976); Souder v. McGuire, 423 F. Supp. 830, 832 (M.D. Pa. 1976); Pena v. New York Div. for Youth, 419 F. Supp. 203, 207–10 (S.D.N.Y. 1976); Welsch v. Likins, 373 F. Supp. 487, 503 (D. Minn. 1974), *aff'd in part, vacated and remanded in part,* 550 F.2d 1122 (8th Cir. 1977); Nelson v. Heyne, 355 F. Supp. 451, 455 (N.D. Ind. 1972), *aff'd,* 491 F.2d 352 (7th Cir.), *cert. denied,* 417 U.S. 976 (1974).

[23]Lojuk v. Quandt, 706 F.2d 1456, 1464–65 (7th Cir. 1983) (electroconvulsive therapy); Rennie v. Klein, 653 F.2d 836, 844 (3d Cir. 1981) (en banc), *aff'g* 462 F. Supp. 1131, 1143 (D.N.J. 1978) (psychotropic medication); Price v. Sheppard, 239 N.W.2d 905, 908–09 (Minn. 1976) (electroconvulsive therapy).

Second, can treatment be considered "punishment" within the meaning of the Eighth Amendment?

Is the Cruel and Unusual Punishment Clause applicable to hospital confinement? Traditionally, Supreme Court Eighth Amendment cases have involved criminal punishments.[24] In *Ingraham v. Wright*,[25] the Supreme Court considered an Eighth Amendment challenge to the use of disciplinary corporal punishment in public schools. Rejecting application of the Eighth Amendment in the school context, the Court construed the proscription against cruel and unusual punishments narrowly as a limitation applicable only to criminal punishments.[26] However, the Court limited its holding by suggesting in a footnote that "[s]ome punishments, though not labelled 'criminal' by the State, may be sufficiently analogous to criminal punishments in the circumstances in which they are administered to justify application of the Eighth Amendment."[27] Significantly, the Court left open the question of "whether or under what circumstances persons involuntarily confined in mental or juvenile institutions can claim the protection of the Eighth Amendment."[28]

How should this question be resolved? The Court's analysis in *Ingraham* is instructive. In finding the Eighth Amendment inapplicable in the public schools, the Court stressed the history of the amendment as traditionally protecting only convicted criminals.[29] The Court also emphasized the safeguards existing in public schools, as contrasted with prisons, that protect children from abuses of corporal punishment—the openness of the schools, community supervision of the public school system, and the availability of common law civil and criminal sanctions for abuses.[30] Although these factors may distinguish public schools from prisons, they do not necessarily distinguish mental institutions from prisons. At the time the Eighth Amendment was adopted, those with mental illness were treated as

---

[24]*See* Ingraham v. Wright, 430 U.S. 651, 666–67 (1977) (citing cases).

[25]430 U.S. 651 (1977).

[26]*Id.* at 664, 671 n.40; *accord* Whitley v. Albers, 475 U.S. 312, 319 (1986); Revere v. Massachusetts Gen. Hosp., 463 U.S. 239, 244 (1983); Bell v. Wolfish, 441 U.S. 520, 535 n.16 (1979).

[27]430 U.S. at 669 n.37.

[28]*Id.* Some lower federal courts had previously applied the Eighth Amendment in these contexts. *E.g.,* United States v. Solomon, 563 F.2d 1121, 1124 (4th Cir. 1977) (dicta) (state mental retardation facility); Harper v. Cserr, 544 F.2d 1121, 1123 (1st Cir. 1976) (mental hospital); Nelson v. Heyne, 491 F.2d 352 (7th Cir.), *cert. denied,* 417 U.S. 976 (1974) (state school for boys); Knecht v. Gillman, 488 F.2d 1136 (8th Cir. 1973) (security medical facility); Wheeler v. Glass, 473 F.2d 983 (7th Cir. 1973) (facility for those with mental retardation); Vann v. Scott, 467 F.2d 1235 (7th Cir. 1972) (Stevens, J.) (facility for runaway juveniles); Rozecki v. Gaughan, 452 F.2d 6 (1st Cir. 1972) (mental hospital for criminal defendants found incompetent to stand trial); Morales v. Turman, 383 F. Supp. 53, 70 (E.D. Tex. 1974), *rev'd on other grounds,* 535 F.2d 864 (5th Cir. 1976), *vacated and remanded,* 430 U.S. 322 (1977) (facilities for juveniles); Welsch v. Likens, 373 F. Supp. 487 (D. Minn. 1974), *aff'd in part, vacated and remanded in part,* 550 F.2d 1122 (8th Cir. 1977) (facility for those with mental retardation); Martarella v. Kelley, 349 F. Supp. 575 (S.D.N.Y. 1972) (facility for juveniles adjudicated "persons in need of supervision"); Inmates of Boys' Training Sch. v. Affleck, 346 F. Supp. 1354, 1366 (D.R.I. 1972) (boys' training school); United States *ex rel.* von Wolfersdorf v. Johnston, 317 F. Supp. 66 (S.D.N.Y. 1970) (lengthy confinement in hospital for incompetency to stand trial).

[29]430 U.S. at 664–68.

[30]*Id.* at 669–71.

criminals and were frequently confined in the same facilities as criminals.[31] In addition, the safeguards in the public schools are largely absent even in modern mental hospitals.[32] Hospitals, often located in remote areas, are closed institutions, largely cut off from public scrutiny. Unlike public school students, who return home to concerned parents each day, mental patients typically are not permitted to leave the institution and may only rarely be visited by family or friends.

Although civil and criminal remedies for abuse may exist in principle, many patients do not have access to lawyers and are unaware of their rights. Finally, like prisoners but unlike students in public schools, mental patients (at least those committed to hospitals) are in custody. When the state places an individual in custody, "the Constitution imposes upon it a corresponding duty to assume some responsibility for his safety and general well-being. . . ."[33] As a result, the considerations cited by the Court to justify denying Eighth Amendment protection to punishment administered in public schools do not apply as clearly to mental hospitals, which in these respects seem more analogous to prisons.

The arguments for applying the Eighth Amendment to mental hospitals thus seem strong.[34] On the other hand, the Supreme Court has declined to apply the Eighth Amendment in cases challenging the conditions of pretrial detention, on the basis that pretrial detainees have not yet been convicted of crime.[35] Jails, mental hospitals, and prisons all share a high potential for abuse. If jails are not subject to Eighth Amendment scrutiny, how can mental hospitals be? This may be largely an academic question, however, in view of the holding in the jail cases that an alternative constitutional limitation—substantive due process— "requires that a pretrial detainee not be punished."[36] Punishment, under this analysis, may constitutionally be applied only after "an adjudication of guilt" in a criminal prosecution.[37] Civil mental patients, as well as criminal defendants hospitalized as incompetent to stand trial or following an acquittal by reason of insanity, have not been adjudicated guilty of a

---

[31]*See* N. KITTRIE, THE RIGHT TO BE DIFFERENT: DEVIANCE AND ENFORCED THERAPY 57 (1971); Gill, *Nothing Less Than the Dignity of Man: The Eighth Amendment in Mental Institutions,* 28 AM. U. L. REV. 109, 117–24 (1978). *See also* Halderman v. Pennhurst State Sch. & Hosp., 446 F. Supp. 1295, 1299–1300 (E.D. Pa. 1977), *aff'd in part,* 612 F.2d 84 (3d Cir. 1979), *rev'd on other grounds,* 451 U.S. 1 (1981), *on remand,* 673 F.2d 647 (3d Cir. 1980), *rev'd on other grounds,* 465 U.S. 89 (1984). This also had been the practice in Europe during the period preceding the American Revolution—starting in the 17th century and continuing until the birth of the asylum in the late 18th and early 19th centuries. *See* M. FOUCAULT, MADNESS AND CIVILIZATION: A HISTORY OF INSANITY IN THE AGE OF REASON 38–64, 221–40 (R. Howard trans. Vintage Books ed., 1973).

[32]*See Halderman,* 446 F. Supp. at 1320–21; Gill, *supra* note 31, at 117–24; Symonds, *Mental Patients' Rights to Refuse Drugs: Involuntary Medication As Cruel and Unusual Punishment,* 7 HASTINGS CONST. L.Q. 701, 722–27 (1980).

[33]Helling v. McKinney, 509 U.S. 25, 32 (1993) (quoting DeShaney v. Winnebago County Dep't Soc. Servs., 489 U.S. 189, 200 (1989)):

> [W]hen the State by the affirmative exercise of its powers so restrains an individual's liberty that it renders him unable to care for himself, and at the same time fails to provide for basic human needs—*e.g.,* food, clothing, shelter, medical care, and reasonable safety—it transgresses the substantive limits on state action set by the Eighth Amendment.

Id. at 2480 (quoting *DeShaney,* 489 U.S. at 200).

[34]*See* Rennie v. Klein, 462 F. Supp. 1131, 1143 (D.N.J. 1978) (assuming that the Eighth Amendment applies in mental hospitals), *aff'd on other grounds,* 653 F.2d 836 (3d Cir. 1981); *Halderman,* 446 F. Supp. at 1320–21 (distinguishing *Ingraham* on the basis of the lack of safeguards in mental institutions similar to those in public schools).

[35]Block v. Rutherford, 468 U.S. 571 (1984); Bell v. Wolfish, 441 U.S. 520 (1979).

[36]*Wolfish,* 441 U.S. at 535 n.16. *See also* City of Revere v. Massachusetts Gen. Hosp., 463 U.S. 239, 244 (1983); Ingraham v. Wright, 430 U.S. 651, 671–72 n.40 (1977).

[37]*Wolfish,* 441 U.S. at 535.

crime; thus, they may not be subjected to punishment consistent with due process.[38] As a result, the critical question becomes identifying the meaning of *punishment* under the Constitution, because once it is determined that punishment has been imposed, it is subject to constitutional scrutiny wherever it has occurred—under the Eighth Amendment if in prison and under due process if elsewhere. Because a punishment that is sufficiently inhumane to be deemed cruel and unusual if imposed on a convicted criminal offender also would violate due process if imposed on a patient,[39] the question of the applicability of the Eighth Amendment to mental hospitals seems largely academic. Whichever constitutional tool is used, the result should be the same.

C. Therapy as Punishment

A second difficulty with applying the Eighth Amendment as a basis for a right to refuse treatment is whether therapy can be considered "punishment." A fairly clear case was presented in *Knecht v. Gillman*,[40] in which the vomit-inducing drug apomorphine was used in an involuntary aversive conditioning program. Inmates were injected with the drug for such "undesirable behavior patterns" as "not getting up, for giving cigarettes against orders, for talking, for swearing, or for lying."[41] After injection, the inmates were exercised. The drug induced vomiting for a period lasting from 15 minutes to an hour and produced a temporary cardiovascular effect. The U.S. Court of Appeals for the Eighth Circuit rejected the state's contention that the program was "treatment" and as such was insulated from Eighth Amendment scrutiny.[42] The court held that, when administered without informed consent, the program constituted cruel and unusual punishment without regard to its characterization as "treatment." The court relied on the Supreme Court's 1958 opinion in *Trop v. Dulles*[43] for the propositions that the government's characterization of an act as nonpenal cannot be conclusive for purposes of resolving the Eighth Amendment question and that a court should look behind the classification and conduct an "inquiry . . . directed to substance."[44]

Similarly, in *Mackey v. Procunier*,[45] the Ninth Circuit Court of Appeals applied the Eighth Amendment to prohibit the use of succinylcholine—a paralyzing "fright drug" that produces sensations of suffocation and drowning—on fully conscious prisoners in a prison aversive conditioning program.[46] The same approach was used by the Seventh Circuit Court

---

[38]*See* Jones v. United States, 463 U.S. 354, 369 (1983) ("As . . . [the insanity acquittee] was not convicted, he may not be punished.").

[39]City of Revere v. Massachusetts Gen. Hosp., 463 U.S. 239, 244 (1983) ("[T]he due process rights . . . [of a person not adjudicated guilty of a crime to be free of punishment] are at least as great as the Eighth Amendment protections available to a convicted prisoner.").

[40]488 F.2d 1136 (8th Cir. 1973).

[41]*Id.* at 1137.

[42]*Id.* at 1139.

[43]356 U.S. 86 (1958) (plurality opinion.)

[44]*Id.* at 95. The court also relied, for the same proposition, on Vann v. Scott, 467 F.2d 1235, 1240 (7th Cir. 1972) (Stevens, J.). *See also* United States v. Ursery, 116 S.Ct. 2135, 2143 (1996) (recognizing that in an appropriate case "a civil penalty . . . may be so extreme and so divorced from the government's damages and expenses as to constitute punishment" within the meaning of the Double Jeopardy Clause.) (quoting United States v. Halper, 490 U.S. 435, 442 (1989)); *Harper*, 490 U.S. at 447–48: "[In determining whether a sanction is civil or criminal for double jeopardy purposes], the labels 'criminal' and 'civil' are not of paramount importance. [T]he labels affixed either to the proceeding or to the relief imposed . . . are not controlling and will not be allowed to defeat the applicable protections of federal constitutional law." (citations omitted).

[45]477 F.2d 877 (9th Cir. 1973).

[46]*Id.* at 878.

of Appeals in a case involving psychotropic drugs administered involuntarily in a juvenile correctional institution "not as part of an ongoing psychotherapeutic program, but for the purpose of controlling excited behavior."[47]

Under this approach, the use of psychotropic medication for control or institutional discipline that is not part of a treatment program could be deemed punishment for Eighth Amendment purposes at least in the absence of an emergency.[48] The same would be true of such uses of electroconvulsive therapy or any of the other intrusive therapies or of behavioral approaches that use painful stimuli. When these treatments are used for therapeutic purposes, however, the Eighth Amendment may be deemed inapplicable even though the effects may be identical.

The Supreme Court's opinion in *Bell v. Wolfish*[49] suggests that, at least in nonprison contexts and for impositions that are not unambiguously punishment, the Eighth Amendment inquiry may turn not on the effect of the intervention but on the intent with which it is administered. The *Wolfish* Court scrutinized the conditions of confinement to which pretrial detainees were subjected. Although noting that under the Due Process Clause a pretrial detainee may not be punished prior to an adjudication of guilt,[50] the Court held that not every disability imposed during pretrial detention amounts to "punishment" within the meaning of the Constitution:

> A Court must decide whether the disability is imposed for the purpose of punishment or whether it is but an incident of some other legitimate governmental purpose. . . . Absent a showing of an express intent to punish on the part of detention facility officials, that determination generally will turn on "[w]hether an alternative purpose to which [the restriction] may rationally be connected is assignable for it and whether it appears excessive in relation to the alternative purpose assigned [to it]." . . . Thus, if a particular condition or restriction . . . is reasonably related to a legitimate governmental objective, it does not, without more, amount to "punishment." Conversely, if a restriction or condition is not reasonably related to a legitimate goal—if it is arbitrary or purposeless—a court permissibly may infer that the purpose of governmental action is punishment. . . .[51]

---

[47]Nelson v. Heyne, 491 F.2d 352, 356 (7th Cir. 1974), *cert. denied*, 417 U.S. 976 (1976). *See also* Souder v. McGuire, 423 F. Supp. 830, 832 (M.D. Pa. 1976) ("[I]nvoluntary administration of drugs which have a painful or frightening effect can amount to cruel and unusual punishment, in violation of the Eighth Amendment.").

[48]*See* Bee v. Greaves, 744 F.2d 1387, 1395 (10th Cir. 1984), *cert. denied*, 469 U.S. 1214 (1985); Pena v. New York Div. for Youth, 419 F. Supp. 203 (S.D.N.Y. 1976); *In re* K.K.B., 609 P.2d 747, 751 (Okla. 1980). A parallel analysis is possible using principles of substantive due process. *See* Riggins v. Nevada, 504 U.S. 127, 135 (1992) (forced administration of antipsychotic medication that was not medically appropriate would violate due process) (dicta); Winick, *New Directions in the Right to Refuse Mental Health Treatment: The Implications of* Riggins v. Nevada, 2 WM. & MARY BILL RTS. L.J. 205, 221–24 (1993) (discussing medical appropriateness principle); *infra* chapter 16, part A (discussing therapeutic appropriateness principle).

[49]441 U.S. 520 (1979).

[50]*Id.* at 535 & n.16; *see supra* note 36 and accompanying text.

[51]441 U.S. at 538–39 (citations omitted); *accord* United States v. Salerno, 481 U.S. 739, 746 (1987) (applying this approach to reject contention that preventive detention was punishment because it furthered the regulatory purpose of community protection); Whitley v. Albers, 475 U.S. 312, 321 (1986); Block v. Rutherford, 468 U.S. 576, 584 (1984). *See also* Kennedy v. Mendoza-Martinez, 372 U.S. 144, 168–69 (1963); Fleming v. Nestor, 363 U.S. 603–14 (1960); Trop v. Dulles, 356 U.S. 86, 96 (1958) (plurality opinion):

> In deciding whether or not a law is penal, this Court has generally based its determination upon the purpose of the statute. If the statute imposes a disability for the purposes of punishment—that is, to reprimand the wrongdoer, to deter others, etc.—it has been considered penal. But a statute has been considered non-penal if it imposes a disability, not to punish, but to accomplish some other legitimate governmental purpose.

See also United States v. Lovett, 328 U.S. 303, 318–30 (1946) (Frankfurter, J., concurring).

Under this approach, virtually all administration of psychotropic drugs,[52] electroconvulsive therapy,[53] behavioral therapy[54] or other therapies as part of a treatment program will
be immune from Eighth Amendment challenge. Unless punitive purposes can be demonstrated,[55] or unless the medication dosage administered is excessively high[56] or the drug or
other therapy used is totally ineffective as treatment,[57] invocation of an Eighth Amendment
basis for a right to refuse treatment will be difficult.[58] This would seem true of therapies
administered for the treatment of mental disorders in hospitals and civil outpatient programs
as well as those provided prisoners and offenders in community programs and forensic
facilities, with at least one exception: the state's use of treatment for purposes of offender
rehabilitation.[59]

D. Rehabilitation of Offenders as Punishment

The Eighth Amendment should be implicated when the purpose of administering
therapy to a convicted offender is not the treatment of a specific mental disorder from which
the individual suffers but rather the desire to change the offender's anti-social personality so
that the individual does not commit future crime.[60] Such "rehabilitation" is one of the

---

[52]*See, e.g.*, Gilliam v. Martin, 589 F. Supp. 680, 682 (W.D. Okla. 1984); Osgood v. District of Columbia, 567
F. Supp. 1026, 1032–33 (D.D.C. 1983); Rennie v. Klein, 482 F. Supp. 1131, 1143 (D.N.J. 1978), *aff'd*, 653 F.2d
836, 844 (3d Cir. 1981) (en banc); Pena v. New York Div. for Youth, 419 F. Supp. 203 (S.D.N.Y. 1976) (enjoining
use of Thorazine in a juvenile facility as punishment, but authorizing its use as part of an ongoing treatment program
supervised by a doctor).

[53]*See, e.g.*, Lojuk v. Quandt, 706 F.2d 1456, 1464 (7th Cir. 1983); Price v. Sheppard, 239 N.W.2d 905, 908–09
(Minn. 1976).

[54]Green v. Baron, 879 F.2d 305 (8th Cir. 1989) (tier program).

[55]For examples of punitive use of psychotropic drugs in institutional settings, see United States *ex rel.* Wilson
v. Coughlin, 472 F.2d 100 (7th Cir. 1972); J. MITFORD, KIND AND USUAL PUNISHMENT: THE PRISON BUSINESS 129
(1973); *supra* chapter 5, notes 92 and accompanying text. For examples of punitive use of electroconvulsive
therapy, see KITTRIE, *supra* note 31, at 307; K. WOODEN, WEEPING IN THE PLAYTIME OF OTHERS: AMERICA'S
INCARCERATED CHILDREN 147 (1976); Robitscher, *Psychosurgery and Other Somatic Means of Altering Behavior*, 2
BULL. AM. ACAD. PSYCHIATRY & L. 12, 12–13 (1974); *supra* chapter 6, notes 53–54 and accompanying text.

[56]*See supra* chapter 5.

[57]*See supra* chapter 5, notes 57–60, 119–23 and accompanying text (psychotropic drugs ineffective for
certain conditions); *supra* chapter 6, notes 18,43 and accompanying text (electroconvulsive therapy ineffective for
certain conditions).

[58]*See* Winick, *Legal Limitations on Correctional Therapy and Research*, 65 MINN. L. REV. 331, 348–50
(1981).

[59]A second potential exception involves treatment of death row inmates found incompetent to be executed in
order to restore their competency so that capital punishment can be imposed. This issue is discussed in *infra* chapter
15, part C 2(b)(3), notes 198–200 and accompanying text.

[60]*See, e.g.*, McConnell, *Stimulus/Response: Criminals Can Be Brainwashed—Now*, PSYCHOLOGY TODAY,
Apr. 1970, at 14, 16, 74; Singer, *supra* note 3, at 433–34, 442. There seems to be an increasing interest in treatment
programs for sex offenders. *See, e.g.*, Sundby v. Fiedler, 827 F. Supp. 581 (W.D. Wis. 1993); Goldsmith v. Dean,
No. 2:93-CV-383 (D. Vt. filed Dec. 1993); *In re* Young, 857 P.2d 989 (Wash. 1993); N. PALLONE, REHABILITATING
CRIMINAL SEXUAL PSYCHOPATHS: LEGISLATIVE MANDATES, CLINICAL QUANDARIES (1990); PREDATORS AND
POLITICS: A SYMPOSIUM ON WASHINGTON'S SEXUALLY VIOLENT PREDATORS STATUTE, 15 U. PUGET SOUND L. REV.
507–871 (1992); Furby et al., *Sex Offender Recidivism: A Review*, 105 PSYCHOL. BULL. 33 (1989).

traditional aims of criminal punishment[61] and therefore may be considered "part of the penalty that criminal offenders pay for their offenses against society."[62] Where the legislature has authorized such offender rehabilitation as part of the criminal penalty, then it clearly would constitute punishment within the meaning of the Eighth Amendment.[63] However, even when the legislative intent is not so clear or when correctional administrators seek to apply such rehabilitative treatment absent legislative authorization, such rehabilitation is sufficiently associated with criminal punishment that the presumption should be that punishment rather than some alternative purpose was intended.

The government could contend that under the "alternative purpose" approach of *Bell v. Wolfish*,[64] such rehabilitation is not imposed as punishment but rather for an alternative regulatory purpose, such as community protection. Such an argument would find support in the Supreme Court's decision in *United States v. Salerno*,[65] upholding the facial validity of the pretrial detention provisions of the Bail Reform Act of 1984.[66] In *Salerno*, the Court decided that pretrial detention without bail was permissible regulation rather than impermissible punishment in violation of substantive due process.[67] The Court stressed the clarity of the legislative history indicating that Congress did not authorize pretrial detention as punishment but rather to solve the "pressing societal problem" of preventing danger to the community by defendants released on bail.[68]

If preventing danger to the community is a regulatory rather than a punitive purpose, can it be contended that because offender rehabilitation is designed to prevent danger to the community, it therefore is not punishment? The problem with this argument is that its acceptance would immunize virtually all punishment from Eighth Amendment scrutiny. All punishment seeks to accomplish community protection, by incapacitating offenders and deterring them and others from committing such offenses in the future. *Salerno* should not be read broadly to apply to the postconviction Eighth Amendment context the approach it used in the preconviction substantive due process context. The *Salerno* Court dealt with pretrial detention applied prior to conviction, not a restriction on liberty imposed after conviction

---

[61] *See, e.g.,* Jones v. United States, 463 U.S. 354, 368 (1983); Pell v. Procunier, 417 U.S. 817, 822–23 (1974); United States v. Brown, 381 U.S. 437, 458 (1965); Trop v. Dulles, 356 U.S. 85, 111 (1958) (Brennan, J., concurring); Williams v. New York, 337 U.S. 241, 248 (1949); L. HALL & S. GLUECK, CASES ON THE CRIMINAL LAW AND ITS ENFORCEMENT 19 (3d ed. 1958); H. PACKER, THE LIMITS OF THE CRIMINAL SANCTION 11–12 (1969); Allen, *Criminal Justice, Legal Values, and the Rehabilitative Ideal,* 50 J. CRIM. L. CRIMINOLOGY & POLICE SCI. 226, 227 (1959). *See also* K. MENNINGER, THE CRIME OF PUNISHMENT (1966) (advocating psychological treatment for offenders); TASK FORCE ON CORRECTIONS, THE PRESIDENT'S COMM'N ON LAW ENFORCEMENT AND ADMINISTRATION OF JUSTICE, TASK FORCE REPORT: CORRECTIONS 53–57 (1967) (advocating educational and vocational training for offenders). The "rehabilitative ideal," although a central goal of correctional policy for the first three quarters of the 20th century, has been in sharp decline since the 1970s. *See generally* F. ALLEN, THE DECLINE OF THE REHABILITATIVE IDEAL: PENAL POLICY AND SOCIAL PURPOSE (1981); Burt, *Cruelty, Hypocrisy, and the Rehabilitative Ideal in Corrections,* 16 INT'L J. L. & PSYCHIATRY 359 (1993).

[62] Whitley v. Albers, 475 U.S. 312, 319 (1986); Rhodes v. Chapman, 452 U.S. 337, 347 (1981). *See 'Behavior Mod' Behind the Walls,* TIME MAGAZINE, March 11, 1974, at 74 (quoting a federal prison official's statement that involvement in prison behavior modification programs is "part of the consequence of committing a crime").

[63] *See* United States v. Salerno, 481 U.S. 739, 747 (1987) ("To determine whether a restriction on liberty constitutes impermissible punishment or permissible regulation, we first look to legislative intent."); Schall v. Martin, 467 U.S. 253, 269 (1984).

[64] 445 U.S. 520 (1979); *see supra* notes 50–52 and accompanying text.

[65] 481 U.S. 739 (1987).

[66] 18 U.S.C. § 3142 (1993).

[67] 481 U.S. at 746–52.

[68] *Id.* at 747. *See also* Schall v. Martin, 467 U.S. 253 (1984) (upholding under a similar analysis the pretrial detention of juveniles).

and because of it. Restrictions on liberty imposed on convicted offenders that are traditionally associated with punishment must be deemed punishment within the meaning of the Eighth Amendment, even if a regulatory purpose can be asserted as an alternative justification. Given the substantive due process injunction against punishment without an adjudication of guilt, a more narrow definition of *punishment* is warranted in the nonprison context (the *Wolfish–Salerno* approach) than should apply in the prison, where punishment (although not cruel and unusual punishment) is permitted. If a convicted criminal defendant sentenced to a lengthy term of imprisonment challenges the sentence imposed as excessive or disproportionate to the offense, and hence cruel and unusual,[69] any justification of detention on the basis of community protection, which always could be asserted, could not be accepted without defeating all Eighth Amendment challenges to criminal sentences.

Pretrial detention or other restrictions on liberty imposed on defendants who have not been convicted of crime, such as crowded conditions of pretrial confinement, in appropriate cases can be seen as nonpunitive attempts by government to accomplish legitimate societal goals, which on balance justify the restrictions imposed. This is the holding of *Salerno* and *Wolfish*. However, when the imposition follows conviction and is of the kind traditionally associated with criminal punishment, Eighth Amendment review should not be eluded so easily. When the rehabilitation of criminal offenders is the purpose of administering correctional therapy to convicted offenders, the limitations imposed by the Eighth Amendment should therefore apply.[70]

Determining that correctional rehabilitation is punishment within the meaning of the Eighth Amendment does not, of course, resolve the constitutional inquiry. To offend the Eighth Amendment, the punishment in question must be deemed cruel and unusual, for example, when it is excessive and disproportionate or indecent and inhumane. Correctional therapies imposed for rehabilitation that involve excessive pain or are unnecessarily degrading can thus be considered cruel and unusual.[71] Indeed, the Supreme Court has suggested that the use as punishment of techniques outside the scope of traditional

---

[69]*See* cases cited in *supra* note 9.

[70]*See* Gobert, *Psychosurgery, Conditioning, and the Prisoner's Right to Refuse "Rehabilitation,"* 61 VA. L. REV. 155, 182 (1975). A parallel analysis can be made for the imposition of intrusive forms of mental health therapy designed to rehabilitate individuals confined in various special offender categories, such as mentally disordered sex offenders and individuals acquitted by reason of insanity. Even though insanity acquittees and some in special sex offender categories have not been convicted of a crime and hence cannot be "punished," *see supra* note 38, the Due Process Clause imposes a similar limitation to that of the Eighth Amendment when such "therapy" is excessively cruel or inhumane. *See supra* notes 35–39 and accompanying text. A related issue is pending before the Supreme Court in Kansas v. Hendricks, 116 S.Ct. 2522 (1996), *granting cert.* in *In re* Hendricks, 912 P.2d 129 (Kan. 1996)— whether commitment of violent sexual predators' following completion of their prison terms constitutes additional punishment for the offense in violation of the Double Jeopardy Clause.

[71]In a parallel context, the Supreme Court has specified when excessive force administered to a prison inmate constitutes cruel and unusual punishment:

> [W]henever prison officials stand accused of using excessive physical force in violation of the Cruel and Unusual Punishment Clause, the core judicial inquiry is that set out in *Whitley*: whether force was applied in a good-faith effort to maintain or restore discipline, or maliciously and sadistically to cause harm. . . . Under the *Whitley* approach, the extent of injury suffered by an inmate is one factor that may suggest "whether the use of force could plausibly have been thought necessary" in a particular situation, "or instead evinced such wantonness with respect to the unjustified infliction of harm as is tantamount to a knowing willingness that it occur." In determining whether the use of force was wanton and unnecessary, it may also be proper to evaluate the need for application of force, the relationship between that need and the amount of force used, the threat "reasonably perceived by the responsible officials," and "any efforts made to temper the severity of a forceful response."

Hudson v. McMillan, 503 U.S. 1, 15 (1992) (citations omitted). To satisfy this standard, the injury inflicted need not be "significant." *Id.*

penalties—a category that presumably is limited to fines, criminal forfeiture, imprisonment, and execution—"is constitutionally suspect."[72]

In the unlikely event that a legislature authorized psychosurgery for those committing certain sex offenses, for example, it could be invalidated under the Eighth Amendment either as disproportionate to the offense,[73] or (given its experimental character[74] and serious and irreversible negative effects on personality[75]) as indecent and inhumane,[76] or as insufficiently related to the goal of transforming the offender into a law-abiding and well-adjusted member of society.[77] If psychosurgery (or for that matter any therapeutic approach) were found to be ineffective as rehabilitation or treatment, it would certainly be subject to Eighth Amendment scrutiny, even if defended as treatment of a specific mental disorder.[78] Ineffective techniques are "arbitrary or purposeless" and "not reasonably related to a legitimate goal [other than punishment]," which under the Supreme Court's analysis in *Bell v. Wolfish* would justify the inference that the government's purpose was punishment rather than treatment.[79] Given the painful, degrading, and dehumanizing effects of psychosurgery, such punishment should easily be deemed cruel and unusual.

If psychosurgery were to be imposed on offenders even though not explicitly authorized by the legislature, this lack of authorization would itself raise Eighth Amendment problems. If imposed by correctional rehabilitators without legislative approval, such psychosurgery could be viewed as an unauthorized sentence. The precursor of the Eighth Amendment, the English Bill of Rights, was especially concerned with imposition of penalties not authorized by statute.[80] As a result, unauthorized "rehabilitation" imposed on offenders can be considered to violate the Eight Amendment.[81]

The courts should subject to especially strict scrutiny offender rehabilitation using any of the more intrusive treatments when not specifically authorized by legislation. Even if

---

[72]Trop v. Dulles, 356 U.S. 86, 100 (1958) (plurality opinion).

[73]*See* Solem v. Helm, 463 U.S. 277 (1983) (life sentence without parole for issuing a $100 bad check under recidivist statute based on six prior nonviolent convictions held disproportionately cruel and unusual); Enmund v. Florida, 458 U.S. 782 (1982) (death penalty unconstitutional for felony murder in certain circumstances); Coker v. Georgia, 433 U.S. 584, 592 (1977) (plurality opinion) (death penalty unconstitutional for rape); Weems v. United States, 217 U.S. 349, 367 (1910) (imprisonment in chains at hard labor for 12 years for falsifying an official document held disproportionately cruel and unusual); Gobert, *supra* note 70, at 183; *supra* note 9 and accompanying text.

[74]*See supra* chapter 8, note 50 and accompanying text.

[75]*See supra* chapter 8, notes 16–25 and accompanying text.

[76]*See* Ingraham v. Wright, 430 U.S. 651, 670 (1977) (" 'unnecessary and wanton infliction of pain' . . . constitutes cruel and unusual punishment") (quoting Estelle v. Gamble, 429 U.S. 97, 103 (1976)); Knecht v. Gillman, 488 F.2d 1136, 1140 (8th Cir. 1973) (invalidating as cruel and unusual punishment aversive conditioning program using an emetic drug, noting that "vomiting (especially in the presence of others) is a painful and debilitating experience."); Selva, *Treatment as Punishment*, 6 NEW ENG. J. PRISON L. 265, 278 (1980) ("The mental distress of a person who has had a psychosurgical operation might, at least, be as great as the distress experienced by an expatriate [the punishment held cruel and unusual in Trop v. Dulles, 356 U.S. 86 (1958) (plurality opinion)]. The mental suffering accompanying . . . psychosurgery . . . would be too degrading and dehumanizing to an individual.").

[77]*See* Knecht v. Gillman, 488 F.2d at 1139–40 ("unproven drug" used in aversive conditioning held cruel and unusual punishment in part because "it is not possible to say that the use of apomorphine is a recognized and acceptable medical practice in institutions" such as the one involved); Schwitzgebel, *Limitations on the Coercive Treatment of Offenders*, 8 CRIM. L. BULL. 267, 305 (1972); Selva, *supra* note 76, at 271, 287–88; Winick, *supra* note 58, at 350.

[78]*See supra* note 75.

[79]441 U.S. 520, 539 (1979); *see supra* note 50 and accompanying text.

[80]Granucci, *supra* note 4, at 860.

[81]*See* Gobert, *supra* note 70, at 182.

"rehabilitation" or "correctional treatment"[82] is mentioned by the statute authorizing the criminal sentence imposed or the one delegating authority to correctional officials, a substantial question would exist as to whether intrusive mental health treatments like psychosurgery were contemplated. In deciding whether a punishment is inconsistent with "the evolving standards of decency that mark the progress of a maturing society"[83] and hence cruel and unusual, the Supreme Court has paid special attention to the evidence provided by the actions of legislatures[84] and juries.[85] Legislatures and juries are reflectors of contemporary community attitudes on the limits of acceptable punishment, but correctional administrators—appointed officials who are not directly responsive to the political process—are not. The judicial deference owed to specific legislative judgments about appropriate punishments is thus unwarranted in considering the constitutionality of punishments selected by correctional officials applying vague delegations of authority.

The courts may avoid the Eighth Amendment analysis just discussed by using an alternative doctrinal approach to invalidate such arguably unauthorized treatments. When a governmental agency purports to have authority to infringe on fundamental rights, courts in other contexts have often invoked the *ultra vires* doctrine to insist on an explicit legislative expression of that authority.[86] In *Kent v. Dulles,*[87] for example, the Supreme Court held that the Passport Act of 1926, which delegated to the Secretary of State the authority to "grant and issue passports . . . under such rules as the President shall designate and prescribe,"[88] was insufficient authority for a regulation prohibiting issuance of passports to Communist Party members. Finding that the regulation impinged on the constitutionally protected right to travel, the Court held that "[w]here activities or enjoyment, natural and often necessary to the well-being of an American citizen . . . are involved, we will construe narrowly all delegated powers that curtail or dilute them."[89] Referring to the Passport Act, the Court could not "find in this broad generalized power an authority to trench so heavily on the rights of the citizen."[90]

Thus, when faced with correctional therapy that raises serious Eighth Amendment concerns, courts may well avoid deciding the Eighth Amendment question by holding that a general legislative delegation[91] is insufficient to support the agency's assertion of authority to impose such treatment. This approach allows courts to avoid unnecessary constitutional

---

[82]*See, e.g.,* DEL. CODE tit. 11, § 6531(e)-(f) (1993); KAN. STAT. § 75-5210(a) (1993); MINN. STAT. § 244.03 (1993); R.I. GEN. L. § 42-56-31 (1993); *see also* A.L.I. MODEL PENAL CODE § 7.01 (1)(b) (Proposed Official Draft, 1962). For delegations that are even more vague, see 18 U.S.C. § 4042(1) (1993) (delegation to Bureau of Prisons to "have charge of the management and regulation of all Federal [prisons]").

[83]*See supra* note 17 and accompanying text.

[84]*See, e.g.,* Gregg v. Georgia, 428 U.S. 153, 173, 179–80 (1976) (plurality opinion); Winick, *Prosecutorial Peremptory Challenge Practices in Capital Cases: An Empirical Study and a Constitutional Analysis,* 81 MICH. L. REV. 1, 3–4 (1982).

[85]*See, e.g.,* Enmund v. Florida, 458 U.S. 782, 794–96 (1982); Coker v. Georgia, 423 U.S. 584, 596 (1977) (plurality opinion); Gregg, 428 U.S. at 181; Woodson v. North Carolina, 428 U.S. 280, 293 (1976) (plurality opinion); Winick, *supra* note 84, at 4, 79; Winick, Witherspoon *in Florida: Reflections on the Challenge for Cause of Jurors in Capital Cases in a State in Which the Judge Makes the Sentencing Decision,* 37 U. MIAMI L. REV. 825, 862–64 (1983).

[86]*See* Regents of the Univ. of Cal. v. Bakke, 438 U.S. 265, 308–09 (1978) (opinion of Powell, J.); Hampton v. Mow Sun Wong, 426 U.S. 88, 105–14 (1976); Kent v. Dulles, 357 U.S. 116, 129 (1958); J. FRIEDMAN, CRISIS AND LEGITIMACY 83–85(1978); B. SCHWARTZ, ADMINISTRATIVE LAW 47–48 (1976).

[87]357 U.S. 116 (1958).

[88]Act of July 3, 1926, Ch. 772, § 1, 44 Stat., pt. 2, 887, *quoted in* Kent v. Dulles, 357 U.S. 116, 123 (1958).

[89]*Id.* at 129.

[90]*Id.*

[91]*See, e.g.,* statutes cited in *supra* note 82.

adjudication and in effect remands the underlying policy question to the legislature for decision with an awareness that its choice implicates fundamental values and will be subjected to constitutional scrutiny.[92]

The Eighth Amendment principles discussed above are not limited to highly controversial therapies like psychosurgery. A similar analysis can be made for other intrusive treatment techniques imposed to rehabilitate offenders. Other intrusive treatments could also be deemed cruel and unusual punishments if they are excessively painful and degrading, ineffective as rehabilitation, disproportionate to the offense, or unauthorized by statute. Moreover, if such treatments are imposed for purposes other than rehabilitation that themselves are traditionally associated with punishment, they should similarly be subject to Eighth Amendment scrutiny. For example, the use of long-acting psychotropic drugs implanted beneath the skin and of electronic stimulation of the brain in conjunction with radio telemetry devices that are surgically implanted have both been suggested as means of incapacitating criminal offenders as an alternative to prison.[93] Because incapacitation is a traditional aim of punishment, subjecting offenders to these treatment techniques should be considered punishment within the meaning of the Eighth Amendment.

E. Treatment as Institutional Discipline

The use of treatments such as psychotropic drugs, electroconvulsive therapy, or behavior therapy for institutional discipline[94] also should be considered punishment within the meaning of the Eighth Amendment. This conclusion is especially clear for such treatment applied in the prison, but it may also apply when administered in civil hospitals. Prison discipline was recognized by the Supreme Court to constitute punishment within the meaning of the Eighth Amendment in *Hutto v. Finney*.[95] Language in two subsequent Supreme Court cases involving restrictions imposed in pretrial detention, however, may support an argument that discipline to further the goal of maintaining institutional security serves a legitimate regulatory purpose other than punishment and thus should not constitute punishment within the meaning of the Constitution.[96] Moreover, the approach taken by the Supreme Court in *United States v. Salerno*,[97] upholding pretrial detention without bail, may also be invoked to support this contention. However, the language in the two cases mentioned above was dicta because neither case involved discipline for the violation of institutional rules. The issues in the cases concerned the validity of a jail prohibition on

---

[92]*See* A. BICKEL, THE LEAST DANGEROUS BRANCH 111–98 (1962); FRIEDMAN, *supra* note 86, at 83; Tribe, *The Emerging Reconnection of Individual Rights and Institutional Design: Federalism, Bureaucracy, and Due Process of Lawmaking,* 10 CREIGHTON L. REV. 433, 442–43 (1977); Winick, *Forfeiture of Attorneys' Fees Under RICO and CCE and the Right to Counsel of Choice: The Constitutional Dilemma and How to Avoid It,* 43 U. MIAMI L. REV. 765, 839–43 (1989).

[93]Lehtinen, *Controlling the Minds and Bodies of Prisoners—Without Prisons,* 6 BARRISTER 11, 11–12, 59 (1979); Lehtinen, *Technological Incapacitation: A Neglected Alternative,* 2 Q. J. OF CORRECTIONS 31, 35–36 (1978).

[94]For examples of the use of these treatment techniques for institutional discipline, see *supra* chapter 5, note 90 and accompanying text (psychotropic drugs); *supra* chapter 6, note 53 and accompanying text (electroconvulsive therapy); *supra* notes 40–42 and accompanying text (aversive conditioning).

[95]437 U.S. 678, 682, 685 (1978).

[96]*See* Block v. Rutherford, 468 U.S. 571, 586 n.8 (1984); Bell v. Wolfish, 441 U.S. 520, 546 (1979).

[97]481 U.S. 739 (1987); *see supra* notes 62–67 and accompanying text.

contact visits[98] and a jail rule against receipt of hardcover books unless mailed directly from publishers or bookstores.[99]

Discipline for the infraction of institutional rules can certainly be related to the need to maintain institutional security, which is not itself a punitive purpose. However, when such discipline follows a rule violation and is imposed because of it—to rehabilitate the inmate or deter him from repeating his behavior, to deter others from misbehavior, and possibly for retribution as well—it constitutes punishment in every meaningful sense of the word,[100] even though it serves the regulatory purpose of maintaining institutional security. Thus, the holding of *Hutto v. Finney* that "punitive isolation" in correctional facilities constitutes punishment within the meaning of the Eighth Amendment[101] and its recognition that other punishments for prison misconduct such as lashing with a strap and the administration of electrical shocks to the body were also within the coverage of the Eighth Amendment[102] must be read to survive the dicta in these subsequent cases.

Hutto involved the prison, the traditional bastion of the Eighth Amendment and a context in which the "alternative purpose" approach of *Bell v. Wolfish,*[103] reapplied in *Salerno,*[104] has not been invoked.[105] The extension of *Hutto* to hospital discipline is not as clear, particularly because, like the jail in *Wolfish* and *Salerno,* the hospital does not house convicted offenders. However, discipline for past infractions in any context seems punitive, even if an alternative regulatory purpose can be asserted. The school paddling administered for disciplinary purposes in *Ingraham v. Wright*[106] was denied Eighth Amendment protection not because it did not meet the definition of *punishment,* but because the locus of its imposition was a school. Pretrial detention without bail, upheld in *Salerno,* simply does not seem inherently punitive, whereas institutional discipline does. The Court in *Ingraham* specifically left open the applicability of its holding to involuntary hospitalization,[107] and its analysis stressed the safeguards existing in public schools,[108] which are largely absent in hospitals.[109] Moreover, the *Ingraham* Court had only an Eighth Amendment contention before it and did not consider whether school discipline could be deemed punishment in violation of substantive due process.[110] If the Eighth Amendment extension from prison to hospital is accepted, paddling in the prison or any other kind of discipline in the hospital would seem to be punishment subject to Eighth Amendment scrutiny. Thus, *Salerno* would

---

[98]*Block,* 468 U.S. at 585–89.

[99]*Wolfish,* 441 U.S. at 544–62.

[100]*See* Ingraham v. Wright, 430 U.S. 651, 685–86 (1977) (White, J., dissenting). The Supreme Court has repeatedly recognized that retribution and deterrence are the traditional aims of punishment. United States v. Halper, 490 U.S. 435, 448 (1989); Kennedy v. Mendoza–Martinez, 372 U.S. 144, 168 (1963). As the Court has noted, "a civil sanction that cannot fairly be said solely to serve a remedial purpose, but rather can only be explained as also serving either retributive or deterrent purposes, is punishment, as we have come to understand the term." *Halper,* 490 U.S. at 448 (dictum). The Court has concluded that " '[r]etribution and deterrence are not legitimate nonpunitive governmental objectives.' " *Id.* (quoting Bell v. Wolfish, 441 U.S. 520, 539, n.20 (1979)).

[101]437 U.S. at 682, 685.

[102]437 U.S. at 682 & nn.4–5.

[103]441 U.S. 520 (1979); *see supra* notes 49–51 and accompanying text.

[104]481 U.S. 739 (1987); *see supra* notes 62–67 and accompanying text.

[105]*See* text following *supra* note 68.

[106]430 U.S. 651 (1977); *see supra* notes 24–28 and accompanying text.

[107]*See supra* notes 27–28 and accompanying text.

[108]*See supra* note 30 and accompanying text.

[109]*See supra* note 32 and accompanying text.

[110]*See Ingraham,* 430 U.S. at 659.

not seem to disqualify institutional discipline from being considered punishment within the meaning of the Eighth Amendment.

In any event, even if not all hospital discipline is deemed punishment, discipline using intrusive treatment techniques should be. Such techniques seem "excessive"[111] in light of other disciplinary alternatives available to maintain institutional security—segregation, transfer to more secure hospital wards, and possibly even physical restraints—supporting the inference that punishment was actually intended.

Treatment methods imposed for institutional discipline should thus be deemed punishment within the cognizance of the Eighth Amendment. Treatment used as punishment cuts against the grain of constitutional values.[112] Treatment, and particularly medical treatment, should generally be left to the individual under a central value of our constitutional heritage—the promotion and preservation of individual autonomy.[113] Only in rare cases should government be permitted to impose treatment, especially when it is intrusive and medical in character. Government should be permitted to impose such treatment over the individual's objection, if at all, only when it can be justified medically.[114] When intrusive treatment is defended, not on medical grounds, but as a means of punishment, it is subject to special scrutiny under the Eighth Amendment, the provision of our Constitution that places explicit limits on punishment.

Medical punishment therefore should be deemed presumptively unconstitutional under the Eighth Amendment. At a minimum, such treatment should be considered cruel and unusual punishment in violation of the Eighth Amendment, and it violates substantive due process, if excessively painful and dehumanizing or disproportionate to the infraction involved. Moreover, such treatments administered for disciplinary purposes also would be unconstitutional if unnecessary, and thus excessive punishments, given the availability of alternative means at the disposal of correctional and hospital authorities for dealing with offender or patient misbehavior—the techniques mentioned above in connection with hospital discipline, as well as prison transfers or forfeiture of good time credit or other prison privileges for offenders. In view of these alternatives, the use of such intrusive treatments as psychotropic drugs or electroconvulsive therapy to deal with troublemakers for whom therapeutic considerations alone would not have mandated such approaches would seem unnecessarily degrading and excessive punishments that violate the Eighth Amendment.

How should treatments used for institutional management or the maintenance of institutional security be considered, if not imposed in a disciplinary context? Should they avoid Eighth Amendment scrutiny on the basis that these are legitimate governmental purposes other than punishment.[115] If the treatments used are excessive for the accomplishment of these purposes, they may be deemed punishments under the approach suggested in

---

[111]*See* United States v. Salerno, 481 U.S. 739, 747 (1987); Bell v. Wolfish, 441 U.S. 520, 538–39 (1979); *supra* note 51 and accompanying text.

[112]*See* Winick, *Competency to be Executed: A Therapeutic Jurisprudence Perspective,* 10 BEHAV. SCI. & L. 317, 330 (1992).

[113]*See generally* Winick, *On Autonomy: Legal and Psychological Perspectives,* 37 VILL. L. REV. 1705 (1993); *supra* chapter 11.

[114]*See* Riggins v. Nevada, 504 U.S. 127, 135 (1992); Washington v. Harper, 494 U.S. 210, 223–27 (1990); Winick, *Ambiguities in the Legal Meaning and Significance of Mental Illness,* 1 PSYCHOL. PUB. POL'Y & L. 534, 549–54 (1995); Winick, *Psychotropic Medication in the Criminal Trial Process: The Constitutional and Therapeutic Implications of* Riggins v. Nevada, 10 N.Y.L. SCH. J. HUM. RTS. 637, 690–91 (1993); *infra* chapter 16, part A (discussing therapeutic appropriateness principle).

[115]*Wolfish,* 441 U.S. at 538–39; *see supra* note 51 and accompanying text.

Bell v. Wolfish.[116] Electroconvulsive therapy or psychosurgery, if used for institutional management or maintenance of security, certainly would be excessive in this sense and would thus violate the Eighth Amendment. Psychotropic drugs present a harder case. Perhaps the use of psychotropic drugs to restore order in an emergency can be defended as a means of achieving the governmental interest in institutional security and thus considered not to be punishment. The availability in the circumstances of alternative means of responding to such an emergency, however, may render medication for this purpose excessive, particularly if the drugs used were highly intrusive and imposed severe negative side effects, like the antipsychotic drugs.[117] This contention, however, may conflict with the Supreme Court's deferential approach in the area of prison security,[118] although the Court seems inclined not to extend this approach beyond the prison.[119] Absent an emergency, however, the use of such drugs to maintain control does not seem " 'reasonably related' . . . to the concededly legitimate goals of . . . [institutional] safety and security"[120] and arguably should be deemed punishment within the cognizance of the Eighth Amendment. Because the use of most drugs for this purpose would violate contemporary standards of decency, it should be invalid as cruel and unusual.[121]

F. Behavior Modification in Corrections

Behavioral approaches in prison contexts raise especially interesting Eighth Amendment questions. Two of the positive reinforcement techniques, the token economy[122] and the tier system,[123] have been used frequently in adult and juvenile correctional institutions as well as in alternative community-based programs for offenders. In the token economy, the individual receives tokens as rewards for instances of desired behavior, and the tokens may be exchanged for various items or privileges that otherwise are unavailable. Inappropriate behavior results in the loss of tokens. A 1974 survey revealed that 14 states used token

---

[116]441 U.S. at 538–39; *see supra* note 51 and accompanying text.

[117]*See supra* chapter 5.

[118]*See* Washington v. Harper, 494 U.S. 210 (1990); *see supra* chapters 1, 15.

[119]*See* Riggins v. Nevada, 504 U.S. 127 (1992); Winick, *supra* note 113, at 690–98; *infra* chapter 16.

[120]Bee v. Greaves, 744 F.2d 1387, 1395 (10th Cir. 1984), *cert. denied,* 469 U.S. 1214 (1985) (quoting *Wolfish,* 441 U.S. at 539).

[121]*See* Nelson v. Heyne, 491 F.2d 352, 356 (7th Cir. 1974), *cert. denied,* 417 U.S. 976 (1976) (use of psychotropic drugs in juvenile correctional institution "for the purpose of controlling excited behavior" held to violate Eighth Amendment); Welsch v. Likens, 373 F. Supp. 487 (D. Minn. 1974), *aff'd in part, vacated and remanded in part,* 550 F.2d 1122 (8th Cir. 1977) (psychotropic drugs used to control behavior of inmates with mental retardation held to violate Eighth Amendment). Even if not a violation of the Eighth Amendment, any medication administered for purposes of institutional security that was not medically appropriate for the individual would offend substantive due process. *See* Riggins v. Nevada, 504 U.S. 127, 135 (1992); Washington v. Harper, 494 U.S. 210, 223–27 (1990); Winick, *supra* note 112, at 330; *infra* chapter 16, part A.

[122]*See* T. AYLLON & N. AZRIN, THE TOKEN ECONOMY, A MOTIVATIONAL SYSTEM FOR THERAPY AND REHABILITATION (1968); A. KAZDIN, THE TOKEN ECONOMY, A REVIEW AND EVALUATION (1977); Wexler, *Token and Taboo: Behavior Modification, Token Economies, and the Law,* 61 CAL. L. REV. 81 (1973); *supra* chapter 4.

[123]*See* Green v. Baron, 879 F.2d 305 (8th Cir. 1989); Canterino v. Wilson, 546 F. Supp. 174 (W.D. Ky. 1982); Clonce v. Richardson, 379 F. Supp. 338, 344 (W.D. Mo. 1974) (Project START); Carlson, *Behavior Modification in the Federal Bureau of Prisons,* 1 NEW ENG. J. PRISONS L. 155, 159–63 (1974); Wexler, *supra* note 122, at 87–88; *supra* chapter 4.

economy systems in their prisons.[124] The Federal Bureau of Prisons has also used token economies in the treatment of delinquents at two facilities.[125]

A variation on the token economy, the tier system, grants privileges on the basis of the prisoner's place in a system of tiers. Inmates earn their way from an orientation level, where privileges are scant or nonexistent, upwards through a ranked series of tiers with increasingly more desirable privileges and conditions. This model was used in the controversial Federal Bureau of Prisons' Project START. In that program the prisoners at entry level were denied such basic privileges as daily showers, exercise, visitors, reading materials, personal property, and commissary privileges—all of which could be regained only by behaving in conformity with program goals.[126] Project START, although discontinued by the Federal Bureau of Prisons, has been used as a model for other prison programs.[127]

The 1974 survey previously referred to indicated that at least seven state prison systems used aversive conditioning in their correctional therapy programs.[128] More extreme examples have been the use of succinylcholine, a paralyzing drug, in a California prison program,[129] and a program for child molesters in a Connecticut prison that paired electric shocks to the prisoner's groin area with arousal experienced while viewing slides of naked children.[130]

To the extent these behavioral approaches are carefully designed, serious attempts to extinguish maladaptive behavior patterns, phobias, compulsive behavior, or other pathologies, they may be deemed treatment as opposed to punishment.[131] On the other hand, inappropriately designed behavioral programs that constitute punishment disguised as treatment should be deemed punishment within the meaning of the Eighth Amendment.[132] If they are designed to extinguish behavior patterns that led to incarceration in order to avoid

[124]See Blatte, State Prisons and the Use of Behavior Control, 4 HASTINGS CTR. REP., Sept. 1974, at 11. See generally Geller, et al., Behavior Modification in a Prison, 4 CRIM. JUST. & BEHAV. 11 (1977); Milan & McKee, The Cellblock Token Economy, Token Reinforcement Procedures in a Maximum Security Correctional Institution for Adult Male Felons, 9 J. APPLIED BEHAV. ANALYSIS 253 (1976); Petrock & Walter, Behavior Modification in Corrections: Implications for Organizational Change, 1 NEW. ENG. J. PRISON L. 203 (1974).

[125]See Carlson, supra note 123, at 158–59. A community-based residential treatment home for court-involved delinquents in Kansas—Achievement Place—which uses a token economy and other behavioral procedures, has been widely copied. See Phillips et al., Achievement Place: Modification of the Behavior of Pre-Delinquent Boys Within a Token Economy, 4 J. APPLIED BEHAV. ANALYSIS 45 (1971).

[126]See Clonce v. Richardson, 379 F. Supp. 338, 344 (W.D. Mo. 1974); Carlson, supra note 123, at 159–63. Another controversial program using a tier system is Maryland's Patuxent Institute for "defective delinquents." Editor's Commentary to Patuxent Institute, 5 BULL. AM. ACAD. PSYCHIATRY & L. v–vi (1977) (symp. issue).

[127]E.g., Green v. Baron, 879 F.2d 305 (8th Cir. 1989); Canterino v. Wilson, 546 F. Supp. 174 (W.D. Ky. 1982); see Gaylin & Blatte, Behavior Modification in Prisons, 13 AM. CRIM. L. REV. 11, 25 (1975).

[128]Blatte, supra note 124, at 11. It may be that, in response to the bad publicity these techniques received in the 1970s, aversive programs are rarely used today in prison programs. See PALLONE, supra note 60, at 95–97; but see Goldsmith v. Dean, No. 2:93-CV-383 (D. Vt. filed Dec. 1993) (drama therapy program with aversive conditioning features).

[129]See Mackey v. Procunier, 477 F.2d 877, 877–78 (9th Cir. 1973).

[130]See Wolfe & Marino, A Program of Behavior Treatment for Incarcerated Pedophiles, 13 AM. CRIM. L. REV. 69, 77–78 (1975).

[131]Green v. Baron, 879 F.2d 305 (8th Cir. 1989) (upholding tier program in security and medical facility to which jail detainee was transferred to stabilize his behavior so he could later attend his criminal trial and assist in his defense).

[132]See, e.g., Converse v. Nelson, No. 95-16776 (Mass. Super. Ct. July 1995) (attacking the Bridgewater State Hospital's Phase System, a tier program). "Because the Phase program does not exhibit any of the characteristics of a competently designed and implemented behavioral management program, it is not likely to produce any therapeutic goals and must be viewed as a punishment program." Affidavit of Joel Dvoskin, filed in Converse, at 12 (July 1995).

recidivism, such as the Connecticut prison program for child molesters, they may be considered "rehabilitation" and thus an aspect of punishment. Even if considered punishment within the meaning of the Eighth Amendment, however, they may be considered constitutionally permissible punishments. Although arguably punishments within the meaning of the Eighth Amendment, if they are authorized by the legislature for rehabilitative purposes they may not sufficiently shock the conscience to receive Eighth Amendment condemnation. Of course, if deemed ineffective[133] or if unnecessarily painful and degrading in light of alternative reinforcers,[134] these programs could be deemed cruel and unusual.

This is especially true for those aversive techniques that inflict serious damage to individuals, including "pain, frustration, increased aggressiveness, arousal, general unspecific anxieties, somatic and physiological malfunctions, and development of various unexpected and often pathological operant behaviors."[135] Several aversive techniques could well constitute cruel and unusual punishment to the extent they are identical to prohibited punitive sanctions.[136] Social isolation, for example, is the functional equivalent of the strip-room and solitary confinement, the abusive use of which has been condemned as violating the Eighth Amendment in cases involving prison and juvenile institutions.[137] The administration of electric shocks to the body, sometimes used in aversive programs, also has been considered cruel and unusual when used for prison discipline.[138] The mild slapping used in some aversive programs seems little different from the corporal punishment held to be cruel and unusual punishment in prison and juvenile cases.[139] Some of these techniques are thus sufficiently offensive to prevailing standards of decency to implicate Eighth Amendment concerns.

If used for therapeutic purposes, however, they may not, under the Supreme Court's "alternative purpose" approach invoked in *Bell v. Wolfish,*[140] be considered "punishment" in the constitutional sense, at least if not excessive in view of the availability of less drastic conditioners. On the other hand, aversive conditioning in correctional facilities is highly controversial, and some commentators have contended that it is ineffective as treatment

---

[133]*See* text accompanying *supra* note 57.

[134]The comparison should be not only with other aversive reinforcers that are less painful or degrading, but also with positive reinforcers, particularly in light of the prevailing clinical view that aversion therapy should not be used unless positive reinforcement has first been attempted unsuccessfully. *See supra* chapter 4.

[135]Bucher & Lovaas, *Use of Aversive Stimulation in Behavior Modification, in* MIAMI SYMPOSIUM ON THE PREDICTION OF BEHAVIOR, 1967: AVERSIVE STIMULATION 77, 78 (M. Jones ed., 1968). *See also supra* chapter 4.

[136]*See supra* note 3.

[137]*See, e.g.,* Hutto v. Finney, 437 U.S. 678 (1978); LaReau v. McDougal, 473 F.2d 974, 978 (2d Cir. 1972), *cert. denied,* 414 U.S. 878 (1973); Wright v. McMann, 387 F.2d 519, 526 (2d Cir. 1967); Gates v. Collier, 379 F. Supp. 881, 894–95 (N.D. Miss. 1972), *aff'd,* 501 F.2d 1291 (5th Cir. 1974); Inmates of Boys Training Sch. v. Affleck, 346 F. Supp. 1354, 1366–67 (D.R.I. 1972); Landman v. Royster, 333 F. Supp. 621, 648 (E.D. Va. 1971); Sostre v. Rockefeller, 312 F. Supp. 863 (S.D.N.Y. 1970), *modified sub nom.* Sostre v. McGinnis, 442 F.2d 178 (2d Cir. 1971), *cert. denied,* 404 U.S. 1049, 405 U.S. 978 (1972).

[138]*See, e.g., Hutto,* 437 U.S. at 682 & n.5; Gates v. Collier, 349 F. Supp. 881, 900 (N.D. Miss. 1972), *aff'd,* 501 F.2d 1291 (5th Cir. 1974); Holt v. Sarver, 309 F. Supp. 362 (E.D. Ark. 1970), *aff'd,* 442 F.2d 304 (8th Cir. 1971).

[139]*See, e.g., Hutto,* 637 U.S. at 682 & n.4; Jackson v. Bishop, 404 U.S. 571, 579–80 (8th Cir. 1968) (Blackmun, J.); Nelson v. Heyne, 355 F. Supp. 451, 454 (N.D. Ind. 1972), *aff'd,* 491 F.2d 352 (7th Cir.), *cert. denied,* 417 U.S. 976 (1974); Landman v. Royster, 333 F. Supp. 621 (E.D. Va. 1971); Harper v. Wall, 85 F. Supp. 783, 786–87 (D.N.J. 1949).

[140]441 U.S. 520 (1979); *see* text accompanying *supra* notes 50–52.

within the prison and constitutes little more than the disguised infliction of punishment.[141] To the extent this criticism is valid, such programs would, of course, merit Eighth Amendment scrutiny.[142]

Most of the positive reinforcement programs—for example, token economies or tier approaches—will not raise Eighth Amendment concerns, with one exception. Positive reinforcement procedures involving substantial entry-level deprivations may trigger Eighth Amendment scrutiny. When token economy or tier programs start offenders off in a situation of severe deprivation that may be remedied only by behaving in conformity with program goals, the reinforcers used may raise special concerns.[143] To the extent that courts have held that prisons must provide certain minimum conditions and meet minimum standards to avoid Eighth Amendment condemnation,[144] these cases may limit the use of these basic rights and privileges as reinforcers in positive reinforcement programs.[145] With this exception, however, the positive reinforcement programs would not seem to implicate the Eighth Amendment.

Verbal approaches like psychotherapy, counseling, and educational programs,[146] as well as such behavioral approaches as systematic desensitization, shaping, modeling, contingency contracting, and cognitive behavior therapy,[147] would seem to present no Eighth Amendment concerns, even if applied in prison rehabilitation programs or for other punitive purposes. These approaches, even if deemed punishments, would not qualify as "cruel and unusual."[148] Even if experienced by some patients and offenders as unpleas-

---

[141]See, e.g., P. HILTS, BEHAVIOR MOD 113–33 (1974); Bandura, *The Ethics and Social Purposes of Behavior Modification, in* 3 ANNUAL REVIEW OF BEHAVIOR THERAPY: THEORY AND PRACTICE 13, 15–16 (C. Franks & G. Wilson eds., 1975); Opton, *Institutional Behavior Modification as a Fraud and Sham,* 17 ARIZ. L. REV. 20 (1975); Opton, *Psychiatric Violence Against Prisoners: When Therapy is Punishment,* 45 MISS. L. REV. 605 (1974); Note, *supra* note 3, at 910–12.

[142]See *supra* notes 56, 130 and accompanying text.

[143]Moreover, unlike most positive reinforcers, which function as motivators and can successfully be resisted, the use of such basic rights and privileges as reinforcers may prove irresistible. See Shah, *Basic Principles and Concepts, in* CORRECTIONAL CLASSIFICATION AND TREATMENT 123, 127 (Am. Correctional Ass'n Comm'n on Classification & Treatment 1975) ("[T]he old saying that you can take a horse to water but you cannot get him to drink, is not necessarily correct. If the horse were fed salt, or allowed to stand in the sun and went without water for a while, one could indeed get him to drink.").

[144]E.g., Hutto v. Finney, 437 U.S. 678 (1978); Ramos v. Lamm, 639 F.2d 559 (10th Cir. 1980), *cert. denied,* 450 U.S. 1041 (1981); James v. Wallace, 533 F.2d 963 (5th Cir. 1976); *see* Rhodes v. Chapman, 452 U.S. 337, 347 (1981) (describing *Hutto* as invalidating as cruel and unusual conditions of confinement in two Arkansas prisons "because they resulted in unquestioned and serious deprivations of basic human needs.").

[145]Wexler, *supra* note 122, at 93–95; Gobert, *supra* note 70, at 184; Winick, *supra* note 58, at 362; *see supra* chapter 4. A parallel analysis applies to these techniques when used in civil mental hospitals and similar institutions in view of cases establishing minimum standards and conditions for such institutions as a matter of due process. *See, e.g.,* Wyatt v. Stickney, 344 F. Supp. 373 (M.D. Ala. 1972), *aff'd in part, rev'd in part, and remanded in part sub nom.* Wyatt v. Aderholt, 503 F.2d 1305 (5th Cir. 1974). An offender or patient wishing to participate in a behavioral program involving the use of basic rights or privileges as reinforcers, provided the conditions of informed consent are satisfied, should, however, be able to waive the right to resist such a program and consent to at least the temporary withholding of such privileges. *See infra* chapter 18; Budd & Baer, *Behavior Modification and the Law: Implications of Recent Judicial Decisions,* 4 J. PSYCHIATRY & L. 171, 205 (1976); *cf.* Gilmore v. Utah, 429 U.S. 1012 (1976) (right to attack validity of death penalty statute under Eighth Amendment held waivable).

[146]See *supra* chapter 3.

[147]See *supra* chapter 4.

[148]Winick, *supra* note 58, at 356–57.

ant,[149] these programs are not "so bad as to be shocking to the conscience of reasonably civilized people."[150]

The Eighth Amendment may thus play a role, although somewhat more limited than the First Amendment[151] or substantive due process,[152] in restricting mental health and correctional treatment. Most treatments will not meet the constitutional definition of punishment, but those that do will be scrutinized under an Eighth Amendment standard that will prohibit them if excessive, ineffective, disproportionate to the offense, unnecessarily painful and degrading, or unauthorized as punishments. In the case of treatments that are found to implicate the First Amendment or substantive due process, the constitutionality of involuntary treatment will turn on scrutiny of governmental purposes for their imposition[153] and the availability of alternative means for accomplishing them.[154] Treatments found to violate the Eighth Amendment standard, however, if imposed involuntarily, will be condemned as unconstitutional without further scrutiny.[155] Whereas intrusive treatment found to be necessary to the attainment of compelling governmental interests thus may not violate the First Amendment or the Due Process Clauses, the Eighth Amendment will prevent its involuntary imposition if it would constitute a form of punishment so shocking to the conscience as to violate basic concepts of human dignity. Although these other constitutional protections require courts to engage in a balancing of relevant interests, the Eighth Amendment stands as an absolute barrier to imposed treatment that constitutes cruel and unusual punishment.

---

[149]*See* Whitley v. Albers, 475 U.S. 312, 319 (1986) (Not every governmental action affecting the interests or well-being of a prisoner is subject to Eighth Amendment scrutiny, however. "After incarceration, only the 'unnecessary and wanton infliction of pain' . . . constitutes cruel and unusual punishment forbidden by the Eighth Amendment.") (quoting Ingraham v. Wright, 430 U.S. 651, 670 (1977) and Estelle v. Gamble, 429 U.S. 97, 103 (1976)); Rhodes v. Chapman, 452 U.S. 337, 349 (1981) (prisons "cannot be free of discomfort").

[150]*See* Holt v. Sarver, 309 F. Supp. 362, 372–73 (D. Ark. 1970), *aff'd,* 442 F.2d 304 (8th Cir. 1971).

[151]*See supra* chapter 10.

[152]*See supra* chapter 11.

[153]*See supra* chapters 10 (First Amendment) and 11 (substantive due process).

[154]*See supra* chapter 16, part B.

[155]*See, e.g.,* Estelle v. Gamble, 429 U.S. 97 (1976); Furman v. Georgia, 408 U.S. 238 (1972) (per curiam); Robinson v. California, 370 U.S. 660 (1962); Trop v. Dulles, 356 U.S. 86 (1958) (plurality opinion).

Chapter 13
RELIGION–BASED REFUSAL OF TREATMENT:
Constitutional Protection for the Free Exercise of Religion

A. The Free Exercise Clause and Treatment Refusal

The First Amendment's protection of the free exercise of religion provides additional support for a right to refuse treatment when refusal is based on religious principles. In addition to the separation of church and state secured by the Establishment Clause, the First Amendment guarantees freedom from laws "prohibiting the free exercise" of religion.[1] Like other fundamental liberties guaranteed by the Bill of Rights, the protections of the Free Exercise Clause of the First Amendment have been incorporated into the Fourteenth Amendment Due Process Clause and thereby made applicable to the states.[2] The purpose of this clause "is to secure religious liberty in the individual by prohibiting any invasion thereof by civil authority."[3] It protects the fundamental principle of voluntarism, rather than governmental compulsion, in matters of religious practice.[4]

Patients whose religious beliefs prohibit medical treatment have long been recognized to have a right under the Free Exercise Clause to refuse treatment, even treatment necessary

---

[1] U.S. CONST. amend. I. The phrase "free exercise of religion" originated in Maryland's Toleration Act of 1649. Levy, *The Bill of Rights, in* ESSAYS ON THE MAKING OF THE CONSTITUTION 258, 295 (L. Levy ed., 2d ed. 1987). An early formulation came in the 1663 Charter of Rhode Island and Providence Plantations, which secured for all inhabitants "the free exercise and enjoyment of their civil and religious rights" by providing that every person might "freelye and fullye hav and enjoye his and theire owne judgments and consciences, in matters of religious concernments. . . ." *Id.*; SOURCES OF OUR LIBERTIES 170 (R. Perry ed., 1959).

[2] The Free Exercise Clause was first applied to the states in 1940 in Cantwell v. Connecticut, 310 U.S. 296 (1940). In dictum, the Court had previously stated that the Fourteenth Amendment protects the individual's freedom to "worship God according to the dictates of his own conscience. . . ." Meyer v. Nebraska, 262 U.S. 390, 399 (1923). *See* Abington Sch. Dist. v. Schempp, 374 U.S. 203, 253–58 (1963) (Brennan, J., concurring); P. KAUPER, RELIGION AND THE CONSTITUTION 53–57 (1964).

[3] *Schempp,* 374 U.S. at 223.

[4] L. TRIBE, AMERICAN CONSTITUTIONAL LAW § 14–3, at 1160 (2d ed. 1988); Adams & Gordon, *The Doctrine of Accommodation in the Jurisprudence of the Religion Clauses,* 37 DEPAUL L. REV. 317, 331 (1988); Giannella, *Religious Liberty, Non-Establishment, and Doctrinal Development—Part I. The Religious Liberty Guarantee,* 80 HARV. L. REV. 1381, 1386 (1967); Hall, *Religion, Equality and Difference,* 65 TEMP. L. REV. 1, 37 (1992); Williams & Williams, *Volitionalism and Religious Liberty,* 76 CORNELL L. REV. 769, 896–99 (1991); Note, *Reinterpreting the Religion Clauses: Constitutional Construction and Construction of the Self,* 97 HARV. L. REV. 1468, 1475 (1984); Note, *Toward a Constitutional Definition of Religion,* 91 HARV. L. REV. 1056, 1058 (1978) [hereinafter Note, *Definition of Religion*].

to save their lives.[5] Similarly, patients or offenders whose religious beliefs preclude a particular type of mental health treatment, or all such treatment, may also be able to assert a right to refuse treatment on the basis of the Free Exercise Clause. A free exercise claim will be raised in only a limited number of right-to-refuse-treatment cases because comparatively few instances of mental health treatment refusal are based on religious objection. Several such cases have been litigated, however, and the courts have consistently recognized that a genuine religious basis for treatment refusal is protected by the Free Exercise Clause and should be honored absent compelling necessity. These cases have arisen in the context of psychotropic medication. In *Winters v. Miller*,[6] for example, a Christian Scientist who objected to the administration of psychotropic drugs at a city mental hospital to which she had been involuntarily committed was held entitled to bring a damages action for violation of a right to freedom of religion under the Free Exercise Clause. Several other lower courts have recognized a right to refuse psychotropic drugs on the basis of religious objections.[7] Moreover, these courts have recognized the right in cases involving individuals who were competent at the time of drug refusal[8] and individuals who, although incompetent at the time, had objected to treatment on religious grounds prior to becoming incompetent.[9]

B. The Definition of ''Religion'' Under the Free Exercise Clause

In order to make a claim under the Free Exercise Clause, the individual must assert a treatment objection that is based on religion. That the individual characterizes such an objection as religious is not dispositive. Indeed, patients may base such a claim on highly individualistic ''religions,'' forcing courts to make difficult and sensitive judgments regarding whether the ''religion'' asserted qualifies for First Amendment protection. The views of the Framers of the Bill of Rights provide little guidance in ascertaining the meaning of *religion* in the First Amendment. Although the Framers were theists and therefore probably equated religion with belief in a Supreme Being,[10] no evidence suggests that they intended to limit the reach of the First Amendment Free Exercise Clause to theistic religions.[11] Early cases construing the clause took a traditional view of religion, stressing the

---

[5]*See, e.g, In re* Milton, 505 N.E. 2d 255, 258 (Ohio 1987) (Free Exercise Clause prohibits state from compelling medical treatment absent an overriding state interest), *cert. denied,* 484 U.S. 820 (1987); *In re* Brown, 478 So.2d 1033, 1039–40 (Miss. 1985) (upholding refusal of blood transfusion based on constitutional right of free exercise of religion); Holmes v. Silver Cross Hosp., 340 F. Supp. 125 (N.D. Ill. 1972) (competent Jehovah's Witness can refuse blood transfusion necessary to save life); *In re* Osborne, 294 A.2d 372 (D.C. App. 1972) (same); *In re* Brooks, 205 N.E.2d 435 (Ill. 1965) (same); *but see* Application of President and Directors of Georgetown College, Inc., 331 F.2d 1000 (D.C. Cir.), *cert. denied,* 377 U.S. 978 (1964) (overriding objection of Jehovah's Witness, not lucid at the time, to refuse blood transfusion necessary to save life); John F. Kennedy Mem. Hosp. v. Heston, 279 A.2d 670 (N.J. 1971) (same). *See generally* Bryn, *Compulsory Lifesaving Treatment for Competent Adults,* 44 FORDHAM L. REV. 1 (1975); Fox, *Constitutional Law—Potential Abandonment of Minor Child Curtails Adult Right to Refuse Life-Saving Medical Treatment—* Norwood v. Munoz, 409 Mass. 116, 564 N.E. 2d 1017 (Mass. 1991), 25 SUFFOLK U. L. REV. 821, 823 (1991); Nobel, *Religious Healing in the Courts: The Liberties and Liabilities of Patients, Parents, and Healers,* 16 U. PUGET SOUND L. REV. 613 (1993); Note, *Developments Medical Technology and the Law,* 103 HARV. L. REV. 1522, 1669 (1990).

[6]446 F.2d 65 (2d Cir.), *cert. denied,* 404 U.S. 985 (1971).

[7]*E.g.,* Osgood v. District of Columbia, 567 F. Supp. 1026 (D.D.C. 1983); *In re* Boyd, 403 A.2d 744 (D.C. 1979); Dyer v. Brooks, No. 953758, 1 MENTAL DISABILITY L. REP. 122 (1976).

[8]Winters v. Miller, 446 F.2d 65 (2d Cir.), *cert. denied,* 404 U.S. 985 (1971).

[9]*In re* Boyd, 403 A.2d 744 (D.C. App. 1979).

[10]Freeman, *The Misguided Search for the Constitutional Definition of ''Religion,''* 71 GEO. L.J. 1519, 1520–21 (1983); Note, *Definition of Religion, supra* note 4, at 1060.

[11]Freeman, *supra* note 10, at 1521; Note, *Definition of Religion, supra* note 4, at 1060.

relationship of individuals to their Creator.[12] In the 1940s the courts began to broaden this traditional view. In a case interpreting the conscientious objector exemption of the Selective Service Act of 1940, Judge Augustus Hand described conscientious objection as "a response of the individual to an inward mentor, call it conscience or God, that is for many persons at the present time the equivalent of what has always been thought a religious impulse."[13] This stress on the psychological functions of a belief in the life of the individual as the defining characteristic of religion, as opposed to the more traditional focus on the external characteristics of a religious denomination, marked a significant shift in emphasis.[14]

In the 1944 case of *United States v. Ballard*,[15] the Supreme Court made it clear that unorthodox faiths met the definition of religion in the First Amendment and that courts should be reluctant to inquire into either the content or the accuracy of the individual's beliefs:[16]

> [Freedom of religion] embraces the right to maintain theories of life and of death and of the hereafter which are rank heresy to followers of the orthodox faiths. . . . Men may believe what they cannot prove. They may not be put to the proof of their religious doctrines or beliefs. Religious experiences which are as real as life to some may be incomprehensible to others. Yet the fact that they may be beyond the ken of mortals does not mean that they can be made suspect before the law.

In the 1961 case of *Torcaso v. Watkins*,[17] the Supreme Court invalidated under the Free Exercise Clause a state statute that required those seeking appointment as a notary public to declare their belief in God. The Court explicitly recognized that the First Amendment protected nontheistic faiths such as Buddhism, Taoism, ethical culture, and secular humanism.[18]

The Court's most extensive consideration of the definition of *religion* occurred in a series of cases involving the statutory conscientious objector exemption from military service. In *United States v. Seeger*,[19] the Court rejected a narrow construction of the statutory test for the exemption that would have required belief "in a relation to a Supreme Being." Instead, the Court held that the test must be whether the individual's belief is "sincere and meaningful" and

> occupies a place in the life of its possessor parallel to that filled by the orthodox belief in God of one who clearly qualifies for the exemption. Where such beliefs have parallel positions in the lives of their respective holders we cannot say that one is 'in a relation to a Supreme Being' and the other is not.[20]

The Court's strained statutory construction presumably was driven by the desire to avoid the constitutional difficulties of honoring Congress' evident intention to exclude

---

[12]*See, e.g.*, Davis v. Beason, 133 U.S. 333, 342 (1890) ("[T]he term 'religion' has reference to one's relations to his Creator, and to the obligations they impose of reverence for his being and character, and of obedience to his will."); *see* Note, *Definition of Religion, supra* note 4, at 1060–61.

[13]United States v. Kauten, 133 F.2d 703, 708 (2d Cir. 1943).

[14]Note, *Definition of Religion, supra* note 4, at 1061.

[15]322 U.S. 78 (1944).

[16]*Id.* at 86–87.

[17]367 U.S. 488 (1961).

[18]*Id.* at 495 n.11.

[19]380 U.S. 163 (1965).

[20]*Id.* at 166.

nontheists from the conscientious objector status.[21] Although the Court was engaged in statutory construction, its holding therefore had strong constitutional overtones.[22] The *Seeger* Court also construed the statute as placing within the ambit of religious belief all sincere beliefs "based upon a power or being, or upon a faith, to which all else is subordinate or upon which all else is ultimately dependent."[23] Referring to the writings of modern theologians such as Paul Tillich in support of its view, the Court construed the concept of a "Supreme Being" broadly as not limited to an anthropomorphic entity.[24] In another conscientious objector case, *Welsh v. United States*,[25] the Court extended *Seeger* by holding that purely ethical and moral considerations could count as religious if held strongly and that a sincere practitioner might be denied the conscientious objector exemption only if his system of beliefs "does not rest at all upon moral, ethic or religious principles but instead rests solely upon considerations of policy, pragmatism, or expediency."[26]

The Court provided further clarification of the concept of religion in *Wisconsin v. Yoder*,[27] in which it found that the Free Exercise Clause protected the right of Amish parents to withdraw their children from school after the eighth grade. The Court made it clear that "purely secular considerations" would not meet the requirement of religious belief within the meaning of the First Amendment.[28] It illustrated the secular–religious dichotomy by referring to Thoreau's rejection of the social values of his time by isolating himself at Walden Pond. In the Court's view, Thoreau's beliefs were "philosophical and personal rather than religious. . . ."[29] This dicta seems to undercut the implication in *Welsh* that purely moral and ethical principles could count as religious, but the point is far from resolved.

Most religious objections to mental health or correctional treatment are grounded in traditional religions for which refusal of treatment is a basic tenet, such as Christian Science.[30] Other faiths, however, can qualify as religions even though they may be unorthodox

---

[21]*See id.* at 188 (Douglas, J., concurring); Note, *Definition of Religion, supra* note 4, at 1064.

[22]*See* International Soc'y for Krishna Consciousness v. Barber, 650 F.2d 430, 439–40 (2d Cir. 1981); Malnak v. Yogi, 592 F.2d 197, 207–10 (3d Cir. 1979) (Adams, J., concurring); Choper, *Defining "Religion" in the First Amendment,* 1982 U. ILL. L. REV. 479, 589; Clancey & Weiss, *The Conscientious Objector Exemption: Problems in Conceptual Clarity and Constitutional Considerations,* 17 ME. L. REV. 143, 145 (1965); Freeman, *supra* note 10, at 1526 n.45; Greenawalt, *All or Nothing at All: The Defeat of Selective Conscientious Objection,* 1971 SUP. CT. REV. 31, 39; Greenawalt, *Religion as a Concept in Constitutional Law,* 72 CAL. L. REV. 753, 760–61 (1984); Rabin, *When Is a Religious Belief Religious: United States v. Seeger and the Scope of Free Exercise,* 51 CORNELL L.Q. 231, 240 (1966); Note, *Definition of Religion, supra* note 4, at 1064.

[23]380 U.S. at 167.

[24]*Id.* at 180–83, 187; *see* P. TILLICH, DYNAMICS OF FAITH 1–4 (1957).

[25]398 U.S. 333 (1970).

[26]*Id.* at 342–43.

[27]406 U.S. 205 (1972).

[28]*Id.* at 215.

[29]*Id.* at 215–16. *See also* Africa v. Pennsylvania, 662 F.2d 1025, 1034–35 (3d Cir. 1981), *cert. denied,* 456 U.S. 908 (1982) (back-to-nature group MOVE held philosophical rather than religious).

[30]*See* M. EDDY, SCIENCE AND HEALTH WITH KEY TO THE SCRIPTURES 165–201 (1875). Many of the right to refuse mental health treatment cases have involved Christian Scientists. *E.g.,* Winters v. Miller, 446 F.2d 65 (2d Cir.), *cert. denied,* 404 U.S. 985 (1971); Osgood v. District of Columbia, 567 F. Supp. 1026 (D.D.C. 1983); *In re* Boyd, 403 A.2d 744 (D.C. 1979).

or nontheistic,[31] provided their adherents are found to meet the parallel belief test of *Seeger*,[32] and their beliefs are not considered merely philosophical and personal[33] or based solely on considerations of policy, pragmatism, or expediency.[34]

C. The Requirements of Sincerity and Centrality

To qualify under the Free Exercise Clause, not only must the belief asserted be religious in nature, but it also must be sincerely held[35] and the practice affected must be central to the individual's religious belief system.[36] The practice in question need not be absolutely required by the particular religion in order to be accorded constitutional protection, but it must be regarded as essential by the individual asserting the free exercise claim.[37] Applying these principles, a district court rejected a free exercise claim by a prisoner challenging the administration of psychotropic medication when the plaintiff failed to demonstrate that he was a sincere adherent of an established religion that prohibited the use of such drugs.[38]

Patients or offenders may thus assert a claim to refuse involuntary mental health treatment on the basis of the Free Exercise Clause if they can demonstrate that the objection

---

[31]*See* Torcaso v. Watkins, 367 U.S. 488, 495 n.11 (1961); *supra* notes 17–18 and accompanying text; Freeman, *supra* note 10, at 1553–54; *see, e.g.*, United States v. Ballard, 322 U.S. 78 (1943) (the "I Am" movement); Malnak v. Yogi, 592 F.2d 197 (3d Cir. 1979) (per curiam) (Transcendental Meditation); Kennedy v. Meacham, 540 F.2d 1057 (10th Cir. 1976) ("Satanic" religion); Remmers v. Brewer, 494 F.2d 1277 (8th Cir.), *cert. denied*, 419 U.S. 1012 (1974) ("Church of the New Song"); Founding Church of Scientology v. United States, 409 F.2d 1146 (D.C. Cir. 1966) (Scientology); Williams v. Warden, 470 F. Supp. 1123 (D. Conn. 1979) ("Christian Adamic" faith).

[32]*See* United States v. Seeger, 380 U.S. 163, 166 (1965); notes 19–24 and accompanying text.

[33]*See* Wisconsin v. Yoder, 406 U.S. 205, 215–16 (1972); *supra* notes 27–29 and accompanying text.

[34]*See* Welsh v. United States, 398 U.S. 333, 342–43 (1970); *supra* notes 25–26 and accompanying text.

[35]*See* TRIBE, *supra* note 4, § 14–12, at 1242; Giannella, *supra* note 4, at 1418; Note, *Definition of Religion*, *supra* note 4, at 1081–82; *see, e.g.*, Theriault v. Silber, 391 F. Supp. 578 (W.D. Tex. 1975) (finding the alleged religion a sham to obtain concessions from prison authorities), *vacated and remanded*, 547 F.2d 1279 (5th Cir. 1977), *reinstated on remand*, 453 F. Supp. 254 (W.D. Tex. 1978); United States v. Kuch, 288 F. Supp. 439, 445 (D.D.C. 1968) (denying religious exemption from federal drug regulations for members of the Neo-American Church, found to be merely a tactical pretense of religion); *In re* Grady, 394 P.2d 728, 729 (Cal. 1964) (remanding for a determination of whether a self-styled "peyote preacher" "actually engaged in good faith in the practice of a religion").

[36]*See* TRIBE, *supra* note 4, §§ 14–12, at 1247–50; Galanter, *Religious Freedoms in the United States: A Turning Point?*, WIS. L. REV. (1966) 217, 274–78; *compare* Wisconsin v. Yoder, 406 U.S. 205, 222–29, 235–36 (1972) (extensive analysis of Amish life and culture, demonstrating that Amish religious beliefs would be seriously burdened by requiring adolescent Amish children to attend school beyond the eighth grade); Sherbert v. Verner, 374 U.S. 398, 406 (1963) (Seventh Day Adventist's religious opposition to work on Saturday found to be "a cardinal principle of her religious faith"); Teterud v. Burns, 522 F.2d 357, 360 (8th Cir. 1975) (Cree Indian prison inmate's belief in wearing long, braided hair found "deeply rooted in religious belief"); *and* Furguan v. Georgia State Bd. of Offender Rehabilitation, 554 F. Supp. 873, 876 (N.D. Ga. 1982) (growing a beard "deeply rooted" in Sunni Muslim faith) *with* United States v. Reynolds, 98 U.S. 145 (1878) (polygamy, although a basic tenet of Mormonism, held not to be essential to the practice of the religion).

[37]The courts have focused on the individual's interpretation of the requirements of his or her religion, rather than the formal tenets of the religion or the practices followed by a majority of its adherents. Thomas v. Review Bd., 450 U.S. 707, 715 (1981) ("[T]he guarantee of free exercise is not limited to beliefs which are shared by all of the members of a religious sect. . . . Courts are not arbiters of scriptural interpretation."); Prushinowski v. Hambrick, 570 F. Supp. 863 (E.D.N.C. 1983); Schlesinger v. Carlson, 489 F. Supp. 612 (M.D. Pa. 1980); Moskowitz v. Wilkinson, 432 F. Supp. 947 (D. Conn. 1977) ("It is [petitioner's] own religious belief that is asserted, not anyone else's. The court need not and should not attempt to determine whether a religious tribunal would hold that the tenets of the Jewish religion do not require petitioner to adhere to his preferred level of observance.").

[38]Sconiers v. Jarvis, 458 F. Supp. 37, 40 (D. Kan. 1978).

is based on a sincerely held religious belief and that the prohibition of treatment is an essential part of their religion. As previously indicated, such claims have been accepted in the context of the refusal of psychotropic drugs.[39] Similar claims, of course, may be raised with respect to any of the mental health treatment techniques, even those regarded as nonintrusive. Unlike the First Amendment right to be free of interference with mental processes[40] or the substantive due process basis for the right to refuse treatment,[41] for which the treatment in question must pass a threshold level of intrusiveness in order to trigger constitutional scrutiny, a free exercise claim may be raised without regard to intrusiveness, as long as the treatment in question is objectionable on religious grounds.

D. The Scrutiny Applied to Free Exercise Claims

Once a religious objection to treatment meeting these requirements is raised, what level of judicial scrutiny will it receive? As with the fundamental constitutional rights previously discussed—the First Amendment right to be free of interference with mental processes[42] and the substantive due process right to bodily integrity, mental privacy, and individual autonomy[43]—strict scrutiny has traditionally been applied to free exercise of religion claims.[44] This appears to be changing, however. Although the Court generally has applied a standard of strict scrutiny to consider free exercise claims, it restricted the category of cases subject to strict scrutiny in its 1990 decision in *Employment Division, Department of Human Resources v. Smith.*[45] In *Smith,* two members of the Native American Church had ingested peyote as part of a religious ceremony and as a result were discharged by their employer. After being denied unemployment compensation by the Oregon Department of Human Services on the ground that they were fired for work-related misconduct, they filed suit asserting that the Department's denial violated their right to the free exercise of religion. In rejecting this claim, the Supreme Court distinguished its prior decision in *Sherbert v. Verner,*[46] which had rejected a state's denial of unemployment compensation benefits to a Seventh Day Adventist who declined to work on Saturdays. The *Smith* Court restricted application of the strict scrutiny standard used in *Sherbert* by holding that strict scrutiny would not apply in all unemployment compensation cases. In *Smith,* the Court declined to read *Sherbert* to require exemption of religious activities from "a generally applicable

---

[39]*See supra* notes 6–9 and accompanying text.

[40]*See supra* chapter 10.

[41]*See supra* chapter 11.

[42]*See supra* chapter 10.

[43]*See supra* chapter 11.

[44]*E.g.*, Bob Jones University v. United States, 461 U.S. 574, 603 (1983) ("The state may justify a limitation on religious liberty by showing that it is essential to accomplish an overriding governmental interest."); United States v. Lee, 455 U.S. 252 (1982) (attempt by Amish employer to obtain exemption from paying Social Security tax for employees rejected; strict scrutiny satisfied); Thomas v. Review Bd., 450 U.S. 707 (1981) (state could justify denial of unemployment compensation to Jehovah's Witness who had left his job at a munitions factory based on religious objections to war only "by showing that it is the least restrictive means of achieving some compelling state interest"; asserted state interests found insufficiently compelling); McDaniel v. Paty, 435 U.S. 618 (1978) (plurality opinion) (applying strict scrutiny); Wisconsin v. Yoder, 406 U.S. 205, 215 (1972) ("Only those interests of the highest order and those not otherwise served can overbalance" legitimate free exercise claims); Walz v. Tax Comm'n, 397 U.S. 664, 774–75 (1970); Sherbert v. Verner, 374 U.S. 398, 403 (1963) ("compelling state interest" test applied); *see* TRIBE, *supra* note 4, § 14–10, at 1251–75.

[45]494 U.S. 872 (1990).

[46]374 U.S. 398 (1963).

criminal law.''⁴⁷ When the statute's object is not to prohibit the exercise of religion, it will be upheld, the Court determined, if its impact in prohibiting religious practices is ''merely the incidental effect of a generally applicable and otherwise valid provision.''⁴⁸ Finding the Oregon criminal prohibition to be a generally applicable and neutral statute that did not target the religious use of drugs, the *Smith* Court found no free exercise violation.

The Court recently reiterated the *Smith* approach in *Church of the Lukumi Babaluaye v. City of Hialeah*,⁴⁹ stating that ''[u]nder the Free Exercise Clause, a law that burdens religious practices need not be justified by compelling governmental interests if it is neutral and of general applicability.''⁵⁰ Applying this standard in *City of Hialeah,* the Court invalidated city ordinances prohibiting religious killings of animals. Because the ordinances did not apply neutrally and generally but targeted only religious-based animal slaughter, the Court found that the *Smith* test was not satisfied. As a result, the Court applied traditional strict scrutiny. The Court rejected the assertion that the city's interests in protecting public health and preventing cruelty to animals would meet the compelling governmental interest requirement because the ordinances were both overbroad and underinclusive inasmuch as ''the proferred objectives are not pursued with respect to analogous non-religious con-duct. . . .''⁵¹ This overbreadth and underinclusiveness also led the Court to conclude that the ''absence of narrow tailoring suffices to establish the invalidity of the ordinances.''⁵² Because the government's interests ''could be achieved by narrower ordinances that burden religion to a far lesser degree,'' the Court found them unconstitutional.⁵³

Will traditional strict scrutiny or the more narrow approach of *Smith* be applied to religious-based refusal of treatment? In the mental health treatment context, typical state statutes or regulations subjected to civil or general practices that remain uncodified require involuntary treatment for mental patients who have been involuntarily committed either to a hospital or for outpatient treatment. Similarly, such involuntary treatment may be required for offenders who have been given criminal sentences for their offenses that include mandated correctional rehabilitation of some kind. Because these requirements do not single out religious-based treatment refusers, but apply neutrally to all patients or offenders without regard to the source of their objection to treatment, the more narrow standard of *Smith* would seem applicable in the right-to-refuse-treatment context.

Smith seems to retreat from the approach previously used in a number of free exercise cases in which the Court applied strict scrutiny without suggesting the existence of this limitation.⁵⁴ The Court limited these prior cases by treating them as situations involving a free exercise claim in conjunction with the assertion of other constitutional claims.⁵⁵ In addition to First Amendment religion claims, these cases, the Court noted, involved claims dealing with freedom of speech and press, both protected by the First Amendment, or the right of parents to direct the education of their children, protected by substantive due process. When the free exercise claim is not supplemented by an additional claim concerning a

⁴⁷*Smith,* 494 U.S. at 884.
⁴⁸*Id.* at 878.
⁴⁹508 U.S. 520 (1993).
⁵⁰*Id.* at 521.
⁵¹*Id.* at 546.
⁵²*Id.*
⁵³*Id.*
⁵⁴Roberts v. United States Jaycees, 468 U.S. 609, 622 (1983); Wooley v. Maynard, 430 U.S. 705 (1977); Wisconsin v. Yoder, 406 U.S. 205 (1972); Follet v. McCormick, 321 U.S. 573 (1944); Murdock v. Pennsylvania, 319 U.S. 105 (1943); Pierce v. Society of Sisters, 268 U.S. 510 (1925); *see also* cases cited in *supra* note 43.
⁵⁵*Smith,* 494 U.S. at 881 (citing cases in *supra* note 54).

fundamental constitutional right, however, the *Smith* Court concluded that strict scrutiny would not be applied if the state law was neutral and of general applicability, rather than targeting religious practice.

Although legal provisions mandating or authorizing involuntary treatment thus may appear to avoid strict scrutiny as a result of *Smith,* the exception carved out by the Court—for instances in which additional constitutional claims supplement the free exercise claim—would seem generally to apply in the right-to-refuse-treatment context. As chapter 10 shows, requiring an individual to accept intrusive treatment may infringe the First Amendment in ways apart from the Free Exercise Clause. Moreover, as chapter 11 demonstrates, such involuntary treatment may infringe on substantive due process. Additionally, in a smaller number of cases, as chapter 12 shows, involuntary treatment as applied to offenders (and perhaps to institutionalized civil patients as well) may infringe the Eighth Amendment's ban on cruel and unusual punishments. When a free exercise claim relates only to nonintrusive treatment, the threshold requirements for application of the First Amendment, substantive due process, or (in most instances) the Eighth Amendment would not be met. As a result, in such cases a free exercise claim will be rejected under *Smith* when treatment is required or authorized on the basis of a neutral and generally applicable state statute or regulation. When, however, the treatment sought to be imposed is sufficiently intrusive to trigger scrutiny under these other constitutional provisions, strict scrutiny will also be applied to the religion claim under the exception noted in *Smith.*[56] However, because strict scrutiny under each of these provisions is essentially the same—requiring compelling governmental interests and the least intrusive means—a First Amendment free exercise of religion claim regarding involuntary treatment will presumably add little to the ultimate constitutional analysis.

---

[56]In such instances, the standards applicable to a right-to-refuse-treatment free exercise claim would appear to be harder to meet than in many other free exercise contexts in which the Court has found strict scrutiny satisfied. Compared with situations in which the government's requirement or prohibition merely imposed an incidental burden on religious practice, the involuntary imposition of mental health treatment in violation of an individual's religious principles that prohibit such treatment would directly and substantially burden religion. *Compare, e.g.,* Bob Jones University v. United States, 461 U.S. 574, 604 (1983) (although denial of tax benefits will have a substantial impact on the operation of private religious schools, it "will not prevent those schools from observing their tenets"); Johnson v. Robison, 415 U.S. 361, 385 (1974) (denial of veterans' educational benefits to alternative service conscientious objectors "involves only an incidental burden upon appellee's free exercise of religion"); Braunfeld v. Brown, 366 U.S. 599, 605 (1961) (Sunday closing laws do not "make unlawful any religious practices;" rather, they operate

> so as to make the practice of [appellants'] religious beliefs more expensive. [Fully] recognizing that the alternatives open to appellants and others similarly situated [may] well result in some financial sacrifice in order to observe their religious beliefs, still the option is wholly different than when the legislation attempts to make a religious practice itself unlawful.

Whether the standards of strict scrutiny will be satisfied in a given case, however, justifying the overriding of a religious objection to treatment, will be considered in chapters 15 and 16.

Chapter 14
ARE MENTAL PATIENTS DIFFERENT?:
Equal Protection Limits on Involuntary Treatment

In general, the law requires informed consent before treatment may be administered.[1] However, those suffering from mental illness traditionally have been exempted from this requirement. Mental patients and occasionally criminal offenders are subjected to mental health treatment without informed consent and sometimes despite their expressed objection.[2] In view of the general practice making treatment voluntary for all other patients, does permitting involuntary treatment for those with mental illness survive scrutiny under the Equal Protection Clause of the Fourteenth Amendment?

The Equal Protection Clause, adopted in 1868 as part of the post-Civil War Reconstruction-era effort to protect the civil rights of the recently freed slaves,[3] has come to represent a general constitutional commitment to the principle of equality. The clause is construed to prevent not only discrimination on the basis of race but also to require that similar

---

[1]Basic principles of tort law require informed consent as a condition for treatment. *E.g.,* Cruzan v. Director, Mo. Dep't of Health, 497 U.S. 261, 269 (1990); Cobbs v. Grant, 502 P.2d 1, 9 (Cal. 1972); Natanson v. Kline, 350 P.2d 1093, 1100 (Kan. 1960); Schloendorff v. Society of N.Y. Hosp., 105 N.E. 92, 93 (N.Y. 1914); P. APPELBAUM ET AL., INFORMED CONSENT: LEGAL THEORY AND CLINICAL PRACTICE (1987); W. KEETON ET AL., PROSSER AND KEETON ON THE LAW OF TORTS § 9, at 39–40, § 32, at 189–92 (5th ed. 1984); Sprung & Winick, *Informed Consent in Theory and Practice: Legal and Medical Perspectives on the Informed Consent Doctrine, and a Proposed Reconceptualization,* 17 CRITICAL CARE MED. 1346 (1989); Winick, *Competency to Consent to Treatment: The Distinction Between Assent and Objection,* 28 HOUS. L. REV. 15 (1991).

[2]*E.g.,* United States v. Charters, 863 F.2d 302 (4th Cir. 1988) (en banc), *cert. denied,* 494 U.S. 1064 (1990) (jail inmates awaiting trial may not refuse antipsychotic drugs); Dautremont v. Broadlawn Hosp., 827 F.2d 291, 298 (8th Cir. 1987) (hospitalized civil patients may be involuntarily treated with psychotropic drugs against their will); State *ex rel.* Jones v. Gerhardstein, 416 N.W.2d 883, 889 (Wis. 1987) ("the state and county concede that psychotropic drugs are involuntarily given to all types of patients"); A. BROOKS, LAW, PSYCHIATRY AND THE MENTAL HEALTH SYSTEM 877 (1974) ("It is widely assumed that the commitment of a person to a mental hospital, voluntary or involuntary, confers on the hospital administrators the authority to 'treat' him in whatever manner they deem appropriate."); Goldiamond, *Toward a Constructional Approach to Social Problems: Ethical and Constitutional Issues Raised by Applied Behavior Analysis,* 2 BEHAVIORISM 1, 13 (1974) ("In practically every section of the hospital except the psychiatric ward, a patient can decline a given form of treatment, can refuse medication, and can leave the hospital AMA (against medical advice)—even when it is thought that his doing so endangers his life and limb".); Note, *Developments in the Law—Civil Commitment of the Mentally Ill,* 87 HARV. L. REV. 1190, 1351 n.151 (1974) ("Most civil commitment statutes . . . either do not discuss a patient's right to refuse unwanted treatments . . . or allow for the overruling of a competent patient's treatment decision for all but the most intrusive types of treatment.") Indeed, some state statutes expressly authorize the treatment of hospital patients without their consent, *e.g.,* CONN. STAT. § 17-206d(b) (1996); LA. REV. STAT. § 28.55(I) (1995), and some courts have expressed the view that hospital failure to treat mental patients involuntarily who have sought to refuse treatment would be unprofessional and actionable. Nason v. Superintendent of Bridgewater State Hosp., 233 N.E.2d 908, 912 n.7 (Mass. 1968); Whitree v. State, 200 N.Y.S.2d 486, 501 (Ct. Cl. 1968).

[3]*See supra* chapter 11, notes 16–23 and accompanying text (discussing origins of the Fourteenth Amendment).

individuals generally be treated alike by the government.[4] Legal classifications may not be arbitrary or discriminatory; they must be generally reasonable. "A reasonable classification is one which includes all persons who are similarly situated with respect to the purpose of the law."[5]

A. The Appropriate Standard of Equal Protection Scrutiny

In considering equal protection challenges to distinctions drawn by state law that treat one group differently than another, the courts use basically a two-tiered standard of review.[6] Under this approach, most classifications are measured under a low-level rational-basis test. In limited circumstances, however, the courts apply strict scrutiny, insisting that differential treatment be justified as necessary to achieve a compelling governmental interest.

In applying the rational-basis standard, courts consider only "whether it is conceivable that the classification bears a rational relation to an end of government which is not prohibited by the Constitution."[7] As long as there is a rational relationship between the treatment of the class and some legitimate governmental purpose, the classification will be upheld.[8] The legislature does not have to "actually articulate at any time the purpose or rationale supporting its classification."[9] There need only be "a reasonably conceivable state of facts that could provide a rational basis for the classification."[10] The courts accord most

---

[4]J. NOWAK & R. ROTUNDA, CONSTITUTIONAL LAW 570 (4th ed. 1991); L. TRIBE, AMERICAN CONSTITUTIONAL LAW 1438 (2d ed. 1988) ("[E]quality can be denied when government classifies so as to distinguish, in its rules or programs, between persons who should be regarded as similarly situated in terms of the relevant equal protection principles.").

[5]Tussman & tenBroek, *The Equal Protection of the Laws,* 37 CAL. L. REV. 341, 346 (1949).

[6]*See generally* NOWAK & ROTUNDA, *supra* note 4, at 575–76; TRIBE, *supra* note 4, at 1451–54; Gunther, *Foreword: The Supreme Court 1971 Term: In Search of Evolving Doctrine on a Changing Court: A Model for a Newer Equal Protection,* 86 HARV. L. REV. 1 (1972); Note, *Developments in the Law—Equal Protection,* 82 HARV. L. REV. 1065 (1969). In cases involving gender-based or illegitimacy-based classifications, the Supreme Court has adopted what can be described as a "middle-tier" approach, requiring that "classifications must be substantially related to achievement of those objectives." Craig v. Boren, 429 U.S. 190, 197 (1976). *See, e.g.,* J.E.B. v. Alabama *ex rel.* T.B., 114 S. Ct. 1419, 1425 (1994) ("'[G]ender-based classifications require 'an exceedingly persuasive justification' in order to survive constitutional scrutiny."); Clark v. Jeter, 486 U.S. 456 (1988) (illegitimate children); Mississippi Univ. for Women v. Hogan, 458 U.S. 718 (1982) (gender); Kirchberg v. Feenstra, 450 U.S. 455 (1981) (gender).

[7]NOWAK & ROTUNDA, *supra* note 4, at 574–75; TRIBE, *supra* note 4, at 1440; Note, *supra* note 2, at 1076–87. *E.g.,* Federal Communications Comm'n v. Beach Communications, Inc., 508 U.S. 307 (1993) (upholding cable television facilities regulation); Pennel v. City of San Jose, 485 U.S. 1 (1988) (upholding rent control ordinance); Lyng v. Castillo, 477 U.S. 635 (1986) (upholding food stamp distribution law); City of Clerburne v. Clerburne Living Ctr., Inc. 473 U.S. 432 (1984) (review of zoning ordinance as applied to a group home for people suffering from mental retardation); New Orleans v. Dukes, 427 U.S. 297 (1976) (per curiam) (upholding grandfather clause in economic regulation of pushcart vendors); Dandridge v. Williams, 397 U.S. 471 (1970) (upholding classifications in a state welfare benefits program); McGowen v. Maryland, 366 U.S. 420 (1961) (upholding a state Sunday closing law riddled with exceptions).

[8]Heller v. Doe, 509 U.S. 312, 318–19 (1993); Nordlinger v. Hahn, 505 U.S. 1, 8–9 (1992); New Orleans v. Dukes, 427 U.S. 297, 303 (1976) (per curiam).

[9]*Nordlinger,* 505 U.S. at 15.

[10]Federal Communications Comm'n v. Beach Communications, Inc., 508 U.S. 307, 313 (1993). The Court in reviewing a classification under the rational-basis standard does not look for a perfect fit between the means used by the legislature and the ends it seeks to achieve. *See* Dandridge v. Williams, 397 U.S. 471, 485 (1970) (quoting Lindsley v. Natural Carbonic Gas Co., 220 U.S. 61, 78 (1911)) (classification does not fail if it is "not made with mathematical nicety or because in practice it results in some inequality").

such classifications a strong presumption of validity[11] and place the burden of establishing otherwise on the party raising the equal protection challenge.[12] When applying this deferential test, the Court will not "judge the wisdom, fairness, or logic of legislative choice,"[13] nor will it "sit as a superlegislature to judge the wisdom or desirability of legislative policy determinations made in areas that neither affect fundamental rights nor proceed along suspect lines."[14] This rational-basis standard is the one generally applied to measure legal classifications claimed to violate equal protection.[15] It is an essentially deferential test, although it occasionally has been applied with what has been described as "bite."[16]

In a limited number of cases, the Court uses a demanding standard of review that has come to be known as "strict scrutiny." This standard, developed in the equal protection revolution of the Warren Court and followed in substance since,[17] is a more searching test requiring a finding that the government was pursuing a compelling end and that the classification used was narrowly tailored to achieve it.[18] This more searching standard is limited to two categories of cases—those involving "fundamental rights"[19] and those affecting "suspect classifications."[20]

Classifications on the basis of race[21] or national origin[22] are "suspect" and call for the most exacting scrutiny. In what has become a celebrated footnote that has had a significant impact on the development of modern constitutional law, Chief Justice Harlan Stone

---

[11]*Heller,* 509 U.S. at 318–19; *see, e.g.,* Federal Communications Comm'n v. Beach Communications, Inc., 508 U.S. 307, 310 (1993); Kadrmas v. Dickinson Public Schs., 487 U.S. 450, 462 (1988); Hodel v. Indiana, 452 U.S. 314, 331–32 (1981).

[12]*Heller,* 509 U.S. at 320; Lehnhausen v. Lake Shore Auto Parts Co., 410 U.S. 356, 364 (1973).

[13]*Heller,* 509 U.S. at 318–19; *Beach Communications,* 508 U.S. at 313; *id.* at 310 ("[A] legislative choice is not subject to courtroom factfinding and may be based on rational speculation unsupported by evidence or empirical data.").

[14]*Heller,* 509 U.S. at 318–19; New Orleans v. Dukes, 427 U.S. 297, 303 (1976) (per curiam).

[15]Rational-basis review is primarily used when analyzing socioeconomic legislation. NOWAK & ROTUNDA, *supra* note 4, at 574; TRIBE, *supra* note 4, at 1439–43; *e.g.,* Federal Communications Comm'n v. Beach Communications, 508 U.S. 307 (1993); United States R.R. Retirement Bd. v. Fritz, 449 U.S. 166 (1980); Railway Express Agency v. New York, 336 U.S. 106 (1949).

[16]Gunther, *supra* note 6, at 18–19; *e.g.,* City of Clerburne v. Clerburne Living Ctr., 473 U.S. 432 (1985); United States Dep't of Agriculture v. Moreno, 413 U.S. 528 (1973); McGinnis v. Royster, 410 U.S. 263 (1973); Reed v. Reed, 404 U.S. 71 (1971).

[17]Gunther, *supra* note 6, at 8–12, 15–16. *See generally* NOWAK & ROTUNDA, *supra* note 4, at 606–718; TRIBE, *supra* note 4, at 1451–1553.

[18]NOWAK & ROTUNDA, *supra* note 4, at 575.

[19]Note, *supra* note 2, at 1120–24, 1124–27; *e.g.,* Attorney General of New York v. Soto-Lopez, 476 U.S. 898 (1986) (right to travel); Hooper v. Bernalillo County Assessor, 472 U.S. 612 (1985) (same); Zablocki v. Redhail, 434 U.S. 374 (1978) (marriage); Kramer v. Union Free Sch. Dist. No. 15, 395 U.S. 621 (1969) (voting); Shapiro v. Thompson, 394 U.S. 618 (1969) (interstate travel); Griffin v. Illinois, 351 U.S. 12 (1956) (equal access to criminal appellate review); Skinner v. Oklahoma *ex rel.* Williamson, 316 U.S. 535 (1942) (procreation).

[20]TRIBE, *supra* note 4, at 1451 ("[T]he idea of strict scrutiny acknowledges that other political choices—those burdening fundamental rights, or suggesting prejudice against other racial minorities—must be subjected to close analysis in order to preserve substantive values of equality and liberty."); Note, *supra* note 2, at 1087–1120, 1124–27; *e.g.,* Bernal v. Fainter, 467 U.S. 216 (1984) (alienage); Palmore v. Sidoti, 466 U.S. 429 (1984) (race); Examining Bd. v. Flores de Otero, 426 U.S. 572 (1976) (alienage); McLaughlin v. Florida, 379 U.S. 184 (1964) (race); Korematsu v. United States, 323 U.S. 214 (1944) (national origin). The strict scrutiny test, however, does not seem to be as stringently enforced when the classification is based on alienage. *See* NOWAK & ROTUNDA, *supra* note 4, at 576, 712–18.

[21]*See, e.g.,* Palmore v. Sidoti, 466 U.S. 429 (1984); McLaughlin v. Florida, 379 U.S. 184 (1964).

[22]*See, e.g.,* Korematsu v. United States, 323 U.S. 214 (1944).

suggested in 1938 the need for a special measure of heightened judicial review in limited categories of cases. He argued that legislation affecting "discrete and insular minorities"[23] should be reviewed with special rigor because prejudice against these groups "tends seriously to curtail the operation of those political processes ordinarily to be relied upon to protect minorities."[24] In subsequent cases, the Supreme Court has applied strict scrutiny to such "suspect classifications" as race and national origin, almost always invalidating challenged legislation found to discriminate on these impermissible bases.[25]

A second category of cases in which the Court applies strict scrutiny involves classifications that burden "fundamental" constitutional rights—those explicitly or implicitly protected by the Constitution and found to be basic to concepts of liberty enshrined in our constitutional history and traditions.[26] These rights have included the right to procreate,[27] to marry,[28] to vote,[29] and to travel.[30] Although government classifications in areas of social and economic regulation generally will receive the deferential scrutiny of the rational-basis test, a special measure of judicial protection is provided when fundamental constitutional rights are involved.

When strict scrutiny is applied, classifications "must be justified by a compelling governmental interest and must be 'necessary . . . to the accomplishment' of their legitimate purpose."[31] In such cases, the Court does not defer to decisions of the other branches of government but independently reviews the degree of relationship between the classification and the end sought.[32] Not every governmental objective will qualify: The end sought must be deemed "compelling" or "overriding."[33] This standard, with its requirement of a close means–ends fit, ensures that "there is little or no possibility that the motive for the classification was illegitimate[ ] prejudice or stereotype."[34] This standard of review is used so that "political choices—those burdening fundamental rights, or suggesting prejudice against racial or other minorities—must be subjected to close analysis in order to preserve substantive values of equality and liberty."[35]

What level of scrutiny should be applied to consider the constitutionality of intrusive mental health treatment administered on an involuntary basis to those with mental illness but not to others? Are the mentally ill a "suspect class," requiring application of strict scrutiny to legal rules that disadvantage them? Do any of the mental health treatments burden fundamental constitutional rights?

An analysis of whether mental illness is a suspect class must start with the approach generally used by the Supreme Court to determine whether a particular class is "suspect." Illustrative of this approach is *Frontiero v. Richardson,*[36] in which the Court faced a claim

---

[23]United States v. Carolene Products, Inc., 304 U.S. 144, 152 n.4 (1938).

[24]*Id.*

[25]*See supra* notes 19–21.

[26]See NOWAK & ROTUNDA, *supra* note 4, at 388.

[27]Skinner v. Oklahoma *ex rel.* Williamson, 316 U.S. 535 (1942).

[28]Zablocki v. Redhail, 434 U.S. 374 (1978).

[29]Hunter v. Underwood, 471 U.S. 222 (1985); Kramer v. Union Free Sch. Dist. No. 15, 395 U.S. 621 (1969).

[30]Attorney General of New York v. Soto-Lopez, 476 U.S. 898 (1986); Hooper v. Bernalillo County Assessor, 472 U.S. 612 (1985).

[31]Palmore v. Sidoti, 466 U.S. 429, 432–33 (1984); *accord* Loving v. Virginia, 388 U.S. 1, 11 (1967); McLaughlin v. Florida, 379 U.S. 184, 196 (1964).

[32]NOWAK & ROTUNDA, *supra* note 4, at 575.

[33]*Id.*

[34]City of Richmond v. J.A. Croson Co., 488 U.S. 469, 493 (1989).

[35]TRIBE, *supra* note 4, at 1451.

[36]411 U.S. 677 (1973) (plurality opinion).

that gender was a suspect classification. Although a Court majority could not be mustered, a plurality would have found gender to be suspect by considering five separate factors. First, the plurality opinion cited our nation's "long and unfortunate history of sex discrimination."[37] Second, the plurality noted that state statutes have traditionally treated women in a stereotypical manner.[38] Third, the opinion noted the "high visibility of the sex characteristic."[39] Fourth, the plurality pointed out that, like race and national origin, sex is an immutable characteristic determined "solely by the accident of birth,"[40] with the result that the imposition of disabilities on the basis of this characteristic "would seem to violate 'the basic concept of our system that legal burdens should bear some relationship to individual responsibility. . . .' "[41] Fifth, the plurality noted that Congress had responded with remedial legislation designed to prevent discrimination on the basis of sex.[42]

A consideration of these factors supports the contention that mental illness is a suspect classification. There has been a long history of discrimination against people with mental illness, state statutes have treated those with mental illness in a stereotypical fashion, mental illness (at least severe mental illness) is relatively visible, and those with mental illness have been the subject of remedial legislation. However, in *City of Clerburne v. Clerburne Living Center*,[43] the Supreme Court suggested that mental illness would not qualify for suspect class treatment.

The *Clerburne* Court, in reviewing a zoning ordinance applied to a group home for people suffering from mental retardation, rejected a contention that mental retardation was a suspect classification qualifying for strict scrutiny or a quasi-suspect class qualifying for intermediate scrutiny. Citing a prior decision rejecting the claim that age was a suspect classification,[44] the Court noted that when individuals in the group affected adversely by the law in question have "distinguishing characteristics relevant to interests the State has the authority to implement," considerations of federalism and separation of powers should make courts reluctant "to closely scrutinize legislative choices as to whether, how, and to what extent those interests should be pursued."[45] The *Clerburne* Court rejected the contention that mental retardation was a suspect class for four reasons. First, noting that those with mental retardation have different levels of disability, the Court pointed to the difficult and technical nature of the question of how this large and diversified group should be treated under the law.[46] Second, noting that government historically had addressed the plight of those with mental retardation in ways that belied the existence of prejudice against this class, the Court declined to impose "more intrusive oversight by the judiciary."[47] Third, the Court indicated that this legislative response demonstrated that those with mental

[37]*Id.* at 684.
[38]*Id.* at 685.
[39]*Id.* at 686.
[40]*Id.*
[41]*Id.* (quoting Weber v. Aetna Cas. & Surety Co., 406 U.S. 164, 175 (1972)).
[42]*Id.* at 687–88.
[43]473 U.S. 432, 445–46 (1985).
[44]Massachusetts Bd. of Retirement v. Murgia, 427 U.S. 307, 313 (1976):

While the treatment of the aged in this Nation has not been wholly free of discrimination, such persons, unlike, say, those who have been discriminated against on the basis of race or national origin, have not experienced a 'history of purposeful unequal treatment' or been subjected to unique disabilities on the basis of stereotyped characteristics not truly indicative of their abilities.

[45]*Clerburne,* 473 U.S. at 441–42.
[46]*Id.* at 442–43.
[47]*Id.* at 443.

retardation have not been politically powerless.[48] Finally, the Court noted the difficulty of distinguishing this group from others with similar immutable characteristics that also can assert similar types of prejudice, such as ''the aging, the disabled, the mentally ill, and the infirm.''[49] The Court therefore concluded that those with mental retardation did not require a special measure of judicial protection[50] and that the low-level rational-basis test would suffice.[51]

Although the Court was discussing mental retardation, its conclusion makes it clear that those with mental illness will not be considered a suspect class. Indeed, compared to mental illness, mental retardation is considerably more immutable. Unlike mental illness, mental retardation is congenital, untreatable, and unchangeable.[52] As a result, the Court's rejection of mental retardation as a suspect or quasi-suspect class indicates that mental illness will not receive suspect class treatment.

Does the imposition of mental health treatment burden any fundamental constitutional right, thereby making strict equal protection scrutiny appropriate even if mental illness is not a suspect class? Because the mental health treatment techniques differ substantially in regard to the nature and duration of their effects, they must be considered separately. Some of the techniques—those at the higher range of the continuum of intrusiveness—burden fundamental rights. Those lower on the continuum do not, however. As chapter 10 demonstrates, intrusive mental health treatment burdens interests protected by the First Amendment, long regarded as a fundamental constitutional right. Moreover, as chapter 11 demonstrates, such intrusive treatment also burdens substantive due process–privacy interests, many of which are also regarded as fundamental. In more limited instances, as chapter 12 demonstrates, when intrusive mental health treatment is applied as punishment, the Eighth Amendment prohibition of cruel and unusual punishments, also a fundamental constitutional right, may be violated. In addition, as discussed in chapter 13, mental health treatment, when imposed over religious objection, may violate the fundamental First Amendment guarantee of free exercise of religion. Even if mental illness is not a suspect classification, when mental health treatment approaches falling along the higher range of the continuum of intrusiveness are imposed involuntarily on those with mental illness but not on others, strict equal protection scrutiny therefore is appropriate because of the resulting burden on fundamental constitutional rights.[53]

Treatments on the lower end of the continuum of intrusiveness, however, will not merit strict scrutiny. For the reasons discussed in chapters 10–13, these do not burden constitutional rights ranked as fundamental. When these treatments are applied to the mentally ill but not to other groups, an equal protection challenge will receive only the minimal scrutiny of the rational-basis test.[54] As long as mental illness bears some rational relationship to a legitimate governmental interest served by involuntary treatment, singling out those with mental illness for such treatment does not offend equal protection.

---

[48]*Id.* at 445.

[49]*Id.* at 446.

[50]Nowak & Rotunda, *supra* note 4, at 589.

[51]*Clerburne*, 473 U.S. at 441.

[52]*See* Ellis, *Decisions by and for People With Mental Retardation: Balancing Considerations of Autonomy and Protection*, 37 Vill. L. Rev. 1779 (1992); Ellis & Luckasson, *Mentally Retarded Criminal Defendants*, 53 Geo. Wash. L. Rev. 414 (1985).

[53]See *supra* notes 27–31.

[54]*See supra* notes 6–15.

B. Applying the Standard

What is the justification for treating those with mental illness differently from those with other types of illnesses, allowing the latter (but not the former) a right to refuse treatment? In what respects do those with mental illness differ from others who are not involuntarily treated? Legislation singling out those with mental illness for special treatment such as civil commitment sometimes is based on the police power interest in protecting others from harm and sometimes on the *parens patriae* interest in promoting the health and welfare of those unable to care for themselves.[55] Are either of these grounds sufficient to justify forcible administration of intrusive treatment to those with mental illness but not to others?

Does mental illness present a risk of harm to others that can justify this disparate treatment? Although some people with mental illness are dangerous to others because their condition substantially impairs their ability for self-control, the overwhelming majority of mentally ill persons are not so impaired and pose no special risk of harm.[56] Moreover, many nonmentally ill people are dangerous, and their dangerousness alone is not thought sufficient to justify the imposition of involuntary mental health treatment.[57] In general, therefore, dangerousness would not seem to be an acceptable basis for distinguishing those with mental illness from others. To the extent that an attempt is made to justify involuntary treatment of a particular patient on the basis of an allegation that he or she is dangerous to others, the issue of dangerousness must be determined at a hearing meeting the requirement of due process.[58] This is the teaching of both *Washington v. Harper*[59] and *Riggins v. Nevada*.[60]

In *Harper,* the court upheld a prison's ability forcibly to medicate a prisoner on the basis of his dangerousness to other prisoners and prison staff, but only after an administrative review board had approved the determination by the prisoner's psychiatrist that he was dangerous when not medicated.[61] *Riggins* reversed a trial judge's determination to continue a criminal defendant on antipsychotic medication to which he had objected when the judge failed to conduct an adequate hearing on the issue or make any findings justifying such medication.[62] Although the court indicated that protecting other jail detainees or staff from harm caused by the defendant's mental illness would have been a sufficient justification for forcible medication, in the absence of judicial findings to this effect, the court held that the continuation of medication violated due process.[63] At least absent an individualized determination that a particular patient was dangerous and that his or her mental illness substantially impaired the ability to control behavior, a presumption that all mental patients are dangerous to others would not withstand strict equal protection scrutiny.

Can the justification for treating mental patients differently with regard to the right to refuse treatment be grounded in any other effects of mental illness that are peculiar to the mental disorders? Does mental illness impair decision-making capacity in ways that prevent those who are mentally ill (but not others) from satisfying the requirements for informed

---

[55]*See* Note, *supra* note 2, at 1351; *infra* chapter 15, part B.

[56]A. STONE, MENTAL HEALTH AND LAW: A SYSTEM IN TRANSITION 27–28 (DHEW Pub. No. (ADM) 76–176, 1975); Monahan, Mental Disorder and Violent Behavior: Perceptions and Evidence, 47 AM. PSYCHOLOGIST 511 (1992).

[57]*See* Note, *supra* note 2, at 1352.

[58]*See infra* chapter 19 (discussing procedural due process requirements in this context).

[59]494 U.S. 210 (1990).

[60]504 U.S. 127 (1992).

[61]494 U.S. at 227.

[62]504 U.S. at 129.

[63]*Id.* at 135.

consent? It seems likely that differential legal approaches with regard to involuntary treatment for those with mental illness compared to those with other illnesses are premised largely on the assumption that those with mental illness are incompetent to engage in treatment decision making. This assumption reflects the 19th-century belief that mental illness destroys decision-making capacity.[64] This model of mental illness persists and continues to influence legal approaches in this area. Indeed, in the 1990 case of *Zinermon v. Burch*,[65] the Supreme Court appeared to accept this assumption. Analyzing the competency of a mental patient to consent to voluntary hospitalization, the Court in dicta suggested that[66]

> even if the state usually might be justified in taking at face value a person's request for admission to a hospital for medical treatment, it might not be justified in doing so without further inquiry as to a mentally ill person's request for admission and treatment at a mental hospital.

The assumption that seems to be embodied in this statement is that physical illness rarely impairs competency but that mental illness typically does have this effect. If this assumption is correct, it may justify a general rule exempting mental patients from the informed consent requirement. But is this assumption correct?

This statement in *Zinermon* went considerably beyond the facts of the case, which involved a grossly incompetent patient who was delusional and hallucinatory and who thought the mental hospital was "heaven."[67] Whereas it is appropriate to require further inquiry into the question of competency when a patient exhibits signs of gross cognitive impairment, most mental patients seeking voluntary hospitalization, even though mentally ill, are not incompetent to make the admission decision for themselves.[68] Indeed, the law generally presumes that even people suffering from mental illness are competent.[69] Requiring an inquiry into competence is justified for patients such as the one in *Zinermon* because the evidence of impairment in decision-making ability that he exhibited on admission destroyed the presumption of competence to which patients generally are entitled. However, requiring such an inquiry for *all* mental patients seeking hospital admission seems

---

[64]Appelbaum & Grisso, *The MacArthur Treatment Competence Study. I: Mental Illness and Competence to Consent to Treatment*, 19 LAW & HUM. BEHAV. 105, 107 (1995).

[65]494 U.S. 113 (1990).

[66]*Id.* at 133 n.18. For an analysis showing that this statement was dicta, see Winick, *Competency to Consent to Voluntary Hospitalization: A Therapeutic Jurisprudence Analysis of* Zinermon v. Burch, 14 INT'L J.L. & PSYCHIATRY 169, 180–81 (1991).

[67]494 U.S. at 130; Winick, *supra* note 66.

[68]*Id.* at 182.

[69]*See, e.g.*, Lotman v. Security Mut. Life Ins. Co., 478 F.2d 868, 873 (3d Cir. 1973); Winters v. Miller, 446 F.2d 65, 68 (2d Cir. 1970), *cert. denied*, 404 U.S. 985 (1971); Rogers v. Okin, 478 F. Supp. 1342, 1361, 1363–64 (D. Mass. 1979), *aff'd in part and vacated in part*, 634 F.2d 650 (1st Cir. 1980) (en banc), *vacated sub nom.* Mills v. Rogers, 457 U.S. 291 (1982); Child v. Wainwright, 148 So.2d 526, 527 (Fla. 1963); Howe v. Commonwealth, 99 Mass. 88, 98–99 (1868); Lane v. Candura, 376 N.E.2d 1232, 1235 (Mass. App. Ct. 1978); Grannum v. Berard, 422 P.2d 812, 814 (Wash. 1967). Not only has this presumption been recognized in case law, but it also finds broad scholarly support. *See, e.g.*, S. BRAKEL ET AL., THE MENTALLY DISABLED AND THE LAW 341 n.167, 375 (3d ed. 1985); 1 PRESIDENT'S COMM'N FOR THE STUDY OF ETHICAL PROBS. IN MED. & BIOMED. & BEHAV. RES., MAKING HEALTH CARE DECISIONS: A REPORT ON THE ETHICAL AND LEGAL IMPLICATIONS OF INFORMED CONSENT IN THE PATIENT– PRACTITIONER RELATIONSHIP 3, 56 (1982) [hereinafter PRESIDENT'S COMM'N]; T. GRISSO, EVALUATING COMPETENCIES: FORENSIC ASSESSMENT AND INSTRUMENTS 314 (1986); Annas & Densberger, *Competence to Refuse Medical Treatment: Autonomy vs. Paternalism*, 15 U. TOL. L. REV. 561, 575 (1984); Appelbaum & Grisso, *Assessing Patients' Capacities to Consent to Treatment*, 319 NEW ENG. J. MED. 1635 (1988); Wexler, *Reflections on the Legal Regulation of Behavior Modification in Institutional Settings*, 17 ARIZ. L. REV. 132, 136 (1975); Winick, *supra* note 1, at 22–23 & n.19, 35–37.

to accept the 19th-century assumption that mental illness *per se* destroys decision-making capacity and that those with mental illness should not receive a presumption of competence.

Not only does the breadth of the *Zinermon* dicta threaten the voluntary hospitalization process,[70] but it also questions one of the most important reforms of modern mental health law and is contrary to our historic political and constitutional commitment to the principle of individual autonomy. In a society structured on respect for individual autonomy and self-determination,[71] it is appropriate that people be presumed competent.[72] Moreover, it is essential that any legal status of incompetency that deprives individuals of freedom to act for themselves be defined narrowly.[73] The Court's broad dicta thus cuts against the grain of cherished constitutional values.

The Court's dicta in *Zinermon* also runs counter to one of the most significant developments in modern mental health law. Under the approach that once prevailed in American law, an adjudication of incompetency rendered an individual generally incompetent.[74] However, the law has rejected this notion of general incompetency in favor of an approach requiring adjudications of specific incompetency.[75] Under the more modern view, a court will determine an individual to be incompetent to perform only particular tasks or roles, such as to decide on hospitalization, to manage property, to consent to treatment, or to stand trial.[76] An adjudication of specific incompetency does not render the individual legally incompetent to perform other tasks or to play other roles. Indeed, modern law presumes that people are competent to make decisions unless they have been adjudicated incompetent.[77] This general presumption of competency applies to those with medical illness and to those with mental illness, and courts have found it applicable even to mental patients who have

---

[70]Winick, *supra* note 66, at 191–99; Winick, *Voluntary Hospitalization After* Zinermon v. Burch, 21 PSYCHIATRIC ANNALS 1 (1991).

[71]Winick, *supra* note 1, at 17–18; Winick, *On Autonomy: Legal and Psychological Perspectives,* 37 VILL. L. REV. 1705 (1992).

[72]Winick, *supra* note 71, at 1736.

[73]*Id.* at 1733.

[74]*See* P. APPELBAUM & T. GUTHEIL, CLINICAL HANDBOOK OF PSYCHIATRY AND THE LAW 219 (2d ed. 1991); P. APPELBAUM ET AL., *supra* note 1, at 82; BRAKEL ET AL., *supra* note 69, at 185, 258, 438–39; D. WEXLER, MENTAL HEALTH LAW 40 (1981); Tepper & Elwork, *Competence to Consent to Treatment as a Psycholegal Construct,* 8 L. & HUM. BEHAV. 205, 207 (1984); Winick, *supra* note 1, at 22–23.

[75]*E.g.,* Rogers v. Commissioner, 458 N.E. 2d 308, 312–13 (Mass. 1983); State *ex rel.* Jones v. Gerhardstein, 416 N.W.2d 883, 894–95 (Wis. 1987); APPELBAUM & GUTHEIL, *supra* note 74, at 219; APPELBAUM ET AL., *supra* note 1, at 82–83; BRAKEL ET AL., *supra* note 69, at 185, 405–07 (table 7.2, col. 1); R. FADEN & T. BEAUCHAMP, A HISTORY AND THEORY OF INFORMED CONSENT 289 (1986); Tepper & Elwork, *supra* note 74, at 207; Winick, *supra* note 1, at 23.

[76]APPELBAUM ET AL., *supra* note 1, at 82–83; T. BEAUCHAMP & J. CHILDRESS, PRINCIPLES OF BIOMEDICAL ETHICS 71–72 (2d ed. 1983); BRAKEL ET AL., *supra* note 69, at 185 & n.73; GRISSO, *supra* note 69, at 314–15. Tepper & Elwork, *supra* note 74, at 207–08; Wexler, *The Structure of Civil Commitment: Patterns, Pressures, and Interactions in Mental Health Legislation,* 7 LAW & HUM. BEHAV. 1, 2 (1983); Winick, *supra* note 1, at 23. Some areas of the law, however, continue to be slow to change. *E.g.,* Tor & Sales, *Guardianship for Incapacitated Persons, in* LAW, MENTAL HEALTH, AND MENTAL DISORDER 202, 203 (B. Sales & D. Shuman eds., 1996) (describing the ''causal link'' approach to guardianship that is still followed in some states, under which certain conditions ''are linked to a generalized incapacity for self-care'').

[77]*See supra* notes 73–75 and accompanying text.

been involuntarily committed under the state's *parens patriae* power on the basis that they are incompetent to make the hospitalization decision for themselves.[78]

Not only did the *Zinermon* dicta run counter to the direction of modern law reform, but the assumption it appeared to make concerning the differential competencies of those with mental illness and those with medical illnesses is highly questionable. The Court's analysis was based on an artificial distinction between medical and mental illness and confusion about the nature of mental illness and its effects on competency.[79] Although mental illness sometimes impairs competency to process information and make rational choices, it often does not do so.[80] The difference between "crazy" and "normal" people is not as great as commonly is supposed.[81] Those who are mentally ill often have a significant capacity for normal and rational thought and behavior,[82] and "normal" people frequently lack contact with reality and cannot always think straight, pay attention, process information, and

---

[78]*See, e.g.,* Rennie v. Klein, 653 F.2d 836, 846 & n.12 (3d Cir. 1981) (en banc), *vacated and remanded on other grounds,* 458 U.S. 1119 (1982); Rogers v. Okin, 634 F.2d 650, 657–59 (1st Cir. 1980), *vacated and remanded on other grounds sub nom.* Mills v. Rogers, 457 U.S. 291 (1982); Winters v. Miller, 446 F.2d 65, 71 (2d Cir. 1971); Davis v. Hubbard, 506 F. Supp. 915, 935–36 (N.D. Ohio 1980); Wyatt v. Stickney, 344 F. Supp. 373, 379 (M.D. Ala. 1972), *aff'd sub nom.* Wyatt v. Aderholt, 503 F.2d 1305 (5th Cir. 1974); Anderson v. State, 663 P.2d 570, 573–74 (Ariz. Ct. App. 1981); People v. Medina, 705 P.2d 961, 973 (Colo. 1985) (en banc); *In re* Boyd, 403 A.2d 744, 747 n.5 (D.C. Ct. App. 1979); Gundy v. Pauley, 619 S.W.2d 730, 731 (Ky. Ct. App. 1981); Rogers v. Commissioner, 458 N.E.2d 308, 314 (Mass. 1983); Rivers v. Katz, 495 N.E.2d 337, 341–42 (N.Y. 1986); *In re* K.K.B., 609 P.2d 747, 749 (Okla. 1980); State *ex rel.* Jones v. Gerhardstein, 416 N.W.2d 883, 890–91, 894–96 (Wis. 1987); S. BRAKEL ET AL., *supra* note 69, at 258; Beck, *Right to Refuse Antipsychotic Medication: Psychiatric Assessment and Legal Decision-Making,* 11 MENTAL & PHYSICAL DISABILITY L. REP. 368, 369 (1987); National Task Force of the National Center for State Courts' Institute on Mental Disability and the Law, *Guidelines for Involuntary Civil Commitment,* 10 MENTAL & PHYSICAL DISABILITY L. REP. 409, § E7, at 466, 468 n.23 (1986) (commentary); Winick, *supra* note 1, at 37–40; Winick, *The Right to Refuse Psychotropic Medication: Current State of the Law and Beyond, in* THE RIGHT TO REFUSE ANTIPSYCHOTIC MEDICATION 7, 17–18 (J. Rapoport & J. Parry eds., 1986). This presumption of competency finds general expression in state statutory provisions as well. *E.g.,* FLA. STAT. § 745.43 (1995) ("Incapacity may not be inferred from the person's voluntary or involuntary hospitalization for mental illness. "); BRAKEL ET AL., *supra* note 69, at 375 & table 7.2; Blackburn, *The "Therapeutic Orgy" and the "Right to Rot" Collide: The Right to Refuse Antipsychotic Drugs Under State Law,* 27 HOUS. L. REV. 447, 471–72 nn. 87–88 (1990).

Similarly, mental illness alone does not justify a determination that a criminal defendant is incompetent to stand trial. *E.g.,* Feguer v. United States, 302 F.2d 214 (8th Cir.), *cert. denied,* 371 U.S. 872 (1962); Martin v. Dugger, 686 F. Supp. 1523, 1572 (S.D. Fla. 1988); R. ROESCH & S. GOLDING, COMPETENCY TO STAND TRIAL 18–24 (1980); Bennett & Sullwold, *Competence to Proceed: A Functional and Context-Determinative Decision,* 29 J. FORENSIC SCI. 1119, 1122 (1984); Winick, *Restructuring Competency to Stand Trial,* 32 UCLA L. REV. 921, 923–24 n.4 (1986). *See also* FLA. R. CRIM. P. 3.215(b) (1995) (adjudication of incompetency to stand trial does not render defendant incompetent for any other purpose).

[79]*See* Winick, *supra* note 66, at 187–91.

[80]"The mere presence of psychosis, dementia, mental retardation, or "some other form of mental illness or disability is insufficient in itself to constitute incompetence." APPELBAUM & GUTHEIL, *supra* note 74, at 220.

[81]McKinnon et al., *Rivers in Practice: Clinicians' Assessments of Patients' Decision-Making Capacity,* 40 HOSP. & COMMUNITY PSYCHIATRY 1159, 1159 (1989); Morse, *A Preference for Liberty: The Case Against Involuntary Commitment of the Mentally Disordered,* 70 CAL. L. REV. 54, 64–65 (1982) [hereinafter *A Preference for Liberty*]; Morse, *Crazy Behavior, Morals and Science: An Analysis of Mental Health Law,* 51 S. CAL. L. REV. 527, 540, 572–74, 632–35 (1978) [hereinafter *Crazy Behavior*]; Winick, *The Right to Refuse Mental Health Treatment: A First Amendment Perspective,* 44 U. MIAMI L. REV. 1, 46–54 (1989).

[82]Rivers v. Katz, 495 N.E. 2d 337, 341–42 (N.Y. 1986); Morse, *Crazy Behavior, supra* note 81, at 573, 588. Mental illness often impairs only limited areas of functioning, leaving patients capable of functioning competently in other areas. Winick, *supra* note 78, at 17–18.

perform important social tasks.[83] Even in the midst of a psychotic episode,[84] mentally ill people function normally some of the time.[85] Moreover, such episodes are intermittent,[86] and between episodes clinicians find it difficult with a high degree of certainty to distinguish "crazy" people from "normal" people.[87] For these reasons, the law's general presumption

---

[83] Morse, *A Preference for Liberty, supra* note 81, at 64–65; Morse, *Crazy Behavior, supra* note 81, at 574, 633–35. Appelbaum and Roth, in discussing competency to consent to research, make a similar point, suggesting that decisions made about research even of

> people of dubious competency, may not differ from the decisions that all of us make in everyday life, such as when buying a used car or choosing a brand of shampoo. . . . [T]he increased technical complexity of our society makes it likely that many decisions in everyday life are made without appreciation of their consequences, without the ability to manipulate in a rational manner the information that is provided, and probably without full knowledge of the relevant details.

Appelbaum & Roth, *Competency to Consent to Research,* 39 ARCHIVES GEN. PSYCHIATRY 951, 957 (1982).

[84] Most of the psychoses develop through several different phases. For example, schizophrenia is typically marked by a "prodromal phase," in which there is a clear deterioration in a previous level of functioning; an "active phase," in which psychotic symptoms are prominent; and a "residual phase," similar to the prodromal phase, "but the current clinical picture is without prominent positive psychotic symptoms (e.g., delusions, hallucinations, disorganized speech or behavior)." AMERICAN PSYCHIATRIC ASS'N, DIAGNOSTIC AND STATISTICAL MANUAL OF MENTAL DISORDERS 274–78, 289 (4th ed. 1994) [hereinafter *DSM–IV*].

[85] Morse, *Crazy Behavior, supra* note 81, at 573.

[86] *See* Lehmann, *Schizophrenia: Clinical Features, in* 2 COMPREHENSIVE TEXTBOOK OF PSYCHIATRY 1153, 1155 (H. Kaplan et al., eds. 3d ed. 1980) ("[A] schizophrenic patient may be incapable at a certain time of carrying on a rational, simple conversation, and yet half an hour later he may write a sensible and remarkably well-composed letter to a relative."). For empirical verification of the intermittent nature of incompetence in the context of competency of mental patients to consent to treatment, see C. LIDZ ET AL., INFORMED CONSENT: A STUDY OF DECISION MAKING IN PSYCHIATRY 198–99 (1984). *See also* Appelbaum & Roth, *Clinical Issues in the Assessment of Competency,* 128 AM. J. PSYCHIATRY 1462, 1465 (1981) (competency fluctuates over time).

[87] Morse, *Crazy Behavior, supra* note 81, at 573; Winick, *supra* note 81, at 54. The distinction between "crazy" and "normal" is elusive, particularly in view of the imprecision of the diagnostic categories used in defining mental illness, Morse, *Failed Explanations and Criminal Responsibility: Experts and the Unconscious,* 68 VA. L. REV. 971, 1049 (1982), as well as of the lack of consistency by clinicians in their application. *See* Ake v. Oklahoma, 470 U.S. 68, 81 (1985) ("Psychiatry is not . . . an exact science, and psychiatrists disagree widely and frequently on what constitutes mental illness, on the appropriate diagnosis to be attached to given behavior and symptoms, on cure and treatment."); Addington v. Texas, 441 U.S. 418, 432 (1979) (recognizing "the uncertainties of psychiatric diagnosis"); O'Connor v. Donaldson, 422 U.S. 563, 587 (1975) (Burger, C.J., concurring) (referring to the "wide divergence of medical opinion regarding the diagnosis of and proper therapy for mental abnormalities). *See generally* J. ZISKIN, COPING WITH PSYCHIATRIC AND PSYCHOLOGICAL TESTIMONY (3d ed. 1981); Ennis & Litwack, *Psychiatry and the Presumption of Expertise: Flipping Coins in the Courtroom,* 62 CAL. L. REV. 693 (1974); Liston et al., *Assessment of Psychotherapy Skills: The Problem of Interrater Agreement,* 138 AM. J. PSYCHIATRY 1069 (1981); Morse, *Crazy Behavior, supra* at 542–60. Even for conditions that by wide or even universal agreement produce distress and interfere in important areas of social and occupational functioning—schizophrenia, for example—and that, therefore, we agree should be considered mental disorders—the clinical determination of who suffers from the disorder raises similar problems. Diagnostic reliability—the probability that two clinicians will agree with each other's diagnosis—may be only 50% to 60% for schizophrenia and 30% to 40% for depression and affective disorder. Westermeyer, *Psychiatric Diagnosis Across Cultural Boundaries,* 142 AM. J. PSYCHIATRY 798, 801 (1985). There is wide disagreement within psychiatry concerning the nature and causes of schizophrenia and many of the other mental illnesses. *See, e.g.,* D. MECHANIC, MENTAL HEALTH AND SOCIAL POLICY 14–17 (1969). There simply is no "litmus test" available for the diagnosis of these conditions. Cancro, *Introduction to Etiologic Studies of the Schizophrenic Disorders, in* PSYCHIATRY 1982 ANNUAL REVIEW 91 (L. Grinspoon ed., 1982) ("There is no independent test to confirm or to reject the diagnosis of schizophrenia. There is no tissue or body fluid which can be sent to the laboratory to ascertain which individuals are false positives or false negatives."). Unlike physical illness, for which objective investigatory procedures are usually available for making and confirming diagnoses, the assessment of mental illness depends almost exclusively on subjective clinical judgment. MECHANIC, *supra,* at 17. The lack of theoretical consensus among clinicians concerning schizophrenia and other conditions inevitably produces varying application of diagnostic criteria.

in favor of competency is usually applied to those with mental illness.[88] Even those who have been involuntarily committed to mental hospitals because their illness renders them incompetent to decide about hospitalization for themselves generally are presumed competent to make other decisions, at least in the absence of evidence that they lack the specific competency in question.[89]

The *Zinermon* Court suggested that the consent to hospitalization of medically ill patients could justifiably be accepted at face value, although the consent of those with mental illness could not.[90] However, such medically ill patients—in hospitals, nursing homes, and the community—frequently suffer from language, educational, emotional, and social problems that severely impair their ability to function competently in processing and understanding medical information and making hospitalization and treatment decisions.[91] Competence is impaired particularly during the pain or stress of an illness that is sufficiently serious to provoke consideration of possible hospitalization and the situational depression and anxiety such an illness often produces. Moreover, medical procedures like general anesthesia sometimes themselves impair cognitive abilities and decision-making capacity for several days or even weeks. Many patients, even though not so impaired as to be considered ''mentally ill,'' generally have great difficulty making important decisions concerning their health, including whether to enter the hospital, because they are essentially irrational or are filled with denial, driven by unconscious needs and desires, paralyzed by fear, or dominated by other strong emotions.

Contrary to the 19th-century model of mental illness and the *Zinermon* Court's assumptions, mental patients sometimes may be severely impaired in their decision-making competence, although they are not always incompetent to make rational treatment decisions and are not categorically and inherently more incompetent than medically ill patients.[92] This conclusion finds support in significant recent research conducted by Thomas Grisso and Paul Appelbaum as part of their work for the MacArthur Foundation Research Network on

---

[88]*See supra* notes 69, 77 and accompanying text.

[89]*See supra* notes 74, 77 and accompanying text.

[90]*Zinermon*, 494 U.S. at 133 n.18.

[91]*See* R. BURT, TAKING CARE OF STRANGERS: THE RULE OF LAW IN DOCTOR–PATIENT RELATIONS 142 (1979); J. FEINBERG, HARM TO SELF 4–5, 23, 27 (1986); Appelbaum et al., *Empirical Assessment of Competency to Consent to Psychiatric Hospitalization,* 138 AM. J. PSYCHIATRY 1170 (1981) (reviewing empirical studies showing poor recall and understanding of patients in a variety of situations who provided informed consent to medical treatment or research); Cassileth et al., *Informed Consent: Why Are Its Goals Imperfectly Realized?,* 203 NEW ENG. J. MED. 896 (1980); Fellner & Marshall, *Kidney Donors—The Myth of Informed Consent,* 126 AM J. PSYCHIATRY 1245 (1970); Ingelfinger, *Informed (But Uneducated) Consent,* 287 NEW ENG. J. MED. 465 (1972); Sprung & Winick, *supra* note 1, at 1351 (discussing studies showing deficiencies in recall and understanding of informed consent on the part of nonmentally ill patients); Stanley, *Informed Consent in Treatment and Research, in* HANDBOOK OF FORENSIC PSYCHOLOGY 63, 72–74 (Weiner & Hess eds., 1987) (reviewing studies of medical patients showing that comprehension of consent information is poor).

[92]*See* Grossman & Summers, *A Study of the Capacity of Schizophrenic Patients to Give Informed Consent,* 31 HOSP. & COMMUNITY PSYCHIATRY 205 (1980) (finding comprehension of consent information in groups of mental patients and medical patients to be fairly equal); McKinnon et al., *supra* note 81, at 1159 (''Clinical evidence suggests that despite alterations in thinking and mood, psychiatric patients are not automatically less capable than others of making health care decisions.''); Soskis, *Schizophrenic and Medical Inpatients as Informed Drug Consumers,* 35 ARCHIVES GEN. PSYCHIATRY 645 (1978) (those with schizophrenia found to be more aware of risks and side effects of their medications than medical patients, but medical patients to be more informed about the name and dose of their medication and of their diagnosis); Soskis & Jaffe, *Communicating With Patients About Antipsychotic Drugs,* 20 COMPREHENSIVE PSYCHIATRY 126 (1970) (understanding in both groups equal); Stanley, *supra* note 91, at 77–78 (reviewing studies finding little difference between psychiatric and medical patients' comprehension of consent information); Stanley et al., *Preliminary Findings on Psychiatric Patients as Research Participants: A Population at Risk?,* 138 AM. J. PSYCHIATRY 669 (1981) (no differences found between groups of mental and medical patients studied).

Mental Health and the Law's study of treatment competency.[93] In 1991, during a preliminary portion of their study, the authors compared two groups of hospitalized mentally ill patients diagnosed as having schizophrenia and major depression, and two groups of nonmentally ill patients, one of which was diagnosed with ischemic heart disease and one that was composed of primary care patients without any diagnosed illness. Patients were administered an objective instrument designed to measure their understanding about decisions concerning medication. Although the group of patients with schizophrenia had significantly poorer understanding of information related to decisions about consent to treatment with medication than did the other groups,[94] the authors concluded that these results did not support "generalized presumptions about the capacities of patients with schizophrenia (or mentally ill patients generally) in comparison to nonmentally ill patients."[95] The patients with schizophrenia were found to display a considerable range of scores, with roughly 30% performing at a level similar to the nonmentally ill groups and an additional 38% performing worse than the mean of the groups but substantially better than the lowest 30%.[96] The performance of the patients with depression was found to be only slightly lower than the nonmentally ill groups.[97] The authors also suggested that premorbid differences in socioeconomic indicators between the mentally ill and nonmentally ill groups may have presented a confounding variable that would preclude conclusions about the linkage between understanding of information and mental illness.[98]

More recent research has now expanded on the preliminary data.[99] The authors performed an elaborate study of the relative competency for treatment decision making of mentally ill persons and physically ill persons. The study involved the administration of three separate instruments. These instruments assessed differing abilities relating to treatment decision making of six groups—patients recently hospitalized for schizophrenia, major depression, and ischemic heart disease, and three groups of non-ill persons in the community matched with the three hospitalized groups on key demographic variables (age, gender, race, and socioeconomic status). The study sought to assess the understanding of treatment disclosures, the perception (or appreciation) of the individual's disorder, and the ability to think rationally about treatment.

The study found that "on the measure of understanding . . . , appreciation . . . , and reasoning . . . , as a group, patients with mental illness more often manifested deficits in performance than did medically ill patients and their non-ill control groups."[100] Indeed, the most highly impaired subgroups were composed almost entirely of patients with mental illness.[101] However, "despite overall lower levels of performance in the groups with mental illness, there was considerable heterogeneity within and across the schizophrenia and

---

[93]Grisso & Appelbaum, *The MacArthur Treatment Competence Study. III: Abilities of Patients to Consent to Psychiatric and Medical Treatments,* 19 LAW & HUM. BEHAV. 175 (1995) [hereinafter *MacArthur Study*]; Grisso & Appelbaum, *Mentally Ill and Non-Mentally Ill Patients' Abilities to Understand Informed Consent Disclosure for Medication: Preliminary Data,* 15 LAW & HUM. BEHAV. 377 (1991) [hereinafter *Preliminary Data*]. For commentary on the MacArthur research, see *Special Theme: A Critical Examination of the MacArthur Treatment Competence Study: Methodological Issues, Legal Implications, and Future Directions,* 2 PSYCHOL. PUB. POL'Y & L. 1 (Winick, guest ed., 1996).

[94]Grisso & Appelbaum, *Preliminary Data, supra* note 93, at 385.

[95]*Id.*

[96]*Id.* at 385–86, 382 (table 2), 385 (table 4).

[97]*Id.* at 382 (table 2).

[98]*Id.* at 386–87.

[99]Grisso & Appelbaum, *MacArthur Study, supra* note 93, at 149.

[100]*Id.* at 169.

[101]*Id.*

depression groups.[102] Although this finding is consistent with other research showing the poorer performance of patients with schizophrenia compared to nonmentally ill patients on a wide array of cognitive tasks,[103] "on any given measure of decisional abilities, the majority of patients with schizophrenia did not perform more poorly than other patients and nonpatients."[104] The general poorer mean performance of the schizophrenia groups "was due to a minority within that group."[105] Apart from this poorer functioning subgroup, however, the groups of hospitalized patients with schizophrenia and major depression did not perform differently than the control groups.

The authors pointed out certain limitations that should be considered in interpreting the findings of the study. For example, the samples used probably underestimated, for all groups of patients, the proportion with serious deficiencies in decisional abilities related to competence to consent to treatment.[106] This is because patients judged to be too acutely disturbed to participate were excluded from the samples. Second, the instruments used do not adequately capture legal standards relating to competency, which vary across jurisdictions and are based on contextualized factors such as the specific disorder, proposed treatments, and probable consequences.[107] An additional limitation (not mentioned by the authors) is that the patients were evaluated several days after hospital admission—perhaps before medication could have a stabilizing and normalizing function. Although subgroups were retreated 2 weeks later, it is not clear whether this was sufficient time, in view of the fluctuating nature of competence and its response to psychopharmacological treatment, that the study presented an accurate picture of the groups with mental illness. As a result, in this sense, the findings probably overestimate the extent of disturbance in the mentally ill subgroups. Even ignoring this likely overestimate of impairment for the mentally ill groups, the findings are striking. Nearly half of the schizophrenia group and 76% of the depression group were found to perform in the "adequate range . . . across all decisionmaking measures," and a significant portion performed at or about the mean for persons without mental illness.[108]

The findings that a high percentage of patients with a mental illness, including schizophrenia, performed in the nonimpaired range and that there were considerable differences among patients in each mental illness diagnostic category suggest that rules of law grounded on the assumption that all mental patients (or all patients diagnosed with schizophrenia) are incompetent to engage in treatment decision making cannot withstand strict scrutiny. Grisso and Appelbaum concluded that those who would deny individuals with mental illness "equal decision making rights no longer can maintain that all persons who are in need of hospitalization for mental disorder lack the requisite ability to make decisions regarding their treatment."[109] The justification for denying such patients a right to refuse treatment, they conclude, "can not be based on the assumption that they uniformly lack decision making capacity."[110] The findings demonstrate the need for individualized determinations of the competency question rather than across the board assumptions that mental illness equates with impaired ability to make treatment decisions.

---

[102]*Id.*

[103]*E.g.,* Gold & Harvey, *Cognitive Defects in Schizophrenia,* 16 PSYCHIATRIC CLINICS N. AM. 295 (1993).

[104]Grisso & Appelbaum, *MacArthur Study, supra* note 93, at 169.

[105]*Id.*

[106]*Id.*

[107]*Id.* at 170.

[108]*Id.* at 171. "When performance on a single measure is examined . . . the rate of adequate performance rose to roughly 76% for patients with schizophrenia and approximately 80% for patients with depression." *Id.*

[109]*Id.*

[110]*Id.*

The MacArthur study, the most extensive ever undertaken of these questions, thus supports the conclusion that individualized determinations rather than blanket approaches treating all mental patients as incompetent are required as a matter of equal protection, at least when intrusive treatments are used. It also supports the conclusion that when nonintrusive treatments are used and when the rational-basis standard of equal protection review therefore will apply, the differences observed between mental patients and others (those with physical illness and community controls) will satisfy minimal equal protection scrutiny of legal practices treating mental patients differently than others in this regard.[111]

All patients have difficulty understanding complex information and making hard decisions such as whether to enter the hospital or to accept certain types of treatment, particularly under the stress of serious illness, and most are willing to defer to their doctors concerning medical decisions.[112] Those with mental illness should therefore enjoy the same general presumption of competency that is applied to those with medical illness. Although there may be differences between mentally ill and nonmentally ill patients, generalizations concerning competency should be avoided. Some patients in both categories are incompetent to engage in treatment decision making, but most members of each probably are competent. In the absence of specific evidence that decision-making ability is severely impaired, the mere existence of mental illness should not therefore necessitate an automatic assumption of incompetency.[113] A broad reading of the *Zinermon* language is thus troubling. Because it is based on an artificial dichotomy between medical and mental illness and confusion about the nature of mental illness, it should be rejected.

Mental illness therefore cannot be equated with incompetency.[114] Legislative classifications treating those with mental illness differently than those with medical illness with regard to the right to refuse treatment cannot be justified on the basis of the general assumption that those with mental illness are incompetent. Some people with mental illness are incompetent in this regard, but many are not. Whereas the rational-basis test of minimal equal protection scrutiny might be satisfied by a legislative assumption that those with mental illness cannot meet the requirements for informed consent and should therefore be treated without consent, this assumption cannot withstand the rigors of strict scrutiny. Because fundamental constitutional rights are burdened by at least the more intrusive mental

---

[111]The authors suggest that the differences between the high frequency of decision-making deficiencies in patients with schizophrenia and to a lesser extent in patients with depression, "may justify differences in the ways in which consent to treatment for mental illness and for medical illness are handled." *Id.* at 171.

[112]*See* LIDZ ET AL., *supra* note 86, at 18, 134; Ende et al., *Measuring Patients' Desire for Autonomy: Decision Making and Information-Seeking Preferences Among Medical Patients,* 4 J. GEN. INTERNAL MED. 23 (1989); Freedman, *A Moral Theory of Informed Consent,* 5 HASTINGS CTR. REP., Aug. 1975, at 32, 34; Glass, *Restructuring Informed Consent: Legal Therapy for the Doctor–Patient Relationship,* 79 YALE L.J. 1533, 1537, 1575 (1970); Lidz & Meisel, *Informed Consent and the Structure of Medical Care, in* 2 PRESIDENT'S COMM'N, *supra* note 69, at 392, 400–01, 403–04; Lynn, *Informed Consent: An Overview,* 1 BEHAV. SCI. & L. 29, 40 (1983); Shultz, *From Informed Consent to Patient Choice: A New Protected Interest,* 95 YALE L.J. 219, 259 (1985); Sprung & Winick, *supra* note 1, at 1349.

[113]The assumption that there is a "directly inverse relationship between the degree of psychopathology and the patient's capacity" is not supported by empirical research. McKinnon et al., *supra* note 81, at 1162; *accord* Stanley & Stanley, *Psychiatric Patients and Research: Protecting Their Autonomy,* 138 COMPREHENSIVE PSYCHIATRY 420, 424 (1981).

[114]*See* APPELBAUM & GUTHEIL, *supra* note 74, at 218, 220 ("The mere presence of psychosis, dementia, mental retardation, or some other form of mental illness or disability is insufficient in itself to constitute incompetence."). Indeed, mental illness cannot be equated with satisfaction of any legal category. *DSM–IV, supra* note 84, at xxiii ("the clinical diagnosis of a DSM–IV mental disorder is not sufficient to establish the existence for legal purposes of a 'mental disorder,' 'mental disability,' 'mental disease,' or 'mental defect.' In determining whether an individual meets a specified legal standard (e.g., for competence, criminal responsibility, or disability), additional information is usually required. . . .").

health therapies, treating all patients with mental illness as incompetent and on this basis depriving them of the right to avoid unwanted treatment extended to all others would seem inconsistent with equal protection. The range of differences regarding competency among those with mental illness, even severe mental illness, suggests the need for case-by-case determinations of the issue rather than categorical treatment.

Indeed, an individualized determination of competence arguably is required as well under the conclusive or irrebuttable presumption doctrine, which reflects both equal protection and due process principles.[115] Using this doctrine in various contexts, the Supreme Court has struck down a number of overly broad legislative classifications on the basis that, by presuming that all members of the burdened class possess those characteristics justifying imposition of the burden without affording the affected individuals any opportunity to rebut this presumption, the state had violated due process of law.[116] Although the Court has restricted the doctrine's applicability,[117] it appears willing to continue to invoke it in areas touching on fundamental rights.[118]

---

[115]See generally NOWAK & ROTUNDA, supra note 4, at 521–24, 751–53; Bezanson, Some Thoughts on the Emerging Irrebuttable Presumption Doctrine, 7 IND. L. REV. 644 (1974); NOWAK, Realigning the Standards of Review Under the Equal Protection Guarantee—Prohibited, Neutral and Permissive Classification, 62 GEO. L.J. 1071, 1104–09 (1974); Simpson, The Conclusive Presumption Cases: The Search for a Newer Equal Protection Continues, 24 CATH. U. L. REV. 217 (1975); Tribe, Structural Due Process, 10 HARV. C.R.-C.L. L. REV. 269 (1975); Note, The Irrebuttable Presumption Doctrine in the Supreme Court, 87 HARV. L. REV. 1534 (1974); Note, Irrebuttable Presumptions as an Alternative to Strict Scrutiny: From Rodriguez to LaFleur, 62 GEO. L.J. 1173 (1974); Note, The Conclusive Presumption Doctrine: Equal Process or Due Protection?, 72 MICH. L. REV. 800 (1974).

[116]E.g., Cleveland Bd. of Educ. v. LaFleur, 414 U.S. 632 (1974) (invalidating regulation compelling public school teachers to take leaves of absence from the 5th and 6th months of pregnancy until 3 months after giving birth); United States Dep't of Agriculture v. Murray, 413 U.S. 508 (1973) (invalidating statute denying eligibility for food stamps to households with individuals over 18 years of age claimed as tax dependents for the previous year by an individual not himself belonging to a household eligible for food stamps); Vlandis v. Kline, 412 U.S. 441 (1973) (invalidating statute classifying students as permanent nonresidents, so as to make them ineligible for reduced tuition at state universities, solely because their legal address was outside the state at the time of application); Stanley v. Illinois, 405 U.S. 645 (1972) (invalidating statute automatically depriving unwed fathers of the custody of their illegitimate children upon the mother's death without affording them an opportunity to demonstrate their fitness as parents); Bell v. Burson, 402 U.S. 535 (1971) (invalidating statute suspending driver's license of driver involved in an accident who would not post security covering the resulting damage, without permitting him an opportunity to present evidence of nonliability to prevent suspension).

[117]Usery v. Turner Elkhorn Mining Co., 428 U.S. 1 (1976) (upholding the Federal Coal Mine Health and Safety Act's irrebuttable presumption that a coal miner shown by x-ray or other clinical evidence to be afflicted with pneumoconiosis was totally disabled by that disease, thereby precluding coal mine operators from attempting to show the contrary); Weinberger v. Salfi, 422 U.S. 749 (1975) (upholding the Social Security Act's 9-month duration-of-relationship requirement for survivors' benefits, which irrebuttably presumes that marriages for a lesser period were fraudulently entered to obtain benefits, without affording an opportunity to demonstrate the bona fide nature of the marriage); see also Michael H. v. Gerald D., 491 U.S. 110 (1989) (upholding a state statute irrebuttably presuming that a child born of the woman and her husband was the legitimate child of the woman and her husband, thereby precluding an individual claiming to be the child's biological father from claiming paternity (although not from claiming a right to visitation)) (plurality opinion of Scalia, J., joined by Rehnquist, C.J., & O'Connor & Kennedy, J.J.). See Chase, The Premature Demise of Irrebuttable Presumptions, 47 U. COLO. L. REV. 653 (1976); Note, The Supreme Court, 1974 Term, 89 HARV. L. REV. 1, 77 (1975).

[118]Compare Turner v. Department of Employment Security, 423 U.S. 44, 46 (1975) (invalidating a statute making pregnant women ineligible for unemployment benefits from 12 weeks before the expected date of childbirth until 6 weeks after, on the ground that "when basic human liberties are at stake," rather than conclusively presuming that women are unable to work during this period, the state must achieve its ends "through more individualized means") with Usery v. Turner Elkhorn Mining Co., 428 U.S. 1 (1976) (upholding an irrebuttable presumption in the Federal Coal Mine and Safety Act concerning the total disability of mine workers afflicted with a particular disease on the basis that the statutory classification involved only entitlement to benefits) and Weinberger v. Salfi, 422 U.S. 749, 771–72 (1975) (distinguishing Stanley and LaFleur as cases involving statutes infringing fundamental rights, whereas the statute at issue involved "a noncontractual claim to receive funds from the public treasury [which] enjoys no constitutionally protected status").

State statutory provisions or other legal practices assuming those with mental illness to be incompetent to engage in treatment decision making conclusively presume that all mentally ill patients are incompetent, when in fact only a small segment of this class cannot engage in rational decision making. As a result, these statutes and practices burden, in an overly broad manner, a fundamental right to refuse intrusive treatment, protected by the First Amendment and substantive due process. The conclusive presumption doctrine may therefore be invoked to require that the state afford an individualized hearing to determine whether mental illness actually impairs the patient's competence in a way that prevents rational treatment decision making, the fact presumed by these state practices.

When intrusive treatment is involved, the equal protection doctrine therefore will provide an additional basis for a right to refuse treatment. Any justification grounded in the assertion that mental illness automatically renders the individual dangerous or incompetent to engage in treatment decision making should be rejected unless a determination is made of the existence of these effects. Even though the police power interest in preventing harm and the *parens patriae* interest in protecting the individual may be compelling governmental interests,[119] a state's equation of mental illness with dangerousness or incompetence would seem not to be carefully tailored to achieve these interests. In the absence of a determination meeting the requirements of procedural due process that the justifications for involuntary treatment are present, such treatment may not be imposed, at least where it is highly intrusive.[120] Treating those with mental illness differently from others in regard to the imposition of intrusive mental health therapy therefore seems inconsistent with equal protection.

On the other hand, when the treatment involved is on the lower range of the continuum of intrusiveness, and as a result does not implicate any fundamental constitutional rights, such presumptions equating mental illness with dangerousness or incompetence would be constitutional. Although imperfect, such presumptions would be rationally related to the state's legitimate interests and hence would be sufficient under the low-level equal protection scrutiny applied when neither fundamental rights nor suspect classifications are involved.

[119]*See infra* chapter 15, part C.
[120]Riggins v. Nevada, 504 U.S. 127 (1992) (forcible administration of antipsychotic medication to a criminal defendant during trial held unconstitutional in the absence of specific findings that such medication was both medically appropriate and the least intrusive means of accomplishing a compelling state interest).

Chapter 15
SCRUTINIZING THE GOVERNMENT'S INTEREST IN INVOLUNTARY TREATMENT

As chapters 10 through 14 demonstrate, several constitutional protections are implicated by involuntary administration of at least the more intrusive forms of mental health treatment. Involuntary psychosurgery, electronic stimulation of the brain, and electroconvulsive therapy raise serious First Amendment[1] and substantive due process concerns.[2] These same constitutional protections also would seem to be implicated by involuntary administration of most types of psychotropic medication. Coercive applications of aversive conditioning using intrusive conditioners that intrude on bodily integrity may raise substantive due process problems. However, most forms of behavior therapy and psychotherapy and other verbal approaches would seem not to raise these constitutional concerns. In more limited circumstances, the use of some of these techniques may raise Eighth Amendment[3] or First Amendment free exercise of religion concerns.[4] Moreover, if administered to mentally ill patients and offenders but not to similarly situated medically ill patients or to offenders generally, they may present equal protection problems.[5]

Under general constitutional principles, the more intrusive treatment techniques therefore would mandate strict judicial scrutiny. To avoid constitutional condemnation, involuntary administration of these techniques must be justified as necessary to achieve one or more compelling governmental interests. Even when the government's interest is found to be compelling, the use of intrusive treatment would not be permissible if that interest could be accomplished through the use of less intrusive alternative measures (including other less intrusive forms of treatment). Because intrusive mental health treatment burdens First Amendment and substantive due process liberty interests that are ''fundamental,'' conventional constitutional doctrine would require application of the demanding standards of traditional strict scrutiny. Will strict scrutiny be applied by the courts in the context of involuntary mental health treatment? The issue has been frequently litigated in the state and lower federal courts, which have reached differing conclusions. On four occasions, the U.S. Supreme Court has considered the issue. Each case challenged the involuntary administration of antipsychotic medication.

A. Supreme Court Consideration of the Right to Refuse Mental Health Treatment

In *Mills v. Rogers*,[6] the Supreme Court granted certiorari to consider the involuntary use of antipsychotic medication for civil patients at the Boston State Hospital. Medication

---

[1]*See supra* chapter 10.
[2]*See supra* chapter 11.
[3]*See supra* chapter 12.
[4]*See supra* chapter 13.
[5]*See supra* chapter 14.
[6]457 U.S. 291 (1982).

practices at the hospital had been the subject of a broad remedial order by the district court, and the court's order had been affirmed in most respects by the First Circuit Court of Appeals.[7] After briefing and oral argument, the Supreme Court vacated and remanded the case for reconsideration in light of an intervening decision of the Supreme Judicial Court of Massachusetts that recognized a right to refuse medication on state law grounds.[8] In its brief opinion, however, the Court noted that the nature of these drugs is to affect mental processes.[9] Without deciding the question, the Court expressed its assumption that these drugs when involuntarily administered intruded on a liberty interest protected by the Due Process Clause of the Fourteenth Amendment.[10]

In *Rennie v. Klein,*[11] which arose in the same period as *Rogers,* the Court vacated the decision of the Third Circuit Court of Appeals in a parallel case challenging medication practices at a New Jersey state hospital.[12] The Court's brief order vacated the Third Circuit's opinion, which had recognized a right of state hospital patients to refuse antipsychotic medication.[13] In vacating the circuit court's decision, the Supreme Court called for reconsideration in light of the Court's 1982 decision in *Youngberg v. Romeo,*[14] another Third Circuit case that had challenged conditions and practices at an institution for those suffering from mental retardation. *Youngberg* had announced a deferential professional judgment standard for scrutinizing the use of physical restraints at the retardation facility,[15] and the Court's remand in *Rennie* implied that the professional judgment standard also might be applied in the right-to-refuse-treatment context.[16]

The Court faced these issues again in 1990 in *Washington v. Harper.*[17] The Court granted certiorari to consider a decision of the Supreme Court of Washington that had placed substantive and procedural due process limitations on a state prison's ability to use antipsychotic medication involuntarily to treat a prisoner who was found to be dangerous when not taking such medication.[18] At the oral argument in *Harper,* the Justices seemed disturbed about the question before them: Could a prison forcibly administer antipsychotic medication to a prisoner found by a prison review board to be mentally ill and dangerous to himself and others? At one level, the answer may have seemed clear. The prisoner had a history of being assaultive, he was concededly mentally ill, a prison psychiatrist treating him had prescribed the drugs, and a security hospital review board had approved the administration of the drug under a regulation limiting forced medication to prevent danger to the prisoner, other inmates, or prison staff.[19]

The Washington Supreme Court had found such involuntary medication to be unconstitutional absent a judicial determination that the prisoner was mentally ill and dangerous and that the treatment was the least intrusive method of dealing with the problem.[20] The main

---

[7]Rogers v. Okin, 478 F. Supp. 1342 (D. Mass. 1979), *aff'd in part, rev'd in part and remanded,* 634 F.2d 650 (1st Cir. 1980), *vacated and remanded sub nom.* Mills v. Rogers, 457 U.S. 291 (1982).

[8]457 U.S. at 306.

[9]*Id.* at 298–99.

[10]*Id.*

[11]458 U.S. 1119 (1982), *vacating* 653 F.2d 836 (3d Cir. 1981) (en banc).

[12]653 F.2d 836 (3d Cir. 1981) (en banc).

[13]*Id.* at 844–45.

[14]457 U.S. 307 (1982).

[15]*Id.* at 323.

[16]*See infra* notes 86–90 and accompanying text.

[17]494 U.S. 210 (1990).

[18]Harper v. Washington, 759 P.2d 358 (Wash. 1988).

[19]*Id.* at 360.

[20]*Id.* at 364–65.

focus of the briefing in the Supreme Court was the procedural due process issue of whether a judicial hearing, as opposed to the administrative hearing authorized by the Washington statute, was required. Although several courts had required a judicial hearing before involuntary antipsychotic medication could be authorized,[21] most had approved a more informal administrative determination of the issue.[22] In addition, the Court's approach in *Parham v. J.R.,*[23] approving an administrative review of the civil commitment of children by their parents, had expressed the Court's distaste for requiring a judicial model as a matter of due process for the resolution of issues requiring clinical judgment and prediction as opposed to the determination of historical questions of fact.[24] It seemed predictable, therefore, that the Court would reverse, but the Justices still seemed disturbed about the effects of the drugs. Although the American Psychiatric Association had submitted an amicus brief in support of the state, defending the use of these drugs and seeking to minimize their risks,[25] the American Psychological Association had filed an amicus brief in support of the prisoner, emphasizing the serious adverse side effects that the drugs produced.[26]

In his questioning, Justice Kennedy in particular seemed to express concern about potential side effects and their constitutional implications, and some of those attending the argument thought that he might vote for the prisoner. Justices Kennedy and O'Connor were then moving toward the vacuum created at the center of the Court with the retirement of Justice Powell, whom Justice Kennedy had replaced, and at least one of their votes seemed essential if the prisoner was to win. As they left the Court, the representatives of the American Psychiatric Association who had attended the argument seemed concerned about the questioning and uncertain about the result.

The opinion was assigned to Justice Kennedy. The Court upheld the prison practice, reversing the decision of the Washington Supreme Court.[27] Writing for five of the Justices, Justice Kennedy's opinion addressed both the substantive and procedural due process issues raised. The Court recognized that involuntary use of antipsychotic drugs involved a serious intrusion on what it characterized as the individual's "significant liberty interest."[28] However, adopting a deferential approach to reviewing the discretion of prison authorities in dealing with the problems of institutional security, the Court upheld the involuntary administration of the drugs in the circumstances presented. The Court applied the limited scope of review developed in prior prison cases, under which invasion of constitutional rights pursuant to prison regulations could be justified if reasonably related to a legitimate

---

[21]*E.g.,* Rogers v. Okin, 634 F.2d 650, 661 (1st Cir. 1980), *vacated and remanded sub nom.* Mills v. Rogers, 457 U.S. 291 (1982); Riese v. St. Mary's Hosp. & Med. Ctr., 243 Cal. Rptr. 241 (Ct. App. 1987), *appeal dismissed,* 774 P.2d 698 (Cal. 1989); Rivers v. Katz, 95 N.E.2d 337 (N.Y. 1986); *see* Winick, *The Right to Refuse Psychotropic Medication: Current State of the Law and Beyond, in* THE RIGHT TO REFUSE ANTIPSYCHOTIC MEDICATION 7, 21–26 (D. Rapaport & J. Parry eds., 1986).

[22]*E.g.,* Rennie v. Klein, 653 F.2d 836, 850 (3d Cir. 1980) (en banc), *vacated and remanded,* 458 U.S. 1119 (1982); United States v. Leatherman, 580 F. Supp. 977 (D.D.C. 1983); *see* Winick, *supra* note 21, at 23–26.

[23]442 U.S. 584 (1979).

[24]*Id.* at 606–09; *see id.* at 607 ("[D]ue process is not violated by use of informal, traditional medical investigative techniques.").

[25]Brief for the American Psychiatric Ass'n and the Washington State Psychiatric Ass'n as *Amici Curiae,* Washington v. Harper, 494 U.S. 210 (1990) (No. 88–599).

[26]Brief for the American Psychological Ass'n as *Amicus Curiae,* Washington v. Harper, 494 U.S. 210 (1990) (No. 88-599).

[27]494 U.S. 210 (1990).

[28]*Id.* at 221.

penalogical objective.[29] The Court also rejected the "least restrictive means" analysis adopted by the Washington Supreme Court.[30] Finally, the Court rejected the contention that procedural due process required a judicial determination of the need for medication, upholding the sufficiency of the administrative model mandated by the Washington regulation.[31] Justice Blackmun wrote a short concurring opinion,[32] and Justice Stevens wrote a dissent, in which Justices Brennan and Marshall joined.[33]

Was *Harper* just a prison case, or did the approach to involuntary antipsychotic medication used by the Court apply more generally to medication practices in civil mental hospitals and other settings? The Court's deferential approach in *Harper* was far from the strict scrutiny applied by the Washington Supreme Court. The protection of the safety of other prisoners and prison staff was unquestionably a compelling state interest, but the prisoner in *Harper* had argued that the state could accomplish this objective by less intrusive means, such as segregation or prison discipline.[34] The Court expressly rejected this least restrictive alternative approach, noting that the Constitution does not require prison authorities to consider and then reject each conceivable response to the problem of institutional security.[35] Yet the *Harper* Court characterized its standard of review as more than merely a rational-basis test.[36] There must be, the Court emphasized, a reasonable, not merely rational, relationship to a legitimate penalogical purpose.[37]

The Court also mentioned that the record in *Harper* reflected that the medication prescribed was in the prisoner's medical interests.[38] Although referring to this finding in its statement of the conditions that would justify forced medication, the prison regulation in *Harper* setting forth standards for involuntary medication had not required such a finding.[39] As a result, the precedential effect of the Court's reference to the medical appropriateness of the administered medication remained unclear. Was the requirement that medication be

---

[29]*Id.* at 223 (citing O'Lone v. Estate of Shabazz, 482 U.S. 342, 349 (1987) and Turner v. Safley, 482 U.S. 78, 89 (1987)).

[30]*Id.* at 225 (" '[T]he absence of ready alternatives is evidence of the reasonableness of a prison regulation,' but this does not mean that prison officials 'have to set up and then shoot down every conceivable alternative method of accommodating the claimant's constitutional complaint.' ") (quoting *Turner,* 482 U.S. at 90–91).

[31]*Id.* at 228.

[32]*Id.* at 236–37 (Blackmun, J., concurring).

[33]*Id.* at 237 (Stevens, J., joined by Brennan & Marshall, J.J., dissenting).

[34]Brief of Respondent at 44, Washington v. Harper, 494 U.S. 210 (1990) (No. 85–599).

[35]*See supra* note 30.

[36]494 U.S. at 224.

[37]*Id.* at 223.

[38]*Id.* at 222–23 ("[T]he fact that the medication must first be prescribed by a psychiatrist, and then approved by a reviewing psychiatrist, ensures that the treatment in question will be ordered only if it is in the prisoner's medical interests, given the legitimate needs of his institutional confinement."); *id.* at 223 n.8 ("We agree with the State's representations at oral argument that, under the Policy, antipsychotic medications can be administered only for treatment purposes, with the hearing committee reviewing the doctor's decision to ensure what has been prescribed is appropriate.").

[39]*Id.* at 215 (quoting Washington Department of Corrections Special Offender Center Policy 600.30). Justice Stevens pointed out this discrepancy:

> Policy 600.30 permits forced administration of psychotropic drugs on a mentally ill inmate based purely on the impact that his disorder has on the security of the prison environment. The provisions of the Policy make no reference to any expected benefit on the inmate's medical condition. . . . Although any application of Policy 600.30 requires a medical judgment as to a prisoner's mental condition and the cause of his behavior, the Policy does not require a determination that forced medication would advance his medical interest. . . . Thus, most unfortunately, there is simply no basis for the Court's assertion that medication under the Policy must be to advance the prisoner's medical interest.

Id. at 243–45 (Stevens, J., joined by Brennan & Marshall, J.J., concurring in part and dissenting in part).

medically indicated an element of the Court's constitutional standard, or merely a factor contained in the record that allowed the majority to feel more comfortable about its decision? Finally, did the Court's rejection of a judicial determination of the appropriateness of forced drugging mean that informal administrative models for such determinations would be approved in other contexts? Although these questions were not resolved in *Harper*, the Court's decision reflected what seemed to be a narrow view of the emerging right to refuse intrusive treatment.

The Court next considered these issues in *Perry v. Louisiana*.[40] The Court's action seemed to signal that the *Harper* approach to right-to-refuse-treatment issues might apply in contexts not involving prison security. In *Perry*, the Court had granted certiorari to consider the assertion of a right to refuse antipsychotic medication by a death row inmate who had been found incompetent to be executed.[41] The state had attempted to treat the prisoner with drugs in order to restore him to competency so that he could be executed, and the prisoner claimed a right to refuse administration of the drugs.[42] After oral argument, the Court vacated the state court's decision ordering forced medication for reconsideration in light of the Supreme Court's ruling in *Harper*.[43] The implication seemed to be that *Harper* supplied the appropriate standard for resolving this and perhaps other right-to-refuse-treatment questions. With the retirement of two of the three dissenters in *Harper*—Justice Brennan in 1991 and Justice Marshall in 1992—and their replacement with the more conservative Justices Souter and Thomas, the narrow approach that *Harper* had adopted to the right to refuse treatment seemed likely to emerge as the Court's general approach in this area.

The Court's 1992 decision in *Riggins v. Nevada*[44] dispels the implication that *Harper* should be construed broadly. Indeed, in its opinion in *Riggins*, the Court moved strongly in the opposite direction from *Harper*, suggesting that outside of the prison context, the right to refuse treatment will be given a considerably more generous reading. *Riggins* involved a criminal defendant being treated with mellaril, an antipsychotic drug, who sought discontinuation of his medication prior to trial so that he might stand trial and raise an insanity defense while in an unmedicated state. After a brief hearing, the trial judge denied the defendant's request and required the continuation of medication. The defendant was convicted at trial and received a death sentence. He appealed, contending that the medication he was forced to take during trial had interfered with his trial performance and ability to communicate with counsel, resulting in a violation of due process.

The Supreme Court reversed Riggins's conviction. The Court's holding was narrow, turning on the absence of sufficient findings by the trial court to justify continuing the defendant's medication over objection. However, in dicta the Court suggested the standards that would apply to measure future assertions of state authority to forcibly medicate a criminal defendant in the pretrial and trial process. Justice O'Connor's opinion for the *Riggins* majority quoted liberally from *Harper*'s description of the serious side effects of

---

[40]498 U.S. 38 (1990).

[41]494 U.S. 1015 (1990), *granting cert. in* State v. Perry, 543 So. 2d 487 (La. 1989) and 545 So. 2d 1049 (La. 1989).

[42]502 So. 2d 543 (La. 1986).

[43]498 U.S. at 38. For analysis of the issue left unresolved in *Perry*, see Winick, *Competency to be Executed: A Therapeutic Jurisprudence Perspective*, 10 BEHAV. SCI. & L. 317, 328–37 (1992). On remand, the Louisiana Supreme Court found *Harper* distinguishable and held that involuntary administration of antipsychotic drugs for restoring a prisoner to competency for execution violated the state and federal constitutions. State v. Perry, 610 So. 2d 746, 749–52 (La. 1992).

[44]Riggins v. Nevada, 504 U.S. 127, 133–34 (1992) (quoting Washington v. Harper, 494 U.S. 210, 229 (1990)).

antipsychotic drugs, the involuntary administration of which, she reiterated, "represents a substantial interference" with liberty protected by the Due Process Clause.[45] Indeed, she pointed out that in the case of an antipsychotic drug like mellaril, the same drug that had been involved in *Harper*, "that interference is particularly severe."[46]

The first hint that the deferential approach of *Harper* would not be applied in *Riggins* came in Justice O'Connor's use of the word *unique* to describe the "circumstances of penal confinement" that had provided the context for *Harper*.[47] Riggins, of course, was not a "convicted prisoner" at the time he was medicated involuntarily; rather, he was in jail awaiting trial. Accordingly, the Court noted that, compared with convicted prisoners, "[t]he Fourteenth Amendment affords at least as much protection to persons whom the State detains for trial."[48] The Court's application of a more stringent standard of review to the practices at issue in *Riggins* was signaled by the Court's quotation of language from *O'Lone v. Estate of Shabazz*[49] stating that prison regulations "are judged under a 'reasonableness' test less restrictive than that ordinarily applied to alleged infringements of fundamental constitutional rights."[50]

The Court then adapted the *Harper* standard to the pretrial setting of *Riggins*, indicating that the state would "certainly" have satisfied due process "if the prosecution had demonstrated and the District Court had found that treatment with antipsychotic medication was medically appropriate and, considering less intrusive alternatives, essential for the sake of Riggins' own safety or the safety of others."[51] In this one critical sentence, the Court appeared to broaden the *Harper* approach in two significant respects. Whereas *Harper* had explicitly rejected the need to show a less restrictive alternative, the *Riggins* Court adopted this test in the pretrial context before it. In addition, although *Harper* had rejected the necessity of a judicial determination of the need for involuntary medication, *Riggins* specifically required that the trial court itself make these necessary findings.[52] Furthermore, although the Court did not specify the standard of proof by which the prosecution would have to make the necessary demonstration, its citation of *Addington v. Texas*[53] (in which the Court held that due process conditions civil commitment on the state's showing by clear and convincing evidence that hospitalization is warranted) suggests that it may have contemplated a similar heightened standard of proof in the pretrial involuntary medication context.

In this same sentence, the Court also made clear that the medical appropriateness of the medication administered to the prisoner in *Harper* was a constitutional requirement for such

---

[45]*Id.* at 135.

[46]*Id.*

[47]*Id.* at 134 (citing *Harper*, 494 U.S. at 227).

[48]*Id.* (citing Bell v. Wolfish, 441 U.S. 520, 545 (1979) and O'Lone v. Estate of Shabazz, 482 U.S. 342, 349 (1987)).

[49]482 U.S. 342 (1987).

[50]*Riggins*, 504 U.S. at 135 (quoting *O'Lone*, 482 U.S. at 349).

[51]*Id.*

[52]It may be difficult to infer from *Riggins*'s adoption of a judicial model for right-to-refuse-treatment issues in the criminal trial process that judicial models also will be required in other right-to-refuse-treatment contexts. In the trial context of *Riggins*, a trial judge is already involved with the matter and would need to deal with the criminal law aspects of the case, including competency to stand trial. As a result, the Court's bifurcation of the medication question by involving an administrative decision maker would not have been sensible. Thus, allowing the court, which is already and inevitably involved with the matter, to resolve the right-to-refuse-treatment issues arising in the criminal trial process does not necessarily indicate a broad rejection of *Harper*'s endorsement of an administrative model for right-to-refuse decision making. As a result, in other contexts, *Harper*'s preference for administrative decision making still would seem applicable. *See infra* chapter 19, part B.

[53]*Riggins*, 504 U.S. at 135 (citing Addington v. Texas, 441 U.S. 418 (1979)).

involuntary treatment.[54] The Court restated its holding in *Harper* that "forcing antipsychotic drugs on a convicted prisoner is impermissible absent a finding of overriding justification and a determination of medical appropriateness."[55] In doing so, the Court elevated to a constitutional prerequisite for involuntary medication the requirement that such medication be shown to be medically appropriate for the patient.

What is the significance of the Court's clarification that medical appropriateness is a constitutionally required condition for involuntary medication? This limitation would prevent the use of medication even to accomplish compelling governmental interests unless it also is in the medical interest of the patient. Unless it can be justified medically, for example, psychotropic medication could not be used in a hospital, a nursing home, a jail, or even a prison where the justification asserted is institutional management, the prevention or control of violence, or as punishment to enforce compliance with institutional rules. Moreover, unless medically justified, such treatment could not be used to attempt to restore incompetent death row inmates to a state of competence so that they may be executed, to "rehabilitate" criminal offenders so as to minimize recidivism, or to punish such offenders in order to deter them or others from committing crime. Although none of these potential uses of medication was before the Court, they would appear to be constitutionally impermissible unless, at a minimum, the medication was needed by the individual for medical purposes.

The *Riggins* Court then considered an additional potential justification for involuntary medication in the pretrial setting. The Court suggested that the state "might have been able to justify [such medication] by establishing that it could not obtain an adjudication of Riggins's guilt or innocence by using less intrusive means."[56] In its description of this potential justification for involuntary medication, as in its statement of the first justification it had suggested, the Court again invoked the less intrusive alternative principle that it previously had rejected in the prison context of *Harper*.[57]

---

[54]*Id.* at 135 ("[W]e determined [in *Harper*] that due process allows a mentally ill inmate to be treated involuntarily with antipsychotic drugs when there is a determination that 'the inmate is dangerous to himself or others and the treatment is in the inmate's medical interest.' ") (quoting *Harper*, 494 U.S. at 227).

[55]*Id.* For further discussion of this principle, see *infra* chapter 16, part A. The constitutional requirement of medical appropriateness parallels a similar requirement of medical ethics. *See Harper*, 494 U.S. at 222–23 n.8; *see also id.* at 244–45 n.11 (Stevens, J., joined by Brennan & Marshall, J.J., concurring in part and dissenting in part) (noting the requirements of medical ethics but suggesting that the existence of medical ethics is not sufficient protection for legal rights); State v. Perry, 610 So. 2d 746, 751–52 (La. 1992). The Hippocratic Oath, which is at the core of medical ethics, imposes a duty of benevolence and nonmalevolence on the physician that is inconsistent with the administration of treatment that is not in her patient's best interests. The Oath provides:

> I swear by Apollo the physician, by Aesculapius, Hygeia, and Panacea, and I take to witness all the gods, all the goddesses, to keep according to my ability and my judgment the following Oath: ... I will prescribe regimen for the good of my patients according to my ability and my judgment and never do harm to anyone. To please no one will I prescribe a deadly drug, nor give advice which may cause his death. ... I will preserve the purity of my life and my art ... In every house where I come I will enter only for the good of my patients, keeping myself far from all intentional ill-doing. ...

Id. (quoting HIPPOCRATES C. 460–400 B.C., STEDMAN'S MEDICAL DICTIONARY 647 (4th unabridged Lawyer's Ed. 1976)); *see* Winick, *supra* note 43, at 332 (discussing the Hippocratic Oath in the context of involuntary treatment administered to restore a death row inmate to competency for execution). For further discussion of ethical issues in the involuntary treatment context, see *infra* chapter 20, part B.

[56]*Riggins*, 504 U.S. at 135.

[57]*Id.* For further discussion of the least intrusive alternative principle, see *infra* chapter 16, part B.

B. The Appropriate Standard of Judicial Scrutiny for the Various Contexts in Which Involuntary Treatment Is Administered

The Court's invocation of the "least intrusive means" standard seems to suggest that strict constitutional scrutiny will be applied in most right-to-refuse-medication contexts. Justice Thomas, in his dissenting opinion in *Riggins,* criticized the Court for adopting a standard of strict scrutiny.[58] The *Riggins* majority responded to this criticism by stating that it had "no occasion to finally prescribe such substantive standards"—referring to those that it had suggested—"since the District Court allowed administration of mellaril to continue without making *any* determination of the need for this course or *any* findings about reasonable alternatives."[59] *Riggins*'s holding thus is quite narrow: The trial court's failure to make any findings concerning the need for involuntary medication rendered its continuation of such medication over objection unconstitutional. The majority's suggestions about possible justifications for involuntary medication in this context accordingly were dicta; thus, the Court clearly was not adopting or finally prescribing any standard. Although dicta, however, the majority's suggestions amounted to a standard of strict scrutiny.[60] The Court's references to plainly compelling state objectives—the protection of the safety of inmates or institutional staff and the need to maintain criminal defendants in a competent state so that they may be tried—and to the requirement that the state administer medication involuntarily only if no "less intrusive means" would suffice, suggest that strict scrutiny was precisely what the majority had in mind.

Should strict scrutiny generally be applied when intrusive treatment is to be imposed involuntarily? Strict scrutiny may be particularly appropriate in the criminal pretrial and trial context presented in *Riggins.* When individuals accused of crime are involuntarily medicated, their due process liberty interests in being free from the substantial intrusion of unwanted treatment are coupled with their due process interests in a fair trial and in controlling their own defenses. A criminal defendant's right to control the defense is, itself, a fundamental constitutional right, invasions of which would warrant heightened scrutiny.[61] Involuntary administration of medication causing side effects that impair a defendant's abilities in this regard thus deserve a considerably more demanding standard of judicial review than the reasonableness test applied in *Harper* and in other prison cases.

Moreover, even apart from this added consideration that is unique to involuntary medication in the criminal trial context, the nature, extent, and duration of the intrusions on

---

[58]*Id.* at 141 (Thomas, J., joined by Scalia, J., dissenting).

[59]*Id.* at 135–36 (majority opinion).

[60]The Court majority in *Riggins* specifically eschews adopting a standard of strict scrutiny, not because the majority disagrees with such a standard but because the majority has "no occasion to finally prescribe such substantive standards." The Court's reasoning and language, however—*e.g.,* its focus on the Nevada court's failure to indicate whether "compelling [state] concerns outweighed Riggins' interest in freedom from unwanted antipsychotic drugs" virtually announces that the compelling state interest test applies. Khiem v. United States, 612 A.2d 160, 178 n.5 (D.C. App. 1992) (Ferren, J., joined by Rogers, C.J., voting to grant rehearing en banc) (citations omitted). *See also* Woodland v. Angus, 820 F. Supp. 1497, 1510 (D. Utah 1993) (construing *Riggins* to require a standard of strict scrutiny).

[61]*See, e.g.,* Rock v. Arkansas, 483 U.S. 44 (1987); Crane v. Kentucky, 476 U.S. 683, 690–91 (1986); Geders v. United States, 425 U.S. 80 (1976); Faretta v. California, 422 U.S. 806 (1975); Brooks v. Tennessee, 406 U.S. 605 (1972); Washington v. Texas, 388 U.S. 14 (1967). *See also* Clinton, *The Right to Present a Defense: An Emerging Constitutional Guarantee in Criminal Trials,* 9 IND. L. REV. 711 (1976); Fentiman, *Whose Right Is It Anyway?: Rethinking Competency to Stand Trial in Light of the Synthetically Sane Insanity Defendant,* 40 U. MIAMI L. REV. 1109, 1120 (1986); Winick, *On Autonomy: Legal and Psychological Perspectives,* 37 VILL. L. REV. 1705, 1748–49 (1992).

bodily privacy and mental processes produced by these drugs make strict constitutional scrutiny appropriate whenever they are sought to be forcibly administered, with the possible exception of administration in a prison when medically appropriate and related to institutional security. Although *Riggins* does not explore the nature of the liberty interest invaded, the intrusions caused by these drugs are sufficiently serious that the liberty interest in avoiding them should be considered fundamental. As demonstrated in chapter 11, involuntary medication invades the "historic liberty interest" in "personal security" and bodily integrity.[62] Moreover, as chapter 11 also demonstrates, the liberty guaranteed by the Due Process Clause includes protection for individual autonomy in making important choices, including personal health decisions.[63] The Court, in its 1990 "right to die" case, *Cruzan v. Director, Missouri Department of Health,* expressed its assumption that such liberty protected an individual's decision "in refusing medical treatment,"[64] and Justice O'Connor, in her concurring opinion in that case, noted that "our notions of liberty are inextricably entwined with our idea of physical freedom and self-determination."[65]

Not only do the serious physical intrusions of antipsychotic medication invade these liberty interests, but as chapters 5, 10, and 11 show, they also infringe on First Amendment values and a separate substantive due process interest in mental privacy.[66] As the Court recognized in both *Riggins* and *Harper,* these drugs "alter the chemical balance in a patient's brain," producing "changes . . . in his or her cognitive processes."[67] Moreover, as Justice Kennedy noted in a lengthy description of their adverse side effects in his concurring opinion in *Riggins,* these drugs may be sedating and may interfere with concentration in ways that diminish the defendant's ability to understand and follow the proceedings, and they may directly affect verbal and nonverbal communication, including speech itself.[68] The Court has never been presented with the opportunity to consider the First Amendment implications of involuntary administration of these drugs,[69] but their serious and direct

---

[62]*See supra* chapter 11, part C1; Ingraham v. Wright, 430 U.S. 651, 673 (1977); Union Pac. Ry. Co. v. Botsford, 141 U.S. 250, 251–52 (1891); Winick, *supra* note 61, at 1733 & n.120; *cf.* Winston v. Lee, 470 U.S. 753 (1985) (applying Fourth Amendment).

[63]*See supra* chapter 11, part C3; Cruzan v. Director, Mo. Dep't of Health, 497 U.S. 261, 278 (1990); Schloendorff v. Society of New York Hosp., 105 N.E. 92, 93 (N.Y. 1914) (Cardozo, J.); Winick, *supra* note 61, at 1732–37.

[64]*Cruzan,* 497 U.S. at 278.

[65]*Id.* at 287 (O'Connor, J., concurring).

[66]*See supra* chapter 10; *supra* chapter 11, part C2; *see, e.g.,* Bee v. Greaves, 744 F.2d 1387, 1392–93 (10th Cir. 1984), *cert. denied,* 469 U.S. 1214 (1985); Winick, *The Right to Refuse Mental Health Treatment: A First Amendment Perspective,* 44 U. MIAMI L. REV. 1 (1989).

[67]Riggins v. Nevada, 504 U.S. 127,134 (1992) (quoting *Harper,* 494 U.S. at 229–30).

[68]*Id.* at 137–38 (Kennedy, J., concurring).

[69]No First Amendment claim was asserted in either *Harper* or *Riggins,* and the dissenting opinion in *Harper* explicitly noted that as a result, the First Amendment implications of these drugs were not before the Court. *Harper,* 494 U.S. at 258 n.32 (Stevens, J., joined by Brennan & Marshall, J.J., concurring in part and dissenting in part). A Tenth Circuit Court of Appeals decision had applied First Amendment limits on the involuntary administration of antipsychotic drugs, but the Court denied a petition for certiorari seeking review of the issue. Bee v. Greaves, 744 F.2d 1387 (10th Cir. 1984), *cert. denied,* 469 U.S. 1214 (1985).

intrusions on mental processes and effects on cognitive and communicative ability make appropriate the strict scrutiny traditionally applied in the First Amendment context.[70]

As a result, the criminal due process concerns presented in *Riggins* may be absent in forcible medication contexts outside of the criminal process, but the nature of the intrusion on liberty alone would justify strict scrutiny of the justifications asserted for imposition of such unwanted treatment in all but the special circumstances presented in the prison. Although *Riggins* does not address whether its strict scrutiny approach would apply more generally, its analysis should extend beyond the criminal trial context in which the case arose.

The strict scrutiny approach of *Riggins* therefore should apply in most contexts in which involuntary treatment is imposed. Involuntary treatment can occur in the prison, in which sentenced offenders are incarcerated; in jail, where pretrial detainees awaiting trial are held; in the forensic facilities in which defendants found incompetent to stand trial are treated to restore them to competence; in psychiatric hospitals in which defendants acquitted by reason of insanity are held; in community corrections settings, in which prisoners released on parole or other release conditions or convicted offenders sentenced to probation are situated; in civil mental hospitals housing civil patients either committed or voluntarily admitted; and in the community, in which released patients or those required to undergo preventive treatment in lieu of hospitalization are treated on an outpatient basis.

The *Riggins* Court's apparent confinement of the more deferential reasonableness approach it had used in *Harper* to the "unique circumstances of penal confinement"[71] suggests that the more demanding scrutiny of *Riggins* may emerge as the general standard

---

[70]*See supra* chapter 10; Winick, *supra* note 66. In a limited number of circumstances outside of the prison, the Court has applied a reduced form of First Amendment scrutiny to First Amendment claims arising in special settings in which the Court was concerned that applying full First Amendment review would be inconsistent with the nature and functioning of the special setting involved. *See* Hazelwood Sch. Dist. v. Kuhlmeier, 484 U.S. 260, 273 (1988) (upholding censorship of high school student newspaper so long as "reasonably related to legitimate pedagogical concerns"); Bethel Sch. Dist. No. 403 v. Fraser, 478 U.S. 675, 682 (1986) (First Amendment rights of public school students "are not automatically coextensive with the rights of adults in other settings"); Brown v. Glines, 444 U.S. 348, 354 (1980) (upholding Air Force regulations requiring prior approval of commanding officer for circulation of petitions on Air Force base, finding that "speech likely to interfere with vital prerequisites for military effectiveness therefore can be excluded from a military base") (quoting Greer v. Spock, 424 U.S. 828, 840 (1976)); Greer v. Spock, 424 U.S. 828 (1976) (upholding military regulations banning speeches and demonstrations of political nature and distribution of literature on a military reservation without prior approval of headquarters); Parker v. Levy, 417 U.S. 733, 758 (1974) (holding that "the different character of the military community and the military mission requires a different application of First Amendment protections"); Tinker v. Des Moines Independent Community Sch. Dist., 393 U.S. 503, 506 (1969) (the First Amendment "must be applied in light of the special characteristics of the school environment").

Perhaps *Harper* can be understood as falling within these limited categories of cases applying reduced constitutional scrutiny because of the special needs of the institution involved. These other cases may be distinguishable from the involuntary administration of intrusive mental health treatment, however. Depriving public school students or members of the armed services of the full exercise of First Amendment rights while in school or in uniform or on a military base still leaves room for the exercise of First Amendment rights outside of school or of the military. By contrast, the intrusion on mental processes produced by highly intrusive mental health treatments like psychosurgery, electronic stimulation of the brain, electroconvulsive therapy, and by prolonged administration of at least certain of the psychotropic drugs is so direct, severe, and long-lasting that considerably more than a postponement in the exercise of First Amendment rights is involved. Although precisely this intrusion was presented in *Harper*, greater incursions on the First Amendment may be tolerable in prisons than in schools, the military, jails, or mental hospitals. As the Court recognized in *Riggins*, the "unique circumstances of prison confinement" justify an especially deferential approach even when the government imposes such severe intrusions on constitutional rights as forced antipsychotic medication. *See Riggins*, 504 U.S. at 134–35.

[71]*Riggins*, 504 U.S. at 135.

applied in the right-to-refuse-treatment area. If this analysis is accepted, the deferential approach applied in *Harper* would be limited to prison contexts in which the asserted justification for involuntary medication relates to the prison's need to maintain institutional security. Perhaps this more deferential standard applies in the context of the need to maintain institutional security in forensic facilities housing defendants acquitted by reason of insanity, many of whom present similar security concerns.[72] In other settings, however, traditional strict scrutiny seems to be the appropriate standard. *Riggins* shows that even in an institution similar to a prison—a jail—the need to protect institutional security does not justify application of the deferential standard used in *Harper* for scrutinizing involuntary medication. Even when the need to protect individual security in a jail is the justification for administration of medication, a more generous standard of constitutional review will be used.

The *Riggins* standard, expressed in the language of traditional strict scrutiny, contrasts sharply with the *Harper* standard of whether the treatment imposed is reasonably related to a legitimate penalogical interest. The need to protect other inmates or staff from physical danger would be a compelling governmental interest in any setting.[73] The *Harper* Court explicitly rejected the requirement that forced medication could be used in the prison only when no less intrusive means for accomplishing this interest existed but suggested in *Riggins* that this standard would apply if protection of safety in the jail had been the asserted justification for involuntary medication.

If the ''less intrusive means'' standard would apply to the forcible use of antipsychotic medication even in a jail, then it seems likely that it also would be applied in forensic facilities for the treatment of defendants found incompetent to stand trial and in the context of the mental hospital. Mental hospitals, even those housing forensic patients, cannot be equated with prisons. They are not, like prisons, filled with inmates who have been convicted of committing crimes of violence.[74] Not all convicted offenders are sentenced to prison. Many first offenders and many offenders convicted of crimes not involving violence are given a term of probation, or if imprisoned, are released on parole after a short imprisonment. The increasingly overcrowded state of U.S. prisons has furthered the tendency to imprison primarily those who, if released, present a serious risk to community safety. Prisons, accordingly, are uniquely dangerous places, and those charged with their administration must be accorded a measure of discretion in dealing with problems of institutional security and the control of violence.

Mental hospitals present no similar risk of violence, and certainly not of violence beyond the control of institutional staff. Many residents of mental hospitals are voluntary patients who are there because they need treatment and accept hospitalization in order to obtain it.[75] Many residents are there who, although involuntarily committed, have been

---

[72]*See* Jones v. United States, 463 U.S. 354 (1983) (concluding that an insanity acquittal justifies a presumption of continued dangerousness and mental illness).

[73]*See Riggins,* 504 U.S. at 135 (classifying ''safety considerations'' as a ''compelling'' concern that would outweigh the defendant's liberty interest in refusing medication); Winick, *supra* note 66, at 93–94.

[74]The prisoner in *Harper* was housed in the Special Offenders Center (SOC), a ''144-bed correctional institution administered by the Department of Corrections'' that was ''established to provide diagnosis and treatment of convicted felons having serious behavioral or mental disorders.'' Harper v. Washington, 759 P.2d 358, 360 (Wash. 1988) (en banc).

[75]*See* Winick, *Competency to Consent to Voluntary Hospitalization: A Therapeutic Jurisprudence Analysis of Zinermon v. Burch,* 14 INT'L J.L. & PSYCHIATRY 169 (1991) (analyzing voluntary hospitalization).

hospitalized because their mental illness has rendered them gravely disabled or incompetent and in need of treatment.[76]

Patients committed to forensic hospitals or to forensic wards of civil mental hospitals because they are incompetent to stand trial similarly are hospitalized because of their treatment needs.[77] The finding of incompetence to stand trial is based on their inability to understand the criminal proceedings and consult with counsel, not their dangerousness.[78] These patients are pretrial detainees like the defendant awaiting trial in *Riggins,* not sentenced prisoners like the incarcerated offender in *Harper.*

Although some civilly committed patients are hospitalized involuntarily because of their dangerousness to self or others, hospitals are not the inherently combustible institutions that prisons are, and a hospital's ability to deal with acute symptomatology differs significantly from that of a prison. Many prisons do not have an adequate number of mental health professionals on staff who are experienced in dealing with mental patients who may act out violently while in a florid state of psychosis.[79] Hospitals, on the other hand, have many professional and support staff with experience in dealing with problems of violence and a variety of alternative approaches for dealing with those problems, such as segregation,[80] physical restraints,[81] and psychotherapeutic[82] and behavioral techniques.[83] Even when medication is thought to be required on an emergency basis to deal with acute symptomatology, a properly staffed mental hospital should be able to deal with such a problem with only a brief use of medication.[84]

Moreover, whatever the approach applied in the mental hospital, patients and offenders in the community should not be subjected to involuntary intrusive mental health treatment absent satisfaction of the more demanding *Riggins* standard of scrutiny. Because emergency commitment provisions of typical state commitment statutes allow for hospitalization of

---

[76]*See* Winick, *supra* note 66, at 98 & n.581. The perhaps common perception that individuals suffering from mental illness are dangerous is not supported by empirical studies. *See* A. STONE, MENTAL HEALTH AND LAW: A SYSTEM IN TRANSITION 27–28 (1976); Monahan, *Mental Disorder and Violent Behavior: Perceptions and Evidence,* 47 AM. PSYCHOLOGIST 511 (1992).

[77]*See* Jackson v. Indiana, 406 U.S. 715 (1972) (recognizing that diagnosis and treatment designed to restore such patients to competency for trial are the only legitimate purpose of such hospitalization and prohibiting continued hospitalization based on trial incapacity once it is determined that the defendant is unlikely to be restored to competence within a reasonable period or is not making satisfactory progress toward that goal).

[78]*See* Dusky v. United States, 362 U.S. 402 (1966) (standard for incompetency to stand trial); *see, e.g.,* FLA. R. CRIM. P. 3.210 (1995).

[79]*See generally* AMERICAN PSYCHIATRIC ASS'N, TASK FORCE REPORT NO. 29: PSYCHIATRIC SERVICES IN JAILS AND PRISONS 2 (1989); Kaufman, *The Violation of Psychiatric Standards of Care in Prisons,* 137 AM. J. PSYCHIATRY 566 (1980); Valdiserri, *Psychiatry Behind Bars,* 12 BULL. AM. ACAD. PSYCHIATRY & L. 93, 93, 97 (1984). *See also* Brief for the American Psychiatric Association and the American Medical Association as *Amici Curiae* in Support of Petitioner at 19, Perry v. Louisiana, 498 U.S. 38 (1990) (No. 89-5120) ("Despite an unquestioned need, the provision of psychiatric care in the Nation's prisons and jails leaves much to be desired.").

[80]*See, e.g.,* THE PSYCHIATRIC USES OF SECLUSION AND RESTRAINT (J. Tardiff ed., 1984) [hereinafter SECLUSION & RESTRAINT]; Soloff, *Physical Controls: The Use of Seclusion and Restraint in Modern Psychiatric Practice, in* CLINICAL TREATMENT OF THE VIOLENT PERSON 119 (L. Roth ed., 1987) [hereinafter CLINICAL TREATMENT].

[81]*See, e.g.,* sources cited in *supra* note 80.

[82]*See, e.g.,* Madden, *Psychotherapeutic Approaches in the Treatment of Violent Persons, in* CLINICAL TREATMENT, *supra* note 80, at 54.

[83]*See, e.g.,* Liberman & Wong, *Behavior Analysis and Therapy Procedures Related to Seclusion and Restraint, in* SECLUSION & RESTRAINT, *supra* note 80, at 35; Wong et al., *Behavioral Analysis and Therapy for Aggressive Psychiatric and Developmentally Disabled Patients, in* CLINICAL TREATMENT, *supra* note 80, at 20.

[84]In limited circumstances, such a brief use of medication to stabilize the patient may be the most reasonable alternative available to deal with an emergency, and if medically appropriate for the patient, it therefore would meet the more demanding scrutiny suggested in *Riggins. See* Winick, *supra* note 66, at 97–99.

mentally ill individuals in the community who present an imminent threat of danger, the need for involuntary medication in community contexts should rarely arise. The exigencies invoked by the *Harper* Court to justify deference in the involuntary administration of medication to control violence in the prison are simply not present in the community.[85]

In addition to modifying *Harper* and limiting its application to the prison, the Court's opinion in *Riggins* suggests that the application of the professional judgment standard of *Youngberg v. Romeo*[86] may be limited in the right-to-refuse-treatment area. In *Youngberg*, the Court had recognized that residents of an institution for those suffering from mental retardation had a due process right to be free from unsafe conditions of confinement and unnecessary physical restraint.[87] In discussing the due process liberty interest in avoiding unnecessary restraint, however, the Court adopted an approach in which the individual's liberty interest was limited to the professional judgment of institutional staff.[88] The Supreme Court subsequently cited *Youngberg* in its order vacating the decision of the Third Circuit in *Rennie v. Klein*,[89] a leading case involving the right of mental patients at a state hospital to refuse antipsychotic medication. The Court vacated *Rennie* for reconsideration in light of its opinion in *Youngberg*, thereby raising the implication that the professional judgment standard of *Youngberg* might apply in the right-to-refuse-treatment context. Indeed, on remand, the Third Circuit limited its prior opinion, adapting the *Youngberg* approach to the state hospital context instead of the least intrusive alternative approach that it had previously applied.[90] Although continuing to recognize that patients had a due process liberty interest in refusing antipsychotic medication, the court found that the interest could be overcome by an exercise of professional judgment on the part of a hospital clinician.[91] In addition, other lower federal court decisions similarly applied the professional judgment approach of *Youngberg* to the right-to-refuse-medication context,[92]

---

[85]Winick, *supra* note 66, at 97.

[86]457 U.S. 307 (1982).

[87]*Id.* at 324.

[88]*See id.* at 323 (finding that liability for violation of this liberty interest would lie only where ''the decision by the professional is such a substantial departure from accepted professional judgment, practice, or standards as to demonstrate that the person responsible actually did not base the decision on such a judgment'').

[89]653 F.2d 836 (3d Cir. 1981) (en banc), *vacated*, 458 U.S. 1119 (1982); *see supra* notes 43, 45 and accompanying text.

[90]On remand, the en banc Third Circuit split several ways concerning the applicability of the least restrictive alternative principle. Of the 10 judges participating in the post-remand en banc decision in *Rennie*, 5 rejected application of the least restrictive alternative principle, at least for short-term administration of drugs. Rennie v. Klein, 720 F.2d 266, 270 (3d Cir. 1983) (en banc); *id.* at 271 (Adams, J., joined by Becker, J., concurring). Four would have applied the principle. *Id.* at 276–77 (Weis, J., joined by Higginbotham & Sloviter, J.J., concurring); *id.* at 277 (Gibbons, J., concurring in opinion of Weis, J., joined by Higginbotham & Sloviter, J.J., concurring). One of the judges did not explicitly discuss the issue. *Id.* at 274 (Seitz, C.J., concurring).

[91]*Id.* at 269–70; *id.* at 273–74 (Seitz, C.J., concurring); *id.* at 276 (Weis, J., joined by Higginbotham and Sloviter, J.J., concurring); *see* M. PERLIN, 2 MENTAL DISABILITY LAW: CIVIL AND CRIMINAL § 5.36, at 320 (1989).

[92]*See, e.g.*, United States v. Watson, 893 F.2d 970, 982 (8th Cir.), *cert. denied*, 491 U.S. 1006 (1990); United States v. Charters, 863 F.2d 302, 307–13 (4th Cir. 1988) (en banc), *cert denied*, 494 U.S. 1016 (1990); Dautremont v. Broadlawns Hosp., 827 F.2d 291, 297–300 (8th Cir. 1987); Bee v. Greaves, 744 F.2d 1387, 1395–96 (10th Cir. 1984), *cert. denied*, 469 U.S. 1214 (1985); Johnson v. Silvers, 742 F.2d 823, 825 (4th Cir. 1984); Project Release v. Prevost, 722 F.2d 960, 977–81 (2d Cir. 1983); United States v. Bryant, 670 F. Supp. 840 (D. Minn. 1987); Stensvad v. Reivitz, 601 F. Supp. 128, 130–31 (W.D. Wis. 1985); R.A.J. v. Miller, 590 F. Supp. 1319, 1321 (N.D. Tex. 1984); United States v. Leatherman, 580 F. Supp. 977, 980 (D.D.C. 1983), *appeal dismissed*, 729 F.2d 863 (D.C. Cir. 1984); Gilliam v. Martin, 589 F. Supp. 680 (W.D. Okla. 1984).

and some commentators concluded that the right to refuse treatment was significantly limited.[93]

Youngberg, however, was not mentioned in the Court's opinion in *Riggins.* This omission seems to suggest that the *Youngberg* professional judgment standard may be inapplicable to the right-to-refuse-treatment question. Riggins, after all, had received the professional judgment of the psychiatrist who had prescribed 800 mg of mellaril for him prior to and during his trial. Indeed, several court-appointed psychiatrists had evaluated Riggins and reported to the trial court concerning his competency and need for ongoing medication during the trial period. Because the professional judgment of these clinicians was that the medication given Riggins was medically appropriate, the professional judgment standard would seem to have been satisfied. The Court, however, treated the issue presented in *Riggins* as a constitutional question requiring a judicial determination, rather than merely a clinical issue left to professional judgment.

Only one aspect of the Court's suggested standards for justifying involuntary medication medical appropriateness raises a clinical question that presumably turns largely on professional judgment. The other components are legal questions that pursuant to *Riggins* are committed to judicial determination. Because Riggins's defense counsel had not challenged the medical appropriateness of the medication administered, the Supreme Court had no occasion to discuss the possible application of the *Youngberg* professional judgment standard to the medical appropriateness issue. With regard to the remaining elements of its suggested standards, however, the Court plainly contemplated a judicial determination of whether the state's interests were sufficient to override the defendant's liberty interest in refusing medication and whether involuntary medication was the least intrusive means of meeting these governmental interests. Although the professional judgment of clinicians may be relevant to these essentially legal issues, *Riggins* clearly suggests that it is not dispositive.

Indeed, application of the *Youngberg* professional judgment approach to the issues presented in *Riggins* would have been an abdication of judicial responsibility for the protection of constitutional rights.[94] The liberty interest involved in *Youngberg*—freedom from short-term use of physical restraints—cannot compare to the more serious and long-lasting intrusion presented by antipsychotic medication, particularly when administered in the extremely high dose involved in *Riggins.* The antipsychotic drugs intrude more on protected constitutional values than does the brief use of restraints, and the values affected may be considered more fundamental.[95] The restraints involved in *Youngberg* were "soft" restraints for the arms only"[96] and were used on the patient "for short periods of time, *i.e.,* five minutes, to prevent him from harming himself or others."[97] Moreover, the use of restraints in *Youngberg* may have served the patient's best interests,[98] and he clearly was incapable of asserting a view of his best interests that diverged from the professional

---

[93]*See, e.g.,* Brooks, *The Right to Refuse Antipsychotic Medications: Law and Policy,* 39 RUTGERS L. REV. 339, 355 (1987).

[94]For an analysis of a wide variety of areas in which the *Youngberg* professional judgment standard has been applied and a criticism of this standard as an inappropriate abdication of judicial responsibility, see Stefan, *Leaving Civil Rights to the "Experts": From Deference to Abdication Under the Professional Judgment Standard,* 102 YALE L.J. 639 (1992).

[95]*See* People v. Medina, 705 P.2d 961, 968 (Colo. 1985) (en banc) ("The effects of these drugs can be far more debilitating to the patient than . . . physical restraints.").

[96]*Youngberg,* 457 U.S. at 310 n.4.

[97]*Id.* at 311 n.8.

[98]*See id.* at 324 (stating that restraints may be used only to ensure safety or provide needed training).

judgment of state physicians. The patient in *Youngberg* was profoundly retarded[99] and as a result grossly incompetent by any standard. By contrast, the detainee involved in *Riggins* had never been declared mentally incompetent.[100] The *Riggins* Court did not discuss these distinctions, but its failure even to mention *Youngberg* suggests limited application of the professional judgment approach in the right-to-refuse-treatment area.

Riggins thus suggests a considerable expansion of the right to refuse intrusive treatment in noncorrectional contexts. Whereas *Harper* suggested a narrow scope for the right to refuse mental health treatment, *Riggins* moved in the opposite direction. The language in Justice O'Connor's opinion in *Riggins* suggests that the Court will construe the right to refuse treatment much more broadly in contexts outside of the prison. Whereas the Court's remand in *Rennie* suggested the possibility that the deferential professional judgment standard of *Youngberg* might apply in the right-to-refuse-treatment area, *Riggins*'s failure to cite *Youngberg* in a context in which it could have been invoked seems to reject this approach. With the exception of treatment imposed in the prison, *Riggins* thus suggests that when government seeks to administer intrusive treatment on an involuntary basis, traditional strict scrutiny or something closely approximating it will be applied to consider the constitutionality of such action. Although the suggested standard in *Riggins* was dicta and the Court did not discuss the nature of the liberty interest it found to be invaded by involuntary antipsychotic medication, an analysis of the constitutional values at issue, protected by the First Amendment and the Due Process Clause, demonstrate the general propriety of applying a strict scrutiny approach.

C. Scrutinizing Governmental Interests Asserted To Justify Involuntary Treatment

Strict scrutiny generally will apply when intrusive treatment is imposed over objection, but the standard of review and whether it is satisfied in a particular context may vary with the circumstances and location of the individual sought to be treated. As contrasting *Washington v. Harper* with *Riggins v. Nevada* demonstrates, the standard of judicial scrutiny that is used to evaluate governmental justifications for involuntary administration of identical treatment is different if the individual sought to be treated is a prisoner incarcerated in a correctional facility rather than a detainee awaiting trial in a jail. Whatever the standard of scrutiny to be applied, courts will reach differing conclusions on the right-to-refuse-treatment question depending on the nature of the governmental interest asserted to justify involuntary treatment.

The following discussion divides those sought to be treated into two categories, civil patients and criminal offenders, and further subdivides each according to the nature of the government's interest in imposing treatment in varied circumstances. It should be emphasized that a determination that one or more constitutional protections are implicated by involuntary mental health treatment merely begins the constitutional analysis. Constitutional rights are not absolute. Rather, when government action restricts constitutional

---

[99]*Id.* at 309.

[100]This factor also may tend to distinguish the situation of hospitalized mental patients (many of whom are not incompetent or have not been determined to be incompetent) to participate in treatment decisions. *See supra* chapter 14, part B (arguing that mental illness may not be equated with incompetency and that absent specific evidence showing incompetence, those with mental illness should be presumed competent). The respect for individual autonomy that lies at the heart of the fundamental constitutional values involved commands at least some deference to the expressed preferences of these patients, even those of marginal competency. *See* Winick, *Restructuring Competency to Stand Trial,* 32 UCLA L. REV. 921, 936–68 (1985).

liberty, "it is necessary to balance 'the liberty of the individual' and 'the demands of an organized society.' "[101] In scrutinizing governmental interests asserted to justify involuntary treatment, courts inevitably engage in a balancing of the interests of the state and of the individual, and the balance is struck differently in different contexts. The level of scrutiny to be applied in the circumstances—strict, intermediate, or low level—tells courts performing this constitutional balancing how to weigh the competing state and individual interests. Even fundamental constitutional rights, the invasion of which requires strict scrutiny, must yield to government regulation advancing a "compelling state interest."[102] In *Jacobson v. Massachusetts*,[103] an early example, the Supreme Court upheld a state program of compulsory vaccination to prevent epidemic over petitioner's free exercise of religion challenge. The Court noted that the protection afforded by the Constitution for individual liberty[104]

> does not import an absolute right in each person to be, at all times and in all circumstances, wholly freed from restraint. There are manifold restraints to which every person is necessarily subject for the common good. . . . "The possession and enjoyment of all rights are subject to such reasonable conditions as may be deemed by the governing authority of the country essential to the safety, health, peace, good order and morals of the community."

When constitutional rights are asserted, courts are thus required to weigh "the individual's interest in liberty against the State's asserted reasons for restraining individual liberty."[105] Governmental intrusions on constitutional liberty must at least be found to be "reasonably related to legitimate government objectives. . . ."[106] When the constitutional liberty interest asserted is a "fundamental right," the government's purpose generally must be "compelling."[107] Moreover, to justify intrusions on fundamental constitutional rights, not only must the government interest be compelling, but the means chosen must be narrowly tailored to accomplish that interest. If less restrictive alternative means are available that would accomplish the government's purpose in a manner that intrudes less on the fundamental constitutional right at issue, the less restrictive alternative must be chosen.[108] This "strict scrutiny"—insisting on "compelling" governmental purposes and use of the "least restrictive alternative" means to accomplish them—is what the language in the Supreme Court's opinion in *Riggins* suggests should generally be applied when intrusive mental health treatment is imposed involuntarily.[109] Whether and when this exacting standard can be satisfied by involuntary mental health treatment can best be analyzed by considering separately the issues raised in the differing contexts of treating civil patients and criminal offenders.

---

[101]Youngberg v. Romeo, 457 U.S. 307, 320 (1982) (quoting Poe v. Ullman, 367 U.S. 497, 522, 542 (1961)) (Harlan, J., dissenting). *See* Faigman, *Madisonian Balancing: A Theory of Constitutional Adjudication,* 88 Nw. U. L. Rev. 641, 645 (1994) ("In the twentieth century, balancing has swiftly overtaken formalism as the preferred method of constitutional adjudication across the entire spectrum.").

[102]Roe v. Wade, 410 U.S. 113, 154–55 (1973).

[103]197 U.S. 11 (1905).

[104]*Id.* at 26–27.

[105]*Youngberg,* 457 U.S. at 320.

[106]*Id.*; Bell v. Wolfish, 441 U.S. 520, 539 (1979); Kelley v. Johnston, 425 U.S. 238, 244–49 (1978).

[107]*See, e.g.,* Roe v. Wade, 410 U.S. 113, 155–56 (1973) (substantive due process right to privacy–autonomy); Wisconsin v. Yoder, 406 U.S. 205 (1972) (First Amendment free exercise of religion); Stanley v. Georgia, 394 U.S. 557 (1969) (First Amendment freedom of thought); *supra* chapters 10–14.

[108]*See infra* chapter 16, part B.

[109]*See supra* notes 51–57 and accompanying text.

1. Governmental Interests in Treating Civil Patients

Civil mental patients may be voluntarily or involuntarily institutionalized or may reside in the community. The latter may reside at home or in a nursing home, a group residential facility, or in some other community placement. For all categories of patients regardless of location, the state may seek to administer treatment on an involuntary basis. Although private practitioners in the community or community mental health centers and other programs rarely treat patients against their will, hospitals often do, and patients sometimes are released from the hospital on condition that they accept treatment in the community, or they are ordered by the court to accept such treatment in lieu of hospitalization. Moreover, criminal, juvenile, and family courts increasingly impose treatment as a condition of diversion from judicial proceedings or as an adjunct to judicial adjudicatory or dispositional processes.

Wherever their location, these civil patients can be seen as being subjected to treatment for one of two principle purposes, which sometimes overlap. These two categories of governmental interests asserted to justify forced treatment are (a) police power purposes—those protecting the public health, safety, welfare, or morals; and (b) the *parens patriae* purpose—government decision making in the best interest of persons who by reason of age or disability are incapable of making such decisions for themselves.[110]

(a) Police Power

Institutions for those suffering from mental illness, often overcrowded and understaffed, may at times be dangerous places for patients and staff alike. Prevention of patient violence is unquestionably a compelling interest that is vital to the operation of such facilities. This interest, treated by the Supreme Court as compelling in the context of the prison and the jail in *Harper and Riggins,* respectively,[111] would similarly qualify as compelling in the context of the hospital and arguably in a variety of community facilities as well.

Accordingly, the police power interest in preventing mentally ill patients from endangering themselves or others has been invoked by the lower courts to justify involuntary mental health treatment, typically the administration of psychotropic drugs. In *Rennie v. Klein,*[112] a class action case involving a class of "dangerous" involuntarily committed patients, the Third Circuit Court of Appeals held that antipsychotic drugs constitutionally may be administered "whenever, in the exercise of professional judgment, such an action is deemed necessary to prevent the patient from endangering himself and others."[113]

In *Rogers v. Okin,*[114] the Boston State Hospital case, the district court recognized a police power justification for involuntary medication. The court held that involuntarily committed mental patients "may be forcibly medicated in an emergency situation in which a failure to do so would result in a substantial likelihood of physical harm to that patient, other patients, or to staff members of the institution."[115] On appeal, the First Circuit Court of

[110]*See* Mills v. Rogers, 457 U.S. 291, 296 (1982); Winick, *Legal Limitations on Correctional Therapy and Research,* 65 MINN. L. REV. 331, 374 (1981); Note, *Developments in the Law—Civil Commitment of the Mentally Ill,* 87 HARV. L. REV. 1190, 1207–45 (1974).
[111]*E.g.,* Riggins v. Nevada, 504 U.S. 127, 135 (1992); Washington v. Harper, 494 U.S. 210, 25–26 (1990).
[112]720 F.2d 266 (3d Cir. 1983) (en banc).
[113]*Id.* at 269.
[114]478 F. Supp. 1342, 1365 (D. Mass. 1979).
[115]*Id.*

Appeals upheld the state's police power interest as sufficient to outweigh the patient's right to refuse medication. The court, however, criticized the district court's formulation as a "simplistic unitary standard for police power emergency drug administration" and adopted instead an ad hoc balancing approach to be applied by qualified state physicians.[116] "The state's purpose in administering drugs forcibly must be to further its police power interests, *i.e.*, the decision must be the result of a determination that the need to prevent violence in a particular situation outweighs the possibility of harm to the medicated individual."[117] The court rejected the district court's attempt to fashion "a single 'more-likely-than-not' standard" in favor of "an individualized balancing of the varying interests of particular patients in refusing antipsychotic medication against the equally varying interests of patients—and the state—in preventing violence."[118]

In *Bee v. Greaves*,[119] involving forcible medication of pretrial detainees held in a jail, the Tenth Circuit Court of Appeals found that in an emergency, a "jail's duty to maintain security and to prevent a violent and dangerous mentally ill prisoner from injuring himself and others" would justify forcible medication with antipsychotic drugs. Although the need for maintaining institutional security may be stronger in a jail setting than in a mental hospital, this government interest would seem compelling in any context. Like the Third Circuit in *Rennie,* the Tenth Circuit applied a balancing test: "Determining that an emergency exists sufficient to warrant involuntary medication with this type of drug requires a professional judgment call that includes a balancing of the jail's concerns for the safety of its occupants and a detainee's interest in freedom from unwanted anti-psychotics."[120] Such a decision "must be the product of professional judgment by appropriate medical authorities, applying accepted medical standards" and "requires an evaluation in each case of all the relevant circumstances, including the nature and gravity of the safety threat, the characteristics of the individual involved, and the likely effects of particular drugs."[121]

Other lower courts also have recognized the state's police power interest in protecting hospital staff and other patients from violence to be sufficiently compelling to justify forced medication, at least in an emergency.[122] Aside from the need to protect the safety of other patients and staff, other police power interests may not be sufficiently compelling to justify forcible intrusive treatment. Thus, the lower courts have found other asserted police power interests insufficient to outweigh the patient's constitutionally protected interest in refusing psychotropic drugs. Considerations of convenience and cost have been rejected,[123] as has the

---

[116]Rogers v. Okin, 634 F.2d 650, 656–57 (1st Cir. 1980).

[117]*Id.* at 656.

[118]*Id.* at 656–57.

[119]744 F.2d 1387, 1394 (10th Cir. 1984), *cert. denied,* 496 U.S. 1214 (1985); *accord* Riggins v. Nevada, 504 U.S. 127, 135 (1992) (dicta).

[120]744 F.2d at 1395–96.

[121]*Id.* at 1396.

[122]*E.g.,* Gilliam v. Martin, 589 F. Supp. 680, 682 (W.D. Okla. 1984); Weiss v. Missouri Dep't of Mental Health, 587 F. Supp. 1157, 1161 (E.D. Mo. 1984); Project Release v. Prevost, 551 F. Supp. 1298, 1309 (E.D.N.Y. 1982), *aff'd,* 722 F.2d 964 (2d Cir. 1983); Davis v. Hubbard, 506 F. Supp. 915, 934–38 (N.D. Ohio 1980); Large v. Superior Court, 714 P.2d 399, 406–08 (Ariz. 1986) (en banc); People v. Medina, 705 P.2d 961, 943–74 (Colo. 1985) (en banc); Rogers v. Commissioner, 458 N.E.2d 308, 321–22 (Mass. 1983); Opinion of the Justices, 465 A.2d 484, 489 (N.H. 1983); Rivers v. Katz, 495 N.E.2d 337, 392 (N.Y. 1986); *In re* K.K.B., 609 P.2d 747, 750 (Okla. 1980).

[123]*Davis,* 506 F. Supp. at 937; Rogers v. Okin, 478 F. Supp. 1342, 1370–71 (D. Mass. 1979); Keyhea v. Rushen, 223 Cal. Rptr. 746, 756 (Ct. App. 1986); *Rogers,* 458 N.E.2d at 320; *Rivers,* 495 N.E.2d at 343 n.6, State *ex rel.* Jones v. Gerhardstein, 416 N.W. 2d 883, 895 (Wis. 1987).

state's interest in allowing doctors to provide treatment without unreasonable intrusion,[124] in providing a therapeutic environment, in increasing the process of deinstitutionalization, in avoiding staff turnover, in minimizing patient length of stay, and in maintaining the ethical integrity of the medical profession.[125] These are undeniably legitimate governmental interests, but they are not sufficiently compelling to overcome the assertion of a fundamental constitutional right. As legitimate state interest, they would be sufficient to outweigh an individual's assertion of a constitutional right to refuse nonintrusive treatment, such as verbal psychotherapy and most of the behavior treatment approaches. However, when intrusive treatment is involved, these interests will not suffice.

Thus, although these other police power interests will be insufficient, the need to protect institutional security, in a proper case, will meet the "compelling" interest standard of strict scrutiny. Because the more intrusive treatments involved (including psychotropic medication) raise First Amendment as well as other fundamental constitutional concerns, however, the prevention of future danger that is merely potential may not be sufficient. Prevention of potential harm may suffice as a justification for involuntary intrusive treatment in the prison, where *Washington v. Harper* has applied a reduced form of constitutional scrutiny out of deference to the special needs of prison administrators to a wide latitude in the maintenance of institutional security.[126] However, outside the prison context, the mere potential of future dangerous conduct predicted to occur as a result of a patient's disordered mental processes should not satisfy First Amendment scrutiny unless the danger to be prevented has some degree of imminence.[127]

In other First Amendment contexts, when the government has attempted to interfere directly with speech or other First Amendment protected activity on the ground that it is thought likely to produce crime, riot, revolution, or some other substantive harm within the government's power to prevent, the Supreme Court has insisted that there be a "clear and present danger" that those substantive evils will occur.[128] Thus, the Court has not "permitted the Government to assume that every expression of a provocative idea will incite a riot" but has instead engaged in "careful consideration of the actual circumstances surrounding such expression, asking whether the expression 'is directed to inciting or producing imminent lawless action and is likely to incite or produce such action.' "[129] Similarly, the government's direct interference with protected First Amendment mental

---

[124]*Davis*, 506 F. Supp. at 937–38; *Okin*, 478 F. Supp. at 1370; Jarvis v. Levine, 418 N.W. 2d 139, 149 (Minn. 1988); *Rivers*, 495 N.E.2d at 343 n.6; *Gerhardstein*, 416 N.W.2d at 895.

[125]*Okin*, 478 F. Supp. at 1369–70; *Rogers*, 458 N.E. 2d at 320; *Rivers*, 495 N.E.2d at 343 n.6.

[126]*See supra* note 70 (analyzing the reduced scrutiny applied in *Harper* and arguing that *Riggins* suggests that such reduced scrutiny will be limited to the prison). The prison is only a possible exception to the general requirement that the risk of danger be imminent because the First Amendment issue was neither raised nor considered by the *Harper* Court. *See supra* note 69.

[127]*See* Texas v. Johnson, 491 U.S. 397, 409 (1989) (citing Brandenburg v. Ohio, 395 U.S. 444, 447 (1969)) ("imminent lawless action"); Landmark Communications, Inc. v. Virginia, 435 U.S. 829, 843 (1978); Winick, *supra* note 66, at 99–100.

[128]*E.g., Landmark Communications*, 435 U.S. at 843 ("the imminence and magnitude of the danger"); *Brandenburg*, 395 U.S. at 447 ("imminent lawless action"); Wood v. Georgia, 370 U.S. 375, 384 (1962) ("the degree of imminence [must be] extremely high"); Pennekamp v. Florida, 328 U.S. 331, 350 (1946) ("clearness and immediacy"); Thomas v. Collins, 323 U.S. 516, 532 (1945) ("grave and impending public danger"); *id.* at 536 ("clear and present, grave and immediate danger"); West Va. State Bd. of Educ. v. Barnette, 319 U.S. 624, 639 (1943) ("grave and immediate danger"); Bridges v. California, 314 U.S. 252, 263 (1941) ("the degree of imminence [must be] extremely high"); Cantwell v. Connecticut, 310 U.S. 296, 308 (1940) ("clear and present danger . . . or other immediate threat"); Schenck v. United States, 249 U.S. 47, 52 (1919) ("clear and present danger").

[129]*Johnson*, 491 U.S. 397 at 409 (quoting *Brandenburg*, 395 U.S. at 447).

processes through administration of psychotropic drugs or other more intrusive treatment designed to prevent future violence that is not imminent should not suffice. Without a requirement of imminence, this police power interest, always potentially present in mental hospitals, could be asserted broadly to justify keeping virtually all patients on high dosages of psychotropic drugs to keep them docile and thus avoid potential violence. Unless there is an emergency, such use of treatment for institutional management should not meet the "compelling" interest test. It might serve the legitimate governmental interests in economy and administrative convenience, but when balanced against fundamental constitutional rights, these interests are insufficient to justify the serious intrusions involved.[130]

The requirement of imminence, although usually not explicitly discussed in the lower court decisions authorizing involuntary medication to prevent harm in an emergency,[131] is fully consistent with them and provides a constitutional basis for their insistence on an emergency as a condition for such use of medication. The clear and present danger requirement in this context suggests that, at least outside the prison, such treatment should be permitted only in an emergency. In addition, the requirement of imminence should prevent the use of involuntary intrusive treatment to protect the community from the potential harm of mental patients hospitalized as a result of a prediction of future dangerousness. These patients typically are held in secure wards. Their isolation from the community should adequately contain the risk of harm to those outside the hospital and prevents it from being considered imminent.[132]

---

[130]For example, in cases involving the fundamental Sixth Amendment right to jury trial, the Supreme Court has rejected contentions that the state's interest in fiscal economy or administrative convenience can justify practices that would seriously burden the right to jury trial. See Burch v. Louisiana, 441 U.S. 130, 139 (1979) (state interest in reducing time and expense of criminal justice administration held insufficient justification for use of nonunanimous six-person juries); Ballew v. Georgia, 435 U.S. 233, 244 (1978) (administrative convenience and state interest in saving money and time by reducing number of jury members in a criminal trial held insufficient justification to deprive defendant of constitutional right to a jury trial); Taylor v. Louisiana, 419 U.S. 522, 535 (1975) ("the administrative convenience of dealing with women as a class is insufficient justification for their wholesale exclusion"). These holdings are consistent with the Court's approach in other contexts rejecting the state interest in saving money as sufficient justification for infringing upon fundamental rights. E.g., United States Trust Co. v. New Jersey, 431 U.S. 1 (1977); Bounds v. Smith, 430 U.S. 817, 825 (1977); Bullock v. Carter, 405 U.S. 134, 147–49 (1972); Mayer v. Chicago, 404 U.S. 189, 196–97 (1971); Shapiro v. Thompson, 394 U.S. 618, 633 (1969); see Winick, supra note 110, at 381.

[131]See cases discussed in supra notes 114–22 and accompanying text. Some of the courts' definitions of the "emergency" in which involuntary medication would be permitted have explicitly adopted an imminence requirement, although without mentioning the First Amendment. See, e.g., Davis v. Hubbard, 506 F. Supp. 915, 934 (N.D. Ohio 1980) (the danger must be "sufficiently grave and imminent"); Anderson v. State, 663 P.2d 570, 573 (Ariz. Ct. App. 1982) (defining an emergency as "an immediate threat of physical injury"); Rivers, 495 N.E.2d at 343 (defining an emergency as "imminent danger to a patient or others in the immediate vicinity"); Rogers v. Commissioner, 458 N.E.2d 308, 321 n.25 (Mass. 1983) (an emergency calls for "immediate action").

[132]This conclusion also is supported by the "least restrictive alternative" principle, an additional requirement of strict scrutiny. See infra chapter 16, part B. Because isolation in a secure facility itself would prevent harm to the community, hospitalization alone constitutes a less restrictive means of accomplishing the state interest in protecting community safety than the use of intrusive treatment. Although such isolation without treatment (when it is refused by the patient) may prolong hospitalization at added cost, the state's interest in fiscal economy alone should not be deemed sufficiently compelling to outweigh the patient's interest in avoiding intrusive treatment. See supra note 130 and accompanying text.

(b) Parens Patriae *Power*

Although the wisdom of Justice Brandeis's warnings about the insidious dangers of benevolence[133] has been repeatedly demonstrated, paternalism is deeply rooted in our history and traditions, indeed, in our genetic makeup.[134] Ground in principles of beneficence, the state's *parens patriae* power allows government to engage in decision making in the best interests of those who are incapable of making decisions for themselves.[135] The government's *parens patriae* power serves as a justification for the civil commitment of those with serious mental retardation and of those suffering from mental illness that renders them unable to appreciate the need for hospitalization. This state power also has been deemed sufficiently compelling to justify forced treatment of patients suffering from mental illness, at least when their condition has rendered them incompetent to make treatment decisions for themselves. Historically, the *parens patriae* power was premised on the presumed incapacity of minors and the actual incapacity of mentally incompetent persons to protect or care for themselves.[136] Because this power is based on the need for the government to protect the well-being of its citizens when they cannot care for themselves, it may legitimately be invoked only in the case of individuals who, because of age or physical or mental disability, cannot determine their own best interests.[137]

Courts have recognized this limitation on the *parens patriae* power in the right-to-refuse-treatment context, holding that assertions of this governmental purpose as a justification for forced medication must be restricted to patients determined to be incompetent to participate in treatment decision making.[138] The courts have also rejected the assertion that the existence of mental illness alone, or indeed even a determination that the patient is subject to involuntary commitment, without an additional finding, can justify the conclusion

---

[133]Experience should teach us to be most on our guard to protect liberty when the Government's purposes are beneficial. Men born to freedom are naturally alert to repel invasion of their liberty by evil-minded rulers. The greatest dangers to liberty lurk in insidious encroachment by men of zeal, well-meaning but without understanding.
Olmstead v. United States, 277 U.S. 438, 479 (1928) (Brandeis, J., dissenting)

[134]*See* Gaylin, *In the Beginning: Helpless and Dependent, in* DOING GOOD: THE LIMITS OF BENEVOLENCE 39 (W. Gaylin et al. eds., 1978).

[135]Mills v. Rogers, 457 U.S. 291, 296 (1982); *see also* J. FEINBERG, HARM TO SELF 6 (1986) (analyzing *parens patriae* power); Winick, *Competency to Consent to Treatment: The Distinction Between Assent and Objection,* 28 HOUS. L. REV. 15, 16 & n.3 (1991) (discussing scope of government's *parens patriae* power); Winick, *supra* note 110, at 374 (examining government's *parens patriae* power to make decisions for those who are unable to make decisions for themselves); Note, *supra* note 110, at 1207–45 (discussing civil commitment under *parens patriae* power of state).

[136]Winick, *supra* note 110, at 375; Winick, *supra* note 61, at 1772; Note, *supra* note 110, at 1212–16; *see, e.g.,* Addington v. Texas, 441 U.S. 418, 426 (1979); O'Connor v. Donaldson, 422 U.S. 563, 583 (1975) (Burger, C.J., concurring).

[137]*E.g.,* Bee v. Greaves, 744 F.2d 1387, 1395 (10th Cir. 1984), *cert. denied,* 469 U.S. 1214 (1985); Rogers v. Okin, 634 F.2d 650, 656–58 (1st Cir. 1980), *vacated and remanded sub nom.* Mills v. Rogers, 457 U.S. 291 (1982); Winters v. Miller, 446 F.2d 65, 68–71 (2d Cir.), *cert. denied,* 404 U.S. 985 (1971); Davis v. Hubbard, 506 F. Supp. 915, 935–36 (N.D. Ohio 1980); Rogers v. Commissioner, 458 N.E.2d 308, 322 (Mass. 1983); Opinion of the Justices, 465 A.2d 484, 489–90 (N.H. 1983); Rivers v. Katz, 495 N.E.2d 337, 340 (N.Y. 1986); *In re* K.K.B., 609 P.2d 747, 750–52 (Okla. 1980).

[138]Rennie v. Klein, 653 F.2d 836, 847 & n.12 (3d Cir. 1981) (en banc), *vacated and remanded,* 458 U.S. 119 (1982); *Okin,* 634 F.2d at 657–59; *Winters,* 446 F.2d at 71; *Davis,* 506 F. Supp. at 935–36; Anderson v. Arizona, 663 P.2d 573 (Ariz. Ct. App. 1982); People v. Medina, 705 P.2d 961, 973 (Colo. 1985) (en banc); *In re* Boyd, 403 A.2d 744, 747 n.5 (D.C. Ct. App. 1979); *Rogers,* 458 N.E.2d at 314; *Rivers,* 495 N.E.2d at 344; *In re* K.K.B., 609 P.2d at 749.

that the patient is incompetent to participate in treatment decisions.[139] On the other hand, when the state civil commitment statute is read to condition commitment on a finding that the individual is incompetent to make treatment decisions and is in need of treatment, the hospital constitutionally may provide treatment involuntarily following the patient's commitment.[140]

In the absence of such a statutory condition, a finding of committability cannot alone justify an assumption of incompetency. Indeed, although the law once made precisely this general assumption,[141] the modern approach is not to equate civil commitment with incompetency for any purpose.[142] Thus, without an additional finding, committed patients no longer are deemed incompetent to manage their own affairs; to marry; to divorce; to make a will; to contract; to vote; to stand trial; to hold a professional, occupational, or motor vehicle license; or to exercise any other civil right.[143] The medical concept of mental illness is no longer considered synonymous with the legal concept of incompetency.[144] An individual may be mentally ill, even overtly psychotic, and yet be capable of decision making in a variety of areas, including evaluating the advantages and disadvantages of particular treatments.[145] Mental illness often impairs only limited areas of functioning,

---

[139]*Rennie,* 653 F.2d at 847 & n.12; *Okin,* 634 F.2d at 657–59; *Winters,* 446 F.2d at 71; *Davis,* 506 F. Supp. at 915, 935–36; *Anderson,* 663 P.2d at 573; *Medina,* 705 P.2d at 973; *Boyd,* 403 A.2d at 747 n.5; *Rogers,* 458 N.E.2d at 314; *Rivers,* 495 N.E.2d at 344; *In re* K.K.B., 609 P.2d at 749; State *ex rel.* Jones v. Gerhardstein, 416 N.W.2d 883, 890–91, 894–96 (Wis. 1987).

[140]Stensvad v. Reivitz, 601 F. Supp, 128 (W.D. Wis. 1985). Although the federal court assumed this to be the law of Wisconsin, the Wisconsin Supreme Court later disagreed with the federal court's assumption. *Gerhardstein,* 416 N.W.2d at 896 (concluding that in Wisconsin, "[a]n involuntary commitment is not equivalent to a finding of incompetency with respect to involuntary treatment decisions").

[141]P. APPELBAUM ET AL., INFORMED CONSENT: LEGAL THEORY AND CLINICAL PRACTICE 82 (1987); S. BRAKEL ET AL., THE MENTALLY DISABLED AND THE LAW 185, 258, 438–39 (3d ed. 1985); D. WEXLER, MENTAL HEALTH LAW: MAJOR ISSUES 40 (1981); Tepper & Elwork, *Competence to Consent to Treatment as a Psycholegal Construct,* 8 LAW & HUM. BEHAV. 205, 207 (1984); Winick, *supra* note 75, at 207.

[142]Winick, The MacArthur Treatment Competence Study: Legal and Therapeutic Implications, 2 PSYCHOL. PUB. POL'Y & L. 137, 151–58 (1996); *e.g.,* Winters v. Miller, 446 F.2d 65, 68 (2d Cir.) (holding that a court finding that a patient was mentally ill does not create a presumption that he is incompetent to make decisions), *cert. denied,* 404 U.S. 985 (1971); Rogers v. Okin, 478 F. Supp. 1342, 1361, 1363–64 (D. Mass. 1979) ("[A]lthough committed, a mental patient is nonetheless presumed competent to manage his affairs, dispose of property, carry on a licensed profession, and even to vote."), *aff'd in part, reversed in part on other grounds,* 634 F.2d 650 (1st Cir. 1980), *vacated sub nom.* Mills v. Rogers, 457 U.S. 291 (1982). Virtually all states now provide by statute that civil commitment does not alone justify the conclusion that a patient may be deprived of civil rights or is incompetent to exercise them. *See* BRAKEL ET AL., *supra* note 141, at 375 & table 7.2; Blackburn, *The "Therapeutic Orgy" and the "Right to Rot" Collide: The Right to Refuse Antipsychotic Drugs Under State Law,* 27 HOUS. L. REV. 447, 471–72 nn.87–88 (1990) (listing statutes).

[143]*See, e.g.,* WIS. STAT. § 51.59(1) (1995); State *ex rel* Jones v. Gerhardstein, 416 N.W.2d 883, 895 (1987).

[144]*Gerhardstein,* 416 N.W. 2d at 890.

[145]Grisso & Appelbaum, *The MacArthur Treatment Competence Study. III: Abilities of Patients to Consent to Psychiatric and Medical Treatment,* 19 LAW & HUM. BEHAV. 175 (1995) (empirical study finding most patients in a sample who were hospitalized for schizophrenia and major depression able to engage in treatment decision making within an acceptable range of competence); Mazade et al., *Mediation as a New Technique For Resolving Disputes in the Mental Health System,* 21 ADMIN. & POL'Y MENTAL HEALTH 431, 437 (1994) (citing studies); McKinnon et al., *Clinicians' Assessments of Patients' Decisionmaking Capacity,* 40 HOSP. & COMMUNITY PSYCHIATRY 1159 (1989) ("Clinical evidence suggests that despite alterations in thinking and mood, psychiatric patients are not automatically less capable than others of making health care decisions."); Winick, *supra* note 142; *see supra* chapter 14, notes 92–97 and accompanying text.

leaving patients capable of functioning competently in other areas.[146] Incompetence in one area of decision making caused by mental illness does not necessarily mean incompetence in others.[147] Instead of treating competence globally, the law now identifies the purpose for which competency is in question and ascertains competency for that particular purpose and no other.[148]

To justify involuntary treatment that invades fundamental constitutional rights on the basis of the government's *parens patriae* power, therefore, the patient's incompetency to make treatment decisions must be separately demonstrated in a manner meeting the requirements of procedural due process.[149] In addition, the state must show that the treatment in question would have been accepted by the individual if he or she were competent, or in the absence of evidence concerning the individual's preferences, that it is in his or her best interests. If these showings are made, the state's *parens patriae* interest would be deemed sufficiently significant to satisfy the compelling state interest requirement of strict scrutiny.

2. Governmental Interests in Treating Criminal Offenders

(a) Parens Patriae *Power*

The government interest in rehabilitating offenders, expressly asserted in the typical statutory delegation of authority to correctional agencies,[150] appears at first blush to be an assertion of both a police power and a *parens patriae* power interest. The government's *parens patriae* power, however, generally is not applicable in the correctional rehabilitation context. Although correctional authorities may attempt to justify rehabilitative programs as being in the best interest of the offenders involved, our constitutional heritage rebels at governmental paternalism when individuals are able to decide their own best interests. As previously demonstrated, because the *parens patriae* power is based on the need for the government to protect the well-being of those unable to care for themselves, it may legitimately be asserted only for individuals whose age or physical or mental disabilities render them incapable of determining their own best interests.[151] Although increasing numbers of sentenced prisoners may suffer from mental illness, few are so cognitively impaired as to be incompetent to make treatment decisions. The few that are so impaired typically are not retained in the prison (which often has few clinical resources) but are transferred to a special forensic facility or a mental hospital for treatment. Except for the small minority of offenders who are mentally incompetent, involuntary rehabilitation that

---

[146]Rennie v. Klein, 462 F. Supp. 1131, 1145 (D. N.J. 1978); Rivers v. Katz, 495 N.E.2d 337, 441–42 (N.Y. 1986); P. APPELBAUM & T. GUTHEIL, CLINICAL HANDBOOK OF PSYCHIATRY AND THE LAW 218, 220 (1991) ("[T]he mere presence of psychosis, dementia, mental retardation, or some other form of mental illness or disability is insufficient in itself to constitute incompetence."); Culver et al., *ECT and Special Problems of Informed Consent,* 137 AM. J. PSYCHIATRY 586, 586 (1980) ("In the view of most psychiatrists serious mental illness does not render a patient incapable of making informed decisions about treatment."); McKinnon et al., *supra* note 145; Morse, *Crazy Behavior, Morals and Science: An Analysis of Mental Health Law,* 51 S. CAL. L. REV. 527, 573, 588 (1978); Weinstock et al., *Competence to Give Informed Consent for Medical Procedures,* 12 BULL. AM. ACAD. PSYCHIATRY & L. 117, 124 (1984); Winick, *supra* note 75, at 188–90; Winick, *supra* note 142.

[147]*See supra* chapter 14, part B.

[148]R. ROESCH & S. GOLDING, COMPETENCY TO STAND TRIAL 10–13 (1980) [hereinafter COMPETENCY]; Bonnie, *The Competence of Criminal Defendants: Beyond* Dusky *and* Drope, 47 U. MIAMI L. REV. 539, 549 (1983).

[149]*See supra* chapter 19 (discussing procedural due process requirements in the right-to-refuse-treatment area). For analysis of the standard for determining competence, see *infra* chapter 18, part A.

[150]*See, e.g.,* 18 U.S.C. § 4001(b)(2) (1985); ALI MODEL PENAL CODE § 401.2(2)(B) (official draft 1985).

[151]*See supra* note 137.

invades fundamental constitutional rights should not be justified on the sole basis of government assertion of the *parens patriae* power. Even criminal offenders (or those accused of crime who have been adjudicated incompetent to stand trial or participate in other aspects of the criminal proceedings or not guilty by reason of insanity) may be competent to participate in treatment decision making.[152] Therefore, the mere existence of mental illness or an adjudication of incompetence to stand trial or an acquittal by reason of insanity should not, without an additional finding, justify the inference that the defendant is incompetent to make treatment decisions.

For several special categories of individuals in the criminal process, therefore, *parens patriae* and police power interests may overlap. In addition to those found incompetent to stand trial or acquitted by reason of insanity, these may include defendants found incompetent to be executed[153] and pretrial detainees or sentenced prisoners transferred to a mental hospital as a result of their mental illness.[154] To analyze right-to-refuse-treatment questions arising in these special circumstances, it is necessary to desegregate police power interests in involuntary treatment from *parens patriae* interests. Because either governmental interest, in appropriate circumstances, may justify involuntary treatment, each should receive separate consideration. The following discussion of defendants found incompetent to stand trial illustrates how the state's *parens patriae* interest should be analyzed in these special categories in which the *parens patriae* interest may overlap with the government's police power interests.

In all jurisdictions, criminal defendants are deemed incompetent to stand trial if, as a result of mental illness, they are found incapable of understanding the proceedings against them or of assisting in their defense.[155] An adjudication of incompetence suspends the criminal proceedings while the defendant is given mental health treatment.[156] The purpose of this court-ordered mental health treatment is to restore these defendants to sufficient competence to stand trial, not necessarily to cure them from their mental illness. In fact, the state's authority to commit incompetent defendants solely on the basis of their incompetence to stand trial is limited by the state's ability to provide treatment that makes it probable that they will attain competence in the foreseeable future.[157] Almost all of those found incompetent to stand trial will be hospitalized for treatment.[158] Indeed, many jurisdictions

---

[152]State *ex rel.* Jones v. Gerhardstein, 416 N.W.2d 883, 891 (Wis. 1987).

[153]*See* Ford v. Wainwright, 477 U.S. 399 (1986); Winick, *supra* note 43.

[154]*See* Vitek v. Jones, 445 U.S. 480 (1980).

[155]Winick, *Incompetency to Stand Trial: An Assessment of Costs and Benefits, and a Proposal for Reform*, 39 RUTGERS L. REV. 243, 243 (1987) [hereinafter *Incompetency to Stand Trial*]; Winick, *Incompetency to Stand Trial: Developments in the Law*, in MENTALLY DISORDERED OFFENDERS: PERSPECTIVES FROM LAW AND SOCIAL SCIENCE 3, 5 (1983) [hereinafter *Incompetency Developments*]. *See generally* ABA, CRIMINAL JUSTICE MENTAL HEALTH STANDARDS, Standards 7–4.1 to 7–4.15 (1989); COMMITTEE ON PSYCHIATRY AND LAW, GROUP FOR THE ADVANCEMENT OF PSYCHIATRY, REPORT NO. 89, MISUSE OF PSYCHIATRY IN THE CRIMINAL COURTS: COMPETENCY TO STAND TRIAL (1974) [hereinafter GAP REPORT]; ROESCH & GOLDING, COMPETENCY, *supra* note 148; H. STEADMAN, BEATING A RAP? DEFENDANT FOUND INCOMPETENT TO STAND TRIAL (1979); Winick, *Reforming Incompetency to Stand Trial and Plead Guilty: A Restated Proposal and a Response to Professor Bonnie*, 85 J. CRIM. L. & CRIMINOLOGY 521 (1995).

[156]Winick, *Incompetency to Stand Trial, supra* note 155, at 243.

[157]Jackson v. Indiana, 406 U.S. 715 (1972). If there is no substantial probability that the defendant will regain competence in the foreseeable future, or if treatment provided for a reasonable period has not succeeded in restoring capacity, substantive due process requires that the state either release the defendant or institute civil commitment proceedings. *Id.* at 738.

[158]A. STONE, MENTAL HEALTH AND LAW: A SYSTEM IN TRANSITION 211 (DHEW Pub. No. (ADM) 76–176, 1975); Roesch & Golding, *Treatment and Disposition of Defendants Found Incompetent to Stand Trial: A Review and a Proposal*, 2 INT'L J.L. & PSYCHIATRY 349 (1979); Winick, *Incompetency Developments, supra* note 155, at 14.

provide for automatic hospitalization following an adjudication that the defendant is incompetent.[159]

Do these criminal defendants found incompetent and hospitalized for treatment designed to restore them to competence to stand trial have a constitutional right to refuse treatment? The treatment for defendants found incompetent to stand trial is almost invariably psychotropic medication.[160] For reasons that are developed further in the next section, the police power interest in restoring such defendants to competence so that they may stand trial and in maintaining them in this state generally is a sufficiently compelling governmental interest to justify involuntary treatment with such drugs, even though they intrude on fundamental constitutional rights.[161] This interest lies at the core of the state's police power—the enforcement of its criminal laws.[162] It is not, however, a *parens patriae* interest. Although the state's police power interest in this context typically will suffice to justify involuntary treatment, there may be occasions (such as in the previously discussed case of *Riggins v. Nevada*) when this police power interest may not be clearly present.

Can the state assert a *parens patriae* interest in such a case? For the government to assert a *parens patriae* interest in treating such defendants involuntarily, it would need to demonstrate that they are incompetent to participate in treatment decisions. Although it is doubtless true that a large percentage of defendants found incompetent to stand trial may also be incompetent to participate in treatment decisions, some such defendants may be competent to decide on treatment, or at least to participate in the decision-making process.[163] The typical formulation of the standard for determining competency to stand trial is whether the defendant "has sufficient present ability to consult with his lawyer with a reasonable degree of rational understanding—and whether he has a rational as well as a factual understanding of the proceedings against him."[164] A defendant lacking this capacity does not necessarily also lack the ability rationally to consult with the defendant's therapist concerning appropriate treatment, to understand treatment information, and to make a treatment decision. Moreover, even those defendants found incompetent to stand trial who also lack competency to participate in treatment decisions at the outset may, after a brief period of hospitalization and stabilization on psychotropic medication, thereafter attain competence to participate in subsequent treatment decisions. As previously indicated, the

---

[159]Roesch & Golding, *supra* note 158, at 357; Winick, *Incompetency Developments, supra* note 155, at 14.

[160]GAP REPORT, *supra* note 155, at 901; Hollister, *Psychotropic Drugs and Court Competency, in* LAW, PSYCHIATRY AND THE MENTALLY DISORDERED OFFENDER 14 (L. Irvine & T. Brelje eds., 1972); Winick, *Psychotropic Medication and Competency to Stand Trial,* 1977 AM. B. FOUND. RES. J. 769, 771–89 [hereinafter *Medication and Competency*]; Winick, *Psychotropic Medication in the Criminal Trial Process: The Constitutional and Therapeutic Implications of* Riggins v. Nevada, 10 N.Y.L. SCH. J. HUM. RTS. 637 (1993) [hereinafter *Psychotropic Medication*].

[161]*See* Riggins v. Nevada, 504 U.S. 127, 135 (1992) (dicta); *infra* notes 173–80 and accompanying text.

[162]*See* Kelley v. Johnson, 425 U.S. 238, 247 (1976).

[163]State *ex rel.* Jones v. Gerhardstein, 416 N.W.2d 883, 891 (Wis. 1987) ("There was expert testimony that individuals who are found incompetent to stand trial . . . may nevertheless be competent to make decisions regarding the acceptance of psychotropic drugs."); *see* State v. Garcia 658 A.2d 947, 969 (Conn. 1995) (recognizing that although "in most circumstances, a defendant who is incompetent to stand trial also will be incompetent to make his own health care decisions," in "unusual circumstances" the trial court may find "that a defendant, although incompetent to stand trial, is competent to make his own health care decisions. . . ."); FLA. R. CRIM. P. 3.215 (1995) (an adjudication of incompetence to stand trial is not an adjudication of incompetence for any other purpose).

[164]Dusky v. United States, 362 U.S. 402, 402 (1960). *Dusky* is followed in substance by all jurisdictions, although statutory terminology varies widely. Winick, *Incompetency Developments, supra* note 155, at 6–8. The Supreme Court recently reendorsed the *Dusky* test as the general standard for determining competency in all aspects of the criminal process. Godinez v. Moran, 509 U.S. 389 (1993).

state's police power interest in restoring these defendants to trial capacity may justify continued treatment with such drugs even over the defendant's objection, but the separate *parens patriae* power should not suffice to justify such treatment absent an additional determination that the defendant is then incompetent to participate in treatment decision making.[165]

In appropriate circumstances *parens patriae* interests thus may justify involuntary treatment for defendants found incompetent to stand trial, as well as for other individuals in several additional special categories of offenders in which police power and *parens patriae* interests may overlap. When involuntary treatment in these contexts is justified on the basis of *parens patriae* interests alone, however, a determination should be required that the individual in question is incompetent to engage in treatment decision making and that the proposed treatment is in the individual's best interests. For individuals in these special categories, as well as for the small number of other offenders who are incompetent to make treatment decisions, the *parens patriae* power thus may provide a sufficient justification for involuntary treatment. For such offenders, the substantive constitutional issues presented by involuntary treatment would seem identical to those analyzed previously with regard to incompetent civil patients,[166] with one exception. As *Washington v. Harper* suggests, the state's interests are more likely to outweigh the individual's interests when the individual in question is an incarcerated prisoner, in view of the reduced standard of constitutional scrutiny applied in the prison context.[167]

(b) Police Power

(i) Prevention of violence in correctional facilities. Aside from *parens patriae* justifications for involuntary mental health treatment, the state in a variety of offender contexts will assert a police power basis for such treatment. Separate police power interests may be invoked. As with patients in civil mental hospitals, the state may assert a police power interest in protecting others from the harmful acts of an individual in the criminal process who suffers from mental illness. This may occur in the prison, the context involved in *Washington v. Harper*.[168] *Harper* recognizes that protecting the safety of others in the prison constitutes a sufficient governmental interest to outweigh a prisoner's assertion of a

---

[165]The Fourth Circuit Court of Appeals in United States v. Charters, 863 F.2d 302, 310 (4th Cir. 1988) (en banc), in declining to insist on a separate determination of incompetency to participate in treatment decisions for a criminal defendant hospitalized for incompetency to stand trial, concluded that "[w]hile in theory there may be a difference between the two mental states [incompetency to stand trial and incompetency to participate in treatment decision making], it must certainly be one of such subtlety and complexity as to tax perception by the most skilled medical or psychiatric professionals." Although this difference may indeed be difficult to diagnose, it nonetheless has important theoretical and legal consequences, and it is appropriate to distinguish these two competencies and not to equate one with the other. Because at least some and perhaps many defendants found incompetent to stand trial are competent to make treatment decisions, it would seem unconstitutional conclusively to presume that all defendants found incompetent to stand trial also are incompetent for this purpose. State *ex rel.* Jones v. Gerhardstein, 416 N.W.2d 883, 891 (Wis. 1987); *see supra* chapter 14, notes 106–08 and accompanying text (discussing conclusive presumption doctrine). The Court in *Charters* was not faced with a *parens patriae* justification for treatment, at least not one distinct from a police power justification grounded in restoration of the defendant to trial capacity. As a result, the court's analysis in this regard may properly be viewed as dicta. In a case in which the only relevant governmental interest asserted to justify involuntary treatment is the *parens patriae* interest, demonstration of the defendant's incapacity to participate in treatment decision making should be deemed a prerequisite.

[166]*See supra* notes 133–49 and accompanying text.

[167]494 U.S. 210 (1990); *see supra* notes 27–39 and accompanying text.

[168]*Id.*

right to refuse forcible administration of antipsychotic medication. This justification also may arise in the jail, a context dealt with in dicta in *Riggins v. Nevada*.[169] The Court's language in *Riggins* suggests a strict scrutiny approach for involuntary medication administered in the jail in order to protect other detainees or jail employees from the harmful acts of a mentally ill detainee. The Court indicated, however, that the need to prevent harm would outweigh the inmate's assertion of a right to refuse medication only if the drug used was medically appropriate for the individual and was the least intrusive means of accomplishing this need.

For offenders residing in the community in halfway houses or other community correctional facilities, forcible treatment to prevent harm to other facility residents or staff also would seem permissible. The standard suggested in dicta in *Riggins* would seem applicable in these contexts rather than the one used in *Harper*. Community correctional facilities would seem to present even fewer institutional security concerns than the jail involved in *Riggins* and certainly fewer than the prison involved in *Harper*. Moreover, although some offenders placed in community facilities are convicted felons, it can be anticipated that only those thought not to be dangerous would be either released from prison to such facilities or placed there in lieu of prison. In addition, individuals in community settings who act out violently as a result of mental illness may be subject to emergency civil commitment, in which case treatment would be imposed, if necessary, in the hospital rather than in the community facility. Nonetheless, if a resident of such a community facility presents an imminent threat of harm to others, forcible medication may be permissible in some circumstances.

As discussed in the context of civil patients, the state should be required to demonstrate that the harm to be prevented has a high degree of imminence before forced intrusive treatment such as psychotropic medication can be justified.[170] Under general First Amendment principles, a clear and present danger should be required for all intrusive treatments that seriously interfere with mental processes.[171] This requirement, however, may not be applicable in the prison. On the facts of *Washington v. Harper*, the prisoner in question was predicted to be violent, but no special showing was made concerning the imminence of such violence. The Court's approval of involuntary antipsychotic medication in *Harper* therefore may suggest a rejection or at least a relaxation of the clear and present danger requirement in the prison context. Even in the context of the prison, however, the issue may be regarded as an open one inasmuch as a First Amendment issue was neither raised nor considered in *Harper*.[172]

Apart from the prevention of violence in a correctional facility, the state may assert a variety of other police power interests to justify involuntary mental health treatment. The state may assert such an interest to justify involuntary treatment of a criminal defendant found incompetent to stand trial so that the defendant can be restored to competence and maintained in a competent state during trial. The state may assert such an interest to justify the involuntary treatment of a death row inmate found incompetent to be executed in order to restore the prisoner to competence so that capital punishment may be administered. The state may assert such a police power interest to justify involuntary treatment of a defendant acquitted by reason of insanity who remains mentally ill in order to prevent future criminal conduct. In addition, the state generally may assert a police power interest in the rehabilita-

---

[169]504 U.S. 127 (1992); *see supra* notes 51–52 and accompanying text.

[170]*See supra* note 127 and accompanying text.

[171]*See supra* notes 127–29 and accompanying text.

[172]*See supra* note 69 and accompanying text.

tion of convicted criminal offenders in order to prevent recidivism. Each of these police power interests is considered separately.

(ii) Restoration and maintenance of competence to stand trial.   When a criminal defendant is found incompetent to stand trial, the criminal proceedings are halted until treatment can restore the defendant to a competent state.[173] Does the state's police power interest in restoring such defendants to competence and maintaining them in a competent state so that they may stand trial constitute a compelling governmental interest sufficient to outweigh the defendant's right to refuse such treatment? As previously mentioned, the most frequently used treatment in the restoration of competence to stand trial is psychotropic medication.[174] Even though drug treatment is sufficiently intrusive to infringe on fundamental constitutional rights and therefore to qualify for strict scrutiny,[175] the government's interest would seem sufficiently weighty to satisfy at least the compelling interest portion of the test. A state's interest in bringing to trial defendants for whom probable cause exists that they have committed criminal offenses touches concerns at the core of its police power.[176] The compelling interest test would therefore seem clearly to be satisfied.[177] In her opinion for the Supreme Court in *Riggins v. Nevada,* Justice O'Connor strongly suggested that this interest would be deemed to override a defendant's interest in resisting unwanted medication.[178] Indeed, she suggested that even if medication were to impose side effects that prejudiced the defendant's performance at trial, ''trial prejudice can sometimes be justified

---

[173]*See supra* notes 156–57 and accompanying text.

[174]*See supra* note 160 and accompanying text.

[175]*See supra* chapters 5 (psychotropic medication), 10 (First Amendment), and 11 (substantive due process).

[176]*See* Kelley v. Johnson, 425 U.S. 238, 247 (1976) (''The promotion of safety of persons and property is unquestionably at the core of the State's police power.'').

[177]Winick, *Medication and Competency, supra* note 160, at 812. A majority of the lower courts have upheld the involuntary administration of psychotropic drugs to restore or maintain a defendant's competency for trial. United States v. Charters, 863 F.2d 302, 304–05 (4th Cir. 1988) (en banc) (rejecting asserted right to refuse medication justified by need to restore competence for trial), *cert. denied,* 494 U.S. 1016 (1990); State v. Garcia, 658 A.2d 947, 962 (Conn. 1995) (''[T]he state's interest in enforcing its criminal laws by bringing a defendant to trial is significant and, under certain circumstances, can override the liberty and privacy interests of the defendant.''); Khiem v. United States, 612 A.2d 160, 168–69 (D.C. 1992) (prosecution had compelling interest in medicating defendant to bring him to trial where he could never be tried absent such medication); People v. Hardesty, 362 N.W.2d 787, 793 (Mich. Ct. App. 1985) (incompetent accused may be made competent through medication even if medication will need to be continued throughout the trial); Ybarra v. State, 731 P.2d 353, 356 (Nev. 1987) (competent defendant was not forced to stand trial while incompetent solely on the basis that he had been drugged); State v. Hayes, 389 A.2d 1379, 1382 (N.H. 1978) (incompetent accused may be made competent through medication); State v. Law, 244 S.W.2d 302, 307 (S.C. 1978) (absent a showing of prejudice, medicated defendant was not denied a fair trial); State v. Lover, 707 P.2d 1351, 1353 (Wash. Ct. App. 1985) (forced medication to gain competence to stand trial is valid if court determines it improves defendant's ability to assist in defense, if it is the least intrusive means to bring defendant to competency, and if the effects of medication can be explained to jury); *see* ABA Criminal Justice Mental Health Standards, Standard 7–4.10(d) (1989) (A defendant committed for incompetence to stand trial ''should have no right to refuse ordinary and reasonable treatment or rehabilitation designed to affect competence. However, a defendant should have the right to refuse any treatment or rehabilitation which may impair the defendant's ability to prepare a defense to the charges, which is experimental, or which has an unreasonable risk of serious, hazardous, or irreversible side effects.''). *But see* Bee v. Greaves, 744 F.2d 1387, 1395 (10th Cir. 1984) (pretrial detainee has liberty interest in avoiding unwanted medication administered to treat him for trial incompetency), *cert. denied,* 496 U.S. 1214 (1985); Fentiman, *supra* note 61, at 1168–69 (arguing that an insanity defendant has a constitutional right to be tried while incompetent without compulsory administration of psychotropic medication).

[178]*Riggins,* 504 U.S. at 135–36 (citing Illinois v. Allen, 397 U.S. 337, 347 (1970) (Brennan, J., concurring) (''Constitutional power to bring an accused to trial is fundamental to a scheme of 'ordered liberty' and prerequisite to social justice and peace.'').

by an essential state interest.''[179] Because the record in *Riggins* contained no findings supporting a conclusion that psychotropic medication was necessary to accomplish an essential state purpose, the Court held that the substantial likelihood of prejudice presented was not justified.[180] The Court's language suggesting that the state could medicate the defendant to restore competence therefore was dicta. However, it seems clear that in the absence of prejudice resulting from medication side effects, the state's interest in treating the defendant to effect a restoration to competence would override the defendant's interest in refusing medication.

When prejudicial effects result from forced drug treatment, however, the question is considerably more troubling. In a concurring opinion in *Riggins*, Justice Kennedy suggested that in such instances the state should be required to demonstrate that continued medication administered over objection would not alter the defendant's demeanor or otherwise hinder the ability to participate in the proceedings.[181] If the state could not carry ''this extraordinary burden,'' Justice Kennedy would not permit continued medication over objection.[182] Justice Kennedy therefore would strike the balance differently than the majority when a likelihood of trial prejudice is presented. The majority's observation that ''trial prejudice can sometimes be justified by an essential state interest''[183] suggests that it may not be willing to insist on Justice Kennedy's additional requirement.

Illinois v. Allen,[184] the case relied on by the *Riggins* majority for the proposition that ''an essential state interest'' may sometimes outweigh the defendant's interest in avoiding prejudice at trial, does not seem analogous to the *Riggins* situation, however. In *Allen*, the Court had upheld the binding and gagging of a defendant who repeatedly had acted in an unruly and disruptive fashion during trial. Although the defendant was mentally ill,[185] he was competent to stand trial.[186] As a result, the *Allen* Court was faced with the need to avoid allowing a competent defendant to frustrate the state's ability to try him by intentionally behaving in a way that would disrupt courtroom decorum.

In the context presented in *Riggins*, by contrast, a defendant asserted a right to refuse medication that he had a constitutionally protected liberty interest in avoiding. In this respect, the two situations cannot be equated because the defendant in *Allen* had no right to behave disruptively at trial. Moreover, the prejudice suffered by the defendant in the *Riggins* situation may be more serious than that resulting from requiring a defendant to stand trial while bound and gagged. The side effects of medication may so alter the defendant's demeanor that the trier of fact forms the impression that his testimony lacks credibility. Moreover, the side effects could possibly affect the content of the defendant's testimony itself. In short, as Justice Kennedy observed, involuntarily imposed medication can have the potential of ''manipulating material evidence'' when it affects the defendant's demeanor to

---

[179]*Id.* at 135–36 (citing Holbrook v. Flynn, 475 U.S. 560, 568–69 (1986) (recognizing that shackling a defendant may be justified by an essential state interest) and Illinois v. Allen, 397 U.S. 337, 344 (1970) (binding and gagging the accused permissible only in extreme situations when it is the ''fairest and most reasonable way'' to control a disruptive defendant)).

[180]*Id.* at 137.

[181]*Id.* at 138 (Kennedy, J., concurring).

[182]*Id.* at 139.

[183]*Id.* at 131.

[184]397 U.S. 337 (1970).

[185]*Compare Riggins*, 504 U.S. 127 (involving the question of whether a defendant could be tried while being medicated) *with Allen*, 397 U.S. 337 (involving the question of whether an obstreperous defendant repeatedly warned about his disruptive behavior could be tried while bound and gagged).

[186]*Allen*, 397 U.S. at 351–52 (Douglas, J., concurring).

the point that it alters the presentation of the defense.[187] Although binding and gagging a defendant as in *Allen* may affect the jury's attitude toward the defendant by emphasizing that the defendant has misbehaved in court, it does not necessarily alter the jury's assessment of the defendant's case as does the resulting side effects of forced medication. A defendant in the *Allen* situation who wishes to testify would presumably be permitted to do so without a gag; a defendant in the *Riggins* situation may not be able to present a defense free of the impairing effects of his medication.

Justice Kennedy's additional requirement thus seems an appropriate measure to protect against an unfair trial. If medication so interferes with the defendant's demeanor or trial functioning that prejudice seems likely, the resulting verdict may be inaccurate. The state's "essential interest" is in obtaining a substantially accurate disposition of the criminal charges.[188] If this becomes unlikely because of the side effects of antipsychotic medication in a particular case, it may be preferable to postpone disposition of the charges or even to avoid adjudication altogether. Unless a reasonably accurate disposition of the criminal charges is possible, the state's interest in trying the defendant on medication should not be considered to outweigh the defendant's right to a fair trial.

Although the full Court may be disinclined to require a demonstration that no substantial risk of drug-induced trial prejudice exists as a condition for permitting an involuntarily medicated defendant to stand trial, as Justice Kennedy proposed, this "extraordinary showing" seems to be an appropriate means of avoiding such prejudice. At the very least, an inquiry into the potential for prejudice may have a salutary effect on medication practices, resulting in lower dose levels in order to minimize the risk of prejudice.[189] It might also induce prosecutors to be more patient in commencing trial to allow sufficient time for the proper regulation of dosage levels in order to minimize the risk of drug-induced trial prejudice.[190] Moreover, this burden may not be as difficult for the prosecution to carry as it might appear. Justice Kennedy expressed serious doubt that the "extraordinary showing" he proposed could be made.[191] However, with the willingness on the part of the trial judge and prosecutor to be flexible and to permit ample opportunity for the treatment psychiatrist to try different medications and to regulate dose levels to minimize adverse side effects, this showing may not be as burdensome as Justice Kennedy supposed.[192]

In most cases, a defendant restored to competence through use of psychotropic drugs will be able to stand trial without drug-induced side effects that impair trial demeanor or functioning. In these instances, the state's interest in effecting a disposition of the criminal charges will be deemed sufficient to outweigh the defendant's liberty interest in avoiding unwanted medication, at least if no less intrusive treatment approaches can bring about this result. When trial prejudice seems likely, however, the substantial interest in avoiding prejudice supplements the defendant's liberty interest in avoiding unwanted intrusions, and these combined interests should outweigh the state's interest in insisting on medication. Whether the Supreme Court strikes the balance in this way, as would Justice Kennedy, or follows the dicta in Justice O'Connor's opinion for the majority in *Riggins* remains to be seen.

---

[187]*Riggins*, 504 U.S. at 139 (Kennedy, J., concurring) (citing Brady v. Maryland, 373 U.S. 83, 87 (1963) (holding that suppression by the prosecution of material evidence favorable to the accused violates due process)).

[188]*See* Brecht v. Abrahamson, 507 U.S. 619, 652 (1993) (O'Connor, J., dissenting) ("'[T]he central goal of the criminal justice system . . . [is the] accurate determination of guilt and innocence.'").

[189]Winick, *Psychotropic Medication, supra* note 160, at 176–77.

[190]*Id.* at 177.

[191]*Riggins*, 504 U.S. at 139 (Kennedy, J., concurring).

[192]*Id.*

(iii) The State's interest in treating death row inmates to restore their competency for execution. The Supreme Court's decision in *Ford v. Wainwright*[193] held that it would be unconstitutional for a state to administer capital punishment to a defendant on death row who had become incompetent to be executed. However, the Court did not address whether the state could coercively treat an incompetent death row inmate in order to restore the prisoner to competency so that the death penalty could be administered. In 1990, the Court granted certiorari in the case of *Perry v. Louisiana*[194] to consider the unresolved question of whether death row inmates possess a right to refuse treatment in this context. After oral argument, the Court decided to avoid resolution of the constitutional question, at least for the time being, and remanded the case to the state court for reconsideration in light of the Supreme Court's intervening decision in *Washington v. Harper*.[195] *Harper* had upheld a state prison's authority to administer medically indicated antipsychotic drugs to a prisoner who was found, when not taking such medication, to be dangerous to other inmates and prison staff. As previously described, the Court applied a relaxed standard of review, rather than traditional strict scrutiny, in deference to the special needs of prison authorities to safeguard the security of inherently volatile institutions.[196]

In a subsequent case in which security considerations were not present, however, the Court in *Riggins v. Nevada* declined to apply the deferential scrutiny of *Harper* but suggested use of a standard of review that closely resembles strict scrutiny.[197] As previously suggested, *Riggins* demonstrates that the deferential approach of *Harper* will be limited to the prison context in which security considerations are the justification for involuntary treatment.

In the context of treating incompetent death row inmates to restore capacity, these security considerations are rarely implicated. Death row inmates are isolated and subjected to intensive security measures that, other than in the most unusual circumstances, significantly diminish any risk to other inmates or prison staff. Moreover, the state's interest in providing treatment is not to safeguard institutional security and prevent injury to inmates or staff as in *Harper,* but rather to enable it to inflict capital punishment. *Harper* is thus not dispositive of the issue raised in *Perry*. Absent the special security concerns that justified a deferential standard of scrutiny in *Harper,* traditional strict scrutiny arguably would be applied in this context. Under this approach, the state's justifications for forcibly administering intrusive treatment like psychotropic drugs to incompetent death row inmates—which unlike in *Harper* would not be in the patient's best interest—may not satisfy the compelling interest standard. Given the security capabilities of death row, the state's police power interest in protecting others would not necessitate forced intrusive treatment.

In addition, a significant question is raised regarding whether intrusive treatment administered essentially for reasons of punishment (to enable the state to carry out the death penalty) would offend contemporary standards of decency and therefore constitute cruel and unusual punishment in violation of the Eight Amendment.[198] Although the Supreme Court has held that states possess a valid penal interest in capital punishment sufficient to withstand an Eighth Amendment challenge,[199] the administration of medication or other intrusive

---

[193]477 U.S. 399 (1986); *see* Winick, *supra* note 43.

[194]494 U.S. 1015 (1990); *see supra* notes 40–43 and accompanying text.

[195]494 U.S. 210 (1990).

[196]*See id.* at 223–34; *supra* notes 28–33 and accompanying text.

[197]504 U.S. 127, 136 (1992); *see supra* note 60 and accompanying text.

[198]*See* Ford v. Wainwright, 477 U.S. 399, 406 (1986) (applying the standard of Trope v. Dulles, 356 U.S. 86, 101 (1958) (plurality opinion)); *supra* chapter 12.

[199]*E.g.,* Gregg v. Georgia, 428 U.S. 153 (1976); Proffitt v. Florida, 428 U.S. 242 (1976).

treatment as punishment raises a different question. "Medical punishment" is a concept alien to American constitutional tradition and does not comport with human dignity. Therefore, it would arguably constitute cruel and unusual punishment.[200]

On remand, the Louisiana Supreme Court in *Perry* distinguished *Harper* and found that involuntary administration of psychotropic drugs in the competency-for-execution context would be unconstitutional.[201] Although the Supreme Court has not resolved this issue, the Louisiana court's decision seems correct and should be followed.[202] Denying the state the ability forcibly to medicate a death row inmate does not seriously undermine the deterrent and retributivist purposes underlying its capital punishment scheme, particularly because so few death row inmates are involved.[203] Moreover, involuntary treatment in this context presents a difficult ethical dilemma for clinicians asked to provide such treatment.[204] When added to the death row inmate's liberty interest in freedom from unwanted medication and in avoiding a form of "medical punishment" in violation of the Eighth Amendment, the interest in avoiding this professional dilemma for clinicians supports rejecting the constitutionality of involuntary treatment in this context. The states' police power interests in imposing intrusive treatment on incompetent death row inmates to facilitate their execution therefore should be held insufficient to outweigh the prisoner's right to refuse such treatment.

(iv) Involuntary treatment for insanity acquittees. Criminal defendants who have been acquitted by reason of insanity almost always are committed to state hospitals for

---

[200]*See* Bee v. Greaves, 744 F.2d 1387, 1395 (10th Cir. 1984), *cert. denied*, 469 U.S. 1214 (1985) (use of psychotropic medication, absent an emergency, for control or institutional discipline not as part of a treatment program may violate Eighth Amendment); Nelson v. Heyne, 491 F.2d 352, 356 (7th Cir. 1974), *cert. denied*, 417 U.S. 976 (1976) (involuntary administration of psychotropic drugs in a juvenile correctional institution "not as part of an ongoing psychotherapeutic program, but for the purpose of controlling excited behavior" held to violate Eighth Amendment); Knecht v. Gillman, 488 F.2d 1136, 1139 (8th Cir. 1973) (involuntary aversive conditioning program using the vomit-inducing drug apomorphine held to constitute cruel and unusual punishment without regard to its characterization as "treatment" when administered without informed consent); Mackey v. Procunier, 477 F.2d 877, 878 (9th Cir. 1973) (use of succinylcholine—a paralyzing "fright drug" producing sensations of suffocation and drowning—on fully conscious prisoners in a prison aversive conditioning program held to be cruel and unusual punishment prohibited by Eighth Amendment); Pena v. New York Div. for Youth, 419 F. Supp. 203 (S.D.N.Y. 1976) (use of psychotropic medication for control or administrative discipline may violate Eighth Amendment); *In re* K.K.B., 609 P.2d 747, 751 (Okla. 1980) (same); Winick, *supra* note 43, at 330.

[201]State v. Perry, 610 So. 2d 746 (La. 1992). The court found that "forcing a prisoner to take antipsychotic drugs to facilitate his execution does not constitute medical treatment." *Id.* at 751. The court also found that the state had not demonstrated that the treatment it sought to impose would "further both the best medical interest of the prisoner and the state's own interest in prison safety." *Id.* Finally, the court concluded that *Harper* had strongly implied that "forced administration of antipsychotic drugs may not be used by the state for the purpose of punishment." *Id.* at 752.

[202]*See* Winick, *supra* note 43, at 329–37 (defending this conclusion on both constitutional and therapeutic jurisprudence grounds).

[203]*See* Miller, *Evaluation of and Treatment to Competency to be Executed: A National Survey and Analysis*, 16 J. PSYCHIATRY & L. 67, 73–74 (1988); Winick, *supra* note 43, at 318 n.8.

[204]*See* Appelbaum, *Competence to be Executed: Another Conundrum for Mental Health Professionals*, 37 HOSP. & COMMUNITY PSYCHIATRY 682 (1986); Ewing, *Diagnosing and Treating "Insanity" on Death Row: Legal and Ethical Perspectives*, 5 BEHAV. SCI. & L. 175 (1987); Miller, *supra* note 203; Radalet & Barnard, *Treating Those Found Incompetent for Execution: Ethical Chaos with Only One Solution*, 16 BULL. AM. ACAD. PSYCHIATRY & L. 297 (1988); Wallace, *Incompetency for Execution: The Supreme Court Challenges the Ethical Standards of the Mental Health Professions*, 8 J. LEGAL MED. 265 (1987); Winick, *supra* note 43, at 318 n.9. In an amicus brief submitted in *Perry*, the American Medical Association and the American Psychiatric Association stated that medical ethics bar physician participation in treatment designed to restore a death row inmate to competence for execution. *See* Winick, *supra* note 43, at 318 n.9.

treatment designed to protect the community from harm and to decrease the likelihood of further criminal conduct.[205] These individuals, although mentally ill, typically are competent to engage in treatment decision making.[206] In order to successfully assert an insanity defense, they must be found competent to stand trial. Although legally insane at the time of the crime, they are not necessarily incompetent at the time of their acquittal and hospitalization. Current mental illness is a prerequisite for commitment, as chapter 14 demonstrates, but mental illness cannot be equated with incompetency to engage in treatment decision making. May these patients refuse treatment designed to diminish their potential recidivism?

The Supreme Court in *Jones v. United States*[207] broadly sanctioned the ability of the states to commit insanity acquittees for lengthy periods in order to treat their mental illness and protect the community from their dangerousness. The Court's opinion, however, did not involve a patient seeking to refuse treatment; rather, it dealt with a procedural due process challenge to automatic commitment and to retention pursuant to procedures that would violate due process if applied in the civil commitment context, in addition to a substantive due process challenge to confinement beyond the time of the maximum sentence the defendant would have received if convicted instead of being acquitted by reason of insanity. The Court upheld the commitment of insanity acquittees under procedures less rigorous than those mandated for civil commitment and permitted the state to confine such individuals in psychiatric hospitals as long as they continue to be both mentally ill and dangerous; however, it did not consider whether such acquittees could be subjected to involuntary intrusive treatment.

The state interest in reducing recidivism in the insanity acquittee context differs from the police power interest in preventing harm to other inmates or institutional staff discussed earlier. Institutionalization itself, provided that it is in a secure facility, ordinarily provides adequate assurance that the community is protected from the potential harmful acts of a dangerous insanity acquittee. The interest in protecting the community against recidivism more closely resembles the state's interest in the rehabilitation of criminal offenders (which is discussed in the next section). There is, however, one important difference. Unlike criminal offenders subjected to rehabilitation, most of whom do not suffer from a serious mental illness, those acquitted by reason of insanity and committed to psychiatric facilities almost invariably are mentally ill.[208] As a result, mental health treatment administered to an insanity acquittee to treat a specific mental disorder would seem more likely to be therapeutically justified, whereas such treatment administered to nonmentally ill prisoners would not.[209] Moreover, although rehabilitative approaches for criminal offenders have not shown a high rate of success in reducing offender recidivism,[210] the use of the mental health treatment techniques in the treatment of specific mental disorders have been relatively efficacious in the treatment of various mental illnesses.[211] The state's interest in applying

---

[205]*See* Jones v. United States, 463 U.S. 354 (1983) (upholding constitutionality of reduced procedural protections and indeterminate commitment for insanity acquittees).

[206]Defendants acquitted by reason of insanity who no longer are mentally ill may not constitutionally be committed to a psychiatric hospital. Foucha v. Louisiana, 504 U.S. 71 (1992); *see* Winick, *Ambiguities in the Legal Meaning and Significance of Mental Illness,* 1 PSYCHOL. PUB. POL'Y & L. 534 (1996).

[207]413 U.S. 354 (1983).

[208]Indeed, if they are not, their continued confinement in a psychiatric facility would violate due process. Foucha v. Louisiana, 504 U.S. 71 (1992).

[209]*See infra* chapter 16, part A (discussing therapeutic appropriateness principle).

[210]*See infra* note 228 and accompanying text.

[211]*See supra* chapters 3 (psychotherapy), 4 (behavior therapy), 5 (psychotropic medication), and 6 (electroconvulsive therapy).

particular mental health treatment techniques to mentally ill insanity acquittees in order to treat their mental illnesses in an effort to reduce the likelihood of their engaging in future criminal conduct, would seem considerably stronger than the state's interest in correctional rehabilitative treatment approaches designed to rehabilitate nonmentally ill prisoners.

The rationale for the insanity defense is that conviction and punishment are inappropriate when defendants suffer from mental illness that resulted in cognitive impairment that rendered them unable to appreciate the wrongfulness of their conduct, and, in a minority of jurisdictions, in volitional impairment that prevented them from conforming their conduct to the requirements of the law.[212] Because the various mental health treatment techniques (particularly if used in conjunction with psychotropic medication) have a high potential for reducing such cognitive and volitional impairments resulting from major mental illnesses such as schizophrenia, the state's interest in applying such treatment to most insanity acquittees would seem to meet the compelling governmental interest standard of strict scrutiny.

However, for intrusive treatment approaches that would trigger First Amendment scrutiny, the clear and present danger requirement[213] would not be satisfied for insanity acquittees held in secure facilities. Isolation alone would eliminate the opportunity for recidivism, preventing the risk of harm to community safety from being deemed imminent. Although mentally ill and dangerous without treatment, insanity acquittees held in a secure facility pose no clear and present danger to the community justifying intrusive treatment that significantly invades mental processes in a way that could abridge the First Amendment. If they are incompetent, there may be *parens patriae* justifications for such treatment, but if they are competent, the risk they pose to community safety would not be sufficiently imminent to justify the resulting invasion of First Amendment rights. Insanity acquittees who are dangerous and refuse treatment may face prolonged isolation, but the fiscal costs alone of such isolation would not meet the compelling state interest test.[214] For less intrusive treatment approaches like verbal psychotherapy or counseling and most forms of behavior therapy, which are not sufficient to call for First Amendment scrutiny,[215] the clear and present danger requirement would not apply. As a result, for these less intrusive treatments,

---

[212]In the wake of the *Hinckley* case, United States v. Hinckley, Crim. No. 81–306 (D.D.C. June 21, 1982), several jurisdictions, including the federal courts, eliminated the volitional prong of the legal insanity test, retaining only a cognitive standard that limited its availability to those unable to understand the nature and consequences of their conduct or appreciate the difference between right and wrong. United States v. Lyons, 739 F.2d 243 (5th Cir. 1984); Insanity Defense Reform Act of 1984, 18 U.S.C. § 17 (1995); N.Y. PENAL LAW § 40.15 (McKinney Supp. 1986); TEX. PENAL CODE ANN. § 8.01(a) (Vernon Supp. 1993); ABA CRIMINAL JUSTICE MENTAL HEALTH STANDARDS, *supra* note 177, Standard 7–6.1(a); R. REISNER & C. SLOBOGIN, LAW AND THE MENTAL HEALTH SYSTEM: CIVIL AND CRIMINAL ASPECTS 501–02 (2d ed. 1985); H. STEADMAN ET AL., BEFORE AND AFTER HINCKLEY: EVALUATING INSANITY DEFENSE REFORM 41 (1993) (discussing Insanity Defense Reform Act's elimination of volitional prong of ALI test and modification of cognitive prong to inability to appreciate); 3 M. PERLIN, MENTAL DISABILITY LAW: CIVIL AND CRIMINAL, § 15.01, at 278–79 (1989); Hermann, *Assault on the Insanity Defense: Limitations on the Effectiveness and Effect of the Defense of Insanity*, 14 RUTGERS L.J. 241 (1983); Keilitz, *Researching and Reforming the Insanity Defense*, 39 RUTGERS L. REV. 289, 296 n.38 (1987).

[213]*See supra* notes 127–29 and accompanying text. Because isolation alone would protect community safety, the "least restrictive alternative" principle applicable when intrusive treatment is imposed in non-prison contexts also arguably would prevent involuntary intrusive treatment for this purpose. *See infra* chapter 16, part B.

[214]*See supra* note 130 and accompanying text. For insanity acquittees refusing treatment who continue to be dangerous, secure preventive detention in a nonhospital setting may be preferable to hospitalization and perhaps constitutionally required. Foucha v. Louisiana, 504 U.S. 71 (1992) (continued confinement in a psychiatric hospital of an insanity acquittee who no longer was mentally ill would not be medically justified and would violate due process).

[215]*See infra* chapter 16, part B.

the state's police power interest in involuntary treatment designed to reduce recidivism by insanity acquittees would meet the requirements of constitutional scrutiny.

(v) Rehabilitation of criminal offenders. The "rehabilitative ideal" was a central goal of correctional policy for the first three-quarters of the 20th century.[216] Although the rehabilitative ideal has been in sharp decline since the mid-1970s,[217] rehabilitation unquestionably remains as one of the traditional aims of criminal punishment.[218] Rehabilitation of criminal offenders designed to prevent future criminal conduct undeniably serves important police power objectives. In other contexts, the government's police power interest—in protecting the public health, safety, welfare, or morals—has long been considered sufficiently "compelling" to outweigh the assertion of a variety of constitutional rights.[219] The most important of these police power objectives is the "promotion of safety of persons and property," an interest characterized by the U.S. Supreme Court as "unquestionably at the core of the State's police power."[220] Rehabilitation is one of the traditional justifications for criminal punishment.[221] Thus, when the government provides treatment to offenders designed to rehabilitate them and thereby prevent future breaches of the public safety, its interest should be considered sufficiently compelling (assuming other requirements of strict scrutiny are satisfied) to outweigh the offender's claim of a constitutional right to object.[222]

Indeed, in the prison context, the Supreme Court has occasionally required only that challenged prison practices further "an important or substantial governmental interest"— something less than a "compelling interest."[223] In *Pell v. Procunier,*[224] for example, the Court cited the "paramount objective" of offender rehabilitation and used such a standard to uphold a prison ban on face-to-face interviews with members of the press that was asserted to violate the First Amendment. "Rehabilitation" was also considered a "substantial governmental interest" in *Procunier v. Martinez,*[225] although the Court made it clear that it would scrutinize carefully the mere assertion of an interest in rehabilitation. The state in *Martinez* had cited "inmate rehabilitation" as justification for the censorship of statements in prison mail that "magnify grievances" or "unduly complain."[226] The Court found this contention wanting, noting that the state did not "specify what contribution the suppression of complaints makes to the rehabilitation of criminals"[227] and that "the weight of professional

---

[216]*See* Allen, *Criminal Justice, Legal Values, and the Rehabilitative Ideal,* 50 J. Crim. L. Criminology & Police Sci. 226 (1959).

[217]*See generally* F. Allen, The Decline of the Rehabilitative Ideal: Penal Policy and Social Purpose (1981); Burt, *Cruelty, Hypocrisy, and the Rehabilitative Ideal in Corrections,* 16 Int'l J.L. & Psychiatry 359 (1993).

[218]*See, e.g.,* Jones v. United States, 463 U.S. 354, 368 (1983).

[219]*See, e.g.,* Jacobson v. Massachusetts, 197 U.S. 11, 25–27 (1905).

[220]Kelley v. Johnson, 425 U.S. 238, 247 (1976).

[221]*See generally* G. Ezorsky, Philosophical Perspectives on Punishment (1972); J. Hall, General Principles of Criminal Law 296–324 (1960); H. Hart, Punishment and Responsibility: Essays in the Philosophy of Law (1968); H. Packer, The Limits of the Criminal Sanction 35–61 (1968); Greenawalt, *Punishment,* 74 J. Crim. L. Criminology 343 (1983).

[222]Winick, *supra* note 110, at 373–76.

[223]Procunier v. Martinez, 416 U.S. 398, 413 (1974).

[224]417 U.S. 817, 823, 827–28 (1974).

[225]416 U.S. 396 (1974). The Court's reference to a "substantial" rather than a "compelling" interest reflects a shift from strict scrutiny to a form of intermediate scrutiny applicable when constitutional rights are infringed within the prison. *See, e.g.,* Washington v. Harper, 404 U.S. 210, 223 (1990) (upholding prison practices if reasonably related to a legitimate penological objective); *see supra* notes 29–30 and accompanying text.

[226]416 U.S. at 399.

[227]*Id.* at 416.

opinion seems to be that inmate freedom to correspond with outsiders advances rather than retards the goal of rehabilitation."[228]

The governmental interest in rehabilitation in furtherance of the police power goal of protecting community safety can thus be regarded as a "compelling" interest and certainly would meet the "substantial" interest test sometimes used in prison contexts. The proposed treatment, however, must be scrutinized to determine whether it actually furthers the asserted governmental interest in rehabilitation. If the "weight of professional opinion" regards the proposed treatment as ineffective, for example, the courts may well reject the asserted justification for its imposition.[229] The effectiveness of rehabilitation programs for offenders remains an unresolved question. Since the 1970s, relatively noncontroversial "counseling" and education programs have been supplemented, both in the prison and in the community, with increasingly more sophisticated rehabilitative programs that use drug treatment, behavior modification techniques, and other controversial therapies.[230] Although the empirical issues remain far from resolved, there is substantial concern that rehabilitative efforts that have been tried within prisons have not worked.[231] A National Academy of Sciences' study of offender rehabilitation concluded that "[t]he entire body of research appears to justify only the conclusion that we do not know of any program or method of rehabilitation that could be guaranteed to reduce the criminal activity of released offenders."[232] Courts, of course, are properly disinclined to second-guess legislatures, which are institutionally better equipped and politically more appropriate than the judiciary to make policy judgments grounded on scientific or technological facts and assumptions. But when the government seeks to impose intrusive treatment techniques on the basis of its interest in rehabilitation and those techniques do not seem likely to work, courts may well find the asserted justification wanting.

Judicial reluctance to approve such intrusive rehabilitation will increase to the extent that the treatment in question is deemed "experimental."[233] Whereas counseling and education programs and even a number of the behavioral approaches have frequently been used in the correctional context,[234] aversive techniques using severe aversive conditioners, and the organic techniques—psychotropic medication, electroconvulsive therapy, electronic stimulation of the brain, and surgical interventions such as castration for sex offenders

---

[228]*Id.* at 412.

[229]Procunier v. Martinez, 416 U.S. at 412–14.

[230]*See generally* J. MITFORD, KIND AND USUAL PUNISHMENT (1973); D. WEXLER, MENTAL HEALTH LAW: MAJOR ISSUES 17–18 (1981); Delgado, *Organically Induced Behavioral Change in Correctional Institutions: Release Decisions and "New Man" Phenomena,* 50 S. CAL. L. REV. 215, 217–18, 223–38 (1977); Halleck, *Psychiatry and Social Control: Two Contradictory Scenarios, in* MENTALLY ILL OFFENDERS AND THE CRIMINAL JUSTICE SYSTEM 24 (N. Beren & B. Toomey eds., 1979); Opton, *Psychiatric Violence Against Prisoners: When Therapy is Punishment,* 45 MISS. L.J., 605 (1974); Rothman, *Behavior Modification in Total Institutions,* 5 HASTINGS CTR. REP. 17 (1975); Spece, *Conditioning and Other Technologies Used to "Treat?" "Rehabilitate?" "Demolish?" Prisoners and Mental Patients,* 45 S. CAL. L. REV. 616 (1972).

[231]*See generally* D. LIPTON ET AL., THE EFFECTIVENESS OF CORRECTIONAL TREATMENT (1975); PANEL ON RESEARCH ON REHABILITATION TECHNIQUES OF THE NATIONAL RESEARCH COUNCIL, NEW DIRECTIONS IN THE REHABILITATION OF CRIMINAL OFFENDERS (S. Martin et al. eds., 1981) [hereinafter NEW DIRECTIONS]; PANEL ON RESEARCH IN REHABILITATIVE TECHNIQUES OF THE NATIONAL RESEARCH COUNCIL, THE REHABILITATION OF CRIMINAL OFFENDERS: PROBLEMS AND PROSPECTS (L. Sechrest et al. eds., 1979); PRESIDENT'S COMM'N ON LAW ENFORCEMENT & ADMINISTRATION OF JUSTICE, THE CHALLENGE OF CRIME IN A FREE SOCIETY 412 (1967); Martinson, *What Works?— Questions and Answers about Prison Reform,* 35 PUB. INTEREST 22 (1974).

[232]NEW DIRECTIONS, *supra* note 231, at 3.

[233]*See* Winick, *supra* note 110, at 403–07.

[234]*Id.* at 352–65.

and psychosurgery—have been rarely used in prison rehabilitation[235] and may be regarded as experimental in this context. To the extent that the prison seeks to use such traditional mental health treatment techniques as psychotropic medication or electroconvulsive therapy to treat a prisoner's mental disorder, the prisoner is either transferred to a hospital setting[236] or treated in a prison psychiatric or medical ward.[237] To the extent that the government relies on its *parens patriae* power, the right-to-refuse-treatment question here would seem analogous to that presented by *parens patriae* treatment in the civil hospital context considered earlier. Such treatment should require, among other things, demonstration that the offender is incompetent to participate in treatment decisions. To the extent, however, that such treatment is given not to cure a prisoner's diagnosed mental disorder, but in some fashion to "rehabilitate" the offender in order to minimize future threats to community safety, such use would appear to be highly experimental and controversial and to raise questions of professional ethics.

Whether such experimental use of intrusive therapies for correctional rehabilitation, as opposed to treatment of a specified mental disorder, meets the compelling interest test presents a question that has not been addressed in the case law. It may be possible, however, for the courts to avoid its resolution by using an approach drawn from administrative law. The question can be asked whether typical correctional statutes, authorizing correctional authorities to "rehabilitate" their charges, serve as sufficient authorization for such experimental use of traditional mental health treatment techniques or of new intrusive rehabilitative techniques that are themselves experimental. When a governmental agency purports to have authority to infringe on fundamental rights, courts have sometimes insisted on an explicit legislative expression of that authority.[238] This doctrine has special force in the First Amendment context, where courts have traditionally ruled that the delegation of power to restrict First Amendment rights requires more than broad legislative directives to guide the restricting authority.[239]

The leading case for this special version of the administrative law delegation doctrine is *Kent v. Dulles.*[240] The *Passport Act of 1926* had given the Secretary of State authority to "grant and issue passports . . . under such rules as the President shall designate and prescribe."[241] At the time of Congress' delegation, a passport was regarded as a mere privilege to which no one had a claim of entitlement[242]; it was not yet a requirement for travel abroad.[243] This began to change after World War II, however, and by the early 1950s most

---

[235]*Id.* at 365–73.

[236]*See* Vitek v. Jones, 445 U.S. 480 (1980).

[237]*See* Kaufman, *supra* note 79.

[238]*E.g.,* Regents of the Univ. of Cal. v. Bakke, 438 U.S. 265, 308–09 (1973) (Powell, J., stating judgment of the Court); Hampton v. Mow Sun Wong, 426 U.S. 88, 105–14 (1976); United States v. Robel, 389 U.S. 258, 275–76 (1967) (Brennan, J., concurring); Greene v. McElroy, 360 U.S. 474, 507 (1959); Kent v. Dulles, 357 U.S. 116, 129 (1958); *see* J. FREEDMAN, CRISIS AND LEGITIMACY: THE ADMINISTRATIVE PROCESS AND AMERICAN GOVERNMENT 83–85 (1978); L. JAFFE, JUDICIAL CONTROL OF ADMINISTRATIVE ACTION 72–73 (abr. ed. 1965); B. SCHWARTZ, ADMINISTRATIVE LAW § 2.9, at 49–50 (2d ed. 1984); L. TRIBE, AMERICAN CONSTITUTIONAL LAW § 5–17, at 365–66 (2d ed. 1988); Stewart, *The Transformation of American Administrative Law,* 88 HARV. L. REV. 1669, 1680–81 (1975); Winick, *Forfeiture of Attorneys' Fees under RICO and CCE and the Right to Counsel of Choice: The Constitutional Dilemma and How to Avoid It,* 43 U. MIAMI L. REV. 765, 853–65 (1989).

[239]*See, e.g.,* City of Lakewood v. Plain Dealer Pub. Co., 486 U.S. 750, 756–57 (1988); Shuttleworth v. City of Birmingham, 394 U.S. 147, 150–51 (1969).

[240]357 U.S. 116 (1958).

[241]Ch. 772, 44 Stat. 887–88 (codified as amended at 22 U.S.C. § 211(a) (1982), *cited in Kent,* 357 U.S. at 123.

[242]SCHWARTZ, *supra* note 238, § 15.14, at 233.

[243]*Kent,* 357 U.S. at 121; SCHWARTZ, *supra* note 238, § 5.14, at 233.

countries required a passport for entry.[244] This increased importance of the passport made its possession essential to the exercise of the constitutional right to travel abroad and led to the recognition that although once a privilege, the passport had become a right.[245]

In 1952, at the height of the Cold War, the Secretary of State invoked the broad power conferred by the Passport Act and adopted regulations prohibiting issuance of passports to members of the Communist Party.[246] The 1952 regulations amounted to a wholesale abrogation of the right of communists to travel outside the United States. Could the broad language of the Passport Act of 1926 support this new assertion of authority, particularly at a time when the passport had been transformed from a privilege to a right?

Confronting the issue in *Kent,* the Supreme Court began its analysis by noting that if a regulation affects the exercise of a constitutionally protected right, the Court "will not readily infer that Congress gave the Secretary of State unbridled discretion to grant or withhold it."[247] The Court further noted that any regulation of such a constitutional liberty "must be pursuant to the law-making function of the Congress,[248] which if delegated, must be delegated pursuant to an adequate standard.[249] Although the delegation doctrine had not been applied strictly in this period to invalidate broad congressional delegations,[250] the Court invoked it with renewed seriousness in *Kent* in view of the constitutional liberties at stake: "Where activities or enjoyment, natural and often necessary to the well-being of an American citizen, such as travel are involved, we will construe narrowly all delegated powers that curtail or dilute them."[251] Referring to the Passport Act, the Court was hesitant "to find in this broad generalized power an authority to trench so heavily on the rights of the citizen."[252] The Court thereby avoided what it characterized as the "important constitutional question"[253] that would have been raised if Congress had given authority to the Secretary of State "to withhold passports to citizens because of their beliefs or associations."[254] Noting that "Congress had made no such provision in explicit terms" in the Passport Act, the Court held that "absent one," the Secretary of State could not enforce the regulations.[255]

This approach therefore requires a more explicit delegation of authority when an agent of Congress asserts power to act in a constitutionally sensitive area than is required in other circumstances.[256] Nevertheless, modern delegation cases allow the delegation of congressional power to the Executive Branch with undetailed expressions of congressional pol-

---

[244]*Kent,* 357 U.S. at 124, 128; Schactman v. Dulles, 225 F.2d 938, 941 (D.C. Cir. 1955); JAFFE, *supra* note 238, at 72.

[245]*Kent,* 357 U.S. at 125–27.

[246]Dep't Reg. No. 108–162, 17 Fed. Reg. 8013 (1952) (effective Aug. 28, 1952) (codified in 22 C.F.R. § 51.135-143 (1957 Supp.)), *cited in Kent,* 357 U.S. at 117–18 & nn.1–2, 124 & n.7.

[247]357 U.S. at 129.

[248]*Id.*

[249]*Id.* (invoking the delegation doctrine by citing to Panama Refining Co. v. Ryan, 293 U.S. 385, 420–30 (1935)).

[250]*See* Winick, *supra* note 238, at 858 n.462 (citing cases).

[251]357 U.S. at 129.

[252]*Id.*

[253]*Id.* at 130.

[254]*Id.*

[255]*Id.*

[256]The function of requiring those delegated power by Congress to adhere to congressional policy is to ensure that "important choices of social policy are made by Congress, the branch of our Government most responsive to the popular will." Industrial Union Dep't, AFL–CIO v. American Petroleum Inst., 448 U.S. 607, 685 (1985) (Rehnquist, J., concurring); *see also* Panama Refining Co. v. Ryan, 293 U.S. 388, 421 (1935); JAFFE, *supra* note 238, at 33–34; Stewart, *supra* note 238, at 1672–73, 1694.

icy.[257] If, however, the statute delegates power to regulate a personal right, more detailed delegation and clearer expression of congressional policy will be required.[258] Although the broad delegation contained in the Passport Act could have been read to cover the asserted authority, the Court properly hesitated to conclude that Congress had intended to confer this power on its agent. The Court did not treat *Kent* simply as a case of statutory construction. The broad language of the Passport Act was not ambiguous, and the congressional history did not negate this application. *Kent* was an administrative law case in which the agency asserted an "unbridled discretion" to act in a constitutionally questionable manner.[259] The Court quite sensibly avoided deciding whether Congress had the constitutional power to withhold passports on the basis of citizens' beliefs or associations, either directly or through authority granted to an agency. A constitutional holding would have been preemptive. Instead the Court, in effect, expressed to Congress its uncertainty as to whether Congress had intended to delegate this constitutionally questionable power to its agent, thereby remanding the issue to Congress for clarification.

The approach of *Kent v. Dulles* may be especially useful in the right-to-refuse-treatment context where involuntary intrusive treatment is sought to be justified under broad delegations of authority to correctional administrators to "rehabilitate" prisoners or under statutes sentencing convicted defendants to their custody "for treatment and supervision."[260] Particularly when faced with correctional treatment that would seriously invade fundamental constitutional rights, courts may well hold that a general legislative delegation of this kind is insufficient to support the agency's assertion of authority to provide intrusive involuntary treatment, particularly of an experimental nature. This technique allows courts to avoid deciding difficult constitutional issues and, in effect, to remand the underlying policy questions to the legislature for decision with the knowledge that its choice implicates fundamental values and is subject to searching constitutional scrutiny.[261] Given the unlikelihood that a legislature delegating such broad authority to correctional administrators contemplated the intrusive kinds of treatment now occasionally used—treatments that probably were not in use at the time the relevant statutes were adopted—such a legislative remand for a "second look" seems especially appropriate. Courts may invoke the delegation doctrine of *Kent v. Dulles* to avoid deciding the difficult substantive constitutional issues presented and instead hold that the asserted discretion of correctional administrators to impose intrusive therapy involuntarily is *ultra vires*.

If courts do not avoid this difficult question through use of the doctrine of *Kent v. Dulles* and determine that the state interest in the rehabilitation of criminal offenders qualifies as "compelling," the question will remain whether other aspects of strict scrutiny also will be

---

[257]*See* JAFFE, *supra* note 238, at 57–72; B. SCHWARTZ, *supra* note 238, § 2.6, at 43–44; Winick, *supra* note 238, at 859 n.468.

[258]*See* United States v. Robel, 389 U.S. 258, 275 (1967) (Brennan, J., concurring); Greene v. McElroy, 360 U.S. 474, 507 (1967).

[259]357 U.S. at 129. In a number of other contexts involving the application of similarly "unbridled discretion" in constitutionally questionable ways, the Court used what can be seen as related approaches to that used in *Kent. See* Thompson v. Oklahoma, 487 U.S. 815, 849–59 (1988) (O'Connor, J., concurring); Furman v. Georgia, 408 U.S. 238 (1972) (per curiam); Delaware v. Prouse, 440 U.S. 648 (1979); Smith v. Goguen, 415 U.S. 566 (1974); Winick, *supra* note 238, at 859–61 n.469, 868–69.

[260]*See* PAROLE COMMISSION AND REORGANIZATION ACT, 18 U.S.C. § 5010(c) (1976) (repealed 1984). *See also* ALI MODEL PENAL CODE §7.01(1)(b) (Proposed Official Draft 1962).

[261]*See* A. BICKEL, THE LEAST DANGEROUS BRANCH: THE SUPREME COURT AT THE BAR OF POLITICS 111–98 (1962); FREEDMAN, *supra* note 238, at 83; Tribe, *The Emerging Reconnection of Individual Rights and Institutional Design: Federalism, Bureaucracy, and Due Process of Law Making,* 10 CREIGHTON L. REV. 433, 442–43 (1977); Winick, *supra* note 238, at 864 & n.480.

satisfied. As indicated earlier, whenever intrusive treatment triggering First Amendment scrutiny is involved, the clear and present danger standard also must be met.[262] Although *Harper* did not apply a clear and present danger test in its consideration of the police power justification of protecting others from harm asserted to justify involuntary medication of the prisoner involved there, no First Amendment issue was raised in the case.[263] In any event, even if the relaxed scrutiny applied generally in prison cases does not include a clear and present danger component, such scrutiny should be reserved for cases involving deference to correctional administrators in matters of institutional safety and security. Where the protection from harm of those outside the institution is asserted as the justification for forced medication, the concern for institutional security is not implicated. Although correctional administrators may be entitled to an extra measure of deference in regard to dealing with institutional security, no such deference is appropriate in the selection of modes of intrusive treatment designed to rehabilitate offenders. When treatment is administered not to protect other inmates or staff but to reduce future recidivism, the considerations justifying relaxed scrutiny do not apply. When that treatment invades interests protected by the First Amendment, the clear and present danger standard therefore should be required to be met.

The state's interest in correctional rehabilitation is similar to the interest in treating insanity acquittees to avoid recidivism discussed above.[264] To meet the clear and present danger test, the harm to be prevented must be imminent.[265] Repeat offenses by imprisoned criminal offenders, however likely they may be in general, cannot satisfy the requirement of imminence because recidivism cannot occur until after discharge from prison. Even for prisoners on parole or discharged to community settings, recidivism would not seem sufficiently imminent to satisfy First Amendment scrutiny unless the particular offender were shown to present a high likelihood of imminent lawless conduct.[266] For treatment approaches that do not call for First Amendment scrutiny, like psychotherapy or counseling approaches and most of the behavior therapies, the interest in correctional rehabilitation should satisfy the compelling interest test of strict scrutiny.

Thus, several police power interests may justify involuntary intrusive treatment. As previously discussed, in appropriate circumstances the police power interest in preserving institutional order and security may suffice, as may the state's interest in providing treatment to criminal defendants found incompetent to stand trial in order to restore them to competence so they may be tried. In addition, the state interest in providing treatment to reduce the potential recidivism of insanity acquittees and criminal offenders sometimes will

---

[262]*See supra* notes 127–29, 213–14 and accompanying text.

[263]*See supra* note 69 and accompanying text.

[264]*See supra,* part C2(b)(4).

[265]*See supra* notes 127–29 and accompanying text.

[266]Even when such a risk is shown to be imminent, alternative approaches may be available to protect against criminality, such as revocation of parole, preventive detention, or civil commitment. *See infra* chapter 16, part B (discussing the ''least restrictive alternative'' principle). In addition, treatment administered for the purpose of avoiding recidivism also must be medically appropriate for the individual. *See infra* chapter 16, part A (discussing therapeutic appropriateness principle). Finally, treatment administered for purposes of offender rehabilitation, a traditional purpose of punishment, can be considered to qualify as punishment within the meaning of the Eighth Amendment. *See supra* chapter 12 (discussing when treatment is punishment under the Eighth Amendment). As a result, such treatment may not be unnecessarily painful or degrading, disproportionate to the offense, unauthorized as punishment, or in other ways an affront to human dignity. *See id.*

suffice to outweigh the individual's right to refuse treatment. Other institutional interests within the purview of the government's police power, however, including the interest in institutional management, administrative convenience, or fiscal economy, should not alone suffice. Although it would make the administration of a correctional facility much easier and less expensive if inmates could be kept in a docile state through the use of heavy dosages of medication, the periodic use of electroconvulsive therapy, or even psychosurgery, these interests cannot outweigh the fundamental constitutional rights invaded by forced intrusive treatments of the kinds mentioned.

This chapter has analyzed the differing state interests that may be asserted to justify involuntary mental health treatment in order to determine which ones satisfy the compelling interest requirement of strict scrutiny. For treatments that are not sufficiently intrusive to trigger strict scrutiny, such as the verbal and most of the behavioral techniques, the state must assert only a legitimate interest, a standard that is considerably easier to satisfy.[267] With the exception of the Eighth Amendment, which places an absolute bar on treatment that would constitute punishment meeting the cruel and unusual standard, constitutional scrutiny of involuntary treatment will require courts to engage in a balancing of interests to determine whether the state's interest outweighs the individual's constitutionally protected liberty.

Apart from scrutiny of governmental interests, courts also will consider whether the treatment proposed is an appropriate means to achieve the state's interest. For intrusive treatment, even when the state's *parens patriae* or police power interests are deemed sufficiently compelling to outweigh the individual's right to refuse treatment, other aspects of strict scrutiny may not be satisfied. The following chapter discusses such requirements— the therapeutic appropriateness principle and the least intrusive means principle. Unless these requirements also are met, intrusive treatment cannot be administered over objection.

---

[267]*E.g.,* United States v. Stine, 675 F.2d 69 (3d Cir.), *cert denied,* 458 U.S. 1110 (1982) (applying rational basis test to uphold psychological counseling imposed as a condition of probation).

Chapter 16
SCRUTINY OF THE MEANS USED TO ACCOMPLISH GOVERNMENTAL INTERESTS

Even when the governmental interest asserted to justify involuntary mental health treatment is found to be compelling, the state also may be required to demonstrate that such treatment is an appropriate means to accomplish that interest. When the individual involved is not mentally ill or when the treatment sought to be imposed is not therapeutically appropriate for the patient, the state's attempt to administer such treatment should be rejected. In addition, even if the individual is mentally ill and the treatment in question can be justified as being in the therapeutic interests of the patient, the Constitution may impose an additional limit on any treatment that invades a fundamental constitutional right, as do those on the higher range of the continuum of intrusiveness developed in chapters 2–8. Outside the context of treatment administered in the prison to prevent harm to other inmates or staff, which the courts scrutinize under a more deferential "reasonableness" standard, the state should be required to show that the treatment in question is necessary to the achievement of its compelling interest. If less intrusive alternative means would suffice, use of the more intrusive treatment is constitutionally impermissible.

A. When Treatment Cannot Be Used to Accomplish State Purposes: The Therapeutic Appropriateness Principle

As indicated in chapter 15, the Supreme Court's 1992 decision in *Riggins v. Nevada* suggests in dicta that antipsychotic medication may not be forcibly administered unless it is medically appropriate for the individual.[1] This appears to be an important newly crystallized constitutional principle, and the Court's opinion clarifies that previous language in the Court's 1990 decision in *Washington v. Harper*[2] should be taken seriously. In *Harper,* the Court upheld a state's use of antipsychotic medication to forcibly treat a mentally ill prisoner found to be dangerous to himself and others when not taking such medication. In the course of its opinion, the Court noted that mellaril, the treatment administered, was in the prisoner's medical interests.[3]

The *Harper* opinion thereby seemed to suggest that medical appropriateness was a condition for involuntary antipsychotic drug treatment. The Court's opinion, however, was ambiguous in this regard and left the matter unclear. Justice Stevens's partial dissent in *Harper* questioned the majority's assumption that only medically appropriate treatment could be authorized under the prison regulation upheld, pointing out that its language did not

---

[1]504 U.S. 127, 135 (1992) (state must show that medication sought to be imposed over objection is "medically appropriate"); *accord* Woodland v. Angus, 820 F. Supp. 1497, 1508 (D. Utah 1993); State v. Garcia, 658 A.2d 947, 961 (Conn. 1995).

[2]494 U.S. 210, 222–23 (1990).

[3]*Id.*

require such a showing.[4] In any event, because the Court had upheld involuntary treatment that the record had shown was in the prisoner's medical interests, its holding did not necessarily require rejection of treatment administered for purposes of institutional security that was not also in the inmate's medical interests. At most, the language in *Harper* concerning medical appropriateness was dicta. It was possible that the medical appropriateness of the drug treatment in *Harper* was merely a factor that allowed the Court to feel more comfortable about authorizing involuntary intrusive treatment. The Court's opinion thus did not resolve the issue of whether the therapeutic appropriateness of a treatment is a constitutional condition for its involuntary administration. Could a state impose involuntary treatment with psychotropic medication as a form of "chemical restraint" in order to deal with an assaultive inmate who was not mentally ill? *Harper* did not clearly answer this question.

Riggins sheds considerable light on this issue and demonstrates that the Court regards therapeutic appropriateness as a necessary condition for exercise of the states' authority to impose intrusive mental health treatment.[5] The *Riggins* Court reversed the conviction of a criminal defendant forcibly administered antipsychotic medication during his trial. The Court assumed that the drugs had altered the defendant's demeanor and probably also his ability to testify and communicate with counsel. The Court found that the record in the trial court had not contained any judicial findings supporting a sufficient governmental interest to justify the administration of medication during trial to an objecting defendant.[6] In dicta, the Court mentioned two state interests that presumably would have sufficed to justify forced medication had the record supported their presence in the case. First, the Court referred to the governmental interest that had been involved in *Harper*—the state's interest in protecting the safety of the individual, other inmates, and institutional staff.[7] Second, the Court mentioned as a possible additional justification for involuntary medication the state's interest in restoring and maintaining a criminal defendant's mental competency so that he could stand trial.[8] Significantly, in referring to each of these two potentially overriding state interests, the Court noted that the state would have to show that the medication sought to be

---

[4]*Id.* at 215 (quoting Washington Department of Corrections Special Offender Center Policy 600.30). Justice Stevens correctly pointed out the discrepancy between the majority's assumption and the language of the prison policy:

> Policy 600.30 permits forced administration of psychotropic drugs on a mentally ill inmate based purely on the impact that his disorder has on the security of the prison environment. The provisions of the Policy make no reference to any expected benefit on the inmate's medical condition. . . . Although any application of Policy 600.30 requires a medical judgment as to a prisoner's medical condition and the cause of his behavior, the Policy does not require a determination that forced medication would advance his medical interest. . . . Thus, most unfortunately, there is simply no basis for the Court's assertion that medication under the Policy must be to advance the prisoner's medical interest.

Id. at 243–45 (Stevens, J., joined by Brennan & Marshall, J.J., concurring in part and dissenting in part).

[5]*See* Winick, *New Directions in the Right to Refuse Mental Health Treatment: The Implications of* Riggins v. Nevada, 2 WM. & MARY BILL OF RTS. J. 205, 220 (1993); Winick, *Psychotropic Medication in the Criminal Trial Process: The Constitutional and Therapeutic Implications of* Riggins v. Nevada, 10 N.Y.L. SCH. J. HUM. RTS. 637, 690–703 (1993).

[6]Riggins v. Nevada, 504 U.S. 127, 138 (1992).

[7]*Id.* at 135.

[8]*Id.*

imposed also would be "medically appropriate."[9] Although this language was dicta, the Court was reiterating its prior dicta in *Harper* and clearly expressing its view that such medication could forcibly be imposed only if the drug's administration was medically justified.

Riggins thus embraces an important new principle first suggested in *Harper*.[10] The Court's language seems to make it clear that the Court regards forcible intrusive mental health treatment as constitutionally impermissible unless, at a minimum, the individual is mentally ill and the proposed intervention is therapeutically appropriate. Therapeutic appropriateness is not a sufficient justification for involuntary treatment; both *Harper* and *Riggins* identify additional standards that must be satisfied as a condition for forced medication. However, the therapeutic appropriateness of treatment for the individual involved is a necessary condition. Absent therapeutic justification, these interventions would offend due process and (in the case of intrusive treatments that invade mental processes) arguably the First Amendment as well.

---

[9]*Id.; accord* Woodland v. Angus, 820 F. Supp. 1497, 1508 (D. Utah 1993) (citing *Riggins*); State v. Garcia, 658 A.2d 947, 961 (Conn. 1995). The constitutional requirement of therapeutic appropriateness parallels a similar requirement of medical ethics. *See Harper*, 494 U.S. at 222 n.8; *id.* at 245 n.11 (Stevens, J., joined by Brennan & Marshall, J.J., concurring in part and dissenting in part); State v. Perry, 610 So. 2d 746, 752 (La. 1992). The Hippocratic Oath, which is at the core of medical ethics, imposes a duty of beneficence and of nonmaleficence on the physician that is inconsistent with the administration of treatment that is not in her patient's best interests. The Oath provides:

> I swear by Apollo the physician, by Aesculapius, Hygeia, and Panacea, and I take to witness all the gods, all the goddesses, to keep according to my ability and my judgment the following Oath: [I] will prescribe regimen for the good of my patients according to my ability and my judgment and never do harm to anyone. To please no one will I prescribe a deadly drug, nor give advice which may cause his death . . . . I will preserve the purity of my life and my art . . . . In every house where I come I will enter only for the good of my patients, keeping myself far from all intentional ill-doing. . . .

Id. (quoting Hippocrates c. 460–400 B.C., STEDMAN'S MEDICAL DICTIONARY 647 (4th Unabridged Lawyer's Ed. 1976)); *see* Winick, *Competency to Be Executed: A Therapeutic Jurisprudence Perspective*, 10 BEHAV. SCI. & L. 317, 332 (1992). The concept of therapeutic appropriateness as a condition for psychiatric hospitalization is also reflected in the official policy of the American Psychiatric Association. *See* AM. PSYCHIATRIC ASS'N TASK FORCE REPORT NO. 34, CONSENT TO VOLUNTARY HOSPITALIZATION 6, 11 (1993) (recommending clinical assessment of the "appropriateness" of a patient for voluntary hospitalization prior to admission and periodically thereafter); *id.* at 11 ("Hospitalization should continue only if it is medically necessary, the patient is receiving active treatment, and hospitalization is the least restrictive alternative available or potentially useful.").

[10]Although first explicitly articulated in *Harper*, the therapeutic appropriateness principle can be seen beneath the surface of earlier Supreme Court mental health cases. In Jackson v. Indiana, 406 U.S. 715 (1972), the Court applied substantive due process to prohibit the continued confinement in a mental hospital of a criminal defendant on the basis of his incompetency to stand trial once it became clear that treatment would not succeed in restoring his competency in this regard. Because the purpose of such confinement was treatment designed to restore competency, continued commitment could not be justified once it became clear that this purpose was unachievable. The defendant in *Jackson* was a mentally deficient deaf mute, but his mental deficiency alone could not justify continued commitment. Although the Court did not put it this way, his continued commitment—confinement in a mental hospital without treatment that could help his condition—was not therapeutically justified. The therapeutic appropriateness principle also can be seen under the surface of O'Connor v. Donaldson, 422 U.S. 563 (1975), in which the Court found unconstitutional commitment to a mental hospital of a mentally ill person for a 15-year period of "enforced custodial care," where the only therapy administered was "milieu therapy," which the Court found to be "a euphemism for confinement in the milieu of the mental hospital." *Id.* at 569. "A finding of mental illness alone," the Court held, "cannot justify a state's locking a person up against his will and keeping him indefinitely in simple custodial confinement." *Id.* at 575. Although the Court didn't say so, such custodial confinement without treatment would not have been therapeutically appropriate. *See also* Parham v. J.R., 442 U.S. 583, 600 (1979) (assuming that "a child [facing commitment to a mental institution] has a protected liberty interest not only in being free of unnecessary bodily restriction, but also in not being confined unnecessarily for medical treatment").

Riggins suggests an answer to the question posed earlier that *Harper* had left open. Due process will prohibit states from using psychotropic medication for inmate control or prevention of violence unless, at a minimum, individuals are mentally ill and the medication sought to be administered is in their medical interests. *Harper* noted this limitation in dicta in the context of forcible medication of a state prisoner with mellaril to reduce the risk to other inmates and staff. It would seem applicable in other contexts as well—in jails (as *Riggins* suggests), mental hospitals, nursing homes, and juvenile facilities. Similarly, this limitation should prohibit the use of such medication for other nontherapeutic purposes, such as institutional management or discipline, at least without a showing that the individual is mentally ill and the treatment is medically appropriate. A number of lower courts had previously recognized this restriction on the use of medication in mental hospitals and juvenile facilities, grounding it in other constitutional limitations.[11] *Riggins* provides clarification concerning the basis for this restriction by its application of what I have argued is best understood as a new constitutional principle of therapeutic appropriateness. Even though the state's purpose in using medication—maintenance of institutional security— would be legitimate and even ''compelling,'' the use of medication is not reasonably related to this purpose if it is not in the individual's medical interests.

This limitation also should apply to an attempt by a prison forcibly to use psychotropic medication or other intrusive mental health treatment techniques, perhaps including some forms of behavior therapy, in order to ''rehabilitate'' offenders and reduce their future potential for recidivism.[12] The rehabilitation of offenders and the reduction in criminality it would bring undoubtedly would qualify as compelling governmental interests.[13] Unless the prison inmate in question is mentally ill and the treatment is therapeutically appropriate for his or her condition, however, any attempt to impose intrusive treatment involuntarily for purposes of ''rehabilitation'' would seem constitutionally impermissible. For the same reasons, although the reduction of recidivism for those acquitted by reason of insanity would seem a compelling government interest, intrusive mental health treatment could not be administered involuntarily to insanity acquittees unless they were mentally ill and the treatment involved can be therapeutically justified.

Similarly, the involuntary administration to offenders of certain forms of mental health treatment as an aspect of criminal punishment should be considered constitutionally impermissible, at least absent satisfaction of these two conditions. A variety of intrusive treatment techniques have been proposed or actually used in correctional contexts,[14]

---

[11]*E.g.*, Nelson v. Heyne, 491 F.2d 352, 357 (7th Cir.), *cert. denied,* 417 U.S. 976 (1974) (Eighth Amendment right to freedom from cruel and unusual punishment); Johnson v. Solomon, 484 F. Supp. 278, 300 (D. Md. 1979) (same); Pena v. New York Div. for Youth, 419 F. Supp. 203, 210–11 (S.D.N.Y. 1976) (due process right to treatment and Eighth Amendment right to freedom from cruel and unusual punishment).

[12]*See* Winick, *Legal Limitations on Correctional Therapy and Research,* 65 MINN. L. REV. 331 (1982) (discussing use of these mental health treatment techniques in correctional settings).

[13]*See* Kelley v. Johnson, 425 U.S. 238, 247 (1976) (''[T]he promotion of safety of persons and property is unquestionably at the core of the State's police power.''); Pell v. Procunier, 417 U.S. 817, 823, 827–28 (1974) (referring to the ''paramount objective'' of offender rehabilitation); Procunier v. Martinez, 416 U.S. 396, 413 (1974) (referring to ''substantial governmental interest'' in rehabilitation of offenders); Winick, *supra* note 12, at 375–76; *supra* chapter 15, part C2(b)(v).

[14]*See* J. MITFORD, KIND AND USUAL PUNISHMENT (1973); STAFF OF SUBCOMM. ON CONSTITUTIONAL RIGHTS OF THE SEN. COMM. ON THE JUDICIARY, 93D CONG., 2D SESS., INDIVIDUAL RIGHTS AND THE FEDERAL ROLE IN BEHAVIOR MODIFICATION (1974); NEW DIRECTIONS IN THE REHABILITATION OF CRIMINAL OFFENDERS (Martin et al. eds., 1981); McConnell, *Stimulus/Response: Criminals Can Be Brainwashed—Now,* PSYCHOLOGY TODAY, Apr. 1970, at 14; Opton, *Psychiatric Violence Against Prisoners: When Therapy is Punishment,* 45 MISS. L.J. 605 (1974); Winick, *supra* note 12.

including psychosurgery,[15] surgical castration,[16] chemical castration using drugs like estrogen or depo-provera,[17] electroconvulsive therapy (ECT),[18] aversive conditioning,[19] and psychotropic medication.[20] Any use by the state of these or any other type of intrusive medical or psychiatric treatment for purposes of punishment would be subject to constitutional scrutiny under the therapeutic appropriateness principle.[21] Unless the recipient of such correctional treatment is mentally ill, such treatment may be constitutionally impermissible. Moreover, even if the criminal offender in question is mentally ill, the treatment administered would seem constitutionally permissible only if it is therapeutically justified. If treatment has no independent therapeutic justification, it would seem improper even if it

---

[15]*Supra* chapter 8; Winick, *supra* note 12, at 372–73; *see* Kaimowitz v. Michigan Dep't of Mental Health, No. 73–19434–AW (Wayne County [Mich.] Cir. Ct., July 10, 1973), *reprinted in* A. BROOKS, LAW, PSYCHIATRY AND THE MENTAL HEALTH SYSTEM 902, 913–14 (1974) (upholding challenge to psychosurgery at a state institution).

[16]*See* Skinner v. Oklahoma *ex rel.* Williamson, 316 U.S. 535 (1942) (invalidating under Equal Protection Clause criminal punishment for certain habitual offenders that included castration); P. LIPTON ET AL., THE EFFECTIVENESS OF CORRECTIONAL TREATMENT 290 (1975) (discussing Danish habitual sex offender program); Klerman & Dworkin, *Can Convicts Consent to Castration?,* 5 HASTINGS CTR. REP., Oct. 1975, at 17 (analyzing a case in which two California child molesters, facing indeterminate sentences, requested castration in the hope that the judge might consider probation); Wettstein, *A Psychiatric Perspective on Washington's Sexually Violent Predators Statute,* 15 U. PUGET SOUND L. REV. 597, 627 (1992); Wexler, *Mental Health Law and the Movement Toward Voluntary Treatment,* 62 CAL. L. REV. 671, 683 (1974) (discussing the case of a Colorado child molester agreeing, during plea bargaining, to submit to castration); Winick, *supra* note 12, at 371–72.

[17]*See* People v. Gauntlett, 352 N.W. 2d 310 (Ct. App.), *modified and remanded,* 353 N.W. 2d 463 (Mich. 1984), *on remand,* 394 N.W. 2d 437 (Ct. App. 1986) (invalidating condition of probation requiring sex offender to submit to depo–provera); Demsky, *The Use of Depo–Provera in the Treatment of Sex Offenders: The Legal Issues,* 5 J. LEGAL ISSUES 295 (1984); Rainear, *The Use of Depo–Provera for Treating Male Sex Offenders: A Review of the Constitutional and Medical Issues,* 16 TOLEDO L. REV. 181 (1984); Winick, *supra* note 12, at 371 n.210; *"Chemical Castration": Another Use for Depo-Provera,* 9 HASTINGS CTR. REP., Aug. 1979, at 10 (discussing "chemical castration" for sex offenders, using depo-provera and a variety of synthetic female hormones, which may cause permanent impotence).

[18]*Supra* chapter 6; Winick, *supra* note 12, at 368–70.

[19]*See supra* chapter 4; Knecht v. Gillman, 488 F.2d 1136 (8th Cir. 1973) (use of apomorphine, a vomit–inducing drug, in a security hospital aversive conditioning program); Mackey v. Procunier, 477 F.2d 877, 877–78 (9th Cir. 1973) (use of succinylcholine, a paralyzing drug, in a California prison aversive conditioning program); Canterino v. Wilson, 546 F. Supp. 174 (W.D. Ky. 1982) (use of punitive tier program in state prison that restricted basic privileges); Taylor v. Manson, Civ. No. H-75-37 (D. Conn. 1975) (constitutional challenge to prison program alleged to coerce inmates to participate in experimental behavior modification program for pedophiles); Price v. Sheppard, 239 N.W. 2d 905 (Minn. 1976) (adopting strict scrutiny standard for aversive conditioning programs); Blatte, *State Prisons and the Use of Behavior Control,* 4 HASTINGS CTR. REP., Sept. 1974 at 11, 11 (survey indicating at least seven state prison systems used aversive conditioning in correctional therapy); McConnell, *supra* note 14, at 74 (advocating coercive use of aversive conditioning and other types of behavior modification); Winick, *supra* note 12, at 359; Wolfe & Marino, *A Program of Behavior Treatment for Incarcerated Pedophiles,* 13 AM. CRIM. L. REV. 69, 77–78 (1975) (program for child molesters in Connecticut prison pairing electric shocks to prisoner's groin area with arousal experienced by viewing slides of naked children).

[20]*See supra* chapter 5; *e.g.,* United States *ex rel.* Wilson v. Coughlin, 472 F.2d 100 (7th Cir. 1973); Nelson v. Heyne, 355 F. Supp. 451 (N.D. Ind. 1972), *aff'd,* 491 F.2d 352 (7th Cir.), *cert. denied,* 417 U.S. 976 (1974); MITFORD, *supra* note 14, at 129; Bomstein, *The Forcible Administration of Drugs to Prisoners and Mental Patients,* 9 CLEARINGHOUSE REV. 379 (1975); Opton, *supra* note 14; Sitnick, *Major Tranquilizers in Prison, Drug Therapy and the Unconsenting Inmate,* 11 WILLIAMETTE L. J. 378 (1975); Winick, *supra* note 12, at 365–68.

[21]In addition to substantive due process, such "treatment" administered as punishment may also offend the Eighth Amendment's ban on cruel and unusual punishments. *See supra* chapter 12; Winick, *supra* note 12, at 330. Moreover, if applied to some but not to other similarly situated offenders, it may violate equal protection. *See supra* chapter 14; *e.g.,* Skinner v. Oklahoma *ex rel.* Williamson, 316 U.S. 535 (1942). The therapeutic appropriateness principle (as well as the Eighth Amendment) also would limit the use of intrusive treatment, such as psychotropic medication, for the purpose of restoring incompetent death row inmates to competence so that they can be executed. State v. Perry, 610 So. 2d 746 (La. 1992); Winick, *supra* note 9.

furthers other important goals of punishment, such as the reduction of recidivism or the incapacitation or deterrence of offenders.

Castration or other intrusive treatment interventions for sex offenders, for example, has been advocated as a means of preventing the offender from committing future sexual offenses or deterring others from doing so. However, such utilitarian justifications should not suffice to sanction use of a medical procedure that is not in the therapeutic interests of the individual. Medical punishment would seem irreconcilable with the therapeutic appropriateness principle.

Most sexual offenders are not mentally ill in the sense that would justify mental hospitalization and imposition of intrusive forms of mental health treatment.[22] For example, merely labeling a class of offenders as *mentally disordered sex offenders* or as *sexually violent predators* does not itself mean that they are mentally ill within the meaning of the Constitution or that their hospitalization or treatment would be medically justified. In *Foucha v. Louisiana*,[23] which can be seen as an application of the therapeutic appropriateness principle,[24] the U.S. Supreme Court declined to treat an accepted diagnostic category— antisocial personality disorder—as a mental illness sufficient to justify the continued psychiatric hospitalization of an insanity acquitee who, although diagnosed as dangerous, had no other illness or disability. Although the insanity acquitee in *Foucha* was diagnosed as having antisocial personality disorder, this did not qualify as a mental illness for which continued involuntary confinement in a mental hospital would have been medically appropriate.

Neither *sexual psychopathy,* the label once given to the propensity to commit sex offenses,[25] nor *antisocial personality disorder,* the condition rejected as a basis for involuntary hospitalization in *Foucha,* are medical conditions for which psychiatric hospitalization or intrusive treatment would be therapeutically justified. In its study on sexual psychopath legislation, the Group for the Advancement of Psychiatry concluded that these laws "lack clinical validity."[26] The study found that sexual psychopathy is "not a psychiatric diagnostic category"[27] but "a meaningless grouping from a diagnostic and

---

[22]S. BRAKEL ET AL., THE MENTALLY DISABLED AND THE LAW 743 (3d ed. 1985) (referring to the "[g]rowing awareness that there is no specific group of individuals who can be labelled sexual psychopaths by acceptable medical standards and that there are no proven treatments for such offenders . . . ."); A. STONE, MENTAL HEALTH AND LAW: A SYSTEM IN TRANSITION 192–94 (DHEW Pub. No. (ADM) 76–176, 1975); LaFond, *Washington's Sexually Violent Predator Law: A Deliberate Misuse of the Therapeutic State for Social Control,* 15 U. PUGET SOUND L. REV. 655, 662 (1992) ("[M]ost experts and policy-makers had concluded that sex offenders were not mentally ill and that involuntary indeterminate treatment was ineffective in changing their criminal behavior. Coercive rehabilitation simply did not work."); Reardon, *Sexual Predators: Mental Illness or Abnormality? A Psychiatrist's Perspective,* 15 U. PUGET SOUND L. REV. 849 (1992).

[23]504 U.S. 71 (1992); *see id.* at 86–89 (O'Connor, J., concurring in part and concurring in the judgment) (It is "clear that acquittees could not be confined as mental patients absent some medical justification for doing so; in such a case the necessary connection between the nature and purpose of confinement would be absent.").

[24]*See* Winick, *Ambiguities in the Legal Meaning and Significance of Mental Illness,* 1 PSYCHOL. PUB. POL'Y & L. 534 (1996) (analyzing *Foucha* and the limitations imposed by the Constitution on the use of the mental illness label to justify involuntary hospitalization and treatment).

[25]*See* ABA MENTAL HEALTH STANDARDS 455–61 (1989) (Introduction and commentary to Standard 7–8.1); GROUP FOR THE ADVANCEMENT OF PSYCHIATRY, PSYCHIATRY AND SEX PSYCHOPATH LEGISLATION: THE 30S TO THE 80S (1989) [hereinafter GAP REPORT]; STONE, *supra* note 22, at 192–94; Dix, *Special Dispositional Alternatives for Abnormal Offenders, in* MENTALLY DISORDERED OFFENDERS: PERSPECTIVES FROM LAW AND SOCIAL SCIENCE 133, 152–53 (Monahan & Steadman eds., 1983); Monahan & Davis, *Mentally Disordered Sex Offenders, in* MENTALLY DISORDERED OFFENDERS: PERSPECTIVES FROM LAW AND SOCIAL SCIENCE, *supra,* at 191, 195–96.

[26]GAP REPORT, *supra* note 25, at 935.

[27]*Id.* at 840.

treatment standpoint."[28] It observed that offenders committed under these statutes are given little treatment or "inappropriate or ineffective treatment."[29] These "mentally disordered sex offender" statutes once were in vogue[30] but now have fallen into disfavor.[31] In those jurisdictions that retain them or that have adopted a newer version under which sex offenders are hospitalized as *sexually violent predators,* they must be regarded as constitutionally suspect under *Foucha* to the extent they authorize involuntary psychiatric hospitalization or intrusive treatment of those committing sex offenses who, apart from their criminal behavior, are not mentally ill. Sexual psychopathy is not regarded by clinicians as a mental disorder; even if it were, it would not satisfy the narrow definition of mental illness that may be implicit in *Foucha.* It has no apparent organic etiology, is not itself a treatable condition (at least absent motivation for treatment on the part of the individual), and does not produce cognitive or volitional incapacity that would justify involuntary hospitalization or treatment.[32] Like *antisocial personality disorder,* found not to be a mental illness justifying commitment to a psychiatric hospital in *Foucha,* this or similar labels should not justify forced hospitalization or intrusive treatment.[33]

---

[28]*Id.* at 936.

[29]*Id.* at 858, 873.

[30]*See id.* at 842–44; BRAKEL ET AL., *supra* note 22, at 739; LaFond, *supra* note 22, at 659; LaFond & Reardon, *Sex Offender Treatment Laws in the United States: Past, Present, and Future* (unpublished paper presented at 18th International Congress on Law and Mental Health, June 24, 1992, Vancouver, Canada); Winick, *supra* note 24.

[31]Although more than half of the states had sexual psychopath legislation in the 1960s, it remains in only four or five states. BRAKEL ET AL., *supra* note 22, at 739–40. "The clear direction of law reform in America is to consider sex offenders as responsible human beings who deserve to be convicted and punished for their crimes." LaFond & Reardon, *supra* note 30, at 2. *See also* ABA MENTAL HEALTH STANDARDS, *supra* note 25, at 459–60 (commentary to Standard 7-8.1) ("[I]n recent years these special statutes for the most part have been either repealed or substantially modified.") (citing statutes); GAP REPORT, *supra* note 25, at 839–40 (advocating repeal and viewing such statutes "[a]s social experiments that have failed and that lack redeeming social value"); LaFond, *supra* note 22, at 659, 662. *But see In re* Blodgett, 510 N.W.2d 910 (Minn.), *cert. denied sub nom.* Blodgett v. Minnesota, 115 S. Ct. 146 (1994) (upholding Minnesota's psychopathic personality statute authorizing civil commitment for treatment in a psychiatric hospital of individuals with "psychopathic personality" even though they are not mentally ill); *In re* Young, 857 P.2d 989 (Wash. 1993) (upholding Washington's recently adopted Sexually Violent Predators statute, which authorizes hospitalization of offenders at expiration of prison terms who meet statutory criteria); LaFond & Reardon, *supra* note 30 (discussing Washington Sexually Violent Predators statute). The sexually violent predators laws, exemplified by the Washington statute, now adopted in four or five states, constitute the latest version of special legislation designed to hospitalize sex offenders. The Supreme Court recently granted review of a case that had held unconstitutional the Kansas sexually violent predators law. *In re* Hendricks, 912 P.2d 129 (Kan.), *cert. granted,* 116 S. Ct. 1540 (1996).

[32]*See* Winick, *supra* note 24.

[33]*See* Foucha v. Louisiana, 504 U.S. 71 (1992) (continued commitment to psychiatric hospital of acquittee whose only present diagnosis was antisocial personality disorder held to violate substantive due process because antisocial personality disorder is not a mental illness); Young v. Weston, 898 F. Supp. 744, 749–51 (W.D. Wash. 1995), *appeal pending,* No. 95–35968 (9th Cir. 1996) (Washington Sexual Predator Statute held to violate substantive due process when the individual's only diagnosis was antisocial personality disorder, which was held not to be a mental illness sufficient for purposes of civil psychiatric hospitalization); LaFond, *supra* note 22, at 693; Winick, *supra* note 24. A different conclusion may be warranted for "mentally disordered sex offender" statutes that require convicted prisoners to participate in nonintrusive treatment programs in prison as an aspect of offender rehabilitation. *See* Sundby v. Fiedler, 827 F. Supp. 580 (W.D. Wis. 1993) (upholding Wisconsin sexual offender treatment program requiring prisoner to participate in treatment and education program). If such treatment occurs within prison, these programs would not offend *Foucha's* prohibition on psychiatric hospitalization of those who are not mentally ill. Moreover, nonintrusive nonmedical treatment, such as verbal psychotherapy, counseling, education, and positive reinforcement programs, may not infringe fundamental liberty interests, as would psychotropic drugs or other organic treatment approaches. *Compare* Winick, *supra* note 12, at 352–65 (discussing verbal and behavioral techniques of correctional therapy) *with id.* at 365–73 (discussing organic techniques); *see* Sundby, 827 F. Supp. at 583 ("Plaintiff's case differs from . . . [*Harper* and others cases] in that the SOTP II policy is a treatment and education program that is carried out without using physical restraints, injections or other bodily

This analysis of the implications of *Foucha* and of the therapeutic appropriateness principle on sexual psychopath legislation requires consideration of two prior Supreme Court decisions, *Allen v. Illinois*[34] and *Minnesota ex rel. Pearson v. Probate Court.*[35] The Court's decision in *Allen,* which was not discussed in *Foucha,* is not inconsistent with the conclusion that *Foucha* places the continued validity of these statutes in question. The *Allen* Court upheld a state "sexually dangerous person" statute that imposed civil commitment and required a clinical evaluation of the individual. The Court rejected the contention that the compelled evaluation violated the individual's Fifth Amendment privilege against self-incrimination. Because civil commitment is not criminal prosecution within the meaning of the Fifth Amendment, the Court found the self-incrimination provision inapplicable. The case did not present any substantive due process challenge to the civil commitment of individuals found to be "sexually dangerous persons," and the Court's opinion did not consider the question. Moreover, the state statute did not define *sexually dangerous persons* as individuals who were mentally ill on the basis of their sexual behavior. Rather, the statute defined individuals subject to civil commitment as those who had suffered from a "mental disorder" for more than one year *and* within this period had demonstrated a "criminal propensity" to commit sexual offenses.[36] Because the statute did not further define *mental disorder,* it seemed to contemplate that individuals suffer from some mental illness apart from their sexual proclivities. Whether individuals qualify for commitment if their only "disorder" was pedophilia or exhibitionism, for example, was therefore not before the Court, and nothing in *Allen* suggests that the Court would approve the constitutionality of a statute so providing.

Although *Allen* thus is not inconsistent with the conclusion that *Foucha* places the constitutionality of sexual psychopath statutes in doubt, this conclusion seems to be in tension with a Supreme Court case from an earlier era, *Minnesota ex rel. Pearson v. Probate Court.*[37] *Pearson* upheld a statute authorizing indefinite commitment of sex offenders with a *psychopathic personality,* defined to cover persons "who, by an habitual course of conduct in sexual matters, have evidenced an utter lack of power to control their sexual impulses, and who, as a result, are likely to attack, or otherwise inflict injury, loss, pain or other evil on the objects of their uncontrolled and uncontrollable desire."[38] *Pearson,* however, preceded our more modern understanding of mental illness and the growing consensus that sexual psychopathy is not a legitimate diagnostic category.[39] Moreover, the *Pearson* Court upheld the statute against void-for-vagueness, equal protection, and procedural due process challenges and did not consider whether it satisfied substantive due process. Substantive due process was a dead letter in 1940, when *Pearson* was decided, soon after the demise of the

---

intrusions.''). When fundamental liberty interests are not implicated, the strict scrutiny approach of *Foucha* may not apply, and such programs, even if of dubious wisdom and questionable efficacy, would seem rationally related to a legitimate governmental interest, and therefore constitutionally permissible. Winick, *supra* note 12, at 373–83. *See Sundby,* 827 F. Supp. at 583 ("The undisputed facts establish that the SOTP II program was designated to help sexual offenders accept their crime, educate them and motivate them to accept treatment. This rehabilitative purpose on the part of defendants is a legitimate phenological interest sufficient to overcome plaintiff's limited liberty interest in refusing treatment.'').

[34]378 U.S. 364 (1986).

[35]309 U.S. 270 (1940).

[36]478 U.S. at 370–71 (citing ILL. REV. STAT. ch. 38 ¶ 105–1.01 (1985)).

[37]309 U.S. 270 (1940).

[38]*Id.* at 273.

[39]*See supra* notes 22–31 and accompanying text. In a closely divided opinion, Minnesota's Supreme Court upheld that state's "psychopathic personality" statute, finding that *Foucha* did not overrule *Pearson. In re* Blodgett, 510 N.W. 2d 910, 914 (Minn.), *cert. denied sub nom.* Blodgett v. Minnesota, 115 S. Ct. 146 (1994). Three judges in dissent, however, concluded that the approach of *Pearson* was outmoded by more recent constitutional developments. *Id.* at 925 (Wahl, J., joined by Keith, C.J., & Tomljanovich, J., dissenting).

controversial *Lochner* doctrine of substantive due process protection for economic liberty and freedom to contract.[40] However, as *Foucha* illustrates, substantive due process has been reinvigorated in the years since *Griswold v. Connecticut,* in which the Court invoked a constitutional right to privacy to invalidate prohibitions on the use of contraceptives.[41] The significant development of substantive due process doctrine that has occurred in the more than 50 years since *Pearson* was decided undercuts that case's continued validity. *Pearson,* to the extent it is seen as a broad endorsement of the constitutionality of sex psychopathy legislation, therefore, seems outmoded, and its approach arguably has been overruled *sub silentio* by *Foucha.*

The principles reflected in *Riggins* and *Foucha* limit the ability of the state to define social problems as medical ones and to seek to remedy them with medical solutions. Only if the individual is mentally ill may intrusive psychiatric or medical treatment techniques be imposed coercively, and only when they are therapeutically appropriate. The state may use a variety of criminal, custodial, or regulatory interventions to deal with social problems, but under the Constitution, involuntary medical treatment should be possible only for those suffering from medical or mental illness and only when it can be justified clinically.

B. When a Particular Treatment Is Impermissible In View of Alternative Approaches: The Least Restrictive Alternative Principle

As described in chapter 15, the Supreme Court in *Riggins v. Nevada*[42] suggested in dicta that the ''less intrusive means'' principle would apply in nonprison contexts to measure the constitutionality of involuntary administration of antipsychotic medication. This ''less intrusive means'' or ''least restrictive alternative'' principle is a component of traditional strict judicial scrutiny applicable when government seeks to intrude on fundamental constitutional rights, like the First Amendment rights analyzed in chapter 10[43] and many of the substantive due process rights discussed in chapter 11.[44] The least restrictive alternative principle allows courts to scrutinize the means chosen by the state to accomplish compelling ends. It enables courts to determine the relationship between the deprivation of an individual's fundamental constitutional right and the achievement of the compelling interest in question. Without a requirement that the means chosen by the state to accomplish its compelling ends was narrowly tailored to achieve them, the mere assertion of a compelling interest would justify the deprivation of fundamental rights. Requiring a ''close fit'' between means and ends ensures that fundamental rights are not unnecessarily abridged. Thus, the state clearly has a compelling interest in preventing violence, but it could not assert this interest to justify a ban on all ''controversial'' speech in public. Although such a ban would advance the state's interest, it would do so at the expense of preventing protected speech. Because freedom of speech is a fundamental right, the state would need to use less drastic means to achieve the goal.

A classic exposition of the least restrictive alternative principle occurred in *Shelton v. Tucker:*[45]

---

[40]*See* Lochner v. New York, 198 U.S. 45 (1905), *overruled by* West Coast Hotel Co. v. Parrish, 300 U.S. 379 (1937). *See generally supra* chapter 11, part A; Strong, *The Economic Philosophy of Lochner: Emergence, Embrasure, and Emasculation,* 15 ARIZ. L. REV. 419 (1973).

[41]381 U.S. 479 (1965); *see supra* chapter 11.

[42]504 U.S. 127 (1992); *see supra* chapter 15, parts A & B.

[43]*See supra* chapter 10, notes 476–497 and accompanying text.

[44]*See supra* chapter 11, notes 249–253 and accompanying text.

[45]364 U.S. 479, 488 (1960).

> [E]ven though the governmental purpose be legitimate and substantial, that purpose cannot be pursued by means that broadly stifle fundamental liberties when the end can be more narrowly achieved. The breadth of legislative abridgement must be viewed in the light of less drastic means for achieving the same basic purpose.

This principle has been evoked frequently by the Court when governmental action has unnecessarily restricted the exercise of fundamental rights, including the freedom of bodily restraint invaded by civil commitment.[46] In the civil commitment context, for example, the principle requires that before the state seeks to hospitalize a nondangerous individual on account of mental illness, it consider whether less restrictive community placements would be sufficient.

Because the interests invaded by at least the more intrusive mental health treatment techniques invade fundamental constitutional rights protected by the First Amendment[47] and the Due Process Clauses,[48] the dicta in *Riggins,* suggesting applicability of the least intrusive means principle in the right-to-refuse-medication area, generally seems plainly correct.[49] Under this principle, not only will courts insist that governmental interests asserted to justify involuntary medication (and other intrusive mental health treatment approaches) be found to be ''compelling,'' but they also will require that the means used to accomplish these interests be necessary to their attainment. If less intrusive means that can accomplish these objectives are available, the state may not use a more intrusive one.

How will the ''less intrusive means'' principle apply in the right-to-refuse-treatment area? Although the *Riggins* Court did not discuss what this principle would require in the criminal trial context that the case presented, an analysis of its likely implications for the criminal competency process illustrates its potential significance there and for the right to refuse treatment generally. At a minimum, when a criminal defendant objects to the administration of medication at trial, the ''less intrusive means'' standard should be read to require that medication be discontinued for a reasonable period of time in order to allow a determination to be made concerning whether the defendant's competency can be maintained in the absence of medication.[50] Because the defendant in *Riggins* never contended that he had a right to terminate medication even if this would render him incompetent, his pretrial motion, made several months before his trial was to commence, in effect sought such a temporary halt in medication in order to allow an assessment of whether its continuation was truly necessary to maintain his competency. Such a trial period without medication would seem to be the most reasonable way of balancing the assertedly conflicting interests of the parties. A trial period of this kind would determine whether an accommodation is possible that satisfies both the defendant's interest in avoiding unwanted medication and the state's interest in bringing the defendant to trial. Moreover, such a trial period without medication is medically appropriate and can have significant therapeutic value. Indeed, the medical literature calls for a reexamination of prolonged maintenance antipsychotic drug therapy and

---

[46]O'Connor v. Donaldson, 422 U.S. 563, 580 (1975); McNeil v. Director, Patuxent Inst., 407 U.S. 245, 348–50 (1972).

[47]*See supra* chapter 10 (First Amendment).

[48]*See supra* chapter 11 (substantive due process).

[49]*See supra* chapter 15, part B (defending applicability of strict scrutiny for intrusive treatment administered outside the prison context).

[50]This was the suggestion of the concurring opinion in the Nevada Supreme Court's decision in *Riggins.* State v. Riggins, 808 P.2d 535, 540 (Nev. 1991). *See also* Winick, *Psychotropic Medication and Competency to Stand Trial,* 1977 Am. B. Found. Res. J. 769, 813–14 (making the same suggestion).

suggests that "drug-free holidays" should be attempted periodically to assess the patient's condition without medication in order to determine its continued necessity.[51]

If the defendant reverts to an incompetent state during a trial period without medication, the "less intrusive means" standard then would require that other less intrusive treatment approaches be considered before medication is resumed.[52] For this purpose, the continuum of intrusiveness framework developed in chapters 2–8 is useful. As these chapters suggest, the various mental health treatment modalities used in the treatment of defendants found incompetent to stand trial can be analyzed as generally falling along a rough continuum of intrusiveness. Psychotherapy and other verbal and educational approaches, as well as most of the behavioral treatment techniques—those using positive reinforcement, modeling, contingency contracting, systematic desensitization, cognitive behavior therapy, and possibly even some of the aversive conditioning approaches—can generally be considered to be less intrusive than medication, particularly antipsychotic and antidepressant medication.[53]

---

[51]*See* Food and Drug Administration–American College of Neuropsychopharmacology Task Force, *Neurological Syndromes Associated with Antipsychotic Drug Use*, 28 ARCHIVES GEN. PSYCHIATRY 463, 465 (1973). *See also* Ayd, *Treatment–Resistant Patients: A Moral, Legal and Therapeutic Challenge*, in RATIONAL PSYCHOPHARMACOTHERAPY AND THE RIGHT TO TREATMENT 37, 49–50 (F. Ayd ed., 1975); Baldessarini & Lipinski, *Risks vs. Benefits of Antipsychotic Drugs*, 289 NEW ENG. J. MED. 427, 428 (1973); Davis, *Overview: Maintenance Therapy in Psychiatry: I. Schizophrenia*, 132 AM. J. PSYCHIATRY 1237, 1242–43 (1975); Gardos & Cole, *Maintenance Antipsychotic Therapy: Is the Cure Worse than the Disease?*, 133 AM. J. PSYCHIATRY 32, 34–36 (1976); Prien & Klett, *An Appraisal of the Long-Term Use of Tranquilizing Medication with Hospitalized Chronic Schizophrenics: A Review of the Drug Discontinuation Literature*, 5 SCHIZOPHRENIA BULL. 64 (1972); Winick, *supra* note 50, at 813–14. Some medical commentators have suggested that perhaps 50% of outpatients with schizophrenia might not be worse off if their medications were withdrawn. *See, e.g.,* Gardos & Cole, *supra* at 34. *But see* Davis, *Antipsychotic Drugs*, in 2 COMPREHENSIVE TEXTBOOK OF PSYCHIATRY 1591, 1609 (B. Kaplan & B. Sadock eds., 5th ed. 1989) (stating that although drug-free holidays have been suggested as a means of reducing the risk of tardive dyskinesia, there are no controlled studies supporting this proposal; moreover, some clinical observations hint at the opposite results); Tanner & Klawans, *Tardive Dyskinesia: Prevention and Treatment*, 9 CLINICAL NEUROPHARMACOLOGY S–76, S–77 (Supp. II 1986) ("Although drug-free periods during neuroleptic treatment regimens have been proposed by some as a means of decreasing the risk of developing tardive dyskinesia, others have reported an increase in tardive dyskinesia in patients having frequent drug-free periods.").

[52]*See, e.g.,* Rogers v. Okin, 634 F.2d 650, 656 (1st Cir. 1980) (before antipsychotic medication may be used on an involuntary basis, "reasonable alternatives to the administration of antipsychotics must be ruled out"), *vacated and remanded sub nom.* Mills v. Rogers, 457 U.S. 291 (1982); Rennie v. Klein, 462 F. Supp. 1131, 1146 (D.N.J. 1978) (under the least restrictive alternative principle, "a patient 'may challenge the forced administration of drugs on the basis that alternative methods should be tried before a more intrusive technique like psychotropic medication is used'") (quoting Winick, *supra* note 50, at 813), *modified, vacated, and remanded*, 653 F.2d 836, 845–48) (3d Cir. 1981) (en banc), *vacated and remanded*, 458 U.S. 1199 (1982); Price v. Sheppard, 239 N.W.2d 905, 913 (Minn. 1976) (before more intrusive treatment methods such as psychosurgery or electroconvulsive therapy may be used, authorizing court must determine necessity and reasonableness of proposed treatment in light of availability of less intrusive treatments). *See also* Bee v. Greaves, 744 F.2d 1387, 1396 (10th Cir. 1984), *cert. denied*, 469 U.S. 1214 (1985); Osgood v. District of Columbia, 567 F. Supp. 1026, 1031 (D.D.C. 1983); People v. Medina, 705 P.2d 961, 974 (Colo. 1985) (en banc); Large v. Superior Court, 714 P.2d 399, 408 (Ariz. 1986) (en banc); *In re* Boyd, 403 A.2d 744, 753 n.15 (D.C. Ct. App. 1979); Rogers v. Commissioner, 458 N.E.2d 308, 321 (Mass. 1983); Rivers v. Katz, 495 N.E.2d 337, 344 (N.Y. 1986).

[53]*Compare supra* chapter 3 (psychotherapy) *and* chapter 4 (behavior therapy) *with* chapter 5 (psychotropic medication). Some treatment techniques can be seen as more intrusive than psychotropic medication. *See supra* chapters 6–8 (ECT, electronic stimulation of the brain, and psychosurgery). Unless a defendant expressed a preference for such a technique instead of medication, the Court's "less intrusive means" standard would not require use of such arguably more intrusive approaches. For example, an incompetent criminal defendant suffering from severe depression may be treated with electroconvulsive therapy (ECT). *See supra* chapter 6. Because ECT is arguably more intrusive than antidepressant medication, *see supra* chapter 6 (discussing the relative intrusiveness of ECT), the "less intrusive means" approach would not require that a defendant objecting to trial on antidepressant drugs be given ECT.

Moreover, these techniques do not involve side effects that would negatively affect a defendant's demeanor at trial or ability to communicate with counsel or participate in the proceedings. As a result, if any of these approaches would succeed in restoring and maintaining the defendant's competence, their use would effectively accommodate the conflicting interests of the defendant and the state, rendering more intrusive psychopharmacological treatment constitutionally impermissible.

Unfortunately, however, many individuals who are sufficiently impaired by mental illness to be found incompetent to stand trial may not respond effectively to these other treatment modalities unless they are accompanied by psychotropic medication. The "less intrusive means" standard should be read to require only that other *feasible* treatment methods be attempted, and if expert testimony clearly predicts that other approaches will not be effective for the defendant, at least in the absence of medication, such other approaches would not be required to be attempted before medication may be used. Where the expert testimony does not clearly eliminate the possibility that other approaches may be efficacious, however, they should be attempted in an effort to determine whether medication is truly necessary to maintain the defendant's competency. Even if one or more of these other approaches seems unlikely to succeed in the absence of medication, however, their combination with medication might enable a lower dose of medication to be used, resulting in less intrusiveness, a lesser burden on constitutional values, and less risk of adverse side effects impairing the defendant's demeanor or trial performance.

If medication is required to enable the defendant to remain in a competent state, the "less restrictive means" standard should be construed to require the psychiatrist to consider, among potentially efficacious drugs, the one presenting the smallest risk of adverse side effects. Moreover, even if a particular drug seems appropriate and the least intrusive drug in the circumstances, the least restrictive means principle should compel consideration of the minimum dose consistent with achieving this effect. Such a dose will minimize not only the extent of the intrusion on the defendant's liberty interests, but also the risk that the medication itself will impair the defendant's trial functioning or demeanor. The trial court should display considerable flexibility in this regard, giving the defendant's treating psychiatrist an adequate opportunity to experiment with different drugs and different dose levels in order to achieve a maximum degree of functioning, while minimizing side effects impairing the defendant's trial ability and demeanor. Thus, even when intrusive treatment is required to maintain a defendant's competence to stand trial, it should be administered in a way that avoids unnecessary intrusions.

This analysis of how the "less intrusive means" standard would apply in the criminal trial context of *Riggins* illustrates how it would apply in other right-to-refuse-treatment contexts. When intrusive mental health treatment is sought to be imposed involuntarily, the principle requires consideration of whether less intrusive treatments, or other approaches that do not involve treatment, may satisfy the government's asserted interest. Thus, if the government asserts a police power interest in protecting other patients or institutional staff from a violent patient, "less restrictive alternatives, such as segregation or the use of less controversial drugs like the tranquilizers or sedatives, should be ruled out before resorting to antipsychotic drugs" to accomplish this purpose.[54] If the government asserts a police power interest in protecting the community from harm, institutionalization alone suffices to meet this interest, at least if the facility is sufficiently secure to prevent escape. The prevention of harm to the community by a dangerous mental patient, criminal offender, or insanity

---

[54]Bee v. Greaves, 744 F.2d 1387, 1396 (10th Cir. 1984), *cert. denied,* 469 U.S. 1214 (1985).

acquittee would constitute a compelling state interest, but if the individual is committed to a secure hospital or to a prison, such commitment would itself eliminate the risk of harm, rendering intrusive treatment unnecessary to accomplish this purpose. While such treatment, if successful, might eliminate the risk of harm and prevent the need for prolonged institutionalization, institutionalization alone protects public safety. For an individual regarding prolonged institutionalization as less intrusive than certain forms of treatment, confinement alone may constitute a less intrusive means of meeting the state's police power interest.[55] If the government asserts a *parens patriae* interest in improving the patient's condition, treatment approaches on the lower end of the continuum of intrusiveness should be considered before those on the higher end are administered.

Thus, a patient suffering from severe depression ordinarily should be given antidepressant medication before ECT is imposed.[56] Only if drug treatment proves unsuccessful should the more intrusive ECT be attempted. For conditions for which behavioral or psychotherapeutic approaches may succeed, these approaches should be attempted before medication is imposed over objection. In situations in which several treatment approaches may be possible, the patient's preferences concerning relative intrusiveness should be taken into account. Only when intrusive treatment is found to be necessary to accomplish the state's compelling interest should it be constitutionally permissible. And when more than one treatment approach might satisfy the asserted state interest, the least intrusive approach should be attempted. Because intrusive treatment burdens fundamental constitutional rights, this high standard should be required to be satisfied before the state may impose it involuntarily.

---

[55]Those preferring treatment to prolonged institutionalization may waive the right to refuse treatment provided the requirements of the informed consent doctrine are satisfied. *See infra* chapter 18 (analyzing the condition for waiver of the right).

[56]When the patient is actively suicidal, ECT may be indicated in preference to at least some of the antidepressant drugs (such as tricyclics) because of the several weeks' delay in their effectiveness. *See supra* chapter 6.

Part III

Evaluating and Implementing the Right to Refuse Treatment

Chapter 17
A THERAPEUTIC JURISPRUDENCE ANALYSIS OF THE RIGHT TO REFUSE MENTAL HEALTH TREATMENT

The chapters in Part II have presented an extensive constitutional analysis of the right to refuse treatment. It concludes that several constitutional rights combine to protect such a right, at least in the case of intrusive mental health treatment. Although the right may be overcome in appropriate circumstances when necessary to the accomplishment of compelling governmental interest, recognition of a general right to refuse in this area inevitably affects the behavior of participants, clinicians, facilities, and governmental agencies. Part III seeks to assess those effects and analyzes the issues that implementation of the right will present. This chapter analyzes the therapeutic implications of recognizing the right. Chapter 18 discusses the conditions for waiver of the right. Chapter 19 discusses when hearings will be required in the treatment refusal context and the differing procedural models that could be used to resolve disputes in this area.

The controversy concerning the recognition and definition of a right to refuse mental health treatment has largely ignored the question of whether such recognition is therapeutically beneficial or detrimental to the patient. Would such recognition lead to refusal of needed treatment so that patients "rot with their rights on," as some have suggested?[1] Will allowing offenders to choose whether to participate in correctional rehabilitation programs increase recidivism? Will patients forced to accept mental health treatment over objection improve and come in time to thank their doctor, retrospectively approving beneficial treatment they never would have accepted voluntarily?[2] On the other hand, might recognition of a right to refuse treatment empower patients and offenders in ways that are therapeutic? Might it provide them with a context in which they could acquire decision-making skills, learn to engage in self-determining behavior, and attain functional capacities that are useful in community adjustment? Will the exercise of choice concerning treatment enhance self-esteem and feelings of self-efficacy in ways that will improve the capacity for

---

[1] *See, e.g.,* Appelbaum & Gutheil, *The Boston State Hospital Case: "Involuntary Mind Control," the Constitution, and the "Right to Rot,"* 137 AM. J. PSYCHIATRY 720 (1980); Gutheil, *In Search of True Freedom: Drug Refusal, Involuntary Medication, and "Rotting with Your Rights On,"* 137 AM. J. PSYCHIATRY 327 (1980) (editorial).

[2] *See, e.g.,* A. STONE, MENTAL HEALTH LAW: A SYSTEM IN TRANSITION 69–70 (DHEW Pub. No. (ADM) 76–176, 1975) (describing this reaction as the "thank you" theory); D. WEXLER, MENTAL HEALTH LAW 45–48 (1981) (analyzing "thank you" theory in context of narcotics abusers); Gove & Fain, *A Comparison of Voluntary and Committed Psychiatric Patients,* 34 ARCHIVES GEN. PSYCHIATRY 669, 675 (1977); Kane et al., *Attitudinal Changes of Involuntarily Committed Patients Following Treatment,* 40 ARCHIVES GEN. PSYCHIATRY 374, 376 (1983); Schwartz et al., *Autonomy and the Right to Refuse Treatment: Patient's Attitudes After Involuntary Medication,* 39 HOSP. & COMMUNITY PSYCHIATRY 1049 (1988) (empirical study showing that medication refusers treated over objection, if rehospitalized, would assent to drug treatment); *but see* Beck & Golowka, *A Study of Enforced Treatment in Relation to Stone's "Thank You" Theory,* 6 BEHAV. SCI. & L. 559, 565 (1988) (empirical study of involuntarily hospitalized patients showing no evidence to support "thank you" theory in 62% of cases).

self-care and competence in general? Will providing patients and offenders with treatment choice enhance the potential that such treatment is efficacious? Will according patients (or offenders) a right to refuse treatment change the therapist–patient (or counselor–offender) relationship in ways that enhance or diminish its therapeutic potential?

These questions have not been examined empirically, but they are critical to resolving the right-to-refuse-treatment dilemma. Whether a right to refuse treatment should be recognized ultimately may be a constitutional question, but judicial and statutory definitions of its parameters and of the procedural requirements necessary to implement it can be critically affected by the answers to these empirical questions. Moreover, because constitutional adjudication itself usually involves the balancing of conflicting interests, the answers to these questions should provide data that are essential to a constitutional analysis of the right to refuse treatment. This chapter attempts a therapeutic jurisprudence analysis of the right to refuse treatment.[3] It examines principles of cognitive and social psychology and psychodynamic theory in order to speculate about the likely impact of recognizing that patients and offenders have a right to refuse treatment and a corresponding opportunity to choose such treatment. This theoretical speculation may generate empirical investigation that, in turn, will aid in a more informed development of the law in this area.

A. The Psychological Value of Choice

An extensive body of psychological literature points to the positive value of allowing individuals to exercise choice concerning a variety of matters affecting them.[4] Patient choice in favor of treatment, for example, appears to be an important determinant of treatment success.[5] Treatment imposed over objection may not work as well. Like most people, patients often do not respond well when told what to do. This may be even more true of criminal offenders, who have demonstrated their unwillingness or inability to behave in accordance with society's rules. Unless people themselves see the merit in achieving a particular goal, they often do not pursue it or do so only half-heartedly. Indeed, sometimes even when the costs of noncompliance with a goal are high, some people may resent the pressure imposed by others and refuse to comply. Sometimes they even may act perversely to frustrate achievement of the goal. By contrast, an individual voluntarily accepting treatment is exercising choice. The law strongly favors allowing individual choice rather than attempting to achieve

---

[3]Therapeutic jurisprudence suggests the need for an assessment of the therapeutic impact of legal rules. The law itself affects therapeutic values—sometimes positively, sometimes negatively. Although other considerations may properly shape legal rules, a sensible policy analysis of law should take into account its consequences for the health and mental health of the individuals and institutions it affects. Therapeutic jurisprudence accordingly calls for theoretical speculation about and empirical investigation of the therapeutic or antitherapeutic effects of the law. *See generally* D. WEXLER & B. WINICK, ESSAYS IN THERAPEUTIC JURISPRUDENCE (1991); B. WINICK, THERAPEUTIC JURISPRUDENCE APPLIED: ESSAYS ON MENTAL HEALTH LAW (1996); LAW IN A THERAPEUTIC KEY: DEVELOPMENTS IN THERAPEUTIC JURISPRUDENCE (D. Wexler & B. Winick eds., 1996); SYMPOSIUM—THERAPEUTIC JURISPRUDENCE: RESTRUCTURING MENTAL DISABILITY LAW, 10 N.Y.L. SCH. J. HUM. RTS. 623–926 (1993); Wexler & Winick, *Therapeutic Jurisprudence as a New Approach to Mental Health Law Policy Analysis and Research,* 45 U. MIAMI L. REV. 979 (1991). David Wexler and I have suggested the need for a therapeutic jurisprudence assessment of the right to refuse treatment. *See* D. WEXLER & B. WINICK, *supra,* at 303, 310–11; Wexler & Winick, *supra,* at 990–92. This chapter attempts such an analysis.

[4]*See* Winick, *On Autonomy: Legal and Psychological Perspectives,* 37 VILL. L. REV. 1705, 1755–68 (1992) (summarizing literature on the psychology of choice).

[5]Winick, *Competency to Consent to Treatment: The Distinction Between Assent and Objection,* 28 HOUS. L. REV. 15, 46–53 (1991).

public or private goals through compulsion.[6] Aside from the political values reflected in this preference, it is strongly supported by utilitarian considerations.

Cognitive and social psychology provide a theoretical explanation for the effect of individual choice on enhancing the potential for success.[7] People directed to perform tasks do not feel personally committed to the goal or personally responsible for its fulfillment.[8] This feeling may apply even for tasks individuals are directed to perform to further their own best interests, such as medical treatment. When physicians do not allow patient participation in treatment decisions and do not explain treatment to them, patients often do not comply with medical advice.[9] Choice, on the other hand, may bring a degree of commitment that mobilizes the self-evaluative and self-reinforcing mechanisms that facilitate goal achievement.[10] To the extent that patients' agreements to accept a course of treatment recommended by therapists constitutes an affirmative expression of patient choice of treatment, such choice itself may be therapeutic. Compliance with a treatment plan is often indispensable to successful treatment.[11] Unless patients show up for scheduled appointments or take their prescribed medication, treatment cannot succeed. This would seem especially true for treatments like psychotherapy, correctional counseling, other forms of verbal therapy,[12] and even for many forms of behavioral therapy.[13] These techniques largely depend on patient

---

[6]Winick, *supra* note 4, at 1707–55.

[7]*See* S. BREHM & J. BREHM, PSYCHOLOGICAL REACTANCE: A THEORY OF FREEDOM AND CONTROL 301 (1981); Carroll, *Consent to Mental Health Treatment: A Theoretical Analysis of Coercion, Freedom, and Control,* 9 BEHAV. SCI. & L 129, 137–38 (1991); Winick, *Harnessing the Power of the Bet: Wagering With the Government as a Means of Accomplishing Social and Individual Change,* 45 U. MIAMI L. REV. 737, 752–72 (1991) [hereinafter *Wagering with the Government*]; Winick, *supra* note 5, at 46–53; Winick, *Competency to Consent to Voluntary Hospitalization: A Therapeutic Jurisprudence Analysis of* Zinermon v. Burch, 14 INT'L J.L. & PSYCHIATRY 169, 192–99 (1991) [hereinafter *Competency to Consent to Voluntary Hospitalization*].

[8]A. BANDURA, SOCIAL FOUNDATIONS OF THOUGHT AND ACTION: A SOCIAL COGNITIVE THEORY 338, 363, 368, 468–69, 470–71, 475–76, 478–79 (1986).

[9]P. APPELBAUM ET AL., INFORMED CONSENT: LEGAL THEORY AND CLINICAL PRACTICE 28 (1987); D. MEICHENBAUM & D. TURK, FACILITATING TREATMENT ADHERENCE: A PRACTITIONER'S GUIDE–BOOK 20, 76–79 (1987); B. MOYERS, HEALING AND THE MIND 50 (1993); *see* Appelbaum & Gutheil, *Drug Refusal: A Study of Psychiatric Inpatients,* 137 AM. J. PSYCHIATRY 340, 341 (1980); Shultz, *From Informed Consent to Patient Choice: A New Protected Interest,* 95 YALE L.J. 219, 293 & n.323 (1985). Treatment adherence in general increases when the patient is given choice and participation in the selection of treatment alternatives and goals. *See* MEICHENBAUM & TURK, *supra* at 157, 159, 175; Kanfer & Gaelick, *Self–Management Methods, in* HELPING PEOPLE CHANGE 334–47 (F. Kanfer & A. Goldstein eds., 1986).

[10]BANDURA, *supra* note 8, at 338, 363, 368, 468, 478–70; BREHM & BREHM, *supra* note 7, at 301; MEICHENBAUM & TURK, *supra* note 9, at 156–57; Carroll, *supra* note 7, at 129, 137–38.

[11]*See generally* MEICHENBAUM & TURK, *supra* note 9.

[12]*See* Council of the Am. Psychiatric Ass'n, *Position Statement on the Question of Adequacy of Treatment,* 123 AM. J. PSYCHIATRY 1458, 1459 (1967) ("[I]t may be said in general that the effectiveness of the psychotherapies is proportional to the degree of cooperation that is present . . . ."); Katz, *The Right to Treatment — An Enchanting Legal Fiction,* 36 U. CHI. L. REV. 755, 777 (1969); Michels, *Ethical Issues of Psychological and Psychotherapeutic Means of Behavior Control: Is the Moral Contract Being Observed?,* 3 HASTINGS CTR. REP., Apr. 1973, at 11, 11; Stromberg & Stone, *A Model State Law on Civil Commitment of the Mentally Ill,* 20 HARV. J. LEGIS. 276, 328 (1983); Winick, *The Right to Refuse Mental Health Treatment: A First Amendment Perspective,* 44 U. MIAMI L. REV. 1, 83–84 (1989).

[13]*See* E. ERWIN, BEHAVIOR THERAPY: SCIENTIFIC, PHILOSOPHICAL AND MORAL FOUNDATIONS 180–81 (1978); MEICHENBAUM & TURK, *supra* note 9, at 150; Bandura, *Behavior Therapy and the Models of Man,* 29 AM. PSYCHOLOGIST 859, 862 (1974); Marks, *The Current Status of Behavioral Psychotherapy: Theory and Practice,* 133 AM. J. PSYCHIATRY 253, 255 (1976); Winick, *Legal Limitations on Correctional Therapy and Research,* 65 MINN. L. REV. 331, 360–61 (1981); Winick, *supra* note 12, at 80.

involvement and active cooperation for their success. However, patient involvement and cooperation would seem essential for even organic forms of treatment.

The conscious, voluntary agreement to accept a course of treatment constitutes the setting of a goal. The setting of explicit goals is itself a significant factor in their accomplishment.[14] This "goal-setting effect" is "one of the most robust . . . findings in the psychological literature."[15] The conscious setting of a goal is virtually indispensable to its achievement.[16] A patient's voluntary agreement to a course of treatment recommended by a therapist constitutes the setting of a goal, the acceptance of a prediction by the therapist that the patient can and will achieve the goal, and at least an implicit undertaking by the patient to attempt the task. The therapist's prediction that the proposed therapy will succeed and the patient's acceptance of this prediction set up expectancies that help to bring about a favorable treatment outcome.[17]

A patient's expectancies concerning treatment success, as well as a number of other cognitive mechanisms, seem to be significantly related to treatment response. The mind plays a crucial role in patients' susceptibility to a variety of medical conditions and their responses to treatment.[18] In its treatment of illness, medicine traditionally has focused almost exclusively on treating the body, often neglecting the role of the mind. Even when fighting organic illnesses with organic treatment techniques, the role of the mind may be significant in producing positive outcomes.[19] Expectancy theory helps to explain the therapeutic power of such phenomena as the placebo effect, the Hawthorne effect, and the

---

[14]Campbell, *The Effects of Goal-Contingent Payment on the Performance of a Complex Task,* 37 PERSONNEL PSYCHOL. 23, 23 (1984); Huber, *Comparison of Monetary Reinforcers and Goal Setting as Learning Incentives,* 56 PSYCHOL. REP. 223 (1985); Kirschenbaum & Flanery, *Toward a Psychology of Behavioral Contracting,* 4 CLINICAL PSYCHOL. REV. 598, 603–09 (1984); Locke et al., *Goal Setting and Task Performance* 1969–80, 90 PSYCHOL. BULL. 125, 125–31 (1981); Terborg & Miller, *Motivation, Behavior, and Performance: A Closer Examination of Goal Setting and Monetary Incentives,* 63 J. APPLIED PSYCHOL. 29, 30–31 (1978).

[15]Campbell, *supra* note 14, at 23; Locke et al., *supra* note 14, at 145.

[16]BANDURA, *supra* note 8, at 469 ("Those who set no goals achieve no change.").

[17]*See id.* at 412–13, 467; Deci & Ryan, *The Empirical Exploration of Intrinsic Motivational Processes,* 13 ADVANCES IN EXPERIMENTAL SOC. PSYCHOLOGY 39, 59 (1980).

[18]*See generally* N. COUSINS, HEALTH FIRST: THE BIOLOGY OF HOPE AND THE HEALING POWER OF THE HUMAN SPIRIT (1990); H. DIENSTFREY, WHERE THE MIND MEETS THE BODY: TYPE A, THE RELAXATION RESPONSE, PSYCHONEUROIMMUNOLOGY, HYPNOSIS, BIOFEEDBACK, NEUROPEPTIDES, AND THE SEARCH FOR IMAGERY, AND THE MIND'S EFFECT ON PHYSICAL HEALTH (1991); H. DUNBAR, EMOTIONS AND BODILY CHANGES (1954) (discussing psychosomatic medicine, a psychological approach to medicine treating the mind and body as one entity); MOYERS, *supra* note 9; Engel, *The Need for a New Medical Model: A Challenge for Biomedicine,* 196 SCIENCE 129 (1977) (proposing a psychosocial view of health, taking into account the interaction of biological, psychological, and social factors in the onset of physical disorders); Frank, *The Faith That Heals,* 137 JOHNS HOPKINS MED. J. 127 (1975) (observing that diverse modes of medical treatment owe their success or failure to the patient's state of mind and expectations, and not solely to the treatment regimen itself).

[19]*See* COUSINS, *supra* note 18, at 192 (commenting on the role of patient's outlook and attitudes on the onset and course of disease); *id.* ("[T]he wise physician makes a careful estimate of the patient's will to live and the ability to put to work all the resources of spirit that can be translated into beneficial biochemical changes."); *id.* ("[F]ew things are more important than the psychological management of the patient" in all medical contexts.); *id.* at 217–20 (discussing survey of oncologists showing their belief that positive patient attitude and participation in treatment were beneficial); MOYERS, *supra* note 9, at 130 (commenting on the role of lifestyle and attitudes on such conditions as cancer and heart disease).

shaman effect.[20] Although as yet imperfectly understood, these phenomena suggest the existence of a powerful relationship between patients' expectations that they will improve and their perceived and even actual improvement. A variety of medical and psychological conditions are treated with hypnosis and positive imaging techniques that ask patients to visualize their bodies fighting illness and their ultimate restoration to health.[21] The positive attitudes and expectations thereby created are thought to allow patients to mobilize their psychic resources in ways that may be critical to the therapeutic process.[22]

How do these positive attitudes and expectancies work to influence treatment success? Social cognitive theory posits that predictions and expectations concerning the achievement of goals, including treatment goals, stimulate feelings of self-efficacy in the individuals, which in turn spark action and effort to further the goal.[23] Setting treatment goals enhances motivation and increases patients' efforts through self-monitoring, self-evaluation, and self-reactive processes.[24] Setting such goals helps to structure and guide patients' behavior over the (often long) course of treatment.[25] It provides direction for patients and focuses their interest, attention, and personal involvement in the treatment.[26] Patients' voluntary acceptance of therapists' treatment recommendation may facilitate an internalization of the

---

[20]See, e.g., J. BOURKE, THE MEDICINE MEN OF THE APACHE 2 (1971) (observing that the ability to inspire belief in patients that he has "the gift" is a prerequisite to being "a diyi" or medicine man); H. BRODY, PLACEBOS AND THE PHILOSOPHY OF MEDICINE: CLINICAL, CONCEPTUAL, AND ETHICAL ISSUES 18–20 (1980) ("[T]he patient's expectations of symptom change is held to be causally connected to the change that occurs"); M. JOSPE, THE PLACEBO EFFECT IN HEALING 93–108, 130 (1978) (analyzing the Hawthorne effect in terms of expectancy theory); O. SIMONTON ET AL., GETTING WELL AGAIN 22 (1978); Beecher, The Powerful Placebo, 159 JAMA 1602 (1955) (documenting the power of the placebo); Evans, Expectancy, Therapeutic Instructions, and the Placebo Response, in PLACEBO: THEORY, RESEARCH, AND MECHANISMS 215, 222–24 (1985) (concluding that the "placebo response is mediated by expectations generated within the context of the doctor–patient relationship"); Frank, Biofeedback and the Placebo Effect, 7 BIOFEEDBACK & SELF-REGULATION 449 (1982) (examining placebo effect in terms of expectancy theory); Horvath, Placebos and Common Factors in Two Decades of Psychotherapy Research, 104 PSYCHOL. BULL. 214, 215 (1988) ("Expectancy factors have been shown to influence therapeutic outcome."); Wolf, Effects of Placebo Administration and Occurrence of Toxic Reactions, 155 JAMA 339 (1974) (documenting beneficial effects of placebos). For an alternative analysis of the placebo effect in terms of classical conditioning, see H. DIENSTFREY, supra note 18, at 86–87; Ader, The Placebo Effect as Conditioned Response, in EXPERIMENTAL FOUNDATIONS OF BEHAVIORAL MEDICINE: CONDITIONING APPROACHES 47 (R. Ader et al. eds., 1988).

[21]See, e.g., P. BROWN, THE HYPNOTIC BRAIN: HYPNOTHERAPY AND SOCIAL COMMUNICATION (1991); G. EPSTEIN, HEALING VISUALIZATIONS: CREATING HEALTH THROUGH IMAGERY (1989); M. ERICKSON, THE COLLECTED PAPERS OF MILTON H. ERICKSON ON HYPNOSIS (E. Ross ed., 1988); Barber, Changing "Unchangeable" Bodily Processes by (Hypnotic) Suggestion: A New Look at Hypnosis, Cognition, Imagining, and the Mind-Body Problem, in IMAGINATION AND HEALING (A. Sheikh ed., 1984); Orne & Dinges, Hypnosis, in 2 COMPREHENSIVE TEXTBOOK OF PSYCHIATRY 1501, 1511–12 (H. Kaplan & B. Sadock eds., 5th ed. 1989); Wilson & Barber, The Fantasy-Prone Personality: Implications for Understanding Imagery, Hynosis, and Parapsychological Phenomena, in IMAGERY: CURRENT THEORY, RESEARCH AND APPLICATION 340 (A. Sheikh & J. Wiley eds., 1983).

[22]See COUSINS, supra note 18, at 237–39 (discussing the psychic interplay and its effects on wound healing, the course of progressive illnesses such as AIDS, and the functioning of the immune system); DIENSTFREY, supra note 18; MOYERS, supra note 9, at 48; Dubos, Introduction, in N. COUSINS, ANATOMY OF AN ILLNESS AS PERCEIVED BY THE PATIENT: REFLECTIONS ON HEALING AND REGENERATION 11, 18, 22–23 (1979); Shultz, supra note 9, at 292–93.

[23]See BANDURA, supra note 8, at 413. See also Rotter, Generalized Expectancies for Internal Versus External Control of Reinforcement, 80 PSYCHOL. MONOGRAPHS 1 (1966) (behavior varies as a function of the individual's generalized expectancies that outcomes are determined by his own actions or by external sources beyond his control); Horvath, supra note 20, at 218 ("The belief that the treatment works in the manner outlined in the rationale motivates the client to perform the tasks of the therapy.").

[24]See BANDURA, supra note 8, at 469–72; MEICHENBAUM & TURK, supra note 9, at 158–61.

[25]See BANDURA, supra note 8, at 469.

[26]See id. at 472.

treatment goal that can produce the personal commitment and expenditure of energy needed to achieve it.[27]

Motivation to succeed is an essential ingredient in goal achievement. Ability to accomplish a goal, although necessary, does not produce success by itself; unless individuals are motivated to succeed, they do not commit the effort needed to bring about success. Psychologist Edward Deci's distinction between intrinsic and extrinsic motivation[28] helps to explain why choice works better than compulsion. Intrinsic motivation involves self-determining behavior and is associated with "an internal perceived locus of causality, feelings of self-determination, and a high degree of perceived competence or self-esteem."[29] With extrinsic motivation, on the other hand, the perceived locus of causality is external, and feelings of competence and self-esteem are diminished.[30] When people are allowed to be self-determining, they function more effectively, with a higher degree of commitment and greater satisfaction.[31] These feelings increase motivation to succeed, stimulate positive expectations and attitudes, and spark effort.[32]

The exercise of treatment choice also may trigger what Leon Festinger described as "cognitive dissonance"—the tendency of individuals to reinterpret information or experience that conflicts with their internally accepted or publicly stated beliefs in order to avoid the unpleasant personal state that such inconsistencies produce.[33] Cognitive dissonance affects not only perception but behavior as well, producing effort in furtherance of the individual's stated goal in order to avoid the dissonance that not achieving it would create.[34] In the treatment context, cognitive dissonance can cause patients to mobilize their energies and resources to accomplish the treatment goal. These motivating effects of cognitive dissonance are even stronger to the extent that patients' commitment to goal achievement is made to respected therapists or counselors or publicly communicated to others whose respect the patients value.[35]

Thus, according to several strands of psychological theory, voluntary choice of treatment, particularly if recommended by a trusted and respected therapist or counselor, engages a number of important intrinsic sources of motivation and creates the positive

---

[27]*Cf. id.* at 477–78 (observing that pledging goal commitments publicly, or to other people, enhances the amount of personal effort expended in their pursuit).

[28]*See* E. Deci, Intrinsic Motivation (1975) [hereinafter Intrinsic Motivation] (reviewing studies in intrinsic motivation and discussing development of its interplay with extrinsic rewards and controls); E. Deci, The Psychology of Self-Determination (1980) [hereinafter The Psychology of Self-Determination]; Deci & Ryan, *supra* note 17, at 41–43, 60–63, 67.

[29]The Psychology of Self-Determination, *supra* note 28, at 41.

[30]*Id.*

[31]*Id.* at 208–10. *See also* C. Kiesler, The Psychology of Commitment: Experiments Linking Behavior to Belief 164–67 (1971) (finding most effective method for behavior therapists to obtain desired results with patients was to give patients perception that they had freedom and control).

[32]*See* Bandura, *supra* note 8, at 390–449; E. Deci, The Psychology of Self-Determination, *supra* note 28, at 208–10; M. Friedman & G. Lackey, Jr., The Psychology of Human Control: A General Theory of Purposeful Behavior 72–74 (1991) (noting that control leads to self-confidence, which in turn leads to positive behavior); Deci & Ryan, *supra* note 17, at 41–42, 60–61.

[33]L. Festinger, A Theory of Cognitive Dissonance 2–3, 18–24, 73 (1957) [hereinafter Cognitive Dissonance]; L. Festinger, Conflict, Decision, and Dissonance 43 (1964). For a review of empirical studies on cognitive dissonance, *see* J. Brehm & A. Cohen, Explorations in Cognitive Dissonance 221–44 (1962).

[34]L. Festinger, Cognitive Dissonance, *supra* note 33, at 19.

[35]*See* Bandura, *supra* note 8, at 477–78; Meichenbaum & Turk, *supra* note 9, at 170, 174; Winick, *Wagering With the Government, supra* note 7, at 763–64.

expectancies that help to bring about treatment success.[36] These intrinsic sources of motivation and positive expectancies are more likely to be activated when individuals make voluntary choices. To the extent that a decision is externally imposed on individuals, or individuals perceive the choice to be coerced, motivation to succeed predictably is reduced.

Indeed, imposing treatment over objection may produce feelings of resentment and psychological reactance that reduce patient compliance and make the treatment's success less likely. The positive expectancies and attitudes that appear to be so significant to treatment response would seem likely to occur only to the extent that a real contractarian relationship exists between therapists and patients. The condition of voluntary choice is satisfied in most outpatient treatment contexts but perhaps rarely in traditional public mental hospitals, where clinicians dictate treatment that is imposed whether or not patients consent,[37] or in prisons in which treatment is given involuntarily[38] or is perceived to be a condition of release. Some jurisdictions, however, recognize a right to refuse treatment that is applicable in public mental health institutions and prisons,[39] and institutionalized individuals in these jurisdictions are able, at least theoretically, to exercise treatment choice. To the extent that these jurisdictions honor a right to refuse, the goal-setting effect, cognitive dissonance, and other psychological mechanisms producing intrinsic motivation would be possible. The ability of patients or prisoners to internalize the goal would seem to be enhanced to the extent they perceive their choices as voluntary and undermined to the extent they perceive them to be coerced. To the extent coercion prevails in public hospitals and prisons, the therapeutic effects of choice discussed here are unlikely to be achieved.

This theoretical explanation of the therapeutic value of choice finds support in empirical research in a variety of areas suggesting that allowing individuals to exercise choice increases the likelihood of success. For instance, research with children has demonstrated that involving them in treatment planning and decision making leads to greater compliance and increases treatment efficacy.[40] Similarly, allowing students to make choices about educational programs causes them to work "harder, faster, and [react] more positively to the situation than when they [are] unable to make such choices."[41] Anecdotal reports and

---

[36]See supra notes 7–35 and accompanying text. See generally BANDURA, supra note 8, at 467, 471–72; E. DECI, INTRINSIC MOTIVATION, supra note 28; E. DECI, THE PSYCHOLOGY OF SELF-DETERMINATION, supra note 28; Carroll, supra note 7, at 129, 137–38; Deci & Ryan, supra note 17, at 41–42, 60–63, 67.

[37]See, e.g., Dautremont v. Broadlawns Hosp., 827 F.2d 291, 298 (8th Cir. 1987) (hospitalized civil patients may be involuntarily treated with psychotropic drugs against their will).

[38]See, e.g., Washington v. Harper, 494 U.S. 210 (1990) (upholding involuntary administration of antipsychotic medication to prisoner).

[39]See, e.g., 2 M. PERLIN, MENTAL DISABILITY LAW: CIVIL AND CRIMINAL §§ 5.01–69 (1989); Winick, supra note 12; Winick, The Right to Refuse Psychotropic Medication: Current State of the Law and Beyond, in THE RIGHT TO REFUSE ANTIPSYCHOTIC MEDICATION 7 (D. Rapoport & J. Parry eds., 1986).

[40]See, e.g., Lewis, Decision Making Related to Health: When Could/Should Children Act Responsibly?, in CHILDREN'S COMPETENCE TO CONSENT 75, 76–77, 78–79 (G. Melton et al. eds., 1983); Melton, Children's Competence to Consent, A Problem in Law and Social Science, in CHILDREN'S COMPETENCE TO CONSENT, supra, at 1, 11; Melton, Decision Making by Children: Psychological Risks and Benefits, in CHILDREN'S COMPETENCE TO CONSENT, supra, at 21, 30–31, 37; Melton, Children's Participation in Treatment Planning: Psychological and Legal Issues, 12 PROFESSIONAL PSYCHOL. 246, 250–51 (1981).

[41]Bringham, Some Effects of Choice on Academic Performance, in CHOICE AND PERCEIVED CONTROL 131, 140 (L. Perlmutter & R. Monty eds., 1979). See also Amabile & Gitomer, Children's Artistic Creativity: Effects of Choice in Task Materials, 10 PERSONALITY & SOC. PSYCHOL. BULL. 209, 213 (1984) (restriction of choice negatively affected creativity); Deci et al., Characteristics of the Rewarder and Intrinsic Motivation of the Rewardee, 40 J. PERSONALITY & SOC. PSYCHOL. 1, 9 (1981) (students in autonomy-oriented classrooms shown to have higher intrinsic motivation and self-esteem than students in control-oriented classrooms).

informed clinical speculation, supported by several empirical studies, suggest that medical and mental health treatment are more effective when provided on a voluntary rather than involuntary basis.[42] An extensive review of the literature on psychotherapy and psychotropic medication, the two most prevalent forms of treatment for those suffering from mental illness, found no persuasive evidence that coercive application of these techniques to involuntarily committed patients was effective.[43]

Although more research is needed before definitive conclusions can be reached concerning the effectiveness of treatment applied coercively,[44] the available evidence supports the conclusion that patient choice increases the likelihood of treatment success and that coercion does not work as well. Choice seems to increase positive outcomes in a variety of treatment contexts, although the question of its impact on patients with psychosis has not been adequately studied. For example, a patient in a florid state of schizophrenia, who is disoriented and hallucinating, may not possess a sufficient degree of competence to make a

---

[42]*See* AM. PSYCHIATRIC ASS'N TASK FORCE REPORT NO. 34: CONSENT TO VOLUNTARY HOSPITALIZATION 1 (1993) (voluntary hospitalization may lead to more favorable outcomes compared to involuntary hospitalization); *id.* at 5 ("The American Psychiatric Association strongly believes that it is preferable whenever possible for patients to be able to initiate their own psychiatric treatment."); APPELBAUM ET AL., *supra* note 9, at 28; S. BRAKEL ET AL., THE MENTALLY DISABLED AND THE LAW 178, 181 n.34 (3d ed. 1985); BREHM & BREHM, *supra* note 7, at 301; MEICHENBAUM & TURK, *supra* note 9, at 175; Appelbaum et al., *Empirical Assessment of Competency to Consent to Psychiatric Hospitalization,* 183 AM. J. PSYCHIATRY 1170, 1170 (1981); Carroll, *supra* note 7, at 129, 137–38; Culver & Gert, *The Morality of Involuntary Hospitalization, in* THE LAW-MEDICINE RELATION: A PHILOSOPHICAL EXPLORATION 159, 171 (S. Spicker et al. eds., 1981); Freedberg & Johnston, *Effects of Various Sources of Coercion on Outcome of Treatment of Alcoholism,* 43 PSYCHOL. REP. 1271, 1271, 1277 (1978); Nicholson, *Correlates of Commitment Status in Psychiatric Patients,* 100 PSYCHOL. BULL. 241, 243–44 (1986); Perlin & Sadoff, *Ethical Issues in the Representation of Individuals in the Commitment Process,* 45 LAW & CONTEMP. PROBS. 161, 190–91 (1982); Rogers & Webster, *Assessing Treatability in Mentally Disordered Offenders,* 13 LAW & HUM. BEHAV. 19, 20–21 (1989); Stein & Test, *Alternatives to Mental Hospital Treatment,* 37 ARCHIVES GEN. PSYCHIATRY 392, 392–93 (1980); Stromberg & Stone, *supra* note 12, at 327, 328; Ward, *The Use of Legal Coercion in the Treatment of Alcoholism: A Methodological Review, in* ALCOHOLISM: INTRODUCTION TO THEORY AND TREATMENT 272 (D. Ward ed., 1980); Note, *Developments in the Law — Civil Commitment of the Mentally Ill,* 87 HARV. L. REV. 1190, 1399 (1974); *see also* Washington v. Harper, 494 U.S. 210, 249 n.15 (1990) ("The efficacy of forced drugging is also marginal; involuntary patients have a poorer prognosis than cooperating patients.") (Stevens, J., dissenting); Rennie v. Klein, 462 F. Supp. 1131, 1144 (D. N.J. 1978) ("[T]he testimony . . . indicated that involuntary treatment is much less effective than the same treatment voluntarily received."); *but see* COMMITTEE OF GOVERNMENT POLICY, GROUP FOR THE ADVANCEMENT OF PSYCHIATRY, FORCED INTO TREATMENT: THE ROLE OF COERCION IN CLINICAL PRACTICE 22–24, 81, 99–101 (1994) [hereinafter GAP REPORT] (anecdotal reports of successful treatment in coercive situations, including treatment of children and adolescents, sex offenders, and employees treated for alcoholism or drug addiction when coercion perceived by patient as fair and appropriate).

[43]Durham & La Fond, *A Search for the Missing Premise of Involuntary Therapeutic Commitment: Effective Treatment of the Mentally Ill,* 40 RUTGERS L. REV. 303, 351–56, 367–68 (1988) [hereinafter *Involuntary Therapeutic Commitment*]. *See also* Durham & La Fond, *The Empirical Consequences and Policy Implications of Broadening the Statutory Criteria for Civil Commitments,* 3 YALE L. & POL'Y REV. 395 (1985) (analyzing adverse effects of a statutory broadening of civil commitment standards).

[44]*See* GAP REPORT; *supra* note 42, at 101 ("Further study of more subtle forms of coercion in traditional adult psychiatry is warranted."); WEXLER & WINICK, *supra* note 3, at 248 n.101 (noting the scarcity and inadequacy of existing studies and suggesting the need for more empirical research on the issue); Hiday, *Coercion in Civil Commitment: Process, Preferences, and Outcome,* 15 INT'L J.L. & PSYCHIATRY 359 (1992) (suggesting the need for empirical research concerning the efficacy of coercive mental health treatment and hospitalization and identifying pertinent research questions).

meaningful choice in favor of treatment.[45] How much understanding and volition are necessary to engage the psychological mechanisms discussed earlier that can contribute to a positive treatment response? Will such a patient's exercise of choice produce the positive expectancies and intrinsic motivation that seem to be related to favorable treatment outcome? Theoretical explanations for the relationship between patient choice and treatment success are based on studies with less impaired populations. Can these findings be generalized to more impaired patients suffering from at least severe cases of major mental illness? These questions remain unexamined empirically.

Even if such patients do not possess sufficient competence to enable their choices to trigger these positive psychological effects, however, allowing them as great a degree of choice as circumstances permit may still be therapeutic. The aim of treatment interventions for acutely psychotic patients is to ameliorate severe symptomatology and restore patient competence as much as possible. After a brief period of medication, for example, most seriously disturbed patients are sufficiently competent that their choices about future treatment presumably have positive therapeutic value.

An additional therapeutic value of choice, especially for disabled and disadvantaged populations like mental patients and criminal offenders, is that having and making choices is developmentally beneficial. Except for young children (and sometimes even including them) the more choice available to individuals, the more they will act as mature, self-determining adults. Indeed, a sense of competency and self-determination provides strong intrinsic gratification and may be a prerequisite for psychological health.[46] Treating individuals as competent adults who are able to make choices rather than as incompetent subjects of our paternalism, pity, or even contempt has a therapeutic effect. This may be especially true for mental patients, who too often are infantilized by the treatment they receive from institutional clinicians and staff.[47] It also may be true for prisoners, particularly those incarcerated for lengthy periods, who develop a form of institutional dependency.[48]

The denial of choice—which occurs in a legal system that rejects a right to refuse treatment—can be antitherapeutic, producing what in therapeutic jurisprudence terminol-

---

[45]See Zinermon v. Burch, 494 U.S. 113 (1990) (patient with schizophrenia who was delusional and hallucinating and who expressed the view that the mental hospital he was entering was "heaven" assumed to be incompetent to consent to voluntary hospitalization). For analysis of competency in various legal contexts, see Winick, Competency to be Executed: A Therapeutic Jurisprudence Perspective, 10 BEHAV. SCI. & L. 317 (1992) (competency to be executed); Winick, supra note 5 (competency to consent to treatment); Winick, Competency to Consent to Voluntary Hospitalization, supra note 7 (competency to consent to hospitalization); Winick, Incompetency to Stand Trial: An Assessment of Costs and Benefits, and a Proposal for Reform, 39 RUTGERS L. REV. 243 (1987) (competency to stand trial). Recognition that patients have a constitutional right to refuse treatment does not, of course, mean that a patient's right is absolute. For analysis of when state interests may outweigh the patient's asserted right to refuse treatment, see supra chapter 15.

[46]Carroll, supra note 7, at 129, 137–38; Deci & Ryan, supra note 17, at 42, 61, 72–73.

[47]See generally E. GOFFMAN, ASYLUMS: ESSAYS ON THE SOCIAL SITUATIONS OF MENTAL PATIENTS AND OTHER INMATES 3–74 (1962) (discussing the phenomena of institutional dependence); DeVillis, Learned Helplessness in Institutions, 15 MENTAL RETARDATION 10 (1977); C. KIESLER & A. SIBULKIN, MENTAL HOSPITALIZATION: MYTHS AND FACTS ABOUT A NATIONAL CRISIS 148 (1987); Cole, Patient's Rights vs. Doctor's Rights: Which Should Take Precedence?, in REFUSING TREATMENT IN MENTAL INSTITUTIONS: VALUES IN CONFLICT (Doudera & Swaze eds., 1982); Doherty, Labeling Effects in Psychiatric Hospitalization: A Study of Diverging Patterns of Inpatient Self-Labeling Process, 32 ARCHIVES GEN. PSYCHIATRY 562 (1975). See also Johnson v. Solomon, 484 F. Supp. 278, 308 (D. Md. 1979) ("Inappropriate and excessive hospitalization fosters deterioration, institutionalization, and possible regression.") (footnotes omitted). In addition to breeding learned helplessness, see DeVillis, supra; infra note 53 and accompanying text, such total institutions condition passivity and helplessness by reinforcing it and by discouraging assertiveness and autonomous behavior.

[48]See GOFFMAN, supra note 47, at 16–17, 25–31, 39, 53–55, 61, 68–70.

ogy is called "law related psychological dysfunction."[49] Exercising self-determination is considered a basic human need.[50] Studies show that allowing individuals to make choices is intrinsically motivating, whereas denying choice "undermines [their] motivation, learning, and general sense of organismic well-being."[51] Indeed, the stress of losing the opportunity to be self-determining may cause "severe somatic malfunctions" and even death.[52] When people feel they have no influence over matters that vitally affect them, they may also develop what Martin Seligman called *learned helplessness.* Seligman's experimental work with animals and humans led him to posit that repetitive events outside an individual's control may produce a generalized feeling of ineffectiveness that debilitates performance and undermines motivation and perceptions of competence.[53] Institutionalized individuals coerced into accepting treatment might come to view themselves as incompetent in ways that could perpetuate and perhaps even worsen their mental health and social problems. This loss of control may produce depression[54] and decrease motivation.[55] Moreover, it may set up expectancies of failure in the individual that undermine commitment and diminish subsequent performance.[56]

Denying people a sense of control over important areas of their lives thus can have very negative consequences. By contrast, when individuals exercise control and make choices, they experience increased opportunities to build skills necessary for successful living. As a result, they may gradually acquire feelings of self-efficacy, which in turn become important determinants of motivation and performance.[57] If given meaningful choices, these individuals may come to view themselves as in control of their lives, rather than as passive victims of forces they can neither understand nor control—a feeling that undoubtedly contributes to a variety of social and health problems. Treating individuals as competent adults who can make choices and exercise a degree of control over their lives rather than as incompetent subjects of governmental paternalism and control has a predictable beneficial effect.

Having a role in making important decisions, such as those involving treatment, can only increase patient satisfaction and confidence in the treatment process,[58] which inevitably

---

[49]*See* WEXLER & WINICK, *supra* note 3, at 313; Wexler & Winick, *supra* note 3, at 979, 994.

[50]E. DECI, THE PSYCHOLOGY OF SELF-DETERMINATION, *supra* note 28, at 208–09 (discussing "intrinsic motivation" as providing energy for various functions of will). *See also* H. HARTMANN, EGO PSYCHOLOGY AND THE PROBLEM OF ADAPTATION (1958) ("independent ego energy"); White, *Motivation Reconsidered: The Concept of Competence,* 66 PSYCHOL. REV. 297 (1959) ("effectance motivation").

[51]DECI, THE PSYCHOLOGY OF SELF-DETERMINATION, *supra* note 28, at 209 (discussing studies).

[52]*Id.*

[53]M. SELIGMAN, HELPLESSNESS: ON DEPRESSION, DEVELOPMENT, AND DEATH (1975); HUMAN HELPLESSNESS: THEORY AND APPLICATIONS (1980); HUMAN HELPLESSNESS: THEORY AND APPLICATIONS (J. Garber & M. Seligman eds., 1980); Maier & Seligman, *Learned Helplessness: Theory and Evidence,* 105 J. EXPERIMENTAL PSYCHOL. 33 (1976); Overmier & Seligman, *Effects of Inescapable Shock Upon Subsequent Escape and Avoidance Responding,* 63 J. COMP. & PHYSIOLOGICAL PSYCHOL. 28 (1976); Seligman, *Learned Helplessness,* 23 ANN. REV. MED. 407 (1972). *See also* Brehm & Brehm, *supra* note 7, at 378 (1981); WALKER, THE BATTERED WOMAN 42–54 (1979) (applying learned helplessness to the battered woman syndrome); Peterson & Bossio, *Learned Helplessness, in* SELF-DEFEATING BEHAVIORS: EXPERIMENTAL RESEARCH, CLINICAL IMPRESSIONS, AND PRACTICAL IMPLICATIONS 235 (C. Peterson & L. Bossio eds., 1989); Thornton & Jacobs, *Learned Helplessness in Human Subjects,* 87 J. EXPERIMENTAL PSYCHOL. 367 (1971).

[54]*See* FRIEDMAN & LACKEY, *supra* note 32, at 73; Peterson & Bossio, *supra* note 53, at 26.

[55]*See* Deci et al., *supra* note 41; Deci & Ryan, *supra* note 17, at 59.

[56]*See* FRIEDMAN & LACKEY, *supra* note 32, at 73.

[57]*See* BANDURA, *supra* note 8, at 390–449; BREHM & BREHM, *supra* note 7, at 301, 376; Carroll, *supra* note 7, at 129, 137–38; Deci & Ryan, *supra* note 17, at 41–42, 60–61.

[58]Wexler, *Doctor–Patient Dialogue: A Second Opinion on Talk Therapy Through Law,* 90 YALE L.J. 458, 469 (1980) (book review).

increases patient compliance and motivation to succeed. Particularly for institutionalized individuals who have developed a form of institutional dependency or learned helplessness, experiencing a measure of control over important decisions can itself be therapeutic. This conclusion is supported by research on nursing home residents, which demonstrated that providing them increased choices and responsibilities produced improvement in their condition.[59] Exercising choice and experiencing a sense of control over important events in their lives can be a tonic for institutionalized mental patients and prisoners.

Thus, the potential for successful treatment in many contexts would appear to increase when individuals choose treatment voluntarily rather than through coercion.[60] Individuals coerced to participate in a treatment program—for example, by court order; as a condition of diversion, probation, or parole; by correctional authorities; or by authorities in psychiatric settings—often just go through the motions, satisfying the formal requirements of the program without deriving any real benefits.[61] Indeed, such coercion may backfire, producing a negative "psychological reactance" that sets up oppositional behavior leading to failure.[62] Coercion may also trigger a form of the "overjustification effect," in which individuals may accomplish a specified goal, but because they attribute their performance to external pressure, they do not experience any lasting attitudinal or behavioral change.[63] In contrast, the voluntary choice of a course of treatment involves a degree of internalized commitment to the goal often not present when treatment is involuntary.[64]

Voluntary treatment therefore seems more likely to be efficacious than coerced treatment. These psychological perspectives on the value of choice in the therapeutic context and on the corresponding disutility of coercion may help to explain why treatment in the typical public mental hospital[65] and correctional rehabilitation in the typical prison[66] often have been ineffective. These psychological insights suggest that the therapist–patient (or counselor–offender) relationship in the typical institution—in which treatment (or correctional rehabilitation) is imposed coercively, or on a basis not perceived by the patient (or offender) as truly voluntary—may frustrate rather than facilitate achievement of the therapeutic goal.

---

[59]Langer & Rodin, *The Effects of Choice and Enhanced Personal Responsibility for the Aged: A Field Experiment in an Institutional Setting*, 34 PERSONALITY & SOC. PSYCHOL. 191 (1976). *See also* E. LANGER, MINDFULNESS (1989) (summarizing experimental work demonstrating the connection between the individual's mindset and actions and concluding that the opportunity to exercise control over one's choices results in increased motivation, less depression, and more independence and confidence).

[60]*See* APPELBAUM ET AL., *supra* note 9, at 28; N. MORRIS, THE FUTURE OF IMPRISONMENT 24 (1974); Carroll, *supra* note 7, at 137–38; Deci & Ryan, *supra* note 17, at 59, 61; Winick, *supra* note 13, at 353, 360, 422; Winick, *supra* note 5, at 46–53; Winick, *supra* note 7, at 192–99; Winick, *Restructuring Competency to Stand Trial*, 32 UCLA L. REV. 921, 980 (1985).

[61]*See* COMMITTEE ON PSYCHIATRY AND LAW OF THE GROUP FOR THE ADVANCEMENT OF PSYCHIATRY, PSYCHIATRY AND SEX PSYCHOPATH LEGISLATION: THE 30s TO THE 80s 889 (1977); AMERICAN FRIENDS SERVICE COMM., STRUGGLE FOR JUSTICE: A REPORT ON CRIME AND PUNISHMENT IN AMERICA 97–98 (1971); Winick, *supra* note 13, at 344–46; Winick, *supra* note 12, at 83–87.

[62]*See* J. BREHM, A THEORY OF PSYCHOLOGICAL REACTANCE (1966); BREHM & BREHM, *supra* note 7, at 300–01.

[63]*See* R. PETTY & J. CACIOPPO, ATTITUDE AND PERSUASION: CLASSIC AND CONTEMPORARY APPROACHES 169–70 (1981); Carroll, *supra* note 7, at 129, 137–38; Deci, *Effects of Externally Mediated Rewards on Intrinsic Motivation*, 18 J. PERSONALITY & SOC. PSYCHOL. 105 (1971).

[64]*See supra* notes 7–10 and accompanying text; Carroll, *supra* note 7, at 129, 137–38; Deci & Ryan, *supra* note 17, at 59, 61.

[65]*See, e.g.*, Durham & LaFond, *Involuntary Therapeutic Commitment, supra* note 43.

[66]*See, e.g.*, D. LIPTON ET AL., THE EFFECTIVENESS OF CORRECTIONAL TREATMENT (1975); PANEL ON RESEARCH ON REHABILITATIVE TECHNIQUES OF THE NATIONAL RESEARCH COUNCIL, THE REHABILITATION OF CRIMINAL OFFENDERS: PROBLEMS AND PROSPECTS 5 (L. Sechrest et al. eds., 1979).

B. Enhancing the Therapeutic Relationship

The psychological perspectives discussed above also suggest that according patients and offenders a right to refuse treatment might produce a restructuring of the therapist–patient (and counselor–offender) relationship in ways that enhance its therapeutic potential. In psychotherapy, the therapist–patient relationship itself plays an essential role in producing positive outcomes.[67] The effectiveness of psychotherapy heavily depends on the quality of the therapeutic relationship. The most effective therapeutic relationships are those in which mutual trust and acceptance are established and maintained and in which the patient perceives that the therapist cares about and is committed to pursuing the patient's interests[68] and well-being.[69] To succeed, therapists must establish their credibility and trustworthiness early in the relationship. Relationships in which therapists treat patients as objects of paternalism whose participation in the therapeutic decision-making process is unnecessary and undesirable do not inspire such trust and confidence and therefore may be counterproductive. Indeed, relationships in which therapists ignore patients' expressed wishes concerning treatment may suggest that they are more concerned with the welfare of the institution rather than the best interests of their patients. Patients are likely to consider a paternalistic approach that ignores their wishes and concerns as offensive and as an affront to their dignity and personhood.[70] Rather than producing trust and confidence, such an approach can inspire resentment and resistance.

Therapists, particularly those in public institutions, too often seem to misperceive the importance of the therapist–patient relationship. Not only do these therapists thereby forgo therapeutic opportunities, but by their actions they may actually create a harmful division between therapist and patient. Too often, there is no real connection or sense of community between therapist and patient. As a result, patients do not develop a sense of trust and confidence in their therapists. Yet such trust and confidence may be a prerequisite for engaging those positive attitudes and expectancies that play an important role in producing a successful treatment response. Some therapists can learn much from the teachings of theologian Martin Buber, whose writings explore the nature of relationships based on mutual dialogue.[71] Buber's notion of an "I–Thou" relationship characterized by mutual respect, openness, and affirmation of the other can be a useful model for restructuring the therapist–

[67]E.g., BREHM & BREHM, supra note 7, at 151–55, 300–01; WEXLER & WINICK, supra note 3, at 173; Deci & Ryan, supra note 17, at 70; Lambert et al., The Effectiveness of Psychotherapy, in HANDBOOK OF PSYCHOTHERAPY AND BEHAVIOR CHANGE 157–211 (S. Garfield & A. Bergin eds., 3d ed. 1986) [hereinafter HANDBOOK].

[68]See authorities cited in supra note 67. The therapist–patient relationship, although especially significant in the context of psychotherapy, is also important in all areas of medical practice. See, e.g., COUSINS, supra note 18, at 18 (discussing confidence by the patient in the doctor and in the patient's own healing resources); MOYERS, supra note 9, at 50 (discussing a "prevention partnership in which a patient is empowered to be a partner with . . . [the doctor] in the healing process"); Appelbaum & Gutheil, supra note 9, at 341 (noting correlation between adherence to drug treatment by psychiatric inpatients and the quality of the doctor–patient relationship).

[69]BREHM & BREHM, supra note 7, at 151–52, 300–02; WEXLER & WINICK, supra note 3, at 173; Beutler et al., Therapist Variables in Psychotherapy Process and Outcome, in HANDBOOK, supra note 67, at 280–81; Orlinsky & Howard, Process and Outcome in Psychotherapy, in HANDBOOK, supra note 67, at 311.

[70]See J. FEINBERG, HARM TO SELF 4–5, 23, 27 (1986); Goldstein, For Harold Lasswell: Some Reflections on Human Dignity, Entrapment, Informed Consent, and the Plea Bargain, 84 YALE L.J. 683, 691 (1975); Meisel & Roth, Toward an Informed Discussion of Informed Consent: A Review and Critique of the Empirical Studies, 25 ARIZ. L. REV. 265, 284 (1983); Winick, supra note 5, at 17.

[71]See M. BUBER, I AND THOU (1937); M. BUBER, BETWEEN MAN AND MAN (1947). For a proposal calling for the restructuring of the attorney–client relationship in the poverty law context that builds upon Buber's work, see Alfieri, The Antinomies of Poverty Law and a Theory of Dialogical Empowerment, 16 N.Y.U. REV. L. & SOC. CHANGE 659 (1987–88).

patient relationship. This model can transform the therapeutic relationship from one of paternalistic monologue to one of true dialogue, thereby increasing its therapeutic potential.

Recognition of a right to refuse treatment can reshape the therapist–patient relationship into a more humane and more effective tool. It can increase the likelihood that therapists will respect the dignity and autonomy of their patients and recognize their essential role in the therapeutic process. This reshaping of the therapist's role can increase the potential for a true therapeutic alliance in which therapists treat their patients as persons.[72] The result can be more patient trust, confidence, and participation in decision making such that patients internalize treatment goals. A therapeutic relationship restructured in this fashion can enhance the patient's intrinsic motivation and the likelihood that the goal-setting effect, commitment, and the reinforcing effects of cognitive dissonance occur.

A real therapist–patient (or counselor–offender) dialogue concerning treatment planning and decision making can only bolster the patient's faith in the therapist and in the therapist's dedication to the patient's best interests. This faith and the expectations it generates may be essential to producing the Hawthorne effect or other interactive mechanisms that can increase the likelihood of therapeutic success.[73] Without trust, the therapeutic opportunities provided by the therapist–patient relationship are drastically reduced.

The need for trust, cooperation, and open communication is particularly important in the context of psychotherapy and other forms of verbal counseling, which are totally dependent on willing patient communication in the therapeutic relationship. What Freud characterized as the "fundamental rule" of psychotherapy requires the patient to communicate openly and candidly with the therapist.[74] Such basic techniques for probing the patient's unconscious as free association and interpretation of dreams necessitate that a patient be forthcoming. Patient cooperation, necessary for these verbal techniques to have any chance of succeeding, assume a high degree of patient trust in the therapist and a relationship that is basically contractarian rather than coercive in nature.

The ability of therapists successfully to manipulate the transference phenomenon similarly depends on a high degree of patient trust. Transference is the process by which patients' feelings, thoughts, and wishes concerning certain important figures in their lives (particularly in the early years) are transferred or displaced to the therapist.[75] This process is an essential device by which therapists help patients to understand their emotional problems and their origins. Transference is a key element in the therapist–patient alliance.[76] Indeed, it has been characterized as "unequivocally the heart of psychoanalysis."[77] Freud himself strongly stressed the role of transference as an ally of the analyst and the motivating force in treatment.[78] According to Freud, a positive transference provides the "strongest motive for

---

[72]See P. RAMSEY, THE PATIENT AS PERSON: EXPLORATIONS IN MEDICAL ETHICS (1970).

[73]See JOSPE, supra note 20, at 93–108, 130; text accompanying supra note 20.

[74]S. FREUD, AN OUTLINE OF PSYCHOANALYSIS, in 23 STANDARD EDITION OF THE COMPLETE PSYCHOLOGICAL WORKS OF SIGMUND FREUD 141 (1964).

[75]See, e.g., AM. PSYCHIATRIC ASS'N, A PSYCHIATRIC GLOSSARY 106 (6th ed. 1988) [hereinafter PSYCHIATRIC GLOSSARY]; Adler, Transference, Real Relationship and Alliance, 61 INT'L J. PSYCHOANALYSIS 547, 547 (1980); Greenson, The Working Alliance and the Transference Neurosis, 34 PSYCHOANALYSIS Q. 155 (1965); Karasu, Psychoanalysis and Psychoanalytic Psychotherapy, in 2 COMPREHENSIVE TEXTBOOK OF PSYCHIATRY 1442, 1446–47 (H. Kaplan & B. Sadock eds., 5th ed. 1989).

[76]See PSYCHIATRIC GLOSSARY, supra note 75, at 106; Adler, supra note 75, at 548 ("[T]ransference and alliance seem inextricably intermeshed.").

[77]Karasu, supra note 75, at 1446.

[78]See Adler, supra note 75, at 548; Friedman, The Therapeutic Alliance, 50 INT'L J. PSYCHOANALYSIS 139 (1969).

the patient's taking a share in the joint work of analysis.''[79] Transference thus is both a crucial therapeutic tool and a motivating force for committing the patient to the therapeutic alliance. It is the "unconscious affective bond that forms the basis for analytic work and underlies the patient's desire to remain in treatment . . . .''[80]

For transference to play this essential role in the therapeutic relationship, the therapist must gain the patient's trust and inspire confidence and respect. A basic sense of trust is a prerequisite to the optimal functioning of the working alliance. Patients "often require an awareness of the person and personality of the analyst as someone appropriately interested, caring, warm, and wishing to be helpful at the beginning of treatment in order to establish the self-object transferences that stabilize the treatment and make optimal therapeutic work possible.''[81] Indeed, "[n]o analysis can proceed without the functioning of a rational, trusting therapeutic alliance.''[82]

The key to successful psychotherapy is the therapeutic alliance itself. The classical analytic concept of the psychotherapist–patient relationship envisioned the therapist as a neutral screen for the patient's transferential projections. However, this concept has more recently been broadened to focus attention on the therapeutic value of the relationship itself. This broadening is often discussed as the "real relationship.''[83] It represents more than a mere acknowledgement of the therapist's humanness: It is also a recognition that the actual, caring, human relationship between therapist and patient is transformative or curative.[84] Thus, the therapeutic relationship itself is a therapeutic agent. To reach its therapeutic potential, the therapist must establish an environment of safety and trust.[85] A voluntary relationship in which the patient sees the therapist as an agent, assisting in the accomplishment of goals that the two of them define rather than as a paternalistic director of the processor as the agent of the institution in which the patient is held, is more likely to create the atmosphere of trust and openness that is necessary for the therapeutic relationship to bring about healing and change.[86]

---

[79]S. FREUD, ANALYSIS TERMINABLE AND INTERMINABLE, *in* 23 THE COLLECTED WORKS OF SIGMUND FREUD 233 (1937), *cited in* Adler, *supra* note 75, at 548.

[80]Karasu, *supra* note 75, at 1446.

[81]Adler, *supra* note 75, at 553. *See also* Viederman, *The Real Person of the Analyst and His Role in the Process of Psychoanalytic Cure,* 39 J. AM. PSYCHOANALYTIC ASS'N 451, 457–58 (1991) (need for first phase of analysis to offer an environment of safety and trust in the therapist–patient relationship in order for the therapeutic potential of transference to be achieved). For a parallel perspective drawn from cognitive psychology, see BREHM & BREHM, *supra* note 7, at 151–53, 300–01; Deci & Ryan, *supra* note 17, at 70.

[82]Karasu, *supra* note 75, at 1449.

[83]*See, e.g.,* Adler, *supra* note 75.

[84]Personal communication from Daniel C. Silverman, M.D., Associate Psychiatrist in Chief, Beth Israel Hospital, Boston, Massachusetts, and Assistant Professor of Psychiatry, Harvard Medical School, Cambridge, Mass., June 3, 1991. *See, e.g.,* Aaron, *The Patient's Experience of the Analyst's Subjectivity,* 1 PSYCHOANALYTIC DIALOGUE 29, 33 (1991) ("The relational approach that I am advocating views the patient–analyst relationship as continually established and re-established through ongoing mutual influences in which both patient and analyst systematically affect, and are affected by, each other. A communication process is established between patient and analyst in which influence flows in both directions.''); *id.* at 41 (analysis viewed as co–participation); *id.* at 43 (analysis viewed as "mutual," with "both patient and analyst functioning as subject and object, as co–participants''); Adler, *supra* note 75, at 552–54; Binstock, *The Therapeutic Relationship,* 21 J. AM. PSYCHOANA-LYTIC ASS'N 543 (1973); Hoffman, *Discussion: Toward a Social–Constructivist View of the Psychoanalytic Situation,* 1 PSYCHOANALYTIC DIALOGUE 74, 75 (1991) (a real personal relationship and a mutual exploration of each one's perception of the analytical relationship creates the opportunity "for a special kind of affective contact with the analyst that is thought to have therapeutic potential'').

[85]Karasu, *supra* note 75, at 1449; Viederman, *supra* note 81, at 548.

[86]*See* GAP REPORT, *supra* note 42, at 7, 100.

A legal system in which the therapist needs the patient's informed consent is thus more conducive to allowing the relationship itself to realize its potential as a therapeutic agent. An informed consent requirement, by encouraging a therapist–patient dialogue, can create a significant therapeutic opportunity. Discussion and negotiation about a patient's objections to treatment can provide an important context for probing conscious and unconscious resistance, for fostering a positive transference, and for earning the patient's trust and confidence.

A therapeutic relationship characterized by voluntariness rather than coercion is particularly important in the institutional contexts—hospital and prison—in which the right-to-refuse-treatment question most often arises. In these contexts, distrust of therapists and concern about their conflicting allegiance to the institutional employer is high. For therapy to be successful, therapists or counselors must distance themselves from the institution's security and management staff and functions and explicitly establish themselves as agents of the patient, not of the institution.[87] Institutional residents, accustomed to being treated as objects—as a means to the accomplishment of institutional ends—will naturally be suspicious and distrustful of therapists who treat them on a coercive basis. Providing therapy or counseling on a truly voluntary basis provides a sharp contrast to the way individuals are treated by other institutional staff and can establish a climate that may allow patients or offenders to view their therapists as allies. It can break down distrust and inspire confidence in and commitment to the therapeutic relationship, which can become an oasis in the desert of institutional life.

Considerations favoring a therapeutic relationship based on voluntariness obviously have special force in the context of verbal psychotherapy or counseling. They also seem applicable in the context of behavior therapy, which uses techniques that require patient cooperation and involvement as well as trust and confidence in the therapist in order to succeed.[88] Moreover, these considerations may apply as well even in the context of the organic treatment techniques, although to a considerably lesser extent. Choosing the appropriate medication, for example, and maximizing the potential that it is used appropriately often require communication with the patient and much cooperation.[89]

In all types of medical decision making, allowing the patient to exercise choice inevitably enriches and improves the quality of the decision-making process.[90] Successful

---

[87]See GAP REPORT, supra note 42, at 7 ("Formation of an alliance is fostered by therapists explicitly defining their role as the agent of the patient, in contrast to working for the patient's parents, the hospital, or another institution that might be perceived by the patient as being in conflict with his or her own needs.").

[88]See supra note 13 and accompanying text.

[89]See Appelbaum & Gutheil, supra note 9, at 341. In addition, many of the organic treatment techniques, like psychotropic drugs, are not administered in isolation, but are part of an integrated treatment plan that involves verbal psychotherapy or counseling. In the case of schizophrenia or severe depression, for example, medication is needed to control symptoms that would prevent the patient from accepting other forms of therapy. Antipsychotic drugs that minimize the visual or auditory hallucinations or agitation that often characterize schizophrenia, and antidepressant drugs that control the severe withdrawal and feelings of worthlessness and profound sadness that often characterize major affective depression, are necessary to render the patient accessible to verbal, social, and occupational therapy approaches. Even if such medication effectively reduces severe symptomatology when administered coercively, the verbal therapy that should follow the reduction in symptoms seems to be more effective to the extent that the individual chooses it voluntarily.

[90]See J. KATZ, THE SILENT WORLD OF DOCTOR AND PATIENT 102–03 (1984) (analyzing the informed consent doctrine as furthering the doctor–patient relationship); COUSINS, supra note 22, at 55 ("[F]ull communication between the patient and physician is indispensable not just in arriving at an accurate diagnosis but in devising an effective strategy for treatment."); Altman, Health Official Urges Focus by Doctors on Caring as Well as Curing: A More Active Role for Patients is Recommended, N.Y. TIMES, Aug. 15, 1993, at A6 ("Doctors need to consider their patients as knowledgeable allies, not as passive recipients of care, and involve them fully in the entire care process, including decision-making about treatment . . . .") (quoting Michael H. Merson, M.D., World Health Organization official).

treatment planning and implementation require a thorough analysis of the patient's problems, of the social context that often perpetuates them, and of the patient's strengths and
weaknesses. Patient trust, cooperation, and full and open communication are essential if the
therapist is to obtain this information from the patient, who frequently is the best if not the
only source. Moreover, the aphorism "two heads are better than one" is especially apt in this
context. Higher quality treatment decision making is more likely when the therapist–patient
dialogue, kept open by allowing the patient a legal right to participate in decision making,
produces the decision rather than the therapist making it unilaterally. Treatment decision
making often involves difficult value choices. How risks and benefits of alternative courses
of treatment are weighed depends on the incentive preferences of the individual. The
therapist does not always share the patient's values and preferences. Moreover, when the
therapist is not the patient's long-term physician—as in mental institutions and prisons—he
or she will be unaware of them, absent dialogue. Doctors may "know best" about the
clinical aspects of risks and benefits of alternative treatments,[91] but they are not more
knowledgeable than their patients concerning the patients' preferences. Although dialogue
may cost more in terms of therapist time, it produces treatment decision making that is more
accurate and thus more likely to be efficacious. In addition, patients are more likely to accept
and comply with treatment when the decision results from a process in which they
participate.[92]

C. Applying the Law Therapeutically in Coercive Contexts

Although the analysis contained in this chapter strongly suggests voluntarily rather than
coerced treatment, there are situations in which coerced treatment is legally permissible, as
chapter 15 demonstrates. In these situations, the manner in which clinicians apply the legal
authority to treat patients coercively may still have positive or negative therapeutic effects.
How can clinicians apply the law therapeutically in these coercive contexts?

There undoubtedly are situations in which a degree of coercion is both therapeutically
appropriate and legally acceptable, but clinicians should use coercion sparingly and involve
the patient in the decision-making process as much as possible. Even when coercion is
necessary, clinicians should seek to apply it in ways that minimize the patient's perception of
coercion. In this respect, the recent research on coercion performed under the auspices of the
MacArthur Network for Mental Health and the Law has special significance.

The MacArthur coercion work proceeded on the premise that before one can properly
study coercion as an independent variable in treatment outcome, a significant issue must be
examined first—coercion as a dependent variable, that is, what makes people feel coerced.[93]
This issue—the determinants and correlates of perceived coercion—has been the subject of
recent research conducted under the auspices of the MacArthur Research Network on
Mental Health and the Law.[94] The study examined attitudes of patients at the time of
admission to mental hospitals. The preliminary results indicated that it is possible to study

---

[91]*But see* KATZ, *supra* note 90, at 166–69 (discussing the uncertainty inherent in medical science).

[92]*See* KATZ, *supra* note 90, at 103; MEICHENBAUM & TURK, *supra* note 9, at 63, 71–76, 84–85.

[93]Monahan et al., *Coercion to Inpatient Treatment: Initial Results and Implications for Assertive Treatment in the Community, in* COERCION AND AGGRESSIVE COMMUNITY TREATMENT: A NEW FRONTIER IN MENTAL HEALTH LAW 1, 14 (D. Dennis & J. Monahan eds., 1996); *see also* Bennet et al., *Inclusion, Motivation, and Good Faith: The Morality of Coercion in Mental Hospital Admission,* 11 BEHAV. SCI & L. 295 (1993); Gardner et al., *Two Scales for Measuring Patients' Perceptions for Coercion During Mental Hospital Admission,* 11 BEHAV. SCI. & L. 307 (1993).

[94]*See* sources cited *supra* note 93.

patients' perceptions of coercion independent of the formal legal status of voluntary or involuntary admission.[95]

The MacArthur coercion study concluded that a number of important variables correlated with patient perceptions of coercion.[96] One of these was motivation—the extent to which the treatment provider was perceived as acting out of concern for the patient. Another was respect—the degree of respect with which the treatment provider dealt with the patient. Others included what in the psychology of procedural justice has come to be known as "voice"—the extent to which the patient was afforded an opportunity to express his or her opinion on the admission decision—and validation—the extent to which the patient's speech was taken seriously. Another important variable was the patient's perception of fairness—whether he or she was treated fairly and whether trickery or deception was used in the admission process. Finally, the extent to which pressure was applied in the admission process was deemed significant (i.e., the degree of persuasion, inducement, threats, or force). Very high levels of perceived coercion were present when providers used the negative pressures of threats and force, whereas positive approaches involving persuasion and inducement were associated with no increase in perceived coercion.[97] Patients in the admissions process who reported that others acted out of concern for them; treated them fairly, with respect, and without deception; provided them with an opportunity for voice; and took what they said seriously were much less likely to experience coercion.[98]

Although empirical research has not yet extensively probed the relationship between the perception of coercion and treatment outcome, the theoretical analysis contained in this chapter strongly suggests that patients who feel coerced do not respond as well as those who do not feel coerced. Therefore, clinicians who find it necessary to impose treatment coercively should heed the admonitions of the MacArthur research and interact with their patients in ways that minimize patients' subjective perceptions of coercion even though, in an objective sense, coercion is being applied. The MacArthur research suggests that positive approaches such as persuasion can be used as a strategy of choice to attempt to convince people to accept treatment.[99] Negative approaches such as threats should be used "only as a last resort to secure needed care."[100] Furthermore, in all circumstances (but especially when negative pressure has been used), patients should be afforded as much process as possible.[101] Clinicians should convey to their patients the notion that they are acting out of concern for them. They should treat their patients fairly—with respect and without deception—giving them an opportunity to tell their side of the story and seriously considering their views in the treatment decision-making process.[102] Clinicians who find it necessary to impose treatment coercively and who heed these admonitions can thereby minimize the risk that coercion will have antitherapeutic effects.

Coercion may sometimes be necessary, particularly in the treatment of severely ill patients. However, in light of the potential antitherapeutic consequences of coercion, clinicians should resort to it only when truly necessary and should involve the patient in the treatment decision-making process as much as possible. As soon as coerced treatment has

---

[95]Monahan et al., *supra* note 93; *see* Lidz et al., *Perceived Coercion in Mental Hospital Admission,* 52 ARCHIVES GEN. PSYCHIATRY 1034 (1995).

[96]Monahan et al., *supra* note 93.

[97]*Id.* at 23.

[98]*Id.* at 24.

[99]*Id.* at 26.

[100]*Id.*

[101]*Id.* at 27.

[102]*Id.*

had the hoped-for effects, the clinician should cede to the patient increasing measures of treatment decision-making autonomy. Whenever possible, clinicians should use persuasion, education, negotiation, and inducement in preference to coercion. Even when coercion is deemed necessary, clinicians should act toward their patients in ways that minimize the perception of coercion and maximize the patient's sense of voice and inclusion and the patient's appreciation that the treatment imposed is benevolently motivated and administered in good faith. Although more research is needed to determine the effectiveness of coercive treatment, enough is now known to reshape clinical practice in the imposition of coercive treatment to reduce its antitherapeutic consequences.

D. The Therapeutic Value of a Right to Refuse Treatment

For all kinds of medical and psychological treatment, there is strong therapeutic value in having a meaningful dialogic process between therapist and patient resulting in mutual decision making. Such a process enhances communication in the therapeutic relationship and increases the quality of clinical decision making. It also fosters patient trust and confidence in the therapist, facilitating positive patient attitudes and expectancies that can play an important role in treatment success.

In a legal system that allows the therapist to make medical decisions unilaterally without patient participation and consent, such a dialogic process would largely be unnecessary and would frequently be dispensed with. Recognizing a right to refuse treatment fosters the possibility of a meaningful dialogic process, thereby enhancing the potential that the therapist–patient relationship itself will be therapeutic. Moreover, in a legal system that denies patients a right to refuse treatment, patients will be deprived of the opportunity to make treatment choices for themselves and of the therapeutic advantages that seem to be associated with choice. A patient deprived of choice against a particular treatment cannot exercise the kind of choice in favor of it that engages the positive expectancies and intrinsic motivation that are important to successful treatment.

The right to refuse treatment, rather than frustrating treatment, may thus actually advance the goal of successful therapy and rehabilitation. Instead of viewing the right to refuse treatment with suspicion and patients who refuse treatment with contempt, therapists should understand that the right to refuse provides an important therapeutic opportunity. Indeed, a right to refuse treatment may be indispensable to a meaningful therapeutic alliance.

This theoretical analysis of the likely impact of recognizing a right to refuse treatment— and a corresponding opportunity of patients and offenders to choose it—strongly suggests that therapeutic values will be furthered by the reshaping of the therapist–patient relationship that can result from recognition of the right. Although empirical work is needed to test these assumptions and their applicability to seriously impaired patients, psychological and psychodynamic theory provide significant support for the recognition of a right to refuse treatment and for its effective implementation.

Chapter 18
WAIVER OF THE RIGHT TO REFUSE TREATMENT:
The Requirement of Informed Consent

Although mental patients and offenders in certain circumstances may possess a constitutional or other legal right to refuse treatment, many decline to assert this right. Legal rights, even those protected by the Constitution, generally may be waived. For example, criminal defendants who enter guilty pleas waive fundamental rights under the Fifth and Sixth Amendments, including the rights to counsel, to trial by jury, to confront adverse witnesses, and to avoid compulsory self-incrimination.[1] In upholding the constitutionality of plea bargaining, the Supreme Court specified the elements of an effective waiver: "Waivers of constitutional rights not only must be voluntary but must be knowing, intelligent acts done with sufficient awareness of the relevant circumstances and likely consequences."[2] This formulation is consistent with the Court's traditional waiver standard, which requires "an intentional relinquishment or abandonment of a known right or privilege."[3] The Court has applied the same waiver standard in noncriminal contexts.[4]

---

[1]*See* Boykin v. Alabama, 395 U.S. 238, 242–43 (1969).

[2]Brady v. United States, 397 U.S. 742, 748 (1970).

[3]Johnson v. Zerbst, 304 U.S. 458, 464 (1938), *cited in* Brady v. United States, 397 U.S. 742, 748 n.6 (1970). *See also* Miranda v. Arizona, 384 U.S. 436, 475–76 (1966). The Court has applied a somewhat more relaxed waiver standard in the case of criminal defendants consenting to warrantless searches that would otherwise violate the Fourth Amendment ban on unreasonable searches and seizures. *See, e.g.,* United States v. Watson, 423 U.S. 411 (1976); Schneckloth v. Bustamonte, 412 U.S. 218 (1973). In these cases the Court stressed the voluntary aspect of waiver, rejecting the arguments that consent was invalid absent a showing by the government that the consenting party understood that it could be freely withheld. *See* 412 U.S. at 227. The Court nonetheless reaffirmed that "consent [may] not be coerced, by explicit or implicit means, by implied threat or covert force." *Id.* at 228. The question whether consent is voluntary or the product of duress or coercion is treated by the Court as "a question of fact to be determined from the totality of all the circumstances." *Id.* at 227. Knowledge of the right to refuse consent is treated merely as "one factor to be taken into account." *Id.* In considering the totality of the circumstances, the prosecutor has the burden of proving that consent "was, in fact, freely and voluntarily given," a burden that "cannot be discharged by showing no more than acquiescence to a claim of lawful authority." Bumper v. North Carolina, 391 U.S. 543, 548–49 (1968). For analyses of waiver in criminal cases, see Dix, *Waiver in Criminal Procedure: A Brief for More Careful Analysis,* 55 Tex. L. Rev. 193 (1977); Tigar, *Foreword: Waiver of Constitutional Rights: Disquiet in the Citadel,* 84 Harv. L. Rev. 1 (1970); Winick, *Restructuring Competency to Stand Trial,* 32 UCLA L. Rev. 921, 951–79 (1985).

[4]*See, e.g.,* Fuentes v. Shevin, 407 U.S. 67 (1972) (standard for waiver of notice in conditional sales contracts); Overmeyer v. Frick Co., 405 U.S. 174 (1972) (upholding the validity of cognovit note).

These elements of constitutional waiver closely parallel the elements of the informed consent doctrine in health law.[5] The requirement of informed consent to medical treatment or research contemplates a therapist who discloses relevant information to the patient or research participant concerning the risks and benefits of a proposed course of treatment or research study and a competent individual who voluntarily decides to accept or refuse the recommendation.[6] The elements of informed consent include disclosure of information, competency, understanding, voluntariness, and decision making.[7] For example, U.S. Department of Health and Human Services regulations concerning the protection of human subjects define *informed consent* as "the knowing consent of an individual or his legally authorized representative, so situated as to be able to exercise free power of choice without undue inducement or any element of force, fraud, deceit, duress, or other form of constraint or coercion."[8] Under these principles, if the decision process is sufficiently free of coercion and undue influence, a patient or offender who receives sufficient information concerning the possible risks and side effects of a proposed therapy and alternative approaches, and who is sufficiently competent and intelligent to comprehend the information, may choose whether to participate in the proposed treatment. Such an informed consent allows treatment to be administered and constitutes a defense to any subsequent legal action asserting violation of the right to refuse treatment.

Specific elements of the informed consent requirements may vary by jurisdiction, depending on differing statutory, regulatory, and case law approaches, but these basic

---

[5]*See generally* J. KATZ, EXPERIMENTATION WITH HUMAN BEINGS 521–88 (1972); LEGISLATIVE AND SOCIAL ISSUES COMM. OF THE AM. ASS'N ON MENTAL DEFICIENCY, CONSENT HANDBOOK (1977) [hereinafter CONSENT HANDBOOK]; Appelbaum & Grisso, *The MacArthur Treatment Competence Study. I: Mental Illness and Competence to Consent to Treatment,* 19 LAW & HUM. BEHAV. 105 (1995); Levine, *The Nature and Definition of Informed Consent in Various Research Settings, in* THE BELMONT REPORT: ETHICAL PRINCIPLES AND GUIDELINES FOR THE PROTECTION OF HUMAN SUBJECTS OF RESEARCH 3–1 (National Commission for the Protection of Human Subjects of Biomedical Research 1978) [hereinafter BELMONT REPORT]; Meisel et al., *Toward a Model of the Legal Doctrine of Informed Consent,* 134 AM. J. PSYCHIATRY 285 (1977); Roth et al., *Tests of Competency to Consent to Treatment,* 134 AM. J. PSYCHIATRY 279 (1977); Sprung & Winick, *Informed Consent in Theory and Practice: Legal and Medical Perspectives on the Informed Consent Doctrine and a Proposed Reconceptualization,* 17 CRITICAL CARE MED. 1346 (1989).

[6]*See generally* P. APPELBAUM ET AL., INFORMED CONSENT: LEGAL THEORY AND CLINICAL PRACTICE (1987); R. FADEN & T. BEAUCHAMP, A HISTORY AND THEORY OF INFORMED CONSENT (1986); J. KATZ, THE SILENT WORLD OF DOCTOR AND PATIENT (1984); CONSENT HANDBOOK, *supra* note 5; 1 PRESIDENT'S COMM'N FOR THE STUDY OF ETHICAL PROBS. IN MED. & BIOMED. & BEHAV. RES., MAKING HEALTH CARE DECISIONS: A REPORT ON THE ETHICAL AND LEGAL IMPLICATIONS OF INFORMED CONSENT IN THE PATIENT–PRACTITIONER RELATIONSHIP (1982) [hereinafter PRESIDENT'S COMM'N REP.]; F. ROZOFSKY, CONSENT TO TREATMENT: A PRACTICAL GUIDE (2d ed. 1990); Meisel & Roth, *What We Do and Do Not Know About Informed Consent,* 246 JAMA 2473, 2473 (1981); Schwartz & Roth, *Informed Consent and Competency in Psychiatric Practice,* 8 AM. PSYCHIATRIC PRESS REV. PSYCHIATRY 409, 409 (1989); Sprung & Winick, *supra* note 5. The common law doctrine of informed consent has been given constitutional recognition. *See, e.g.,* Cruzan v. Director, Mo. Dep't of Health, 497 U.S. 261, 269 (1990); *id.* at 287 (O'Connor, J., concurring); *id.* at 300 (Brennan, J., dissenting, joined by Marshall & Blackmun, JJ.); *id.* at 330 (Stevens, J., dissenting). For discussion of informed consent as a defense to tort suits for unauthorized treatment, see KEETON ET AL., PROSSER AND KEETON ON THE LAW OF TORTS § 32 (5th ed. 1984) [hereinafter PROSSER AND KEETON].

[7]*See, e.g.,* APPELBAUM ET AL., *supra* note 6, at 57; FADEN & BEAUCHAMP, *supra* note 6, at 274–75; Appelbaum & Grisso, *Assessing Patients' Capacities to Consent to Treatment,* 319 NEW ENG. J. MED. 1635, 1637 (1988); Appelbaum & Grisso, *supra* note 5, at 106; Meisel & Roth, *Toward an Informed Discussion of Informed Consent: A Review and Critique of the Empirical Studies,* 25 ARIZ. L. REV. 265, 271–72 (1983); Roth et al., *supra,* note 5, at 279; Schwartz & Roth, *supra* note 6, at 412–17; Sprung & Winick, *supra* note 5, at 1346. Some of these elements— competency and understanding, for example—are somewhat overlapping.

[8]45 C.F.R. § 46.116 (1994).

principles are common to most formulations.[9] The key elements of informed consent—competency, knowledge, and voluntariness—and the ability of mental patients and criminal offenders to satisfy these requirements are discussed below.

A. Competency

Generally, people make important decisions for themselves, including decisions concerning their own health. Individual choice is thwarted only when individuals are believed to be unable to make decisions about their own well-being. In such cases, the state may invoke its *parens patriae* power, using an incompetency label to veto such choices and substituting the decision of another concerning what is best for them.[10] Once the state applies the incompetency label, the individual generally is precluded from making choices concerning the activity in question. Such individuals often perceive this paternalistic response as offensive and as an affront to their dignity and personhood.[11] Some, however, do not feel this way and welcome the benevolently motivated intrusion on their decision-making authority

---

[9]*See supra* note 7.

[10]The *parens patriae* power allows government to engage in decision making in the best interests of persons who by reason of age or disability are incapable of making such decisions for themselves. *See* Mills v. Rogers, 457 U.S. 291, 296 (1982); Winick, *Legal Limitations on Correctional Therapy and Research,* 65 MINN. L. REV. 331, 374 (1981); Note, *Developments in the Law—Civil Commitment of the Mentally Ill,* 87 HARV. L. REV. 1190, 1207–45 (1974); *supra* chapter 15, parts C1(b), C2(a). Historically, the *parens patriae* power was premised on the presumed incapacity of minors and the actual incapacity of the mentally incompetent to protect or care for themselves. Winick, *supra,* at 375; Note, *supra,* at 1212–16; *see, e.g.,* Addington v. Texas, 441 U.S. 418, 426 (1979); O'Connor v. Donaldson, 422 U.S. 563, 583 (1975) (Burger, C.J., concurring). Because the *parens patriae* power is based on the need for the government to protect the well-being of its citizens when they cannot care for themselves, the government may legitimately invoke this power only in the case of individuals who, because of age or physical or mental disability, are incapable of determining their own best interests. *See, e.g.,* Bee v. Greaves, 744 F.2d 1387, 1395 (10th Cir. 1984), *cert. denied,* 469 U.S. 1214 (1985); Winters v. Miller, 446 F.2d 65, 68–71 (2d Cir.), *cert. denied,* 404 U.S. 985 (1971); Davis v. Hubbard, 506 F. Supp. 915, 935–36 (N.D. Ohio 1980); Rogers v. Commissioner, 458 N.E.2d 308, 322 (Mass. 1983); Opinion of the Justices, 465 A.2d 484, 489–90 (N.H. 1983); Rivers v. Katz, 495 N.E.2d 337, 342 (N.Y. 1986); *In re* K.K.B., 609 P.2d 747, 750–52 (Okla. 1980). Courts have frequently recognized this limitation in cases involving patients asserting a right to refuse psychotropic medication sought to be administered without their consent, restricting assertions of the *parens patriae* power to patients determined to be incompetent to participate in treatment decisions. Rennie v. Klein, 653 F.2d 836, 847 & n.12 (3d Cir. 1981) (en banc), *vacated and remanded,* 458 U.S. 1119 (1982); Rogers v. Okin, 634 F.2d 650, 657–59 (1st Cir. 1980), *vacated and remanded sub nom.* Mills v. Rogers, 457 U.S. 291 (1982); *Winters,* 446 F.2d at 71; *Davis,* 506 F. Supp. at 935–36; Anderson v. State, 663 P.2d 570, 571 (Ariz. Ct. App. 1982); People v. Medina, 705 P.2d 961, 973 (Colo. 1985) (en banc); *In re* Boyd, 403 A.2d 744, 748 n.5 (D.C. Ct. App. 1979); Gundy v. Pauley, 619 S.W.2d 730, 731 (Ky. 1981); *Rogers,* 458 N.E.2d at 314; *Rivers,* 495 N.E.2d at 343–44; *In re* K.K.B., 609 P.2d at 749. The Supreme Court's decision in Washington v. Harper, 494 U.S. 210, 236 (1990), upholding the authority of a state prison to administer antipsychotic medication to a competent prisoner, is not inconsistent with this proposition, as it involved an exercise of the state's police power interest in protecting the safety of other inmates and staff from an assaultive prisoner.

Although incompetency is thus a prerequisite to exercise of the government's *parens patriae* power, the government does not always substitute its judgment for that of an incompetent patient. *See* Cruzan v. Director, Mo. Dep't of Health, 497 U.S. 261, 286 (1990) ("[W]e do not think the Due Process Clause requires the State to repose judgment on these matters [of life-prolonging treatment] with anyone but the [incompetent] patient herself.").

[11]*See* J. FEINBERG, HARM TO SELF 4–5, 23, 27 (1986); Goldstein, *For Harold Lasswell: Some Reflections on Human Dignity, Entrapment, Informed Consent, and the Plea Bargain,* 84 YALE L.J. 683, 691 (1975); Meisel & Roth, *supra* note 7, at 284.

or come retrospectively to do so.[12] Such paternalism frustrates the value society places on autonomy and self-determination but does so on the ground of beneficence.[13] The justification presumably is that the injury caused by denying such people autonomy would be exceeded by the harm produced by honoring the choices of incompetent people.

Thus, competency is treated as a prerequisite to informed consent,[14] and its absence is a prerequisite to invocation of the state's *parens patriae* power. If patients are competent, their treatment decisions must be respected, even if they refuse treatment, no matter how foolish their decisions appear to be.[15] Alternatively, any decisions made by incompetent patients are deemed invalid and without legal effect.[16]

---

[12]*See, e.g.,* A. STONE, MENTAL HEALTH LAW: A SYSTEM IN TRANSITION 69–70 (1975) (describing this reaction as the "thank you" theory); D. WEXLER, MENTAL HEALTH LAW: MAJOR ISSUES 45–48 (1981) (analyzing the "thank you" theory in context of narcotics abusers); Gove & Fain, *A Comparison of Voluntary and Committed Psychiatric Patients,* 34 ARCHIVES GEN. PSYCHIATRY 669, 675 (1977); Kane et al., *Attitudinal Changes of Involuntarily Committed Patients Following Treatment,* 40 ARCHIVES GEN. PSYCHIATRY 374, 376 (1983); Schwartz et al., *Autonomy and the Right to Refuse Treatment: Patients' Attitudes After Involuntary Medication,* 39 HOSP. & COMMUNITY PSYCHIATRY 1049–54 (1988) (empirical study showing that medication refusers treated over objection, if rehospitalized, would assent to drug treatment). *But see* Beck & Golowka, *A Study of Enforced Treatment in Relation to Stone's "Thank You" Theory,* 6 BEHAV. SCI. & L. 559, 565 (1988) (empirical study of involuntarily hospitalized patients showing no evidence to support "thank you" theory in 62% of cases). Some patients—those who are profoundly retarded or irreversibly ill with loss of brain function, for example—remain unconscious of the state's paternalistic intervention. *See, e.g., Cruzan,* 497 U.S. at 266 (patient in a persistent vegetative state); Superintendent of Belchertown State Sch. v. Saikewicz, 370 N.E.2d 417, 419 (Mass. 1977) (profoundly retarded patient).

[13]*See* T. BEAUCHAMP & J. CHILDRESS, PRINCIPLES OF BIOMEDICAL ETHICS 170–71 (2d ed. 1983); Meisel, *The "Exceptions" to the Informed Consent Doctrine: Striking a Balance Between Competing Values in Medical Decisionmaking,* 1979 WIS. L. REV. 413, 425.

[14]*Cruzan,* 497 U.S. at 262 (recognizing that "an incompetent person is not able to make an informed and voluntary choice to exercise a hypothetical right to refuse treatment or any other right''); 4 RESTATEMENT (SECOND) OF TORTS § 892 (1979); S. BRAKEL ET AL., THE MENTALLY DISABLED AND THE LAW 340 (3d ed. 1985); CONSENT HANDBOOK, *supra* note 5, at 6; Meisel et al., *supra* note 5, at 287; Roth et al., *supra* note 5; Winick, *supra* note 10, at 383. This assumption is rarely questioned. *But see* Winick, *Incompetency to Stand Trial: An Assessment of Costs and Benefits, and a Proposal for Reform,* 39 RUTGERS L. REV. 243, 244 (1987) (questioning the assumption in the context of competency to stand trial); Winick, *supra* note 3, at 925 (1985) (same).

[15]*See, e.g.,* Tune v. Walter Reed Army Med. Hosp., 602 F. Supp. 1452, 1455 (D.D.C. 1985); Bouvia v. Superior Court, 225 Cal. Rptr. 297, 301 (Cal. Ct. App. 1986); In re Estate of Brooks, 205 N.E.2d 435, 442 (Ill. 1965); Downer v. Veilleux, 322 A.2d 82, 91 (Me. 1974); Lane v. Candura, 376 N.E.2d 1232, 1235–36 (Mass. App. Ct. 1978); In re Conroy, 486 A.2d 1209, 1225 (N.J. 1985); In re Quackenbush, 383 A.2d 785, 789 (N.J. 1978); New York City Health & Hosps. Corp. v. Stein, 335 N.Y.S.2d 461, 465 (Sup. Ct. 1972); In re Yetter, 62 Pa.D.&C.2d 619, 623 (1973); BRAKEL ET AL., *supra* note 14, at 340; PRESIDENT'S COMM'N FOR THE STUDY OF ETHICAL PROBLEMS IN MED. & BIOMED. AND BEHAV. RES., DECIDING TO FORGO LIFE SUSTAINING TREATMENT: ETHICAL, MEDICAL AND LEGAL ISSUES IN TREATMENT DECISIONS 40 (1983) [hereinafter DECIDING TO FORGO]; Perry, *A Problem With Refusing Certain Forms of Psychiatric Treatment,* 20 SOC. SCI. MED. 645, 646 (1985); Sprung & Winick, *supra* note 5, at 1348. In appropriate circumstances, the government may insist that even a competent individual accept treatment in furtherance of an overriding police power interest in protecting public health or safety. *See, e.g.,* Washington v. Harper, 494 U.S. 210, 227 (1990) (involuntary antipsychotic medication upheld for prisoner found dangerous to others within prison when not taking medication); Jacobson v. Massachusetts, 197 U.S. 11, 26–27 (1905) (compulsory vaccination to prevent the spread of communicable smallpox upheld as "of paramount necessity" to the state's fight against epidemic).

[16]4 RESTATEMENT (SECOND) OF TORTS § 892A(2)(a) (1979). *E.g.,* Relf v. Weinberger, 372 F. Supp. 1196, 1200 (D.D.C. 1974); Demers v. Gerety, 515 P.2d 645, 649–50 (Ct. App. 1973), *rev'd on other grounds,* 589 P.2d 180

Although the competency question is thus of critical importance, no general agreement exists concerning the appropriate legal standard for ascertaining competency to provide informed consent.[17] Several tests have been used (sometimes in combination) to determine the patient's ability (a) to make and express a decision; (b) to actually understand the information disclosed about the treatment and alternatives to treatment; (c) to engage in decision making in a rational manner (*i.e.,* to manipulate rationally the available information and appreciate the implications of alternative choices); and (d) to make a reasonable treatment decision.[18] The standards used to define *competency* and their application vary considerably.

Some cases suggest that patient assent without understanding is not valid.[19] Many judicial statements invoke Judge Cardozo's oft-quoted maxim that ''[e]very human being of adult years and sound mind has a right to determine what shall be done with his own body,''[20] and assume that the decision of a person of *unsound* mind is legally ineffective.[21] How ''unsound'' the individual's mind must be, and the precise relationship between such ''unsoundness'' and decision-making ability, are rarely elucidated, however. The 1982 President's Commission Report on health care decision making defines *competency to make medical decisions* as requiring a patient to possess a set of values and goals and the ability to communicate with others, understand information, and reason and deliberate.[22] This demanding test for competency is similar to tort law definitions of *consent* as a defense to

---

(N.M. 1978); Sprung & Winick, *supra* note 5, at 1348. In such cases, the decision is made by a substitute decision maker, often a close relative, attempting to decide what the patient would have chosen if competent, or acting in the patient's best interests. *See, e.g., Cruzan,* 497 U.S. at 279–84; *In re* Conroy, 486 A.2d 1209, 1229–33 (N.J. 1985); APPELBAUM ET AL., *supra* note 6, at 91; BRAKEL ET AL., *supra* note 14, at 453; FADEN & BEAUCHAMP, *supra* note 6, at 36; T. GRISSO, EVALUATING COMPETENCIES: FORENSIC ASSESSMENTS AND INSTRUMENTS 316 (1986); 1 PRESIDENT'S COMM'N REP., *supra* note 6, at 62; Appelbaum & Grisso, *supra* note 7, at 1637; Parry, *A Unified Theory of Substitute Consent: Incompetent Patients' Right to Individualized Health Care Decision-Making,* 11 MENTAL & PHYSICAL DISABILITY L. REP. 378, 378 (1987).

[17]APPELBAUM ET AL., *supra* note 6, at 59, 83; FADEN & BEAUCHAMP, *supra* note 6, at 288, 291; GRISSO, *supra* note 16, at 314; Appelbaum & Grisso, *supra* note 5, at 106; Schwartz & Roth, *supra* note 6, at 415; Tepper & Elwork, *Competence to Consent to Treatment as a Psychological Construct,* 8 LAW & HUM. BEHAV. 205, 206 (1984); Waltz & Scheuneman, *Informed Consent to Therapy,* 64 NW. U. L. REV. 628, 636–37 (1969); Note, *Informed Consent and the Dying Patient,* 83 YALE L.J. 1632, 1653 (1974).

[18]APPELBAUM ET AL., *supra* note 6, at 88; GRISSO, *supra* note 16, at 314; Appelbaum & Grisso, *supra* note 5, at 109–11; Appelbaum & Grisso, *supra* note 7, at 1636; Appelbaum & Roth, *Competency to Consent to Research,* 39 ARCHIVES GEN. PSYCHIATRY 951, 951 (1982); Drane, *The Many Faces of Competency,* 15 HASTINGS CTR. REP., Apr. 1985, at 17; Roth et al., *supra* note 5, at 279; Schwartz & Roth, *supra* note 6, at 415; Sprung & Winick, *supra* note 5, at 1350–51; Tepper & Elwork, *supra* note 17, at 208–10, 214–216. *See also* Rivers v. Katz, 495 N.E.2d 337, 344 n.7 (N.Y. 1986) (eight-factor test).

[19]*E.g.,* Demers v. Gerety, 515 P.2d 645, 649 (Ct. App. 1973) (consent by patient administered sleeping medication found not valid), *rev'd on other grounds,* 589 P.2d 180 (N.M. 1978); Grannum v. Berard, 422 P.2d 812, 814 (Wash. 1967) (patient must have the mental capacity necessary to consent to surgery); APPELBAUM ET AL., *supra* note 6, at 59 (referring to cases suggesting that assent to medical care by a patient who has not actually understood the disclosed information is not valid); GRISSO, *supra* note 16, at 315; Meisel, *The Expansion of Liability for Medical Accidents: From Negligence to Strict Liability by Way of Informed Consent,* 56 NEB. L. REV. 51, 119–21 (1977) (consent of patients who have not actually understood the disclosure of information is not valid authorization for treatment); Meisel & Roth, *supra* note 7, at 284 (patients may provide informed consent only if they understand the information the doctor is obliged to furnish).

[20]Schloendorff v. Society of New York Hosp., 105 N.E. 92, 93 (N.Y. 1914).

[21]APPELBAUM ET AL., *supra* note 6, at 59.

[22]1 PRESIDENT'S COMM'N REP., *supra* note 6, at 57.

intentional tort, which generally contemplate assent by one who is capable of expressing a rational will.[23] The Restatement of Torts provides that to be effective, consent must be given by one who "is capable of appreciating the nature, extent and probable consequences of the conduct consented to."[24]

Case law and commentary thus treat patient competency as a prerequisite to informed consent and, without analysis, often incorporate tort law notions of consent to define *competency* broadly, sometimes even insisting on a demonstration of actual understanding. Is such a demanding standard of competency appropriate? If inability to appreciate and understand is the appropriate standard when the state seeks to override patients' refusal of treatment on the basis that they are incompetent, should this demanding test also be used when patients assent to treatment in accordance with their therapists' recommendation? In current legal definitions of competency, no distinction is made between patients who assent to treatment and those who object to it. In a number of contexts, however, medical practice seems to differentiate between assenting and objecting patients, at least tacitly applying a different standard of competency to each and scrutinizing the competence of patient decision making primarily (if not exclusively) in cases of objection.[25]

I have previously suggested that the law could learn much from medical practice regarding competency and should similarly differentiate between assent and objection.[26] At least in noncoercive situations, the law should require less in the way of competence when patients assent to conventional treatment than when they refuse treatment. This distinction would allow patient choice in favor of treatment to be respected in a wider range of cases and reserve serious inquiry into competency primarily for cases in which physicians or others seek to override a patient's choice against treatment. Rather than applying a rigid, unilateral approach to competency that treats all cases alike, I proposed a flexible, sliding-scale approach that takes account of the important distinction between assent and objection. I argued that recognizing this distinction is not only consistent with medical practice but would best serve the policies underlying the informed consent doctrine and the therapeutic interests of patients.

Although the law does not formally recognize such a distinction, in practice it seems to reflect the distinction made by medical practitioners between patients who assent and those who object to treatment. A basic insight of legal realism is that law on the books often differs considerably from law in action. Sometimes assessing how law actually functions in practice provides insights that cause us to seek to change law on the books to bring it in line with law in action. This seems to be the case with the law of informed consent. In practice, assent and hence a waiver of rights are frequently allowed in a variety of contexts without an assessment of competency, even when competency is in question. In practice, the law generally reserves scrutiny of competency primarily for cases of refusal.[27] These practices tacitly acknowledge a difference between patients who assent to hospitalization and treatment and those who

---

[23]APPELBAUM ET AL., *supra* note 6, at 59–60; 1 F. HARPER ET AL., THE LAW OF TORTS § 3.10, at 304 (2d. ed. 1986); PROSSER AND KEETON, *supra* note 6, § 18, at 114–15.

[24]4 RESTATEMENT (SECOND) OF TORTS § 892A & cmt. b (1979).

[25]Grisso & Appelbaum, *The MacArthur Treatment Competence Study. III: Abilities of Patients to Consent to Psychiatric and Medical Treatment,* 19 LAW & HUM. BEHAV. 149, 171 (1995); Winick, *Competency to Consent to Treatment: The Distinction Between Assent and Objection,* 28 HOUS. L. REV. 15, 37–40 (1991).

[26]*See generally* Winick, *supra* note 25.

[27]*See* Winick, *supra* note 25, at 16.

object to them.[28] Objecting patients retain a qualified right to refuse the intervention in question. Although this right to refuse may be outweighed in appropriate circumstances by countervailing state interests,[29] some kind of scrutiny is usually needed to satisfy the requirements of due process—often including a hearing—before treatment may be imposed over objection[30] or a patient is hospitalized involuntarily.[31] However, when patients assent

---

[28]1 PRESIDENT'S COMM'N REP., *supra* note 6, at 61–62; Annas & Densberger, *Competence to Refuse Medical Treatment: Autonomy v. Paternalism,* 15 U. TOL. L. REV. 561, 573 (1984); Geller, *State Hospital Patients and Their Medication—Do They Know What They Take?,* 139 AM. J. PSYCHIATRY 611, 615 (1982); Macklin, *Some Problems in Gaining Informed Consent from Psychiatric Patients,* 31 EMORY L.J. 345, 364–65 (1982); Roth et al., *supra* note 5, at 282–83; Sprung & Winick, *supra* note 5, at 1350–51; Wexler, *Reflections on the Legal Regulation of Behavior Modification in Institutional Settings,* 17 ARIZ. L. REV. 132, 135–37 (1975); Winick, *supra* note 3, at 963–68.

The National Commission for the Protection of Human Subjects of Biomedical and Behavioral Research has recommended explicit recognition of this difference between assent and objection in the context of research involving those with mental illness and mental retardation. In a number of recommendations, the National Commission suggested more liberal rules for permitting research on those who assent, compared with those who object, and more relaxed scrutiny of research involving those who assent. NATIONAL COMM'N FOR THE PROTECTION OF HUMAN SUBJECTS OF BIOMED. BEHAV. RES., RESEARCH INVOLVING THOSE INSTITUTIONALIZED AS MENTALLY INFIRM 117–21 (Recommendations 2–4). (DHEW Pub. No. (OS) 78-0006, 1978) [hereinafter MENTALLY INFIRM]. The Commission used the term *assent* as follows:

> [A]uthorization by a person whose capacity to understand and judge is somewhat impaired by illness or institutionalization, but who remains functional. The standard for "assent" requires that the subject know what procedures will be performed in the research, choose freely to undergo those procedures, communicate this choice unambiguously, and be aware that subjects may withdraw from participation. This standard for assent is intended to require a lesser degree of comprehension by the subject than would generally support informed consent. . . .

Id. at 9–10. *See also* Wyatt v. Aderholt, 368 F. Supp. 1382, 1383 (M.D. Ala. 1974) (stating that incompetent residents of state institution may be sterilized with approval of review committee only if they have "formed, without coercion, a genuine desire to be sterilized"); *In re* Moe, 432 N.E.2d 712, 720 (Mass. 1982) (concluding that expressed preferences of incompetent individuals with mental retardation must be considered in making substituted judgment determination concerning sterilization); *In re* Roe, 421 N.E.2d 40, 57 (Mass. 1981) (stated preferences of incompetent mentally ill person must be treated as a critical factor in making substituted judgment determinations concerning antipsychotic medication); NATIONAL COMM'N, PSYCHOSURGERY 64–65 (DHEW Pub. No. (OS) 77-0001, 1977) (Recommendation 3) (recommending that psychosurgery may be performed on patients incapable of giving informed consent where the patient's guardian gives informed consent, the patient does not object, and a court approves, except that psychosurgery may never be performed over objection even for an incompetent patient whose guardian consents) [hereinafter PSYCHOSURGERY]; NATIONAL COMM'N, RESEARCH INVOLVING CHILDREN 16 (DHEW Pub. No. (OS) 77-0004, 1977) (suggesting that assent to participation in research should be required for children 7 years of age or older in addition to parental permission; with limited exceptions, the child's objection should be binding).

This difference between assent and objection by incompetent individuals also has been recognized in contract law. A mentally incompetent person, having "nothing which the law recognizes as a mind," Dexter v. Hall, 82 U.S. (15 Wall.) 9, 20 (1872), was traditionally deemed to lack the capacity to contract. J. DAWSON ET AL., CASES AND COMMENTS ON CONTRACTS 496 (4th ed. 1982); E. FARNSWORTH, CONTRACTS § 4.6 (1982); Cook, *Mental Deficiency and the Law of Contract,* 21 COLUM. L. REV. 424, 425 (1921); Weihofen, *Mental Incompetency to Contract or Convey,* 39 S. CAL. L. REV. 211, 215–17 (1966). Under the modern view, however, agreements entered into by individuals who are incompetent are not void, but only voidable at the instance of the incompetent; they may disaffirm the contract but may honor it if they wish, thereby binding the other party. BRAKEL ET AL., *supra* note 14, at 438; DAWSON ET AL., *supra* at 497; FARNSWORTH, *supra,* § 4.7; Kronman, *Paternalism and the Law of Contracts,* 92 YALE L.J. 763, 787–88 (1983); Weihofen, *supra,* at 231–32.

[29]*See supra* chapter 15, part C (analyzing when state interests in involuntary treatment outweigh an individual's assertion of a right to refuse treatment).

[30]*See infra* chapter 19 (analyzing procedural due process requirements in treatment-refusal contexts).

[31]*See* Addington v. Texas, 441 U.S. 418, 425 (1979); Note, *supra* note 10, at 1265–1316; *see also* Vitek v. Jones, 445 U.S. 480, 483–84 (1980) (procedural due process requires adversary hearing for involuntary transfer of prisoner to mental hospital).

to such an intervention, even if their assent is not fully competent, such scrutiny is rare.[32] Instead, unless patients are grossly incompetent[33] (and sometimes even when they are), hospital admission and treatment typically proceed in accordance with the patients' expressed wishes.

In addition to the assent–objection distinction, medical and legal practices with regard to the determination of competency also seem to vary based on the risk–benefit ratio of the treatment involved. When treatment carries a questionable risk–benefit ratio, we are more inclined to insist on a hearing whether or not the patient assents.[34] On the other hand, when the risk–benefit ratio is considered so favorable that "reasonable" patients might elect the intervention, the patient's assent usually is accepted without further inquiry. Even if inquiry is required, a relatively low standard of competency is used in cases in which a favorable risk–benefit ratio exists.[35]

Can these distinctions drawn by medical and legal practice (although not acknowledged in the law on the books) be defended? The approach to competency reflected in medical and judicial practices can be justified by autonomy values and by the understanding that patients who assent to conventional treatment recommended by their therapists do not ordinarily require additional protection to ensure that their choices are not harmful. The principle of autonomy is central to American ethical and political theory.[36] U.S. constitutional history and traditions also reflect a strong preference for autonomy and individual self-determination.[37] Indeed, the principle of autonomy permeates American law[38] and is a major basis for the doctrine of informed consent.[39]

---

[32]*See* GRISSO, *supra* note 16, at 316; 1 PRESIDENT'S COMM'N REP., *supra* note 6, at 61; Geller, *supra* note 28, at 615; Roth et al., *supra* note 5, at 283; Winick, *supra* note 10, at 402.

[33]*See, e.g.,* Zinermon v. Burch, 494 U.S. 113, 118 (1990) (involving a patient volunteering for hospitalization who thought he was entering heaven).

[34]*See* CONSENT HANDBOOK, *supra* note 5, at 7–8, 21–23, 38–54; BELMONT REPORT, *supra* note 5, at 13; 1 PRESIDENT'S COMM'N REP., *supra* note 6, at 60; Friedman, *Legal Regulation of Applied Behavior Analysis in Mental Institutions and Prisons,* 17 ARIZ. L. REV. 39, 87 (1975); Roth et al., *supra* note 5, at 283; Winick, *supra* note 10, at 402.

[35]*See* FADEN & BEAUCHAMP, *supra* note 6, at 292; 1 PRESIDENT'S COMM'N REP., *supra* note 6, at 60; Gaylin, *The Competence of Children: No Longer All or None,* 12 HASTINGS CTR. REP., Apr. 1982, at 33, 35; Roth et al., *supra* note 5, at 283; Sprung & Winick, *supra* note 5, at 1352–53. The justification for this practice has been articulated as follows:

> [T]he prudent course is to take into account the potential consequences of the patient's decision. When the consequences for well-being are substantial, there is a greater need to be certain that the patient possesses the necessary level of capacity. When little turns on the decision, the level of decisionmaking capacity required may be appropriately reduced (even though the constituent elements remain the same) and less scrutiny may be required about whether the patient possesses even the reduced level of capacity. Thus a particular patient may be capable of deciding about a relatively inconsequential medication, but not about the amputation of a gangrenous limb.

1 PRESIDENT'S COMM'N REP., *supra* note 6, at 60.

[36]*See* Winick, *On Autonomy: Legal and Psychological Perspectives,* 37 VILL. L. REV. 1705, 1707–15 (1992).

[37]*See id.* at 1715–53.

[38]*See id.* at 1715–55.

[39]*See, e.g.,* Canterbury v. Spence, 464 F.2d 772, 780 (D.C. Cir.), *cert. denied,* 409 U.S. 1064 (1972); *In re Guardianship of Browning,* 568 So. 2d 4, 10 (Fla. 1990); Natanson v. Kline, 350 P.2d 1093, 1104 (Kan. 1960); *In re Conroy,* 486 A.2d 1209, 1223 (N.J. 1985); Schloendorff v. Society of New York Hosp., 105 N.E. 92, 93 (N.Y. 1914); APPELBAUM ET AL., *supra* note 6, at 22, 26–28; 1 PRESIDENT'S COMM'N REPORT, *supra* note 6, at 2–4; Appelbaum et al., *Empirical Assessment of Competency to Consent to Psychiatric Hospitalization,* 138 AM. J. PSYCHIATRY 1170, 1170 (1981); Beauchamp, *Paternalism and Behavioral Control,* 60 THE MONIST 62, 68–69 (1977); Macklin & Sherwin, *Experimenting on Human Subjects: Philosophical Perspectives,* 25 CASE W. RES. L. REV. 434, 443 (1075); Meisel, *supra* note 13, at 441; Shultz, *From Informed Consent to Patient Choice: A New Protected Interest,* 95 YALE L.J. 1533, 1537 (1985); Sprung & Winick, *supra* note 5, at 1346; Winick, *supra* note 36, at 1732–35.

Principles of autonomy justify use of a sliding-scale approach to defining competency that takes into account the distinction between assent and objection. Although vetoing patients' choices to accept particular treatments and overriding their objections to treatment would frustrate autonomy values, the imposition of unwanted treatment seems more offensive to the autonomy principle. In a society in which drugs and other forms of medical treatment are highly regulated, people cannot necessarily expect to receive every treatment they may want. However, the imposition of intrusive medical treatment that invades the historic liberty interest in bodily integrity and personal security constitutes a breach of human dignity and an affront to principles of self-determination. Involuntary treatment constitutes a deprivation of this cherished liberty interest. Although being denied something people may wish (chosen treatment) is an affront to their sense of autonomy, taking away something they have (the control over their own bodies) seems categorically more offensive to principles of individual self-determination.

In addition to autonomy interests, principles of beneficence also call for the use of a sliding-scale approach. The law should adopt a less demanding standard of competency in the case of patients assenting to conventional treatment recommended by their therapists than in the case of patients objecting to such treatment or assenting to experimental or highly risky treatment. When the consequences of honoring treatment objections are grave (*e.g.,* objection to the amputation of a gangrenous leg where death is otherwise thought likely to follow) or when the treatment assented to is risky (*e.g.,* psychosurgery),[40] a more demanding standard of competency should be applied. Concern for protecting the individual's well-being is heightened in proportion to the gravity and likelihood of the risk. When the threat to patient well-being seems small, the need for protective measures is correspondingly less. Application of a more demanding standard of competency in cases in which the risk seems to be grave—insisting, for example, that patients are very knowledgeable about the consequences of their decisions—does not mean that particular patients cannot meet this higher standard and be deemed competent to make the decision.

Deference to autonomy values should justify allowing patients to make choices even if the consequences of those choices are detrimental to them so long as they understand those consequences and their choice is voluntary. Concern for the welfare of patients may justify an inquiry into their understanding when the consequences are grave, although not necessarily a veto of their choices. However, when the consequences are reasonable and even seem likely to be beneficial, this inquiry is not justified by considerations of beneficence. Because it would intrude on autonomy values and expend scarce resources without achieving significant benefits, such an inquiry generally should be considered unnecessary when patients assent to conventional therapy recommended by their therapists.

How would the sliding-scale approach to defining and assessing competency work? The clearest and least controversial case of incompetency exists when individuals cannot or will not express their preferences.[41] In such cases, imposing treatment does not threaten autonomy values as does rejecting patients' assents to treatment or overriding their objections to it. When individuals clearly and voluntarily express a choice, however, disregarding that choice presents the greatest threat to autonomy values, at least in the absence of specific signs of incompetence.[42] In principle, of course, incompetent expres-

---

[40]*See supra* chapter 8 (discussing psychosurgery).

[41]*E.g.,* Cruzan v. Director, Mo. Dep't of Health, 497 U.S. 261, 266 (1990) (patient in a persistent vegetative state); *see also* Macklin, *supra note* 28, at 358; Roth et al., *supra* note 5, at 280.

[42]Winick, *supra* note 25, at 42.

sions of autonomy should not be accepted.[43] Assent by those who are so impaired that they are unaware of or cannot understand their actions represents little genuine autonomy. Moreover, individuals who are incompetent to make meaningful choices may require protection from themselves. Competence therefore should not be equated with the ability to articulate a choice. But how much more than the ability to express a choice should be required? The answer should vary with the circumstances. Because the competing values at stake are respect for autonomy and a desire to promote the health of the individual, the competency question should turn on an assessment of the degree of autonomy present and the risk–benefit ratio of the therapeutic intervention involved. Although patients should be allowed to choose conventional treatment without demonstrating a high degree of competency, a greater showing of competency is appropriate when the intervention chosen is of questionable value and carries great risk. A sliding-scale approach to the competency standard thus allows a proper accommodation of the sometimes conflicting principles of autonomy and beneficence.

How should incompetency be determined? In addition to defining competency differently on the basis of the assent–objection distinction and the relative riskiness of the intervention in question, the law should use a presumption of competence in determining the competency question. The law's commitment to the principle of autonomy gives rise to a general presumption in favor of competency.[44] Unless outweighed by other values in a particular context, our preference for autonomy leads to a presumption that individual choices are competent and should be respected, at least in the absence of clear evidence suggesting incompetency. This presumption has the effect of preventing inquiry into the individual's competence unless special circumstances exist.

Should this basic presumption of competency apply to individuals who are mentally ill? For reasons developed in chapter 14, I have argued that it should, at least for those who do not base their preferences on reasons that seem clearly irrelevant, on beliefs that seem clearly irrational, or on outright delusions or hallucinations.[45] Although mental illness sometimes impairs competency to process information and make rational choices, it often does not.[46] As chapter 14 demonstrates, the difference between those with mental illness and "normal" people with regard to the ability to engage in rational decision making is not as great as

---

[43]*See* BEAUCHAMP & CHILDRESS, *supra* note 13, at 61, 63; FEINBERG, *supra* note 11, at 316; 1 PRESIDENT'S COMM'N REP., *supra* note 6, at 48, 56–57; BELMONT REPORT, *supra* note 5, at 4–5; Appelbaum et al., *supra* note 39, at 1174–75.

[44]*See, e.g.,* Lotman v. Security Mut. Life Ins. Co., 478 F.2d 868, 873 (3d Cir. 1973); Winters v. Miller, 446 F.2d 65, 68 (2d Cir.), *cert. denied,* 404 U.S. 985 (1971); Rogers v. Okin, 478 F. Supp. 1342, 1361, 1363–64 (D. Mass. 1979), *aff'd in part, vacated in part,* 634 F.2d 650 (1st Cir. 1980), *vacated sub nom.* Mills v. Rogers, 457 U.S. 291 (1982); Child v. Wainwright, 148 So. 2d 526, 527 (Fla. 1963); Howe v. Commonwealth, 99 Mass. 88, 98–99 (1868); Lane v. Candura, 376 N.E. 2d 1232, 1235 (Mass. App. Ct. 1978); Grannum v. Berard, 422 P.2d 812, 814 (Wash. 1967); BRAKEL ET AL., *supra* note 14, at 258, 341 n.167, 375; 1 PRESIDENT'S COMM'N REP., *supra* note 6, at 2–3, 56; GRISSO, *supra* note 16, at 312; Annas & Densberger, *supra* note 28, at 575; Appelbaum & Grisso, *supra* note 7, at 1635; Goldstein, *On the Right of the "Institutionalized Mentally Infirm" to Consent to or Refuse to Participate as Subjects in Biomedical and Behavioral Research, in* MENTALLY INFIRM, *supra* note 28, at 2–12 to 2–13, 2–25 to 2–26, 2–29, 2–31 to 2–32 (App. DHEW Pub. No. (OS) 78-0007, 1978); Parry, *supra* note 16, at 384; Schwartz & Roth, *supra* note 6, at 417; Sprung & Winick, *supra* note 5, at 1348; Wexler, *Reflections on the Legal Regulation of Behavior Modification in Institutional Settings,* 17 ARIZ. L. REV. 132, 136 (1975). Moreover, virtually all states have a statutory presumption in favor of competency. BRAKEL ET AL., *supra* note 14, at 175 & table 7.2; Blackburn, *The "Therapeutic Orgy" and the "Right to Rot" Collide: The Right to Refuse Antipsychotic Drugs Under State Law,* 27 HOUS. L. REV. 447, 471–72 nn.87–88 (1990)*; see, e.g.,* FLA. STAT. § 765.204 (1995).

[45]*See supra* chapter 14, part B; *see also* Winick, *supra* note 25, at 37.

[46]*See supra* chapter 14, part B.

commonly is supposed.[47] Those with mental illness have a significant capacity for normal and rational thought and behavior,[48] and ''normal'' people frequently lose contact with reality and lack the ability to think straight, to pay attention, to process information, and to perform at least some key social tasks. Even in the midst of a psychotic episode,[49] mentally ill people function normally some of the time.[50] Moreover, such episodes are intermittent, and between episodes clinicians find it difficult to distinguish clearly between people with mental illness and ''normal'' people.[51] Mentally ''normal'' but physically ill patients in hospitals, nursing homes, and the community frequently suffer from linguistic, educational, emotional, and social problems that severely impair their ability to function competently in processing information and making treatment choices.[52] This may occur particularly during the pain or stress of a serious illness and the situational anxiety and depression it often produces. Moreover, medical procedures like general anesthesia sometimes impair cognitive abilities and decision-making capacity for several days or even weeks. Many patients, although not so impaired as to be considered ''mentally ill,'' generally have great difficulty making important decisions concerning their health because they are essentially irrational or are filled with denial, driven by unconscious needs and desires, paralyzed by fear, or dominated by other emotions.

In short, although the decision-making competency of those with mental illness is sometimes severely impaired, they are not categorically more incompetent than physically ill patients.[53] All patients have difficulty understanding complex information and making difficult decisions, particularly under the stress of illness. Most patients, whether mentally ill or medically ill, willingly defer to their doctors concerning appropriate treatment.[54]

---

[47]*Id.;* Winick, *supra* note 25, at 37.

[48]*Id.*

[49]Winick, *supra* note 25, at 38.

[50]Morse, *Crazy Behavior, Morals and Science, An Analysis of Mental Health Law,* 51 S. CAL. L. REV. 527, 573 (1978); Winick, *supra* note 25, at 38.

[51]Morse, *supra* note 50, at 573.

[52]*See* R. BURT, TAKING CARE OF STRANGERS: THE RULE OF LAW IN DOCTOR–PATIENT RELATIONS 142 (1979); FEINBERG, *supra* note 11, at 340–43; Cassileth et al., *Informed Consent—Why Are Its Goals Imperfectly Realized?,* 302 NEW ENG. J. MED. 896, 899 (1980).

[53]*See* Grisso & Appelbaum, *supra* note 25, at 171 (empirical study of decision-making impairment of those hospitalized for mental illness compared to those hospitalized for heart disease and a matched group of non-ill individuals finding significant differences in treatment decision-making ability, but finding that nearly half of the group with schizophrenia and 76% of the group with depression performed in an ''adequate range'' and ''a significant portion performed at or above the mean for persons without mental illness'' and concluding that the ''justification for a blanket denial of the right to consent to or refuse treatment for persons hospitalized because of mental illness cannot be based on the assumption that they lack decision-making capacity''); McKinnon et al., Rivers *In Practice: Clinicians' Assessments of Patients' Decision-Making Capacity,* 40 HOSP. & COMMUNITY PSYCHIATRY 1159, 1159 (1989) (''Clinical evidence suggests that despite alterations in thinking and mood, psychiatric patients are not automatically less capable than others of making health care decisions.''); Winick, *The MacArthur Treatment Competence Study: Legal and Therapeutic Implications,* 2 PSYCHOL. PUB. POL'Y & L. 137 (1996) (analyzing relative competence of patients with mental illness and ''normal'' people); *supra* chapter 14, part B.

[54]*See* Lidz & Meisel, *Informed Consent and the Structure of Medical Care,* in 2 PRESIDENT'S COMM'N REP., *supra* note 6, at 392, 400–01, 403–04; Lynn, *Informed Consent: An Overview,* 1 BEHAV. SCI. & L. 29, 40 (1983); Meisel, *supra* note 13, at 457–60; Shultz, *supra* note 39, at 259; Sprung & Winick, *supra* note 5, at 1349.

For these reasons, the law's general presumption in favor of competency often is and should be applied to those with mental illness.[55] Both medically ill and mentally ill individuals should enjoy this presumption. Even those who have been committed to mental hospitals involuntarily because they are incompetent to decide should be presumed competent to make other decisions, at least in the absence of evidence that their illness has deprived them of the specific competency in question.[56] The law should presume that voluntary[57] expressions of individual choice in favor of a treatment recommendation by the individual's therapist are competent, and an evaluation of competency should be unnecessary in the absence of specific indications that the individual's choice is a product of mental illness.

A *presumption* is a procedural device that sometimes prevents the need for further inquiry into the subject. In practice, it is difficult to ascertain an individual's ability to process information and engage in rational decision making and easy for evaluators to confuse the quality of the decision-making process with the reasonableness of the result reached.[58] Competency is often difficult to determine.[59] To prevent excessive paternalism, it is appropriate to presume, in the absence of evidence of gross incompetence, that individuals who are able to express a choice in favor of conventional treatment recommended by their therapists are competent. Individuals who express choices exercise at least some autonomy, and respect for the principle of autonomy makes it generally appropriate to presume competence of the decision maker. Moreover, when that choice is consistent with a reasonable treatment intervention recommended by a clinician who has a fiduciary duty to act in the patient's best interests, the need to inquire about competency to avoid a threat to the patient's welfare is significantly reduced.

In cases of assent to conventional treatment recommended by the patient's clinician, presuming competency would largely avoid the necessity of a formal determination of the issue. In appropriate cases, however, such a presumption would not prevent further inquiry, and it does not always decide a case; it is rebuttable. As with presumptions generally, the presumption of competency places a production burden on those who question the patient's competence. To rebut the presumption and justify an inquiry into competency, I would require some evidence suggesting that the patient's expressed choice was the product of pathological delusions or hallucinations or was based on intrinsically irrational beliefs or

---

[55]*See* Winick, *supra* note 25, at 38–39.

[56]*See id.* at 39.

[57]My argument assumes that the patient's assent to a treatment recommendation, although perhaps only marginally competent, is voluntary (*i.e.,* obtained without force, fraud, deceit, duress, or coercion). For further analysis of the requirement of voluntariness, see *infra* part C of this chapter.

[58]*See* 1 PRESIDENT'S COMM'N REP., *supra* note 6, at 61; Annas & Densberger, *supra* note 28, at 571 & n.39 ("the 'outcome approach' trap"); Roth et al., *supra* note 5, at 281.

[59]BEAUCHAMP & CHILDRESS, *supra* note 13, at 73; Appelbaum & Grisso, *supra* note 7, at 1637; Murphy, *Incompetency and Paternalism,* 60 ARCHIV FÜR RECHTS-UND SOCIALPHILOSOPHIE 465, 478–79 (1974).

clearly irrelevant reasons.[60] In short, the presumption should be overcome only by evidence of gross impairment of decision-making ability. In the absence of such evidence, the question of competency should not be raised as long as the patient's choice is voluntary and clearly expressed. Other than in contexts in which a conflict of interest between therapist and patient is possible,[61] the therapist's recommendation provides strong evidence that the risk—benefit ratio of the patient's choice is acceptable and that the patient's decision thus is reasonable.

Therapeutic considerations also support the distinction between assent and objection and the use of the presumption in favor of competence suggested here.[62] The informed consent doctrine reflects a balance between autonomy values and society's interest in the promotion of individual health.[63] Although these values sometimes conflict, they coalesce in favor of an approach that generally defers to patient choice. As chapter 17 demonstrates, there is considerable therapeutic value in allowing patients to make choices concerning their own treatment and corresponding disadvantages in coercing such treatment. Thus, restructuring informed consent doctrine to allow a presumption of competency when patients clearly manifest treatment choices and applying a less demanding standard of competency

[60]See Murphy, supra note 59, at 473–74; Tepper & Elwork, supra note 17, at 216–18; Winick, supra note 25, at 44; see, e.g., Zinermon v. Burch, 494 U.S. 113, 118 (1990) (delusional patient seeking voluntary hospitalization who thought he was entering heaven assumed to be incompetent to consent to hospitalization); Department of Human Servs. v. Northern, 563 S.W.2d 197, 211–12 (Tenn. App. 1978) (finding that the delusional denial by gangrenous patient that she could live without amputation rendered her incompetent to refuse recommended surgery). When the patient is delusional, but her delusions are not the primary reason for her treatment decision, however, she should not be found incompetent. E.g., In re Yetter, 62 Pa. D. & C.2d 619, 623 (1973).

A diagnosis of schizophrenia—the condition most likely to produce decision-making impairment—should not alone be sufficient to rebut the presumption. See Grisso & Appelbaum, supra note 25, at 171, 173. Although such a diagnosis should "increase one's attention to the possibility of deficiencies in abilities relating to legal competence," the diagnosis itself "is only moderately related to serious deficiencies in those abilities." Id. at 173. Such deficits are more likely to be present in cases involving "greater degrees of thought disturbance (e.g., conceptual disorganization, active delusions, and hallucinations)." Id. Even such cases, however, are merely "at greater risk" of incompetence. Id. "The relation is not strong enough to presume that serious thought disturbance 'identifies' deficits in understanding, reasoning, or appreciation of a type sufficient to presume that the person is not able to make treatment decisions." Id. These factors, which Grisso and Appelbaum suggest identify a patient as "at risk" for incompetence, should rebut the presumption of competence that I argue is generally appropriate, and should justify further inquiry into competency. In their absence, however, the patient, even if diagnosed with schizophrenia, should be deemed competent.

[61]See WHO IS THE CLIENT? THE ETHICS OF PSYCHOLOGICAL INTERVENTION IN THE CRIMINAL JUSTICE SYSTEM (J. Monahan ed., 1980); In the Service of the State: The Psychiatrist as Double Agent, 8 HASTINGS CTR. REP., Apr. 1978 (Suppl.), at 1; Shestack, Psychiatry and the Dilemmas of Dual Loyalties, 60 ABA J. 1521, 1522–24 (1974). The fact that the physician is an employee of the treating institution does not alone create a conflict of interest in violation of due process, at least when he or she is independent and has a professional duty to act in the best interests of the patient and can place fiduciary duty to the patient over any interests of the institutional employer. See Washington v. Harper, 494 U.S. 210, 231–32 (1990); Parham v. J.R., 442 U.S. 584, 615–16, 618 (1979). The treatment recommendation of an institutional physician should therefore ordinarily support an inference that the recommendation in question is in the best interests of the patient. In some institutions—prisons, security hospitals, and some (perhaps many) understaffed civil mental hospitals—practices have sadly evidenced a conflict of interest on the part of staff physicians who sometimes prescribe psychotropic medication in amounts exceeding therapeutic needs for purposes of institutional management and control. See BRAKEL ET AL., supra note 14, at 341–42. In such facilities, the presumption in favor of accepting the competency of a patient's assent to such a recommendation should not apply, and further inquiry would be appropriate. The extent to which institutional physicians can and do act in their patients' interests without conflicting loyalties to their employers is a complex analytical and empirical question that deserves much further investigation.

[62]See supra chapter 17.

[63]See Meisel, supra note 13; Sprung & Winick, supra note 5, at 1346.

when patients assent to treatment than when they object, serve both individual autonomy and therapeutic values.

Accordingly, patients and offenders who assent to recommended treatment should be presumed to be competent, and a low standard of competency should be applied.[64] Only where evidence of gross impairment suggests incompetency, or when the treatment chosen is experimental or carries great risk, should there be further inquiry. Given the choice to participate in therapies that they have a right to refuse, many patients and most criminal offenders are able to meet the requirements for competency to waive this right. In principle, for offenders at least, the element of competency should be easily met in most situations. Mental patients, by contrast, may be severely impaired in their ability to comprehend treatment information and make treatment choices, although many are not. Although the question of competency must be inquired into more frequently in the case of mental patients, those expressing assent to recommended treatment generally should be presumed competent, and no inquiry should be undertaken. Only when assent seems clearly to be a product of mental illness should competency be questioned. Although some such patients ultimately will be found incompetent to assent to treatment and therefore to waive their right to refuse treatment, a large majority will and should be deemed competent to do so.

B. Knowledge

A second element of the informed consent doctrine that patients and offenders who desire to assent to treatment must satisfy is the requirement of knowledge. Unless a therapist discloses certain information to a patient before administering treatment, or the patient otherwise possesses such knowledge, the patient is entitled to damages even if treatment was performed correctly.[65] The exact scope of disclosure demanded of the therapist is not clear, but most courts require that the patient be told the diagnosis, the nature of the proposed treatment, the risks and benefits of the procedure, the available alternative procedures and their risks and benefits, and the consequences of not having the suggested treatment.[66] A therapist does not have to disclose risks that the patient already is aware of or is likely to know.[67]

---

[64]The Supreme Court's decision in Zinermon v. Burch, 494 U.S. 113 (1990), seems to question the propriety of the distinction urged here between assent and objection by suggesting the need for an inquiry into the competence of patients seeking to effect a voluntary admission to a mental hospital. Read broadly, *Zinermon* would transform existing practices concerning voluntary hospitalization and would be basically inconsistent with my thesis. *Zinermon,* however, need not be read so broadly. For the reasons developed in Winick, *Competency to Consent to Voluntary Hospitalization: A Therapeutic Jurisprudence Analysis of* Zinermon v. Burch, 14 INT'L J.L. & PSYCHIA-TRY 169 (1991), *Zinermon*'s discussion of the need for an inquiry into the competency of patients seeking voluntary hospitalization is largely dicta, and a broad reading of it would be unwise and should be rejected. *See also* AMERICAN PSYCHIATRIC ASS'N TASK FORCE REPORT NO. 34: CONSENT TO VOLUNTARY HOSPITALIZATION (1993); Winick, *How to Handle Voluntary Hospitalization After* Zinermon v. Burch, 21 ADMIN. & POL'Y IN MENTAL HEALTH 395 (1994); *supra* chapter 14, part B.

[65]APPELBAUM ET AL., *supra* note 6, at 114; FADEN & BEAUCHAMP, *supra* note 6, at 27–28; Sprung & Winick, *supra* note 5, at 1347.

[66]Canterbury v. Spence, 464 F.2d 772, 787 (D.C. Cir.), *cert. denied,* 409 U.S. 1064 (1972); Cobbs v. Grant, 502 P.2d 1 (Cal. 1972); Natanson v. Kline, 350 P.2d 1093, 1106 (Kan. 1960); Wilkinson v. Vesey, 295 A.2d 676 (R.I. 1972); Appelbaum & Grisso, *supra* note 5, at 106; Capron, *Informed Consent in Catastrophic Disease Research and Treatment,* 123 U. PA. L. REV. 340, 346 (1974); Sprung & Winick, *supra* note 5, at 1346–54.

[67]*Canterbury,* 464 F.2d at 787; Sard v. Hardy, 379 A.2d 1014 (Md. 1977); *Wilkinson,* 295 A.2d at 676; Scaria v. St. Paul Fire & Marine Ins. Co., 227 N.W.2d 647 (Wis. 1975).

Two standards have emerged to define the therapist's duty to disclose information. Under the "professional standard," the scope of the therapist's duty to provide information is based on the custom of therapists practicing in the same or in a similar community.[68] The therapist is not held liable unless the omission of information deviates from the prevalent professional practice in the community. The question is not what risks a reasonable person would disclose to the patient under the circumstances, but rather what a reasonable clinician would disclose.[69] Under this standard, patients must demonstrate what the routine practice of disclosure was by therapists in the community and that the disclosure made did not conform to the customary practice. Expert testimony frequently is required to establish the professional standard of disclosure prevalent in the community.

The second standard of disclosure, the "lay standard" or "material risk" approach, requires the therapist to disclose all information that a reasonable person in the patient's position would consider material to decision making.[70] The patient's right of self-determination concerning treatment "shapes the boundaries of the duty to reveal. . . ."[71] The scope of the therapist's communications to the patient "must be measured by the patient's need, and that need is the information material to the decision."[72] Accordingly, whether a particular risk must be communicated to the patient depends on "its materiality to the patient's decision: all risks potentially affecting the decision must be unmasked."[73]

Whether a risk is material is a function of its severity and the likelihood of its occurrence. It is "obviously prohibitive and unrealistic to expect therapists to discuss with their patients every risk of proposed treatment—no matter how small or remote."[74] Risks that are not serious and are unlikely to occur are not as material to a patient's decision as more serious and common risks. If a serious injury might occur from a given treatment method, the therapist must inform the patient of all but extremely remote risks. However, if the potential injury is slight, then the patient should be informed of only those risks that might well occur.[75] What risks are considered "extremely remote" may vary with the jurisdiction. For example, disclosure was held to be required for a 3% chance of death or paralysis[76] and a 1% chance of loss of hearing,[77] but not for a 1.5% chance of loss of an eye,[78] a 0.4% to 0.2% chance of esophageal perforation,[79] or a 1/8,000,000 chance of aplastic anemia.[80] The severity of risk that must be disclosed also may vary from "death or serious bodily harm"[81] to less severe risks. The severity of risk may be more important than the probability of the risk occurring.[82] Moreover, a greater obligation is imposed on the therapist to disclose even

---

[68]E.g., Di Fillippo v. Preston, 173 A.2d 333 (Del. 1961); Natanson v. Kline, 350 P.2d 1093, 1106 (Kan. 1960); Wilson v. Scott, 412 S.W.2d 299 (Tex. 1967).

[69]FADEN & BEAUCHAMP, supra note 6, at 30–31.

[70]E.g., Canterbury v. Spence, 464 F.2d 772, 787 (D.C. Cir.), cert. denied, 409 U.S. 1064 (1972); Cobbs v. Grant, 502 P.2d 1 (Cal. 1972); Getchell v. Mansfield, 489 P.2d 953 (Okla. 1971); Wilkinson v. Vesey, 295 A.2d 676 (R.I. 1972); Appelbaum & Grisso, supra note 5, at 106; Waltz & Scheuneman, supra note 17, at 639–40.

[71]Canterbury v. Spence, 464 F.2d at 786.

[72]Id.

[73]Id. at 787; FADEN & BEAUCHAMP, supra note 6, at 133–38.

[74]Cobbs v. Grant, 502 P.2d 1 (Cal. 1972).

[75]Holland v. Sisters of St. Joseph of Peach, 522 P.2d 208 (Ore. 1974).

[76]Bowers v. Talmage, 159 So. 2d 888 (Fla. Dist. Ct. App. 1963).

[77]Wilson v. Scott, 412 S.W.2d 299 (Tex. 1967).

[78]Yeates v. Harms, 393 P.2d 982 (Kan. 1964).

[79]Starnes v. Taylor, 158 S.E.2d 339 (N.C. 1968).

[80]Stottlemire v. Cawood, 213 F. Supp. 897 (D.D.C. 1963).

[81]Cobbs v. Grant, 502 P.2d 1, 11 (Cal. 1972).

[82]Longmore v. Hoey, 512 S.W.2d 307 (Tenn. Ct. App. 1974).

remote risks if alternative procedures are available that would afford lesser risks or greater probabilities of success.[83] Under these general standards, it would seem clear that the risks and side effects described in chapters 3–8 for the various mental health treatment techniques must be disclosed. Patients given antipsychotic drugs, for example, should be told about extrapyramidal side effects and the serious risk of tardive dyskinesia,[84] and patients facing electroconvulsive therapy should be told about memory loss and the possibility of other cognitive deficits.[85]

In the early 1970s it appeared that many courts were moving away from the traditional professional standard toward the patient-based standard.[86] However, beginning in the mid-1970s, some states enacted statutes adopting the professional standard,[87] in part to "provide certainty and clarity"[88] to the law and in part to address the medical malpractice insurance crisis of this time period.[89] A slight majority of the states continue to follow the professional standard approach.[90]

The rules governing disclosure of information are almost exclusively fashioned by judges in the context of tort suits for malpractice or battery. As indicated, considerable variation among jurisdictions exists. Thus, the amount of information that must be disclosed in a particular context in order to permit an effective informed consent depends on state law. Although most jurisdictions continue to apply the professional standard rather than the patient-based standard for measuring the duty to disclose, therapists sensitive to the therapeutic value of patient choice[91] may prefer the patient-based standard inasmuch as it tends to increase patients' sense of participation in the decision-making process and the likelihood that patients internalize the choices made as their own.

The manner in which the risk probabilities of a procedure are communicated to patients can significantly affect patient understanding and hence whether consent is truly informed.[92] For example, the use of words such as "rare," rather than of mathematical probabilities such as 1/1,000,000, is subject to interpretation by patients based on various demographic factors.[93] Studies show that patients often do not comprehend or remember the information disclosed,[94] supporting the need for the use of simple language and techniques to foster understanding. Thus, Grisso and Appelbaum's study of patient abilities to consent to psychiatric and medical treatment suggested that all patients manifested superior understanding of treatment information when information was disclosed a second time and part by

---

[83]Miller, *Informed Consent II*, 244 JAMA 2347, 2347–48 (1980).

[84]*See supra* chapter 5.

[85]*See supra* chapter 6.

[86]1 PRESIDENT'S COMM'N REP., *supra* note 6, at 15–39.

[87]*Id.*

[88]*See, e.g.,* IDAHO CODE § 39–4301(2) (1993); *see* Merz & Fischhoff, *Informed Consent Does Not Mean Rational Consent*, 11 J. LEGAL MED. 321, 329 (1990).

[89]Merz & Fischhoff, *supra* note 88, at 329.

[90]*Id.* at 330.

[91]*See supra* chapter 17 (analyzing the therapeutic value of allowing patient self-determination in treatment decision making).

[92]Mazur & Merz, *Patients' Interpretations of Verbal Expressions of Probability: Implications for Securing Informed Consent to Medical Interventions,* 12 BEHAV. SCI. & L. 417 (1994).

[93]*Id.* at 420.

[94]S. MCLEAN, A PATIENT'S RIGHT TO KNOW 75–77 (1989) (discussing Canterbury v. Spence 464 F.2d 772 (D.C. Cir.), *cert. denied,* 409 U.S. 1064 (1972) as illustrative of a patient's not being fully able to grasp information disclosed by a physician); Sprung & Winick, *supra* note 5, at 1351 (discussing the results of studies of patient understanding of informed consent).

part, rather than being disclosed as a whole and only once.[95] Instead of requiring patients to read a lengthy and technical description of risks, an attempt should be made to explain or ''teach'' the information to the patient.[96] Attempts to convey information that result in better patient understanding can increase patient trust and confidence in the therapist, as well as patient motivation and treatment compliance.[97]

Even if therapists do not provide adequate disclosure of information to patients, patients cannot recover for damages unless they suffered injury because the nondisclosed risk occurred and injury was caused by not informing patients of the risks.[98] If patients submit to the procedure with knowledge of the risk, no causal connection exists and no liability is imposed.[99] Courts have disagreed concerning the standard to be used to determine the existence of a causal relationship between the therapist's failure to disclose the risk and the patient's injury. Some courts have used a subjective test—whether the particular patient would have rejected the procedure if adequate disclosure was provided.[100] Other courts have criticized this approach, however, because ''at the time of the trial the uncommunicated hazard has materialized [and] it would be surprising if the patient-plaintiff did not claim that had he been informed of the dangers he would have declined treatment.''[101] These courts have rejected the subjective test in favor of an objective one based on ''what a prudent person in the patient's position would have decided if suitably informed of all perils bearing significance.''[102] On the issue of whether the patient, having been properly informed, would have consented to the treatment, all but two states now apply an objective test.[103]

Fearing lawsuits, many therapists obtain signed informed consent forms for diagnostic procedures or treatment without accomplishing the purpose underlying the use of the forms and without obtaining true informed consent. For these therapists, the goal of informed consent forms is no longer to provide information for patients but rather to avoid liability. Unfortunately, the consent form has at times replaced the process it was intended to substantiate.[104] A signed form may constitute evidence that a patient consented to a procedure but does not prove that the consent was truly informed.[105] Some courts evaluate forms as they would an oral consent and ''unless a person has been adequately apprised of the material risks and therapeutic alternatives incident to a proposed treatment, any consent given, be it oral or written, is necessarily ineffectual.''[106] In fact, written consent is rarely required when oral consent has been given.[107] Ironically, the use of written general consent forms by many hospitals may be ineffective[108] unless the consent form specifies the nature and risks of the particular procedure to be performed.[109]

---

[95]Grisso & Appelbaum, *supra* note 25, at 173.

[96]*See id.*; Winick, *supra* note 53, at 149–51.

[97]*See supra* chapter 17.

[98]Canterbury v. Spence, 464 F.2d at 790; Waltz & Scheuneman, *supra* note 17, at 646; Schuck, *Rethinking Informed Consent*, 103 YALE L.J. 899, 918 (1994). *See also id.* (discussing ''decision causation,'' injury based on the patient's having made a decision other than the one he or she would have made had disclosure been complete).

[99]*Canterbury*, 464 F.2d at 790; Waltz & Scheuneman, *supra* note 17, at 648.

[100]Wilkinson v. Vesey, 295 A.2d 676 (R.I. 1972); Longmore v. Hoey, 512 S.W.2d 307 (Tenn. Ct. App. 1974).

[101]Cobbs v. Grant, 502 P.2d 1, 11 (Cal. 1972).

[102]*Canterbury*, 464 F.2d at 791; Waltz & Scheuneman, *supra* note 17, at 648.

[103]Schuck, *supra* note 98, at 919. The two states are Oklahoma and Oregon. *Id.*

[104]1 PRESIDENT'S COMM'N REP., *supra* note 6, at 69–111; Sprung & Winick, *supra* note 5, at 1348.

[105]Demers v. Gerety, 515 P.2d 645 (N.M. Ct. App. 1973).

[106]Sard v. Hardy, 379 A.2d 1014 (Md. 1977).

[107]Hernandez v. United States, 465 F. Supp. 1071 (D. Kan. 1979).

[108]Rogers v. Lumbermens Mut. Cas. Co., 119 So. 2d 649 (La. Ct. App. 1960).

[109]Luna v. Nering, 426 F.2d 95 (5th Cir. 1970).

Therapists too often misperceive the informed consent requirement, treating it as a technical hurdle to avoid liability. In fact, the doctrine and its disclosure requirement present significant therapeutic opportunities. The process of obtaining consent can be an important aspect of forging the therapeutic alliance and setting up expectancies of favorable treatment outcomes that can increase patient motivation and compliance and facilitate treatment success. Rather than going through the motions of technical compliance with legal requirements, therapists should use the process of obtaining consent to obtain the patient trust and confidence that may be essential to the basic mission of the therapeutic relationship. Properly understood, the principle of informed consent is "the cardinal canon of loyalty" joining patient and therapist together in the therapeutic process.[110] The disclosure of information in particular provides an opportunity to meet patient concerns that might otherwise prevent the patient from engaging whole-heartedly in the therapeutic process and to bolster patient confidence in the therapist and in the treatment recommended. Particularly in the treatment of those with mental illness, the informed consent process, properly undertaken, can be an important therapeutic tool.

Although therapists are required to make information available to patients, they need not force information on unwilling patients.[111] Patients can and frequently do waive their right to information and defer to their therapists. In order for patients to waive their right to render an informed consent, they must know that they have the right to do so.[112] They must know (a) that the therapist has a duty to disclose information about the treatment, (b) that they have a legal right to make a decision about treatment, (c) that the therapist cannot render treatment without first obtaining consent, and (d) that the right of decision includes the right to consent to or refuse treatment.[113] Traditional notions of waiver emphasize that a waiver must be freely and voluntarily given in order to be valid.[114] The primary objective of informed consent is to promote self-determination, and permitting patients to make such decisions fosters this value.[115] Compelling patients to receive information that they do not wish to have or to make decisions that they do not wish to make violates patient dignity.[116] The exercise of a waiver allows patients to relinquish their right to an informed consent when they wish to do so.[117] Like people generally, patients often do not wish to assert their right to receive information that would allow for optimal decision making. Particularly when functioning within the context of a professional relationship in which the professional is an expert in the area in question, many individuals are happy to defer to the expert and do not wish to engage in an extensive second-guessing of the expert's recommendation. Indeed, a willingness to waive further information and accept the professional's recommendation is a sign that the individual has trust and confidence in the expert and that the professional relationship is healthy. As long as patients are aware that they have a right to further information, waiver of the right is often appropriate and should not be discouraged by the law.

Thus, for a variety of good reasons, patients may delegate decision-making authority to therapists or request not to be informed. Waiver frees therapists from a further disclosure

---

[110]P. RAMSEY, THE PATIENT AS PERSON: EXPLORATIONS IN MEDICAL ETHICS 5–7 (1970).

[111]3 PRESIDENT'S COMM'N REP., *supra* note 6, at 193–251; *see, e.g.,* Ferrera v. Galluchio, 152 N.E.2d 249 (N.Y. 1958).

[112]Meisel, *supra* note 13, at 454.

[113]*Id.*; *see* APPELBAUM ET AL., *supra* note 6, at 70.

[114]*Id.* at 71; Meisel, *supra* note 13, at 457.

[115]*Id.* at 459.

[116]*Id.*; *see* Goldstein, *supra* note 11, at 191.

[117]FADEN & BEAUCHAMP, *supra* note 6, at 38.

duty.[118] In effect, patients may make an informed decision not to make another informed decision.[119] For tort purposes, a properly obtained waiver of informed consent constitutes a bar to recovery.[120]

Whatever the extent of therapists' duty to disclose treatment information, a duty that varies from jurisdiction to jurisdiction, this requirement would seem to be easily satisfied in the context of criminal offenders and mental patients. As long as sufficient information is disclosed in a reasonably clear manner to competent patients or offenders, this element of the informed consent doctrine should be easily satisfied for those seeking to assent to mental health treatment and thereby to waive a right to refuse it.

C. Voluntariness

The third requirement for informed consent is voluntariness. The patient's choice must be free of coercion, force, fraud, duress, or other forms of compulsion. The requirement of voluntariness is troubling in both the hospital and the correctional contexts. In its report on "*Research Involving Prisoners,*" for example, the National Commission for the Protection of Human Subjects of Biomedical and Behavioral Research considered "whether prisoners are, in the words of the Nuremberg Code, 'so situated as to be able to exercise free power of choice'—that is, whether prisoners can give truly voluntary consent to participate in research."[121] Some of the commissioners argued that prisons, by their very purpose and character, make sufficiently free consent to research impossible.[122] Similarly, several participants at a National Minority Conference on Human Experimentation held under the auspices of the National Commission objected in principle to the notion of truly voluntary consent by prisoners.[123] The National Commission, however, ultimately rejected the idea that prisons are so inherently coercive that voluntary consent is impossible and concluded that at least some prison research could be undertaken with appropriate safeguards.[124] The Commission proposed a number of requirements to ensure "a high degree of voluntariness on the part of the prospective participants," including "adequate living conditions, provisions for effective redress of grievances, separation of research participation from parole considerations, and public scrutiny."[125] The U.S. Department of Health and Human Services regulations, initially adopted as a result of the Commission's work, include an additional protection for prisoners subjected to biomedical and behavioral research. The regulation requires an assurance that parole boards not take into account a prisoner's participation in such research in making parole decisions and that prisoners be clearly informed in advance that such participation will not affect parole."[126]

---

[118]*Id.*; *see* Cobbs v. Grant, 502 P.2d 1 (Cal. 1972).

[119]FADEN & BEAUCHAMP, *supra* note 6, at 38.

[120]*See, e.g.,* Palmer v. Biloxi Regional Med. Ctr., Inc., 564 So. 2d 1346 (Miss. 1990) (recovery precluded by the patient's waiver of right to receive information).

[121]NATIONAL COMM'N FOR THE PROTECTION OF HUMAN SUBJECTS OF BIOMED. AND BEHAV. RES., RESEARCH INVOLVING PRISONERS 5 (1976) [hereinafter RESEARCH].

[122]Branson, *Prison Research, National Commission Says "No, Unless . . . ,"* 7 HASTINGS CTR. REP., Feb. 1977, at 15, 17 (remarks of Commissioner King).

[123]RESEARCH, *supra* note 121, at 42, 44. This was also the view of the American Correctional Association. American Correctional Ass'n, *Position Statement: The Use of Prisoners and Detainees as Subjects of Human Experimentation, Feb. 20, 1976, in* PRISONER RESEARCH, *supra* note 121, at 22–1 to 22–2 app.

[124]Palmer, *Biomedical and Behavioral Research on Prisoners: Public Policy Issues in Human Experimentation, in* RESEARCH, *supra* note 121, at 14–21 app.; *see* Branson, *supra* note 122, at 16.

[125]RESEARCH, *supra* note 121, at 16.

[126]45 C.F.R. § 46.305(a)(6) (1994).

In the *Kaimowitz* Michigan psychosurgery case,[127] the court considered the impact on voluntariness of institutionalization and of the inducement created when release is tied to consent. The court held that involuntarily confined mental patients are unable as a matter of law to consent to experimental psychosurgery. The court's analysis has broad implications for the ability of all institutionalized populations to provide informed consent and therefore deserves careful analysis. The court stated:[128]

> Although an involuntarily detained mental patient may have sufficient I.Q. to intellectually comprehend his circumstances . . . the very nature of his incarceration diminishes the capacity to consent to psychosurgery.
>
> . . . The fact of institutional confinement has special force in undermining the capacity of the mental patient to make a competent decision on this issue, even though he be intellectually competent to do so.
>
> . . . It is impossible for an involuntarily detained mental patient to be free of ulterior forms of restraint or coercion when his very release from the institution may depend upon his cooperating with institutional authorities and giving consent to experimental surgery.
>
> Involuntarily confined mental patients live in an inherently coercive institutional environment. Indirect and subtle psychological coercion has a profound effect upon the patient population. . . . They are not able to voluntarily give informed consent because of the inherent inequality of their position.

The court's rationale seems equally applicable to prisoners, whose institutional environment is marked by the same subtle and not so subtle psychological coercion. Similarly, the prisoner who consents in the hope of obtaining parole or the offender who agrees to community treatment to avoid incarceration seem indistinguishable from the involuntarily confined patient in *Kaimowitz* who consented to psychosurgery in the hope of obtaining a release from confinement. It is doubtful, however, that the sweeping approach of *Kaimowitz* will be followed by other courts. In fact, the *Kaimowitz* court sought to limit its holding to experimental psychosurgery by stating that consent could be given to conventionally accepted procedures.[129] Notwithstanding this disclaimer, some commentators have suggested that the court's reasoning should be applied to all treatment procedures, whether experimental or not.[130]

Although the *Kaimowitz* court may have reached the correct result on the facts of that case,[131] the potential breadth of the court's holding concerning the effects of institutionalization and the promise of release on the capacity to give informed consent could give rise to absurd and constitutionally dubious results. Institutionalization may substantially diminish the ability of some patients and prisoners to decide freely on therapy, and the lure of release or of avoiding hospitalization or incarceration may be so potent that, for at least some patients and offenders, refusal to consent is virtually impossible. These factors, however,

---

[127]Kaimowitz v. Michigan Dep't of Mental Health, No. 73-19434-AW (Cir. Ct. Wayne [Mich.] July 10, 1973), *reprinted in* A. BROOKS, LAW, PSYCHIATRY AND THE MENTAL HEALTH SYSTEM 902, 913–14 (1974); *see supra* chapter 8.

[128]*Kaimowitz,* slip op. at 25–29; BROOKS, *supra* note 127, at 913–15.

[129]*Kaimowitz,* slip op. at 40; BROOKS, *supra* note 127, at 920.

[130]*See* AMERICAN CIVIL LIBERTIES UNION, NATIONAL PRISON PROJECT, PRISONERS' RIGHTS 1979, 417–26, 612 (1979).

[131]*See generally* Burt, *Why We Should Keep Prisoners from the Doctors,* 5 HASTINGS CTR. REP., Feb. 1975, at 25.

should not preclude all patients and offenders from being considered capable of making these decisions voluntarily. If institutionalization *per se* diminishes decision-making abilities so that patients or prisoners are incompetent to elect psychosurgery, how can patients or prisoners be considered competent to make other important decisions? Can they decide to have elective surgery or other medical treatment when needed, to choose particular work assignments that may be more hazardous than others, or to agree to accept certain conditions of conditional release or parole? Moreover, if the prospect of release renders confined individuals incompetent to elect psychosurgery, how can patients or prisoners be permitted to elect the variety of other hospital or prison programs that may result in early release?

The absurdity of a *per se* rule based on the impact of institutionalization or the lure of release is demonstrated by its sweeping effect. A common example of use of the early-release lure to modify prisoner behavior is the virtually universal practice of providing "good time" credit. As the Supreme Court noted in *McGinnis v. Royster*,[132] "the granting of good-time credit toward parole eligibility takes into account a prisoner's rehabilitative performance."[133] The New York statute involved in *Royster* authorized such good time credit "for good conduct and efficient and willing performance of duties assigned."[134] Under a U.S. Bureau of Prisons rule, an award of "extra good time" may be made for (among other things) "[v]oluntary acceptance and satisfactory performance of an unusually hazardous assignment."[135] Yet if the *Kaimowitz* approach is broadly construed, the decision of prisoners to accept such assignments or participate in such programs could be considered involuntary as a matter of law.

The approach in *Kaimowitz* also seems unduly paternalistic. Patients or offenders who genuinely desire to participate in a therapy program could be deemed legally incapable of doing so. Yet to deny access to a particular therapeutic program that patients or offenders "voluntarily" and competently elect may, in effect, impose additional confinement and may even violate their right to treatment[136] and their constitutional right of privacy.[137] For these

---

[132]410 U.S. 263 (1973).

[133]*Id.* at 271.

[134]*Id.* at 266–67 n.5 (quoting Royster v. McGinnis, 332 F. Supp. 973, 974–75 (S.D.N.Y. 1971)).

[135]28 C.F.R. § 523.16 (1994). *See also* 28 C.F.R. § 2.60 (1994) (rule of U.S. Parole Commission permitting advancement of presumptive release date for "superior program achievement" in "educational, vocational, industry, or counseling programs").

[136]*See* Donaldson v. O'Connor, 493 F.2d 502 (5th Cir. 1974), *aff'd in part and rev'd in part on other grounds*, 422 U.S. 563 (1975); Wyatt v. Stickney, 344 F. Supp. 373, (M.D. Ala. 1972), *aff'd sub nom.* Wyatt v. Aderholt, 503 F.2d 1305 (5th Cir. 1974).

[137]In certain circumstances the right of privacy protects health decisions made between individuals and their physicians from governmental interference. *See* Aden v. Younger, 129 Cal. Rptr. 535, 546–48 (Cal. Ct. App. 1976); Wexler, *Mental Health Law and the Movement Toward Voluntary Treatment*, 62 CAL. L. REV. 671, 681–84 (1974). *But see* Rutherford v. United States, 399 F. Supp. 1208 (W.D. Okla. 1975), *aff'd on other grounds*, 542 F.2d 1137 (10th Cir. 1976), *rev'd on other grounds*, 442 U.S. 544 (1979), *rev'd* on remand, 616 F.2d 455 (10th Cir. 1980).

and other reasons, broad application of the *Kaimowitz* doctrine has been roundly criticized by commentators and at least implicitly rejected in a number of subsequent cases.[138]

In the analogous situation of plea bargaining, the courts have rejected the notion that the opportunity or even the assurance of a shorter sentence necessarily renders a guilty plea involuntary. In *Brady v. United States*,[139] the defendant attacked the validity of his guilty plea, arguing that it was entered to avoid the possibility of the death penalty. Under the statute involved, the death penalty could be imposed following a jury determination of guilt but could not be imposed when a defendant waived trial and pleaded guilty. Stressing that "[t]he voluntariness of Brady's plea can be determined only by considering all of the relevant circumstances surrounding it,"[140] the Court rejected the coercion claim:[141]

> Even if we assume that Brady would not have pleaded guilty except for the death penalty provision . . . , this assumption merely identifies the penalty provision as a "but for" cause of his plea. That the statute caused the plea in this sense does not necessarily prove that the plea was coerced and invalid as an involuntary act. . . .
>
> Of course, the agents of the State may not produce a plea by actual or threatened physical harm or by mental coercion overbearing the will of the defendant. But nothing of the sort is claimed in this case. . . . Brady's claim is of a different sort: that it violates the Fifth Amendment to influence or encourage a guilty plea by opportunity or promise of leniency and that a guilty plea is coerced and invalid if influenced by the fear of a possible higher penalty for the crime charged if a conviction is obtained after the State is put to its proof.
>
> . . . We decline to hold, however, that a guilty plea is compelled and invalid under the Fifth Amendment whenever motivated by the defendant's desire to accept the certainty or probability of a lesser penalty. . . .

The *Brady* Court adopted as its standard of voluntariness the rule that a guilty plea "must stand unless induced by threats . . . misrepresentation . . . , or perhaps by promises that are by their nature improper," such as bribes.[142] Under this standard, the Court held that "a plea of guilty is not invalid merely because entered to avoid the possibility of a death penalty."[143]

If avoidance of the possibility of a death sentence is not so inherently coercive as to invalidate a guilty plea, then it is difficult to see how the possibility or promise of early release could be considered so inherently coercive as to invalidate a patient's or offender's choice of therapy. Of course, there may be cases in which the forces of institutionalization

[138]*See* PSYCHOSURGERY, *supra* note 28, at 19, 22; R. SCHWITZGEBEL, LEGAL ASPECTS OF THE ENFORCED TREATMENT OF OFFENDERS 56–57 (1979); Murphy, *Total Institutional and the Possibility of Consent to Organic Therapies*, 5 HUMAN RIGHTS 25, 18–25 (1975); Singer, *Consent of the Unfree, Part II*, 1 LAW & HUMAN BEHAV. 101, 148–61 (1977); Wexler, *supra* note 131, at 677–84; Winick, *supra* note 10, at 342–46. *See also* N. MORRIS, THE FUTURE OF IMPRISONMENT 24–26 (1974). Singer, in the most extensive discussion of these issues, concludes that "the confined, assuming competency, can indeed consent to any and all kinds of experimentation or behavior change, including psychosurgery." Singer, *supra*, at 101. With the exception of cases in which offenders, as a means of inducing their consent, have been charged with an offense in excess of what the facts of the alleged crime would warrant, and with the further exception of prison systems in which the conditions of confinement are not minimally acceptable or in which the release system is inequitable, Singer concludes that "participation motivated by early release . . . would be both morally and legally viable." *Id.* at 162. He finds the argument that institutionalization *per se* should invalidate consent to be without factual evidence to sustain it. *Id.* Moreover, he expresses concern that acceptance of the argument might lead to unwarranted intrusions upon other rights of prisoners. *Id.*

[139]397 U.S. 742 (1970).
[140]*Id.* at 749.
[141]*Id.* at 750–51.
[142]*Id.* at 755 (quoting Shelton v. United States, 246 F.2d 571, 572 n.2 (5th Cir. 1957)).
[143]397 U.S. at 755.

render an individual incapable of making such voluntary choices or in which threats or promises are so potent that their consent is virtually assured. Nevertheless, this does not mean that institutionalization or the opportunity of early release or of avoidance of confinement renders consent impossible.

Virtually no choice is totally free of coercion.[144] Israel Goldiamond has performed a useful behavioral analysis of voluntariness and coercion, defining situations of coercion and noncoercion through the use of a contingency analysis.[145] In this model, coercion is most severe when there are no genuine choices and the consequences contingent on behavior are critical.[146] Certainly plea bargaining is coercive under this model,[147] sometimes extremely so. Nevertheless, courts have accepted the basic legitimacy of plea bargaining, deeming this degree of coercion constitutionally tolerable.[148]

One court has even held that informed consent may be valid where the conditions of confinement thereby avoided are themselves unconstitutional. In *Bailey v. Lally*,[149] inmates at the Maryland House of Corrections challenged the constitutionality of a state-sponsored program of medical experimentation in which they had participated. General conditions at the prison were concededly bad; in fact, similar conditions had been declared unconstitutional in prior cases. The medical research program in question offered at least a partial escape from those conditions into a live-in medical unit that provided a clean, less restrictive environment with air conditioning, adequate heating, hot water, color television, and separate bathroom facilities. Volunteers had the opportunity to earn extra money and could hope that parole authorities would take their participation into consideration, but they were not advised that their participation would affect parole. Nevertheless, the district court held that this was not legally impermissible coercion. Although acknowledging that the prison conditions may have made participation "very attractive," the court noted that many inmates declined to participate in the program.[150] Moreover, prisoners who did participate were not directly pressured to do so and were not subjected to the unconstitutional conditions as a means of inducing their consent. Rather, the court found that the prisoners "had a viable choice" as well as "the option to withdraw" from the experimental program.[151] Approving the procedures used for obtaining informed consent, the court noted that the doctors involved made "diligent, continuing efforts" to inform prisoners concerning the various studies.[152]

---

[144]*See* Goldiamond, *Protection of Human Subjects and Patients: A Social Contingency Analysis of Distinctions Between Research and Practice, and its Implications,* 4 BEHAVIORISM 1, 27 (1976) ("[C]oercion is not absolute; there are degrees of coercion as well as of freedom."); Jaffee, *Law as a System of Control, in* EXPERIMENTATION WITH HUMAN SUBJECTS 203, 216 (P. Freund ed., 1969). For an extensive philosophical analysis of the concept of coercion, see *Coercion, in* YEARBOOK OF THE AM. SOC'Y FOR POLITICAL & LEGAL PHILOSOPHY 1–328 (J. Pennock & J. Chapman eds., 1972); *see also* J. RAZ, THE MORALITY OF FREEDOM (1986); A. WERTHEIMER, COERCION (1987); Murphy, *Consent, Coercion and Hard Choices,* 67 VA. L. REV. 79 (1981); Wertheimer, *A Philosophical Examination of Coercion for Mental Health Issues,* 11 BEHAV. SCI. & L. 239 (1993).

[145]Goldiamond, *supra* note 144, at 20–34; Goldiamond, *Singling Out Behavior Modifications for Legal Regulation: Some Effects on Patient Care, Psychotherapy and Research in General,* 17 ARIZ. L. REV. 105, 121–25 (1975).

[146]Goldiamond, *supra* note 144, at 23.

[147]*See* Langbein, *Torture and Plea Bargaining,* 46 U. CHI. L. REV. 3, 12–13 (1978); Nemerson, *Coercive Sentencing,* 64 MINN. L. REV. 669, 675–78 (1980).

[148]*See, e.g.,* Corbitt v. New Jersey, 439 U.S. 212, 222–23 (1978); Bordenkircher v. Hayes, 434 U.S. 357, 364 (1978); Blackledge v. Allison, 431 U.S. 63, 71 (1977). The Supreme Court even has suggested that plea bargaining, properly conducted, is worth encouraging. *See* Santabello v. New York, 404 U.S. 257, 260 (1971).

[149]481 F. Supp. 203 (D. Md. 1979).

[150]*Id.* at 220.

[151]*Id.*

[152]*Id.* at 219.

By providing information orally rather than merely relying on a written consent form and by emphasizing the right of prisoners to withdraw from the program at any time, the doctors "took the necessary measures to assure that the prisoners were exercising their free choice."[153] The court thus declined to deem the prisoners' consent involuntary.

In *Knecht v. Gillman*,[154] the U.S. Court of Appeals for the Eighth Circuit found that the involuntary use of apomorphine in a behavior modification program constituted cruel and unusual punishment. The court indicated, however, that use of this technique on inmates "who knowingly and intelligently consent"[155] would be permitted if an adequate system was instituted that would ensure that informed consent was obtained. The inmates affected in *Knecht* were certainly subject to the inherent coercion of institutionalization and to the inducement of potentially early release if they participated; nevertheless, the court considered them legally capable of giving consent.

These cases suggest that most patients or offenders will be deemed, in principle, capable of consenting to even the most intrusive of treatment programs—programs that they otherwise could have a constitutional right to refuse. Because the inherent psychological pressures faced by institutionalized individuals choosing treatment or rehabilitation are simply not avoidable, courts seek only to protect against unfair additional or related pressures.[156] An analogy to plea bargaining is useful. The inherent coerciveness of plea bargaining is mitigated by the presence and advice of counsel during the plea bargaining process[157] and by the practice of giving pleas in open court where the judge must review the extent of the defendant's knowledge of the rights about to be waived and the voluntariness of that waiver.[158] Similar protection could easily be fashioned in the context of consent to the most intrusive of treatments. Indeed, some type of pretreatment hearing and independent review may be required by the guarantee of procedural due process.[159] With these procedural qualifications, courts probably will uphold the validity of consent given by patients or offenders in connection with mental health or correctional therapies. Although institutionalization and the lure of release may provide pressures that render some choices made in response legally coerced, most patients and offenders can still satisfy the requirement of voluntariness and provide informed consent to treatment.

In appropriate circumstances, therefore, patients and offenders who have a right to refuse treatment may waive this right and choose to accept treatment. The concept of competence to consent to conventional treatment may and should be defined to require only a low threshold of competence when the patient is seeking to consent to treatment recommended by the patient's therapist. Indeed, a presumption in favor of competence should be applied in this context that is rebuttable only by evidence suggesting that the patient's expressed choice was the product of delusions, hallucinations, or obvious irrationality. As

---

[153]*Id.* at 220.

[154]488 F.2d 1136 (8th Cir. 1973); *see supra* chapter 12, notes 42–44 and accompanying text.

[155]488 F.2d at 1138.

[156]Murphy, *supra* note 138, at 38; Wexler, *supra* note 28, at 133.

[157]*See* Brady v. United States, 397 U.S. 742, 758 (1970). *Compare* Tollett v. Henderson, 411 U.S. 258, 265 (1973) *and* McMann v. Richardson, 397 U.S. 759, 771 (1970) *with* Fontaine v. United States, 411 U.S. 213, 215 (1973).

[158]*See* Brady v. United States, 397 U.S. 742, 758 (1970); Boykin v. Alabama, 395 U.S. 238, 241–44 (1969); McCarthy v. United States, 394 U.S. 459, 467 (1969); FED. R. CRIM. P. 11.

[159]*See infra* chapter 19.

long as the individual is given sufficient information to enable a reasonable decision to be made and the decision made is voluntary, waiver of a right to refuse treatment will be legally valid. In circumstances in which the potentially coercive effects of institutionalization or the promise of release make voluntariness suspect, an inquiry into voluntariness may be appropriate, as is the use of procedural measures that mitigate these coercive pressures. The inherent coerciveness of institutionalization or the promise of release should not, however, necessarily render voluntariness legally impossible.

When the treatment in question is especially risky and intrusive—when it is high on the continuum of intrusiveness—special procedures and more demanding standards of coercion, knowledge, and voluntariness may be appropriate. For most forms of mental health treatment, however, the conditions for waiver of a right to refuse should not be set so high as to overly burden waiver. Indeed, the therapeutic value of allowing patients to exercise choice in favor of treatment discussed in chapter 17 suggests that the law should encourage and facilitate choices in favor of treatment that the individual seeks voluntarily to make.

The process of ensuring the adequacy of waiver of a right to refuse treatment can itself present an important therapeutic opportunity. Therapists must play the primary role in obtaining informed consent, and in many cases, the exclusive role. The elements of informed consent—competency, knowledge, and voluntariness—should be defined and applied to maximize both the autonomy values underlying the doctrine and the therapeutic opportunities that satisfying the legal requirement presents. Therapists should understand this therapeutic potential and administer the informed consent process so as to foster the therapeutic alliance and increase the likelihood that the treatment achieves the hoped-for effect. Their information-disclosure practices should convey information desired by patients in a manner that treats patients as full participants in treatment decision making. Information should be presented simply and clearly so that patients can comprehend it. In this respect, therapists also should understand the psychological aspects of coercion. Even if legal standards of voluntariness are satisfied, treatment efficacy is enhanced to the degree that patients experience their choices as voluntary rather than coerced. Coercion, with its potential for a negative psychological reactance, is at its greatest when people feel unfairly treated. When patients have trust in their therapists and believe that their therapists have their best interests at heart, they are likely to experience pressure to accept treatment as noncoercive. The informed consent process provides an opportunity for therapists to establish trust and confidence, thereby facilitating a positive therapeutic outcome. Handled properly, the informed consent process thus can have significant therapeutic value.

Chapter 19
PROCEDURAL DUE PROCESS AND INVOLUNTARY THERAPY:
The Right to a Hearing

When patients or offenders refuse to accept treatment voluntarily, the state may be required to provide a hearing before treatment may be imposed over objection. As chapters 15 and 16 demonstrate, in appropriate circumstances the constitutional right of individuals to refuse mental health treatment may be outweighed by countervailing governmental interests. Even for intrusive treatment that burdens fundamental constitutional rights, a state's attempt to impose treatment involuntarily will satisfy the requirements of strict scrutiny when the state seeks to further a compelling interest, and the treatment in question is both therapeutically appropriate and the least intrusive means of accomplishing the state's interest. State interests in imposing treatment that meet the compelling interest standard include the police power interest in protecting institutional staff and other institutional residents from violence and the *parens patriae* interest in furthering the best interests of those so impaired that they are unable to participate meaningfully in treatment decisions. To accomplish these purposes, the state also must show that the treatment sought to be imposed is therapeutically appropriate for the individuals in question. Moreover, to the extent that the least intrusive means principle applies in the treatment context at issue, the state also must show that less intrusive alternative approaches would not accomplish the state's compelling purpose. Even for treatments on the lower end of the continuum of intrusiveness that do not implicate fundamental constitutional rights, the state may need to justify coerced treatment on the basis that it is rationally related to a legitimate governmental interest if other (albeit nonfundamental) liberty interests protected by the Constitution are infringed.

Whether these standards of strict or minimal scrutiny are satisfied in an individual case must be determined through a process meeting the Constitution's requirements of fairness. For example, whether the particular patient is violent and whether other methods of containing such violence are available and feasible in the circumstances are largely questions of fact. Similarly, whether the patient is incompetent to make treatment decisions, whether the treatment proposed is therapeutically appropriate and in the patient's best interests, and whether there are no less intrusive approaches available in the circumstances also are largely questions of fact. Although the meaning of these standards is a legal question, once the law has defined them (through legislation, administrative regulation, or judicial pronouncements), their application to the circumstances of a particular patient presents largely factual questions. As a result, the state must make factual showings relating to the individual sought to be treated involuntarily, and these showings must be made through a process meeting the procedural due process requirements of the Fifth and Fourteenth Amendments. Whether these factual predicates for involuntary treatment are satisfied in a particular case thus will require some kind of hearing.

A. When Procedure Is Constitutionally Required

The Due Process Clause of the Fourteenth Amendment imposes on the states the requirement that notice and some kind of hearing occur when the state seeks to deprive an individual of liberty or property.[1] The Fifth Amendment imposes a parallel requirement on the federal government.[2] Not every grievous loss inflicted on a person by the government is sufficient to invoke these procedural requirements; due process requirements apply only if the interests infringed on may be classified as either *liberty* or *property*.[3]

As explained in chapter 11, the concept of *liberty* within the meaning of the Due Process Clauses of the Fifth and Fourteenth Amendments has been construed expansively to protect a variety of rights guaranteed explicitly or implicitly by the Constitution.[4] It "denotes not merely freedom from bodily restraint but also the right of the individual . . . generally to enjoy those privileges long recognized . . . as essential to the orderly pursuit of happiness by free men."[5] This broad definition of *liberty* has been cited frequently.[6] Moreover, liberty interests requiring due process protection may be created not only by the Constitution, but by state or local law as well. Even if not protected by the Constitution, liberty interests may arise from positive law, as occurs when a state affords mental patients a right to refuse treatment grounded in the state constitution, a state statute, or state common law.[7]

The Supreme Court in *Mills v. Rogers* "assume[d] for purposes of [its] discussion that involuntarily committed mental patients do retain liberty interests protected directly by the Constitution . . . and that these interests are implicated by the involuntary administration of antipsychotic drugs."[8] In *Washington v. Harper*[9] and *Riggins v. Nevada,*[10] the Court explicitly recognized that antipsychotic drugs administered over objection implicate a significant liberty interest protected by due process. Because the patient in *Harper* was a sentenced prisoner, the Court's analysis also recognizes that this liberty interest survives criminal conviction and sentencing.[11] Although the Court in these cases never identified the precise liberty interest it found the drugs would invade, it seems clear that, at a minimum, the

---

[1]U.S. CONST. amend. XIV. *See generally* J. NOWAK & R. ROTUNDA, CONSTITUTIONAL LAW 525–29 (4th ed. 1991); L. TRIBE, AMERICAN CONSTITUTIONAL LAW 664 (2d ed. 1988); Winick, *Competency to Consent to Voluntary Hospitalization: A Therapeutic Jurisprudence Analysis of* Zinermon v. Burch, 14 INT'L J.L. & PSYCHIATRY 169, 175 (1991); Winick, *Legal Limitations on Correctional Therapy and Research,* 65 MINN. L. REV. 331, 392–402 (1981) [hereinafter *Legal Limitations*].

[2]U.S. CONST. amend. V.

[3]*See, e.g.,* Greenholtz v. Inmates of Neb. Penal & Correctional Complex, 442 U.S. 1, 7 (1979); Meachum v. Fano, 427 U.S. 215, 224 (1976); NOWAK & ROTUNDA, *supra* note 1, at 487; TRIBE, *supra* note 1, at 664.

[4]*See supra* chapter 11, part B.

[5]Meyer v. Nebraska, 262 U.S. 390, 399 (1923).

[6]*See, e.g.,* Ingraham v. Wright, 430 U.S. 651, 673 (1977); Board of Regents v. Roth, 408 U.S. 564, 572 (1972).

[7]*See* Mills v. Rogers, 457 U.S. 291, 300 (1982); Vitek v. Jones, 445 U.S. 480, 488 (1980); Wolff v. McDonnell, 418 U.S. 539, 557 (1974); Project Release v. Prevost, 722 F.2d 960, 979 (2d Cir. 1983); Rennie v. Klein, 653 F.2d 836, 841–42 (3d Cir. 1981) (en banc), *vacated and remanded on other grounds,* 458 U.S. 1119 (1982). Moreover, when state law conditions the state's ability to impose involuntary treatment on satisfaction of specified criteria, it may create an entitlement interest to freedom from such treatment that can create a property interest that itself would require due process protections when the state seeks to take it away. *See Greenholtz,* 442 U.S. at 7; Goss v. Lopez, 419 U.S. 565, 572 (1975); *Roth,* 408 U.S. at 569.

[8]457 U.S. at 299 n.16.

[9]494 U.S. 210, 221–22 (1990); *see supra* chapter 15, part A.

[10]504 U.S. 127, 134 (1992); *see supra* chapter 15, part A.

[11]*Compare* Meachum v. Fano, 427 U.S. 215 (1976) (a criminal sentence extinguishes the prisoner's liberty interest in being placed in one correctional facility rather than another) *with* Washington v. Harper, 494 U.S. 210 (1990) (sentenced prisoner retains liberty interest in avoiding unwanted antipsychotic medication) *and* Vitek v. Jones, 449 U.S. 480 (1980) (sentenced prisoner retains liberty interest in avoiding transfer to mental hospital for drug and behavioral treatment).

liberty interest in personal security and bodily integrity is implicated.[12] Other intrusive treatments—other drugs, electroconvulsive therapy, electronic stimulation of the brain, and psychosurgery—also would invade this liberty interest.[13] Moreover, even less intrusive treatments may implicate this interest or other liberty interests protected by due process.[14] To the extent that requiring participation in such treatment necessitates the individual's presence for any significant period in a place other than where he or she would prefer to be, this can be seen as an infringement of the historic liberty interest in freedom from bodily restraint.[15] In addition, state law in a number of states has been read to create liberty interests independent of the federal Constitution in freedom from involuntary treatment.[16] These liberty interests are not extinguished by involuntary civil commitment pursuant to typical state commitment statutes, which generally do not require a finding of incompetence to participate in treatment decisions or a determination that the patient will be dangerous to hospital staff or other patients.[17] These liberty interests also are not extinguished by criminal conviction and a prison sentence,[18] as *Harper* explicitly recognizes.

B. The Process That Is Due

Given the existence of a liberty interest implicated by intrusive (and in certain instances even nonintrusive) mental health treatment, what are "the minimum procedures required by the Constitution for determining that the individual's liberty interest actually is outweighed

---

[12]*See supra* chapter 15, part B. The Court previously had held that the transfer of a prisoner to a mental hospital for treatment in a mandatory behavior modification program that included administration of psychotropic drugs implicated the "right to be free from, and to obtain judicial relief for, unjustified intrusions on personal security." Vitek v. Jones, 445 U.S. 480, 492 (1980) (quoting Ingraham v. Wright, 430 U.S. 651, 673 (1977)).

[13]*See supra* chapters 5–8; *see, e.g.,* Price v. Sheppard, 239 N.W.2d 905 (Minn. 1976) (electronconvulsive therapy and psychosurgery).

[14]*See supra* chapters 3–4; *see, e.g.,* Clonce v. Richardson, 379 F. Supp. 338 (W.D. Mo. 1974) (tier program, a form of behavioral conditioning).

[15]*See supra* chapter 11, notes 1–41 and accompanying text; Foucha v. Louisiana, 504 U.S. 71, 80 (1992) (Hospital confinement infringes on individual's freedom from bodily restraint, an interest "at the core of the liberty protected by the Due Process Clause."); Parham v. J.R., 442 U.S. 584, 600 (1979); Humphrey v. Cady, 405 U.S. 504, 509 (1972); *see also* Zinermon v. Burch, 494 U.S. 113, 131 (1990) (noting that an individual has a "substantial liberty interest in avoiding confinement in a mental hospital"). To qualify as a restraint on liberty in this sense, the restraint in question must be significant or substantial in both a temporal and spatial way. *See* Colb, *Freedom From Incarceration: Why Is This Different From All Other Rights?*, 69 N.Y.U. L. REV. 781, 841 (1994). Interferences with liberty that are merely *de minimus* do not qualify. Thus, requiring a driver to stop at a red light or to come to the motor vehicle bureau to wait in line to obtain a driver's license would be an insufficiently substantial restraint on liberty to invoke the constitutional requirements of due process. *See id.* at 839, 841.

[16]*E.g.,* Project Release v. Prevost, 722 F.2d 960, 979 (2d Cir. 1983) (applying New York law); Large v. Superior Court, 714 P.2d 399, 405–09 (Ariz. 1986) (en banc); Kehyea v. Rushen, 223 Cal. Rptr. 746 (Cal. Ct. App. 1986); Gundy v. Pauley, 619 S.W.2d 730, 731 (Ky. Ct. App. 1981); Guardianship of Roe, III, 421 N.E.2d 40, 51 n.9 (Mass. 1981); Opinion of the Justices, 465 A.2d 484, 495, 489 (N.H. 1983); Rivers v. Katz, 495 N.E.2d 337 (N.Y. 1986).

[17]*Rennie,* 653 F.2d at 843, 846; Rogers v. Okin, 634 F.2d 650, 658–59 (1st Cir. 1980) (en banc); Winters v. Miller, 446 F.2d 65 (2d Cir.), *cert. denied,* 404 U.S. 985 (1971); Davis v. Hubbard, 506 F. Supp. 915, 935 (N.D. Ohio 1980); Rivers v. Katz, 495 N.E.2d 337, 344 (N.Y. 1986); *see* Youngberg v. Romeo, 457 U.S. 307, 316 (1982) ("[T]he mere fact that Romeo has been committed under proper procedures does not deprive him of all substantive liberty interests under the Fourteenth Amendment.").

[18]Washington v. Harper, 494 U.S. 210, 221–22 (1990) (sentenced prisoner retains a liberty interest in freedom from unwanted antipsychotic medication); Vitek v. Jones, 445 U.S. 480, 491–94 (1980) (criminal commitment does not extinguish the prisoner's liberty interest in avoiding transfer to a mental hospital where involuntary psychiatric treatment would be imposed); *see supra* note 11 and accompanying text.

in a particular instance''?[19] That liberty interests are implicated does not mean that a formal, adversarial hearing will be required.[20] ''The very nature of due process negates any concept of inflexible procedures universally applicable to every imaginable situation.''[21] Due process instead ''is a flexible concept that varies with the particular situation.''[22] In determining what process is due in a particular situation, the Supreme Court has engaged in a broad balancing approach; it applied a test developed in *Mathews v. Eldridge*[23] and considered three distinct factors:

> First, the private interest that will be effected by the official action; second, the risk of an erroneous deprivation of such interests through the procedures used, and the probable value, if any, of additional or substitute procedural safeguards; and finally, the Government's interest, including the function involved and fiscal and administrative burdens that the additional or substitute procedural requirement would entail.[24]

The *Mathews* test asks whether additional or substitute procedural requirements would sufficiently diminish the risk of erroneous determination to be worth the fiscal, administrative, and social costs that the procedural requirement would impose. Although *Mathews* seems to focus only on the value of various procedural protections in increasing the accuracy of adjudication, due process also serves important dignitary or participatory values that are achieved by allowing individuals to participate in decisions affecting their liberty or property.[25] The *Mathews* calculus does not explicitly take into account the substantial

---

[19]Mills v. Rogers, 457 U.S. 291, 299 (1982).

[20]*E.g., Harper,* 494 U.S. at 231 (upholding informal administrative process for authorizing involuntary medication of prisoner); Parham v. J.R., 442 U.S. 584, 606–07 (1979) (upholding informal clinical review of parents' admission of child to mental hospital or mental retardation facility); Goss v. Lopez, 419 U.S. 565, 579 (1975) (upholding informal hearing for 10-day suspension from public school).

[21]Cafeteria Workers v. McElroy, 367 U.S. 886, 895 (1961).

[22]Zinermon v. Burch, 494 U.S. 113, 127 (1990); Parham v. J.R., 442 U.S. 584, 608 n.16 (1979); Morrissey v. Brewer, 408 U.S. 471, 481 (1972).

[23]424 U.S. 319 (1976).

[24]*Id.* at 335. This standard is regularly invoked in due process cases, including those involving mental illness. *See, e.g., Zinermon,* 494 U.S. at 127; Washington v. Harper, 494 U.S. 210, 229 (1990); *Parham,* 442 U.S. at 599–600; Vitek v. Jones, 445 U.S. 480 (1980); Addington v. Texas, 441 U.S. 418 (1979). The Supreme Court, however, has recently rejected the *Mathews* test as a standard for determining the requirements of due process in criminal trial contexts. Medina v. California, 504 U.S. 437 (1992); *see* Winick, *Presumptions and Burdens of Proof in Determining Competency to Stand Trial: An Analysis of* Medina v. California *and of the Supreme Court's New Due Process Methodology in Criminal Cases,* 47 U. MIAMI L. REV. 817 (1993).

[25]*See* Marshall v. Jerrico, Inc., 446 U.S. 238, 242 (1980) (one of the ''central concerns of procedural due process'' is ''the promotion of participation and dialogue by affected individuals in the decision making process''); Carey v. Piphus, 435 U.S. 247, 266 (1978); Codd v. Velger, 429 U.S. 624, 636 (1977) (Stevens, J., dissenting); Goldberg v. Kelly, 397 U.S. 254, 264–65 (1970); Joint Anti-Fascist Refugee Comm. v. McGrath, 341 U.S. 123, 171–72 (1951) (Frankfurter, J., concurring); J. MASHAW, DUE PROCESS IN THE ADMINISTRATIVE STATE 177–80 (1985) (discussing ''the claim that the dignity and self-respect of the individual can be protected only through processes of government in which there is meaningful participation by affected interests''); TRIBE, *supra* note 1, at 666 (''[I]ntrinsic'' values of due process include a ''chance to participate'' by affected individuals, ''an opportunity that expresses their dignity as persons.''); LaTour, *Determinants of Participant and Observer Satisfaction With Adversary and Inquisitorial Modes of Adjudication,* 36 J. PERSONALITY & SOC. PSYCHOL. 153 (1978) (empirical showing that adversarial procedures are favored because they give disputants more ''process control''); Mashaw, *The Supreme Court's Due Process Calculus for Administrative Adjudication in* Mathews v. Eldridge: *Three Factors in Search of a Theory of Value,* 44 U. CHI. L. REV. 28, 50 (1976) (''[A] lack of participation causes alienation and a loss of that dignity and self-respect that society properly deems independently valuable.''); Michelman, *Formal and Associational Aims in Procedural Due Process,* XVIII NOMOS 126, 127–28 (1977) (Due process vindicates values of ''participation.''); Summers, *Evaluating and Improving Legal Processes—A Plea for ''Process Values,''* 60 CORNELL L. REV. 1, 20–21 (1974); Winick, *Forfeiture of Attorneys' Fees Under RICO and CCE and the Right to Counsel of Choice: The Constitutional Dilemma and How to Avoid It,* 43 U. MIAMI L. REV. 765, 801–03 (1989).

participatory values served by due process hearings, but this benefit should not be ignored in performing the *Mathews* cost–benefit analysis.

In balancing these factors, the Supreme Court has displayed an increased willingness to permit informal procedures that depart substantially from the trial-type hearing traditionally associated with due process.[26] In view of the predictive, subjective, and clinical nature of many of the judgments involved in the right-to-refuse-treatment context, informal and flexible administrative procedures rather than adversarial trial-like hearings generally will suffice.[27] For example, in *Parham v. J.R.*,[28] the Supreme Court rejected the contention that due process requires a judicial-type hearing when parents seek to commit their minor children to mental hospitals or mental retardation facilities. Applying the *Mathews* balancing test, the Court accepted the sufficiency of an administrative determination made by an independent clinical fact finder using "informal traditional medical investigative techniques."[29] These procedures involved the filing of an application for hospital admission followed by hospital staff examination, observation, and periodic review. A formal judicial hearing, the Court found, would be considerably more costly than an informal clinical determination of the admission decision, would be more burdensome to the family relationship and to the therapeutic goals of hospitalization, and would not necessarily result in reduced risk of erroneous commitment.

The Supreme Court's decision in *Washington v. Harper*[30] further illustrates the Court's preference for an administrative model in this area. In *Harper*, the Court found that a convicted prisoner's interest in avoiding unwanted antipsychotic medication, which it recognized to be a liberty interest protected by the Due Process Clause of the Fourteenth Amendment,[31] was "adequately protected, and perhaps better served, by allowing the decision to medicate to be made by medical professionals rather than a judge."[32] Prior to administering drugs involuntarily to any inmate, Washington prison procedures required that the inmate receive notice and a hearing before a tribunal composed of medical professionals and prison authorities, at which time the inmate could challenge the decision to administer drug treatment.[33] Although the Washington Supreme Court held this procedure to violate due process and required a judicial hearing to be held, the Supreme Court found that this informal hearing procedure satisfied the requirements of due process.[34] The Court observed that the "fallibility of medical and psychiatric diagnosis" cannot always be avoided by "shifting the decision from a trained specialist . . . to an untrained judge . . . after a judicial-type hearing. Even after a hearing, the nonspecialist decisionmaker must make a medical–psychiatric decision."[35] In addition, the Court noted that because medical personnel are conducting the review, the rules of evidence and standard of proof that would be applied in a trial-type hearing would not be helpful.[36] The Court also expressed the concern

---

[26]*E.g., Harper,* 494 U.S. at 231; Parham v. J.R., 442 U.S. 584 (1979); Board of Curators v. Horowitz, 435 U.S. 78 (1978); Goss v. Lopez, 419 U.S. 565 (1975); *see supra* note 20 and accompanying text.

[27]*See Harper,* 494 U.S. at 231–32; *Parham,* 442 U.S. at 606–07.

[28]442 U.S. 584 (1979).

[29]*Id.* at 607; *see id.* at 614–17 (describing informal administrative procedures used to make hospital admission decisions).

[30]494 U.S. 210 (1990).

[31]*Id.* at 221–22.

[32]*Id.* at 232.

[33]*Id.* at 215–16.

[34]*Id.* at 225.

[35]*Id.*

[36]*Id.* at 235.

that "requiring judicial hearings will divert scarce prison resources, both money and the staff's time, from the care and treatment of mentally ill inmates."[37]

The Court rejected the contention that the prison review board violated due process because it was composed of prison medical personnel and administrators.[38] Although the dissent argued that the members of the review board suffered from an inherent conflict of interest,[39] the majority was impressed by the fact that the clinicians on the board could not be involved in the inmate's treatment and had a professional duty to act independently.[40] Finding "no indication that any institutional biases affected or altered the decision to medicate respondent against his will," the majority was satisfied that existing procedures ensured "independence of the decisionmaker."[41] Moreover, the Court endorsed an internal system of review, citing studies indicating that outside decision makers most often concur with the treating physician's recommendation to medicate involuntarily.[42]

Of course, *Harper* was a prison case, and as *Riggins v. Nevada*[43] shows, the Court's deferential approach in prison contexts may not extend outside the prison.[44] Indeed, in the criminal pretrial context presented in *Riggins,* the Court called for a judicial determination by the criminal trial court to resolve the issues presented when a state seeks to administer antipsychotic medication over the criminal defendant's objection.[45] Does *Riggins* in this respect suggest that the *Harper* Court's approval of an informal administrative model for right-to-refuse-medication determinations will be limited to the prison? This conclusion seems highly unlikely. It is difficult to infer from *Riggins*'s adoption of a judicial model for right-to-refuse-treatment issues in the criminal trial process that judicial models also will be required in other right-to-refuse-treatment contexts. In the trial context of *Riggins,* a trial judge is already involved with the matter and would need to deal with the criminal law aspects of the case, including competency to stand trial. As a result, it would not have been sensible for the *Riggins* Court to have bifurcated the medication question by involving an administrative decision maker. Thus, allowing the criminal court, which is already and inevitably involved with the matter, to resolve the right-to-refuse-treatment issues arising in the criminal trial process does not necessarily indicate a broad rejection of *Harper*'s endorsement of an administrative model for right-to-refuse decision making. As a result, *Harper*'s preference for administrative decision making still would seem applicable in other contexts.[46]

Even before *Harper* endorsed informal administrative models in this area, the trend in the lower federal courts seemed clearly to be going in this direction. These court cases approved the use of flexible and informal mechanisms for making right-to-refuse-treatment determinations, rather than adversarial trial-type hearings. The cases in this area almost

---

[37]*Id.* at 232.

[38]*Id.* at 215–16.

[39]*Id.* at 251–52 (Stevens, J., dissenting, joined by Brennan & Marshal, JJ.).

[40]*Id.* at 233.

[41]*Id.*

[42]*Id.* at 234 n.13 (citing studies).

[43]504 U.S. 127 (1992).

[44]*See supra* chapter 15, part B.

[45]504 U.S. at 135–36.

[46]For descriptions of how such informal mechanisms work in practice, see Susman, *Resolving Hospital Conflicts: A Study on Therapeutic Jurisprudence,* 22 J. PSYCHIATRY & L. 107 (1994) (describing Maryland's Clinical Review Panel, an informal model for reviewing treatment refusals, headed by an independent psychiatrist); Zito et al., *The Treatment Review Panel: A Solution to Treatment Refusal?,* 12 BULL. AM. ACAD. PSYCHIATRY & L. 349 (1984) (presenting an overview of Minnesota's Treatment Review Panel process, detailing its clinical significance, and discussing administrative and legal implications).

always have involved psychotropic drugs, the treatment technique that has been at the center of the right-to-refuse-treatment controversy. Because psychotropic medication is a fairly intrusive therapy, approval of the use of informal administrative models in the medication context indicates that such models will suffice for other treatment techniques falling lower on the continuum of intrusiveness. Thus, these lower court medication cases deserve careful consideration.

In *Rogers v. Okin*,[47] the First Circuit Court of Appeals held that determinations necessary to justify forced psychotropic medication must be made, at least initially, by clinicians pursuant to a "professional judgment-call," requiring a balancing of the varying interests and an "individualized estimation" of the relevant factors.[48] At a minimum, the court concluded, "the determination that medication is necessary must be made by a qualified physician as to each individual patient to be medicated."[49] The court left the question of what additional procedures might be warranted to the district court on remand, noting that the district court "should leave this difficult necessarily *ad hoc* balancing to state physicians and limit its own role to designing procedures for insuring that the patients' interests in refusing antipsychotics are taken into consideration" and that the drugs are not forcibly administered "absent a finding by a qualified physician that those interests are outweighed in a particular situation. . . ."[50]

For treatment based on an assertion of the *parens patriae* power, the *Rogers* court found that state law required that "absent an emergency, a judicial determination of incapacity to make treatment decisions" must be made.[51] In an emergency, however, which the court found to include situations when "the immediate administration of drugs is reasonably believed to be necessary to prevent further deterioration in the patient's mental health," such determinations could be made by state officials.[52] The court rejected the district court's prior determination that the state was required to seek individualized guardian approval for decisions to treat incompetent patients with antipsychotic drugs.[53] Although the court left such treatment decisions to the professional judgment of state physicians in the first instance, it noted that due process might require "some mechanism for periodic review by non-treating physicians of the full treatment history of patients to insure that the treating physicians are in fact attempting to make treatment decisions as the patients themselves would were they competent."[54] The court thus broadly approved an informal mechanism for making these clinically oriented determinations, identifying the various interests that must be weighed by state physicians exercising professional judgment, and suggesting the possibility that independent clinical review might be appropriate. With the exception of the determination of incompetency to make treatment decisions in nonemergency situations, however, the court declined to require judicial determinations.

In *Rennie v. Klein*,[55] the Third Circuit Court of Appeals also rejected a "rigid, traditionally adversary proceeding."[56] The court upheld a New Jersey regulation com-

---

[47]634 F.2d 650 (1st Cir. 1980) (en banc).

[48]*Id.* at 656.

[49]*Id.*

[50]*Id.* at 657.

[51]*Id.* at 661.

[52]*Id.* at 659–60.

[53]*Id.* at 660–61. Such treatment guardians are used in this context in a number of states. *E.g.*, FLA. STAT. § 394.459(3)(a) (1993).

[54]634 F.2d at 661.

[55]653 F.2d 836 (3d Cir. 1981) (en banc).

[56]*Id.* at 848.

mitting involuntary medication determinations to the professional judgment of state physicians subject to managerial review. The regulation set forth elaborate procedures for determining right-to-refuse-medication controversies and for their review. Under these procedures, when patients objected to administration of antipsychotic medication, the attending physician was required to explain to them the nature of their condition, the reasons for prescribing the drug, and the risks and benefits of the proposed treatment and of treatment alternatives. If a patient persisted in refusing treatment, the matter then was discussed at a meeting of the patient's treatment team, composed of the treating physician and other hospital personnel. Patients could attend this meeting, unless their conditions did not allow such participation. If the meeting did not resolve the matter, the medical director of the hospital or a designee was required personally to examine the patient and review the record. If the director agreed with the treating physician's recommendation, medication was administered. In connection with this review, the medical director was authorized (but not required) to retain an independent psychiatrist to evaluate the patient's need for medication. In addition, the director was required to conduct a weekly review of the treatment program of each patient subjected to involuntary medication in order to determine its continued necessity. The State Division of Mental Health and Hospitals also routinely had all cases of compulsory medication reviewed by a division director or other physician in the division's central office.[57]

The district court in *Rennie* found that these in-house review procedures failed to meet the requirements of due process.[58] The court found the medical director's review of the attending psychiatrist's recommendation to be inadequate because "institutional pressures" would deprive the medical director of sufficient independence to satisfy due process.[59] The district court required expansion of the state's procedures in four respects. First, the court required use of consent forms advising patients of their rights and describing the drug effects. Second, it ordered establishment of a system of patient advocates—lawyers, psychologists, social workers, registered nurses, paralegals, or other qualified lay persons— to represent patients refusing treatment. Third, the court required the retention of independent psychiatrists to make the ultimate determination and to render a written decision. Finally, the court mandated the holding of formal adversarial hearings before the independent psychiatrist on 5 days' notice, at which the patient would be represented by a patient advocate and (at the patient's expense, if desired) a retained attorney.

On appeal, the Third Circuit reversed the district court's decision in *Rennie,* finding that the New Jersey procedures were adequate to meet due process requirements.[60] Applying the balancing test mandated by *Mathews v. Eldridge,*[61] the Third Circuit was satisfied that the state's procedures, "if carefully followed, pose only a minor risk of erroneous deprivation."[62] Moreover, the court was not convinced "that this risk would be significantly reduced by superimposing the district court's own requirements on those already required by the state."[63] The circuit court found the "adversary contest" mandated by the district court to be "ill-suited to the type of medical determination that must be made."[64]

[57]*See id.* at 848–49.

[58]Rennie v. Klein, 476 F. Supp. 1294, 1310–14 (D.N.J. 1979).

[59]*Id.* at 1310.

[60]Rennie v. Klein, 653 F.2d 836 (3d Cir. 1981) (en banc).

[61]424 U.S. 319 (1976); *see supra* notes 23–24 and accompanying text.

[62]653 F.2d at 850.

[63]*Id.*

[64]*Id.*

The Third Circuit also rejected the district court's requirement of independent psychiatrists and patient advocates, finding no due process violation in the use of decision makers employed by and responsible to the state.[65] The court was particularly impressed with the state requirement that an outside psychiatrist be retained in certain circumstances, which it found "tends to blunt the district court's concern that institutional pressures will prevent an independent decision."[66] Moreover, the court found that the district court's order would "impose substantial financial burdens on the state and even greater expenditures of staff time at the hospitals."[67] The court was unwilling to divert limited state resources available for the care of the mentally ill "to finance nonessential administrative procedures" that "would not provide help for the patient's most critical needs."[68] The Third Circuit thus found that the procedures imposed by the regulation were consistent with constitutional requirements and that the district court had erred in mandating additional procedures, which it found to be "ill-suited" to the resolution of issues that are essentially "medical in nature" and unduly expensive.[69] Following remand, the Third Circuit reaffirmed its determination that the New Jersey regulations "afforded sufficient due process protection with respect to forcibly medicating the mentally ill without the need for interposing external judicial requirements."[70]

The Second Circuit Court of Appeals also applied a flexible due process approach in *Project Release v. Prevost,* approving New York's three-tiered administrative review process for involuntary medication decision making.[71] Relying on *Parham, Rogers,* and *Rennie,* the Second Circuit held that at a minimum, a "procedural scheme must . . . provide sufficient opportunity for professional input."[72] New York's procedures involved three levels of review by medical personnel other than the treating physician. In addition, patients were permitted legal counsel or other interested persons to represent them at all levels of the appeal process, as well as the assistance of a statewide advocacy office.[73] The court found that this system of administrative review satisfies due process requirements.[74] A similar approach was taken by a district court in upholding the procedures used for involuntary medication by St. Elizabeths Hospital in Washington, DC.[75] The hospital procedures permitted treatment over objection only after consultation with a patient advocate and the patient's family and completion of an independent administrative review. The court found these procedures to satisfy due process and rejected the contention that a judicial determination of incompetence was required because "[t]o require the courts to pass on such issues would embroil them in a never-ending controversy concerning medical judgments for which courts have neither the institutional resources nor the necessary expertise."[76]

---

[65]*Id.*

[66]*Id.*

[67]*Id.* at 851.

[68]*Id.*

[69]*Id.* at 850–51. The court relied on *Parham's* distaste for adversary proceedings and preference for informal medical investigative techniques for resolving essentially medical questions. *Id.* at 851.

[70]Rennie v. Klein, 720 F.2d 266, 270 (3d Cir. 1983) (en banc).

[71]Project Release v. Prevost, 722 F.2d 960 (2d Cir. 1983).

[72]*Id.* at 980.

[73]*Id.*

[74]*Id.* at 980–81.

[75]United States v. Leatherman, 580 F. Supp. 977 (D.D.C. 1983).

[76]*Id.* at 979–80. *See also* R.A.J. v. Miller, 590 F. Supp. 1319, 1322 (N.D. Tex. 1984) (upholding a "two tiered medical review process, which assures that professional judgment will be exercised," and which included the right to review by independent consulting psychiatrists of treatment decisions for competent patients).

The approach of these lower federal court decisions in cases decided prior to *Harper* demonstrate flexible administrative models that meet the requirements of procedural due process for right-to-refuse-medication decision making. *Harper*'s rejection of the necessity of a judicial model and approval of the administrative review process used in the Washington prison makes it clear that the Supreme Court would find a variety of informal administrative models acceptable in the treatment refusal area. Review of the treating clinician's determinations concerning the patient's satisfaction of the substantive requirements for authorizing involuntary treatment (*e.g.,* incompetency, therapeutic appropriateness, best interests, absence of less intrusive means, dangerousness) may occur through a variety of procedural mechanisms. These may include an administrative review board, another clinician, or an administrator with access to independent clinical consultation. The review may take the form of a formal or informal hearing or may be managerial in nature. The reviewer or reviewing body must exercise independent judgment, but *Harper* and *Parham* make it clear that being employed by the institution seeking to impose treatment does not itself necessarily compromise independence in violation of due process.[77]

Although flexible administrative models will meet federal constitutional due process requirements, not all courts have approved their use in the involuntary treatment context. On the basis of state law, several state courts have required more formal adversarial judicial determinations in right-to-refuse-medication cases. In *Rivers v. Katz*,[78] the New York Court of Appeals invoked the state constitution to invalidate portions of the state's administrative procedures for administering psychotropic drugs that previously had been upheld against federal constitutional attack in *Project Release v. Prevost*. In a case involving an assertion of the *parens patriae* justification for involuntary treatment, the court in *Rivers* required a judicial determination of the patient's competence to participate in treatment decision making. This determination must be made at a *de novo* hearing following exhaustion of administrative review at which the patient is afforded the right to counsel and the state bears the burden of demonstrating by clear and convincing evidence that the patient is incompetent and that the proposed treatment is in the patient's best interests and is the least intrusive treatment available.[79]

Similarly, the Colorado Supreme Court has found that state law requires a judicial hearing in right-to-refuse-treatment cases.[80] The court held that such a hearing must include the right to counsel, to cross-examine adverse witnesses, and to present evidence. In addition, the court placed the burden of proof by clear and convincing evidence on the physician seeking to administer treatment. In a state court counterpart of the *Rogers* case, the Massachusetts Supreme Judicial Court relied on state constitutional law, common law, and statutes to require a judicial determination of incompetency and application of a substituted judgment standard to decide whether the patient would have consented to the medication if competent.[81] The court authorized medication in an emergency without prior court approval, but only to prevent the ''immediate, substantial and irreversible deterioration of a serious mental illness.''[82] A judicial adjudication of incompetency must follow, the court held, if continued drug treatment is expected. Other state cases have also required a judicial model

---

[77]Washington v. Harper, 494 U.S. 210, 233 (1990); Parham v. J.R., 442 U.S. 584, 594.

[78]495 N.E.2d 337 (N.Y. 1986).

[79]*Id.* at 344.

[80]People v. Medina, 705 P.2d 961, 971–73 (Colo. 1985) (en banc); *In re* M.K.M; 765 P.2d 1075 (Colo. Ct. App. 1988); *In re* M.P., 500 N.E. 2d 216 (Ind. Ct. App. 1986).

[81]Rogers v. Commissioner, 458 N.E.2d 308 (Mass. 1983).

[82]*Id.* at 311, 322.

for right-to-refuse-medication decision making rather than the administrative model approved by federal courts as adequate under the federal Constitution.[83]

Experience under these judicial procedures and under the more informal administrative models approved in the federal cases should provide an empirical basis for assessing the relative merits of these differing approaches. Absent evidence impairing the integrity of decision making under the more informal administrative models,[84] however, it would seem unlikely that courts would read the Due Process Clause of the federal Constitution to require more formal procedures. A body of empirical research has begun to emerge that examines the right-to-refuse decision-making process under these differing models.[85] Does a model using judicial decision making increase accuracy? The results of some of these studies may suggest not. Deciding competency issues under the requirement of *Rivers,* New York judges deferred to hospital recommendations of involuntary treatment of incompetent patients in 87% of cases, and Massachusetts judges performing under the requirements of *Rogers*

---

[83]*See In re* Application for the Commitment of an Alleged Mentally Disordered Person, 854 P.2d 1207 (Ariz. Ct. App. 1993) (individuals cannot be involuntary medicated unless a court has adjudicated them incompetent to make treatment decisions); Keyhea v. Rushen, 223 Cal. Rptr. 746, 753–55 (Ct. App. 1986) (based on statute); Riese v. St. Mary's Hosp. & Medical Ctr., 271 Cal. Rptr. 199 (Ct. App. 1988), *dismissed,* 774 P.2d 698 (Cal. 1989) (patients have a statutory right to exercise informed consent to use of antipsychotic drugs absent a judicial determination of incompetence); Goedecke v. State, 603 P.2d 123, 125 (Colo. 1979) (based on common law and statute); Doe v. Hunter, 667 A.2d 90 (Conn. Super. Ct. 1995) (mental health treatment recipient entitled to a competency determination on ability to make a mental health treatment decision, even if already determined generally incompetent and under the care of a guardian); *In re* M.P., 510 N.E.2d 645 (Ind. 1987) (statutory right to refuse pending judicial review); Guardianship of Roe, 421 N.E.2d 40, 51 & n.9 (Mass. 1981) (state constitution and common law require judicial approval of involuntary administration of psychotropic drugs to non-institutionalized mentally ill person); Jarvis v. Levine, 418 N.W.2d 139 (Minn. 1988) (state constitutional right to privacy); *In re* K.K.B., 609 P.2d 747, 751–52 (Okla. 1980) (based on state constitutional right to privacy); State *ex rel.* Jones v. Gerhardstein, 416 N.W. 2d 883, 898 (Wis. 1987) (requiring adversarial judicial hearing to determine incompetency for civilly committed patients prior to administration of psychotropic medication based on federal and state constitutional guarantee of equal protection). *See generally* Perlin, *Decoding Right to Refuse Treatment Law,* 16 INT'L J.L. & PSYCHIATRY 151 (1993) (reviewing the trend toward a liberal interpretation of procedural due process protections on behalf of patients in state court proceedings).

[84]*See* Bersoff, *Judicial Deference to Nonlegal Decisionmakers: Imposing Simplistic Solutions on Problems of Cognitive Complexity in Mental Disability Law,* 46 SMU L. REV. 329, 351–62 (1992) (discussing studies that demonstrate bias of clinician toward the treatment values of the medical model); Kirk & Bersoff, *How Many Procedural Safeguards Does It Take to Get a Psychiatrist to Leave the Lightbulb Unchanged?: A Due Process Analysis of the MacArthur Treatment Competence Study,* 2 PSYCHOL. PUB. POL'Y & L. 45 (1996).

[85]*See, e.g.,* Appelbaum & Hoge, *Empirical Research on the Effects of Legal Policy on the Right to Refuse Treatment, in* THE RIGHT TO REFUSE ANTIPSYCHOTIC MEDICATION 87 (D. Rapoport & J. Parry eds., 1988); Cournos et al., *A Comparison of Clinical and Judicial Procedures for Reviewing Requests for Involuntary Medication in New York,* 39 HOSP. & COMMUNITY PSYCHIATRY 851, 855 (1988); Hoge et al., *The Right to Refuse Treatment Under* Rogers v. Commissioner: *Preliminary Empirical Findings and Comparisons,* 15 BULL. AM. ACAD. PSYCHIATRY & L. 163 (1987); Veliz & James, *Medicine Court:* Rogers *in Practice,* 144 AM. J. PSYCHIATRY 62 (1987); Young et al., *Treatment Refusals Among Forensic Inpatients,* 15 BULL. AM. ACAD. PSYCHIATRY & L. 5 (1987); Susman, *supra* note 46. *See also* Zito, *Toward a Therapeutic Jurisprudence Analysis of Medication Refusal in the Court Review Model,* 11 BEHAVIORAL SCI. & L. 151 (1993) (therapeutic jurisprudence analysis of judicial model for treatment refusal, finding, through patient interviews, that the process is antitherapeutic and concluding that judicial review should be the last resort); Zito et al., *Clinical Characteristics of Hospitalized Psychotic Patients Who Refuse Antipsychotic Drug Therapy,* 152 AM. J. PSYCHIATRY 822 (1985); Zito et al., *One Year Under* Rivers: *Drug Refusal in a New York State Psychiatric Facility,* 12 INT'L J.L. & PSYCHIATRY 295 (1989) [hereinafter *One Year Under* Rivers].

deferred to such hospital recommendations in 90% to 95% of cases.[86] These results are consistent with studies in other contexts showing that judges tend to defer to clinical evaluators on issues they regard as largely clinical in nature, such as competency.[87] To the extent that judges "rubber stamp" the recommendations of clinicians on such issues, rather than giving them independent consideration, the superiority of judicial compared to administrative determinations in this area may be questioned. Review by an independent clinician or by an administrative body that includes or has access to such a clinician may result in more reliable right-to-refuse-treatment decision making than processes relying on judges.

Determinations concerning the existence in individual cases of the substantive predicates required by the Constitution for authorizing involuntary administration of medication can thus, consistent with due process, be remitted to procedures using the professional judgment of treating physicians, with some opportunity for administrative review. Such administrative review, if performed independently, should not diminish the accuracy of the fact-finding process and may even improve accuracy. Whether increased accuracy results from administrative compared to judicial fact finding in this area warrants additional empirical research.

Increased accuracy may relate to two issues in particular that are deserving of empirical examination. First, what factors ensure a sufficient degree of independence on the part of the fact finder and reviewer? Does employment by the same institutional employer (hospital or prison) that seeks involuntary treatment compromise independence? The Supreme Court in *Harper* assumed not,[88] but the dissenters criticized this assumption on the ground that reviewing clinicians who sometimes function as treating clinicians may over-identify with the position of treating clinicians or may feel that deference to them may help to ensure that they receive similar deference when their roles are reversed.[89] Use of entirely independent clinicians would reduce these institutional pressures, but whether the added cost that this would impose would be justified may turn on whether research demonstrates the validity of the dissent's concerns.

Second, can clinical reviewers be counted on to apply the correct legal standards, such as competency? In the context of determining competence to stand trial, existing research

---

[86]Hoge et al., *supra* note 85, at 165 (petitions approved in 95.1% of cases filed in Massachusetts); Veliz & James, *supra* note 85, at 64 (90% of patients given judicial hearings in Massachusetts found incompetent in accordance with hospital recommendation); Zito et al., *One Year Under* Rivers, *supra* note 85, at 300 (hospital recommendations approved in 87% of cases in New York). *See also* Washington v. Harper, 494 U.S. 210, 234 n.13 (1990). ("[T]he practical effect of mandating an outside decisionmaker such as an independent psychiatrist or judge in these circumstances may be chimerical. Review of the literature indicates that outside decisionmakers concur with the treating physician's decision to treat a patient involuntarily in most, if not all, cases."); *accord* Bloom et al., *An Empirical View of Patients Exercising Their Right to Refuse Treatment*, 7 INT'L J.L. & PSYCHIATRY 315, 325 (1984) (independent physician concurring in 95% of cases); Hickman et al., *Right to Refuse Psychotropic Medication: An Interdisciplinary Proposal*, 6 MENTAL & PHYSICAL DISABILITY L. REP. 122, 130 (1982) (100% of cases).

[87]Bonnie, *The Competence of Criminal Defendants: Beyond Dusky and Drope*, 47 U. MIAMI L. REV. 539, 550 (1993); Golding et al., *Assessment and Conceptualization of Competency to Stand Trial: Preliminary Data on the Interdisciplinary Fitness Interview*, 8 LAW & HUM. BEHAV. 121 (1984); Hart & Hare, *Predicting Fitness to Stand Trial: The Relative Power of Demographic, Criminal and Clinical Variables*, 5 FORENSIC REPORTS 53, 56, 59 (1992); Winick, *Reforming Competency to Stand Trial and Plead Guilty: A Restated Proposal and a Response to Professor Bonnie*, 85 J. CRIM. L. & CRIMINOLOGY 571, 620 (1995). *But see* Hiday, *Court Decisions in Civil Commitment*, 4 INT'L J.L. & PSYCHIATRY 159, 166–67 (1981) (noting that a study in one state suggests that the courts may be moving toward acting more independently in civil commitment decision making).

[88]Washington v. Harper, 494 U.S. 210, 233–35 (1990).

[89]*Id.* at 251–54 (Stevens, J., joined by Brennan & Marshall, J.J., concurring in part, and dissenting in part).

suggests that clinical evaluators frequently confuse the legal standard for competency with the existence of psychosis or the test for legal insanity.[90] Competency is a legal, not a clinical, question; for clinicians to assess competency with a high degree of accuracy, it is necessary that a clear definition of competency be provided[91] and that training in its application be undertaken. Further accuracy can be ensured by developing and validating competency assessment instruments to assist clinical evaluators[92] and by developing and refining clinical protocols or guidelines for competency assessment.[93] Different approaches for training clinical evaluators should also be developed and tested.

Apart from accuracy concerns, a proper procedural due process analysis should take into account dignitary or participatory values.[94] Those values should be considered in designing informal administrative models that will be used in the right-to-refuse-treatment context. Existing literature suggests greater litigant satisfaction and increased compliance with the results of more adversarial (rather than inquisitorial) procedural models.[95] This would suggest that patients would find more acceptable informal administrative models in which they have an opportunity to participate through counsel or a counsel substitute, compared to systems that involve exclusively managerial review.[96] Greater patient satisfac-

---

[90]See Winick, *supra* note 87, at 620. *See also* Appelbaum & Grisso, *The MacArthur Treatment Competence Study. I: Mental Illness and Competence to Consent to Treatment,* 19 LAW & HUM. BEHAV. 105, 111 (1995) (noting that courts often confuse the legal standard as well).

[91]See Winick, *Competency to Consent to Treatment: The Distinction Between Assent and Objection,* 28 HOUS. L. REV. 15, 41–44 (1991); Winick, *The Side Effects of Incompetency Labeling and the Implications for Mental Health Law,* 1 PSYCHOL. PUB. POL'Y & L. 30–33 (1995); Winick, *On Autonomy: Legal and Psychological Perspectives,* 37 VILL. L. REV. 1705, 1774–75 (1992).

[92]See Grisso & Appelbaum, *The MacArthur Treatment Competence Study. III: Abilities of Patients to Consent to Psychiatric and Treatment,* 19 LAW & HUM. BEHAV. 149, 173 (1995) (discussing the development of an instrument for this purpose). Although undeniably useful in focusing clinical evaluators' attention on the proper factors to be considered, assessment instruments and other psychometric tests can never fully capture legal concepts, and can never fully replace the exercise of clinical judgment in the individual case. *See* Kapp & Mossman, *Measuring Decisional Capacity: Cautions on the Construction of a "Capacimeter,"* 2 PSYCHOL. PUB. POL'Y & L. 73 (1996); Roesch et al., *Conceptualizing and Assessing Competency to Stand Trial: Implications and Applications of the MacArthur Treatment Competence Model,* 2 PSYCHOL. PUB. POL'Y & L. 96 (1996).

[93]See Kapp & Mossman, *supra* note 92.

[94]See *supra* note 25. For an analysis of the participatory value of hearings from a legal perspective, see Winick, *supra* note 25, at 801–06.

[95]See, e.g., E. LIND & T. TYLER, THE SOCIAL PSYCHOLOGY OF PROCEDURAL JUSTICE 26–34 (1988) (discussing studies that show connection between perceived fairness and litigant satisfaction with procedural rules); J. THIBAULT & L. WALKER, PROCEDURAL JUSTICE: A PSYCHOLOGICAL ANALYSIS 83–84, 94–95, 118 (1975) (finding adversarial system superior to other judicial systems because of level of control retained by individuals); LaTour, *supra* note 25, at 1531–33 (noting that defendants studied were more satisfied with verdicts under adversarial system rather than inquisitorial system, in part because of the perception of greater control over process as a result of ability to select an attorney). *See also* Hoge & Feucht-Haviar, *Long-Term, Assenting Psychiatric Patients: Decisional Capacity and the Quality of Care,* 23 BULL. AM. ACAD. PSYCHIATRY & L. 343 (1995); Poythress, *Procedural Preferences, Perceptions of Fairness, and Compliance with Outcomes,* 18 LAW & HUM. BEHAV. 361 (1994); Thibault et al., *Procedural Justice as Fairness,* 26 STAN L. REV. 1271 (1974).

[96]Ensinger & Ligouri, *The Therapeutic Significance of the Civil Commitment Hearing: An Unexplored Potential,* 6 J. PSYCHIATRY & L. 5, 15 (1978) (suggesting that counsel's efforts at the hearing and in preparing for it together with the client can increase the patient's understanding of the process and diminish the potential trauma of the hearing). Although counsel and other advocacy services can play an all-important role in increasing the patient's sense of "voice" in the process, in many jurisdictions counsel in mental health cases often are "woefully inadequate—disinterested, uninformed, roleless and often hostile." Perlin & Dorfman, *Is it More Than "Dodging Lions and Wastin' Time?": Adequacy of Counsel, Questions of Competence, and the Judicial Process in Individual Right to Refuse Treatment Cases,* 2 PSYCHOL. PUB. POL'L & L. 114, 117 (1996) (criticizing performance of counsel and suggesting that poor and ineffective performance by counsel can have antitherapeutic consequences for patients).

tion and treatment compliance may therefore result if informal administrative approaches developed in the right-to-refuse-treatment context include some adversarial features.[97]

One feature present in adversarial models that could be included in informal procedures is the presentation of evidence. It may be beneficial for patients to hear the testimony of the physician recommending involuntary treatment so that they can better understand their doctors' professional opinions and their reasons for recommending medication.[98] Hearing such testimony may convince the patient to accept the physician's recommendation or at least to understand it as benevolently motivated. Even if the patient persists in wishing to avoid medication, an adverse ruling by the tribunal or decision maker may thereby produce greater patient acceptance and compliance. Patients also should be permitted to present evidence and to testify, thereby increasing their sense of "voice" in the proceedings and ultimately their sense of fairness and acceptance of the outcome.[99] Thus, even when informal procedural models are used, there may be considerable value in adapting at least some adversarial processes.

In addition, the composition of the adjudicative body may also contribute to perceived fairness and ultimate acceptance. Even if the independence of clinical reviews or members of administrative bodies as a matter of law is not *per se* destroyed as a result of their employment by the same institution seeking to administer involuntary treatment, the patient's perception of fairness and participation may well be increased when the clinician is entirely independent. Patient perceptions of the process used may be an important determinant of the success of any treatment ultimately imposed, and this consideration therefore

---

[97]*Cf.* Tyler, *The Psychological Consequences of Judicial Procedures: Implications for Civil Commitment Hearings,* 46 SMU L. REV. 433, 433–44 (1992). In his analysis of the therapeutic value of civil commitment procedures, Tyler notes that the empirical findings contained in the procedural justice literature

> are consistent with the suggestion of the therapeutic jurisprudence literature that hearings which lack the characteristics which people associate with due process are likely to be experienced as unfair. Such unfairness, in turn, is likely to have negative consequences for the subsequent therapeutic process. However, it does not point to judicial hearings as the only possible source of procedures that people will experience as unfair. It is also possible that professionals could develop procedures containing some of the elements [of participation, dignity, and trust]. If they did so, then professional decision-making procedures might also be therapeutic.

Id. (footnote omitted).

[98]*See* Cournos et al., *supra* note 85, at 855 (finding such benefits in judicial hearings); Susman, *supra* note 46, at 117–18 (suggesting that patient acceptance of unfavorable decisions in medication refusal review determinations could be enhanced if patients are given the rationale for the clinical reviewers' decision); Tyler, *supra* note 97, at 441 (suggesting that "people value evidence that the authorities with whom they are dealing are concerned about their welfare and want to treat them fairly"); *cf.* Ensinger & Ligouri, *supra* note 96, at 24–25 (recommending that by working together with the client, in preparing for a hearing and in their participation with the client at the hearing, the roles of counsel and the psychiatrist can promote the client's appreciation of the need and reasons for the recommended treatment and demonstrate that the determinations actually are made in the client's interests).

[99]Lind et al., *Voice, Control, and Procedural Justice: Instrumental and Non-Instrumental Concerns in Fairness Judgments,* 59 J. PERSONALITY & SOC. PSYCHOL. 952 (1990); Stransky, Comment, *Civil Commitment and the Right to Refuse Treatment: Resolving Disputes from a Due Process Perspective,* 50 U. MIAMI. L. REV. 413 (1996); Tyler, *supra* note 97.

should not be ignored in determining the design of procedural systems for treatment-refusal decision making.[100]

Although attention has focused on judicial and administrative models for resolving right-to-refuse-treatment controversies, alternative dispute resolution mechanisms also should be considered. Both judicial and administrative models involve decision making by an individual or body that is not a party to the treatment-refusal dispute. By contrast, negotiation and mediation leave the dispute in the hands of the parties. Negotiation should always be considered when the clinician and patient are in disagreement concerning the course of treatment. As chapter 17 demonstrates, clinician–patient negotiations can be very therapeutic for the patient. Rather than being treated as incompetent objects of government paternalism, patients should be treated as persons whose desires and objectives are given great weight in decisions that vitally affect them. In contrast with a dispute resolved by a third person or body, negotiation can be empowering. It gives patients an opportunity to exercise choice and decision-making ability. Any decision arrived at through negotiation would seem more likely to be acceptable to the patient than one imposed coercively by a court or administrative body.[101] Moreover, it would seem more likely that the patient would comply with the result of such a consensual process than when the patient is ordered by a judge or administrative authority to undergo treatment.[102]

As chapter 17 suggests, negotiation also may present significant therapeutic opportunities for clinicians. The negotiation process may provide a vehicle for therapists to probe resistance and to make advantageous use of transference and countertransference. It therefore may be better for clinicians to engage their patients in an extended dialogue concerning treatment refusal rather than to regard treatment refusal as a problem and to transfer the ''problem'' to a court or administrative body for resolution. Patients who say no to treatment may actually be saying no to something else. Clinicians must be certain that they hear and fully understand patients' objections. Such an extended dialogue may resolve many treatment-refusal issues without the need for the intervention of a third party acting as decision maker.

---

[100]In his study of the Maryland procedure for resolving medication refusal controversies, Susman postulated that patient perceptions of the fairness of the procedure:

> may in fact aid treatment and recovery; fairness may enhance the authority of doctors, nurses, and other staff members, as well as increase the legitimacy of psychiatric hospitals and the psychiatric profession. Furthermore, fair processes in the hospital context may increase compliance with medical decisions among patients and may improve the prospects of patients for reintegrating into the community upon release from the hospital.

Susman, *supra* note 46, at 122–23. *See also* Tyler, *supra* note 97, at 439 (finding that patient perceptions of the fairness of the civil commitment process can be more important than the outcome of the proceedings in fostering patient satisfaction and sense of participation, and these favorable attitudes will foster the patients' concept of the legitimacy of legal authorities, which, in turn, will ''facilitate the subsequent therapeutic process'').

[101]For example, in one study patients found psychiatrists' legally mandated disputing procedures to be less fair than nurses' negotiating processes. Susman, *supra* note 46, at 113–14. In another study, researchers determined that patients' perceptions of fair procedures seemed to be an important determinant of perceived coercion. Monahan et al., *Coercion to Inpatient Treatment: Initial Results and Implications for Assertive Treatment in the Community,* in COERCION AND AGGRESSIVE COMMUNITY TREATMENT: A NEW FRONTIER IN MENTAL HEALTH LAW 13 (D. Dennis & J. Monahan eds., 1996). *See also* Pruitt et al., *Longterm Success in Mediation,* 17 LAW & HUM. BEHAV. 313, 315 (1993); Tyler, *The Psychology of Disputant Concerns in Mediation,* 3 NEGOTIATION J. 367, 368 (1987).

[102]Lind et al., *Procedure and Outcome Effects on Reactions to Adjudicated Resolutions of Conflicts of Interest,* 39 J. PERSONALITY & SOC. PSYCHOL. 643, 652–53 (1980); Musante et al., *The Effects of Control on Perceived Fairness of Procedures and Outcomes,* 19 J. EXPERIMENTAL SOC. PSYCHOL. 223, 224 (1983); Tyler, *The Role of Perceived Injustice in Defendants' Evaluations of Their Courtroom Experience,* 18 LAW & SOC'Y REV. 51, 52, 74 (1984).

When the clinician and patient are at an impasse following such extended negotiation, the use of mediation may prove successful. Mediation is an alternative dispute resolution mechanism that has emerged in recent years in response to growing dissatisfaction with traditional judicial models of resolving disputes.[103] Unlike arbitration, which involves a third party (albeit not a judge) acting as decision maker, a mediator functions merely as part of the negotiation process. The mediator facilitates negotiation and sometimes permits the parties to reach a negotiated settlement to their dispute when they themselves are unable to do so without assistance. The mediator sometimes conducts joint sessions with both parties but often speaks with them separately and shuttles back and forth between them, ascertaining areas of agreement and disagreement and conveying proposals and counterproposals to narrow the disagreement and ultimately to forge agreement.

Mediation has been used extensively in the resolution of family, matrimonial, labor, and commercial disputes,[104] and this technique may hold much promise in the context of disputes arising between mental patients and the hospital or other facility in which they reside.[105] For example, mediation has proven to be effective in dispute resolution in the public schools.[106] In this context, mediation has been shown to be an effective means of teaching problem-solving and dispute resolution skills and of fostering self-esteem and the student's sense of mastery.[107] Although the relationship between a student and the public school bears some analogy to that between the patient and the hospital, the analogy between schools and mental hospitals is not a perfect one. There are many similarities, however, suggesting the potential of mediation in mental hospital and similar contexts. Like public school students, mental patients can profit from enhanced problem-solving and dispute resolution skills, which are essential to a successful posthospital community adjustment. Moreover, participation in the mediation process may foster independence and increase self-esteem in ways that improve patient competency and community-living skills.[108]

Mediation has not yet been frequently used in mental health dispute resolution contexts, perhaps because of the assumption that mental patients lack the competency to engage in the mediation process.[109] This assumption, however, is questionable in the case of many

---

[103]J. KELTNER, MEDIATION: TOWARD A CIVILIZED SYSTEM OF DISPUTE RESOLUTION 322 (1987); Pruitt et al., *supra* note 101, at 314; Kressel & Pruitt, *Themes in the Mediation of Social Conflict,* 41 J. SOC. ISSUES 179, 198 (1985). *See generally* P. GULLIVER, DISPUTES AND NEGOTIATIONS (1979).

[104]*See, e.g.,* R. WALTON & R. MCKERSIE, A BEHAVIORAL THEORY OF LABOR NEGOTIATIONS (1965); Abram et al., *Arbitral Therapy,* 46 RUTGERS L. REV. 175 (1994); Brett & Goldberg, *Mediator-Advisors: A New Third-Party Role, in* NEGOTIATING IN ORGANIZATIONS 284 (M. Bazerman & R. Lewichi eds., 1983); Hiltrop, *Factors Associated With Successful Labor Mediation, in* MEDIATION RESEARCH 241–62 (K. Kressel & D. Pruitt eds., 1989); Jacobson, *A Component Analysis of Behavioral Marital Therapy: The Relative Effectiveness of Behavior Exchange and Communication/Problem-Solving Training,* 52 J. CONSULTING & CLINICAL PSYCHOL. 295 (1984); Jacobson & Follette, *Clinical Significance of Improvement Resulting From Two Behavioral Marital Therapy Components,* 16 BEHAV. THERAPY 249 (1985); Pruitt et al., *supra* note 101, at 314; Welton et al., *The Role of Caucusing in Community Mediation,* 32 J. CONFLICT RESOL. 181 (1988).

[105]*See* Abisch, *Mediational Lawyering in the Civil Commitment Context: A Therapeutic Jurisprudence Solution to the Counsel Role Dilemma,* 1 PSYCHOL. PUB. POL'Y & L. 120 (1995); Mazade et al., *Mediation as a New Technique for Resolving Disputes in the Mental Health System,* 21 ADMIN. & POL'Y MENTAL HEALTH 431 (1994).

[106]*See* Maxwell, *Mediation in the Schools: Self-Regulation, Self-Esteem, and Self-Discipline,* 7 MEDIATION Q. 149 (1989).

[107]*Id.*

[108]Mazade, *supra* note 105, at 441.

[109]*Id.* at 436–37.

patients.[110] Moreover, even for patients diagnosed with a psychotic disorder, the condition may only be episodic and may not impair decision-making competency in certain areas.[111] Furthermore, former patients report that even when in a psychotic state, they were able to discuss and negotiate about aspects of their lives that were unrelated to the specific thought content of their psychotic episode.[112] In addition, it has been suggested that those in a mental health crisis often are willing and able to discuss with others the precipitating causes of their problems and how to resolve them.[113] Obviously, some patients are too incompetent to participate meaningfully in a mediation process. Although mediation may be inappropriate for them, it may once again become appropriate soon after the crisis has been resolved and should be considered for treatment-refusal problems arising then.

In general, research on the psychology of procedural modes of dispute resolution have suggested that parties prefer adversary to nonadversarial models, feeling more satisfied with the outcomes of such procedural mechanisms and more compliant with the decision reached.[114] In large part, this is explained as a result of the individuals' increased sense of participation or "voice" in adversarial compared with nonadversarial methods of dispute resolution.[115] Tyler has suggested that these benefits of adversarial modes of dispute resolution may apply as well to mediation.[116] He suggests that disputants are more likely to accept and comply with mediated agreements if they perceive that the mediation was fairly conducted and provided them an opportunity to state their concerns to an attentive mediator.[117]

Mediation in the right-to-refuse-treatment context thus may prove a beneficial alternative to other types of dispute resolution. It may produce more satisfaction and compliance on the part of patients and ultimately may enhance therapeutic outcomes.[118] In addition, mediation may enhance the satisfaction of clinicians by providing a mechanism for hearing their views "without the need for protection against professional liability, malpractice, or fears of under-treating."[119] Mediation also may resolve many disputes that otherwise would require more formal and expensive methods of resolution. Mediation thus has much to commend it and should be attempted in treatment-refusal contexts.

---

[110]*See supra* chapter 14, part B (mental illness does not equate with incompetency); *supra* chapter 18, part A (mental patients should be presumed competent and frequently possess similar decision-making capacities as nonmental patients); P. APPELBAUM & T. GUTHEIL, CLINICAL HANDBOOK OF PSYCHIATRY AND THE LAW 218, 220 (1981) ("[T]he mere presence of psychosis, dementia, mental retardation, or some other form of mental illness or disability is insufficient in itself to constitute incompetence."); Grisso & Appelbaum, *supra* note 92, at 173 (study finding most hospitalized mental patients to perform within an adequate range of treatment decision-making capacity); Mazade, *supra* note 105, at 437; McKinnon et al., Rivers *In Practice: Clinicians' Assessment of Patients' Decision-Making Capacity,* 40 HOSP. & COMMUNITY PSYCHIATRY 1159, 1159–60 (1989).

[111]*See supra* chapter 14, notes 80–87 and accompanying text.

[112]Mazade, *supra* note 105, at 437. *See also* Grisso & Appelbaum, *supra* note 92, at 168 (reporting that only 5% of respondents were unable to express a choice among treatment options).

[113]*Id.*

[114]*See supra* note 101 and accompanying text. *See also* Monahan et al., *supra* note 101; Susman, *supra* note 46, at 123–26 (concluding that patient satisfaction with process relates to treatment outcomes).

[115]*See* M. BAYLES, PROCEDURAL JUSTICE: ALLOCATING TO INDIVIDUALS (1990); T. TYLER, WHY PEOPLE OBEY THE LAW (1990); Lind et al., *supra,* note 99, at 953; Poythress, *supra* note 95, at 363; Sheppard, *Justice Is No Simple Matter: Case for Elaborating Our Model of Procedural Fairness,* 49 J. PERSONALITY & SOC. PSYCHOL. 953, 954 (1985); Thibault et al., *supra* note 95, at 1274.

[116]Tyler, *The Psychology of Disputant Concerns in Mediation,* 3 NEGOTIATION J. 367 (1987).

[117]*Id.; see also* Pruitt et al., *supra* note 101, at 316.

[118]Susman, *supra* note 46, at 121.

[119]Mazade, *supra* note 105, at 442.

Of course, mediation is a consensual mode of dispute resolution. Unless the parties wish to engage in it, mediation cannot possibly succeed. In other contexts, however, litigants frequently are required to participate in mediation as a prerequisite for seeking judicial resolution of certain matters.[120] When mediation is resisted or is unsuccessful, use of more formal mechanisms ultimately will be required when the dispute persists. Because it is consensual in nature, mediation will meet due process requirements if the patient participates on a voluntary basis. In effect, although patients may have a procedural due process right to a hearing (before either a judge or an informal administrative tribunal), they may waive this right as long as the decision to waive is competent, knowing, and voluntary.[121]

When the conditions for waiver cannot be satisfied, or when negotiation and mediation prove unsuccessful, right-to-refuse-treatment disputes must be resolved by more formal judicial or administrative processes. When administrative models are used in treatment-refusal decision making, a patient unhappy with a determination that involuntary treatment may be imposed may have additional remedies. Institutions may have an internal review process that permits review by the institution's administrator or by a review board or committee. Following exhaustion of any administrative remedies, the patient also may have an opportunity for limited judicial review of the administrative determination approving involuntary treatment.[122] Such judicial review would be limited to a consideration of whether required procedures were followed and the appropriate standards were applied. It would not review the substance of the decision reached other than perhaps to determine whether the record contained substantial evidence to support it and whether the decision constituted an abuse of discretion.

The discussion in this chapter has focused mainly on procedural due process requirements when psychotropic medication is imposed involuntarily. Because less intrusive treatment approaches may impose lesser intrusions on constitutional liberty and because the costs of error are correspondingly lower, even less formality may be required when verbal or behavioral approaches are sought to be imposed over objection. On the other hand, involuntary administration of treatment approaches that fall higher on the continuum of intrusiveness than medication may require more elaborate procedural hearings. More intrusive therapies impose increasingly greater deprivations on the individuals affected, thus increasing the risk of harm from erroneous deprivations.[123] In view of the grave intrusions on fundamental rights presented by psychosurgery, for example, and the irreversible nature of the procedure, courts probably will insist on a highly formal evidentiary hearing, perhaps by a court, in order to authorize involuntary psychosurgery—assuming an individual in a particular context does not have an absolute right to refuse the treatment.[124] Interventions like psychotropic drugs may invade fundamental constitutional rights, but they often do not

---

[120]See KELTNER, *supra* note 103, at 324; Wall & Rude, *Judicial Mediation of Settlement Negotiations, in* MEDIATION RESEARCH, *supra* note 104, at 190–212.

[121]See *supra* chapter 18 (discussing informed consent doctrine as an aspect of constitutional waiver and analyzing the requirements for providing informed consent).

[122]See Project Release v. Prevost, 722 F.2d 960, 981 n.25 (2d Cir. 1983). *But see* Rivers v. Katz, 495 N.E.2d 337, 344 (N.Y. 1986) (*de novo* review).

[123]See Winick, *Legal Limitations, supra* note 1, at 400–02.

[124]See, *e.g.,* Price v. Sheppard, 239 N.W.2d 905, 913 (Minn. 1976) (requiring elaborate procedures for involuntary administration of ECT and psychosurgery under which that institution's medical director must petition court for a determination of a proposed treatment's necessity, balanced against its intrusiveness, and the court must issue an order balancing treatment's necessity against its intrusiveness before proposed treatment may be administered).

impose permanent effects.[125] As a result, more formal procedures may be required for imposing psychosurgery, electronic stimulation of the brain, or electroconvulsive therapy. The balance struck for most behavioral techniques will likely require even less in the way of formality than will be required for involuntary medication.[126] To the extent that process is required before the imposition of traditional verbal therapy or rehabilitative approaches, such process would be extremely informal. The nature of the hearing required in each case will vary substantially, depending on the extent of intrusion on protected constitutional rights and the court's evaluation of the usefulness and costs of particular procedural safeguards. Moreover, the amount of procedure required may change over time as professional and community attitudes toward the various therapeutic interventions change and as the risks and benefits of each become better understood.

---

[125]*See supra* chapter 5. Some of the medications, however, especially some of the antipsychotics, do produce permanent effects in some patients, such as tardive dyskinesia. *Id.*

[126]*See* Clonce v. Richardson, 379 F. Supp. 338, 352 (W.D. Mo. 1974) (forcible transfer of a prisoner into a behavior modification program requires only minimal due process procedures).

Chapter 20
THE FUTURE OF THE RIGHT TO REFUSE TREATMENT

A. Advance Directive Instruments and the Right To Refuse Treatment: Encouraging Patients and Clinicians to Engage in Advance Planning

The Supreme Court's landmark "right-to-die" case, *Cruzan v. Director, Missouri Department of Health,*[1] presents the right-to-refuse-treatment question in a new light. By taking an interdisciplinary approach to the issues explored here, this book presents a multidimensional look at the right to refuse treatment. Now *Cruzan* introduces a new dimension—time—that expands our ability to see the right in a clearer and more enriched manner. *Cruzan* allows reframing of the right to refuse issue and creates new possibilities for resolving and in many cases avoiding right to refuse mental health treatment problems.

Rather than viewing treatment refusal issues as disputes requiring judicial or administrative resolution, the logic of *Cruzan* allows them to be seen as opportunities for advance planning, which in many cases may avoid dispute resolution. Moreover, the possibility that *Cruzan* creates for advance planning in the area of mental health treatment and hospitalization presents new therapeutic opportunities as well.

Cruzan and its state court counterparts[2] have recognized that a patient enjoys a constitutionally protected liberty interest in making future health care decisions.[3] Although these cases involved the right of a terminally ill patient to discontinue life-prolonging treatment or nourishment, their language and rationale suggest that the right recognized includes a broad liberty interest in making choices to accept or refuse treatment that should extend to both medical and mental health treatment and hospital admission decision mak-

---

[1]497 U.S. 261 (1990); see *supra* chapter 11, notes 244–47 and accompanying text.

[2]*See, e.g.,* New Mark v. Williams, 588 A.2d 1108 (Del. 1991); *In re* Guardianship of Browning, 568 So.2d 4 (Fla. 1990); *In re* Dubreil, 603 So. 2d 538 (Fla. Ct. App. 1992), *rev'd,* 629 So.2d 819 (Fla. 1993); *In re* Doe, 418 S.E.2d 3 (Ga. 1991); *In re* Estate of Greenspan, 558 N.E.2d 1194 (Ill. 1990); *In re* Doe, 583 N.E.2d 1263 (Mass.), *cert. denied sub nom.* Doe v. Gross, 503 U.S. 950 (1992); Mack v. Mack, 618 A.2d 744 (Md. 1993); *In re* Rosebush, 491 N.W.2d 633 (Mich. Ct. App. 1992); McKay v. Bergstedt, 801 P.2d 617 (Nev. 1990); In re Guardianship of L.W., 482 N.W.2d 60 (Wis. 1992); Gleason v. Abrams, 593 A.2d 1232 (N.J. Super. Ct. App. Div. 1991); Grace Plaza of Great Neck, Inc. v. Elbaum, 588 N.Y.S.2d 853 (App. Div.), *aff'd,* 623 N.E.2d 513 (N.Y. 1993).

[3]Cruzan v. Director, Mo. Dep't of Health, 497 U.S. 261, 278 (1990). In *Cruzan,* the Court assumed that individuals possess a "constitutionally protected liberty interest in refusing unwanted medical treatment. . . ." *Id.* Moreover, the *Cruzan* Court cited three earlier decisions involving psychiatric patients to support the right to refuse treatment: Washington v. Harper, 494 U.S. 210 (1990), Vitek v. Jones, 445 U.S. 480 (1980), and Parham v. J.R., 442 U.S. 584 (1979). First, in *Harper,* the Court recognized that mentally ill convicted prisoners possess "a significant liberty interest in avoiding the unwanted administration of antipsychotic drugs under the Due Process Clause of the Fourteenth Amendment." 494 U.S. at 221–22, *quoted in Cruzan,* 497 U.S. at 278. Second, the *Cruzan* Court cited *Vitek* for the proposition that a prisoner's "transfer to a mental hospital coupled with mandatory behavior modification implicated liberty interests." *Cruzan,* 497 U.S. at 278. Finally, quoting *Parham,* the Court noted that "a child, in common with adults, has a substantial liberty interest in not being confined unnecessarily for medical treatment." *Id.* at 278–79.

ing.[4] Moreover, these cases have recognized that not only do competent patients have the constitutional right to make future health care decisions, but incompetent patients do as well; however, the right of incompetent persons was traditionally exercised by a surrogate. The thrust of recent legal developments is that such surrogate decision making should reflect the patient's values, rather than some objective view of the best interests of the patient.[5] Under *Cruzan,* patients are given an opportunity to express their desires about future treatment.[6] Depending on the clarity of their expression, these preferences will either bind the surrogate or provide strong guidance for the exercise of surrogate decision making.

Under these developments, patients are empowered to make decisions in advance concerning future health care needs arising at a time when they may be incapacitated. They may do so pursuant to living wills or other advance oral or written directive instruments. As long as there is clear and convincing evidence concerning the patient's desires,[7] *Cruzan* implies that the patient may choose in advance to discontinue life-prolonging treatment or nourishment that may be attempted in the future.[8] A further implication of *Cruzan* is that the state's interest in prolonging life, however important it may be, will not outweigh a patient's expressed desire to discontinue life support treatment or nourishment. As between the state and the patient, the Constitution leaves this important matter largely to individual choice.

These principles should apply equally to the acceptance or refusal of treatment that is not life prolonging. If patients possess a due process right to choose whether to accept or reject medical treatment, then a competent expression of the patient's desires should be respected even if, at a future time of incapacity, the state asserts a *parens patriae* interest in promoting and protecting the patient's best interests.[9] The state interest in prolonging life, which *Cruzan* suggested would be subordinate to the individual's interest in choosing whether to discontinue life-sustaining treatment or nourishment, would seem as strong or stronger than the state's *parens patriae* interest in administering treatment to a patient whose life is not at risk. Given the finality of death, the state interest in preserving life would be

---

[4]*See* J. AHRONHEIM ET AL., ETHICS IN CLINICAL PRACTICE 16–19 (1994); Perling, Comment, *Health Care Advance Directives: Implications for Florida Mental Health Patients,* 48 U. MIAMI L. REV. 193, 206 (1993); Winick, *Advance Directive Instruments for Those With Mental Illness,* 51 U. MIAMI L. REV. 1 (1996).

[5]AHRONHEIM ET AL. *supra* note 4, at 17–18; A. BUCHANAN & D. BROCK, DECIDING FOR OTHERS: THE ETHICS OF SURROGATE DECISIONMAKING 350–57 (1989) (reviewing the moral and ethical arguments supporting the use of advance directives and surrogate decision making). *See also* Barnes, *Florida Guardianship and the Elderly: The Paradoxical Right to Unwanted Assistance,* 40 U. FLA. L. REV. 949, 988 (1988); Emanuel & Emanuel, *Proxy Decision Making for Incompetent Patients,* 267 JAMA 2067, 2071 (1992); Gutheil & Appelbaum, *The Substituted Judgment Approach: Its Difficulties and Paradoxes in Mental Health Settings,* 13 L. MED. & HEALTH CARE 61, 64 (1985); Wettstein & Roth, *The Psychiatrist as Legal Guardian,* 145 AM. J. PSYCHIATRY 600, 604 (1988).

[6]In *Cruzan,* the Court upheld the constitutionality of Missouri's requirement that, to be effective, there must be clear and convincing evidence that the patient desires to refuse life–sustaining treatment or nourishment if she should be in a vegetative state. 497 U.S. at 288. The Court, however, specifically declined to determine whether a state might be required to defer to the decision of a surrogate appointed by the patient. 497 U.S. at 287 n.12. Nancy Cruzan had not left any written instructions regarding her care in the event of incompetency. As a result, the case presented no occasion for the Court to consider the question. Although the law is not yet developed in this area, the state may enjoy a wider latitude in regulating surrogate decision making pursuant to health care proxies or powers of attorney than treatment decision making made by the individual in an advance directive instrument.

[7]A. MEISEL, THE RIGHT TO DIE 316–21 (1989); B. WEINER & R. WETTSTEIN, LEGAL ISSUES IN MENTAL HEALTH CARE 299 (1993); Parry, *The Court's Role in Decisionmaking Involving Incompetent Refusals of Life–Sustaining Care and Psychiatric Medications,* 14 MENTAL & PHYSICAL DISABILITY L. REP. 468, 474 (1990); Perling, *supra* note 4, at 205, 219; Sales, *The Health Care Proxy for Mental Illness: Can It Work and Should We Want It To?,* 21 BULL. AM. ACAD. PSYCHIATRY & L. 161 (1993).

[8]A. BERGER, DYING AND DEATH IN LAW AND MEDICINE 113–16 (1993); Winick, *supra* note 4.

[9]*See supra* chapter 15, part C (discussing the states' *parens patriae* power).

totally frustrated by honoring a patient's decision to discontinue life-sustaining treatment. By contrast, honoring a patient's decision to reject treatment that is not itself necessary to keep the patient alive still leaves open other ways in which the state may attempt to achieve its *parens patriae* interest in promoting individual health, including future attempts by the state to persuade or induce the patient to accept treatment thought to be beneficial. As a constitutional matter, competent patients are more appropriate decision makers concerning their own health than is the state.[10] The state's *parens patriae* interests might allow the state to insist on treatment for an incompetent patient who has not expressed a previous competent desire concerning treatment, based on a surrogate decision maker's perception of the patient's best interests. However, when a patient, when competent, has expressed a preference, the state's *parens patriae* interests would generally seem insufficient to outweigh the patient's prior judgment about his or her own best interests.[11]

This analysis of *Cruzan* and its implications suggests that mental patients during a period of competency should be able to make advance determinations concerning hospitalization and treatment issues. The due process liberty interest recognized in *Cruzan* would apply to all *persons,* the term used in the Due Process Clauses of both the Fifth and Fourteenth Amendments to describe the beneficiaries of their protection against governmental deprivation.[12] Both those suffering from mental illness and those suffering from life-threatening medical conditions may exercise this liberty interest as long as they are competent at the time of their expression of choice, even though both may be incompetent at the time when that choice is given effect.

Patients with mental illness who have been restored to competency following a period of hospitalization or treatment or who never have been incompetent should be encouraged to reflect on their experiences and determine in advance how they would like to be treated during any future period of incompetency. To meet the clear and convincing evidence standard approved in *Cruzan,* patients should be encouraged to express their desires in writing and to designate an appropriate health care surrogate or proxy to assist in effectuating their desires. In the absence of such an expressed desire, a state's *parens patriae* civil commitment statute or involuntary treatment authority would presumably prevail,[13] allowing the state to determine what the patient would have wished if competent.

The advance health care directive bears a strong analogy to the will.[14] Just as individuals have the ability to dispose of their property upon death by expressing their intentions in a will, patients may control future health treatment through the use of advance directive instruments. When competent individuals execute a will, their estate will be disposed of in accordance with the will's directions, even if they subsequently become incompetent to

---

[10]*See* T. BEAUCHAMP & J. CHILDRESS, PRINCIPLES OF BIOMEDICAL ETHICS 67–74 (3d ed. 1989); Winick, *On Autonomy: Legal and Psychological Perspectives,* 37 VILL. L. REV. 1705, 1755–71 (1992).

[11]*See* Winick, *Competency to Consent to Treatment: The Distinction Between Assent and Objection,* 28 HOUS. L. REV. 15, 19 (1991) [hereinafter *Competency for Treatment*] (noting that, although mental illness may impair competency, mentally ill persons have a significant capacity for rational thought); Winick, *Reforming Incompetency to Stand Trial and Plead Guilty: A Restated Proposal and a Response to Professor Bonnie,* 85 J. CRIM. L. & CRIMINOLOGY 571, 585 (1995). *See also* A. STONE, MENTAL HEALTH AND LAW: A SYSTEM IN TRANSITION 102 (DHEW Pub. No. (ADM) 76–176, 1975); Perling, *supra* note 4, at 195; Szasz, *The Psychiatric Will: A New Mechanism for Protecting Persons Against "Psychosis" and Psychiatry,* 37 AM. PSYCHOLOGIST 762, 766 (1982).

[12]U.S. CONST. amends. V, XIV. For Supreme Court recognition that persons with mental illness have a constitutionally protected liberty interest in refusing unwanted mental health treatment, see Riggins v. Nevada, 504 U.S. 127, 133 (1992); Washington v. Harper, 494 U.S. 210, 221–22 (1990).

[13]Clayton, *From* Rogers *to* Rivers: *The Rights of the Mentally Ill to Refuse Medication,* 13 AM. J. L. & MED. 7, 29 (1987).

[14]MEISEL, *supra* note 7, at 312–13.

execute or amend a will. On the other hand, when individuals do not execute a will, the state's law on intestate succession applies. In the mental health context, by analogy, the state's *parens patriae* hospitalization or treatment law and practice will prevail in the absence of an advance directive concerning hospitalization or treatment. When patients express their desires in such an instrument, however, it generally will be effective in determining future hospitalization or treatment during a future period of incompetency.

When the state's interest in hospitalization or treatment is grounded in its police power[15] rather than its *parens patriae* power, an advance directive would not control. Just as a will provision that violated public policy would be unenforceable,[16] a mental health advance directive seeking to refuse hospitalization or treatment that would be required to prevent harm to others would be unenforceable. The subordination of the patient's liberty interest in engaging in future mental health care decision making to the state's police power is no different from when the state's interest in public health or safety is permitted to override the desire of a patient suffering from infectious tuberculosis to refuse treatment or quarantine or the desire of an individual to refuse compulsory vaccination designed to prevent the spread of epidemic.[17] The autonomy justification for respecting and enforcing advance mental health directives is insufficient to outweigh the state's interest in protecting the safety of those who would be subjected to a serious risk of harm from the patient's actions. Just as the state would be able to hospitalize or treat competent mental patients presenting a serious risk of danger to others over their present objection,[18] the state would be able to insist on hospitalization or treatment for this purpose over the objection of patients expressed in the past.

Thus, in the future, the right-to-refuse-treatment question may in part be determined by the use of advance directive instruments. Although statutory commitment or involuntary treatment laws applied to accomplish police power interests will prevail over patient choices made in such instruments, these laws should prevail in the *parens patriae* context only in the absence of such instruments. In addition to avoiding the need for formal resolution of treatment disputes, this development may have significant therapeutic value. It will cause patients to reflect on their desires in light of the hospitalization or treatment they have experienced and to take responsibility for future decision making. When patients have strong feelings about these issues, they generally should be respected. Patients who do not have such feelings can either leave their affairs in the event of future incapacity to surrogate decision making under the state's *parens patriae* power or designate a surrogate or proxy to make such decisions for them—one who knows them and is better able than the state to reflect their interests and preferences.

The very process of thinking about future decision making should have a therapeutic effect for a number of reasons. Particularly for mental patients, who in the past have too frequently been infantilized by the treatment they have received in mental hospitals, the exercise of decision making and the taking of responsibility for decisions vitally affecting themselves would be empowering and would have predictable beneficial effects.[19] More-

---

[15]*See, e.g.*, Washington v. Harper, 394 U.S. 210 (1990) (upholding state's authority to forcibly administer antipsychotic drugs to a prisoner to protect safety of other prisoners and prison staff); *see supra* chapter 15, part C (discussing state police power interests in involuntary treatment).

[16]McGovern et al., Wills, Trusts and Estates 69–77 (1988).

[17]*See* Jacobson v. Massachusetts, 197 U.S. 11 (1905) (state's police power interest in preventing epidemic held to outweigh competent individual's asserted right to refuse compulsory vaccination for smallpox).

[18]*See* Washington v. Harper, 494 U.S. 210 (1990) (state's police power interests in protecting other prisoners and staff held to outweigh competent prisoner's attempt to refuse antipsychotic medication).

[19]Winick, *supra* note 10, at 1755–71.

over, the very process of making decisions about the future might well have an impact on the patient's future behavior and condition (*i.e.,* it may have the effect of diminishing the chances of future incompetency).

The process of preparing an advance directive instrument also can provide an important therapeutic opportunity that creative clinicians can exploit. Preparing the instrument will focus patients' attention on future goals and how to attain them. The goal-setting effect—the finding that the setting of concrete goals itself helps to bring about their achievement—can be harnessed through the process of planning the instrument.[20] Because patients' goals will be specified in writing and executed formally, the advance directive instrument can be a particularly effective means of achieving the benefits of goal setting. Therapists should become involved with their patients in the process of preparing the instrument because the process itself will provide an opportunity to engage patients and to explore and eliminate potential resistance in a context that, precisely because it involves the future, may be less threatening to them than the process of treatment decision making concerning a present problem.

An advance directive can function as an important safety valve for the right-to-refuse-treatment issue. Patients feeling strongly about determining the course of their treatment, or having particularly negative or positive feelings about a specific treatment or intervention, will have the option of making advance decisions that will effectuate their wishes. Doing so in a way that the law will honor will provide a measure of predictability that may reduce stress and anxiety that might otherwise be devastating. Being able to plan in advance about important matters with the assurance that those plans will be respected and effectuated brings a measure of ease that can permit the patient to pursue happiness and attempt to secure the blessings of liberty in a way that the anxiety and fear produced by uncertainty in such matters might well prevent. Patients may thereby be liberated to maximize their potential for a healthy adjustment to life. Dealing with such an important matter in an effective way also predictably will promote patients' self-esteem and self-efficacy, which may increase their decision-making capacity generally and their ability to act effectively.

Acting and being treated as self-determining individuals with authority over their own fate, instead of as powerless and incompetent victims of forces beyond their understanding and control, can be therapeutically advantageous.[21] Restoration of mental patients to as high a degree of community functioning as is possible in the circumstances should be a significant goal of any sensible system of mental hospitalization and treatment, and this goal will be furthered by allowing patients to make decisions. By contrast, being treated as an incompetent subject of paternalism can foster feelings of incompetency, reinforcing expectancies that might well keep such patients in the psychiatric sick role.[22]

---

[20]Campbell, *The Effects of Goal–Contingent Payment on the Performance of a Complex Task,* 37 PERSONNEL PSYCHOL. 23, 23 (1984); Locke et al., *Goal Setting and Task Performance* 1969–80, 90 PSYCHOL. BULL. 125, 125–31 (1981); Terburg & Miller, *Motivation, Behavior, and Performance: A Closer Examination of Goal Setting and Monetary Incentives,* 63 J. APPLIED PSYCHOL. 29, 30–31 (1978); *supra* chapter 17, notes 13–17 and accompanying text.

[21]Winick, *The Right to Refuse Mental Health Treatment: A Therapeutic Jurisprudence Analysis,* 17 INT'L J. L. & PSYCHIATRY 99, 106–08 (1994); Note, *Developments in the Law—Medical Technology and the Law,* 103 HARV. L. REV. 1519, 1643 (1990); *see supra* chapter 17.

[22]*See* J. STRAUSS & W. CARPENTER, SCHIZOPHRENIA 128–29 (1981); Bersoff, *Autonomy for Vulnerable Populations: The Supreme Court's Reckless Disregard for Self-Determination and Social Science,* 37 VILL. L. REV. 1569, 1571 (1992); Fennell, *Inscribing Paternalism in the Law: Consent to Treatment and Mental Disorder,* 17 J. L. & SOC'Y 29, 29 (1990); Winick, *The Side Effects of Incompetency Labeling and the Implications for Mental Health Law,* 1 PSYCHOL. PUB. POL'Y & L. 6, 8, 12–13 (1995). *See also* J. KATZ, THE SILENT WORLD OF DOCTOR AND PATIENT 2 (1984).

Moreover, recognizing that patients have the power to direct the future course of their treatment will predictably make psychiatrists and other clinicians negotiate with them about treatment and increase the likelihood that they will be treated with dignity and respect, rather than as mere objects of paternalism.[23] Patients who can choose in advance a course of treatment are likely to feel better about it, to be more willing to comply with the treatment regimen, and to be less resistant to it—all of which can help to maximize the potential for therapeutic success.[24] Even for those whose feelings about future treatment are not so strong as to lead them to execute an advance directive, the provision of the opportunity to do so, even though forgone, may well lead to greater feelings of acceptance for any therapeutic intervention subsequently imposed by the state pursuant to its *parens patriae* power. Patients who choose not to deal with the matter through an advance directive when that option is made known to them may experience less resentment and psychological reactance to a course of treatment later imposed through surrogate decision making.[25] Psychological reactance may be high when individuals feel that their decision-making authority has unfairly been intruded upon.[26] Being reminded that they had the ability to make other arrangements but neglected to do so may diffuse such negative reactions.

One potential problem with the use of advance directives in the mental health context arises when patients who have given advance directives later seek to change their minds.[27] Obviously, if the change of mind occurs during a period of competency, the advance directive instrument may be revoked or revised. This would be similar to the way individuals who change their minds about dispositions made in a will may act. As long as they are still competent, they may revoke or amend their wills as often as they like.

If patients' change of mind occurs during a period of questionable competency or of incompetency, how should the law respond? Under general principles, incompetent individuals would be unable to revoke or revise the previously executed advance directive instrument. But should they be bound to a prior decision that may no longer be in their best interests? If their new circumstances were envisioned at the time the instrument was executed, the instrument provides the best evidence of how they would wish to be treated should the anticipated circumstances materialize. In the absence of a police power interest sufficient to trump the individuals' prior expression of choice,[28] that expression—competent when made—should be respected, even if it may not serve their best interests. Deference for individual autonomy should mandate respect for competent decisions even if thought to be unwise or imprudent.[29]

If, on the other hand, the individual did not anticipate the changed circumstances—the development of a new form of treatment perhaps, or of a means of eliminating or successfully treating the adverse side effects of an existing treatment objected to as a result of

---

[23]*See* Winick, *supra* note 21, at 111–12; *supra* chapter 17.

[24]*See* Winick, *supra* note 21, at 115–16; *supra* chapter 17; *see also* KATZ, *supra* note 22, at 102–03; D. MEICHENBAUM & D. TURK, FACILITATING TREATMENT ADHERENCE: A PRACTITIONER'S GUIDE-BOOK 63, 71–76, 84–85 (1987).

[25]S. BREHM & J. BREHM, PSYCHOLOGICAL REACTANCE: A THEORY OF FREEDOM AND CONTROL 301 (1981).

[26]Monahan et al., *Coercion to Inpatient Treatment: Initial Results and Implications for Assertive Treatment in the Community, in* COERCION AND AGGRESSIVE COMMUNITY TREATMENT: A NEW FRONTIER IN MENTAL HEALTH LAW 13, 24, 27 (D. Dennis & J. Monahan eds., 1996).

[27]*See, e.g.,* J. ELSTER, ULYSSES AND THE SIRENS 38 (1979); Reinert, *A Living Will for a Commitment Hearing,* 31 HOSP. & COMMUNITY PSYCHIATRY 857 (1980). *See generally* Rosenson & Kasten, *Another View of Autonomy: Arranging for Consent in Advance,* 17 SCHIZOPHRENIA BULL. 1 (1991).

[28]*See* text accompanying *supra* notes 15–18.

[29]*See* Winick, *Competency for Treatment, supra* note 11, at 21 & n.17.

the individual's concerns about these effects—there may be good reason not to respect individuals' previously expressed direction. Indeed, if we were satisfied that individuals would have modified the original direction in a particular way had they anticipated the changed circumstance, then that modification should be made. Careful drafting of advance directive instruments that anticipate possible changes in circumstances and express the individuals' wishes in the event they occur would deal with many of these problems. Lawyers and health care professionals assisting patients in the preparation of these instruments should thus attempt to help them anticipate various changes that might occur and decide how to deal with them.

When changed circumstances were not or could not have been anticipated, how should the law respond? The law of wills again provides a useful analogy. Under the doctrine of *cy-pres,* a court may modify a provision in an individual's will that seems inconsistent with the testator's intentions when originally expressed in light of unanticipated circumstances.[30] Thus, a will provision making a bequest to a now defunct organization or charity (*e.g.,* the League of Nations) may be modified by the probate court to have the bequest go to another organization fulfilling a similar purpose (*e.g.,* the United Nations). Applying a form of the *cy-pres* doctrine, courts can modify advance directive health care instruments in a similar way.[31]

In many cases, individuals seeking to change their minds concerning a previously executed advance directive will not clearly be either competent or incompetent. How should the law deal with such cases of questionable competence? How should the law define competency in this context, and how should it be determined? The distinction between patient assent and objection developed in chapter 18 may prove useful in this context as well.[32]

When patients of questionable competency attempt to assert a change of mind in favor of voluntary hospitalization or voluntary treatment that is recommended by their therapists, the law should use a low threshold standard of competency and find their assent to such an intervention to be effective to revoke any prior advance directive against such interventions, unless that assent seems to be the product of hallucinations, delusions, or outright irrationality. Patients should be considered competent as long as they understand at a basic level that they have a problem and are able clearly and voluntarily to express a choice in favor of a recommended treatment intervention, such as mental hospitalization or customary mental health treatment that concerned professionals believe to be in their best interests.[33] Although impaired by mental illness, these patients are able to express a preference that does not, on its face, seem ''crazy'' or the product of a pathological delusion. Patients should be deemed competent as long as they understand that the facility to which admission is sought is a psychiatric hospital, that the treatment sought is for mental illness, that care and treatment

---

[30]*See, e.g.,* Granberry v. Islay Invs., 889 P.2d 970 (Cal. 1995); Yale Univ. v. Blumenthal, 621 A.2d 1304 (Conn. 1993); *In re* Estate of Crawshaw, 819 P.2d 613 (Kan. 1991); Franklin Found. v. Attorney General, 623 N.E.2d 1109 (Mass. 1993); *In re* Estes Estate, 523 N.W.2d 863 (Mich. Ct. App. 1994); *In re* Gonzalez, 621 A.2d 94 (N.J. Super. Ct. Ch. Div. 1992); *In re* Coffey, 590 N.Y.S. 2d 357 (App. Div. 1992); *In re* Estate of Wilson, 451 N.Y.S. 2d 891 (App. Div. 1982). *See also* MCGOVERN ET AL., *supra* note 16, at 333–38, 534–35, 550.

[31]No case thus far appears to apply the *cy-pres* doctrine in the advance health care directive context, perhaps because the use of such directives is still in its early stages.

[32]*See* Winick, *Competency to Consent to Voluntary Hospitalization: A Therapeutic Jurisprudence Analysis of* Zinermon v. Burch, 14 INT'L J. L. & PSYCHIATRY 169 (1991); Winick, *Competency for Treatment, supra* note 11; see supra chapter 18.

[33]*See* Winick, *Competency for Treatment, supra* note 11, at 19; Winick, *supra* note 32, at 172; *supra* chapter 18, part A.

will be provided, and that release or discontinuation of treatment can occur if they change their minds. Moreover, patients possessing this low threshold of competency who seek to assent to a recommended intervention previously rejected in an advance directive instrument should be presumed competent, and a formal inquiry into competency should be unnecessary unless the assent seems to be a product of outright irrationality, delusions, or severe depression.[34]

For the reasons developed in chapter 18, this approach would serve both autonomy interests and therapeutic values. Indeed, under psychological theory, permitting patients to choose a therapeutic intervention recommended by their therapists increases the potential efficacy of such an intervention.[35] Moreover, recommendations of clinicians who owe patients a fiduciary duty, when agreed to by patients, provide reasonable assurance that the chosen treatment will promote patients' health.

Autonomy values and therapeutic interests may not align as closely when patients' changes of mind constitute attempts to object to hospitalization or treatment to which they had assented in a prior advance directive. From the perspective of autonomy values, two conflicting expressions of autonomy exist—the previous (presumably competent) one and the subsequent one (of perhaps more dubious competency). Although ordinarily a more recent expression of autonomy would be a more accurate reflection of patients' current preferences, there may be reason to question whether patients' present objections are a product of mental illness rather than of genuine autonomy. When the objection is to a therapeutic intervention—hospitalization or conventional treatment—recommended by the patients' therapists, there also may be reason to at least question whether the refusal of such treatment might be antitherapeutic and inconsistent with their welfare.

For these reasons, scrutiny of such patients' competency should be greater than that for patients seeking to change their minds and assenting to hospitalization or treatment, and a higher standard of competency should be used. If pursuant to this standard, patients are found to be competent, then their presently expressed objection should take precedence over the previously expressed assent. If patients' present objections are found to be incompetent, then the previously expressed assent should take precedence, unless it appears that an unanticipated change in circumstances would have led patients to choose otherwise had they anticipated it.[36]

Although many details concerning the use, modification, and revocability of advance health care directives remain to be worked out, these instruments present an exciting new mechanism for dealing with at least some right-to-refuse-treatment issues, and one that will surely expand in importance in the future. *Cruzan*'s endorsement of the living will has led to

---

[34]This narrow definition was recently recommended by the American Psychiatric Association Task Force on Consent to Voluntary Hospitalization as a test for competency to consent to voluntary hospital admission. CONSENT TO VOLUNTARY HOSPITALIZATION (Am. Psychiatric Ass'n Task Force Report No. 34, 1993); *see* Winick, *How to Handle Voluntary Hospitalization After* Zinermon v. Burch, 21 ADMIN. & POL'Y MENTAL HEALTH 395, 402–03 (1994).

[35]*See* Winick, *supra* note 21; *supra* chapter 17.

[36]*See supra* notes 19–24 and accompanying text.

statutory acceptance of advance health care instruments generally.[37] Although their extension to the context of mental health treatment has not yet been fully accepted and raises problems,[38] the use of such instruments by mental patients would be both constitutionally protected and therapeutically advantageous in many areas.[39]

B. Professional Ethics and the Right To Refuse Mental Health Treatment

This book has presented a framework of legal limitations on involuntary mental health and correctional treatment and has outlined the direction in which the law appears to be moving. Although the law obviously plays an important role in limiting the activities of those involved with mental health treatment and offender rehabilitation, it acts against a background of ethical and professional controls that frequently operate much more directly and effectively on the actors in the treatment and rehabilitation process.[40] Legal limitations in this area will derive from legislative, regulatory, and judicial sources that necessarily lack the insight and experience of those in the field. As a result, the law is likely to develop generalized approaches and to respond most sharply to exposed abuses in a manner that will make clinicians and correctional rehabilitators feel misunderstood and unduly restricted. Professional and ethical controls are always to be preferred. This preference, if not the threat of the legal controls that this book describes, should prompt the various disciplines involved in mental health treatment and correctional rehabilitation to implement reforms before they are imposed from without.

Although much work must be done by the relevant professional disciplines, a foundation already exists. Codes of professional ethics do not clearly recognize a right of

---

[37]*See, e.g.,* 42 U.S.C.A. §§ 1395cc(f) & 1396a(w) (West 1992 & Supp. 1993). This federal statute, called the Patient Self–Determination Act (the "PSDA") (an amendment to the Social Security Act establishing the Medicare and Medicaid programs), applies to entities participating in the Medicare and Medicaid programs. *Id.* Any service provider participating in Medicare or Medicaid are considered entities. *Id.* § 1396a(w)(1). The PSDA defines advance directives to be a written instrument, recognized under state law, relating to an incapacitated individual's health care. *Id.* § 1395cc(f)(3). The PSDA seeks to facilitate and promote the use of advance directive instruments by requiring covered providers to inform patients with regard to state law with respect to such instruments and to educate the public about their use. For state statutes authorizing use of such advance directive instruments, *see e.g.,* ALA. CODE §§ 22-8A-1-22-8A-10 (1993); ARIZ. REV. STAT. ANN. §§ 36-3201-36-3210 (1992); CAL. HEALTH & SAFETY CODE §§ 7185-7195 (West. 1995); FLA. STAT. §§ 765.01–15 (1995); GA. CODE ANN. §§ 31-32-1-31-32-12 (1993); ILL. REV. STAT. ch. 110-5, 701-710 (1993); MINN. STAT. §§ 145B.01-145B.17 (1993); MO. REV. STAT. §§ 459.010-459.055 (1995). *See also* MEISEL, *supra* note 7, at 314–19; Perling, *supra* note 4, at 209.

[38]For example, one significant concern is an individual's ability to anticipate future circumstances and account for all contingencies. *See* Appelbaum, *Advance Directives for Psychiatric Treatment,* 42 HOSP. & COMMUNITY PSYCHIATRY 983, 983 (1991). As the use of these instruments becomes more widespread, lawyers and health care professionals experienced with their use can help guide individuals through the process of planning and drafting the instrument. Advance directive instrument forms with optional provisions and riders will be developed that will prove useful, as will checklists to guide individuals preparing them. These forms, of course, must be tailored to the particular circumstances of the individual. Anticipating future circumstances and changes in treatment modalities may be difficult, but the process itself can have therapeutic value.

[39]Because these instruments may, for the reasons discussed here, have therapeutic value, the negative attitude toward them that some psychiatrists have, *see, e.g.,* Chodoff & Peele, *The Psychiatric Will of Dr. Szasz,* 13 HASTINGS CTR. REP. 187 (1983); Reinert, *supra* note 27, at 858, may be inappropriate. Viewed properly, these instruments can provide an important therapeutic opportunity, and their use therefore should be welcomed by therapists.

[40]*See* Jaffe, *Law as a System of Control, in* EXPERIMENTATION WITH HUMAN SUBJECTS 203, 205 (P. Freund ed., 1969); Winick, *Legal Limitations on Correctional Therapy and Research,* 65 MINN. L. REV. 331, 420 (1981). *See generally* A. THOMPSON, GUIDE TO ETHICAL PRACTICE IN PSYCHOTHERAPY (1990).

mental patients to refuse treatment,[41] although some professional organizations consider a patient's informed consent an ethical prerequisite to treatment.[42] A body of scholarship concerning the ethical limitations on forced treatment has begun to emerge[43] and consideration has been given to specific ethical problems, such as those presented by the role of the therapist as a "double agent" with loyalties both to patient and governmental employer.[44] Rigorous application of clear standards in this area, however, has yet to emerge.

When the therapeutic implications of recognizing a right to refuse treatment are recognized,[45] the arguments in favor of formal protection for such a right in codes of professional ethics become compelling. Principles of beneficence and nonmaleficence are central to the ethical standards regulating health and mental health professionals.[46] The maxim *primum non nocere*—above all, do no harm—is at the core of the Hippocratic tradition in medicine and is the foundation of medical ethics.[47] These principles point strongly in the direction of recognizing and protecting a right of patients to refuse treatment. As chapter 17 demonstrates, giving patients choice in general facilitates positive treatment outcomes. Moreover, those denied choice concerning treatment do not do as well. Indeed, treatment may be frustrated as a result of a psychological reactance to coercion.[48] Some patients coerced to undergo treatment may even develop a form of institutional dependence that undermines their ability to function independently.[49] Some patients may develop learned helplessness and become amotivational, dysfunctional, and depressed.[50]

Clinicians' fiduciary duty to their patients requires that they place their patients' interests above the interests of their institutional employer in convenience, economy, and ease of administration. At least to the extent that patients are competent to engage in treatment decision making, they should therefore be given choice and sufficient information to make a reasonable choice. Patients should be treated with dignity and respect—as

---

[41]Annas et al., *The Right of Privacy Protects the Doctor–Patient Relationship,* 263 JAMA 858, 861 (1994); Quinn, *The Best Interests of Incompetent Patients: The Capacity for Interpersonal Relationships as a Standard for Decisionmaking,* 76 CAL. L. REV. 897, 906 (1988).

[42]*E.g.,* AM. MEDICAL ASS'N, COUNCIL ON ETHICAL & JUDICIAL AFFAIRS, CODE OF MEDICAL ETHICS, ANNOTATED CURRENT OPINIONS 69 (1992); Ass'n for Advancement of Behavior Therapy, *Ethical Issues for Human Services,* 8 BEHAV. THERAPY 763 (1977). *See* A. THOMPSON, *supra* note 40, at 20–29; Kapp, *Placebo Therapy and the Law: Prescribe With Care,* 8 AM. J. L. & MED. 371, 391 (1983). *See also* Bandura, *The Ethical and Social Purposes of Behavior Modification, in* ANNUAL REVIEW OF BEHAVIOR THERAPY: THEORY AND PRACTICE 16 (C. Franks & G. Wilson eds., 1975); Davison & Stuart, *Behavior Therapy and Civil Liberties,* 30 AM. PSYCHOLOGIST 755 (1975).

[43]*See, e.g.,* AHRONHEIM ET AL., *supra* note 4, at 130–37; T. PERLIN, CLINICAL MEDICAL ETHICS: CASES IN PRACTICE 195–226 (1992); LEGAL & ETHICAL ISSUES, IV TASK PANEL REPORTS SUBMITTED TO THE PRESIDENT'S COMM'N ON MENTAL HEALTH 1359 (1978); Halleck, *Legal and Ethical Aspects of Behavior Control,* 131 AM. J. PSYCHIATRY 381 (1974); Robinson, *Harm, Offense and Nuisance: Some First Steps in the Establishment of an Ethics of Treatment,* 29 AM. PSYCHOLOGIST 233 (1974).

[44]*See, e.g.,* LEGAL & ETHICAL ISSUES, IV TASK PANEL REPORTS SUBMITTED TO THE PRESIDENT'S COMM'N ON MENTAL HEALTH 1474–76 (1978); WHO IS THE CLIENT? THE ETHICS OF PSYCHOLOGICAL INTERVENTION IN THE CRIMINAL JUSTICE SYSTEM (J. Monahan ed., 1980); American Psychological Ass'n, *Board of Social & Ethical Responsibility for Psychology: Report of the Task Panel on the Role of Psychology in the Criminal Justice System,* 33 AM. PSYCHOL. 1099 (1978); *In the Service of the State: The Psychiatrist as Double Agent,* 8 HASTINGS CTR. REP., Apr. 1978; Shestack, *Psychiatry and the Dilemmas of Dual Loyalty,* 60 A.B.A. J. 1521 (1974).

[45]*See supra* chapter 17.

[46]*See, e.g.,* BEAUCHAMP & CHILDRESS, *supra* note 10, at 106; T. BEAUCHAMP & L. WALTERS, CONTEMPORARY ISSUES IN BIOETHICS 28 (2d ed. 1982); R. FADEN & T. BEAUCHAMP, A HISTORY AND THEORY OF INFORMED CONSENT 10 (1986).

[47]FADEN & BEAUCHAMP, *supra* note 46, at 10; THOMPSON, *supra* note 40, at 121.

[48]*See* BREHM & BREHM, *supra* note 25, at 110–15; *supra* chapter 17, notes 7–10 and accompanying text.

[49]*See supra* chapter 17, notes 47–48 and accompanying text.

[50]*See id.*

persons, not as objects, as ends in themselves, not as means to the ends of others.[51] Clinicians should not allow themselves to be used as instruments of punishment, and they should not use treatment for punitive purposes.[52] Clinicians are the patients' agents and should strive to accomplish patients' self-defined interests and goals. If the clinician–patient relationship is based on this foundation, patient trust and confidence in the therapist will be fostered,[53] enhancing expectancies of positive results which in turn will help to produce positive therapeutic outcomes.[54] Moreover, it will create positive attitudes by patients toward treatment and increase treatment compliance.[55] Indeed, such a reshaping of the clinician–patient relationship may be essential to enabling a true therapeutic alliance to occur.[56]

Considerations of beneficence and nonmaleficence support recognition in professional ethics of a right to refuse treatment most strongly in the context of those treatments on the lower end of the continuum of intrusiveness. Psychotherapy and the behavioral approaches will be largely ineffective unless the patient cooperates and genuinely desires to change.[57] Hence, considerations of therapeutic efficacy and of respect for patient dignity and autonomy combine to favor a voluntary rather than a coercive approach to these techniques. If, as chapter 17 strongly suggests, patients do better when they are permitted to exercise choice about treatment than when treatment is applied coercively, professional ethics should support voluntary rather than involuntary treatment. The more intrusive techniques may be less dependent on patient cooperation and motivation, but even these techniques would seem more effective to the extent that the patient voluntarily chooses to undergo them. Although the psychological value of patient choice and the advantages of deferring to individual autonomy are lessened to the extent that the patient lacks competence to make treatment choices, perhaps justifying a degree of involuntary treatment consistent with principles of beneficence and nonmaleficence, as soon as such treatment has succeeded in restoring a degree of patient competence, the long-range goals of treatment would seem to be furthered by recognizing and deferring to patient choice. Because the goal of any sensible system of mental health hospitalization and treatment is to restore the patient to as high a degree of functional capacity as is possible, ethical considerations should dictate that clinicians treat their patients in a way that would facilitate attainment of this goal and not act in ways that would frustrate it. Excessive paternalism breeds dependence and reinforces incompetence. By contrast, treating patients as competent and permitting them to engage in decision making generally will promote independence and build competence. Ethical principles therefore should at least communicate a strong preference for voluntary treatment.

Professional ethics also should recognize the therapeutic appropriateness principle, requiring that any treatment imposed be in the patient's therapeutic interests.[58] This principle, also supported by principles of beneficence and nonmaleficence, is basic to the Hippocratic tradition and is reflected in the codes of professional ethics of the relevant

---

[51]See BEAUCHAMP & CHILDRESS, *supra* note 10, at 74; P. RAMSEY, THE PATIENT AS PERSON: EXPLORATIONS IN MEDICAL ETHICS 48 (1970); THOMPSON, *supra* note 40, at 119.

[52]See Winick, *Competency to be Executed: A Therapeutic Jurisprudence Perspective,* 10 BEHAV. SCI. & L. 317, 318 n.9 (1992) (citing conclusion of American Medical Association and American Medical Association that physician participation in treatment to restore competence for execution would be unethical).

[53]See Winick, *supra* note 21, at 105, 111–15; supra chapter 17, part B.

[54]See Winick, *supra* note 21, at 102–04; *supra* chapter 17, part A.

[55]See Winick, *supra* note 21, at 106–08; *supra* chapter 17.

[56]See Winick, *supra* note 21; *supra* chapter 17, part B.

[57]THOMPSON, *supra* note 40, at 121–30; *see supra* chapters 3 (psychotherapy) and 4 (behavior therapy).

[58]See *supra* chapter 16, part A.

disciplines.[59] In its recent task force report "Consent to Voluntary Hospitalization," the American Psychiatric Association recommended that the medical appropriateness of hospitalization should be regarded as a precondition for admission to a psychiatric hospital.[60]

In addition, the least intrusive alternative principle[61] similarly is supported by considerations of beneficence and nonmaleficence.[62] It is good clinical practice to attempt less intrusive and less risky procedures before a more invasive and dangerous one is tried. For example, before aversive conditioning is applied, leading behavioral therapists suggest that less intrusive and often more effective positive reinforcement approaches be attempted.[63] Similarly, good clinical practice would indicate a trial on antidepressant medication before a more risky and intrusive course of electroconvulsive therapy is imposed.[64] The clinician should be parsimonious in the selection of treatment, preferring the least invasive or intrusive approach that seems likely to be efficacious in the circumstances. This leastintrusive means principle also is reflected in codes of professional ethics.[65]

Principles of professional ethics therefore should parallel the legal and constitutional restrictions discussed in this book. I sincerely hope that this book will provoke further development of professional and ethical standards concerning involuntary applications of mental health treatment. Such standards inevitably will be more effective than legal controls and more acceptable to therapists and rehabilitators. If the professional community does not recognize these ethical principles and respond to the problems created by involuntary treatment, the law must and inevitably will.

---

[59]See, e.g., AM. HOSP. ASS'N, A PATIENT'S BILL OF RIGHTS, Principles 1, 2, 3, 5, 7, 10 (1992); AM. PSYCHIATRIC ASS'N, OPINIONS OF THE ETHICS COMM. ON THE PRINCIPLES OF MEDICAL ETHICS WITH ANNOTATIONS ESPECIALLY APPLICABLE TO PSYCHIATRY, Principles 1, 2, 4 (1992) [hereinafter MEDICAL ETHICS APPLICABLE TO PSYCHIATRY]; AM. NURSES' ASS'N, THE CODE FOR PROFESSIONAL NURSES, Guidelines 1, 5, 17 (1960); AM. PSYCHOLOGICAL ASS'N, ETHICAL PRINCIPLES OF PSYCHOLOGISTS AND CODE OF CONDUCT, standards 1.02, 1.14, 1.15, 8.03, 8.05 (1992) [hereinafter ETHICAL PRINCIPLES OF PSYCHOLOGISTS]. For example, the American Psychological Association mandates that "[p]sychologists take reasonable steps to avoid harming their patients or clients . . . and to minimize harm where it is foreseeable and unavoidable." ETHICAL PRINCIPLES OF PSYCHOLOGISTS, supra, Standard 1.14. The American Medical Association further defines "the psychiatrist's ethics and professional responsibilities [to] preclude him/her gratifying his/her own needs by exploiting the patient. This becomes particularly important because of the essentially private, highly personal, and sometimes intensely emotional nature of the relationship established with the psychiatrist." MEDICAL ETHICS APPLICABLE TO PSYCHIATRY, supra, Principle 1.

[60]See AM. PSYCHIATRIC ASS'N, TASK FORCE REPORT NO. 34, CONSENT TO VOLUNTARY HOSPITALIZATION 6, 11 (1993) (recommending clinical assessment of the "appropriateness" of a patient for voluntary hospitalization prior to admission and periodically thereafter); id. at 11 ("Hospitalization should continue only if it is medically necessary, the patient is receiving active treatment, and hospitalization is the least restrictive alternative available or potentially useful.").

[61]See AHRONHEIM ET AL., supra note 4, at 229; supra chapter 16, part B.

[62]See T. BEAUCHAMP & J. CHILDRESS, supra note 10, at 20 ("[W]henever there is a choice between different but equally efficacious methods of treatment patients' benefits should be maximized and their costs and risks minimized. Any other approach would rightly be regarded as an unethical practice."); id. at 159 ("Principles of beneficence and non–maleficence require balancing of possible benefits against possible harms in order to maximize benefits and minimize risks of harm.").

[63]A. BECK, COGNITIVE THERAPY AND THE EMOTIONAL DISORDERS (1976); Bergin & Lambert, The Effectiveness of Psychotherapy, in HANDBOOK OF PSYCHOTHERAPY AND BEHAVIOR CHANGE 156 (A. Bergen & S. Garfield eds., 4th ed. 1994); Hollow & Beck, Cognitive and Cognitive–Behavioral Therapies, in BECK, supra, at 428.

[64]A TASK FORCE REPORT OF THE AM. PSYCHIATRIC ASS'N, THE PRACTICE OF ELECTROCONVULSIVE THERAPY: RECOMMENDATIONS FOR TREATMENT, TRAINING, AND PRIVILEGING 50 (1990).

[65]See, e.g., ETHICS PRINCIPLES OF PSYCHOLOGISTS, supra note 59, Standard 5.03; MEDICAL ETHICS APPLICABLE TO PSYCHIATRY, supra note 59, Principle 6.1.

TABLE OF AUTHORITY

Administrative Regulations

Constitutional Provisions

Statutes, Regulations, and Rules of Procedure

Cases

INDEX

ABOUT THE AUTHOR

Bruce J. Winick, JD, is Professor of Law and Scholar in Residence at the University of Miami School of Law in Coral Gables, FL. His other books include *Therapeutic Jurisprudence Applied: Essays on Mental Health Law* (Carolina Academic Press, forthcoming 1997), *Law in a Therapeutic Key: Developments in Therapeutic Jurisprudence* (with David B. Wexler, Carolina Academic Press, 1996), *Essays in Therapeutic Jurisprudence* (with David B. Wexler, Carolina Academic Press, 1991), and *Current Issues in Mental Disability Law* (co-edited with Alexander D. Brooks, 1987). He is co-editor of the American Psychological Association Press book series, Law and Public Policy: Psychology and the Social Sciences. He also serves on the editorial boards of *Law & Human Behavior* and *Psychology, Public Policy, and Law* and is a reviewer for the *American Journal of Psychiatry*. He has served as legal consultant to the American Psychiatric Association Task Force on Consent to Voluntary Hospitalization and has chaired the Association of American Law Schools Section on Law and Medicine. Prior to joining the faculty of the University of Miami in 1974, Professor Winick served as New York City's director of Court Mental Health Services and as general counsel of the New York City Department of Mental Health and Mental Retardation Services. He received his law degree from the New York University School of Law.